BRIEF CONTENTS

CONTENTS

Part Two   THE MEASUREMENT OF FINANCIAL POSITION AND PERFORMANCE: KEY REPORTING ISSUES   183

Chapter 6   SHORT-TERM LIQUID ASSETS   184

ABOUT THE AUTHORS

Sidney J. Gray, BEc, Ph.D., FCCA, CPA, ACIS, MIMgt

Dr. Gray received his BEc degree from the University of Sydney and his Ph.D. degree from the University of Lancaster. Dr. Gray teaches and researches international accounting, international business strategy, and cross-cultural management at the University of New South Wales, Sydney, Australia, where he is a Professor and Head of the School of International Business. He was formerly a Professor at the University of Warwick in England and the University of Glasgow in Scotland.

Dr. Gray has published in many leading journals around the world including *Journal of Accounting Research, Abacus, Journal of International Business Studies, Journal of International Financial Management and Accounting, Accounting and Business Research, European Accounting Review, The International Journal of Accounting,* and the *Journal of Business Finance and Accounting.* He is the author/co-author of more than 20 books and monographs and 100 articles. Dr. Gray is a co-founder and Associate Editor of the *Journal of International Financial Management and Accounting.*

Dr. Gray is active in many academic and professional organisations. He has served as President of the International Association for Accounting Education and Research, Chairman of the British Accounting Association, and Secretary General of the European Accounting Association. He has served as a member of the Accounting Standards Committee of the U.K. and Ireland and as a member of the Consultative Group to the International Accounting Standards Committee. In 1994, he received from the American Accounting Association the award of Outstanding International Accounting Educator.

Belverd E. Needles, Jr., Ph.D., MBA, BBA, CPA, CMA

Dr. Needles received his BBA and MBA degrees from Texas Tech University and his Ph.D. degree from the University of Illinois. Dr. Needles teaches auditing and financial accounting at DePaul University, Chicago, USA, where he is the Arthur Andersen LLP Alumni Distinguished Professor and is an internationally known expert in international accounting and accounting education. He has published numerous articles in leading journals in these fields and is the author or editor of more than 20 books and monographs.

Dr. Needles is active in many academic and professional organisations. He is President of the International Association for Accounting Education and Research and Past President of the Federation of Schools of Accountancy. He has served as the elected U.S. representative to the European Accounting Association and Chair of the International Accounting Section of the American Accounting Association. He has served as Director of Continuing Education of the American Accounting Association. He serves on the Information Technology Executive Committee of the American Institute of CPAs. For the past five years he has served as the U.S. representative on the Education Committee of the International Federation of Accountants.

Dr. Needles has received the Distinguished Alumni Award from Texas Tech University, the Illinois CPA Society Outstanding Educator Award, the Joseph A. Silvoso Faculty Award of Merit from the Federation of Schools of Accountancy, the Ledger & Quill Award of Merit, and the Ledger & Quill Teaching Excellence Award. In 1992, he was named Educator of the Year by the national honorary society Beta Alpha Psi. He was also named Outstanding Accounting Educator by the American Institute of CPAs. In 1996, he received from the American Accounting Association the award of Outstanding International Accounting Educator.

PREFACE

Financial Accounting: A Global Approach is a first course in financial accounting for students with no previous training in accounting or business. The text is based on international accounting standards and, as such, is relevant in every country where international business and investments are important. In this book, we provide a comprehensive and accessible introduction to financial accounting with a strong real-world orientation achieved through examples and cases drawn from the annual reports of companies from all over the world. We have designed this text for use in a traditional one-quarter or one-semester course, and it may be used equally well in a two-quarter course in financial accounting. The text lends itself to a variety of instructional models, including open and self-learning strategies.

Fundamental to *Financial Accounting: A Global Approach* is the belief that a knowledge of financial reporting in the context of international accounting standards is essential to a majority of business students in the world today. Since most business students do not take more than one financial accounting course, it is necessary that these standards be integrated into the first course. Basic to our approach are the following objectives:

1. To provide global perspective, relevance, and authoritativeness through the use of international accounting standards.
2. To write a basic, yet thorough, treatment of introductory accounting for business and management students, including accounting majors, that focuses on the role of accounting information in decision making.
3. To emphasise conceptual, practical, and real-world content.
4. To provide a strong self-learning pedagogical approach through the learning-by-objectives framework integrated in the text, assignment material, and ancillaries.
5. To develop comprehensive and flexible assignment materials.

GLOBAL PERSPECTIVE, RELEVANCE, AND AUTHORITATIVENESS

We have built many features into *Financial Accounting: A Global Approach* to provide global perspective, relevance, and authoritativeness:

■ When writing this text, we were careful to be as neutral as feasible regarding national viewpoints. Monetary symbols—such as dollar, pound, and yen signs—do not appear in the text, except where real company cases are cited, so that the student will read his or her own currency into the discussion.

■ We do not intend this book to be a primer on international accounting standards as promulgated by the International Accounting Standards Committee, but we do intend the text to be compatible with them. When specific international standards are relevant to the beginning level of this book, we discuss them.

- Examples and assignment materials are international in scope and feature companies from countries all over the world.
- Both authors have extensive experience in teaching and practising global financial reporting and in the standard setting process. We have both served on the Consultative Group to the International Accounting Standards Committee. For more information on our academic credentials and experience, please see the brief biographies that appear on pages xiv–xv.
- Further strengthening the global perspective, relevance, and authoritativeness of the text is the **International Advisory Board**, which consists of accounting scholars from more than twenty countries. This distinguished group meets periodically with the authors and has reviewed chapters of the text to suggest improvements, to enhance the text's relevance for use in each member's country, and to provide international cases and examples. International Advisory Board members are listed at the end of this preface.

BASIC YET THOROUGH TREATMENT FOR BUSINESS AND MANAGEMENT STUDENTS

Financial Accounting: A Global Approach is a basic text in that it assumes students have no previous knowledge of accounting or financial reporting; it furnishes comprehensive coverage of the principal accounting and reporting topics. Our goal is to provide students with a text that will enable them to become intelligent users of financial information for decision making in a global context.

CONCEPTUAL, PRACTICAL, AND REAL-WORLD CONTENT

Financial Accounting: A Global Approach emphasises the use of accounting information in decision making, both by internal management and by external users. We demonstrate the conceptual underpinnings of financial reporting and accounting, as well as their application in a real-world environment, through the following features:

Actual Financial Statements We have incorporated examples from the annual reports of real companies or articles about them extensively in the text and assignment material. In addition to including the complete annual report of Nestlé in Appendix A, we examine the financial statements of other well-known companies such as Cadbury Schweppes and Volvo. These are only a few examples of the scores of real companies that appear in the text.

Decision Points Every chapter begins with a Decision Point based on excerpts from a real company's annual report or from an article in a business journal. A sampling of the companies featured in the Decision Points includes Daimler-Benz, Sime Darby, Danone, Reuters, and Philips. Decision Points present a situation requiring a decision by management or other users of financial information and then show how the decision can be made using accounting information.

Business Bulletins Business Bulletins are short items related to the chapter topics that show the relevance of accounting in such areas as Business Practice, Technology in Practice, Ethics in Practice, and International Practice.

Marginal Notes These brief annotations, found in the text margins and indicated by a globe icon, provide useful information on specific accounting practices used in various countries, often detailing how accounting methods vary from country to country.

Other Real-World Topics   We highlight information from annual reports of real companies and from articles about them in business journals such as *Business Week*, *The Economist*, *Forbes*, *The Financial Times*, and the *Wall Street Journal*, to enhance students' appreciation of the usefulness and relevance of accounting information. In total, more than one hundred publicly held companies appear in the text as examples.

Real Companies in Assignments   We feature real companies in the assignment materials as discussed below.

International Accounting   In recognition of the global economy in which all businesses operate today, we introduce international accounting examples in Chapter 1 and integrate them throughout the text. Some examples of companies mentioned in the text and assignments are Sony, Glaxo Wellcome, BMW, Groupe Michelin, and McDonald's.

INTEGRATED LEARNING OBJECTIVES

Integrated learning objectives significantly improve the teaching and learning of accounting. They enhance the role of the overall package, and particularly that of the textbook, by achieving complete and thorough communication between teacher and student. Each learning objective is, in effect, a mini chapter that is linked to the assignment material by the learning objective references. This feature improves accessibility for students for whom English is a second language and facilitates self-learning by students, especially those in distance learning situations.

ABUNDANT AND FLEXIBLE ASSIGNMENT MATERIAL

Acknowledging the need for an expanded skill set in students and greater pedagogical flexibility for faculty members, we have organised the end-of-chapter assignments and accompanying material to provide great variety and flexibility. The assignments are described in the paragraphs that follow.

Knowledge and Understanding

This section contains fifteen to twenty-four review questions that cover the essential topics of the chapter.

Application

This section contains about fifteen single-topic exercises that stress the application of all topics in the chapter. It also contains four problems that provide more extensive applications of chapter topics, often covering more than one learning objective. Selected problems in each chapter contain writing components.

Critical Thinking and Communication

This section consists of cases, usually based on real companies, that require critical thinking and communication skills in the form of writing. Each case has a specific purpose:

Conceptual Mini Case   Designed so that a written solution is appropriate, but which may also be used in other kinds of communication modes, these short cases address conceptual accounting issues and are based on real companies and situations.

Cultural Mini Case   Created to emphasise the effects of cultural and environmental differences on accounting and the interpretation of financial reports, these short cases use examples of companies from around the world.

Ethics Mini Case   In recognition of the need for accounting and business students to be exposed in all their courses to ethical considerations, every chapter has a short case, often based on a real company, in which the student must address an ethical dilemma directly related to the chapter content.

Decision-Making Case   In the role of decision maker, the student is asked to extract relevant data from a longer case, make computations as necessary, and arrive at a decision. The decision maker may be a manager, an investor, an analyst, or a lender.

Basic Research Activity   These exercises enhance student learning and participation in the classroom by acquainting students with business periodicals, use of annual reports and business references, and use of the library. Through field activities at actual businesses, some are designed to improve interviewing and observation skills.

Financial Reporting and Analysis

Interpretation Cases from Business   These short cases, abstracted from business articles and annual reports of well-known corporations and organisations such as Unilever, Mitsubishi, Peugeot, Toys "R" Us, Volvo, and Ford, require students to extract relevant data, make computations, and interpret the results.

Nestlé Case   This case requires the reading and analysis of the actual annual report of Nestlé, a Swiss multinational company, contained in Appendix A.

SUPPLEMENTARY SUPPORT MATERIALS FOR STUDENTS AND TEACHERS

Internet Web Site   The Needles Accounting Resource Center (http://www.hmco.com/college/needles/home.html) provides access to a wealth of resources for the teacher and the student. For example, additional country-specific cases provided by the International Advisory Board may be found on the Web site. PowerPoint slides depicting the figures in the text are also available on the site.

Tutor's Manual   A Tutor's Manual with solutions to all of the end-of-chapter assignments in the text, as well as a bank of test questions, is available.

PowerPoint Slides   PowerPoint slides of the figures in the text are available in disk format or on the Web site.

INTERNATIONAL ADVISORY BOARD

Niamh Brennan
University College Dublin

Alain Burlaud
CNAM

Leandro Canibano
Universidad Autonoma de Madrid

Lynne Chow
Hong Kong Polytechnic University

Adolf Coenenberg
University of Augsburg

Daniel Darmanin
University of Malta

Geoffrey Everingham
University of Capetown

Kazuo Hiramatsu
Kwansei Gakuin University

Martin Hoogendoorn
University of Amsterdam

In Ki Joo
Yonsei University

Tatiana Krylova
Moscow State University

Christian Lefebvre
Katholieke Universiteit Leuven

Malcolm Miller
University of New South Wales

Libuse Mullerova
University of Economics, Prague

Ramaswamy Narayanaswamy
Indian Institute of Management,
Bangalore

Anthony Papas
Athens University of Economics

Clare Roberts
University of Aberdeen

Susela Devi Selvaraj
University of Malaya

Shuaib Shuaib
University of Kuwait

Yunwei Tang
Shanghai University of Finance
and Economics

Lina Valcarcel
University of the Philippines

Alfred Wagenhofer
University of Graz

Trevor Wilkins
National University of Singapore

Roger Willett
University of Otago

Anne Wu
National Chengchi University

Part One

Accounting as an Information System

*A*ccounting is an information system for measuring, processing, and communicating information that is useful in making economic decisions. Part One focuses on the users and uses of accounting information and presents the fundamental concepts and techniques of the basic accounting system, including the presentation and analysis of financial statements.

Chapter 1   Accounting Information, Decision Making, and the Uses of Financial Statements explores the nature and environment of accounting, with special emphasis on the users and uses of accounting information. It introduces the basic financial statements, the concept of accounting measurement, and the effects of business transactions on financial position. This chapter concludes with a discussion of ethical considerations in accounting.

Chapter 2   Measuring Business Transactions continues the exploration of accounting measurement by focusing on the problems of recognition, valuation, and classification and how they are solved in the measuring and recording of business transactions.

Chapter 3   Measuring Business Profit defines the accounting concept of business profit, discusses the role of adjusting and closing entries in the measurement of profit, and demonstrates the preparation of financial statements.

Chapter 4   Accounting for Trading Operations introduces the trading company and the trading income statement. The periodic and perpetual inventory systems receive equal treatment. Internal control for trading companies is the final topic of the chapter.

Chapter 5   Financial Statement Objectives, Presentation, and Analysis introduces the objectives and qualitative aspects of financial information. It demonstrates how much more useful classified financial statements are than simple financial statements in presenting information to statement users. This chapter also includes an introduction to financial statement analysis.

Chapter 1

ACCOUNTING INFORMATION, DECISION MAKING, AND THE USES OF FINANCIAL STATEMENTS

LEARNING OBJECTIVES

1. Define *accounting*, identify business goals and activities, and describe the role of accounting in making informed decisions.
2. Identify the many users of accounting information in society.
3. Explain the importance of business transactions, money measure, and separate entity to accounting measurement.
4. Describe the corporate form of business organisation.
5. Define *financial position*, state the accounting equation, and show how they are affected by simple transactions.
6. Identify the basic financial statements.
7. State the relationship of accounting standards to financial statements and the independent auditor's report, and identify the factors that influence accounting standards.
8. Define *ethics* and describe the ethical responsibilities of accountants.

McDonald's Corporation

Top management of McDonald's, the U.S.-based global food service retailer, state in the McDonald's 1995 Annual Report that they have an established growth strategy of improving customer satisfaction, increasing market share, and enhancing profitability and returns. Their vision is to dominate the global food service industry by adopting strategies designed "... to create financial success—for the company, for franchisees, for partners, for suppliers and ultimately, for shareholders".[1]

What financial knowledge do the company's managers need to promote these goals? Managers must have a thorough knowledge of accounting to understand how the operations for which they are responsible contribute to the overall financial health of the business. This requires a mastery of the terminology and concepts that underlie accounting, of the way in which financial information is generated, and of the way in which that information is interpreted and analysed. The purpose of this textbook is to assist you in acquiring that mastery.

OBJECTIVE 1

Define accounting, identify business goals and activities, and describe the role of accounting in making informed decisions

ACCOUNTING AS AN INFORMATION SYSTEM

Today's accountant focuses on the ultimate needs of decision makers who use accounting information, whether those decision makers are inside or outside the business. **Accounting** is *an information system that measures, processes, and communicates financial information about an enterprise.* An **enterprise** is any commercial, industrial, or business entity, whether in the public or private sector.

As stated by the **International Accounting Standards Committee (IASC)**, a private sector organisation bringing together national professional accountancy bodies from more than eighty-five countries, accounting carries out a vital service by providing the financial information about an enterprise "that is useful to a wide range of users in making economic decisions".[2]

As shown in Figure 1-1, accounting is a link between business activities and decision makers. First, accounting measures business activities by recording data about

---

BUSINESS BULLETIN   Business Practice

Accounting in some form or other has been essential to commerce for more than five thousand years. Accounting, in a version close to what we know today, gained widespread use in the 1400s, especially in Italy, where it was instrumental to the development of shipping, trade, construction, and other forms of commerce. This system of double-entry bookkeeping was documented by the famous Italian mathematician, scholar, and philosopher Luca Pacioli. In 1494, Pacioli published his most important work, *Summa de Arithmetica, Geometrica, Proportioni et Proportionalita,* which contained a detailed description of accounting as practised in that age. This book became the most widely read book on mathematics in Italy and firmly established Pacioli as the "Father of Accounting".

FIGURE 1-1 *Accounting as an Information System*

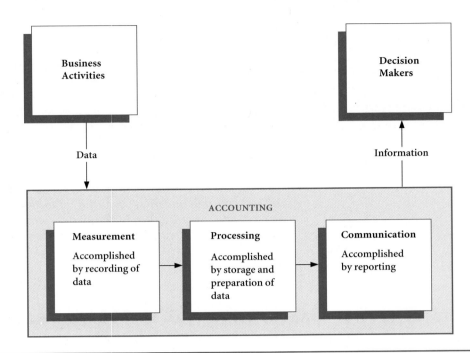

them for future use. Second, the data are stored until needed and then processed to become useful information. Third, the information is communicated, through various reports, to decision makers. We might say that data about business activities are the input to the accounting system and that useful information for decision makers is the output.

Business Goals and Activities

A **business** is an economic unit that aims to sell goods and services to customers at prices that will provide an adequate return to its owners. For example, listed below are some companies and the principal goods or services they sell:

Volvo	Cars, trucks, and buses
Nike	Athletic footwear and clothing
Sony	Consumer electronics
Unilever	Foods, detergents, and personal products
Hilton Hotels	Hotels and resorts service
British Airways	Passenger airline service

Despite their differences, all these businesses have similar financial goals and engage in similar activities, as shown in Figure 1-2. Each must take in enough money from customers to pay all the costs of doing business, with enough left over as profit for the owners to want to stay in the business. This need to earn enough profit to attract and hold investment capital is the goal of **profitability**. In addition, businesses must meet the goal of liquidity. **Liquidity** means having enough funds available to pay debts when they are due. For example, Volvo may meet the goal of profitability by

FIGURE 1-2 *Business Goals and Activities*

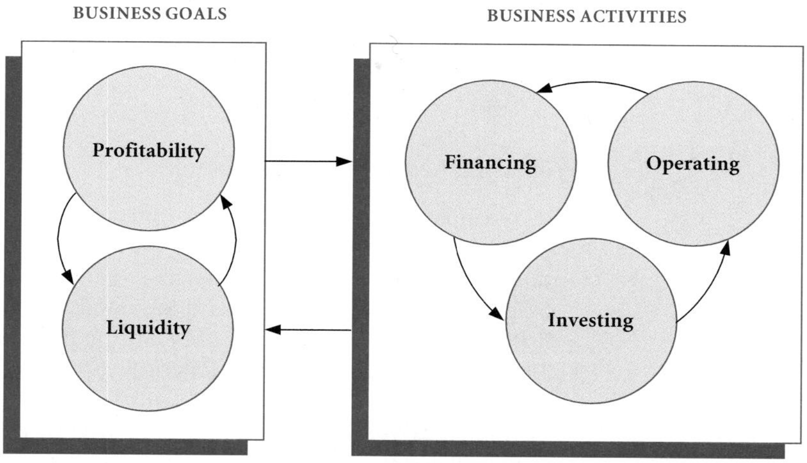

BUSINESS GOALS   BUSINESS ACTIVITIES

Profitability

Liquidity

Financing   Operating

Investing

selling many cars at a price that earns a profit, but if its customers do not pay for their cars quickly enough to enable Volvo to pay its suppliers and employees, the company may fail to meet the goal of liquidity. Both goals must be met if a company is to survive and be successful.

All businesses pursue their goals by engaging in similar activities. First, each business must engage in **financing activities** to obtain adequate funds, or capital, to begin and to continue operating. Financing activities include obtaining capital from owners and from lenders, such as banks. They also include repaying lenders and paying a return to the owners. Second, each business must engage in **investing activities** to spend the capital it receives in ways that are productive and will help to achieve its objectives. Investing activities include buying land, buildings, equipment, and other resources that are needed in the operation of the business, and selling these resources when they are no longer needed. Third, each business must engage in **operating activities**. In addition to the selling of goods and services to customers, operating activities include such actions as employing managers and workers, buying and producing goods and services, and paying taxes to the government.

Financial and Management Accounting

Accounting's role of assisting decision makers by measuring, processing, and communicating information is usually divided into the categories of management accounting and financial accounting. Although there is considerable overlap in the functions of management accounting and financial accounting, the two can be distinguished by who the principal users of their information will be. **Management accounting** provides internal decision makers who are charged with achieving the goals of profitability and liquidity with information about financing, investing, and operating activities. Managers and employees who conduct the activities of the business need information that tells them how they have done in the past and what they can expect in the future. For example, McDonald's needs an operating report on each outlet that tells how much was sold at that outlet, and what costs were incurred, and it needs a budget for each outlet that projects the sales and costs for the next year. **Financial accounting** generates reports and communicates them to external decision makers so that they can evaluate how well the business has achieved its goals. These reports to external users are called **financial statements.** McDonald's, for instance, will send its financial statements to its owners, its banks and other lenders, and government regulators. Financial statements report directly on the goals of profitability and liquidity and are used extensively both inside and outside a business to evaluate the business's success. It is important for every person involved with a business to understand financial statements. They are a central feature of accounting and are the primary focus of this book.

Processing Accounting Information

To avoid misunderstandings, it is important to distinguish accounting itself from the ways in which accounting information is processed by bookkeeping, the computer, and management information systems.

People often fail to understand the difference between accounting and bookkeeping. **Bookkeeping** is the process of recording financial transactions and keeping financial records. Mechanical and repetitive, bookkeeping is only a small—although important—part of accounting. Accounting, on the other hand, includes the design of an information system that meets the user's needs. The major goals of accounting are the analysis, interpretation, and use of information.

The **computer** is an electronic tool that is used to collect, organise, and communicate vast amounts of information with great speed. Accountants were among the earliest and most enthusiastic users of computers, and today they use microcomputers in all aspects of their work. It may appear that the computer is doing the accountant's job; in fact, it is only a tool that is instructed to do routine bookkeeping and to perform complex calculations.

With the widespread use of the computer today, a business's many information needs are organised into what is called a **management information system (MIS).** A management information system consists of the interconnected subsystems that provide the information needed to run a business. The accounting information system is the most important subsystem because it plays the key role of managing the flow of economic data to all parts of a business and to interested parties outside the business.

OBJECTIVE 2

Identify the many users of accounting information in society

DECISION MAKERS: THE USERS OF ACCOUNTING INFORMATION

Figure 1-3 depicts the people who use accounting information to make decisions: those who manage a business plus a variety of interested parties, including investors, employees, lenders, suppliers and other trade creditors, customers, governments and their agencies, and the public.[3]

Management describes the people who have overall responsibility for operating a business and for meeting its profitability and liquidity goals. In a small business, management may include the owners. In a large business, management more often consists of people who have been employed to run the business. Managers must decide what to do, how to do it, and whether the results match their original plans. Successful managers consistently make the right decisions based on timely and valid information. To make good decisions, managers need answers to such questions as: What was the company's net profit during the past month, quarter, or year? Is the rate of return to the owners adequate? Does the company have enough cash? Which products or services are most profitable? Because so many key decisions are based on accounting data, management is one of the most important users of accounting information. Management has the primary responsibility for the preparation and presentation of the company's financial statements, not only for its own use, but for other users who may rely on the financial statements as their major source of financial information about the business.

FIGURE 1-3   *The Users of Accounting Information*

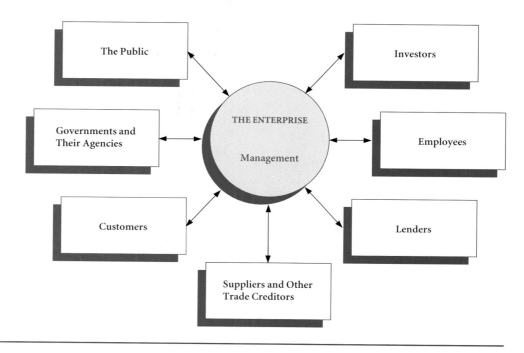

In Germany, investors as users of financial statements have not received the attention and priority that they have in the U.K. and the U.S. But recently, many large German companies such as Daimler-Benz, Bayer, and Hoechst have adopted a shareholder value orientation and have placed a higher priority on communicating more closely with their shareholders and potential investors.

Investors are the owners, or potential owners, of the business. They are the providers of the capital at risk and are hence interested in the returns from their investments and the risks involved. Investors need accounting information to help them decide whether to buy, hold, or sell shares in a company. When investors own shares they become shareholders (or stockholders), and as such they are also interested in information which helps them to assess the dividend paying ability of the business. Note here that accounting terminology in the English language sometimes differs between North American and British English. The term "shareholders" is British English in contrast to its equivalent "stockholders" which is North American English. Throughout this book, we will follow mainly the terminology adopted by the International Accounting Standards Committee (IASC) in its International Accounting Standards, which is a mixture of North American and British terminology. Table 1-1 sets out some key IASC terms and identifies some possible alternatives (see also the appendix on international accounting terms for a more extensive selection of terms).

Employees are those who work in the business, and their representative groups. They are interested in financial information which will help them to assess the ability of their employers to survive and prosper, and to provide employment opportunities, remuneration, and retirement benefits.

Most companies borrow money for both long-term and short-term operating needs. **Lenders** are interested in financial information that enables them to determine whether their loans, and the interest charges applicable, will be paid when due. They study a company's liquidity and cash flow as well as its profitability. Banks and other lenders will also wish to analyse a company's financial position before making a loan.

Suppliers and other trade creditors are interested in financial information that will help them to assess whether the amounts owing to them will be paid when due. Trade creditors are likely to be more interested in the short-term financial viability of the business unless they have a major customer relationship.

TABLE 1-1 *IASC Accounting Terminology*

IASC Terms	Alternatives
Financial statements	Accounts (British)
Income statement	Profit and loss account (British)
Balance sheet	Statement of financial position (North American)
Revenue	Turnover (British)
Net profit	Net income (North American)
Long-term assets	Fixed assets (British)
Land and buildings	Real estate (North American)
Inventories	Stocks (British)
Receivables	Debtors (British)
Payables	Creditors (British)
Loans	Debt (British)
Shareholders	Stockholders (North American)
Shares	Stock (North American)
Share capital	Common stock (North American)
Shareholders' equity	Stockholders' equity (North American)

The company's **customers** also have an interest in financial information because this will help them assess the prospects of an enterprise. This is especially the case when they have a long-term relationship with, or are dependent upon, the company.

Governments and their agencies are interested in the activities of companies owing to their concern with the allocation of resources and economic policy, with taxation policy and collection, and with company regulation. Accounting information is often a crucial input especially in the case of taxation where the authorities usually require detailed reports to be prepared based on the accounting records. In the context of regulation, companies are required in most countries to report regularly to governmental agencies by sending them their financial statements.

Members of the **public** are affected in a variety of ways by enterprise activities. The success and financial prospects of a business are relevant to the economy including employment, use of local suppliers, development of roads, housing, the environment, communications and so on. Accounting information is likely to be useful in keeping the public, and their representatives, informed.

While accounting information and financial statements are likely to be useful to a wide range of users, they cannot provide all of the information that users may need to make economic decisions. This is because financial reports are largely concerned with reflecting the financial effects of past events. They do not necessarily provide nonfinancial or future-oriented information, though companies are increasingly including information of this kind voluntarily in their reports to shareholders.

It is also important to note that financial statements are prepared and presented for external user purposes by enterprises all over the world. While these financial statements may appear broadly similar from country to country, there are many differences which have been caused by a variety of economic, social, political, legal, and cultural factors. Different countries have evolved, in an accounting sense, in different ways, and it is often the case that they have had different users in mind, or at least different ideas about the relative importance of different user groups, when setting national regulations. For example, in countries such as Canada, the United States, and the United Kingdom, the investor group has had the highest priority consistent with the importance placed on stock markets in contrast to France, Germany, and Japan where the interests of lenders and government agencies, especially taxation agencies, have dominated. It is in this context that the International Accounting Standards Committee (IASC) was established in 1973 with the aim of narrowing differences internationally by harmonising accounting practice on a global basis (see the appendix on the IASC for additional information).

<table>
<tr><td>

OBJECTIVE 3

Explain the importance of business transactions, money measure, and separate entity to accounting measurement

</td></tr>
</table>

ACCOUNTING MEASUREMENT

Accounting is an information system that measures, processes, and communicates financial information. In this section, you begin the study of the measurement aspects of accounting. Here you learn what accounting actually measures and study the effects of certain transactions on a company's financial position.

To make an accounting measurement, the accountant must answer four basic questions:

1. What is measured?
2. When should the measurement be made?
3. What monetary amount should be placed on what is measured?
4. How should what is measured be classified?

All these questions deal with basic assumptions and generally accepted accounting principles, and their answers establish what accounting is and what it is not. Accountants in industry, professional associations, auditing, government, and academic circles debate the answers to these questions constantly, and the answers change as new knowledge and practice require. But the basis of today's accounting practice rests on a number of widely accepted concepts and criteria, which are described in this book. Questions 2, 3, and 4 are examined in the chapter on measuring and recording business transactions. Here we focus on the first question presented above: What is measured?

What Is Measured?

The world contains an unlimited number of things to measure and ways to measure them. For example, consider a machine that makes bottle caps. How many measurements of this machine could you make? You might start with size and then go on to weight, cost, or one of many other units of measurement. Some of these measurements are relevant to accounting; some are not. Every system must define what it measures, and accounting is no exception. Basically, financial accounting uses money measures to gauge the impact of business transactions on separate business entities. The concepts of business transactions, money measure, and separate entity are discussed in the next sections.

Business Transactions as the Object of Measurement

Business transactions are economic events that affect the financial position of a business entity. Business entities can have hundreds or even thousands of transactions every day. These business transactions are the raw material of accounting reports.

A transaction can be an exchange of value (a purchase, sale, payment, receipt, or loan) between two or more independent parties. A transaction also can be an economic event that has the same effect as an exchange transaction but does not involve an exchange. Some examples of "nonexchange" transactions are losses from fire, flood, explosion, and theft; physical wear and tear on machinery and equipment; and the day-by-day accumulation of interest.

Money Measure

All business transactions are recorded in terms of money. This concept is termed **money measure**. Of course, information of a nonfinancial nature may be noted, but it is through the recording of monetary amounts that the diverse transactions and activities of a business are measured. Money is the only factor that is common to all business transactions, and thus it is the only practical unit of measure that can produce financial data that are alike and can be compared.

The monetary unit a business uses depends on the country in which the business operates. For example, in the United States, the basic unit of money is the dollar. In Japan, it is the yen; in Switzerland, the franc; in Indonesia, the rupiah; and in the United Kingdom, the pound. If there are transactions between countries, exchange rates must be used to translate from one currency to another. An **exchange rate** is the value of one currency in terms of another. For example, an English person purchasing goods from a U.S. company and paying in U.S. dollars must exchange British pounds for U.S. dollars before making payment. In effect, the currencies are goods that can be bought and sold. Table 1-2 illustrates the exchange rates for several currencies in terms of the rate per U.S. dollar. It shows the exchange rate for British pounds as 0.61 pounds per dollar on a particular date. Like the price of any good or service, these prices change daily according to supply and demand for the currencies.

The Concept of Separate Entity

For accounting purposes, a business is a **separate entity**, distinct not only from its lenders and customers but also from its owner or owners. It should have a completely separate set of records, and its financial records and reports should refer only to its own financial affairs. For example, the Jones Florist Company should have a bank account that is separate from the account of Satomi Jones, the owner. Satomi Jones may own a home, a car, and other property, and she may have personal debts, but these are not the Jones Florist Company's resources or debts. Satomi Jones also may own another business, say a stationery shop. If she does, she should have a completely separate set of records for each business.

<table>
<tr><td>**OBJECTIVE 4**

Describe the corporate form of business organisation</td><td>## THE CORPORATION AS A SEPARATE ENTITY

There are three basic forms of business enterprise. Besides the corporate form, there are the sole proprietorship form and the partnership form. Whichever form is used, the business should be viewed for accounting purposes as a separate entity, and all its records and reports should be developed separate and apart from those of its owners.</td></tr>
</table>

Corporations Differentiated from Sole Proprietorships and Partnerships

A **sole proprietorship** is a business owned by one person. The individual receives all profits or losses and is liable for all obligations of the business. Sole proprietorships represent the largest number of businesses in most countries, but typically they are the smallest in size. A **partnership** is like a proprietorship in most ways except that it has two or more co-owners. The partners share the profits and losses of the partnership according to an agreed-upon formula. Generally, any partner can bind the partnership to another party, and, if necessary, the personal resources of each partner can be called on to pay obligations of the partnership. A partnership must be dissolved if the ownership changes, as when a partner leaves or dies. If the business is to continue as a partnership after this occurs, a new partnership must be formed. Both the sole

TABLE 1-2 *Listing of Selected Foreign Exchange Rates*

Country	Price per U.S. Dollar
Canada (dollar)	1.34
Germany (mark)	1.52
Japan (yen)	113.59
Switzerland (franc)	1.27
United Kingdom (pound)	0.61

From *Financial Times,* November 2, 1996. Used by permission of Financial Times.

proprietorship and the partnership are convenient ways of separating the business owners' commercial activities from their personal activities. But legally there is no economic separation between the owners and the businesses.

A **corporation** or **company**, on the other hand, is a business unit that is legally separate from its owners (the shareholders). The shareholders, whose ownership is represented by shares, do not directly control the corporation's operations. Instead they elect a board of directors to run the corporation for their benefit. In exchange for their limited involvement in the corporation's actual operations, shareholders enjoy limited liability. That is, their risk of loss is limited to the amount they paid for their shares. If they wish, shareholders can sell their shares without affecting corporate operations. Because of this limited liability, shareholders are often willing to invest in riskier, but potentially more profitable, activities. Also, because ownership can be transferred without dissolving the corporation, the life of a corporation is unlimited and not subject to the whims or health of a proprietor or a partner.

The characteristics of corporations make them very efficient in amassing capital, which enables them to grow extremely large. Even though corporations are fewer in number than sole proprietorships and partnerships, they typically contribute much more to the economy in monetary terms. For example, General Electric of the United States, the world's largest company in terms of market value in 1996, generates more revenues than many countries in the world. Because of the economic significance of corporations, this book will emphasise accounting for the corporate form of business.

Formation of a Corporation

To form a corporation, most countries require individuals to sign an application and file it with the proper government official. This application contains the **articles of incorporation**. If approved by the regulators, these articles become, in effect, a contract, called the company charter, between the government and the incorporators. The company is then authorised to do business.

Organisation of a Corporation

The authority to manage the corporation is delegated by the shareholders to the board of directors and by the board of directors to the corporate officers (see Figure 1-4). That is, the shareholders elect a board of directors, which sets company policies and chooses the corporate officers, who in turn carry out the corporate policies by managing the business.

FIGURE 1-4   *The Corporate Form of Business*

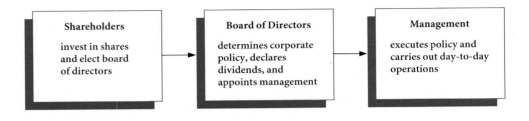

Shareholders

A unit of ownership in a corporation is called a **share**. The articles of incorporation state the maximum number of shares that the corporation will be allowed, or autho- rised, to issue. The number of shares held by shareholders is the outstanding capital; this may be less than the number authorised in the articles of incorporation. To invest in a corporation, a shareholder transfers cash or other resources to the corporation. In return, the shareholder receives shares representing a proportionate share of own-

BUSINESS BULLETIN   **Business Practice**

While many businesses are very large and span the globe, as shown in the list- ing below of top global corporations by market value, there are also many millions of small businesses which are family owned or have relatively few shareholders.

Top Global Corporations by Market Value (May 31, 1996)

Rank				Market Value
1996	1995			Billions of U.S. Dollars
1	3	General Electric	U.S.	137.34
2	2	Royal Dutch/Shell	Neth./Britain	128.29
3	1	NTT	Japan	115.70
4	6	Coca-Cola	U.S.	115.07
5	8	Bank of Tokyo-Mitsubishi	Japan	110.29
6	4	Exxon	U.S.	105.27
7	5	AT&T	U.S.	99.72
8	7	Toyota Motor	Japan	85.78
9	13	Philip Morris	U.S.	82.09
10	16	Merck	U.S.	78.62
11	14	Roche Holding	Switzerland	73.31
12	20	Microsoft	U.S.	71.04
13	22	Johnson & Johnson	U.S.	64.88
14	10	Fuji Bank	Japan	62.99
15	21	Intel	U.S.	62.09

Source: "Top Global Corporations by Market Value (May 31, 1996)", *Business Week,* July 8, 1996 by permission of Business Week. © 1996.

ership in the corporation. Afterwards, the shareholder may transfer the shares at will. Corporations may have more than one kind of capital, but the first part of this book will refer only to share capital held by the owners.

Board of Directors

As noted, the shareholders elect the board of directors, which in turn decides on the major business policies of the corporation. Among the specific duties of the board are authorising contracts, setting executive salaries, and arranging major loans with banks. The payment of dividends is also an important function of the board of directors. Dividends are distributions of resources, generally in the form of cash, to the shareholders. Paying dividends is one way of rewarding shareholders for their investment when the corporation has been successful in earning a profit. (The other way is through a rise in the market value of the shares.) Although there is usually a delay between the time a dividend is declared and the date of the actual payment, we shall assume in the early chapters of this book that declaration and payment are made on the same day.

The board of directors will vary in composition from company to company, but in most cases it will contain several officers of the corporation and several outsiders. Today, in many countries, the formation of an **audit committee** with several outside directors is encouraged to make sure that the board will be objective in evaluating management's performance. One function of the audit committee is to engage the company's independent auditors and review their work. Another is to make sure that proper systems exist to safeguard the company's resources and ensure that reliable accounting records are kept.

Management

The board of directors appoints managers to carry out the corporation's policies and run day-to-day operations. Besides being responsible for running the business, management has the duty of reporting the financial results of its administration to the board of directors and the shareholders. Though management must, at a minimum, make a comprehensive annual report, it may and generally does report more often. The annual reports of large public corporations are available to the public. Excerpts from many of them will be used throughout this book.

OBJECTIVE 5

Define financial position, state the accounting equation, and show how they are affected by simple transactions

FINANCIAL POSITION AND THE ACCOUNTING EQUATION

Financial position refers to the economic resources that are controlled by a company and the claims against those resources at a point in time. Another term for claims is equities. Therefore, a company can be viewed as economic resources and equities:

$$\text{Economic resources} = \text{equities}$$

Every company has two types of equities, nonowners' (i.e. lenders' and creditors') equities and owners' equity. Thus,

$$\text{Economic resources} = \text{nonowners' equities} + \text{owners' equity}$$

In accounting terminology, economic resources are called assets and nonowners' equities are called liabilities. So the equation can be written like this:

$$\text{Assets} = \text{liabilities} + \text{owners' equity}$$

This equation is known as the **accounting equation**. The two sides of the equation always must be equal, or "in balance".

Assets

Assets are economic resources controlled by a business that are expected to benefit future operations. Certain kinds of assets—for example, cash and money owed to the company from customers (called accounts receivable)—are monetary items. Other assets—inventories (goods held for sale), land, buildings, and equipment—are nonmonetary physical things. Still other assets—the rights granted by patent, trademark, or copyright—are nonphysical.

Liabilities

Liabilities are present obligations of a business to pay cash, transfer assets, or provide services to other entities in the future. Among these obligations are debts of the business, amounts owed to suppliers for goods or services bought on credit (called accounts payable), borrowed money (for example, money owed on loans payable to banks), salaries and wages owed to employees, taxes owed to the government, and services to be performed.

As debts, liabilities are claims recognised by law. That is, the law gives lenders the right to force the sale of a company's assets if the company fails to pay its debts. Lenders have rights over owners and must be paid in full before the owners receive anything, even if payment of a debt uses up all the assets of a business.

Owners' Equity

Owners' equity represents the claims by the owners of a business to the assets of the business. It equals the residual interest, or residual equity, in the assets of an entity that remains after deducting the entity's liabilities. Theoretically, it is what would be left over if all the liabilities were paid and sometimes is said to equal **net assets.** By rearranging the accounting equation, we can define owners' equity this way:

$$\text{Owners' equity} = \text{assets} - \text{liabilities}$$

The owners' equity of a corporation is called **shareholders' equity,** and so the accounting equation becomes

$$\text{Assets} = \text{liabilities} + \text{shareholders' equity}$$

Shareholders' equity has two parts, share capital and retained earnings:

$$\text{Shareholders' equity} = \text{share capital} + \text{retained earnings}$$

Share capital is the amount invested in the business by the shareholders. Their ownership in the business is represented by shares of capital.

Typically, share capital is divided between nominal value and share premium. Nominal value is an amount per share that is entered in the corporation's capital account and is the minimum amount that can be reported as share capital. Share premium results when shares are issued at an amount greater than nominal value, i.e. at a premium. In the initial chapters of this book, share capital will be shown as shares that have been issued at nominal value.

Retained earnings represent the equity of the shareholders generated from the profit-producing activities of the business and kept for use in the business. As you can see in Figure 1-5, retained earnings are affected by three kinds of transactions: revenues, expenses, and dividends.

Simply stated, **revenues** and **expenses** are the increases and decreases in shareholders' equity that result from operating a business. For example, the cash a customer pays (or agrees to pay in the future) to a company in return for a service provided by the company is a revenue to the company. The assets (cash or accounts receivable) of the company increase, and the shareholders' equity in those assets also increases. On the other hand, the cash a company pays out (or agrees to pay in the future) in the process of providing a service is an expense. In this case, the assets

FIGURE 1-5 *Three Types of Transactions That Affect Retained Earnings*

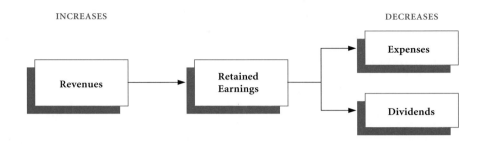

(cash) decrease or the liabilities (accounts payable) increase, and the shareholders' equity decreases. Generally speaking, a company is successful if its revenues exceed its expenses. When revenues exceed expenses, the difference is called **net profit**; when expenses exceed revenues, the difference is called **net loss**. **Dividends** are distributions to shareholders of assets (usually cash) generated by past earnings. It is important not to confuse expenses and dividends, both of which reduce retained earnings.

Some Illustrative Transactions

Let us now examine the effect of some of the most common business transactions on the accounting equation. Suppose that James and John Shannon open a property agency called Shannon Property on December 1. During December, their business engages in the transactions described in the following paragraphs.

Owner's Investment

James and John Shannon file articles of incorporation and receive their charter. To begin their new business, they invest 50,000 in Shannon Property in exchange for 5,000 shares at 10 nominal value. The first balance sheet of the new company would show the asset Cash and the Share Capital of the owners:

	Assets	=	Shareholders' Equity (SE)	
	Cash		Share Capital	Type of SE Transaction
1.	50,000		50,000	Shareholders' Investments

At this point, the company has no liabilities, and assets equal shareholders' equity. The labels Cash and Share Capital are called **accounts** and are used by accountants to accumulate amounts that result from similar transactions. Transactions that affect shareholders' equity are identified by type so that similar types may later be grouped together in financial statements.

Purchase of Assets with Cash

After a good location is found, the company pays cash to purchase land for 10,000 and a small building on the land for 25,000. This transaction does not change the total assets, liabilities, or shareholders' equity of Shannon Property, but it does change the composition of the company's assets—it decreases Cash and increases Land and Building:

	Assets			=	Shareholders' Equity
					Share Capital
	Cash	Land	Building		
Bal.	50,000				50,000
2.	−35,000	+10,000	+25,000		
Bal.	15,000	10,000	25,000		50,000

50,000

Purchase of Assets by Incurring a Liability

Assets do not always have to be purchased with cash. They may also be purchased on credit, that is, on the basis of an agreement to pay for them later. Suppose the company buys some office supplies for 500 on credit. This transaction increases the assets (Supplies) and increases the liabilities of Shannon Property. This liability is designated by an account called Accounts Payable:

	Assets				=	Liabilities +	Shareholders' Equity
						Accounts Payable	Share Capital
	Cash	Supplies	Land	Building			
Bal.	15,000		10,000	25,000			50,000
3.		+500				+500	
Bal.	15,000	500	10,000	25,000		500	50,000

50,500   50,500

Note that this transaction increases both sides of the accounting equation to 50,500.

Payment of a Liability

If the company later pays 200 of the 500 owed for the supplies, both assets (Cash) and liabilities (Accounts Payable) decrease, but Supplies is unaffected:

	Assets				=	Liabilities +	Shareholders' Equity
						Accounts Payable	Share Capital
	Cash	Supplies	Land	Building			
Bal.	15,000	500	10,000	25,000		500	50,000
4.	−200					−200	
Bal.	14,800	500	10,000	25,000		300	50,000

50,300   50,300

Notice that both sides of the accounting equation are still equal, although now at a total of 50,300.

Revenues

Shannon Property earns revenues in the form of commissions by selling houses for clients. Sometimes these commissions are paid to Shannon Property immediately in the form of cash, and sometimes the client agrees to pay the commission later. In either case, the commission is recorded when it is earned and Shannon Property has a right to a current or future receipt of cash. First, assume that Shannon Property sells a house and receives a commission of 1,500 in cash. This transaction increases both assets (Cash) and shareholders' equity (Retained Earnings):

	Assets				= Liabilities +	Shareholders' Equity		
	Cash	Supplies	Land	Building	Accounts Payable	Share Capital	Retained Earnings	Type of SE Transaction
Bal.	14,800	500	10,000	25,000	300	50,000		
5.	+1,500						+1,500	Commissions Earned
Bal.	16,300	500	10,000	25,000	300	50,000	+1,500	
			51,800				51,800	

Now assume that Shannon Property sells a house, in the process earning a commission of 2,000, and agrees to wait for payment of the commission. Because the commission has been earned now, a bill or invoice is sent to the client, and the transaction is recorded now. This revenue transaction increases both assets and shareholders' equity as before, but a new asset account, Accounts Receivable, shows that Shannon Property is awaiting receipt of the commission:

	Assets					= Liabilities +	Shareholders' Equity		
	Cash	Accounts Receivable	Supplies	Land	Building	Accounts Payable	Share Capital	Retained Earnings	Type of SE Transaction
Bal.	16,300		500	10,000	25,000	300	50,000	1,500	
6.		+2,000						+2,000	Commissions Earned
Bal.	16,300	2,000	500	10,000	25,000	300	50,000	3,500	
			53,800					53,800	

The use of separate accounts for revenues, like Commissions Earned, will be introduced in the chapter on measuring business transactions.

Collection of Accounts Receivable

Let us assume that a few days later Shannon Property receives 1,000 from the client in transaction 6. At that time, the asset Cash increases and the asset Accounts Receivable decreases:

	Assets					= Liabilities +	Shareholders' Equity	
	Cash	Accounts Receivable	Supplies	Land	Building	Accounts Payable	Share Capital	Retained Earnings
Bal.	16,300	2,000	500	10,000	25,000	300	50,000	3,500
7.	+1,000	−1,000						
Bal.	17,300	1,000	500	10,000	25,000	300	50,000	3,500
			53,800				53,800	

Notice that this transaction does not affect shareholders' equity because the commission revenue was already recorded in transaction 6. Also, notice that the balance of Accounts Receivable is 1,000, indicating that 1,000 is still to be collected.

Expenses

Just as revenues are recorded when they are earned, expenses are recorded when they are incurred. Expenses can be paid in cash when they occur, or they can be paid later. If payment is going to be made later, a liability—for example, Accounts Payable or Wages Payable—increases. In both cases, shareholders' equity decreases. Assume that Shannon Property pays 1,000 to rent some equipment for the office and 400 in wages to a part-time helper. These transactions reduce assets (Cash) and shareholders' equity (Retained Earnings):

		Assets				= Liabilities +	Shareholders' Equity		
	Cash	Accounts Receivable	Supplies	Land	Building	Accounts Payable	Share Capital	Retained Earnings	Type of SE Transaction
Bal.	17,300	1,000	500	10,000	25,000	300	50,000	3,500	
8.	−1,000							−1,000	Equipment Rental Expense
9.	−400							−400	Wages Expense
Bal.	15,900	1,000	500	10,000	25,000	300	50,000	2,100	
			52,400				52,400		

Now assume that Shannon Property has not paid the 300 bill for electricity expenses incurred for December. In this case, the effect on shareholders' equity is the same as when the expense is paid in cash, but instead of a reduction in assets, there is an increase in liabilities (Accounts Payable):

		Assets				= Liabilities +	Shareholders' Equity		
	Cash	Accounts Receivable	Supplies	Land	Building	Accounts Payable	Share Capital	Retained Earnings	Type of SE Transaction
Bal.	15,900	1,000	500	10,000	25,000	300	50,000	2,100	
10.						+300		−300	Electricity Expense
Bal.	15,900	1,000	500	10,000	25,000	600	50,000	1,800	
			52,400				52,400		

The use of separate accounts for expenses will be introduced in the chapter on measuring business transactions.

Dividends

A dividend of 600 is declared, and it is paid by taking 600 out of the company's bank account and paying it to the shareholders for deposit in their personal bank accounts. The payment of dividends reduces assets (Cash) and shareholders' equity (Retained Earnings). Note that although these dividends reduce retained earnings in the same way as the expenses in transactions 8, 9, and 10, they perform a different function. They are distributions of assets (Cash) to the shareholders, whereas the function of the expenses is to pay for services that helped produce the revenues in transactions 5 and 6.

		Assets				= Liabilities +		Shareholders' Equity	
	Cash	Accounts Receiv- able	Supplies	Land	Building	Accounts Payable	Share Capital	Retained Earnings	Type of SE Transaction
Bal.	15,900	1,000	500	10,000	25,000	600	50,000	1,800	
11.	−600							−600	Dividends
Bal.	15,300	1,000	500	10,000	25,000	600	50,000	1,200	
			51,800					51,800	

Summary

A summary of these eleven illustrative transactions is presented in Exhibit 1-1 (on page 20).

OBJECTIVE 6

Identify the basic financial statements

COMMUNICATION THROUGH FINANCIAL STATEMENTS

Financial statements are the primary means of communicating important accounting information to users. It is helpful to think of these statements as models of the business enterprise because they show the business in financial terms. As is true of all models, however, financial statements are not perfect pictures of the real thing, but rather the accountant's best effort to represent what is real. Three major financial statements are used to communicate accounting information about a business: the income statement, the balance sheet, and the cash flow statement.

Exhibit 1-2 illustrates the relationship among the three financial statements by showing how they would appear for Shannon Property after the eleven sample transactions shown in Exhibit 1-1. It is assumed that the time period covered is the month of December, 20xx. Notice that each statement is headed in a similar way. Each heading identifies the company and the kind of statement. The income statement and the cash flow statement give the time period to which they apply; the balance sheet gives the specific date to which it applies. Much of this book deals with developing, using, and interpreting more complete versions of these basic statements.

The Income Statement

The **income statement** summarises the revenues earned and expenses incurred by a business over a period of time. Many people consider it the most important financial report because it shows whether or not a business achieved its profitability goal of earning an acceptable net profit. In Exhibit 1-2, Shannon Property had revenues in the form of commissions earned of 3,500 (2,000 of revenue earned on credit and 1,500 of cash). From this amount, total expenses of 1,700 were deducted (equipment rental expense of 1,000, wages expense of 400, and electricity expense of 300), to arrive at a net profit of 1,800. To show that it applies to a period of time, the statement is dated "For the Month Ended December 31, 20xx". Deducted from this net profit are the dividends for the month of 600, leaving an ending balance of 1,200 of earnings retained in the business.

The Balance Sheet

The purpose of a **balance sheet** is to show the financial position of a business on a certain date, usually the end of the month or year. For this reason, it often is called the *statement of financial position* and is dated as of a certain date. The balance sheet presents a view of the business as the controller of resources, or assets, that are equal to

EXHIBIT 1-1   *Summary of Effects of Illustrative Transactions on Financial Position*

| | Assets | | | | | = Liabilities + | Shareholders' Equity | | |
	Cash	Accounts Receivable	Supplies	Land	Building	Accounts Payable	Share Capital	Retained Earnings	Type of Shareholders' Equity Transaction
1.	50,000						50,000		Shareholders' Investments
2.	−35,000			+10,000	+25,000				
Bal.	15,000			10,000	25,000		50,000		
3.			+500			+500			
Bal.	15,000		500	10,000	25,000	500	50,000		
4.	−200					−200			
Bal.	14,800		500	10,000	25,000	300	50,000		
5.	+1,500							+1,500	Commissions Earned
Bal.	16,300		500	10,000	25,000	300	50,000	1,500	
6.		+2,000						+2,000	Commissions Earned
Bal.	16,300	2,000	500	10,000	25,000	300	50,000	3,500	
7.	+1,000	−1,000							
Bal.	17,300	1,000	500	10,000	25,000	300	50,000	3,500	
8.	−1,000							−1,000	Equipment Rental Expense
9.	−400							−400	Wages Expense
Bal.	15,900	1,000	500	10,000	25,000	300	50,000	2,100	
10.						+300		−300	Electricity Expense
Bal.	15,900	1,000	500	10,000	25,000	600	50,000	1,800	
11.	−600							−600	Dividends
	15,300	1,000	500	10,000	25,000	600	50,000	1,200	
	51,800					51,800			

EXHIBIT 1-2 *Income Statement, Balance Sheet, and Cash Flow Statement for Shannon Property*

Shannon Property
Income Statement
For the Month Ended December 31, 20xx

Revenues		
Commissions Earned		3,500
Expenses		
Equipment Rental Expense	1,000	
Wages Expense	400	
Electricity Expense	300	
Total Expenses		1,700
Net Profit		**1,800**

Shannon Property
Cash Flow Statement
For the Month Ended December 31, 20xx

Cash Flows from Operating Activities		
Net Profit		1,800
Noncash Expenses and Revenues		
Included in Income		
Increase in Accounts Receivable	(1,000)*	
Increase in Supplies	(500)	
Increase in Accounts Payable	600	(900)
Net Cash Flows from Operating		
Activities		900
Cash Flows from Investing Activities		
Purchase of Land	(10,000)	
Purchase of Building	(25,000)	
Net Cash Flows from		
Investing Activities		(35,000)
Cash Flows from Financing Activities		
Investments by Shareholders	50,000	
Dividends	(600)	
Net Cash Flows from		
Financing Activities		49,400
Net Increase (Decrease) in Cash		**15,300**
Cash at Beginning of Month		0
Cash at End of Month		15,300

Shannon Property
Balance Sheet
December 31, 20xx

Assets		Liabilities	
Cash	15,300	Accounts Payable	600
Accounts			
Receivable	1,000	**Shareholders' Equity**	
Supplies	500		
Land	10,000	Share Capital 50,000	
Building	25,000	**Retained**	
		Earnings 1,200	
		Total Shareholders'	
		Equity	51,200
		Total Liabilities and	
Total Assets	51,800	Shareholders' Equity	51,800

Note: Retained earnings, December 31, 20xx, is calculated as follows:

Retained Earnings, December 1, 20xx	0
Net Profit for the Month	1,800
	1,800
Less Dividends	600
Retained Earnings, December 31, 20xx	1,200

*Parentheses indicate a negative amount.

the claims against those assets. The claims consist of the company's liabilities and the shareholders' equity in the company. In Exhibit 1-2, Shannon Property has several categories of assets, which total 51,800. These assets equal the total liabilities of 600 (Accounts Payable) plus the ending balance of shareholders' equity of 51,200.

The Cash Flow Statement

Whereas the income statement focuses on a company's profitability goal, the **cash flow statement** is directed towards the company's liquidity goal. It shows the cash produced by operating a business as well as important investing and financing transactions that take place during an accounting period. Exhibit 1-2 shows the cash flow statement for Shannon Property. Notice that the statement explains how the Cash account changed during the period. Cash increased by 15,300. Operating activities produced net cash flows of 900, and financing activities produced net cash flows of 49,400. Investment activities used cash flows of 35,000.

This statement is related directly to the other statements. Notice that net profit comes from the income statement. The other items in the statement represent changes in the balance sheet accounts: Accounts Receivable, Supplies, Accounts Payable, Land, Building, Share Capital, and Retained Earnings. Here we focus on the importance and overall structure of the statement. Its construction and use are discussed in detail in the chapter on cash flow statements.

OBJECTIVE 7

State the relationship of accounting standards to financial statements and the independent auditor's report, and identify the factors that influence accounting standards

ACCOUNTING STANDARDS

To ensure that financial statements will be understandable to their users, a set of generally accepted accounting principles (GAAP) comprising criteria, rules, and procedures, and generally called **accounting standards**, has been developed to provide guidelines for financial accounting and reporting.

As we discussed earlier, in the context of identifying the users of accounting information, there are differences in the way in which financial statements are prepared and presented by enterprises around the world. Moreover, in some countries, such as France, Germany, and Japan, accounting standards are set by law, whereas in others, such as Australia, Canada, Sweden, the United Kingdom, and the United States, the accounting profession is much more involved in the standard setting process. For example, in the United States, the Financial Accounting Standards Board (FASB) sets accounting standards which are then enforced by the Securities and Exchange Commission (SEC), which is a government agency responsible for protecting the interests of investors.

The International Accounting Standards Committee (IASC) is seeking to harmonise regulations, accounting standards, and procedures around the world by establishing a set of international accounting standards that everybody can agree to. To date, more than thirty-five International Accounting Standards have been approved. Given that the main purpose of financial statements is to provide information that is useful for making economic decisions, the IASC believes that the needs of most users will be served by these accounting standards. Of course, national standard setters and governments may also wish to specify some different or additional requirements for their own special purposes, but this should not detract from the general need to provide information relevant to economic decision making.

However, accounting standards are not like the unchangeable laws of nature found in chemistry or physics. They are developed by accountants, businesses, and regulators to serve the needs of decision makers, and they can be altered as better methods evolve or as circumstances change.

In this book, we present the essentials of accounting practice based on international accounting standards. We also try to explain the reasons or theory on which the practice is based and adopt a global perspective which recognises different countries' practices where relevant. Both theory and practice are part and parcel of the study of accounting. However, you should realise that accounting is a discipline that is always growing, changing, and improving. Just as years of research are necessary before a new surgical method or lifesaving drug can be introduced, it may take years for research and new discoveries in accounting to become common practice. As a result, you may come across practices that seem contradictory. In some cases, we point out new directions in accounting. Your teacher also may mention certain weaknesses in current theory or practice.

Financial Statements, Accounting Standards, and the Independent Auditor's Report

Because financial statements are prepared by the management of a company and could be falsified for personal gain, all companies that sell shares to the public and many companies that apply for sizeable loans have their financial statements audited by an independent accountant. These independent accountants, often described as **certified public accountants (CPAs)** or **chartered accountants (CAs)**, are licensed for the same reason that lawyers and doctors are—to protect the public by ensuring the quality of professional service. One important attribute of CPAs or CAs is independence: they have no financial or other compromising ties with the companies they audit. This gives the public confidence in their work. The firms listed in Table 1-3 are the world's largest accounting firms, with activities which include not only auditing but also tax advice and management consultancy.

An independent auditor conducts an **audit**, which is an examination of a company's financial statements and the accounting systems, controls, and records that produced them. The purpose of the audit is to ascertain that the financial statements have been prepared in accordance with accounting standards and show a true and fair view. If the independent accountant is satisfied that the standards have been met, his or her report will contain an opinion to that effect.

However, accounting and auditing are not exact sciences. The application of accounting standards necessitates the making of estimates. Hence the auditor can render an opinion or judgement only on the financial statements. The accountant's report does not preclude minor or immaterial errors in the financial statements. It does imply, though, that on the whole, investors and lenders can rely on those statements. Historically, auditors have enjoyed a strong reputation for competence and independence. As a result, banks, investors, and lenders are willing to rely on an

TABLE 1-3 *Global Accounting Firms*

	Global Revenue (in $ Millions) (1996)	% Change over 1995	U.S. Revenue (in $ Millions) (1996)	% Change over 1995
Andersen Worldwide	9,500	16.8	4,511	16.9
KPMG Peat Marwick	7,450	8.0	2,310	10.4
Ernst & Young	7,760	13.0	3,571	20.1
Coopers & Lybrand	6,600	9.7	2,115	11.1
Deloitte & Touche	6,500	9.5	2,925	13.8
Price Waterhouse	5,020	12.6	2,016	13.9

Reprinted by special permission of *Public Accounting Report.* Copyright 1995 by Strafford Publications, Inc., Postal Drawer 13729, Atlanta, GA 30324-0729. 404/881-1141.

auditor's opinion when deciding to invest in a company or to make loans to a firm that has been audited. The independent audit is an important factor in the worldwide growth of financial markets.

Factors That Influence Accounting Standards

While a variety of economic, social, political, legal, and cultural factors influence the formulation of accounting standards, the most important factors would seem to be the enterprise's sources of finance and the nature of capital markets, taxation, the accounting profession, the nature of accounting regulation, national cultures and traditions, and international economic and political relationships (see Figure 1-6).

Sources of Finance and Capital Markets

The sources of finance for an enterprise exert an important influence because the more capital that is raised from the public or external shareholders the more pressure there will be for public accountability and information disclosure. This is the case especially in countries such as the United States and the United Kingdom where stock markets are highly developed and substantial numbers of corporations are owned by a broad base of shareholders. In this way, investor interests have been perceived by management to be significant and have become the predominant influence on financial statements. In contrast, banks are a much more important source of finance in countries such as Germany, Japan, and Switzerland, and hence their concerns have tended to influence the preparation of financial statements more than those of investors.

Taxation

Another major influence on accounting standards is taxation, such as in France, Germany, and Japan, where the financial statements of business enterprises prepared

FIGURE 1-6   *Factors That Influence Accounting Standards*

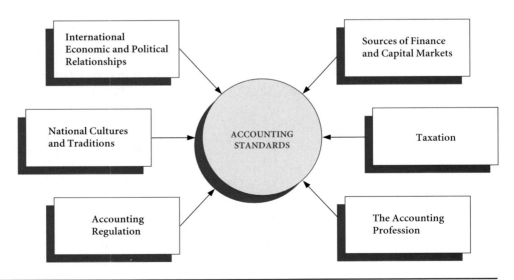

for shareholders are also used as the basis of taxation, irrespective of the size and ownership of business. Not surprisingly, the tax rules have tended to dominate the preparation of financial statements. In the United States, the United Kingdom, Canada, and Australia, however, the published accounting reports are adjusted to comply with the tax rules and submitted separately from the reports to shareholders.

The Accounting Profession

Where there is a more developed accounting profession, there tends to be a more business and decision-making oriented accounting system in place, such as in North America and western Europe. This can be contrasted with the more government-controlled, centralised, and uniform systems that have been the historical experience, for example, of Russia, China, and other emerging economies. Where accounting judgements as a basis for economic decision making are required, the need for professional accountants and their influence on accounting standards tend to be high.

Accounting Regulation

The nature of accounting regulation is an important influence on accounting standards and is linked to the status of the accounting profession. Where the accounting profession has a high status because it is perceived to contribute to better business decision making, such as in the Anglo-Saxon countries, accountants tend to have more influence in the development of accounting regulation. On the other hand, where government concerns and company law are more influential, such as in France and Germany, more emphasis is placed on detailed and uniform rules and regulations to determine accounting standards. In Europe, the company law harmonisation programme of the EU has meant that legal rules have become relatively more important in setting accounting standards in recent years. However, the accounting profession in the form of the International Accounting Standards Committee (IASC) is now leading the process of international accounting harmonisation as more countries have recognised the importance of financial statements for decision-making purposes and the useful role that accountants can play in this process.

National Cultures and Traditions

A major influence on accounting standards is national culture. Culture means the values and attitudes which are widely held in a society or by groups in a society, such as accountants. While accountants around the world have many similarities, they tend to have different approaches to the measurement of assets and to the disclosure of information about business activities. In Figure 1-7 the accounting practices of some groups of countries are shown in a very generalised way in terms of cultural tendencies to be more or less cautious in the practice of accounting measurement and more or less transparent in the disclosure of information to the public. These cultural tendencies are ways of accounting which have developed over many years and which have become the accounting tradition of a country.

While accountants are inherently conservative, some are more so than others. Accountants in countries such as Germany and Japan tend to be more cautious in recognising profit and the value of assets, reflecting the interests of lenders, in contrast to the more optimistic approach of the United Kingdom and the United States in reporting results to shareholders.

As regards information disclosure, countries such as Germany, Japan, and Switzerland tend to have less disclosure, reflecting their traditional value of secrecy compared to the Anglo-Saxon countries which are more transparent in response to external shareholder and market pressures.

FIGURE 1-7   *Cultural Influences on Accounting Standards*

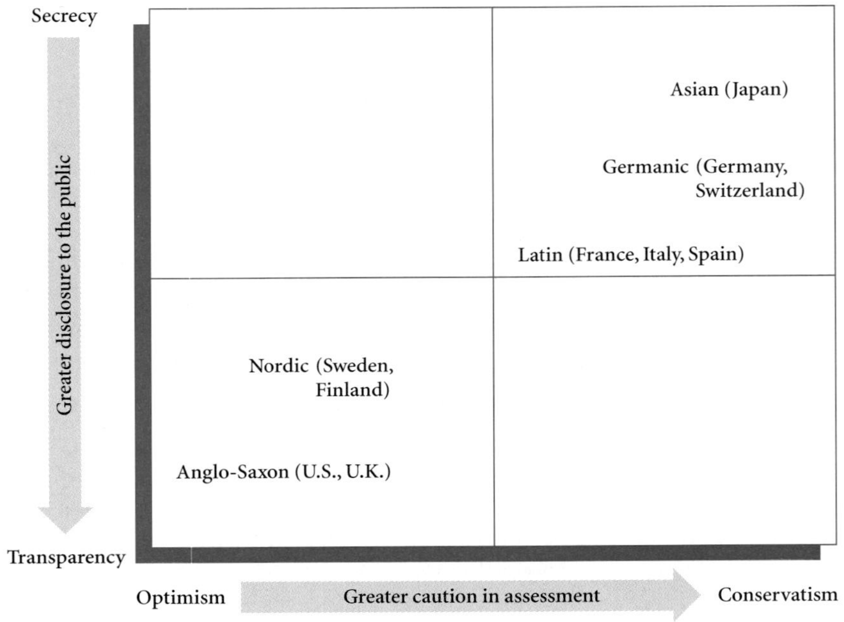

Source: Adapted from S. J. Gray, "Towards a Theory of Cultural Influence on the Development of Accounting Systems International", *Abacus* (March 1988), p. 12.

International Economic and Political Relationships

In Malaysia and Singapore, International Accounting Standards are usually adopted as the basis for local accounting standards. In Malta, company law now requires International Accounting Standards to be followed in preparing company financial statements.

Accounting traditions have developed over long periods of time and, in many countries such as in Africa and Asia, have incorporated influences arising from periods of colonisation and war. These traditions are now changing because of the growing internationalisation of economic and political relationships around the world. The formation of economic groupings such as the European Union (EU), the North American Free Trade Agreement (NAFTA), and the Asia Pacific Economic Cooperation Forum (APEC) coupled with dramatic political changes in Russia and Eastern Europe, China, South America, and Africa have resulted in tremendous increases in international trade and foreign direct investment. New stock markets have sprung up in many countries, and existing markets have been developing rapidly in response to deregulation, privatisation, and the internationalisation of finance and investment. Accounting reports in a cross-border context have become more important, together with the need to promote better international financial understanding. It is in this context that the International Accounting Standards Committee (IASC) is seeking to harmonise accounting standards so that financial statements prepared and presented by companies will be acceptable and understood everywhere in the world irrespective of their country of origin. It is the purpose of this book to contribute to this process of developing a common understanding of accounting and financial statements for decision-making purposes.

OBJECTIVE 8

Define ethics and describe the ethical responsibilities of accountants

PROFESSIONAL ETHICS AND THE ACCOUNTING PROFESSION

Ethics is a code of conduct that applies to everyday life. It addresses the question of whether actions are right or wrong. Ethical actions are the product of individual decisions. You are faced with many ethical situations every day. Some may be potentially illegal—the temptation to take office supplies from your employer to use at home, for example. Others are not illegal but are equally unethical—for example, deciding not to tell a fellow student who missed class that a test has been announced for the next class meeting. When an organisation is said to act ethically or unethically, it means that individuals within the organisation have made a decision to act ethically or unethically. When a company uses false advertising, cheats customers, pollutes the environment, treats employees poorly, or misleads investors by presenting false financial statements, members of management and other employees have made a conscious decision to act unethically. In the same way, ethical behavior within a company is a direct result of the actions and decisions of the company's employees.

Professional ethics is a code of conduct that applies to the practice of a profession. Like the ethical conduct of a company, the ethical actions of a profession are a collection of individual actions. As members of a profession, accountants have a responsibility, not only to their employers and clients but to society as a whole, to uphold the highest ethical standards. It is the responsibility of every person who becomes an accountant to uphold the high standards of the profession, regardless of the field of accounting the individual enters.

To ensure that its members understand the responsibilities of being professional accountants, the professional bodies of most countries have adopted codes of professional conduct that must be followed by independent accountants. Fundamental to these codes is responsibility to the public, including clients, lenders, investors, and anyone else who relies on the work of the accountant. In resolving conflicts among these groups, the accountant must act with integrity, even to the sacrifice of personal benefit. **Integrity** means that the accountant is honest and candid, and subordinates personal gain to service and the public trust. The accountant must also be objective. **Objectivity** means that he or she is impartial and intellectually honest. Naturally, the accountant must be independent. **Independence** means avoiding all relationships that impair or even appear to impair the accountant's objectivity. One way in which the auditor of a company maintains independence is by having no direct financial interest in the company and not being an employee of the company. The accountant must exercise **due care** in all activities, carrying out professional responsibilities with competence and diligence. For example, an accountant must not accept a job for which he or she is not qualified, even at the risk of losing a client to another firm, and careless work is not acceptable.

Management accountants also have ethical responsibilities: to be competent in their jobs, to keep information confidential except when authorised or legally required to disclose it, to maintain integrity and avoid conflicts of interest, and to communicate information objectively and without bias.

CHAPTER REVIEW

Review of Learning Objectives

1. **Define *accounting*, identify business goals and activities, and describe the role of accounting in making informed decisions.** Accounting is an information system that measures, processes, and communicates information, primarily financial in nature, about an enterprise for the purpose of making economic decisions. Management accounting focuses on the preparation of information primarily for internal use by management. Financial accounting is concerned with the development and use of accounting reports that are communicated to those external to the business organisation as well as to management. Accounting is not an end in itself but a tool that provides the information that is necessary to make reasoned choices among alternative uses of scarce resources in the conduct of business and economic activities.

2. **Identify the many users of accounting information in society.** Accounting plays a significant role in society by providing information to managers and to a variety of interested parties including investors, employees, lenders, suppliers and other trade creditors, customers, governments and their agencies, and the public.

3. **Explain the importance of business transactions, money measure, and separate entity to accounting measurement.** To make an accounting measurement, the accountant must determine what is measured, when the measurement should be made, what value should be placed on what is measured, and how what is measured should be classified. Accounting standards define the objects of accounting measurement as business transactions, money measure, and separate entities.

Relating these three concepts, financial accounting uses money measure to gauge the impact of business transactions on a separate business entity.

4. **Describe the corporate form of business organisation.** Corporations, whose ownership is represented by shares, are separate entities for both legal and accounting purposes. The shareholders own the corporation and elect the board of directors, whose duty it is to determine corporate policy. The corporate officers or management of the corporation are appointed by the board of directors and are responsible for the operation of the business in accordance with the board's policies.

5. **Define *financial position*, state the accounting equation, and show how they are affected by simple transactions.** Financial position is the economic resources that are controlled by a company and the claims against those resources at a point in time. The accounting equation shows financial position in the equation form Assets = liabilities + owners' equity. For a corporation, the accounting equation is Assets = liabilities + shareholders' equity. Business transactions affect financial position by decreasing or increasing assets, liabilities, or shareholders' equity in such a way that the accounting equation is always in balance.

6. **Identify the basic financial statements.** Financial statements are the means by which accountants communicate the finan-cial condition and activities of a business to those who have an interest in the business. The basic financial statements are the income statement, the balance sheet, and the cash flow statement.

7. **State the relationship of accounting standards to financial statements and the independent auditor's report, and identify the factors that influence accounting standards.** Acceptable accounting practice consists of those criteria, rules, and procedures that comprise accounting standards at a particular time. Accounting standards are essential to the preparation and interpretation of financial statements and the indepen-dent auditor's report. Among the factors that influence the formulation of accounting standards are the sources of finance and the nature of capital markets, taxation, the accounting profession, the nature of accounting regulation, national cul-tures and traditions, and international economic and political relationships.

8. **Define *ethics* and describe the ethical responsibilities of accountants.** All accountants are required to follow a code of professional ethics, the foundation of which is responsibility to the public. Accountants must act with integrity, objectivity, and independence, and they must exercise due care in all their activities.

Review of Concepts and Terminology

The following concepts and terms were introduced in this chapter.

LO 1   *Accounting:* An information system that measures, processes, and communicates financial information about an enterprise.

LO 5   *Accounting equation:* Assets = liabilities + owners' equity or, for corporations, Assets = liabilities + share-holders' equity.

LO 7   *Accounting standards:* The rules and procedures that define accepted accounting practice at a particular time.

LO 5   *Accounts:* The labels used by accountants to accumulate the amounts produced from similar transactions.

LO 4   *Articles of incorporation:* An official document filed with and approved by a government that authorises the incor-porators to do business as a corporation.

LO 5   *Assets:* Economic resources controlled by a business that are expected to benefit future operations.

LO 7   *Audit:* An examination of a company's financial state-ments in order to render an independent professional opinion that they have been presented fairly, or show a true and fair view, and have been prepared in conformity with accounting standards.

LO 4   *Audit committee:* A subgroup of the board of directors of a corporation that is charged with ensuring that the board will be objective in reviewing management's performance; it engages the company's independent auditors and reviews their work.

LO 6   *Balance sheet:* The financial statement that shows the assets, liabilities, and shareholders' equity of a business at a point in time. Also called a *statement of financial position*.

LO 1   *Bookkeeping:* The process of recording financial transac-tions and keeping financial records.

LO 1   *Business:* An economic unit that aims to sell goods and services to customers at prices that will provide an ade-quate return to its owners.

LO 3   *Business transactions:* Economic events that affect the financial position of a business entity.

LO 6   *Cash flow statement:* The financial statement that shows the inflows and outflows of cash from operating activities, investing activities, and financing activities over a period of time.

LO 7   *Certified public accountants (CPAs)/chartered accoun-tants (CAs):* Public accountants who have met the strin-gent licensing requirements set by individual countries.

LO 1   *Computer:* An electronic tool for the rapid collection, organisation, and communication of large amounts of information.

LO 4   *Corporation/company:* A business unit granted a charter recognising it as a separate legal entity having its own rights, privileges, and liabilities distinct from those of its owners.

LO 2   *Customers:* The people who purchase a company's goods and services.

LO 5   *Dividends:* Distributions to shareholders of assets (usually cash) generated by past earnings.

LO 8   *Due care:* The act of carrying out professional responsibil-ities competently and diligently.

LO 2   *Employees:* The people who work in a business.

LO 1   *Enterprise:* Any commercial, industrial, or business entity, whether in the public or private sector.

LO 8   *Ethics:* A code of conduct that addresses whether everyday actions are right or wrong.

LO 3   *Exchange rate:* The value of one currency in terms of another.

LO 5   *Expenses:* Decreases in shareholders' equity that result from operating a business.

LO 1   *Financial accounting:* The process of generating and communicating accounting information in the form of financial statements.

LO 5   *Financial position:* The economic resources that are controlled by a company and the claims against those resources at a point in time.

LO 1   *Financial statements:* The primary means of communicating accounting information to users. They include the income statement, balance sheet, and cash flow statement.

LO 1   *Financing activities:* Activities undertaken by management to obtain adequate funds to begin, and continue, operating a business.

LO 2   *Governments and their agencies:* The people concerned with the allocation of resources and economic policy, taxation, and regulation.

LO 6   *Income statement:* The financial statement that summarises the revenues earned and expenses incurred by a business over a period of time.

LO 8   *Independence:* The avoidance of all relationships that impair or appear to impair an accountant's objectivity.

LO 8   *Integrity:* Honesty, candidness, and the subordination of personal gain to service and the public trust.

LO 1   *International Accounting Standards Committee (IASC):* The organisation of professional accounting bodies that is formulating and promoting the worldwide acceptance and observance of international accounting standards; it has approved more than thirty-five international accounting standards.

LO 1   *Investing activities:* Activities undertaken by management to spend the capital received in such a way that the money will be productive and helpful in achieving the business's objectives.

LO 2   *Investors:* The owners, or potential owners, of the business who have provided the capital at risk.

LO 2   *Lenders:* The people, including banks, who lend money for both short-term and long-term operating needs.

LO 5   *Liabilities:* Present obligations of a business to pay cash, transfer assets, or provide services to other entities in the future.

LO 1   *Liquidity:* Having enough funds available to pay debts when they are due.

LO 2   *Management:* The people who have overall responsibility for operating a business and meeting its goals.

LO 1   *Management accounting:* The process of producing accounting information for the internal use of a company's management.

LO 1   *Management information system (MIS):* The interconnected subsystems that provide the information needed to run a business.

LO 3   *Money measure:* The recording of all business transactions in terms of money.

LO 5   *Net assets:* Shareholders' equity, or assets minus liabilities.

LO 5   *Net profit:* The difference between revenues and expenses when revenues exceed expenses.

LO 5   *Net loss:* The difference between expenses and revenues when expenses exceed revenues.

LO 8   *Objectivity:* Impartiality and intellectual honesty.

LO 1   *Operating activities:* Activities undertaken by management in the course of running the business.

LO 5   *Owners' equity:* The residual interest in the assets of a business entity that remains after deducting the entity's liabilities. Also called *residual equity* or, for corporations, *shareholders' equity.*

LO 4   *Partnership:* A business owned by two or more people.

LO 8   *Professional ethics:* A code of conduct that applies to the practice of a profession.

LO 1   *Profitability:* The ability to earn enough income to attract and hold investment capital.

LO 2   *Public:* The people affected by enterprise activities including the development of roads, housing, the environment, communications, and so on.

LO 5   *Retained earnings:* The equity of the shareholders generated from the income-producing activities of the business and kept for use in the business.

LO 5   *Revenues:* Increases in shareholders' equity that result from operating a business.

LO 3   *Separate entity:* A business that is treated as distinct from its lenders, customers, and owners.

LO 4   *Share:* A unit of ownership in a corporation.

LO 5   *Share capital:* The part of shareholders' equity that represents the amount invested in the business by the owners (shareholders).

LO 5   *Shareholders' equity:* The owners' equity of a corporation, consisting of share capital and retained earnings.

LO 4   *Sole proprietorship:* A business owned by one person.

LO 2   *Suppliers and other trade creditors:* The people who supply goods and services for cash or credit.

Review Problem

The Effect of Transactions on the Accounting Equation

LO 5   Sonja Rudek finished business school in June and immediately set up her own management consultancy practice. During the first month of operation, she completed the following transactions:

a. Began the business by exchanging 2,000 cash for 1,000 shares in the company.
b. Purchased a business library for 900 cash.
c. Purchased office supplies for 400 on credit.
d. Accepted 500 in cash for completing a contract.
e. Billed clients 1,950 for services rendered during the month.
f. Paid 200 of the amount owed for office supplies.
g. Received 1,250 in cash from one client who had been billed for services rendered.
h. Paid rent expense for the month in the amount of 1,200.
i. Declared and paid a dividend of 400.

REQUIRED   Show the effect of each of these transactions on the balance sheet equation by completing a table similar to Exhibit 1-1. Identify each shareholders' equity transaction.

Answer to Review Problem

	Cash	Accounts Receivable	Office Supplies	Business Library	Accounts Payable	Share Capital	Retained Earnings	Type of SE Transaction
		Assets			= Liabilities +	Shareholders' Equity (SE)		
a.	2,000					2,000		Shareholders' Investment
b.	−900			+900				
bal.	1,100			900		2,000		
c.			+400		+400			
bal.	1,100		400	900	400	2,000		
d.	+500						+500	Service Revenue
bal.	1,600		400	900	400	2,000	500	
e.		+1,950					+1,950	Service Revenue
bal.	1,600	1,950	400	900	400	2,000	2,450	
f.	−200				−200			
bal.	1,400	1,950	400	900	200	2,000	2,450	
g.	+1,250	−1,250						
bal.	2,650	700	400	900	200	2,000	2,450	
h.	−1,200						−1,200	Rent Expense
bal.	1,450	700	400	900	200	2,000	1,250	
i.	−400						−400	Dividends
bal.	1,050	700	400	900	200	2,000	850	

3,050   =   3,050

CHAPTER ASSIGNMENTS

Knowledge and Understanding

Questions

1. Why is accounting considered an information system?
2. What is the role of accounting in the decision-making process?
3. Distinguish between management accounting and financial accounting.
4. Distinguish among these terms: *accounting, bookkeeping,* and *management information systems.*
5. Which decision makers use accounting information?
6. A business is an economic unit whose goal is to sell goods and services to customers at prices that will provide an adequate return to the business owners. What functions must management perform to achieve that goal?
7. Why are investors interested in reviewing the financial statements of a company?
8. Apart from management many people and organisations have an interest in the business entity. Briefly describe them.
9. Why has society as a whole become one of the largest users of accounting information?
10. Use the terms *business transaction, money measure,* and *separate entity* in a single sentence that demonstrates their relevance to financial accounting.
11. How do sole proprietorships, partnerships, and corporations differ?
12. In a corporation, what are the functions of shareholders, the board of directors, and management?

13. Define *assets, liabilities,* and *shareholders' equity.*
14. Arnold Smith's corporation has assets of 22,000 and liabilities of 10,000. What is the amount of the shareholders' equity?
15. What three elements affect retained earnings? How?
16. Give examples of the types of transactions that (a) increase assets and (b) increase liabilities.
17. Why is the balance sheet sometimes called the statement of financial position?
18. Contrast the purpose of the balance sheet with that of the income statement.
19. A statement for an accounting period that ends in June can be headed "June 30, 20xx" or "For the Year Ended June 30, 20xx". Which heading is appropriate for (a) a balance sheet and (b) an income statement?
20. How does the income statement differ from the cash flow statement?
21. What are accounting standards? Why are they important to the users of financial statements?
22. What is the significance of "international" accounting standards?
23. Why are auditors important?
24. What factors most influence accounting standards?
25. Discuss the importance of professional ethics in the accounting profession.

Application

Exercises

LO 1 *Accounting*
LO 2 *Terminology*
LO 7

E 1-1. Indicate the IASC term and its North American or British origin for the following accounting terms:

	IASC	Origin
1. Financial statements	_____	_____
2. Profit and loss account	_____	_____
3. Turnover	_____	_____
4. Balance sheet	_____	_____
5. Net income	_____	_____
6. Stocks	_____	_____
7. Payables	_____	_____
8. Stockholders	_____	_____
9. Shares	_____	_____
10. Common stock	_____	_____

LO 3 *Business Transactions*

E 1-2. Theresa owns and operates a general store. State which of the actions below are business transactions. Explain why any other actions are not regarded as transactions.

1. Theresa reduces the price of a gallon of milk to match the price offered by a competitor.
2. Theresa pays a high school student cash for cleaning up the driveway behind the store.
3. Theresa fills her son's car with gasoline in payment for restocking the vending machines and the snack food shelves.
4. Theresa pays interest to herself on a loan she made three years ago to the business.

LO 3 *Accounting Concepts*
LO 4

E 1-3. Financial accounting uses money measures to gauge the impact of business transactions on a separate business entity. State whether each of the following words or phrases relates most closely to (a) a business transaction, (b) a separate entity, or (c) a money measure.

1. Corporation
2. Mexican peso
3. Sale of products
4. Receipt of cash
5. Sole proprietorship
6. U.S. dollar
7. Partnership
8. Shareholders' investments
9. Japanese yen
10. Purchase of supplies

LO 3 *Money Measure*

E 1-4. You have been asked to compare the sales and assets of four companies that make computer chips in order to determine which company is the largest in each category. You have gathered the following data, but they cannot be used for direct comparison because each company's sales and assets are in its own currency:

Company (Currency)	Sales	Assets
Inchip (U.S. dollar)	20,000,000	13,000,000
Britchip (British pound)	38,000,000	25,000,000
Mitzu (Japanese yen)	3,500,000,000	2,500,000,000
Works (German mark)	35,000,000	39,000,000

Assuming that the exchange rates in Table 1-2 are current and appropriate, convert all the figures to U.S. dollars and determine which company is the largest in sales and which is the largest in assets.

LO 5 *The Accounting Equation*

E 1-5. Use the accounting equation to answer each question below. Show any calculations you make.

1. The assets of Newport Corporation are 650,000, and the shareholders' equity is 360,000. What is the amount of the liabilities?
2. The liabilities and shareholders' equity of Fitzgerald Corporation are 95,000 and 32,000, respectively. What is the amount of the assets?
3. The liabilities of Emerald Corporation equal one-third of the total assets, and shareholders' equity is 120,000. What is the amount of the liabilities?
4. At the beginning of the year, Pickett Corporation's assets were 220,000 and its shareholders' equity was 100,000. During the year, assets increased 60,000 and liabilities decreased 10,000. What is the shareholders' equity at the end of the year?

E 1-6.

LO 5 *Effect of Transactions on the Accounting Equation*

During the month of April, Andres Corporation had the following transactions:

a. Paid salaries for April, 5,400.
b. Purchased equipment on credit, 9,000.
c. Purchased supplies with cash, 300.
d. Additional investment by shareholders, 12,000.
e. Received payment for services performed, 1,800.
f. Made partial payment on equipment purchased in transaction **b**, 3,000.
g. Billed customers for services performed, 4,800.
h. Received payment from customers billed in transaction **g**, 900.
i. Received electricity bill, 210.
j. Approved and paid dividends of 4,500.

On a sheet of paper, list the letters **a** through **j**, with columns labelled Assets, Liabilities, and Shareholders' Equity. In the columns, indicate whether each transaction caused an increase (+), a decrease (−), or no change (NC) in assets, liabilities, and shareholders' equity.

E 1-7.

LO 5 *Effect of Transactions on the Accounting Equation*

The total assets and liabilities at the beginning and end of the year for Pizarro Company are listed below.

	Assets	Liabilities
Beginning of the year	110,000	45,000
End of the year	200,000	120,000

Determine Pizarro Company's net profit for the year under each of the following alternatives:

1. The shareholders made no investments in the business, and no dividends were paid during the year.
2. The shareholders made no investments in the business, but dividends of 22,000 were paid during the year.
3. The shareholders made investments of 13,000, but no dividends were paid during the year.
4. The shareholders made investments of 10,000 in the business, and dividends of 22,000 were paid during the year.

E 1-8.

LO 5 *Identification of Accounts*
LO 6

1. Indicate whether each of the following accounts is an asset (A), a liability (L), or a part of shareholders' equity (SE).

   a. Cash   e. Land
   b. Salaries Payable   f. Accounts Payable
   c. Accounts Receivable   g. Supplies
   d. Share Capital

2. Indicate whether each account would be shown on the income statement (IS) or the balance sheet (BS).

   a. Repair Revenue   d. Cash
   b. Car   e. Rent Expense
   c. Fuel Expense   f. Accounts Payable

E 1-9.

LO 6 *Preparation of a Balance Sheet*

Listed in random order below are the balance sheet figures for the Glick Company as of June 30, 20xx.

Accounts Payable	20,000
Building	45,000
Share Capital	50,000
Supplies	5,000
Accounts Receivable	25,000
Cash	10,000
Equipment	20,000
Retained Earnings	35,000

Sort the balances and prepare a balance sheet similar to the one in Exhibit 1-2.

E 1-10.

LO 6 *Preparation of Financial Statements*

Strickland Corporation engaged in the following activities during the year: Service Revenue, 52,800; Rent Expense, 4,800; Wages Expense, 33,080; Advertising Expense, 5,400; Electricity Expense, 3,600; and Dividends, 2,800. In addition, the year-end balances of selected accounts were as follows: Cash, 6,200; Accounts Receivable, 3,000; Supplies, 400; Land, 4,000; Accounts Payable, 1,800; and Share Capital, 4,000.

Prepare the income statement and balance sheet for Strickland Corporation (assume the year ends on June 30, 20x2). (**Note:** You must solve for the year-end balances of retained earnings for 20x1 and 20x2.)

E 1-11.

LO 6 *Revenues, Expenses, and Cash Flows*

Sheila, a lawyer, bills her clients at a rate of 100 per hour. During July, she worked 150 hours for clients and billed them appropriately. By the end of July, 80 of these hours remained unpaid. At the beginning of the month, clients owed Sheila 8,000, of which 5,600 was paid during July.

Sheila has one employee, a secretary who is paid 20 per hour. During July, the secretary worked 170 hours, of which 16 hours were to be paid in August. The rest were paid in July. Also, during July, Sheila paid the secretary for 8 hours worked in June.

Determine for the month of July: (1) the amount of revenue from clients, (2) wages expense for the secretary, (3) cash received from clients, and (4) cash paid to the secretary.

E 1-12.

LO 6 *Cash Flow Statement*

Diamond Corporation began the year 20xx with cash of 86,000. In addition to earning a net profit of 50,000 and paying cash dividends of 30,000, Diamond borrowed 120,000 from the bank and purchased equipment for 180,000 with cash. Also, Accounts Receivable increased by 12,000 and Accounts Payable increased by 18,000.

Determine the amount of cash available at December 31, 20xx, by preparing a cash flow statement similar to the one in Exhibit 1-2.

Problem Set

P 1-1.

LO 5 *Effect of Transactions on the Accounting Equation*

The Creative Frames Shop was started by Rosa Partridge in a small shopping centre. In the first weeks of operation, she completed the following transactions:

a. Deposited 21,000 in cash in the name of the company, in exchange for 2,100 shares of the corporation.
b. Paid the current month's rent, 1,500.
c. Purchased store equipment on credit, 10,800.
d. Purchased framing supplies for cash, 5,100.
e. Received framing revenues, 2,400.
f. Billed customers for services, 2,100.
g. Paid electricity expense, 750.
h. Received payment from customers in transaction **f**, 600.
i. Made payment on store equipment purchased in transaction **c**, 5,400.
j. Approved and paid dividends of 1,200.

REQUIRED

1. Arrange the following asset, liability, and shareholders' equity accounts in an equation similar to Exhibit 1-1: Cash, Accounts Receivable, Framing Supplies, Store Equipment, Accounts Payable, Share Capital, and Retained Earnings.
2. Show by addition and subtraction, as in Exhibit 1-1, the effects of the transactions on the accounting equation. Show new balances after each transaction, and identify each shareholders' equity transaction by type.

P 1-2.

LO 5 *Effect of Transactions on the Accounting Equation*

The Quality Courier Corporation was founded by Johnny Hui on March 1 and engaged in the following transactions:

a. Deposited 12,000 in cash in the name of Quality Courier Corporation, in exchange for 12,000 shares of the corporation.
b. Purchased a motorbike on credit, 3,200.
c. Purchased delivery supplies for cash, 400.
d. Billed a customer for a delivery, 200.
e. Received delivery fees in cash, 600.
f. Made a payment on the motorbike, 1,400.
g. Paid repair expense, 240.
h. Received payment from customer billed in transaction **d**, 100.
i. Declared and paid dividends of 300.

REQUIRED

1. Arrange the following asset, liability, and shareholders' equity accounts in an equation similar to Exhibit 1-1: Cash, Accounts Receivable, Delivery Supplies, Motorbike, Accounts Payable, Share Capital, and Retained Earnings.
2. Show by addition and subtraction, as in Exhibit 1-1, the effects of the transactions on the accounting equation. Show new balances after each transaction, and identify each shareholders' equity transaction by type.

P 1-3.

LO 6 *Preparation of Financial Statements*

At the end of its first month of operation, March 20xx, Ellis Plumbing Corporation had the following account balances:

Cash	58,600
Accounts Receivable	10,800
Delivery Truck	38,000
Tools	7,600
Accounts Payable	8,600

In addition, during the month of March, the following transactions affected shareholders' equity:

Initial investment by J. Ellis	40,000
Further investment by J. Ellis	60,000
Contract revenue	23,200
Repair revenue	5,600
Salaries expense	16,600
Rent expense	1,400
Fuel expense	400
Dividends	4,000

REQUIRED

Using Exhibit 1-2 as a model, prepare an income statement and a balance sheet for Ellis Plumbing Corporation. (**Note:** The final balance of Shareholders' Equity is 106,400.)

P 1-4.

LO 5
LO 6 *Effect of Transactions on the Accounting Equation and Preparation of Financial Statements*

Arrow Copying Service began operations and engaged in these transactions during August 20xx:

a. Myra Lomax deposited 10,000 in cash in the name of the corporation, in exchange for 1,000 shares of the corporation.
b. Paid current month's rent, 900.
c. Purchased copier for cash, 5,000.
d. Copying job payments received in cash, 1;780.
e. Copying job billed to major customer, 1,360.
f. Paid cash for paper and other copier supplies, 380.
g. Paid wages to part-time employees, 560.
h. Purchased additional copier supplies on credit, 280.
i. Received partial payment from customer in transaction **e**, 600.
j. Paid current month's electricity bill, 180.
k. Made partial payment on supplies purchased in transaction **h**, 140.
l. Declared and paid dividends of 1,400.

REQUIRED

1. Arrange the asset, liability, and shareholders' equity accounts in an equation similar to Exhibit 1-1, using these account titles: Cash, Accounts Receivable, Supplies, Copier, Accounts Payable, Share Capital, and Retained Earnings.
2. Show by addition and subtraction, as in Exhibit 1-1, the effects of the transactions on the accounting equation. Show new balances after each transaction, and identify each shareholders' equity transaction by type.
3. Using Exhibit 1-2 as a guide, prepare an income statement and a balance sheet for Arrow Copying Service.

Critical Thinking and Communication

Conceptual Mini-Case

CMC 1-1.

LO 2 *Concept of an Asset*
LO 5

Club Méditerranée, a French company, is the world's leading vacation village operator. It has facilities on five continents serving 1.4 million customers from around the world. A staff of 25,000, composed of resort professionals, called "Gentils Organisateurs" or G.O.'s, and service employees, runs Club Med's exceptional locations. In a recent annual report the Chairman, Serge Trigano, states:

> While many have copied or tried to copy tangible aspects of our business—such as all-inclusive holidays, buffet meal service or mini-clubs—none has been able to reproduce our intangible advantages—the unique human qualities of our resort staffs, the club's spirit of conviviality, cheerfulness and generosity. These are the values that in the future will increasingly distinguish Club Med from its competition. Whether working at resort villages or in administrative offices, our teams are stronger and more professional than ever. They are eager to compete, to succeed, and to attract customers. It is now up to us to capitalise on these assets.[4]

Are employees normally considered assets in financial statements? Discuss the importance of employees as Club Med assets. How can financial statements be useful to employees?

Cultural Mini-Case

CLMC 1-1.

LO 1 *International Accounting*
LO 2 *Terminology*

In setting international accounting standards, the IASC has adopted the English language for official purposes. However, the terminology used is a mixture of North American and British terminology. From the condensed balance sheet of **British Petroleum** given below, restate the terms numbered 1–7 into those generally followed by the IASC.

British Petroleum
Consolidated Balance Sheet as at December 31, 1995

	£Million
1. Fixed Assets	
Intangible Assets	878
Tangible Assets	19,538
Investments	2,193
	22,609
Current Assets	
2. Stocks	2,814
3. Debtors	6,534
Investments	101
Cash	294
	9,743
Creditors—amounts falling due within one year	
4. Finance Debt	738
5. Other Creditors	8,963
Net Current Assets	42
Total Assets less Current Liabilities	22,651
Creditors—amounts falling due after more than one year	
6. Finance Debt	4,760
Other Creditors	1,619
Provisions for Liabilities and Charges	4,350
Net Assets	11,922
7. Shareholders' Interest	11,922

Ethics Mini-Case

EMC 1-1.

LO 8 *Professional Ethics*

Discuss the ethical choices in the situations below. In each instance, determine the alternative courses of action, describe the ethical dilemma, and state what you would do.

1. You are the payroll accountant for a small business. A friend asks you how much another employee is paid per hour.
2. As an accountant for the branch office of a wholesale supplier, you discover that several of the receipts the branch manager has submitted for reimbursement as selling expense actually stem from nights out with his spouse.
3. You are an accountant in the purchasing department of a construction company. When you arrive home from work on December 22, you find a large ham in a box marked "Happy Holidays—It's a pleasure to work with you". The gift is from a supplier who has bid on a contract your employer plans to award next week.
4. As an auditor with one year's experience at a local firm, you are expected to complete a certain part of an audit in twenty hours. Because of your lack of experience, you know you cannot finish the job within that time. Rather than admit this, you are thinking about working late to finish the job and not telling anyone.

5. You are a tax accountant at a local firm. You help your neighbour fill out her tax return, and she pays you 200 in cash. Because there is no record of this transaction, you are considering not reporting it on your tax return.
6. The accounting firm for which you work has just won a new client, a firm in which you own 200 shares that you received as an inheritance from your grandmother. Because it is only a small number of shares and you think the company will be very successful, you are considering not disclosing the investment.

Decision-Making Case

DMC 1-1.

LO 6   *Effect of Transactions on the Balance Sheet*

Instead of hunting for a holiday job after finishing her first year at university, Lucy Henderson started a lawn maintenance service business. On June 1, she deposited 1,350 in a new bank account in the name of her corporation, Henderson Lawn Care. The 1,350 consisted of a 500 loan from her father and 850 of her own money. In return for her investment, Lucy issued 850 shares to herself.

Using the money in this bank account, Lucy rented lawn equipment, purchased supplies, and hired high school students to mow and trim the lawns of neighbours who had agreed to pay her for the service. At the end of each month, she mailed bills to her customers.

On August 31, Lucy was ready to dissolve her business and go back to university. Because she had been so busy, she had not kept any records other than her chequebook and a list of amounts owed by customers.

Her chequebook had a balance of 1,760, and her customers owed her 435. She expected these customers to pay her during September. She planned to return unused supplies to Suburban Landscaping Company for a full credit of 25. When she brought back the rented lawn equipment, Suburban Landscaping also would return a deposit of 100 she had made in June. She owed Suburban Landscaping 260 for equipment rentals and supplies. In addition, she owed the students who had worked for her 50, and she still owed her father 350. Although Lucy feels she did quite well, she is not sure just how successful she was.

REQUIRED

1. Prepare one balance sheet dated June 1 and another dated August 31 for Henderson Lawn Care.
2. Compare the two balance sheets and comment on the performance of Henderson Lawn Care. Did the company make a profit or a loss? (Assume that Lucy used none of the company's assets for personal purposes.)
3. If Lucy wants to continue her business next holidays, what kind of information from her record-keeping system would make it easier for her to tell whether or not she is earning a profit?

Basic Research Activity

RA 1-1.

LO 1   *Need for Knowledge of*
LO 2   *Accounting*

From the business section of your local paper or a national daily, clip out an article about a company. List all of the financial and accounting terms used in the article. Bring the article to class and be prepared to discuss how a knowledge of accounting would help a user understand the content of the article.

Financial Reporting and Analysis

Interpretation Cases from Business

ICB 1-1.

LO 6   *Nature of Cash, Assets, and Net Profit*

BMW is a German car and motorcycle company. Information for 1995 and 1994 from the company's 1995 annual report is presented at the top of the next page.[5] (All numbers are in millions.)

Three students who were looking at BMW's annual report were overheard to make the following comments:

Student A: What a great year BMW had in 1995! The company earned net profit of 2,154 because its total assets increased from 38,693 to 40,847.

Student B: But the change in total assets isn't the same as net profit! The company had a net profit of only 197 because cash increased from 2,683 to 2,880.

Student C: I see from the annual report that BMW paid cash dividends of 277 in 1995. Don't you have to take that into consideration when analysing the company's performance?

REQUIRED

1. Comment on the interpretations of Students A and B, and then answer Student C's question.
2. Calculate BMW's net profit for 1995. (**Note:** Reconstruct the calculation of retained earnings.)

BMW
Condensed Balance Sheets
December 31, 1995 and 1994
(Millions of Deutsche Marks)

	1995	1994
Assets		
Cash	2,880	2,683
Other Assets	37,967	36,010
Total Assets	40,847	38,693
Liabilities		
Total Liabilities	32,647	30,771
Shareholders' Equity		
Share Capital	2,580	2,559
Retained Earnings	5,620	5,363
Total Liabilities and Shareholders' Equity	40,847	38,693

ICB 1-2.

LO 1 *The Goal of Profitability*

Volvo, the Swedish car, truck, and bus company, had a difficult year in 1992. In the company's annual report, the chief executive said in part, "The results in 1992 for Volvo's core businesses are profoundly unsatisfactory. The operating loss in Volvo Cars was considerable and Volvo Trucks also reported a loss. The measures to return Volvo to favourable profitability have the highest priority."[6]

REQUIRED

1. Discuss the meaning of profitability. What other goal must a business achieve? Why is the goal of profitability important to Volvo's president?
2. What is the accounting measure of profitability, and on which statement is it determined?

Nestlé Case

NC 1-1.

LO 6 *The Basic Financial Statements*

Refer to the financial statements in the appendix on Nestlé, the Swiss-based global food and beverage company, to answer the following questions. Keep in mind that every company, while following basic principles, adapts financial statements and terminology to its own special needs. Therefore, the complexity of the financial statements and the terminology in the Nestlé statements will sometimes differ from those in the text.

1. What names does Nestlé give its basic financial statements? (Note that the use of the word "Consolidated" in the names of the financial statements simply means that these statements combine those of several companies owned by Nestlé.)
2. Prove that the accounting equation works for Nestlé in 1996 by finding the amounts for the following equation: Assets = liabilities + shareholders' equity.
3. What were the total revenues of Nestlé for 1996?
4. Was Nestlé profitable in 1996? How much was net profit in that year, and did it increase or decrease from 1995?
5. How did the company's cash and equivalents change from 1995 to 1996? By how much?

ENDNOTES

1. McDonald's Corporation, *Annual Report,* 1995, p. 2.
2. International Accounting Standards Committee, *Framework for the Preparation and Presentation of Financial Statements* (London: IASC, 1996), para. 12.
3. Ibid., para. 9–11.
4. Club Méditerranée, *Annual Report,* 1994–95, p. 3.
5. BMW, *Annual Report,* 1995.
6. Volvo, *Annual Report,* 1992.

Chapter 2

MEASURING BUSINESS

TRANSACTIONS

LEARNING OBJECTIVES

1. Explain, in simple terms, the ways of solving the measurement issues of recognition, valuation, and classification.
2. Describe the chart of accounts and recognise commonly used accounts.
3. Define *double-entry system* and state the rules for double entry.
4. Apply the steps for transaction analysis and processing to simple transactions.
5. Record transactions in the general journal.
6. Post transactions from the general journal to the ledger.
7. Prepare a trial balance and describe its value and limitations.

DECISION POINT

UNITED AIRLINES AND BOEING

In October 1990, UAL Corporation in the United States, United Airlines' parent company, announced that it had ordered up to 128 Boeing widebody jets: 68 of the long-awaited 777 models and 60 of the 747-400 models. This order, which was estimated to come to more than $22 billion, was the largest order ever placed for commercial aircraft. The agreement included firm orders for half the aircraft and options to buy the other half. Boeing was manufacturing the aircraft for UAL, and the new planes were to be delivered beginning in 1995. How should this important order have been recorded, if at all, in the records of UAL and of Boeing? When should the forthcoming purchase and sale have been recorded in the companies' records?

The order obviously was an important event, one that carried long-term consequences for both companies. But, as you will understand from this chapter, it was not recorded in the accounting records of either company. At the time the order was placed, the aircraft were yet to be manufactured and would not begin to be delivered for five years. For half the aircraft, UAL was given an option that could be accepted or refused. Even for the "firm" orders, Boeing cautioned in its 1989 annual report that "an economic downturn could result in airline equipment requirements less than currently anticipated resulting in requests to negotiate the rescheduling or possible cancellation of firm orders". The aircraft were not assets of UAL, and the company had not incurred a liability. No aircraft had been delivered or even built, so UAL was not obligated to pay at that point. And Boeing could not record any revenue until the aircraft were manufactured and delivered to UAL, until title to (ownership of) the aircraft shifted from Boeing to UAL. As it turned out, some orders and options were cancelled or extended in 1993 because of the adverse effects of the economy on UAL Corporation.[1]

To understand and use financial statements, it is important to know how to analyse events to determine the extent of their impact on those statements.

OBJECTIVE 1

Explain, in simple terms, the ways of solving the measurement issues of recognition, valuation, and classification

MEASUREMENT ISSUES

In the chapter on uses of accounting information and the basic financial statements, we defined business transactions as economic events that affect the financial position of a business entity. To measure a business transaction, the accountant must decide when the transaction occurred (the recognition issue), what monetary amount to place on the transaction (the valuation issue), and how the components of the transaction should be categorised (the classification issue).

These three issues—recognition, valuation, and classification—underlie almost every major decision in financial accounting today. They lie at the heart of accounting for pension plans, of mergers of giant companies, and of international transactions; and they allow the accountant to project and plan for the effects of inflation. In discussing the three basic issues, we follow international accounting standards and use an approach that promotes an understanding of the basic ideas of accounting. Keep in mind, however, that controversy does exist, and that some solutions to problems are not as cut-and-dried as they appear.

The Recognition Issue

The **recognition** issue refers to the difficulty of deciding when a business transaction should be recorded. Often the facts of a situation are known, but there is disagreement about when the event should be recorded. Suppose, for instance, that a company orders, receives, and pays for an office desk. Which of the following actions constitutes a recordable event?

1. An employee sends a purchase requisition to the purchasing department.
2. The purchasing department sends a purchase order to the supplier.
3. The supplier ships the desk.
4. The company receives the desk.
5. The company receives the bill from the supplier.
6. The company pays the bill.

The answer to this question is important because amounts in the financial statements are affected by the date on which a purchase is recorded. According to accounting tradition, the transaction is recorded when title to the desk passes from the supplier to the purchaser, creating an obligation to pay. Thus, depending on the details of the shipping agreement, the transaction is recognised (recorded) at the time of either action 3 or action 4. This is the guideline that we generally use in this book. However, in many small businesses that have simple accounting systems, the transaction is not recorded until the bill is received (action 5) or paid (action 6) because these are the implied points of title transfer. The predetermined time at which a transaction should be recorded is the **recognition point**.

The recognition issue is not always solved easily. Consider the case of an advertising agency that is asked by a client to prepare a major advertising campaign. People may work on the campaign several hours a day for a number of weeks. Value is added to the plan as the employees develop it. Should this added value be recognised as the campaign is being produced or at the time it is completed? Normally, the increase in value is recorded at the time the plan is finished and the client is billed for it. However, if a plan is going to take a long period to develop, the agency and the client may agree that the client will be billed at key points during its development.

The Valuation Issue

In the U.K. there is a more flexible approach to valuation compared to most countries. Land and buildings are frequently revalued to market value as and when company directors decide this is appropriate. The monetary amounts representing assets in balance sheets are thus often a mixture of historical costs and more up-to-date market values.

Valuation is perhaps the most controversial issue in accounting. The **valuation** issue focuses on assigning a monetary amount to a business transaction. International accounting standards indicate that the most commonly adopted value to assign to all business transactions—and therefore to all assets, liabilities, and components of shareholders' equity, including revenues and expenses, acquired by a business—is the original cost (usually called *historical cost*). **Cost** is defined here as the exchange price associated with a business transaction at the point of recognition. According to this guideline, the purpose of accounting is not to account for value in terms of worth, which can change after a transaction occurs, but to account for value in terms of cost at the time of the transaction. For example, the cost of an asset is recorded when the asset is acquired, and the value is held at that level until the asset is sold, expires, or is consumed. In this context, *value* means the cost at the time of the transaction. The practice of recording transactions at cost is referred to as the **historical cost principle**.

Suppose that a person offers a building for sale at 120,000. It may be valued for tax purposes at 75,000, and it may be insured for 90,000. One prospective buyer may offer 100,000 for the building, and another may offer 105,000. At this point, several different, unverifiable opinions of value have been expressed. Finally, suppose the seller and a buyer settle on a price and complete the sale for 110,000. All of these figures are values of one kind or another, but only the last is generally considered sufficiently reliable to be used in the records. The market value of the building may vary over the years, but it will remain on the new buyer's records at 110,000 until it is sold again. At that point, the accountant will record the new transaction at the new exchange price, and a profit or loss will be recognised.

The historical cost principle is used because the cost is verifiable. It results from the actions of independent buyers and sellers who come to an agreement on price. An exchange price is an objective price that can be verified by evidence created at the time of the transaction. It is this final price, verified by agreement of the two parties, at which the transaction is recorded.

However, historical cost is not the only measurement approach recognised and used internationally.[2] For example, inventories are usually stated at the lower of cost and net realisable value, i.e. the cash or cash equivalents that could be currently obtained by selling the inventories in an orderly disposal. Marketable securities may be stated at market value. Property, plant, and equipment may be stated at **fair value**, i.e. the amount for which an asset could be exchanged between knowledgeable, willing parties in an arm's-length transaction. Sometimes the fair value may be based on the cost of replacing the asset rather than its net realisable value. In some countries, revaluations to fair value of property, plant, and equipment are permitted such as in Australia, the Netherlands, and the United Kingdom, whereas in others such as Canada, Germany, Japan, and the United States the historical cost principle must be used. Table 2-1 shows the different measurement approaches followed in a selection of countries.

Clearly, the valuation issue is not one that can be resolved easily given the diversity of practice. The International Accounting Standards Committee (IASC) has adopted historical cost as its benchmark principle. However, revaluation to fair value, subsequent to the initial recognition of an asset at cost, is an allowed alternative measurement approach.

The Classification Issue

The **classification** issue has to do with assigning all the transactions in which a business engages to appropriate categories, or accounts. For example, a company's ability to borrow money can be affected by the way in which its debts are categorised. Or a company's net profit can be affected by whether purchases of small items such as tools are considered repair expenses (a component of shareholders' equity) or equipment (assets). Proper classification depends not only on correctly analysing the effect of each transaction on the business, but also on maintaining a system of accounts that reflects that effect. The rest of this chapter explains the classification of accounts and the analysis and recording of transactions.

TABLE 2-1 *Valuation of Property, Plant, and Equipment*

	At Historical Cost	At a Revaluation
Australia	Normal practice	Permitted
Brazil	Required	Not permitted
Canada	Required	Not permitted
China	Required	Not permitted
France	Required	Not permitted
Germany	Required	Not permitted
Italy	Required	Not permitted
Japan	Required	Not permitted
Netherlands	Normal practice	Permitted
Spain	Required	Not permitted
Sweden	Normal practice	Permitted
Switzerland	Normal practice	Permitted
United Kingdom	Normal practice	Permitted
United States	Required	Not permitted

OBJECTIVE 2

Describe the chart of accounts and recognise commonly used accounts

ACCOUNTS AND THE CHART OF ACCOUNTS

In the measurement of business transactions, large amounts of data are gathered. These data require a method of storage. Business people should be able to retrieve transaction data quickly and in usable form. In other words, there should be a filing system to sort out or classify all the transactions that occur in a business. This filing system consists of accounts. Recall that accounts are the basic storage units for accounting data and are used to accumulate amounts from similar transactions. An accounting system has a separate account for each asset, each liability, and each component of shareholders' equity, including revenues and expenses. Whether a company keeps records by hand or by computer, management must be able to refer to accounts so that it can study the company's financial history and plan for the future. A very small company may need only a few dozen accounts; a multinational corporation may need thousands.

In a manual accounting system, each account is kept on a separate page or card. These pages or cards are placed together in a book or file called the **general ledger**. In the computerised systems that most companies have today, accounts are maintained on magnetic tapes or disks. However, as a matter of convenience, accountants still refer to the group of company accounts as the general ledger, or simply the *ledger*.

To help identify accounts in the ledger and to make them easy to find, the accountant often numbers them. A list of these numbers with the corresponding account names is called a **chart of accounts**. A very simple chart of accounts appears in Exhibit 2-1. Notice that the first digit refers to the major financial statement classifications. An account number that begins with the digit 1 is an asset, an account number that begins with a 2 is a liability, and so forth. The second and third digits refer to individual accounts. Notice the gaps in the sequence of numbers. These gaps allow the accountant to expand the number of accounts. The accounts in Exhibit 2-1 will be used in this chapter and in the next two chapters, through the sample case of the Joan Miller Advertising Agency.

In France, a uniform chart of accounts, known as the Plan Comptable, *is required to be used by most French enterprises. In the U.S. and U.K., by way of contrast, the design of the accounting system is a matter for individual enterprises.*

Shareholders' Equity Accounts

In the chart of accounts in Exhibit 2-1, the revenue and expense accounts are separated from the shareholders' equity accounts. The relationships of these accounts to each other and to the basic financial statements are shown in Figure 2-1. The distinctions among them are important for legal and financial reporting purposes.

First, the shareholders' equity accounts represent legal claims by the shareholders against the assets of the company. Share Capital is a capital account (companies may have more than one type of capital) that represents shareholders' claims arising from their investments in the company, and Retained Earnings represents shareholders' claims arising from profitable operations. Both are claims against the general assets of the company, not against specific assets. They do not represent pools of funds that

---

BUSINESS BULLETIN   Business Practice

Today, most businesses, even the smallest, use computerised accounting systems. In small businesses, these systems are called *general ledger packages* and run on personal computers. The starting point for these systems is a chart of accounts that reflects the activities in which the business engages. Every company develops a chart of accounts for its own needs. Seldom do two companies have exactly the same chart of accounts. A small business may get by with a simple chart of accounts like that in Exhibit 2-1. A large, complicated business like Boeing will have twelve or more digits in its account numbers and thousands of accounts in its chart of accounts.

EXHIBIT 2-1 *Chart of Accounts for a Small Business*

Account Number	Account Name	Description
	Assets	
111	Cash	Money and any medium of exchange, including coins, currency, cheques, postal and express money orders, and money on deposit in a bank
112	Notes Receivable	Amounts due from others in the form of promissory notes (written promises to pay definite sums of money at fixed future dates)
113	Accounts Receivable	Amounts due from others from credit sales (sales on account)
114	Fees Receivable	Amounts arising from services performed but not yet billed to customers
115	Art Supplies	Prepaid expense; art supplies purchased and not used
116	Office Supplies	Prepaid expense; office supplies purchased and not used
117	Prepaid Rent	Prepaid expense; rent paid in advance and not used
118	Prepaid Insurance	Prepaid expense; insurance purchased and not expired; unexpired insurance
141	Land	Property owned for use in the business
142	Buildings	Structures owned for use in the business
143	Accumulated Depreciation, Buildings	Sum of the periodic allocation of the cost of buildings to expense
144	Art Equipment	Art equipment owned for use in the business
145	Accumulated Depreciation, Art Equipment	Sum of the periodic allocation of the cost of art equipment to expense
146	Office Equipment	Office equipment owned for use in the business
147	Accumulated Depreciation, Office Equipment	Sum of the periodic allocation of the cost of office equipment to expense
	Liabilities	
211	Notes Payable	Amounts due to others in the form of promissory notes
212	Accounts Payable	Amounts due to others for purchases on credit

(continued)

EXHIBIT 2-1   *Chart of Accounts for a Small Business (continued)*

Account Number	Account Name	Description
		Liabilities (*continued*)
213	Unearned Art Fees	Unearned revenue; advance deposits for artwork to be provided in the future
214	Wages Payable	Amounts due to employees for wages earned and not paid
215	Income Taxes Payable	Amounts due to government for income taxes owed and not paid
221	Mortgage Payable	Amounts due on loans that are backed by the company's property and buildings
		Shareholders' Equity
311	Share Capital	Shareholders' investments in a company for which they receive shares
312	Retained Earnings	Shareholders' claims against company assets derived from profitable operations
313	Dividends	Distributions of assets (usually cash) that reduce retained earnings
314	Profit Summary	Temporary account used at the end of the accounting period to summarise the revenues and expenses for the period
		Revenues
411	Advertising Fees Earned	Revenues derived from performing advertising services
412	Art Fees Earned	Revenues derived from performing art services
		Expenses
511	Wages Expense	Amounts earned by employees
512	Electricity Expense	Amount of electricity used
513	Telephone Expense	Amounts of telephone services used
514	Rent Expense	Amounts of rent on property and buildings used
515	Insurance Expense	Amounts for insurance used
516	Art Supplies Expense	Amounts for art supplies used
517	Office Supplies Expense	Amounts for office supplies used
518	Depreciation Expense, Buildings	Amounts of buildings' cost allocated to expense
519	Depreciation Expense, Art Equipment	Amount of art equipment costs allocated to expense
520	Depreciation Expense, Office Equipment	Amount of office equipment costs allocated to expense
521	Interest Expense	Amount of interest on debts

FIGURE 2-1 *Relationships of Shareholders' Equity Accounts*

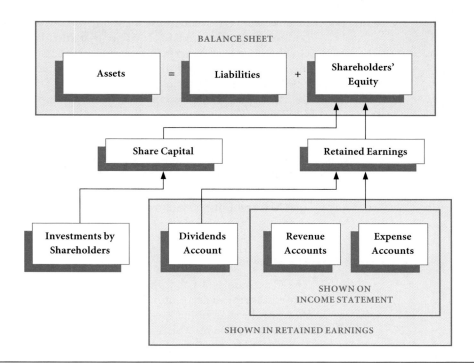

have been set aside. Dividends are included among the shareholders' equity accounts because they are distributions of assets that reduce ownership claims on retained earnings and are shown on the statement of retained earnings.

Second, the law requires that capital investments and dividends be separated from revenues and expenses for income tax reporting, financial reporting, and other purposes.

Third, management needs a detailed breakdown of revenues and expenses for budgeting and operating purposes. From these accounts, which are included on the income statement, management can identify the sources of all revenues and the nature of all expenses.

Account Titles

The names of accounts often confuse beginning accounting students because some of the words are new or have technical meanings. Also, the same asset, liability, or shareholders' equity account can have different names in different companies and countries. (Actually, this is not so strange. People, too, often are called different names by their friends, families, and associates.) For example, Fixed Assets, Plant and Equipment, Capital Assets, and Long-Lived Assets are all names for long-term asset accounts. Even the most acceptable names change over time, and, out of habit, some companies use names that are out of date.

In general, an account title should describe what is recorded in the account. When you come across an account title that you do not recognise, you should examine the context of the name—whether it is classified as an asset, liability, or shareholders' equity component, including revenue or expense, on the financial statements—and look for the kind of transaction that gave rise to the account.

<table>
<tr><td>

OBJECTIVE 3

Define double-entry system *and state the rules for double entry*

</td></tr>
</table>

THE DOUBLE-ENTRY SYSTEM: THE BASIC METHOD OF ACCOUNTING

The double-entry system, the backbone of accounting, evolved during the Renaissance. As noted previously, the first systematic description of double-entry bookkeeping appeared in 1494 in a mathematics book written by Luca Pacioli. Goethe, the famous German poet and dramatist, referred to double-entry bookkeeping as "one of the finest discoveries of the human intellect". And Werner Sombart, an eminent economist-sociologist, believed that "double-entry bookkeeping is born of the same spirit as the system of Galileo and Newton".

What is the significance of the double-entry system? The system is based on the *principle of duality*, which means that every economic event has two aspects—effort and reward, sacrifice and benefit, source and use—that offset or balance each other. In the **double-entry system**, each transaction must be recorded with at least one debit and one credit, so that the total amount of debits and the total amount of credits equal each other. Because of the way it is designed, the whole system is always in balance. All accounting systems, no matter how sophisticated, are based on the principle of duality.

The T Account

The T account is a good place to begin the study of the double-entry system. In its simplest form, an account has three parts: (1) a title, which describes the asset, the liability, or the shareholders' equity account; (2) a left side, which is called the **debit** side; and (3) a right side, which is called the **credit** side. This form of an account, called a **T account** because it resembles the letter *T*, is used to analyse transactions. It looks like this:

Title of Account
Debit (left) side	Credit (right) side

Any entry made on the left side of the account is a debit, or debit entry; and any entry made on the right side of the account is a credit, or credit entry. The terms *debit* (abbreviated Dr., from the Latin *debere*) and *credit* (abbreviated Cr., from the Latin *credere*) are simply the accountant's words for "left" and "right" (not for "increase" or "decrease"). We present a more formal version of the T account later in this chapter, where we examine the ledger account form.

The T Account Illustrated

In the chapter on accounting information and the uses of financial statements, Shannon Property had several transactions that involved the receipt or payment of cash. (See the exhibit "Summary of Effects of Illustrative Transactions on Financial Position" in the chapter on uses of accounting information and the basic financial statements for a summary of the numbered transactions listed below.) These transactions can be summarised in the Cash account by recording receipts on the left (debit) side of the account and payments on the right (credit) side of the account:

		Cash		
(1)	50,000		(2)	35,000
(5)	1,500		(4)	200
(7)	1,000		(8)	1,000
			(9)	400
			(11)	600
	52,500			37,200
Bal.	15,300			

The cash receipts on the left total 52,500. (The total is written in small figures so that it cannot be confused with an actual debit entry.) The cash payments on the right side total 37,200. These totals are simply working totals, or **footings**. Footings, which are calculated at the end of each month, are an easy way to determine cash available. The difference in amounts between the total debit footing and the total credit footing is called the **balance**, or *account balance*. If the balance is a debit, it is written on the left side. If it is a credit, it is written on the right side. Notice that Shannon Property's Cash account has a debit balance of 15,300 (52,500 − 37,200). This is the amount of cash the business has available at the end of the month.

Analysing and Processing Transactions

The two rules of double-entry bookkeeping are that every transaction affects at least two accounts and that total debits must equal total credits. In other words, for every transaction, one or more accounts must be debited and one or more accounts must be credited, and the total amount of the debits must equal the total amount of the credits. Look again at the accounting equation:

$$\text{Assets} = \text{liabilities} + \text{shareholders' equity}$$

You can see that if a debit increases assets, then a credit must be used to increase liabilities or shareholders' equity because they are on opposite sides of the equal sign. Likewise, if a credit decreases assets, then a debit must be used to decrease liabilities or shareholders' equity. These rules can be shown as follows:

Assets			=	Liabilities			+	Shareholders' Equity	
Debit for increases (+)	Credit for decreases (−)			Debit for decreases (−)	Credit for increases (+)			Debit for decreases (−)	Credit for increases (+)

1. Increases in assets are debited to asset accounts. Decreases in assets are credited to asset accounts.
2. Increases in liabilities and shareholders' equity are credited to liability and shareholders' equity accounts. Decreases in liabilities and shareholders' equity are debited to liability and shareholders' equity accounts.

One of the more difficult points to understand is the application of double-entry rules to the shareholders' equity components. The key is to remember that dividends and expenses are deductions from shareholders' equity. Thus, transactions that *increase* dividends or expenses *decrease* shareholders' equity. Consider this expanded version of the accounting equation:

Shareholders' Equity

$$\text{Assets} = \text{liabilities} + \text{share capital} + \text{retained earnings} - \text{dividends} + \text{revenues} - \text{expenses}$$

This equation may be rearranged by shifting dividends and expenses to the left side:

Assets		+	Dividends		+	Expenses		=	Liabilities		+	Share Capital		+	Retained Earnings		+	Revenues	
+ (debits)	− (credits)		+ (debits)	− (credits)		+ (debits)	− (credits)		− (debits)	+ (credits)		− (debits)	+ (credits)		− (debits)	+ (credits)		− (debits)	+ (credits)

Note that the rules for double entry for all the accounts on the left of the equal sign are just the opposite of the rules for all the accounts on the right of the equal sign. Assets, dividends, and expenses are increased by debits and decreased by credits. Liabilities, share capital, retained earnings, and revenues are increased by credits and decreased by debits.

FIGURE 2-2 *Analysing and Processing Transactions*

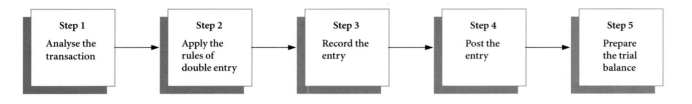

With this basic information about double entry, it is possible to analyse and process transactions by following the five steps illustrated in Figure 2-2. To show how the steps are applied, assume that on June 1, Shell Oil Company borrows 100,000 from its bank on a promissory note. The transaction is analysed and processed in the following way:

1. *Analyse the transaction to determine its effect on assets, liabilities, and shareholders' equity.* In this case, both an asset (Cash) and a liability (Notes Payable) increase. A transaction is usually supported by some kind of **source document**—an invoice, a receipt, a cheque, or a contract. (Note that *check* is the North American usage of **cheque**, which is a written order for a bank to pay money as instructed.) Here, a copy of the signed note would be the source document.
2. *Apply the rules of double entry.* Increases in assets are recorded by debits. Increases in liabilities are recorded by credits.
3. *Record the entry.* Transactions are recorded in chronological order in a journal. One form of journal, which is explained in more detail later in this chapter, records the date, the debit account, and the debit amount on one line and the credit account and credit amount indented on the next line, as follows:

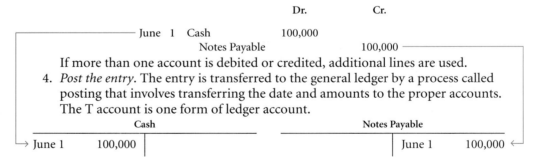

If more than one account is debited or credited, additional lines are used.
4. *Post the entry.* The entry is transferred to the general ledger by a process called posting that involves transferring the date and amounts to the proper accounts. The T account is one form of ledger account.

For purposes of analysis, accountants often bypass step **3** and record entries directly in T accounts because doing so clearly and quickly shows the effects of transactions on the accounts. Some of the assignments in this chapter use the same approach to emphasise the analytical aspects of double entry. In formal records, step **3** is not omitted.

BUSINESS BULLETIN **Technology in Practice**

In computerised accounting systems, it is essential that transactions be recorded properly because most of the subsequent processing is done automatically. Thus, the most important steps in the process are analysing the transaction and applying the rules of double entry. The acronym GIGO describes what happens if transactions are incorrectly analysed and recorded: **g**arbage **i**n, **g**arbage **o**ut.

5. *Prepare the trial balance to confirm the balance of the accounts.* Periodically, accountants prepare a trial balance to confirm that the accounts are still in balance after the recording and posting of transactions. Preparation of the trial balance is explained at the end of this chapter.

OBJECTIVE 4

Apply the steps for transaction analysis and processing to simple transactions

Transaction Analysis Illustrated

In the next few pages, we examine the transactions for Joan Miller Advertising Agency during the month of January. In the discussion, we illustrate the principle of duality and show how transactions are recorded in the accounts.

January 1: Joan Miller commences business and invests 10,000 in her own advertising agency in exchange for 10,000 shares at a nominal value of 1 for each share.

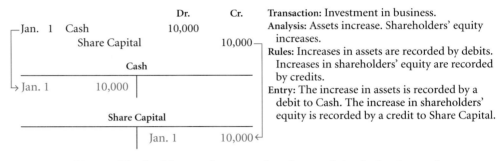

Transaction: Investment in business.
Analysis: Assets increase. Shareholders' equity increases.
Rules: Increases in assets are recorded by debits. Increases in shareholders' equity are recorded by credits.
Entry: The increase in assets is recorded by a debit to Cash. The increase in shareholders' equity is recorded by a credit to Share Capital.

Analysis: If Joan Miller had invested assets other than cash in the business, the appropriate asset accounts would be debited.

January 2: Rents an office, paying two months' rent, 800, in advance.

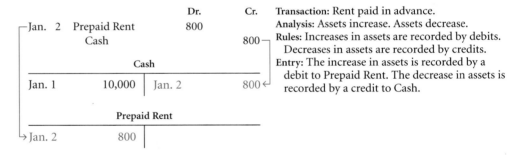

Transaction: Rent paid in advance.
Analysis: Assets increase. Assets decrease.
Rules: Increases in assets are recorded by debits. Decreases in assets are recorded by credits.
Entry: The increase in assets is recorded by a debit to Prepaid Rent. The decrease in assets is recorded by a credit to Cash.

January 3: Orders art supplies, 1,800, and office supplies, 800.

Analysis: No entry is made because no transaction has occurred. According to the recognition issue, there is no liability until the supplies are shipped or received and there is an obligation to pay for them.

January 4: Purchases art equipment, 4,200, with cash.

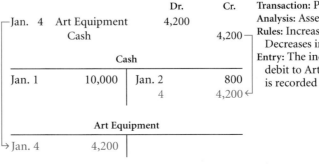

Transaction: Purchase of equipment.
Analysis: Assets increase. Assets decrease.
Rules: Increases in assets are recorded by debits. Decreases in assets are recorded by credits.
Entry: The increase in assets is recorded by a debit to Art Equipment. The decrease in assets is recorded by a credit to Cash.

January 5: Purchases office equipment, 3,000, from Morgan Equipment; pays 1,500 in cash and agrees to pay the rest next month.

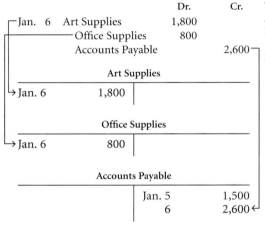

		Dr.	Cr.
Jan. 5	Office Equipment	3,000	
	Cash		1,500
	Accounts Payable		1,500

Cash

Jan. 1	10,000	Jan. 2	800
		4	4,200
		5	1,500

Office Equipment

Jan. 5	3,000	

Accounts Payable

	Jan. 5	1,500

Transaction: Purchase of equipment and partial payment.

Analysis: Assets increase. Assets decrease. Liabilities increase.

Rules: Increases in assets are recorded by debits. Decreases in assets are recorded by credits. Increases in liabilities are recorded by credits.

Entry: The increase in assets is recorded by a debit to Office Equipment. The decrease in assets is recorded by a credit to Cash. The increase in liabilities is recorded by a credit to Accounts Payable.

January 6: Purchases art supplies, 1,800, and office supplies, 800, from Taylor Supply Company, on credit.

		Dr.	Cr.
Jan. 6	Art Supplies	1,800	
	Office Supplies	800	
	Accounts Payable		2,600

Art Supplies

Jan. 6	1,800	

Office Supplies

Jan. 6	800	

Accounts Payable

	Jan. 5	1,500
	6	2,600

Transaction: Purchase of supplies on credit.

Analysis: Assets increase. Liabilities increase.

Rules: Increases in assets are recorded by debits. Increases in liabilities are recorded by credits.

Entry: The increase in assets is recorded by debits to Art Supplies and Office Supplies. The increase in liabilities is recorded by a credit to Accounts Payable.

January 8: Pays for a one-year life insurance policy, 480, with coverage effective January 1.

		Dr.	Cr.
Jan. 8	Prepaid Insurance	480	
	Cash		480

Cash

Jan. 1	10,000	Jan. 2	800
		4	4,200
		5	1,500
		8	480

Prepaid Insurance

Jan. 8	480	

Transaction: Insurance purchased in advance.

Analysis: Assets increase. Assets decrease.

Rules: Increases in assets are recorded by debits. Decreases in assets are recorded by credits.

Entry: The increase in assets is recorded by a debit to Prepaid Insurance. The decrease in assets is recorded by a credit to Cash.

January 9: Pays Taylor Supply Company 1,000 of the amount owed.

		Dr.	Cr.
Jan. 9	Accounts Payable	1,000	
	Cash		1,000

Cash

Jan. 1	10,000	Jan. 2	800
		4	4,200
		5	1,500
		8	480
		9	1,000

Accounts Payable

Jan. 9	1,000	Jan. 5	1,500
		6	2,600

Transaction: Partial payment on a liability.
Analysis: Assets decrease. Liabilities decrease.
Rules: Decreases in assets are recorded by credits. Decreases in liabilities are recorded by debits.
Entry: The decrease in liabilities is recorded by a debit to Accounts Payable. The decrease in assets is recorded by a credit to Cash.

January 10: Performs a service for a car dealer by placing advertisements in the newspaper and collects a fee, 1,400.

		Dr.	Cr.
Jan. 10	Cash	1,400	
	Advertising Fees Earned		1,400

Cash

Jan. 1	10,000	Jan. 2	800
10	1,400	4	4,200
		5	1,500
		8	480
		9	1,000

Advertising Fees Earned

		Jan. 10	1,400

Transaction: Revenue earned and cash collected.
Analysis: Assets increase. Shareholders' equity increases.
Rules: Increases in assets are recorded by debits. Increases in shareholders' equity are recorded by credits.
Entry: The increase in assets is recorded by a debit to Cash. The increase in shareholders' equity is recorded by a credit to Advertising Fees Earned.

January 12: Pays the secretary two weeks' wages, 600.

		Dr.	Cr.
Jan. 12	Office Wages Expense	600	
	Cash		600

Cash

Jan. 1	10,000	Jan. 2	800
10	1,400	4	4,200
		5	1,500
		8	480
		9	1,000
		12	600

Office Wages Expense

Jan. 12	600		

Transaction: Payment of wages expense.
Analysis: Assets decrease. Shareholders' equity decreases.
Rules: Decreases in assets are recorded by credits. Decreases in shareholders' equity are recorded by debits.
Entry: The decrease in shareholders' equity is recorded by a debit to Office Wages Expense. The decrease in assets is recorded by a credit to Cash.

January 15: Accepts an advance fee, 1,000, for artwork to be done for another agency.

		Dr.	Cr.
Jan. 15	Cash	1,000	
	Unearned Art Fees		1,000

Cash

Jan. 1	10,000	Jan. 2	800
10	1,400	4	4,200
15	1,000	5	1,500
		8	480
		9	1,000
		12	600

Unearned Art Fees

		Jan. 15	1,000

Transaction: Payment received for future services.
Analysis: Assets increase. Liabilities increase.
Rules: Increases in assets are recorded by debits. Increases in liabilities are recorded by credits.
Entry: The increase in assets is recorded by a debit to Cash. The increase in liabilities is recorded by a credit to Unearned Art Fees.

January 19: Performs a service by placing several major advertisements for Ward Department Stores. The fee, 2,800, is billed now but will be collected next month.

		Dr.	Cr.
Jan. 19	Accounts Receivable	2,800	
	Advertising Fees Earned		2,800

Accounts Receivable

Jan. 19	2,800		

Advertising Fees Earned

		Jan. 10	1,400
		19	2,800

Transaction: Revenue earned, to be received later.
Analysis: Assets increase. Shareholders' equity increases.
Rules: Increases in assets are recorded by debits. Increases in shareholders' equity are recorded by credits.
Entry: The increase in assets is recorded by a debit to Accounts Receivable. The increase in shareholders' equity is recorded by a credit to Advertising Fees Earned.

January 26: Pays the secretary two more weeks' wages, 600.

		Dr.	Cr.
Jan. 26	Office Wages Expense	600	
	Cash		600

Cash

Jan. 1	10,000	Jan. 2	800
10	1,400	4	4,200
15	1,000	5	1,500
		8	480
		9	1,000
		12	600
		26	600

Office Wages Expense

Jan. 12	600		
26	600		

Transaction: Payment of wages expense.
Analysis: Assets decrease. Shareholders' equity decreases.
Rules: Decreases in assets are recorded by credits. Decreases in shareholders' equity are recorded by debits.
Entry: The decrease in shareholders' equity is recorded by a debit to Office Wages Expense. The decrease in assets is recorded by a credit to Cash.

January 29: Receives and pays the electricity bill, 100.

		Dr.	Cr.
Jan. 29	Electricity Expense	100	
	Cash		100

Transaction: Payment of electricity expense.

Analysis: Assets decrease. Shareholders' equity decreases.

Rules: Decreases in assets are recorded by credits. Decreases in shareholders' equity are recorded by debits.

Entry: The decrease in shareholders' equity is recorded by a debit to Electricity Expense. The decrease in assets is recorded by a credit to Cash.

Cash

Jan. 1	10,000	Jan. 2	800
10	1,400	4	4,200
15	1,000	5	1,500
		8	480
		9	1,000
		12	600
		26	600
		29	100

Electricity Expense

Jan. 29	100	

January 30: Receives (but does not pay) the telephone bill, 70.

		Dr.	Cr.
Jan. 30	Telephone Expense	70	
	Accounts Payable		70

Transaction: Expense incurred, to be paid later.

Analysis: Liabilities increase. Shareholders' equity decreases.

Rules: Increases in liabilities are recorded by credits. Decreases in shareholders' equity are recorded by debits.

Entry: The decrease in shareholders' equity is recorded by a debit to Telephone Expense. The increase in liabilities is recorded by a credit to Accounts Payable.

Accounts Payable

Jan. 9	1,000	Jan. 5	1,500
		6	2,600
		30	70

Telephone Expense

Jan. 30	70	

January 31: Declares and pays a dividend of 1,400.

		Dr.	Cr.
Jan. 31	Dividends	1,400	
	Cash		1,400

Transaction: Declaration and payment of dividends.

Analysis: Assets decrease. Shareholders' equity decreases.

Rules: Decreases in assets are recorded by credits. Decreases in shareholders' equity are recorded by debits.

Entry: The decrease in shareholders' equity is recorded by a debit to Dividends. The decrease in assets is recorded by a credit to Cash.

Cash

Jan. 1	10,000	Jan. 2	800
10	1,400	4	4,200
15	1,000	5	1,500
		8	480
		9	1,000
		12	600
		26	600
		29	100
		31	1,400

Dividends

Jan. 31	1,400	

EXHIBIT 2-2   *Summary of Sample Accounts and Transactions for Joan Miller Advertising Agency*

Assets	=	Liabilities	+	Shareholders' Equity

Cash

Jan. 1	10,000	Jan. 2	800
10	1,400	4	4,200
15	1,000	5	1,500
		8	480
		9	1,000
		12	600
		26	600
		29	100
		31	1,400
	12,400		10,680
Bal.	1,720		

Accounts Receivable

Jan. 19	2,800	

Art Supplies

Jan. 6	1,800	

Office Supplies

Jan. 6	800	

Prepaid Rent

Jan. 2	800	

Prepaid Insurance

Jan. 8	480	

Art Equipment

Jan. 4	4,200	

Office Equipment

Jan. 5	3,000	

Accounts Payable

Jan. 9	1,000	Jan. 5	1,500
		6	2,600
		30	70
	1,000		4,170
		Bal.	3,170

Unearned Art Fees

		Jan. 15	1,000

Share Capital

		Jan. 1	10,000

Dividends

Jan. 31	1,400	

Advertising Fees Earned

		Jan. 10	1,400
		19	2,800
		Bal.	4,200

Office Wages Expense

Jan. 12	600	
26	600	
Bal.	1,200	

Electricity Expense

Jan. 29	100	

Telephone Expense

Jan. 30	70	

Summary of Transactions

The transactions for January are shown in Exhibit 2-2 in their accounts and in relation to the accounting equation.

RECORDING AND POSTING TRANSACTIONS

The formal processing of transactions in the general journal, the general ledger, and the trial balance is now illustrated.

BUSINESS BULLETIN   Ethics in Practice

American Collegiate Sales Corporation (ACS) in the United States used student representatives to market grooming aids, casual clothes, and other such products on college campuses. These representatives organised parties at which they displayed the products. Students who bought products paid the representative, who in turn ordered the products and paid ACS for them. When the products arrived, the student representative delivered them to the buyers. The representative paid ACS less than he or she charged the buyer. The difference represented the earnings of the representatives, who were not employees of ACS. Investors admired ACS because the company had enjoyed several years of rapid growth in sales and earnings.

Early in its most current financial year ACS predicted further increases in sales of 30 per cent. By December, however, it was apparent that the forecasted sales goals would not be met. So, during the last two weeks of December, ACS shipped 20 million of goods to the sales representatives to be held for future sales parties. The company billed the student representatives and recorded the shipments as sales. In this way, ACS was able to meet its sales goal for the year and maintain the high value of its shares.

The shipments, however, were improperly recorded as sales. The goods had not been ordered by or sold to actual customers, and the student representatives had the right to return all the products unconditionally. It was misleading to call them sales. In technical terms, this type of arrangement is called a *consignment*. To report consignment shipments as legitimate sales is certainly unethical and can be, as in this case, illegal when the intent is to deceive. As it turned out, most of the 20 million of products were returned during January and February, and ACS went into bankruptcy. Officials of the company were later convicted of fraud.

OBJECTIVE 5

Record transactions in the general journal

The General Journal

As you have seen, transactions can be entered directly into the accounts. But this method makes identifying individual transactions or finding errors very difficult because the debit is recorded in one account and the credit in another. The solution is to record all transactions chronologically in a **journal**. The journal is sometimes called the *book of original entry* because it is where transactions first enter the accounting records. Later, the debit and credit portions of each transaction can be transferred to the appropriate accounts in the ledger.

A separate **journal entry** is used to record each transaction, and the process of recording transactions is called **journalising**.

Most businesses have more than one kind of journal. The simplest and most flexible type is the **general journal**, the one we focus on in this chapter. Entries in the general journal include the following information about each transaction:

1. The date
2. The names of the accounts debited and the amounts on the same lines in the debit column
3. The names of the accounts credited and the amounts on the same lines in the credit column
4. An explanation of the transaction
5. The account identification numbers, if appropriate

We have recorded two transactions for Joan Miller Advertising Agency in Exhibit 2-3. As shown in that exhibit, the procedure for recording transactions in the general journal is as follows:

EXHIBIT 2-3   *The General Journal*

		General Journal			Page 1
Date		Description	Post. Ref.	Debit	Credit
20xx Jan.	6	Art Supplies		1,800	
		Office Supplies		800	
		Accounts Payable			2,600
		Purchase of art and office			
		supplies on credit			
	8	Prepaid Insurance		480	
		Cash			480
		Paid one-year life insurance			
		premium			

1. Record the date by writing the year in small figures on the first line at the top of the first column, the month on the next line of the first column, and the day in the second column opposite the month. For subsequent entries on the same page for the same month and year, the month and year can be omitted.
2. Write the exact names of the accounts debited and credited under the heading "Description". Write the name of the account debited next to the left margin of the second line, and indent the name of the account credited. The explanation is placed on the next line and further indented. It should be brief but sufficient to explain and identify the transaction. A transaction can have more than one debit or credit entry; this is called a **compound entry**. In a compound entry, all debit accounts are listed before any credit accounts. (The January 6 transaction of Joan Miller Advertising Agency is an example of a compound entry; see Exhibit 2-3.)
3. Write the debit amounts in the appropriate column opposite the accounts to be debited, and write the credit amounts in the appropriate column opposite the accounts to be credited.
4. At the time the transactions are recorded in the general journal, nothing is placed in the Post. Ref. (posting reference) column. (This column is sometimes called *Folio*.) Later, if the company uses account numbers to identify accounts in the ledger, fill in the account numbers to provide a convenient cross-reference from the general journal to the ledger and to indicate that the entry has been posted to the ledger. If the accounts are not numbered, use a checkmark (✔).
5. It is customary to skip a line after each journal entry.

OBJECTIVE 6

Post transactions from the general journal to the ledger

The General Ledger

The general journal is used to record the details of each transaction. The general ledger is used to update each account.

The Ledger Account Form

The T account is a simple, direct means of recording transactions. In practice, a somewhat more complicated form of the account is needed in order to record more information. The **ledger account form**, which contains four columns for monetary amounts, is illustrated in Exhibit 2-4.

EXHIBIT 2-4 *Accounts Payable in the General Ledger*

General Ledger

			Post. Ref.	Debit	Credit	Balance	
Date		Item				Debit	Credit
20xx							
Jan.	5		J1		1,500		1,500
	6		J1		2,600		4,100
	9		J1	1,000			3,100
	30		J2		70		3,170

Accounts Payable — Account No. 212

The account title and number appear at the top of the account form. The date of the transaction appears in the first two columns, just as it does in the journal. The Item column is used only rarely to identify transactions, because explanations already appear in the journal. The Post. Ref. column is used to note the journal page on which the original entry for the transaction can be found. The amount of the entry is entered in the appropriate Debit or Credit column, and a new account balance is calculated in the final two columns after each entry. The advantage of this form of account over the T account is that the current balance of the account is readily available.

Posting to the Ledger

After the transactions have been entered in the journal, they must be transferred to the general ledger. The process of transferring journal entry information from the journal to the ledger is called **posting**. Posting is usually done after several entries have been made—for example, at the end of each day or less frequently, depending on the number of transactions.

Through posting, each amount in the Debit column of the journal is transferred into the Debit column of the appropriate account in the ledger, and each amount in the Credit column of the journal is transferred into the Credit column of the appropriate account in the ledger, as shown in Exhibit 2-5. These are the steps in the posting process:

1. In the ledger, locate the debit account named in the journal entry.
2. Enter the date of the transaction and, in the Post. Ref. column of the ledger, the journal page number from which the entry comes.
3. Enter in the Debit column of the ledger account the amount of the debit as it appears in the journal.
4. Calculate the account balance and enter it in the appropriate balance column.
5. Enter in the Post. Ref. column of the journal the account number to which the amount has been posted.
6. Repeat the same five steps for the credit side of the journal entry.

Notice that step **5** is the last step in the posting process for each debit and credit. In addition to serving as an easy reference between the journal entry and the ledger account, this entry in the Post. Ref. column of the journal indicates that all steps for the item have been completed. This allows accountants who have been called away from their work to easily find where they were before the interruption.

EXHIBIT 2-5   *Posting from the General Journal to the Ledger*

OBJECTIVE 7

Prepare a trial balance and describe its value and limitations

THE TRIAL BALANCE

For every amount debited in the ledger, an equal amount must be credited. This means that the total of debits and credits in the ledger must be equal. To test this, the accountant periodically prepares a **trial balance**. Exhibit 2-6 shows a trial balance for Joan Miller Advertising Agency. It was prepared from the accounts in Exhibit 2-2, on page 54.

The trial balance may be prepared at any time but is usually prepared on the last day of the month. Here are the steps in preparing a trial balance:

1. List each ledger account that has a balance, with debit balances in the left column and credit balances in the right column. Accounts are listed in the order in which they appear in the ledger.
2. Add each column.
3. Compare the totals of the columns.

EXHIBIT 2-6 *Trial Balance*

Joan Miller Advertising Agency
Trial Balance
January 31, 20xx

Cash	1,720	
Accounts Receivable	2,800	
Art Supplies	1,800	
Office Supplies	800	
Prepaid Rent	800	
Prepaid Insurance	480	
Art Equipment	4,200	
Office Equipment	3,000	
Accounts Payable		3,170
Unearned Art Fees		1,000
Share Capital		10,000
Dividends	1,400	
Advertising Fees Earned		4,200
Office Wages Expense	1,200	
Electricity Expense	100	
Telephone Expense	70	
	18,370	18,370

In carrying out steps **1** and **2**, remember that the account form in the ledger has two balance columns, one for debit balances and one for credit balances. In accounts in which increases are recorded by debits, the **normal balance** (the usual balance) is a debit balance; where increases are recorded by credits, the normal balance is a credit balance. Table 2-2 summarises the normal account balances of the major account categories. According to the table, the ledger account Accounts Payable (a liability) typically has a credit balance and is copied into the trial balance as a credit balance.

Once in a while, a transaction leaves an account with an "abnormal" balance. For example, when a company overdraws its account at the bank, its Cash account (an asset) will show a credit balance instead of a debit balance. The "abnormal" balance should be copied into the trial balance columns as it stands, as a debit or a credit.

TABLE 2-2 *Normal Account Balances of Major Account Categories*

	Increases Recorded by		Normal Balance	
Account Category	Debit	Credit	Debit	Credit
Asset	x		x	
Liability		x		x
Shareholders' Equity:				
Share Capital		x		x
Dividends	x		x	
Revenues		x		x
Expenses	x		x	

> # BUSINESS BULLETIN   Technology in Practice
>
> In computerised accounting systems, posting is done automatically and the trial balance can be easily prepared as often as needed. Any accounts with abnormal balances are highlighted for investigation. Some general ledger software packages for small businesses list the trial balance amounts in a single column, with credit balances shown as minuses. In such cases, the trial balance is in balance if the total is zero.

The trial balance proves whether or not the ledger is in balance. *In balance* means that equal debits and credits have been recorded for all transactions, so that total debits equal total credits. But the trial balance does not prove that the transactions were analysed correctly or recorded in the proper accounts. For example, there is no way of determining from the trial balance that a debit should have been made in the Art Equipment account rather than the Office Equipment account. And the trial balance does not detect whether transactions have been omitted, because equal debits and credits will have been omitted. Also, if an error of the same amount is made in both a debit and a credit, it will not be discovered by the trial balance. The trial balance proves only that the debits and credits in the accounts are in balance.

If the debit and credit columns of the trial balance are not equal, look for these errors: (1) a debit was entered in an account as a credit, or vice versa; (2) the balance of an account was computed incorrectly; (3) an error was made in carrying the account balance to the trial balance; or (4) the trial balance was summed incorrectly.

Other than simply adding the columns incorrectly, the two most common mistakes in preparing a trial balance are (1) recording an account with a debit balance as a credit, or vice versa, and (2) transposing two numbers when transferring an amount to the trial balance (for example, entering 23,459 as 23,549). The first of these mistakes causes the trial balance to be out of balance by an amount divisible by 2. The second causes the trial balance to be out of balance by a number divisible by 9. Thus, if a trial balance is out of balance and the addition has been verified, determine the amount by which the trial balance is out of balance and divide it first by 2 and then by 9. If the amount is divisible by 2, look in the trial balance for an amount equal to the quotient. If you find the amount, it is probably in the wrong column. If the amount is divisible by 9, trace each amount to the ledger account balance, checking carefully for a transposition error. If neither of these techniques identifies the error, first recompute the balance of each account in the ledger, then, if the error still has not been found, retrace each posting from the journal to the ledger.

CHAPTER REVIEW

Review of Learning Objectives

1. **Explain, in simple terms, the ways of solving the measurement issues of recognition, valuation, and classification.** To measure a business transaction, the accountant must determine when the transaction occurred (the recognition issue), what monetary amount should be placed on the transaction (the valuation issue), and how the components of the transaction should be categorised (the classification issue). In general, recognition occurs when title passes, and a transaction is valued at the exchange price, the cost at the time the transaction is recognised. Classification refers to the categorising of transactions according to a system of accounts.

2. **Describe the chart of accounts and recognise commonly used accounts.** An account is a device for storing data from transactions. There is one account for each asset, liability, and component of shareholders' equity, including revenues and expenses. The general ledger is a book or file consisting of all of a company's accounts arranged according to a chart of accounts. Commonly used asset accounts are Cash, Notes Receivable, Accounts Receivable, Prepaid Expenses, Land, Buildings, and Equipment. Common liability accounts are Notes Payable, Accounts Payable, Wages Payable, and Mortgages Payable. Shareholders' equity accounts are Share

Capital, Retained Earnings, Dividends, and revenue and expense accounts.

3. **Define *double-entry system* and state the rules for double entry.** In the double-entry system, each transaction must be recorded with at least one debit and one credit so that the total amount of the debits equals the total amount of the credits. The rules for double entry are (1) that increases in assets are debited to asset accounts; decreases in assets are credited to asset accounts; and (2) that increases in liabilities and shareholders' equity are credited to those accounts; decreases in liabilities and shareholders' equity are debited to those accounts.

4. **Apply the steps for transaction analysis and processing to simple transactions.** The procedure for analysing transactions is (1) analyse the effect of the transaction on assets, liabilities, and shareholders' equity; (2) apply the appropriate double-entry rule; (3) record the entry; (4) post the entry; and (5) prepare a trial balance.

5. **Record transactions in the general journal.** The general journal is a chronological record of all transactions. That record contains the date of each transaction, the names of the accounts and the amounts debited and credited, an explana-

tion of each entry, and the account numbers to which postings have been made.

6. **Post transactions from the general journal to the ledger.** After transactions have been entered in the general journal, they are posted to the general ledger. Posting is done by transferring each amount in the Debit column of the general journal to the Debit column of the appropriate account in the general ledger, and transferring each amount in the Credit column of the general journal to the Credit column of the appropriate account in the general ledger. After each entry is posted, a new balance is entered in the appropriate Balance column.

7. **Prepare a trial balance and describe its value and limitations.** A trial balance is used to check that the debit and credit balances in the ledger are equal. It is prepared by listing each account with its balance in the Debit or Credit column. Then, the two columns are added and compared to test their balances. The major limitation of the trial balance is that even if debit and credit balances are equal, this does not necessarily mean that the transactions were analysed correctly or recorded in the proper accounts.

Review of Concepts and Terminology

The following concepts and terms were introduced in this chapter.

LO 3   *Balance:* The difference between the total debit footing and the total credit footing of an account. Also called *account balance.*

LO 2   *Chart of accounts:* A scheme that assigns a unique number to each account to facilitate finding the account in the ledger; also, the list of account numbers and titles.

LO 3   *Cheque:* A written order for a bank to pay money as instructed.

LO 1   *Classification:* The process of assigning transactions to the appropriate accounts.

LO 5   *Compound entry:* A journal entry that has more than one debit or credit entry.

LO 1   *Cost:* The exchange price associated with a business transaction at the point of recognition.

LO 3   *Credit:* The right side of an account.

LO 3   *Debit:* The left side of an account.

LO 3   *Double-entry system:* The accounting system in which each transaction is recorded with at least one debit and one credit so that the total amount of debits and the total amount of credits equal each other.

LO 1   *Fair value:* The amount for which an asset could be exchanged between knowledgeable, willing parties in an arm's-length transaction.

LO 3   *Footings:* Working totals of columns of numbers. To *foot* means to total a column of numbers.

LO 5   *General journal:* The simplest and most flexible type of journal.

LO 2   *General ledger:* The book or file that contains all or groups of the company's accounts, arranged in the order of the chart of accounts. Also called *ledger.*

LO 1   *Historical cost principle:* The practice of recording a transaction at its original cost and maintaining this cost in the records until the asset, liability, or component of

shareholders' equity is sold, expires, is consumed, is liquidated, or is otherwise disposed of.

LO 5   *Journal:* A chronological record of all transactions; the place where transactions first enter the accounting records. Also called *book of original entry.*

LO 5   *Journal entry:* The notations in the journal that are used to record a single transaction.

LO 5   *Journalising:* The process of recording transactions in a journal.

LO 6   *Ledger account form:* The form of account that has four columns: one column for debit entries, one column for credit entries, and two columns (debit and credit) for showing the balance of the account.

LO 7   *Normal balance:* The usual balance of an account; also the side (debit or credit side) that increases the account.

LO 6   *Posting:* The process of transferring journal entry information from the journal to the ledger.

LO 1   *Recognition:* The determination of when a business transaction should be recorded.

LO 1   *Recognition point:* The predetermined time at which a transaction should be recorded; usually, the point at which title passes to the buyer.

LO 3   *Source document:* An invoice, cheque, receipt, or other document that supports a transaction.

LO 3   *T account:* The simplest form of an account, used to analyse transactions.

LO 7   *Trial balance:* A comparison of the total of debit and credit balances in the ledger to check that they are equal.

LO 1   *Valuation:* The process of assigning a monetary amount to a business transaction.

Review Problem

Transaction Analysis, General Journal, Ledger Accounts, and Trial Balance

LO 4
LO 5
LO 6
LO 7

After graduation from veterinary school, Laura Choi entered private practice. The transactions of the business through May 27 are as follows:

20xx

May 1   Laura Choi invested 2,000 of her savings in 2,000 shares of her new company, Pet Clinic.
       3   Paid 300 for two months' rent in advance for an office.
       9   Purchased medical supplies for 200 in cash.
      12   Purchased 400 of equipment on credit, making a 25 per cent down payment.
      15   Delivered a calf for a fee of 35.
      18   Made a partial payment of 50 on the equipment purchased May 12.
      27   Paid an electricity bill of 40.

REQUIRED

1. Record these entries in the general journal.
2. Post the entries from the journal to the following accounts in the ledger: Cash (111); Medical Supplies (115); Prepaid Rent (117); Equipment (144); Accounts Payable (212); Share Capital (311); Veterinary Fees Earned (411); and Electricity Expense (512).
3. Prepare a trial balance as of May 31.

Answer to Review Problem

1. Record the journal entries.

		General Journal			Page 1
Date		Description	Post. Ref.	Debit	Credit
20xx May	1	Cash	111	2,000	
		Share Capital	311		2,000
		Invested 2,000 in 2,000 shares			
	3	Prepaid Rent	117	300	
		Cash	111		300
		Paid two months' rent in advance for an office			
	9	Medical Supplies	115	200	
		Cash	111		200
		Purchased medical supplies for cash			
	12	Equipment	144	400	
		Accounts Payable	212		300
		Cash	111		100
		Purchased equipment on credit, paying 25 per cent down			
	15	Cash	111	35	
		Veterinary Fees Earned	411		35
		Collected fee for delivery of a calf			
	18	Accounts Payable	212	50	
		Cash	111		50
		Partial payment for equipment purchased May 12			
	27	Electricity Expense	512	40	
		Cash	111		40
		Paid electricity bill			

2. Post the transactions to the ledger accounts.

General Ledger

Cash — Account No. 111

Date		Item	Post. Ref.	Debit	Credit	Balance Debit	Balance Credit
20xx							
May	1		J1	2,000		2,000	
	3		J1		300	1,700	
	9		J1		200	1,500	
	12		J1		100	1,400	
	15		J1	35		1,435	
	18		J1		50	1,385	
	27		J1		40	1,345	

Medical Supplies — Account No. 115

Date		Item	Post. Ref.	Debit	Credit	Balance Debit	Balance Credit
20xx							
May	9		J1	200		200	

Prepaid Rent — Account No. 117

Date		Item	Post. Ref.	Debit	Credit	Balance Debit	Balance Credit
20xx							
May	3		J1	300		300	

Equipment — Account No. 144

Date		Item	Post. Ref.	Debit	Credit	Balance Debit	Balance Credit
20xx							
May	12		J1	400		400	

Accounts Payable — Account No. 212

Date		Item	Post. Ref.	Debit	Credit	Balance Debit	Balance Credit
20xx							
May	12		J1		300		300
	18		J1	50			250

Share Capital — Account No. 311

Date		Item	Post. Ref.	Debit	Credit	Balance Debit	Balance Credit
20xx							
May	1		J1		2,000		2,000

(continued)

Veterinary Fees Earned   Account No. 411

| Date | Item | Post. Ref. | Debit | Credit | Balance | |
					Debit	Credit
20xx May 15		J1		35		35

Electricity Expense   Account No. 512

| Date | Item | Post. Ref. | Debit | Credit | Balance | |
					Debit	Credit
20xx May 27		J1	40		40	

3. Complete the trial balance.

Pet Clinic
Trial Balance
May 31, 20xx

Cash	1,345	
Medical Supplies	200	
Prepaid Rent	300	
Equipment	400	
Accounts Payable		250
Share Capital		2,000
Veterinary Fees Earned		35
Electricity Expense	40	
	2,285	2,285

CHAPTER ASSIGNMENTS

Knowledge and Understanding

Questions

1. What three issues underlie most accounting measurement decisions?
2. Why is recognition an issue for accountants?
3. A customer asks the owner of a store to save an item for him and says that he will pick it up and pay for it next week. The owner agrees to hold it. Should this transaction be recorded as a sale? Explain your answer.

4. Why is it practical for accountants to rely on original or historical cost for valuation purposes?
5. Under the historical cost principle, changes in value after a transaction is recorded are not usually recognised in the accounts. Comment on this possible limitation of using historical cost in accounting measurements.
6. What is an account, and how is it related to the ledger?

7. State whether each of the following accounts is an asset account, a liability account, or a shareholders' equity account:
   a. Notes Receivable   e. Prepaid Rent
   b. Land   f. Insurance Expense
   c. Dividends   g. Service Revenue
   d. Bonds Payable
8. In the shareholders' equity accounts, why do accountants maintain separate accounts for revenues and expenses?
9. Why is the system of recording entries called the double-entry system? What is significant about this system?
10. "Double-entry accounting refers to entering a transaction in both the journal and the ledger." Comment on this statement.
11. "Debits are bad, and credits are good." Comment on this statement.
12. What are the rules of double entry for (a) assets, (b) liabilities, and (c) shareholders' equity?
13. Why are the rules of double entry the same for liabilities and shareholders' equity?
14. What is the meaning of the statement, "The Cash account has a debit balance of 500"?
15. Explain why debits, which decrease shareholders' equity, also increase expenses, which are a component of shareholders' equity.
16. What five steps are involved in analysing and processing a transaction?

17. Is it a good idea to forgo the journal and enter a transaction directly into the ledger? Explain your answer.
18. In recording entries in a journal, which is written first, the debit or the credit? How is indentation used in the general journal?
19. What is the relationship between the journal and the ledger?
20. Describe each of the following:
    a. Account   f. Journalising
    b. Journal   g. Posting
    c. Ledger   h. Footings
    d. Book of original entry   i. Compound entry
    e. Post. Ref. column
21. What does a trial balance prove?
22. What is the normal balance of Accounts Payable? Under what conditions could Accounts Payable have a debit balance?
23. Can errors be present even though a trial balance balances? Explain your answer.
24. List the following six items in sequence to illustrate the flow of events through the accounting system:
    a. Analysis of the transaction
    b. Debits and credits posted from the journal to the ledger
    c. Occurrence of the business transaction
    d. Preparation of the financial statements
    e. Entry made in the journal
    f. Preparation of the trial balance

Application

Exercises

E 2-1.

LO 1   *Recognition*

Which of the following events would be recognised and recorded in the accounting records of the Sabatini Corporation on the date indicated?

Feb. 17   Sabatini Corporation offers to purchase some land for 280,000. There is a high likelihood that the offer will be accepted.

Mar. 7   Sabatini Corporation receives notice that its rent will be increased from 1,000 per month to 1,200 per month effective April 1.

Apr. 28   Sabatini Corporation receives its electricity bill for the month of April. The bill is not due until May 10.

May 2   Ray Sabatini, a major shareholder in Sabatini Corporation, dies. Ray's son, Andrew, inherits all of Ray's shares in the company.

May 14   Andrew, who inherited Ray's shares in Sabatini Corporation, sells 2,000 shares to Bob Rader for 120,000.

May 19   Sabatini Corporation places a firm order for new office equipment costing 42,000.

June 27   The office equipment ordered on May 19 arrives. Payment is not due until September 1.

E 2-2.

LO 1   *Application of Recognition Point*

Gina Health Shop uses a large amount of supplies in its business. The following table summarises selected transaction data for orders of supplies purchased:

Order	Date Shipped	Date Received	Amount
a	April 28	May 7	300
b	May 8	13	750
c	10	16	400
d	15	21	600
e	25	June 1	750
f	June 3	9	500

Determine the total purchases of supplies for May alone under each of the following assumptions:

1. Gina Health Shop recognises purchases when orders are shipped.
2. Gina Health Shop recognises purchases when orders are received.

E 2-3.

LO 2

LO 7

Classification of Accounts

Listed below are the ledger accounts of the Kedzie Service Corporation:

a. Cash
b. Wages Expense
c. Accounts Receivable
d. Share Capital
e. Service Revenue
f. Prepaid Rent
g. Accounts Payable
h. Investments in Shares and Bonds
i. Bonds Payable
j. Income Taxes Expense
k. Land
l. Supplies Expense
m. Prepaid Insurance

n. Electricity Expense
o. Fees Earned
p. Dividends
q. Wages Payable
r. Unearned Revenue
s. Office Equipment
t. Rent Payable
u. Notes Receivable
v. Interest Expense
w. Notes Payable
x. Supplies
y. Interest Receivable

Complete the following table, using Xs to indicate each account's classification and normal balance (whether a debit or credit increases the account):

			Type of Account					
				Shareholders' Equity			Normal Balance (increases balance)	
					Retained Earnings			
Item	Asset	Liability	Share Capital	Dividends	Revenue	Expense	Debit	Credit
a.	x						x	

E 2-4.

LO 4

Transaction Analysis

Analyse each of the following transactions, using the form shown in the example below the list.

a. Benny James established Benny's Barber Shop by investing 2,400 in exchange for 2,400 shares.
b. Paid two months' rent in advance, 840.
c. Purchased supplies on credit, 120.
d. Received cash for barbering services, 300.
e. Paid for supplies purchased in **c**.
f. Paid electricity bill, 72.
g. Declared and paid a dividend of 100.

Example

The asset Cash was increased. Increases in assets are recorded by debits. Debit Cash 2,400. A component of shareholders' equity, Share Capital, was increased. Increases in shareholders' equity are recorded by credits. Credit Share Capital 2,400.

E 2-5.

LO 4

Recording Transactions in T Accounts

Open the following T accounts: Cash; Repair Supplies; Repair Equipment; Accounts Payable; Share Capital; Dividends; Repair Fees Earned; Salary Expense; and Rent Expense. Record the following transactions for the month of June directly in the T accounts; use the letters to identify the transactions in your T accounts. Determine the balance in each account.

a. Michelle Donato opened Eastmoor Repair Service by investing 4,300 in cash and 1,600 in repair equipment in return for 5,900 shares in the company.
b. Paid 400 for current month's rent.
c. Purchased repair supplies on credit, 500.
d. Purchased additional repair equipment for cash, 300.
e. Paid salary to a helper, 450.
f. Paid 200 of amount purchased on credit in **c**.
g. Accepted cash for repairs completed, 960.
h. Declared and paid a dividend of 100.

E 2-6.

LO 7

Trial Balance

After recording the transactions in E 2-5, prepare a trial balance in proper sequence for Eastmoor Repair Service at June 30, 20xx.

E 2-7.

LO 4   *Analysis of Transactions*

Explain each transaction (**a** through **h**) entered below.

	Cash					Accounts Receivable						Equipment			
a.	60,000	b.	15,000		c.	6,000	g.	1,500		b.	15,000	h.	900
g.	1,500	e.	3,000							d.	9,000		
h.	900	f.	4,500										

	Accounts Payable					Service Revenue					Wages Expense	
f.	4,500	d.	9,000				c.	6,000		e.	3,000	

	Share Capital		
		a.	60,000

E 2-8.

LO 4   *Analysis of Unfamiliar*
LO 5   *Transactions*

Managers and accountants often encounter transactions with which they are unfamiliar. Use your analytical skills to analyse and record in general journal form the transactions below, which have not yet been discussed in the text.

May 1   Purchased inventory on account, 1,600.
    2   Purchased marketable securities for cash, 4,800.
    3   Returned part of inventory purchased in **a** for full credit, 500.
    4   Sold inventory on account, 1,600 (record sale only).
    5   Purchased land and a building for 600,000. Payment is 120,000 cash and a thirty-year mortgage for the remainder. The purchase price is allocated 200,000 to the land and 400,000 to the building.
    6   Received an order for 24,000 in services to be provided. With the order was a deposit of 8,000.

E 2-9.

LO 5   *Recording Transactions in*
LO 6   *the General Journal and*
          Posting to the Ledger
          Accounts

Open a general journal form like the one in Exhibit 2-3, and label it Page 10. After opening the form, record the following transactions in the journal.

Dec. 14   Purchased an item of equipment for 6,000, paying 2,000 as a cash down payment.
    28   Paid 3,000 of the amount owed on the equipment.

Prepare three ledger account forms like the one shown in Exhibit 2-4. Use the following account numbers: Cash, 111; Equipment, 143; and Accounts Payable, 212. Then post the two transactions from the general journal to the ledger accounts, at the same time making proper posting references.

Assume that the Cash account had a debit balance of 8,000 on the day before these transactions took place.

E 2-10.

LO 6   *Preparation of a Ledger*
          Account

Below is a T account showing cash transactions for the month of July.

	Cash		
July 1	18,800	July 3	1,800
9	2,400	7	400
16	8,000	13	3,400
23	400	15	10,000
29	12,800	27	1,200

Prepare the account in ledger form for Cash (Account 111). (See Exhibit 2-4 for an example.)

E 2-11.

LO 7   *Preparing a Trial Balance*

The accounts of the Barnes Service Corporation as of October 31, 20xx are listed below in alphabetical order. The amount of Accounts Payable is omitted.

Accounts Payable	?	Land	10,400
Accounts Receivable	6,000	Notes Payable	40,000
Building	68,000	Prepaid Insurance	2,200
Cash	18,000	Retained Earnings	22,900
Equipment	24,000	Share Capital	40,000

Prepare a trial balance with the proper heading (see Exhibit 2-6) and with the accounts listed in the chart of accounts sequence (see Exhibit 2-1). Calculate the balance of Accounts Payable.

E 2-12.

LO 7   *Effect of Errors on a Trial Balance*

Which of the following errors would cause a trial balance to have unequal totals? Explain your answers.

a. A payment to a lender was recorded as a debit to Accounts Payable for 172 and a credit to Cash for 127.
b. A payment of 200 to a lender for an account payable was debited to Accounts Receivable and credited to Cash.
c. A purchase of office supplies of 560 was recorded as a debit to Office Supplies for 56 and a credit to Cash for 56.
d. A purchase of equipment for 600 was recorded as a debit to Supplies for 600 and a credit to Cash for 600.

E 2-13.

LO 7   *Correcting Errors in a Trial Balance*

This was the trial balance for Gilliam Services at the end of September:

Gilliam Services
Trial Balance
September 30, 20xx

Cash	3,840	
Accounts Receivable	5,660	
Supplies	120	
Prepaid Insurance	180	
Equipment	8,400	
Accounts Payable		4,540
Share Capital		4,000
Retained Earnings		7,560
Dividends		700
Revenues		5,920
Salaries Expense	2,600	
Rent Expense	600	
Advertising Expense	340	
Electricity Expense	26	
	21,766	22,720

The trial balance does not balance because of a number of errors. Gilliam's accountant compared the amounts in the trial balance with the ledger, recalculated the account balances, and compared the postings. He found the following errors:

a. The beginning balance of Cash was understated by 400.
b. A cash payment of 420 was credited to Cash for 240.
c. A debit of 120 to Accounts Receivable was not posted.
d. Supplies purchased for 60 were posted as a credit to Supplies.
e. A debit of 180 to Prepaid Insurance was not posted.
f. The Accounts Payable account had debits of 5,320 and credits of 9,180.
g. The Notes Payable account, with a credit balance of 2,400, was not included in the trial balance.
h. The debit balance of Dividends was listed in the trial balance as a credit.
i. A 200 debit to Dividends was posted as a credit.
j. The actual balance of Electricity Expense, 260, was listed as 26 in the trial balance.

Prepare a corrected trial balance.

E 2-14.

LO 7   *Preparing a Trial Balance*

The Ferraro Construction Corporation builds foundations for buildings and parking lots. The following alphabetical list shows the account balances as of November 30, 20xx.

Accounts Payable	11,700		Office Van	6,600
Accounts Receivable	30,360		Prepaid Insurance	13,800
Cash	?		Retained Earnings	30,000
Construction Supplies	5,700		Revenue Earned	52,200
Dividends	23,400		Share Capital	90,000
Electricity Expense	1,260		Supplies Expense	21,600
Equipment	73,500		Wages Expense	26,400
Notes Payable	60,000			

Prepare a trial balance for the company with the proper heading and with the accounts in balance sheet sequence. Determine the correct balance for the Cash account on November 30, 20xx.

Problem Set

LO 4	*Transaction Analysis,*	P 2-1.
LO 7	*T Accounts, and Trial Balance*	

Elena Garcia established a small business, Garcia Training Centre, to teach individuals how to use spreadsheet analysis, word processing, and other techniques on microcomputers.

a. Garcia began by transferring the following assets to the business in exchange for 39,200 shares at a nominal value of 1 each:

Cash	18,400
Furniture	6,200
Microcomputer	14,600

b. Paid the first month's rent on a small storefront, 560.
c. Purchased computer software on credit, 1,500.
d. Paid for an advertisement in the local newspaper, 200.
e. Received enrolment applications from five students for a five-day course to start next week. Each student will pay 400 if he or she actually begins the course.
f. Paid wages to a part-time helper, 300.
g. Received cash payments from three of the students enrolled in **e**, 1,200.
h. Billed the two other students in **e**, who attended but did not pay in cash, 800.
i. Paid the electricity bill for the current month, 220.
j. Made a payment on the software purchased in **c**, 500.
k. Received payment from one student billed in **h**, 400.
l. Purchased a second microcomputer for cash, 9,400.
m. Declared and paid a dividend of 600.

REQUIRED

1. Set up the following T accounts: Cash; Accounts Receivable; Software; Furniture; Microcomputers; Accounts Payable; Share Capital; Dividends; Tuition Revenue; Wages Expense; Electricity Expense; Rent Expense; and Advertising Expense.
2. Record the transactions listed above by entering debits and credits directly in the T accounts, using the transaction letter to identify each debit and credit.
3. Prepare a trial balance using the current date.

		P 2-2.
LO 1	*Transaction Analysis*	
LO 4	*and Concepts*	
LO 5		

Monique Lacroix opened a photography and portrait studio on July 1. The studio completed the following transactions during the month:

July 1   Opened the business by depositing 51,000 in a bank account in the name of the business in exchange for 5,100 shares at a nominal value of 10 each.
3   Paid two months' rent in advance for a studio, 2,700.
5   Transferred to the business personal photography equipment valued at 12,900 in exchange for 1,290 shares of 10 each.
7   Ordered additional photography equipment, 7,500.
8   Purchased office equipment for cash, 5,400.
10   Received and paid for the photography equipment ordered on July 7, 7,500.
12   Purchased photography supplies on credit, 2,100.
13   Received cash for previously unbilled portraits, 1,140.
17   Billed customers for portraits, 2,250.
19   Paid for half the supplies purchased on July 12, 1,050.
25   Paid the electricity bill for July, 360.
26   Paid the telephone bill for July, 210.
28   Received payments from the customers billed on July 17, 750.
29   Paid wages to assistant, 1,200.
30   Received an advance deposit from a customer for work to be done, 150.
31   Declared and paid a dividend of 3,600.

REQUIRED

1. Record these transactions in the general journal.
2. Discuss how recognition applies to the transactions of July 7 and 8 and how classification applies to the transactions of July 13 and 30.

		P 2-3.
LO 1	*Transaction Analysis,*	
LO 4	*T Accounts,*	
LO 5	*General Journal,*	
LO 7	*and Trial Balance*	

Bob Reeves won a concession to rent bicycles in the local park during the summer. In the month of May, Reeves completed the following transactions for his bicycle rental business:

May 3   Began business by placing 14,400 in a bank account in the name of the corporation in exchange for 14,400 shares at a nominal value of 1 each.
6   Purchased supplies on account for 300.

May 7 Purchased ten bicycles for a total of 5,000, paying 2,400 down and agreeing to pay the rest in thirty days.

8 Received 940 in cash for rentals during the first week of operation.

9 Hired a part-time assistant to help out on weekends at 8 per hour.

10 Purchased a small shed to hold the bicycles and to use for other operations for 5,800 in cash.

11 Paid 800 in cash for shipping and installation costs (considered an addition to the cost of the shed) to place the shed at the park entrance.

14 Received 1,000 in cash for rentals during the second week of operation.

15 Paid a maintenance person 150 to clean the grounds.

16 Paid the assistant 160 for a weekend's work.

19 Paid 300 for the supplies purchased on May 6.

20 Paid 110 on a previously unrecorded repair bill on bicycles.

21 Received 1,100 in cash for rentals during the third week of operation.

23 Paid the assistant 160 for a weekend's work.

24 Billed a company 220 for bicycle rentals for an employees' outing.

26 Paid the 200 fee for May to the Park District for the right to the bicycle concession.

28 Received 820 in cash for rentals during the week.

30 Paid the assistant 160 for a weekend's work.

31 Declared and paid a dividend of 1,000.

REQUIRED

1. Record these transactions in the general journal. Use the accounts listed below.
2. Set up the following T accounts and post all the journal entries: Cash; Accounts Receivable; Supplies; Shed; Bicycles; Accounts Payable; Share Capital; Dividends; Rental Revenue; Wages Expense; Maintenance Expense; Repair Expense; and Concession Fee Expense.
3. Prepare a trial balance for Reeves Rentals as of May 31, 20xx.
4. Discuss how recognition applies to the transactions of May 24 and 28 and how classification applies to the transactions of May 11 and 15.

P 2-4.

LO 4 *Transaction Analysis,*
LO 5 *General Journal, Ledger*
LO 6 *Accounts, and Trial*
LO 7 *Balance*

Fulton Security Service provides ushers and security personnel for athletic events and other functions. Here is Fulton's trial balance at the end of October:

Fulton Security Services
Trial Balance
October 31, 20xx

Cash (111)	26,600	
Accounts Receivable (113)	18,800	
Supplies (115)	1,120	
Prepaid Insurance (118)	1,200	
Equipment (144)	15,600	
Accounts Payable (212)		10,600
Share Capital (311)		20,000
Retained Earnings (312)		22,320
Dividends (313)	4,000	
Security Services Revenue (411)		56,000
Wages Expense (511)	32,000	
Electricity Expense (512)	3,200	
Rent Expense (514)	6,400	
	108,920	108,920

During November, Fulton engaged in the following transactions:

Nov. 1 Received cash from customers billed last month, 8,400.

3 Made a payment on accounts payable, 6,200.

5 Purchased a new one-year insurance policy in advance, 7,200.

7 Purchased supplies on credit, 860.

8 Billed a client for security services, 4,400.

10 Made a rent payment for November, 1,600.

Nov. 11 Received cash from customers for security services, 3,200.
   12 Paid wages to the security staff, 2,800.
   14 Ordered equipment, 1,600.
   15 Paid the current month's electricity bill, 800.
   17 Received and paid for the equipment ordered on November 14, 1,600.
   19 Returned for full credit some of the supplies purchased on November 7 because they were defective, 240.
   21 Paid for the supplies purchased on November 7, less the return on November 19, 620.
   23 Billed a customer for security services performed, 3,600.
   30 Paid wages to the security staff, 2,100.
   30 Declared and paid a dividend of 2,000.

REQUIRED
1. Record these transactions in the general journal.
2. Open ledger accounts for the accounts shown in the trial balance. Enter the October 31 trial balance amounts in the ledger.
3. Post the journal entries to the ledger.
4. Prepare a trial balance as of November 30, 20xx.

Critical Thinking and Communication

Conceptual Mini-Case

CMC 2-1.
LO 1 *Recognition, Valuation, Classification Issues*

Stauffer Chemical Company, a United States-based company, relies on agricultural chemicals, such as fertiliser and pesticides, for more than half its profits. One year, Stauffer was hammered by bad weather, depressed farm prices, and decreased farm output caused by a federal price-support programme. In an article in the *Wall Street Journal*, it was reported that Stauffer had overstated its 1982 earnings by 31.1 million by improperly accounting for certain sales. In settling a lawsuit brought by the Securities and Exchange Commission (SEC), the company agreed, without admitting or denying the charges, to restate the 1982 financial results, lowering the 1982 profit by 25 per cent. The *Wall Street Journal* summarised the situation as follows:

> In the summer of 1982, "aware that agricultural chemical sales for its 1982–83 season would probably fall off sharply," Stauffer undertook a plan to accelerate sales of certain products to dealers during fiscal 1982, according to the SEC. . . .
>
> Stauffer, the SEC charged, offered its dealers incentives to take products during the fourth quarter of 1982. As a result, the company reported $72 million of revenue that ordinarily wouldn't have been booked until early 1983. By March 1983, according to the commission, Stauffer realized that it would have to "offer its distributors relief" from the oversupply of unsaleable products. Stauffer offered dealers refunds for as much as 100% of unsold products taken in 1982, compared with 32% the previous year.
>
> Stauffer ended up refunding nearly 40% of its 1982 agricultural chemical sales, but failed to disclose the "substantial uncertainties" surrounding the sales in the annual report it filed with the SEC in April 1983. The omission was "materially false and misleading," according to the SEC.
>
> "Their business was down and they wanted to accelerate sales," said a government official familiar with the year-long SEC investigation.[3]

REQUIRED
1. Prepare the journal entry that Stauffer made in 1982 that the SEC feels should not have been made until 1983.
2. Three issues that must be addressed when recording a transaction are recognition, valuation, and classification. Which of these issues were of most concern to the SEC in the Stauffer case? Explain how each applies to the transaction in **1**.

Cultural Mini-Case

CLMC 2-1.
LO 1 *Valuation*

Guinness, based in the United Kingdom, is one of the world's leading drinks companies, producing and marketing international best-selling brands such as Johnnie Walker, Bell's and Dewar's scotch whiskies, Gordon's and Tanqueray gins, and Guinness stout beer. In its statement of accounting policies, Guinness reports that "The accounts are prepared under the historical cost convention, modified to include the revaluation of land and buildings". As regards land and buildings, these are "stated at cost or valuation less depreciation. In the case of distilleries, breweries, and related specialised properties, valuations are principally on a depreciated replacement cost basis. Hotel and leisure business properties are valued on the basis of an open market valuation for existing use".[4]

REQUIRED
1. Explain what is meant by the "historical cost convention".
2. What are the advantages and disadvantages of adopting a revaluation approach to measurement?
3. Discuss the relevance of the methods used by Guinness to value their land and buildings.

Ethics Mini-Case

EMC 2-1.

LO 1   *Recognition Point and*
Ethical Considerations

One of **Chan Office Supplies Corporation**'s sales representatives, Jerry Hasbrow, is compensated on a commission basis and receives a substantial bonus for meeting his annual sales goal. The company's recognition point for sales is the day of shipment. On December 31, Jerry realises that he needs sales of 2,000 to reach his sales goal and receive the bonus. He calls a purchaser for a local insurance company, whom he knows well, and asks him to buy 2,000 worth of copier paper today. The purchaser says, "But Jerry, that's more than a year's supply for us." Jerry says, "Buy it today. If you decide it's too much, you can return however much you want for full credit next month." The purchaser says, "Okay, ship it." The paper is shipped on December 31 and recorded as a sale. On January 15, the purchaser returns 1,750 worth of paper for full credit (approved by Jerry) against the bill. Should the shipment on December 31 be recorded as a sale? Discuss the ethics of Jerry's action.

Decision-Making Case

DMC 2-1.

LO 4   *Transaction Analysis and*
LO 5   *Evaluation of*
LO 6   *a Trial Balance*
LO 7

Benjamin Obi hired a lawyer to help him start **Obi Repairs Corporation**. On June 1, Mr Obi deposited 23,000 in a bank account in the name of the corporation in exchange for 2,300 shares at 10 each. When he paid the lawyer's bill of 1,400, the lawyer advised him to hire an accountant to keep his records. However, Mr Obi was so busy that it was June 30 before he asked you to straighten out his records. Your first task is to develop a trial balance based on the June transactions.

After the investment and payment to the lawyer, Mr Obi borrowed 10,000 from the bank. He later paid 520, which included interest of 120, on this loan. He also purchased a pickup truck in the company's name, paying 5,000 down and financing 14,800. The first payment on the truck is due July 15. Mr Obi then rented an office and paid three months' rent, 1,800, in advance. Credit purchases of office equipment for 1,400 and repair tools for 1,000 must be paid by July 13.

In June, Obi Repairs Corporation completed repairs of 2,600, of which 800 were cash transactions. Of the credit transactions, 600 was collected during June, and 1,200 remained to be collected at the end of June. Wages of 800 were paid to employees. On June 30, the company received a 150 bill for June electricity expense and a 100 check from a customer for work to be completed in July.

REQUIRED
1. Record the June transactions in the general journal (no dates are required).
2. Set up and determine the balance of each T account by posting the general journal entries to T accounts and determining the balance of each account.
3. Prepare a June 30 trial balance for Obi Repairs Corporation.
4. Benjamin Obi is unsure how to evaluate the trial balance. His Cash account balance is 24,980, which exceeds his original investment of 23,000 by 1,980. Did he make a profit of 1,980? Explain why the Cash account is not an indicator of business earnings. Cite specific examples to show why it is difficult to determine net profit by looking solely at figures in the trial balance.

Basic Research Activity

RA 2-1.

LO 4   *Transactions in a*
LO 5   *Business Article*

Obtain a recent issue of a business journal or newspaper. Find an article on a company you recognise or on a company in a business that interests you. Read the article carefully, noting any references to transactions that the company engages in. These may be normal transactions (sales, purchases) or unusual transactions (a merger, the purchase of another company). Bring a copy of the article to class and be prepared to describe how you would analyse and record the transactions you have noted.

Financial Reporting and Analysis

Interpretation Cases from Business

ICB 2-1.

LO 4   *Transactions*
LO 5   *Analysis*

Mitsubishi Electric is a Japanese company that manufactures and markets a broad range of electrical and electronic products and systems including home electronics, communications satellites, and Internet support services. The company states: "As a transnational company, we have always been a world leader who has been able to anticipate emerging trends, and continue to generate new and innovative ideas through our global network of R & D programmes. As a result of this approach we have created an environment in which we can create new technologies, new products and new markets."[5]

Selected data from Mitsubishi's 1996 statement of cash flows are shown below (in millions of yen):

Investing Activities

Capital expenditures (including property, plant, and equipment)	(307,028)
Proceeds from sale of property, plant, and equipment	7,683
Purchase of current investments and investment securities	(137,791)
Proceeds from sale of current investments and investment securities	62,254

Financing Activities

Proceeds from long-term debt	119,768
Repayment of long-term debt	(192,559)
Dividends paid to shareholders	(21,467)

REQUIRED

1. Record each of the above entries in the general journal (assuming that each is done in a single transaction and that there are no gains or losses on the transactions).
2. From 1995 to 1996, Mitsubishi's cash balance declined by only 197,375 million yen. How is this possible when investing and financing activities resulted in a net cash outflow of 422,646 million yen?

ICB 2-2.

LO 4   *Transactions*
LO 5   *Analysis*

McDonald's, a United States-based global food service retailer, reported the following selected aggregate cash transactions in the investing and financing activities sections of its statement of cash flows in its 1995 annual report (amounts in millions of dollars):[6]

Property and equipment expenditures	(2,063.7)
Purchases of restaurant businesses	(110.1)
Sales of restaurant businesses	151.6
Long-term financing issuances	1,250.2
Long-term financing repayments	(532.2)

REQUIRED

1. Prepare journal entries to record the above transactions (assuming that each is a single transaction and that there are no gains or losses on the transactions).
2. Given that McDonald's cash flow from operations is 2,296.2 million dollars, why should additional long-term finance be needed?

Nestlé Case

NC 2-1.

LO 4   *Transactions Analysis*
LO 5

Refer to the Consolidated Balance Sheet in the appendix on Nestlé to answer the following questions. Prepare T accounts for the accounts Liquid Assets (cash and cash equivalents), Trade and Other Debtors (accounts receivable), Trade and Other Creditors (accounts payable), and Provisions for Taxation (taxes payable). Properly place the balance of the account at December 31, 1996, in the T accounts. Below are some typical transactions in which Nestlé would engage. Analyse each transaction, enter in the T accounts, and determine the balance of each account. Assume all entries are in millions of Swiss francs.

a. Received cash from customers billed previously, 35.
b. Paid cash for income taxes previously owed, 24.
c. Paid cash to suppliers for amounts owed, 120.

ENDNOTES

1. The *Wall Street Journal*, October 16, 1990, p. A3, and The Boeing Co., *Annual Report*, 1989.
2. See International Accounting Standards Committee, *Framework for the Preparation and Presentation of Financial Statements* (London: IASC, 1996).
3. Wynter, Leon E., "Stauffer Profit Overstated in '82, SEC Says in Suit", *Wall Street Journal*, August 14, 1984. Reprinted by permission of *Wall Street Journal*, © 1984 Dow Jones & Company, Inc. All Rights Reserved Worldwide.
4. Guinness, *Annual Report*, 1995, p. 48.
5. Mitsubishi Electric, *Annual Report*, 1996, preface.
6. McDonald's Corporation, *Annual Report*, 1995.

Chapter 3

MEASURING BUSINESS
PROFIT

LEARNING OBJECTIVES

1. Define *net profit* and its two major components, *revenues* and *expenses*.
2. Explain the difficulties of profit measurement caused by (a) the accounting period issue, (b) the going concern issue, and (c) the matching issue.
3. Define *accrual accounting* and explain two broad ways of accomplishing it.
4. State four principal situations that require adjusting entries.
5. Prepare typical adjusting entries.
6. Prepare financial statements from an adjusted trial balance.
7. Explain the purposes of closing entries.
8. Prepare the required closing entries.

SUPPLEMENTAL OBJECTIVE

9. Analyse cash flows from accrual-based information.

DECISION POINT
REUTERS

Reuters, based in the United Kingdom, aims to be the leading supplier of information and news to the financial community and the world's media. Its main competitors in the information market are Bloomberg, Dow Jones Telerate, and Knight-Ridder. In media, Associated Press, Worldwide Television News, and Agence France Presse are the main international competitors. Reuters has 14,348 employees, and payroll is its largest expense.[1]

During most of the year, payroll is recorded as an expense when it is paid. However, at the end of the year employees may have earned compensation (wages and salaries) that will not be paid until after the end of the year. If these wages and salaries are not accounted for correctly, they will appear in the wrong year—the year in which they are paid instead of the year in which the company benefited from them. How does accounting solve this problem?

According to the concepts of accrual accounting and the matching rule, which you will learn in this chapter, the accountant must determine the amount of wages and salaries earned but not paid and record an adjusting entry for this amount as an expense of the current year and a liability to be paid the next year. In this way, expenses are correctly stated on the income statement and liabilities are correctly stated on the balance sheet. In the case of Reuters, the effect is significant. At the end of 1995, Reuters had a liability for accruals including compensation of 333 million British pounds. If an adjusting entry had not been made to record this liability and its related expense in 1995, profit (before taxes) would have been overstated by this amount. Profit after deducting this expense in 1995 was 599 million British pounds. Without the adjusting entry, readers of the financial statements would have been misled into thinking that Reuters' profit was much greater than it actually was.

THE MEASUREMENT OF BUSINESS PROFIT

For a business to succeed, or even to survive, it must earn a profit. The elements directly related to profit are revenues and expenses. *Net profit* is reported on the income statement and is used by management, shareholders, and others to monitor business performance. Readers of income statements need to understand how the accountant defines net profit and be aware of its strengths and weaknesses as a measure of company performance.

OBJECTIVE 1

Define net profit *and its two major components,* revenues *and* expenses

Net Profit

Net profit is the net increase in shareholders' equity that results from the operations of a company and is accumulated in the Retained Earnings account. Net profit, in its simplest form, is measured by the difference between revenues and expenses when revenues exceed expenses:

$$\text{Net profit} = \text{revenues} - \text{expenses}$$

When expenses exceed revenues, a **net loss** occurs.

Revenues

Revenues are the gross inflow of economic benefits during the period arising in the course of the ordinary activities of a business when these activities result in increases in shareholders' equity.[2] Revenues result from selling goods, rendering services, or performing other business activities. In the simplest case, revenues equal the price of goods sold and services rendered over a specific period of time. When a business delivers a product or provides a service to a customer, it usually receives either cash or a promise to pay cash in the near future. The promise to pay is recorded in either Accounts Receivable or Notes Receivable. The revenue for a given period equals the total of cash and receivables from goods and services provided to customers during that period.

Liabilities generally are not affected by revenues, and some transactions that increase cash and other assets are not revenues. For example, a bank loan increases liabilities and cash but does not produce revenue. The collection of accounts receivable, which increases cash and decreases accounts receivable, does not produce revenue either. Remember that when a sale on credit takes place, the asset account Accounts Receivable increases; at the same time, a shareholders' equity revenue account increases. So counting the collection of the receivable as revenue later would be counting the same sale twice.

Not all increases in shareholders' equity arise from revenues. Shareholders' investments increase shareholders' equity but are not revenue.

Expenses

Expenses are the decreases in economic benefits during the period in the form of outflows or depletion of assets or incurrences of liabilities that result in decreases in shareholders' equity. Expenses result from the costs of selling goods, rendering services, or performing other business activities. In other words, expenses are the costs of the goods and services used up in the course of earning revenues. Often called the *cost of doing business*, expenses include the costs of goods sold, the costs of activities necessary to carry on a business, and the costs of attracting and serving customers. Examples are salaries, rent, advertising, telephone service, and depreciation (allocation of cost) of a building or office equipment.

Just as not all cash receipts are revenues, not all cash payments are expenses. A cash payment to reduce a liability does not result in an expense. The liability, however, may have come from incurring a previous expense, such as advertising, that is to be paid later. There may also be two steps before an expenditure of cash becomes an expense. For example, prepaid expenses or plant assets (such as machinery and equipment) are recorded as assets when they are acquired. Later, as their usefulness expires in the operation of the business, their cost is allocated to expenses. In fact, expenses sometimes are called *expired costs*.

Not all decreases in shareholders' equity arise from expenses. Dividends decrease shareholders' equity, but they are not expenses.

Temporary and Permanent Accounts

Revenues and expenses can be recorded directly in shareholders' equity as increases and decreases to retained earnings. In practice, however, management and others want to know the details of the increases and decreases in shareholders' equity produced by revenues and expenses. For this reason, a separate account for each revenue and expense is needed to accumulate the amounts. Because the balances of these income statement accounts apply only to the current accounting period, they are called **temporary accounts**. Temporary accounts, or *nominal accounts*, show the accumulation of revenues and expenses over the accounting period. At the end of the accounting period, their balances are transferred to shareholders' equity. Thus, nominal accounts start each accounting period with zero balances and then accumulate the specific revenues and expenses of that period. On the other hand, the balance sheet accounts—that is, assets, liabilities, and shareholders' equity—are called **permanent accounts**, or *real accounts*, because their balances extend beyond the end of an accounting period. The process of transferring totals from the temporary revenue and expense accounts to the permanent shareholders' equity accounts is described in the section on completion of the accounting cycle.

<table>
<tr><td>

OBJECTIVE 2a

Explain the difficulties of profit measurement caused by the accounting period issue

</td><td>

The Accounting Period Issue

The **accounting period issue** addresses the difficulty of assigning revenues and expenses to a short period of time, such as a month or a year. Not all transactions can be easily assigned to specific time periods. Purchases of buildings and equipment, for example, have effects that extend over many years. Accountants solve this problem by estimating the number of years the buildings or equipment will be in use and the cost that should be assigned to each year. In the process, they make an assumption about **periodicity:** that the net profit for any period of time less than the life of the business, although tentative, is still a useful estimate of the net profit for the period.

Generally, to make comparisons easier, the time periods are of equal length. And the time period should be noted in the financial statements. Financial statements may be prepared for any time period. Accounting periods of less than one year—for example, a month or a quarter—are called *interim periods*. The twelve-month accounting period used by a company is called its **accounting year.** Many companies use the calendar year, January 1 to December 31, for their accounting year. Others find it convenient to choose an accounting year that ends during a slack season rather than a peak season. In this case, the accounting year corresponds to the company's yearly cycle of business activity.

</td></tr>
</table>

<table>
<tr><td>

OBJECTIVE 2b

Explain the difficulties of profit measurement caused by the going concern issue

</td><td>

The Going Concern Issue

The process of measuring business profit requires that certain expense and revenue transactions be allocated over several accounting periods. The number of accounting periods raises the issue of *going concern*: how long will the business entity last? Many businesses last less than five years; in any given year, thousands go bankrupt. To prepare financial statements for an accounting period, the accountant must make an assumption about the ability of the business to survive. Specifically, unless there is evidence to the contrary, the accountant assumes that the business will continue to operate for the foreseeable future, that the business is a **going concern.** Justification for all the techniques of profit measurement rests on the assumption of continuity.[3] For example, the assumption of continuity allows the cost of certain assets to be held on the balance sheet to a future year when it will become an expense on the income statement.

Another example has to do with the value of assets on the balance sheet. In the chapter on measuring business transactions, we pointed out that the accountant records assets at cost and may well not record subsequent changes in their value. But the value of assets to a going concern is much higher than the value of assets to a firm facing bankruptcy. In the latter case, the accountant may be asked to set aside the assumption of going concern and to prepare financial statements based on the assumption that the firm will go out of business and sell all of its assets at liquidation value—that is, for what they will bring in cash.

</td></tr>
</table>

<table>
<tr><td>

OBJECTIVE 2c

Explain the difficulties of profit measurement caused by the matching issue

</td><td>

The Matching Issue

Revenues and expenses can be accounted for on a cash received and cash paid basis. This practice is known as the **cash basis of accounting.** In certain instances, an individual or a business may use the cash basis of accounting for income tax purposes. Under this method, revenues are reported in the period in which cash is received, and expenses are reported in the period in which cash is paid. Taxable profit, therefore, is calculated as the difference between cash receipts from revenues and cash payments for expenses.

</td></tr>
</table>

In some countries, such as Austria, France, Germany, Spain, Portugal, and Switzerland, a cautious approach to the recognition of work completed on long-term contracts is often adopted. This means that a smaller amount of revenues is recorded in the current accounting period than would otherwise be the case.

Although the cash basis of accounting works well for some small businesses and many individuals, it does not meet the needs of most businesses. As explained above, revenues can be earned in a period other than the one in which cash is received, and expenses can be incurred in a period other than the one in which cash is paid. To measure net profit adequately, revenues and expenses must be assigned to the appropriate accounting period. The accountant solves this problem by applying the **matching rule**:

Revenues must be assigned to the accounting period in which the goods are sold or the services performed, and expenses must be assigned to the accounting period in which they are used to produce revenue.

Direct cause-and-effect relationships seldom can be demonstrated for certain, but many costs appear to be related to particular revenues. The accountant recognises these expenses and the related revenues in the same accounting period. Examples are the costs of goods sold and sales commissions. When there is no direct means of connecting expenses and revenues, the accountant tries to allocate costs in a systematic way among the accounting periods that benefit from the costs. For example, a building is converted from an asset to an expense by allocating its cost over the years that benefit from its use.

OBJECTIVE 3

Define accrual accounting and explain two broad ways of accomplishing it

ACCRUAL ACCOUNTING

To apply the matching rule, accountants have developed accrual accounting. **Accrual accounting** is the basis under which "the effects of transactions and other events are recognised when they occur (and not as cash or its equivalent is received or paid) and they are recorded in the accounting records and reported in the financial statements of the periods to which they relate".[4] That is, accrual accounting consists of all the techniques developed by accountants to apply the matching rule. It is done in two general ways: (1) by recording revenues when earned and expenses when incurred and (2) by adjusting the accounts.

Recognising Revenues When Earned and Expenses When Incurred

We illustrated the first method of accrual accounting several times in the chapter on measuring business transactions. For example, when Joan Miller Advertising Agency made a sale on credit by placing advertisements for a client (in the January 19 transaction), revenue was recorded at the time of the sale by debiting Accounts Receivable and crediting Advertising Fees Earned. This is how the accountant recognises the revenue from a credit sale before the cash is collected. Accounts Receivable serves as a holding account until payment is received. The process of determining when a sale takes place is called **revenue recognition**.

When Joan Miller Advertising Agency received the telephone bill on January 30, the expense was recognised both as having been incurred and as helping to produce revenue in January. The transaction was recorded by debiting Telephone Expense and crediting Accounts Payable. Until the bill is paid, Accounts Payable serves as a holding account. Notice that recognition of the expense does not depend on the payment of cash.

Adjusting the Accounts

An accounting period, by definition, ends on a particular day. The balance sheet must list all assets and liabilities as of the end of that day, and the income statement must

EXHIBIT 3-1   *Trial Balance for Joan Miller Advertising Agency*

Joan Miller Advertising Agency
Trial Balance
January 31, 20xx

Cash	1,720	
Accounts Receivable	2,800	
Art Supplies	1,800	
Office Supplies	800	
Prepaid Rent	800	
Prepaid Insurance	480	
Art Equipment	4,200	
Office Equipment	3,000	
Accounts Payable		3,170
Unearned Art Fees		1,000
Share Capital		10,000
Dividends	1,400	
Advertising Fees Earned		4,200
Office Wages Expense	1,200	
Electricity Expense	100	
Telephone Expense	70	
	18,370	18,370

contain all revenues and expenses applicable to the period ending on that day. Although operating a business is a continuous process, there must be a cutoff point for the periodic reports. Some transactions invariably span the cutoff point; thus, some accounts need adjustment.

For example, some of the accounts in the end-of-the-period trial balance for Joan Miller Advertising Agency (Exhibit 3-1) do not show the correct balances for preparing the financial statements. The January 31 trial balance lists prepaid rent of 800. At 400 per month, this represents rent for the months of January and February. So on January 31, one-half of the 800, or 400, represents rent expense for January; the remaining 400 represents an asset that will be used in February. An adjustment is needed to reflect the 400 balance in the Prepaid Rent account on the balance sheet and the 400 rent expense on the income statement. As you will see on the following pages, several other accounts in the Joan Miller Advertising Agency trial balance do not reflect their correct balances. Like the Prepaid Rent account, they need to be adjusted.

OBJECTIVE 4

State four principal situations that require adjusting entries

THE ADJUSTMENT PROCESS

Accountants use **adjusting entries** to apply accrual accounting to transactions that span more than one accounting period. Adjusting entries have at least one balance sheet (or permanent) account entry and at least one income statement (or temporary) account entry. Adjusting entries never involve the Cash account. They are needed when deferrals or accruals exist. A **deferral** is the postponement of the recognition of an expense already paid or incurred, or of a revenue already received. Deferrals are used in two instances:

1. Costs have been recorded that must be apportioned between two or more accounting periods. Examples are prepaid rent, prepaid insurance, supplies, and costs of a building. The adjusting entry in this case involves an asset account and an expense account.
2. Revenues have been recorded that must be apportioned between two or more accounting periods. An example is payments collected for services yet to be rendered. The adjusting entry involves a liability account and a revenue account.

An **accrual** is the recognition of a revenue or expense that has arisen but has not yet been recorded. Accruals are required in these two cases:

1. There are unrecorded revenues. An example is fees earned but not yet collected or billed to customers. The adjusting entry involves an asset account and a revenue account.
2. There are unrecorded expenses. Examples are the wages earned by employees in the current accounting period but after the last pay period. The adjusting entry involves an expense account and a liability account.

Once again, we use Joan Miller Advertising Agency to illustrate the kinds of adjusting entries that most businesses must make.

OBJECTIVE 5

Prepare typical adjusting entries

Apportioning Recorded Expenses between Two or More Accounting Periods (Deferred Expenses)

Companies often make expenditures that benefit more than one period. These expenditures are usually debited to an asset account. At the end of the accounting period, the amount that has been used is transferred from the asset account to an expense account. Two of the more important kinds of adjustments are for prepaid expenses and the depreciation of plant and equipment.

Prepaid Expenses

Some expenses customarily are paid in advance. These expenditures are therefore called **prepaid expenses.** Among them are rent, insurance, and supplies. At the end of an accounting period, a portion (or all) of these goods or services will have been used up or will have expired. An adjusting entry reducing the asset and increasing the expense, as shown in Figure 3-1, is always required. The amount of the adjustment equals the cost of the goods or services used up or expired. If adjusting entries for prepaid expenses are not made at the end of the period, both the balance sheet and the income statement will present information that is incorrect: the assets of the company will be overstated, and the expenses of the company will be understated. This

FIGURE 3-1 *Adjustment for Prepaid (Deferred) Expense*

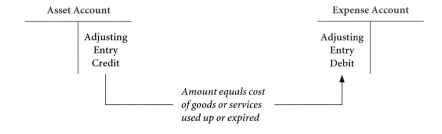

means that shareholders' equity on the balance sheet and net profit on the income statement will be overstated.

At the beginning of the month, Joan Miller Advertising Agency paid two months' rent in advance. This expenditure resulted in an asset consisting of the right to occupy the office for two months. As each day in the month passed, part of the asset's cost expired and became an expense. By January 31, one-half had expired and should be treated as an expense. Here is the analysis of this economic event:

Prepaid Rent (Adjustment a)

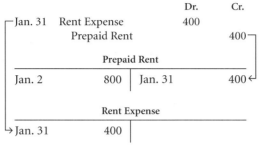

Transaction: Expiration of one month's rent.

Analysis: Assets decrease. Shareholders' equity decreases.

Rules: Decreases in assets are recorded by credits. Decreases in shareholders' equity are recorded by debits.

Entries: The decrease in shareholders' equity is recorded by a debit to Rent Expense. The decrease in assets is recorded by a credit to Prepaid Rent.

The Prepaid Rent account now has a balance of 400, which represents one month's rent paid in advance. The Rent Expense account reflects the 400 expense for the month of January.

Besides rent, Joan Miller Advertising Agency prepaid expenses for insurance, art supplies, and office supplies, all of which call for adjusting entries.

On January 8, the agency purchased a one-year life insurance policy, paying for it in advance. Like prepaid rent, prepaid insurance offers benefits (in this case, protection) that expire day by day. By the end of the month, one-twelfth of the protection had expired. The adjustment is analysed and recorded like this:

Prepaid Insurance (Adjustment b)

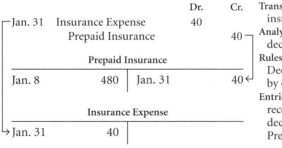

Transaction: Expiration of one month's life insurance.

Analysis: Assets decrease. Shareholders' equity decreases.

Rules: Decreases in assets are recorded by credits. Decreases in shareholders' equity are recorded by debits.

Entries: The decrease in shareholders' equity is recorded by a debit to Insurance Expense. The decrease in assets is recorded by a credit to Prepaid Insurance.

The Prepaid Insurance account now shows the correct balance, 440, and Insurance Expense reflects the expired cost, 40 for the month.

Early in the month, Joan Miller Advertising Agency purchased art supplies and office supplies. As Joan Miller did artwork for various clients during the month, art supplies were consumed. Also, her secretary used office supplies. There is no need to account for these supplies every day because the financial statements are not prepared until the end of the month and the recordkeeping would involve too much work. Instead, Joan Miller makes a careful inventory of the art and office supplies at the end of the month. This inventory records the number and cost of those supplies that are still assets of the company—that are yet to be consumed.

Suppose the inventory shows that art supplies costing 1,300 and office supplies costing 600 are still available. This means that of the 1,800 of art supplies originally purchased, 500 worth were used up (became an expense) in January. Of the original 800 of office supplies, 200 worth were consumed. These transactions are analysed and recorded as follows:

Art Supplies and Office Supplies (Adjustments c and d)

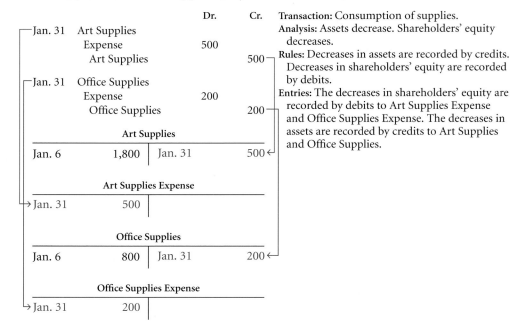

			Dr.	Cr.	Transaction: Consumption of supplies.

Jan. 31 Art Supplies Expense 500

Art Supplies 500

Transaction: Consumption of supplies.
Analysis: Assets decrease. Shareholders' equity decreases.
Rules: Decreases in assets are recorded by credits. Decreases in shareholders' equity are recorded by debits.

Jan. 31 Office Supplies Expense 200

Office Supplies 200

Entries: The decreases in shareholders' equity are recorded by debits to Art Supplies Expense and Office Supplies Expense. The decreases in assets are recorded by credits to Art Supplies and Office Supplies.

Art Supplies

| Jan. 6 | 1,800 | Jan. 31 | 500 |

Art Supplies Expense

| Jan. 31 | 500 | |

Office Supplies

| Jan. 6 | 800 | Jan. 31 | 200 |

Office Supplies Expense

| Jan. 31 | 200 | |

The asset accounts Art Supplies and Office Supplies now reflect the correct balances, 1,300 and 600, respectively, of supplies that are yet to be consumed. In addition, the amount of art supplies used up during the accounting period is shown as 500 and the amount of office supplies used up is shown as 200.

Depreciation of Plant and Equipment

When a company buys a tangible long-term asset—a building, equipment, trucks, cars, a computer, store fixtures, or office furniture—it is, in effect, prepaying for the usefulness of that asset for as long as it benefits the company. Because a long-term asset is a deferral of an expense, the accountant must allocate the cost of the asset over its estimated useful life. The amount allocated to any one accounting period is called **depreciation**, or *depreciation expense*. Depreciation, like other expenses, is incurred during an accounting period to produce revenue.

It is often impossible to tell how long an asset will last or how much of the asset is used in any one period. For this reason, depreciation must be estimated. Accountants have developed a number of methods for estimating depreciation and for dealing with the related complex problems. Here we look at the simplest case.

Suppose, for example, that Joan Miller Advertising Agency estimates that its art equipment and office equipment will last five years (60 months) and will be worthless at the end of that time. The monthly depreciation of art equipment and office equipment is 70 (4,200 ÷ 60 months) and 50 (3,000 ÷ 60 months), respectively. These amounts represent the costs allocated to the month, and they are the amounts by which the asset accounts must be reduced and the expense accounts increased (reducing shareholders' equity).

Art Equipment and Office Equipment (Adjustments e and f)

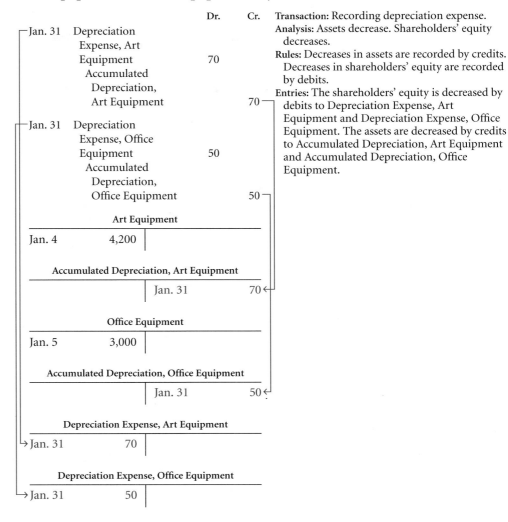

	Dr.	Cr.	
Jan. 31 Depreciation Expense, Art Equipment	70		Transaction: Recording depreciation expense.
Accumulated Depreciation, Art Equipment		70	
Jan. 31 Depreciation Expense, Office Equipment	50		
Accumulated Depreciation, Office Equipment		50	

Analysis: Assets decrease. Shareholders' equity decreases.

Rules: Decreases in assets are recorded by credits. Decreases in shareholders' equity are recorded by debits.

Entries: The shareholders' equity is decreased by debits to Depreciation Expense, Art Equipment and Depreciation Expense, Office Equipment. The assets are decreased by credits to Accumulated Depreciation, Art Equipment and Accumulated Depreciation, Office Equipment.

Art Equipment

Jan. 4   4,200

Accumulated Depreciation, Art Equipment

                          Jan. 31   70

Office Equipment

Jan. 5   3,000

Accumulated Depreciation, Office Equipment

                          Jan. 31   50

Depreciation Expense, Art Equipment

Jan. 31   70

Depreciation Expense, Office Equipment

Jan. 31   50

Accumulated Depreciation—A Contra Account

Notice that in the analysis above, the asset accounts are not credited directly. Instead, as shown in Figure 3-2, new accounts—Accumulated Depreciation, Art Equipment and Accumulated Depreciation, Office Equipment—are credited. These **accumulated depreciation accounts** are contra-asset accounts used to total the past depreciation expense on a specific long-term asset. A **contra account** is a separate account that is paired with a related account—in this case an asset account. The balance of the contra account is shown on the financial statement as a deduction from the related account. There are several types of contra accounts. In this case, the balance of Accumulated Depreciation, Art Equipment is shown on the balance sheet as a deduction from the associated account Art Equipment. Likewise, Accumulated Depreciation, Office Equipment is a deduction from Office Equipment. Exhibit 3-2 shows the plant and equipment section of the balance sheet for Joan Miller Advertising Agency after these adjusting entries have been made.

A contra account is used for two very good reasons. First, it recognises that depreciation is an estimate. Second, a contra account preserves the original cost of an asset: in combination with the asset account, it shows both how much of the asset has been allocated as an expense and the balance left to be depreciated. As the months

FIGURE 3-2 *Adjustment for Depreciation*

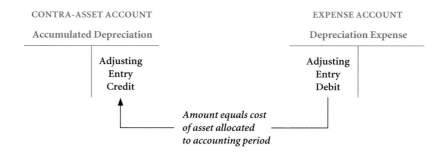

pass, the amount of the accumulated depreciation grows, and the net amount shown as an asset declines. In six months, Accumulated Depreciation, Art Equipment will show a balance of 420; when this amount is subtracted from Art Equipment, a net amount of 3,780 will remain. This net amount is called the carrying amount, or *book value*, of the asset.

Other names are also used for accumulated depreciation; among them is the term *allowance for depreciation*. However, *accumulated depreciation* is the newer, better term.

Apportioning Recorded Revenues between Two or More Accounting Periods (Deferred Revenues)

Just as expenses can be paid before they are used, revenues can be received before they are earned. When revenues are received in advance, the company has an obligation to deliver goods or perform services. Therefore, **unearned revenues** are shown in a liability account. For example, publishing companies usually receive payment in advance for magazine subscriptions. These receipts are recorded in a liability account. If the company fails to deliver the magazines, subscribers are entitled to have their money returned to them. As the company delivers each issue of the magazine, it earns a part of the advance payments. This earned portion must be transferred from the

EXHIBIT 3-2 *Plant and Equipment Section of the Balance Sheet*

Joan Miller Advertising Agency
Partial Balance Sheet
January 31, 20xx

Plant and Equipment		
Art Equipment	4,200	
Less Accumulated Depreciation	70	4,130
Office Equipment	3,000	
Less Accumulated Depreciation	50	2,950
Total Plant and Equipment		7,080

FIGURE 3-3 *Adjustment for Unearned (Deferred) Revenue*

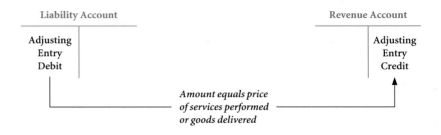

Unearned Subscriptions account to the Subscription Revenue account, as shown in Figure 3-3.

During the month of January, Joan Miller Advertising Agency received 1,000 as an advance payment for artwork to be done for another agency. Assume that by the end of the month, 400 of the artwork was done and accepted by the other agency. Here is the transaction analysis:

Unearned Art Fees (Adjustment g)

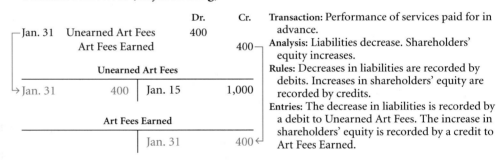

The liability account Unearned Art Fees now reflects the amount of work still to be performed, 600. The revenue account Art Fees Earned reflects the services performed and the revenue earned for those services during the month, 400.

Recognising Unrecorded Revenues (Accrued Revenues)

Accrued revenues are revenues for which a service has been performed or goods delivered but for which no entry has been recorded. Any revenues that have been earned but not recorded during the accounting period call for an adjusting entry that debits an asset account and credits a revenue account, as shown in Figure 3-4. For example, the interest on a note receivable is earned day by day but may not be received until another accounting period. Interest Receivable should be debited and Interest Income should be credited for the interest accrued at the end of the current period.

Suppose that Joan Miller Advertising Agency has agreed to place a series of advertisements for Marsh Gas Company and that the first appears on January 31, the last day of the month. The fee of 200 for this advertisement, which has been earned but not recorded, should be recorded this way:

FIGURE 3-4   *Adjustment for Unrecorded (Accrued) Revenue*

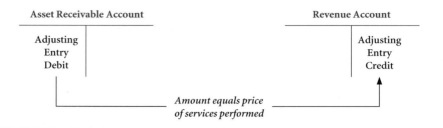

Accrued Advertising Fees (Adjustment h)

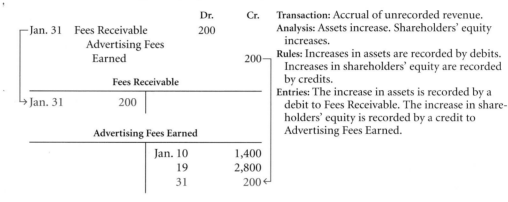

		Dr.	Cr.
Jan. 31	Fees Receivable	200	
	Advertising Fees		
	Earned		200

Fees Receivable

| Jan. 31 | 200 | |

Advertising Fees Earned

	Jan. 10	1,400
	19	2,800
	31	200

Transaction: Accrual of unrecorded revenue.
Analysis: Assets increase. Shareholders' equity increases.
Rules: Increases in assets are recorded by debits. Increases in shareholders' equity are recorded by credits.
Entries: The increase in assets is recorded by a debit to Fees Receivable. The increase in shareholders' equity is recorded by a credit to Advertising Fees Earned.

Now both the asset and the revenue accounts show the correct balance: the 200 in Fees Receivable is owed to the company, and the 4,400 in Advertising Fees Earned has been earned by the company during the month. Marsh will be billed for the series of advertisements when it is completed.

Recognising Unrecorded Expenses (Accrued Expenses)

At the end of an accounting period, there are usually expenses that have been incurred but not recorded, and they require adjusting entries. For example, each day interest accumulates on borrowed money. At the end of the accounting period, an adjusting entry is made to record this accumulated interest, which is an expense of the period, and the corresponding liability to pay the interest (see Figure 3-5). Other unrecorded expenses are taxes, wages, and salaries. As the expense and the corresponding liability accumulate, they are said to *accrue*—hence the term **accrued expenses**.

FIGURE 3-5   *Adjustment for Unrecorded (Accrued) Expense*

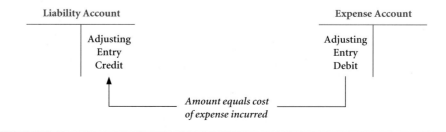

Accrued Wages

Suppose the calendar for January looks like this:

January

Su	M	T	W	Th	F	Sa
	1	2	3	4	5	6
7	8	9	10	11	12	13
14	15	16	17	18	19	20
21	22	23	24	25	26	27
28	29	30	31			

By the end of business on January 31, the secretary at Joan Miller Advertising Agency will have worked three days (Monday, Tuesday, and Wednesday) beyond the last biweekly pay period, which ended on January 26. The employee has earned the wages for these days, but she will not be paid until the regular payday in February. The wages for these three days are rightfully an expense for January, and the liabilities should reflect the fact that the company owes the secretary for those days. Because the secretary's wage rate is 600 every two weeks, or 60 per day (600 ÷ 10 working days), the expense is 180 (60 × 3 days).

Accrued Wages (Adjustment i)

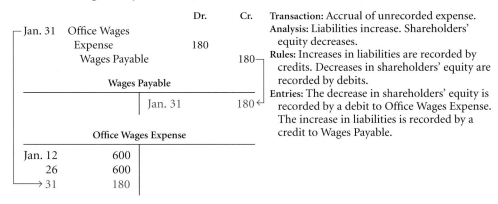

The liability of 180 is now reflected correctly in the Wages Payable account. The actual expense incurred for office wages during the month, 1,380, is also correct.

Estimated Income Taxes

As a corporation, Joan Miller Advertising Agency is subject to income taxes. Although the actual amount owed cannot be determined until after net profit is computed at the end of the year, each month should bear its part of the total year's expense, in accordance with the matching concept. Therefore, the amount of income taxes expense for the current month must be estimated. Assume that after analysing the first month's operations and conferring with her accountant, Joan Miller estimates January's share of the income taxes for the year to be 400. This estimated expense can be analysed and recorded as follows:

Estimated Income Taxes (Adjustment j)

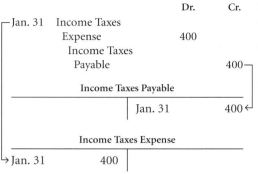

		Dr.	Cr.
Jan. 31	Income Taxes		
	Expense	400	
	Income Taxes		
	Payable		400

Income Taxes Payable

	Jan. 31 400

Income Taxes Expense

| Jan. 31   400 | |

Transaction: Accrual of estimated income taxes.
Analysis: Liabilities increase. Shareholders' equity decreases.
Rules: Increases in liabilities are recorded by credits. Decreases in shareholders' equity are recorded by debits.
Entries: The decrease in shareholders' equity is recorded by a debit to Income Taxes Expense. The increase in liabilities is recorded by a credit to Income Taxes Payable.

Expenses for January will now reflect the estimated income taxes attributable to that month, and the liability for these estimated income taxes will appear on the balance sheet.

DECISION POINT

JOAN MILLER ADVERTISING AGENCY

In one example used in this chapter, on January 31, an accrual of 180 is made for wages payable. Joan Miller might ask, "Why go to the trouble of making this adjustment? Why worry about it? Doesn't everything come out in the end, when the secretary is paid in February? Because wages expense in total is the same for the two months, isn't the net profit in total unchanged?" Give three reasons why adjusting entries can help Joan Miller assess the performance of her business.

Adjusting entries are important because they help accountants compile information that is useful to management and shareholders. First, adjusting entries are necessary to measure income and financial position in a relevant and useful way. Joan Miller should know how much the agency has earned each month and what its liabilities and assets are on the last day of the month. For instance, if the three days' accrued wages for the secretary are not recorded, the agency's profit will be overstated by 180, or 11.3 per cent (180 ÷ 1,590). Second, adjusting entries allow financial statements to be compared from one accounting period to the next. Joan Miller can see whether the company is making progress towards earning a profit or if the company has improved its financial position.

To return to our example, if the adjustment for accrued wages is not recorded, not only will the net profit for January be overstated by 180, but the net profit for February (the month when payment will be made) will be understated by 180. This error will make February's earnings, whatever they may be, appear lower than they actually are. Third, even though one adjusting entry may seem insignificant, the cumulative effect of all adjusting entries can be great. Look back over all the adjustments made by Joan Miller Advertising Agency for prepaid rent and insurance, art and office supplies, depreciation of art and office equipment, unearned art fees, accrued advertising fees, accrued wages, and estimated income taxes. These are normal adjustments. Their effect on net profit in January is to increase expenses by 1,840 and revenues by 600, for a net effect of minus 1,240, or 78 per cent (1,240 ÷ 1,590) of net profit. If adjusting entries had not been made, Joan Miller would have had a false impression of her company's performance.

OBJECTIVE 6

Prepare financial statements from an adjusted trial balance

Using the Adjusted Trial Balance to Prepare Financial Statements

In the chapter on measuring business transactions, a trial balance was prepared before any adjusting entries were recorded. Here, we prepare an **adjusted trial balance**, a list of the accounts and balances after the adjusting entries have been recorded and posted. The adjusted trial balance for Joan Miller Advertising Agency is shown on the left side of Exhibit 3-3. Notice that some accounts, such as Cash and Accounts

EXHIBIT 3-3 *Relationship of Adjusted Trial Balance to Income Statement*

Joan Miller Advertising Agency
Adjusted Trial Balance
January 31, 20xx

Cash	1,720	
Accounts Receivable	2,800	
Fees Receivable	200	
Art Supplies	1,300	
Office Supplies	600	
Prepaid Rent	400	
Prepaid Insurance	440	
Art Equipment	4,200	
Accumulated Depreciation, Art Equipment		70
Office Equipment	3,000	
Accumulated Depreciation, Office Equipment		50
Accounts Payable		3,170
Unearned Art Fees		600
Wages Payable		180
Income Taxes Payable		400
Share Capital		10,000
Dividends	1,400	
Advertising Fees Earned		4,400
Art Fees Earned		400
Office Wages Expense	1,380	
Electricity Expense	100	
Telephone Expense	70	
Rent Expense	400	
Insurance Expense	40	
Art Supplies Expense	500	
Office Supplies Expense	200	
Depreciation Expense, Art Equipment	70	
Depreciation Expense, Office Equipment	50	
Income Taxes Expense	400	
	19,270	19,270

Joan Miller Advertising Agency
Income Statement
For the Month Ended January 31, 20xx

Revenues		
Advertising Fees Earned		4,400
Art Fees Earned		400
Total Revenues		4,800
Expenses		
Office Wages Expense	1,380	
Electricity Expense	100	
Telephone Expense	70	
Rent Expense	400	
Insurance Expense	40	
Art Supplies Expense	500	
Office Supplies Expense	200	
Depreciation Expense, Art Equipment	70	
Depreciation Expense, Office Equipment	50	
Income Taxes Expense	400	
Total Expenses		3,210
Net Profit		1,590

Receivable, have the same balances they have in the trial balance (see Exhibit 3-1 on page 79) because no adjusting entries affected them. Other accounts, such as Art Supplies, Office Supplies, Prepaid Rent, and Prepaid Insurance, have different balances from those in the trial balance because adjusting entries did affect them. If the adjusting entries have been posted to the accounts correctly, the adjusted trial balance should have equal debit and credit totals.

From the adjusted trial balance, the financial statements can be easily prepared. The income statement is prepared from the revenue and expense accounts, as shown in Exhibit 3-3. Then, as shown in Exhibit 3-4, the balance sheet is prepared. Notice that the net profit from the income statement is combined with dividends to give the net change in Joan Miller Advertising Agency's Retained Earnings account. The resulting balance of Retained Earnings at January 31 is used on the balance sheet, as are the asset and liability accounts. Finally, closing entries are made to the accounts and the financial statements are prepared for users. This final step completes the **accounting cycle** (see Figure 3-6), which is the sequence of steps followed in the accounting process to measure business transactions and transform them into financial statements.

<table>
<tr><td>OBJECTIVE 7</td><td>CLOSING ENTRIES</td></tr>
<tr><td>*Explain the purposes of
closing entries*</td><td></td></tr>
</table>

Closing entries are journal entries made at the end of an accounting period. They accomplish two purposes. First, closing entries set the stage for the next accounting period by clearing revenue, expense, and dividend accounts of their balances. Remember that the income statement reports net profit (or loss) for a single accounting period and shows revenues and expenses for that period only. For the income statement to present the activity of a single accounting period, each new period must begin with zero balances in the revenue and expense accounts. These zero balances are obtained by using closing entries to clear the balances in the revenue and expense accounts at the end of each accounting period. The Dividends account is closed in a similar manner.

Second, closing entries summarise a period's revenues and expenses. This is done by transferring the balances of revenues and expenses to the **Profit Summary** account. This temporary account, which appears in the chart of accounts between the Dividends account and the first revenue account, provides a place to summarise all revenues and expenses. It is used only in the closing process and never appears in the financial statements.

The balance of Profit Summary equals the net profit or loss reported on the income statement. The net profit or loss is then transferred to the Retained Earnings account. This is done because even though revenues and expenses are recorded in revenue and expense accounts, they actually represent increases and decreases in shareholders' equity. Closing entries transfer the net effect of increases (revenues) and decreases (expenses) to shareholders' equity. An overview of the closing process is illustrated in Figure 3-7.

As explained earlier, revenue and expense accounts are temporary, or nominal, accounts because they begin each period with a zero balance, accumulate a balance during the period, and are then cleared by means of closing entries. On the other hand, balance sheet accounts are considered to be permanent accounts because they carry their end-of-period balances into the next accounting period.

EXHIBIT 3-4 *Relationship of Adjusted Trial Balance to Balance Sheet*

Joan Miller Advertising Agency
Adjusted Trial Balance
January 31, 20xx

Cash	1,720	
Accounts Receivable	2,800	
Fees Receivable	200	
Art Supplies	1,300	
Office Supplies	600	
Prepaid Rent	400	
Prepaid Insurance	440	
Art Equipment	4,200	
Accumulated Depreciation,		
Art Equipment		70
Office Equipment	3,000	
Accumulated Depreciation,		
Office Equipment		50
Accounts Payable		3,170
Unearned Art Fees		600
Wages Payable		180
Income Taxes Payable		400
Share Capital		10,000
Dividends	1,400	
Advertising Fees Earned		4,400
Art Fees Earned		400
Office Wages Expense	1,380	
Electricity Expense	100	
Telephone Expense	70	
Rent Expense	400	
Insurance Expense	40	
Art Supplies Expense	500	
Office Supplies Expense	200	
Depreciation Expense,		
Art Equipment	70	
Depreciation Expense,		
Office Equipment	50	
Income Taxes Expense	400	
	19,270	19,270

Joan Miller Advertising Agency
Balance Sheet
January 31, 20xx

Assets

Cash		1,720
Accounts Receivable		2,800
Fees Receivable		200
Art Supplies		1,300
Office Supplies		600
Prepaid Rent		400
Prepaid Insurance		440
Art Equipment	4,200	
Less Accumulated		
Depreciation	70	4,130
Office Equipment	3,000	
Less Accumulated		
Depreciation	50	2,950
Total Assets		14,540

Liabilities

Accounts Payable	3,170	
Unearned Art Fees	600	
Wages Payable	180	
Income Taxes Payable	400	
Total Liabilities		4,350

Shareholders' Equity

Share Capital	10,000	
Retained Earnings	190	
Total Shareholders' Equity		10,190
Total Liabilities and Shareholders' Equity		14,540

From Income Statement in Exhibit 3-3

Note: Retained Earnings Account
for the Month Ended January 31, 20xx

Retained Earnings, January 1, 20xx	0
Net Profit	1,590
Subtotal	1,590
Less Dividends	1,400
Retained Earnings, January 31, 20xx	190

FIGURE 3-6   *Overview of the Accounting Cycle*

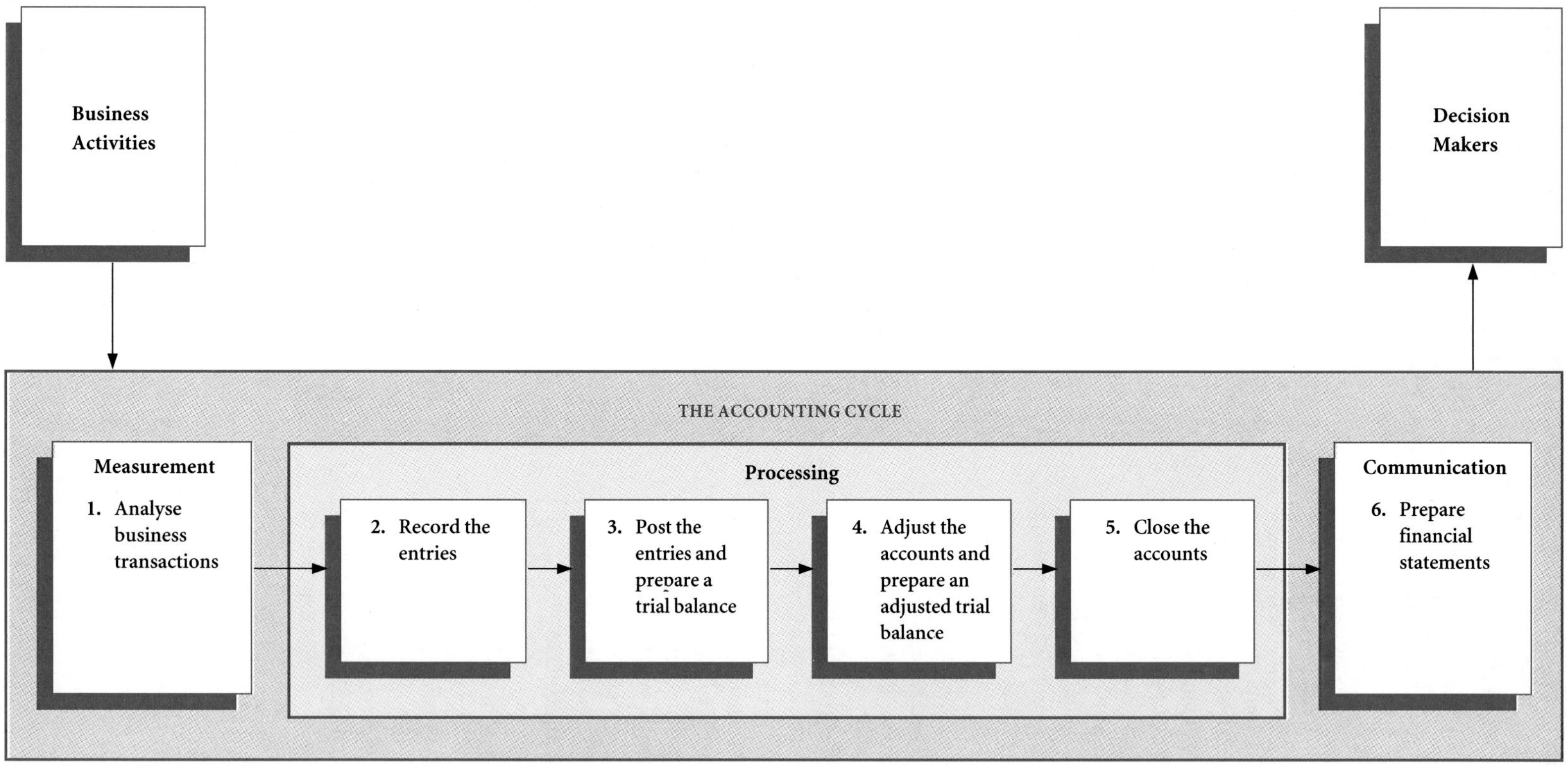

Business Activities

Decision Makers

THE ACCOUNTING CYCLE

Measurement

1. Analyse business transactions

Processing

2. Record the entries

3. Post the entries and prepare a trial balance

4. Adjust the accounts and prepare an adjusted trial balance

5. Close the accounts

Communication

6. Prepare financial statements

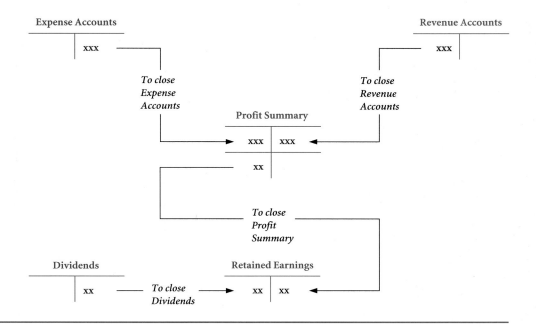

FIGURE 3-7 *Overview of the Closing Process*

OBJECTIVE 8

Prepare the required closing entries

Required Closing Entries

There are four important steps in closing the accounts:

1. Closing the credit balances from income statement accounts to the Profit Summary account
2. Closing the debit balances from income statement accounts to the Profit Summary account
3. Closing the Profit Summary account balance to the Retained Earnings account
4. Closing the Dividends account balance to the Retained Earnings account

Each step is accomplished by a closing entry. The data for recording the closing entries are found in the adjusted trial balance. Exhibit 3-5 shows the relationships of the four kinds of entries to the adjusted trial balance.

BUSINESS BULLETIN   **Technology in Practice**

In a computerised accounting system, adjusting entries may be entered just like any other transactions. However, since some adjusting entries, such as those for insurance expense and depreciation expense, may be similar for each accounting period, and others, such as those for accrued wages and income taxes, may always involve the same accounts, the computer may be programmed to display the adjusting entries automatically so that all the accountant has to do is verify the amounts or enter the correct amounts. Then the adjusting entries are entered and posted and the adjusted trial balance is prepared with the touch of a button.

EXHIBIT 3-5 *Preparing Closing Entries from the Adjusted Trial Balance*

Joan Miller Advertising Agency Adjusted Trial Balance January 31, 20xx		
Cash	1,720	
Accounts Receivable	2,800	
Fees Receivable	200	
Art Supplies	1,300	
Office Supplies	600	
Prepaid Rent	400	
Prepaid Insurance	440	
Art Equipment	4,200	
Accumulated Depreciation, Art Equipment		70
Office Equipment	3,000	
Accumulated Depreciation, Office Equipment		50
Accounts Payable		3,170
Unearned Art Fees		600
Wages Payable		180
Income Taxes Payable		400
Share Capital		10,000
Dividends	1,400	
Advertising Fees Earned		4,400
Art Fees Earned		400
Office Wages Expense	1,380	
Electricity Expense	100	
Telephone Expense	70	
Rent Expense	400	
Insurance Expense	40	
Art Supplies Expense	500	
Office Supplies Expense	200	
Depreciation Expense, Art Equipment	70	
Depreciation Expense, Office Equipment	50	
Income Taxes Expense	400	
	19,270	19,270

Entry 1:

Jan. 31 Advertising Fees Earned 411 4,400
  Art Fees Earned 412 400
    Profit Summary 314 4,800
    To close the revenue accounts

Entry 2:

Jan. 31 Profit Summary 314 3,210
    Office Wages Expense 511 1,380
    Electricity Expense 512 100
    Telephone Expense 513 70
    Rent Expense 514 400
    Insurance Expense 515 40
    Art Supplies Expense 516 500
    Office Supplies Expense 517 200
    Depreciation Expense, Art Equipment 519 70
    Depreciation Expense, Office Equipment 520 50
    Income Taxes Expense 521 400
    To close the expense accounts

Profit Summary			
Jan. 31	3,210	Jan. 31	4,800
Jan. 31	1,590	Bal.	—

Entry 3:

Jan. 31 Profit Summary 314 1,590
    Retained Earnings 312 1,590
    To close the Profit Summary account

Entry 4:

Jan. 31 Retained Earnings 312 1,400
    Dividends 313 1,400
    To close the Dividends account

Step 1: Closing the Credit Balances from Income Statement Accounts to the Profit Summary Account

On the credit side of the adjusted trial balance in Exhibit 3-5, two revenue accounts show balances: Advertising Fees Earned and Art Fees Earned. To close these two accounts, a journal entry must be made debiting each in the amount of its balance and crediting the total to the Profit Summary account. The effect of posting the entry is shown in Exhibit 3-6. Notice that the entry (1) sets the balances of the revenue accounts to zero and (2) transfers the total revenues to the credit side of the Profit Summary account.

EXHIBIT 3-6   *Posting the Closing Entry of the Credit Balances from the Income Statement Accounts to the Profit Summary Account*

Advertising Fees Earned					Account No. 411	
Date	Item	Post. Ref.	Debit	Credit	Balance Debit	Balance Credit
Jan. 10		J2		1,400		1,400
19		J2		2,800		4,200
31	Adj. (h)	J3		200		4,400
31	Closing	J4	4,400			—

Profit Summary					Account No. 314	
Date	Item	Post. Ref.	Debit	Credit	Balance Debit	Balance Credit
Jan. 31	Closing	J4		4,800		4,800

4,400
400
4,800

Art Fees Earned					Account No. 412	
Date	Item	Post. Ref.	Debit	Credit	Balance Debit	Balance Credit
Jan. 31	Adj. (g)	J3		400		400
31	Closing	J4	400			—

Step 2: Closing the Debit Balances from Income Statement Accounts to the Profit Summary Account

Several expense accounts show balances on the debit side of the adjusted trial balance in Exhibit 3-5. A compound entry is needed to credit each of these expense accounts for its balance and to debit the Profit Summary account for the total. The effect of posting the closing entry is shown in Exhibit 3-7. Notice how the closing entry (1) reduces the expense account balances to zero and (2) transfers the total of the account balances to the debit side of the Profit Summary account.

Step 3: Closing the Profit Summary Account to the Retained Earnings Account

After the entries closing the revenue and expense accounts have been posted, the balance of the Profit Summary account equals the net profit or loss for the period. Since revenues are represented by the credit to Profit Summary and the expenses are represented by the debit to Profit Summary, a net profit is indicated by a credit balance (where revenues exceed expenses); a net loss, by a debit balance (where expenses exceed revenues). At this point, the Profit Summary balance, whatever its nature, must be closed to the Retained Earnings account, as shown in Exhibit 3-5. The effect of posting the closing entry, when the company has a net profit, is shown in Exhibit 3-8. Notice the dual effect of (1) closing the Profit Summary account and (2) transferring the balance, net profit in this case, to Retained Earnings.

Step 4: Closing the Dividends Account to the Retained Earnings Account

The Dividends account shows the amount by which retained earnings is reduced during the period by cash dividends. The debit balance of the Dividends account is closed to the Retained Earnings account, as shown in Exhibit 3-5. The effect of this closing entry, as shown in Exhibit 3-9, is to (1) close the Dividends account and (2) transfer the balance to the Retained Earnings account.

The Accounts after Closing

After all the steps in the closing process have been completed and all closing entries have been posted to the accounts, the stage is set for the next accounting period. The

EXHIBIT 3-7   *Posting the Closing Entry of the Debit Balances from the Income Statement Accounts to the Profit Summary Account*

Office Wages Expense   Account No. 511

Date	Item	Post. Ref.	Debit	Credit	Balance Debit	Balance Credit
Jan. 12		J2	600		600	
26		J2	600		1,200	
31	Adj. (i)	J3	180		1,380	
31	Closing	J4		1,380	—	

Electricity Expense   Account No. 512

Date	Item	Post. Ref.	Debit	Credit	Balance Debit	Balance Credit
Jan. 29		J2	100		100	
31	Closing	J4		100	—	

Telephone Expense   Account No. 513

Date	Item	Post. Ref.	Debit	Credit	Balance Debit	Balance Credit
Jan. 30		J2	70		70	
31	Closing	J4		70	—	

Rent Expense   Account No. 514

Date	Item	Post. Ref.	Debit	Credit	Balance Debit	Balance Credit
Jan. 31	Adj. (a)	J3	400		400	
31	Closing	J4		400	—	

Insurance Expense   Account No. 515

Date	Item	Post. Ref.	Debit	Credit	Balance Debit	Balance Credit
Jan. 31	Adj. (b)	J3	40		40	
31	Closing	J4		40	—	

Art Supplies Expense   Account No. 516

Date	Item	Post. Ref.	Debit	Credit	Balance Debit	Balance Credit
Jan. 31	Adj. (c)	J3	500		500	
31	Closing	J4		500	—	

Office Supplies Expense   Account No. 517

Date	Item	Post. Ref.	Debit	Credit	Balance Debit	Balance Credit
Jan. 31	Adj. (d)	J3	200		200	
31	Closing	J4		200	—	

Profit Summary   Account No. 314

Date	Item	Post. Ref.	Debit	Credit	Balance Debit	Balance Credit
Jan. 31	Closing	J4		4,800		4,800
31	Closing	J4	3,210			1,590

1,380
100
70
400
40
500
400
50
70
200
3,210

Depreciation Expense, Art Equipment   Account No. 519

Date	Item	Post. Ref.	Debit	Credit	Balance Debit	Balance Credit
Jan. 31	Adj. (e)	J3	70		70	
31	Closing	J4		70	—	

Depreciation Expense, Office Equipment   Account No. 520

Date	Item	Post. Ref.	Debit	Credit	Balance Debit	Balance Credit
Jan. 31	Adj. (f)	J3	50		50	
31	Closing	J4		50	—	

Income Taxes Expense   Account No. 521

Date	Item	Post. Ref.	Debit	Credit	Balance Debit	Balance Credit
Jan. 31	Adj. (j)	J3	400		400	
31	Closing	J4		400	—	

revenue, expense, and Dividends accounts (temporary accounts) have zero balances. Retained Earnings has been increased to reflect the agency's net profit and decreased for dividends. The balance sheet accounts (permanent accounts) show the correct balances, which are carried forward to the next period.

EXHIBIT 3-8 *Posting the Closing Entry of the Profit Summary Account to the Retained Earnings Account*

Profit Summary					Account No. 314	
		Post.			Balance	
Date	Item	Ref.	Debit	Credit	Debit	Credit
Jan. 31	Closing	J4		4,800		4,800
31	Closing	J4	3,210			1,590
31	Closing	J4	1,590			—

Retained Earnings					Account No. 312	
		Post.			Balance	
Date	Item	Ref.	Debit	Credit	Debit	Credit
Jan. 31	Closing	J4		1,590		1,590

SUPPLEMENTAL

OBJECTIVE 9

Analyse cash flows from accrual-based information

Cash flow statements are becoming increasingly important around the world. In many countries, including Australia, China, Fiji, Malaysia, Malta, Nigeria, Singapore, the U.K. and U.S., cash flow statements are now required to be presented to shareholders along with an income statement and balance sheet.

CASH FLOWS, ACCRUAL ACCOUNTING, AND MANAGEMENT OBJECTIVES

The purpose of accrual accounting is to measure the earnings of a business during an accounting period. This measurement of net profit is directly related to management's profitability goal. A company must earn a sufficient net profit to survive over the long term. Management also has the short-range goal of achieving sufficient liquidity to meet its needs for cash, to pay its ongoing obligations, and to plan for borrowing money from the bank. An important measure of liquidity is cash flow. Cash flow is the amount of cash paid out or received during an accounting period and the resulting availability of cash. It is important for managers to be able to use accrual-based financial information to analyse cash flows in order to plan payments to lenders and assess the need for short-term borrowing.

Every revenue or expense account on the income statement has one or more related accounts on the balance sheet. For instance, Supplies Expense is related to Supplies, Wages Expense to Wages Payable, and Service Revenues to Unearned Revenues. As shown in this chapter, these accounts are related through adjusting entries whose purpose is to apply the matching rule in the measurement of net profit. The cash flows generated or paid by company operations may also be determined by analysing these relationships. For example, suppose that after receiving the financial statements in Exhibits 3-3 and 3-4, Joan Miller wants to know how much cash was expended for art supplies. On the income statement, Art Supplies Expense is 500, and on the balance sheet, Art Supplies is 1,300. Because January was the first month of operation for the company, there was no prior balance of supplies, so the amount of cash expended for supplies during the month was 1,800. The cash flow used to purchase art supplies (1,800) was much greater than the amount expensed in determining profit (500). In planning for February, Joan Miller can anticipate that the cash needed may be less than the amount expensed because, given the large inventory of art supplies, probably a month or more will pass before it is necessary to buy additional

EXHIBIT 3-9 *Posting the Closing Entry of the Dividends Account to the Retained Earnings Account*

Dividends					Account No. 313	
		Post.			Balance	
Date	Item	Ref.	Debit	Credit	Debit	Credit
Jan. 25		J2	1,400		1,400	
31	Closing	J4		1,400	—	

Retained Earnings					Account No. 312	
		Post.			Balance	
Date	Item	Ref.	Debit	Credit	Debit	Credit
Jan. 31	Closing	J4		1,590		1,590
31	Closing	J4	1,400			190

supplies. Understanding these cash flow effects enables Joan to better predict her business's need for cash during February.

The general rule for determining the cash flow received from any revenue or paid for any expense (except depreciation, which is a special case not covered here) is to determine the potential cash payments or cash receipts and deduct the amount not paid or received. The application of the general rule varies with the type of asset or liability account, as shown below:

Type of Account	Potential Payment or Receipt			Not Paid or Received		Result
Prepaid Expense	Ending Balance	+	Expense for the Period	− Beginning Balance	=	Cash Payments for Expenses
Unearned Revenue	Ending Balance	+	Revenue for the Period	− Beginning Balance	=	Cash Receipts from Revenues
Accrued Liability	Beginning Balance	+	Expense for the Period	− Ending Balance	=	Cash Payments for Expenses
Accrued Receivable	Beginning Balance	+	Revenue for the Period	− Ending Balance	=	Cash Receipts from Revenues

For instance, assume that on May 31 a company had a balance of 480 in Prepaid Insurance and that on June 30 the balance was 670. If the insurance expense during June was 120, the amount of cash expended on insurance during June can be calculated as follows:

Prepaid Insurance at June 30	670
Insurance Expense during June	120
Potential cash payments for insurance	790
Less Prepaid Insurance at May 31	480
Cash payments for insurance during June	310

The beginning balance is deducted because it was paid in a prior accounting period. Note that the cash payments equal the expense plus the increase in the balance of the Prepaid Insurance account [120 + (670 − 480) = 310]. In this case, the cash paid was almost three times the amount of insurance expense. In future months, cash payments are likely to be less than the expense.

A NOTE ABOUT JOURNAL ENTRIES

Throughout this chapter and the chapter on measuring business transactions, we have presented a full analysis of each journal entry. The analyses showed you the thought process behind each entry. By now, you should be fully aware of the effects of transactions on the accounting equation and the rules of debit and credit. For this reason, in the rest of the book, journal entries are presented without full analysis.

CHAPTER REVIEW

Review of Learning Objectives

1. **Define *net profit* and its two major components, *revenues* and *expenses*.** Net profit is the net increase in shareholders' equity that results from the operations of a company. Net profit equals revenues minus expenses, unless expenses exceed revenues, in which case a net loss results. Revenues equal the price of goods sold and services rendered during a specific period. Expenses are the costs of goods and services used up in the process of producing revenues.

2. **Explain the difficulties of profit measurement caused by (a) the accounting period issue, (b) the going concern issue, and (c) the matching issue.** The accounting period issue recognises that net profit measurements for short periods of time are necessarily tentative. The going concern issue recognises that even though businesses face an uncertain future, without

evidence to the contrary, accountants must assume that a business will continue indefinitely. The matching issue has to do with the difficulty of assigning revenues and expenses to a period of time. It is approached by applying the matching rule: revenues must be assigned to the accounting period in which the goods are sold or the services performed, and expenses must be assigned to the accounting period in which they are used to produce revenue.

3. **Define *accrual accounting* and explain two broad ways of accomplishing it.** Accrual accounting consists of all the techniques developed by accountants to apply the matching rule. The two general ways of accomplishing accrual accounting are (1) by recognising revenues when earned and expenses when incurred and (2) by adjusting the accounts.

4. **State four principal situations that require adjusting entries.** Adjusting entries are required (1) when recorded expenses have to be apportioned between two or more accounting periods, (2) when recorded revenues must be apportioned between two or more accounting periods, (3) when unrecorded revenues exist, and (4) when unrecorded expenses exist.

5. **Prepare typical adjusting entries.** The preparation of adjusting entries is summarised in the following table:

| Type of Adjusting Entry | Type of Account | | Examples |
	Debited	Credited	
Deferrals			
1. Apportioning recorded expenses (expired, not recorded)	Expense	Asset (or contra asset)	Prepaid Rent Prepaid Insurance Supplies Buildings Equipment
2. Apportioning recorded revenues (earned, not recorded)	Liability	Revenue	Commissions Received in Advance
Accruals			
1. Accrued revenues (earned, not received)	Asset	Revenue	Commissions Receivable Interest Receivable
2. Accrued expenses (incurred, not paid)	Expense	Liability	Wages Payable Interest Payable

6. **Prepare financial statements from an adjusted trial balance.** An adjusted trial balance is prepared after adjusting entries have been posted to the ledger accounts. Its purpose is to test the balance of the ledger after the adjusting entries are made and before the financial statements are prepared. The income statement is prepared from the revenue and expense accounts. The balance sheet is prepared from the asset and liability accounts in the adjusted trial balance and from the retained earnings account.

7. **Explain the purposes of closing entries.** Closing entries have two purposes. First, they clear the balances of all temporary accounts (revenue and expense accounts and Dividends) so that they have zero balances at the beginning of the next accounting period. Second, they summarise a period's revenues and expenses in the Profit Summary account so that the net profit or loss for the period can be transferred as a total to Retained Earnings.

8. **Prepare the required closing entries.** Closing entries are prepared by first transferring the revenue and expense account balances to the Profit Summary account. Then the balance of the Profit Summary account is transferred to the Retained Earnings account. And, finally, the balance of the Dividends account is transferred to the Retained Earnings account.

Supplemental Objective

9. **Analyse cash flows from accrual-based information.** Cash flow information bears on management's liquidity goal. The general rule for determining the cash flow effect of any revenue or expense (except depreciation, which is a special case not covered here) is to determine the potential cash payments or cash receipts and deduct the amount not paid or received.

Review of Concepts and Terminology

The following concepts and terms were introduced in this chapter.

LO 6 **Accounting cycle:** The sequence of steps followed in the accounting process to measure business transactions and transform them into financial statements.

LO 2 **Accounting period issue:** The difficulty of assigning revenues and expenses to a short period of time.

LO 2 **Accounting year:** Any twelve-month accounting period used by an economic entity.

LO 4 **Accrual:** The recognition of an expense or revenue that has arisen but has not yet been recorded.

LO 3 **Accrual accounting:** The basis under which the effects of transactions and other events are recognised when they occur, and not as cash or its equivalent is received or paid by the business.

LO 5 **Accrued expenses:** Expenses that have been incurred but are not recognised in the accounts; unrecorded expenses.

LO 5 **Accrued revenues:** Revenues for which a service has been performed or goods delivered but for which no entry has been made; unrecorded revenues.

LO 5 **Accumulated depreciation accounts:** Contra-asset accounts used to accumulate the depreciation expense of a specific long-lived asset.

LO 6 **Adjusted trial balance:** A trial balance prepared after all adjusting entries have been posted to the accounts.

LO 4 **Adjusting entries:** Entries made to apply accrual accounting to transactions that span more than one accounting period.

LO 2 **Cash basis of accounting:** Accounting for revenues and expenses on a cash received and cash paid basis.

LO 7 **Closing entries:** Journal entries made at the end of an accounting period that set the stage for the next accounting period by clearing the temporary accounts of their balances, and that summarise a period's revenues and expenses.

LO 5 **Contra account:** An account whose balance is subtracted from an associated account in the financial statements.

LO 4 **Deferral:** The postponement of the recognition of an expense that already has been paid or incurred, or of a revenue that already has been received.

LO 5 **Depreciation:** The portion of the cost of a tangible long-term asset allocated to any one accounting period. Also called *depreciation expense.*

LO 1 **Expenses:** The decreases in economic benefits during the period in the form of outflows or depletions of assets or incurrences of liabilities that result in decreases in shareholders' equity. Expenses are the cost of goods and services used up in the course of earning revenues. Often called the *cost of doing business.*

LO 2 **Going concern:** The assumption, unless there is evidence to the contrary, that a business entity will continue to operate for the foreseeable future.

LO 2 **Matching rule:** Revenues must be assigned to the accounting period in which the goods are sold or the services performed, and expenses must be assigned to the period in which they are used to produce revenue.

LO 1 **Net loss:** The net decrease in shareholders' equity that results when expenses exceed revenues. It is accumulated in the Retained Earnings account.

LO 1   **Net profit:** The net increase in shareholders' equity that results from business operations and is accumulated in the Retained Earnings account; revenues less expenses when revenues exceed expenses.

LO 2   **Periodicity:** The recognition that net profit for any period less than the life of the business, although tentative, is still a useful estimate of net profit for that period.

LO 1   **Permanent accounts:** Balance sheet accounts; accounts whose balances can extend past the end of an accounting period. Also called *real accounts*.

LO 5   **Prepaid expenses:** Expenses paid in advance that have not yet expired; an asset account.

LO 7   **Profit Summary:** A temporary account used during the closing process that holds a summary of all revenues and expenses before the net profit or loss is transferred to the Retained Earnings account.

LO 3   **Revenue recognition:** In accrual accounting, the process of determining when a sale takes place.

LO 1   **Revenues:** The gross inflow of economic benefits during the period arising in the course of the ordinary activities of a business when these activities result in increases in shareholders' equity. Revenues result from selling goods, rendering services, or performing other business activities.

LO 1   **Temporary accounts:** Accounts that show the accumulation of revenues and expenses over the accounting period; at the end of the accounting period, these account balances are transferred to shareholders' equity. Also called *nominal accounts*.

LO 5   **Unearned revenues:** Revenues received in advance for which the goods have not yet been delivered or the services performed; a liability account.

Review Problem

Determining Adjusting Entries, Posting to T Accounts, Preparing Adjusted Trial Balance, and Preparing Financial Statements

LO 5
LO 6   This was the unadjusted trial balance for Certified Answering Service on December 31, 20x2:

Certified Answering Service
Trial Balance
December 31, 20x2

Cash	2,160	
Accounts Receivable	1,250	
Office Supplies	180	
Prepaid Insurance	240	
Office Equipment	3,400	
Accumulated Depreciation, Office Equipment		600
Accounts Payable		700
Unearned Revenue		460
Share Capital		2,000
Retained Earnings		2,870
Dividends	400	
Answering Service Revenue		2,900
Wages Expense	1,500	
Rent Expense	400	
	9,530	9,530

The following information is also available:

a. Insurance that expired during December amounted to 40.
b. Office supplies available at the end of December totaled 75.
c. Depreciation for the month of December totaled 100.
d. Accrued wages at the end of December totaled 120.
e. Services performed in December but not yet billed on December 31 totaled 300.
f. Revenues earned for services performed that were paid in advance totaled 160.
g. Income taxes are estimated to be 250.

REQUIRED   1. Prepare T accounts for the accounts in the trial balance and enter the balances.
2. Determine the required adjusting entries and record them directly to the T accounts. Open new T accounts as needed.
3. Prepare an adjusted trial balance.
4. Prepare an income statement and a balance sheet for the month ended December 31, 20x2.

Answer to Review Problem

1. T accounts set up and amounts from trial balance entered
2. Adjusting entries recorded

Cash			
Bal.	2,160		

Accounts Receivable			
Bal.	1,250		

Service Revenue Receivable			
(e)	300		

Office Supplies			
Bal.	180	(b)	105
Bal.	75		

Prepaid Insurance			
Bal.	240	(a)	40
Bal.	200		

Office Equipment			
Bal.	3,400		

Accumulated Depreciation, Office Equipment			
		Bal.	600
		(c)	100
		Bal.	700

Accounts Payable			
		Bal.	700

Unearned Revenue			
(f)	160	Bal.	460
		Bal.	300

Wages Payable			
		(d)	120

Income Taxes Payable			
		(g)	250

Share Capital			
		Bal.	2,000

Retained Earnings			
		Bal.	2,870

Dividends			
Bal.	400		

Answering Service Revenue			
		Bal.	2,900
		(e)	300
		(f)	160
		Bal.	3,360

Wages Expense			
Bal.	1,500		
(d)	120		
Bal.	1,620		

Rent Expense			
Bal.	400		

Insurance Expense			
(a)	40		

Office Supplies Expense			
(b)	105		

Depreciation Expense, Office Equipment			
(c)	100		

Income Taxes Expense			
(g)	250		

3. Adjusted trial balance prepared

Certified Answering Service
Adjusted Trial Balance
December 31, 20x2

Cash	2,160	
Accounts Receivable	1,250	
Service Revenue Receivable	300	
Office Supplies	75	
Prepaid Insurance	200	
Office Equipment	3,400	
Accumulated Depreciation, Office Equipment		700
Accounts Payable		700
Unearned Revenue		300
Wages Payable		120
Income Taxes Payable		250
Share Capital		2,000
Retained Earnings		2,870
Dividends	400	
Answering Service Revenue		3,360
Wages Expense	1,620	
Rent Expense	400	
Insurance Expense	40	
Office Supplies Expense	105	
Depreciation Expense, Office Equipment	100	
Income Taxes Expense	250	
	10,300	10,300

4. Financial statements prepared

Certified Answering Service
Income Statement
For the Month Ended December 31, 20x2

Revenues		
Answering Service Revenue		3,360
Expenses		
Wages Expense	1,620	
Rent Expense	400	
Insurance Expense	40	
Office Supplies Expense	105	
Depreciation Expense, Office Equipment	100	
Income Taxes Expense	250	
Total Expenses		2,515
Net Profit		845

Certified Answering Service
Balance Sheet
December 31, 20x2

Assets

Cash		2,160
Accounts Receivable		1,250
Service Revenue Receivable		300
Office Supplies		75
Prepaid Insurance		200
Office Equipment	3,400	
Less Accumulated Depreciation	700	2,700
Total Assets		6,685

Liabilities

Accounts Payable		700
Unearned Revenue		300
Wages Payable		120
Income Taxes Payable		250
Total Liabilities		1,370

Shareholders' Equity

Share Capital	2,000	
Retained Earnings	3,315	
Total Shareholders' Equity		5,315
Total Liabilities and Shareholders' Equity		6,685

CHAPTER ASSIGNMENTS

Knowledge and Understanding

Questions

1. Why does the accountant use the term *net profit*?
2. Define the terms *revenues* and *expenses.*
3. Why are income statement accounts called *temporary accounts*?
4. Why does the need for an accounting period cause problems?
5. What is the significance of the going concern assumption?
6. "The matching rule is the most significant concept in accounting." Do you agree with this statement? Explain your answer.
7. What is the difference between the cash basis and the accrual basis of accounting?
8. In what two ways is accrual accounting accomplished?
9. Why do adjusting entries have to be made?
10. What are the four situations that require adjusting entries? Give an example of each.
11. "Some assets are expenses that have not expired." Explain this statement.
12. What do plant and equipment, office supplies, and prepaid insurance have in common?
13. What is the difference between accumulated depreciation and depreciation expense?

14. What is a contra account? Give an example.
15. Why are contra accounts used to record depreciation?
16. How does unearned revenue arise? Give an example.
17. Where does unearned revenue appear on the balance sheet?
18. What accounting problem does a magazine publisher who sells three-year subscriptions have?
19. Under what circumstances does a company have accrued revenues? Give an example. What asset arises when the adjustment is made?
20. What is an accrued expense? Give three examples.
21. "Why worry about adjustments? Doesn't it all come out in the wash?" Discuss these questions.
22. Why is the income statement usually the first statement prepared from the adjusted trial balance?
23. What are the two purposes of closing entries?
24. What is the difference between adjusting entries and closing entries?
25. What is the purpose of the Profit Summary account?
26. To what management goals do the measurements of net profit and cash flow relate?

Application

Exercises

E 3-1.

LO 2 *Applications of Accounting*
LO 3 *Concepts Related to Accrual*
LO 4 *Accounting*

The accountant for Marina Company makes the following assumptions or performs the following activities:

1. In estimating the life of a building, assumes that the business will last indefinitely.
2. Records a sale when the customer is billed.
3. Postpones the recognition of a one-year insurance policy as an expense by initially recording the expenditure as an asset.
4. Recognises the usefulness of financial statements prepared on a monthly basis even though they are based on estimates.
5. Recognises, by making an adjusting entry, wages expense that has been incurred but not yet recorded.
6. Prepares an income statement that shows the revenues earned and the expenses incurred during the accounting period.

Tell which of the following concepts of accrual accounting most directly relates to each of the assumptions and actions above: (a) periodicity, (b) going concern, (c) matching rule, (d) revenue recognition, (e) deferral, and (f) accrual.

E 3-2.

LO 5 *Revenue Recognition*

Lifestyle Corporation publishes a monthly magazine featuring local restaurant reviews and upcoming social, cultural, and sporting events. Subscribers pay for subscriptions either one year or two years in advance. Cash received from subscribers is credited to an account called Magazine Subscriptions Received in Advance. On December 31, 20x2, the end of the company's accounting year, the balance of this account was 1,000,000. Expiration of subscriptions was as follows:

During 20x2	200,000
During 20x7	500,000
During 20x4	300,000

Prepare the adjusting journal entry for December 31, 20x2.

E 3-3.

LO 5 *Adjusting Entries for*
Prepaid Insurance

An examination of the Prepaid Insurance account shows a balance of 4,112 at the end of an accounting period, before adjustment. Prepare journal entries to record the insurance expense for the period under each of the following independent assumptions:

1. An examination of the insurance policies shows unexpired insurance that cost 1,974 at the end of the period.
2. An examination of the insurance policies shows that insurance that cost 694 has expired during the period.

E 3-4.

LO 5 *Supplies Account: Missing*
Data

Each column below represents a supplies account:

	a	b	c	d
Supplies available October 1	396	651	294	?
Supplies purchased during the month	78	?	261	2,892
Supplies consumed during the month	291	1,458	?	2,448
Supplies available October 31	?	654	84	1,782

1. Determine the amounts indicated by the question marks in the columns.
2. Make the adjusting entry for Column **a**, assuming supplies purchased are debited to an asset account.

E 3-5.

LO 5 *Adjusting Entry for Accrued*
Salaries

Salim Engineering has a five-day workweek and pays salaries of 70,000 each Friday.

1. Make the adjusting entry required on July 31, assuming that August 1 falls on a Wednesday.
2. Make the entry to pay the salaries on August 3.

E 3-6.

LO 5 *Revenue and Expense*
Recognition

Paris Company produces computer software that is sold by Bond Systems. Paris receives a royalty of 15 per cent of sales. Royalties are paid by Bond Systems and received by Paris semiannually on May 1 for sales made July through December of the previous year and on November 1 for sales made January through June of the current year. Royalty expense for Bond Systems and royalty income for Paris in the amount of 12,000 were accrued on December 31, 20x1. Cash in the amounts of 12,000 and 20,000 was paid and received on May 1 and November 1, 20x2, respectively. Software sales during the July to December, 20x2 period totaled 300,000.

1. Calculate the amount of royalty expense for Bond Systems and royalty income for Paris during 20x2.
2. Record the appropriate adjusting entries made by each of the companies on December 31, 20x2.

E 3-7.		Prepare year-end adjusting entries for each of the following:
LO 5	*Adjusting Entries*	1. Office Supplies had a balance of 168 on January 1. Purchases debited to Office Supplies during the year amount to 830. A year-end inventory reveals supplies of 570 available. 2. Depreciation of office equipment is estimated to be 4,260 for the year. 3. Property taxes for six months, estimated at 1,750, have accrued but have not been recorded. 4. Unrecorded interest receivable on government bonds is 1,700. 5. Unearned Revenue has a balance of 1,800. Services for 600 received in advance have now been performed. 6. Services totalling 400 have been performed; the customer has not yet been billed.

E 3-8.

LO 5 *Accounting for Revenue Received in Advance*

Antonia Soria, a lawyer, was paid 72,000 on April 1 to represent a client in property negotiations over the next twelve months.

1. Record the entries required in Soria's records on April 1 and at the end of the accounting year, June 30.
2. How would this transaction be reflected in the income statement and balance sheet on June 30?

E 3-9.

LO 5 *Identification of Accruals*

East Asia Refrigeration Company has the following liabilities at year end:

Notes Payable	30,000	Wages Payable	4,900
Accounts Payable	20,000	Interest Payable	1,400
Contract Revenue Received in Advance	18,000	Income Taxes Payable	2,500

1. Which of these accounts probably was created at the end of the accounting year as a result of an accrual? Which probably was adjusted at year end?
2. Which adjustments probably reduced net profit? Which probably increased net profit?

E 3-10.

LO 6 *Preparation of Financial Statements*

Prepare the monthly income statement and balance sheet for Rogers Security Services from the data provided in this adjusted trial balance:

Rogers Security Services
Adjusted Trial Balance
August 31, 20xx

Cash	4,590	
Accounts Receivable	2,592	
Prepaid Insurance	380	
Prepaid Rent	200	
Security Supplies	152	
Security Equipment	3,200	
Accumulated Depreciation, Security Equipment		320
Vehicle	7,200	
Accumulated Depreciation, Vehicle		720
Accounts Payable		420
Wages Payable		80
Unearned Security Services Revenue		920
Income Taxes Payable		800
Share Capital		4,000
Retained Earnings		11,034
Dividends	2,000	
Security Services Revenue		14,620
Wages Expense	5,680	
Rent Expense	1,200	
Gas, Oil, and Other Vehicle Expense	580	
Insurance Expense	380	
Security Supplies Expense	2,920	
Depreciation Expense, Security Equipment	320	
Depreciation Expense, Vehicle	720	
Income Taxes Expense	800	
	32,914	32,914

E 3-11.
SO 9 *Relationship of Cash to Expenses Paid or Revenues Received*

After adjusting entries had been made, the balance sheets of Pandan Company showed the following asset and liability amounts at the end of 20x1 and 20x2:

	20x1	20x2
Prepaid Insurance	1,450	1,200
Wages Payable	1,100	600
Unearned fees	950	2,100

From the 20x2 income statement, the following amounts were taken:

Insurance Expense	2,150
Wages Expense	9,250
Fees Earned	3,300

Calculate the amount of cash paid for insurance and wages and received for fees during 20x2.

E 3-12.
SO 9 *Cash Flow Analysis of Deferrals and Accruals*

The following amounts are taken from the balance sheets of Neutral Bay Corporation:

	December 31	
	20x1	20x2
Prepaid Expenses	45,000	56,000
Accrued Liabilities	103,000	88,000

During 20x2, expenses related to Prepaid Expenses were 103,000, and expenses related to Accrued Liabilities were 197,000. Determine the amount of cash payments related to Prepaid Expenses and to Accrued Liabilities for 20x2.

E 3-13.
SO 9 *Determining Cash Flows*

Horowitz Newspaper Agency delivers morning, evening, and Sunday city newspapers to subscribers who live in the suburbs. Customers can pay a yearly subscription fee in advance (at a savings) or pay monthly after delivery of their newspapers. The following data are available for the Subscriptions Receivable and Unearned Subscriptions accounts at the beginning and end of October 20xx:

	October 1	October 31
Subscriptions Receivable	7,600	9,200
Unearned Subscriptions	22,800	19,600

The income statement shows subscription revenue for October of 44,800. Determine the amount of cash received from customers for subscriptions during October. Why is it important for management to make a calculation like this?

E 3-14.
SO 9 *Relationship of Expenses to Cash Paid*

The income statement for Jarvis Company included the following expenses for 20xx:

Rent Expense	5,200
Interest Expense	7,800
Salaries Expense	83,000

Listed below are the related balance sheet account balances at year end for last year and this year:

	Last Year	This Year
Prepaid Rent	—	900
Interest Payable	1,200	—
Salaries Payable	5,000	9,600

1. Calculate the cash paid for rent during the year.
2. Calculate the cash paid for interest during the year.
3. Calculate the cash paid for salaries during the year.

Problem Set

P 3-1.
LO 5 *Preparation of Adjusting Entries*

On May 31, the end of the current accounting year, the following information was available to help Costa Corporation's accountants make adjusting entries:

a. The Supplies account showed a beginning balance of 4,348. Purchases during the year were 9,052. The end-of-year inventory revealed supplies available that cost 2,794.
b. The Prepaid Insurance account showed the following on May 31:

Beginning Balance	7,160
February 1	8,400
April 1	14,544

The beginning balance represents the portion of a one-year policy that remained unexpired at the beginning of the current accounting year. The February 1 entry represents a new one-year policy, and the April 1 entry represents additional coverage in the form of a three-year policy.

c. The table below contains the cost and annual depreciation for buildings and equipment, all of which were purchased before the current year.

Account	Cost	Annual Depreciation
Buildings	572,000	29,000
Equipment	748,000	70,800

d. On March 1, the company completed negotiations with a client and accepted payment of 33,600, which represented one year's services paid in advance. The 33,600 was credited to Unearned Service Revenue.

e. The company calculated that as of May 31, it had earned 8,000 on a 22,000 contract that would be completed and billed in September.

f. Among the liabilities of the company is a note payable in the amount of 600,000. On May 31, the accrued interest on this note amounted to 30,000.

g. On Saturday, June 2, the company, which is on a six-day workweek, will pay its regular salaried employees 24,600.

h. On May 29, the company completed negotiations and signed a contract to provide services to a new client at an annual rate of 35,000.

i. Management estimates income taxes for the year to be 50,000.

REQUIRED   Prepare adjusting entries for each item listed above.

P 3-2.

LO 5   *Determining Adjusting Entries, Posting to T Accounts, and Preparing Adjusted Trial Balance*

Here is the trial balance for Crown Advisory Services on July 31:

Crown Advisory Services
Trial Balance
July 31, 20xx

Cash	8,250	
Accounts Receivable	4,125	
Office Supplies	1,331	
Prepaid Rent	660	
Office Equipment	4,620	
Accumulated Depreciation, Office Equipment		770
Accounts Payable		2,970
Notes Payable		5,500
Unearned Fees		1,485
Share Capital		5,000
Retained Earnings		7,001
Dividends	11,000	
Fees Revenue		36,300
Salaries Expense	24,700	
Rent Expense	2,200	
Electricity Expense	2,140	
	59,026	59,026

The following information is also available:

a. Ending inventory of office supplies, 132.
b. Prepaid rent expired, 220.
c. Depreciation of office equipment for the period, 330.
d. Accrued interest expense at the end of the period, 275.
e. Accrued salaries at the end of the month, 165.
f. Fees still unearned at the end of the period, 583.
g. Fees earned but unrecorded, 1,100.
h. Estimated income taxes, 2,000.

REQUIRED   1. Open T accounts for the accounts in the trial balance plus the following: Fees Receivable; Interest Payable; Salaries Payable; Income Taxes Payable; Office Supplies Expense; Depreciation Expense, Office Equipment; Interest Expense; and Income Taxes Expense. Enter the balances.
2. Determine the adjusting entries and post them directly to the T accounts.
3. Prepare an adjusted trial balance.

P 3-3.

LO 5 *Determining Adjusting*
LO 6 *Entries and Tracing Their*
      Effects to Financial
      Statements

The Foremost Janitorial Service is owned by Ron Hudson. After six months of operations, the September 30, 20xx trial balance for the company was prepared.

Foremost Janitorial Service
Trial Balance
September 30, 20xx

Cash	4,524	
Accounts Receivable	3,828	
Prepaid Insurance	760	
Prepaid Rent	1,400	
Cleaning Supplies	2,792	
Cleaning Equipment	3,480	
Truck	7,200	
Accounts Payable		340
Unearned Janitorial Fees		960
Share Capital		14,190
Dividends	1,000	
Janitorial Fees		14,974
Wages Expense	4,800	
Gas, Oil, and Other Truck Expenses	680	
	30,464	30,464

The balance of the Share Capital account reflects investments made by Ron Hudson. The following information is also available:

a. Cleaning supplies of 234 are available.
b. Prepaid Insurance represents the cost of a one-year policy purchased on April 1.
c. Prepaid Rent represents a 200 payment made on April 1 towards the last month's rent of a three-year lease plus 200 rent per month for each of the past six months.
d. The cleaning equipment and trucks are depreciated at the rate of 20 per cent per year (10 per cent for each six-month period).
e. The unearned revenue represents a six-month payment in advance made by a customer on August 1.
f. During the last week of September, Ron completed the first stage of work on a project that will not be billed until the contract is completed. The price of this stage is 800.
g. On Saturday, October 3, Ron will owe his employees 1,080 for one six-day workweek.
h. Income taxes for the six months are estimated to be 1,500.

REQUIRED   1. Open T accounts for the accounts in the trial balance plus: Fees Receivable; Accumulated Depreciation, Cleaning Equipment; Accumulated Depreciation, Truck; Wages Payable; Income Taxes Payable; Rent Expense; Insurance Expense; Cleaning Supplies Expense; Depreciation Expense, Cleaning Equipment; Depreciation Expense, Truck; and Income Taxes Expense.
2. Determine the adjusting entries and post them directly to the T accounts.
3. Prepare an adjusted trial balance, an income statement, and a balance sheet.

P 3-4.

LO 5 *Determining Adjusting*
LO 6 *Entries and Tracing Their*
      Effects to Financial
      Statements

The trial balance for Century Dance School at the end of its current accounting year appears at the top of the next page. Loretta Harper, the owner, made no investments in the business during the year. The following information is available to help in the preparation of adjusting entries:

a. An inventory of supplies reveals 276 still available.
b. Prepaid Rent reflects the rent for July plus the rent for the last month of the lease.
c. Prepaid Insurance consists of a two-year policy purchased on February 1, 20x2.
d. Depreciation on equipment is estimated at 2,400.
e. Accrued wages are 195 on July 31.
f. Two-thirds of the unearned dance fees had been earned by July 31.
g. Management estimates income taxes for the year to be 9,000.

Century Dance School
Trial Balance
July 31, 20x2

Cash (111)	5,084	
Accounts Receivable (113)	3,551	
Supplies (115)	510	
Prepaid Rent (117)	1,200	
Prepaid Insurance (118)	1,080	
Equipment (144)	18,300	
Accumulated Depreciation, Equipment (147)		1,200
Accounts Payable (212)		1,140
Unearned Dance Fees (213)		2,700
Share Capital (311)		4,500
Retained Earnings (312)		3,000
Dividends (313)	26,000	
Dance Fees (411)		62,985
Wages Expense (511)	9,600	
Electricity Expense (512)	3,600	
Rent Expense (514)	6,600	
	75,525	75,525

REQUIRED

1. Record the adjusting entries in the general journal.
2. Open ledger accounts for the accounts in the trial balance plus: Wages Payable (214); Income Taxes Payable (215); Insurance Expense (515); Supplies Expense (516); Depreciation Expense, Equipment (519); Income Taxes Expense (520). Record the balances shown in the trial balance.
3. Post the adjusting entries from the general journal to the ledger, showing the correct references.
4. Prepare an adjusted trial balance, an income statement, and a balance sheet.

P 3-5.
LO 6 *Preparation of Financial*
LO 7 *Statements and*
LO 8 *End-of-Period Entries*

Benzinger Truck Rental owns thirty small trucks that it rents by the day. Its adjusted trial balance at the end of the current accounting year is shown below.

Benzinger Truck Rental
Trial Balance
December 31, 20x2

Cash	1,384	
Accounts Receivable	1,944	
Supplies	238	
Prepaid Insurance	720	
Trucks	24,000	
Accumulated Depreciation, Trucks		14,400
Accounts Payable		542
Wages Payable		400
Share Capital		2,000
Retained Earnings		6,388
Dividends	11,400	
Truck Rentals		91,092
Wages Expense	46,800	
Insurance Expense	1,440	
Supplies Expense	532	
Depreciation Expense, Trucks	4,800	
Other Expenses	21,564	
Income Taxes Expense	4,000	
Income Taxes Payable		4,000
	118,822	118,822

REQUIRED

1. Prepare an income statement and a balance sheet.
2. From the information given, record the closing entries.

Critical Thinking and Communication

Conceptual Mini-Case

CMC 3-1.

LO 2   *Importance of Adjustments*
LO 3
LO 4

Never Flake Company, which once operated in the northeastern United States, provided a rust prevention coating for the underside of new cars. The company offered its product through new car dealers, who promoted it as an option that would make cars last longer in the severe northeastern winters. A key selling point was Never Flake's warranty, which stated that it would repair any damage due to rust at no charge as long as the buyer owned the car.

During the 1970s and most of the 1980s, Never Flake was very successful, but in 1988 the company suddenly declared bankruptcy. Company officials said that the firm had only $5.5 million in assets against liabilities of $32.9 million. Most of the liabilities represented potential claims under the company's lifetime warranty. It seemed that owners were keeping their cars longer in the 1980s than they had in the 1970s. Therefore, more damage was being attributed to rust. Discuss what accounting decisions could have helped Never Flake to survive under these circumstances.

Cultural Mini-Case

CLMC 3-1.

LO 1   *Profit Measurement,*
LO 2   *Matching*
LO 3

Daimler-Benz, one of Germany's largest manufacturing, companies, produces cars, commercial vehicles, rail systems, diesel engines, aircraft, space systems, and other products. Revenues in 1995 were 103.549 billion Deutsche marks; of these 63.2 per cent were international.[5]

German law requires that the completed contract method be used to record revenues and expenses associated with long-term contracts. Thus, the recognition of revenues and expenses to determine net profit is not carried out until the company completes the contract, which may take a period of years. In the United States and the United Kingdom, the percentage of completion method is used: contract revenue is matched with the contract costs incurred in reaching the stage of completion at the end of the accounting period. This results in the reporting of profit that can be attributed to the proportion of work completed. The percentage of completion method has been adopted as the International Accounting Standard for long-term contracts.[6]

REQUIRED

1. Explain the matching issue involved in this case.
2. What are the advantages and disadvantages of each method for long-term contracts?
3. Why do you think the percentage of completion method has been adopted as the International Accounting Standard?

Ethics Mini-Case

EMC 3-1.

LO 2   *Importance of Adjustments*
LO 3
LO 4

Central Appliance Company has achieved fast growth by selling service contracts on large appliances, such as refrigerators. For a fee, the company will provide all parts and labour on an appliance after the regular warranty runs out. For example, by paying a fee of 200, a person can add two years to the regular one-year warranty on a dishwasher. In 1996, the company sold service contracts in the amount of 1.8 million, all of which applied to future years. Management wanted all the sales recorded as revenues in 1996, contending that the amount of the contracts could be determined and the cash had been received. Discuss whether you agree with this logic. How would you record these cash receipts? What assumptions should be made? Would you consider it unethical to follow management's recommendation? Who might be hurt or helped by this action?

Decision-Making Case

DMC 3-1.

LO 1   *Adjusting Entries and*
LO 5   *Dividend Policy*

Karen Jamison, the owner of a newsletter for managers of hotels and restaurants, has prepared condensed amounts from the financial statements for 20x2, as follows:

Revenues	346,000
Expenses	282,000
Net Profit	64,000
Total Assets	172,000
Liabilities	48,000
Shareholders' Equity	124,000
Total Liabilities and Shareholders' Equity	172,000

Given these figures, Jamison is planning a cash dividend of 50,000. However, Jamison's accountant has found that the following items were overlooked:

a. Although the balance of the Printing Supplies account is 32,000, only 14,000 in supplies is available at the end of the year.

b. Depreciation of 20,000 on equipment has not been recorded.

c. Wages in the amount of 9,400 have been earned by employees but not recognised in the accounts.

d. No provision has been made for estimated income taxes payable of 10,800.

e. A liability account called Unearned Subscriptions has a balance of 16,200, although it is determined that one-third of these subscriptions have been mailed to subscribers.

REQUIRED

1. Prepare the necessary adjusting entries.
2. Recast the condensed financial statement figures after making the necessary adjustments.
3. Discuss the performance of Jamison's business after the adjustments have been made. **Note:** compare net profit to revenues and total assets before and after the adjustments. Do you think that paying the dividend is advisable?

Basic Research Activity

RA 3-1.

LO 4 *Service Businesses and Adjusting Entries*

Consult the business pages of your local telephone directory. Find the names of five different kinds of service businesses. List the types of adjusting entries you think each business regularly makes. Be prepared to discuss any adjustments you think may be unique to each business.

Financial Reporting and Analysis

Interpretation Cases from Business

ICB 3-1.

LO 2 *Analysis of an Asset Account*
LO 5

Orion Pictures Corporation, based in the United States, finances, produces, and distributes motion pictures and television programming. In Orion's 1993 annual report, the balance sheet contains an asset called Film Inventories. This asset, which consists of the cost associated with producing films less the amount expensed, was $498,890,000 in 1993. The annual report reveals that the amount of film inventories expensed (amortised) during 1993 was $161,173,000 and the amount spent for new film productions was only $7,348,000 because of the company's financial problems.[7]

REQUIRED

1. What is the nature of the asset Film Inventories?
2. Prepare an entry to record the amount spent on new film production during 1993 (assume all expenditures are paid for in cash).
3. Prepare an adjusting entry to record the expense for film productions in 1993.
4. Can you suggest a method by which Orion Pictures Corporation might have determined the expense in **3** in accordance with the matching rule?

ICB 3-2.

LO 1 *Accounting process and cycle*
LO 2
LO 3
LO 4
LO 6
LO 7

Unilever, an Anglo-Dutch multinational, produces foods, detergents, personal care products, and speciality chemicals. Its many brand names include Lipton and Brooke Bond tea, Boursin cheese, Birds Eye frozen foods, Surf washing powder, Lux soap, Jif cleaner, Brut and Fabergé deodorants, Ponds and Pears skin care products, and Signal toothpaste. The company has operations in more than ninety countries spanning every continent of the world. Unilever's revenues in 1995 were US $49.732 billion with 52 per cent from Europe, 19 per cent from North America, and 29 per cent from Africa, Latin America, Asia, and the Pacific.[8] The company's operations are decentralised to a significant extent, and managing them is a tremendous challenge. How would the accounting process of measuring business transactions and profit be the same for Unilever as for Joan Miller Advertising Agency? How would it differ?

Nestlé Case

NC 3-1.

LO 4 *Analysis of Balance Sheet*
LO 5 *and Adjusting Entries*

Refer to the consolidated balance sheet in the Nestlé appendix. Examine the accounts listed in the current assets, tangible fixed assets, and current liabilities sections. Which accounts most likely have had year-end adjusting entries? State the nature of the adjusting entries. For more information about the tangible fixed assets, refer to the notes to the consolidated financial statements.

ENDNOTES

1. Reuters Holdings, *Annual Report*, 1995.
2. International Accounting Standard IAS18, *Revenue* (London: IASC, revised 1993), para. 7.
3. International Accounting Standards Committee, *Framework for the Preparation and Presentation of Financial Statements* (London: IASC, 1996), para. 23.
4. Ibid., para. 22.
5. Daimler-Benz, *Annual Report*, 1995.
6. International Accounting Standard IAS11, *Construction Contracts* (London: IASC, revised 1993).
7. Orion Pictures Corporation, *Annual Report*, 1993.
8. Unilever, *Annual Report*, 1995.

Chapter 4

ACCOUNTING FOR
TRADING OPERATIONS

LEARNING OBJECTIVES

1. Identify the management issues related to trading businesses.
2. Compare the income statements for service and trading enterprises and define the components of the trading income statement.
3. Distinguish between the perpetual and the periodic inventory systems and explain the importance of taking a physical inventory.
4. Contrast and record transactions related to sales and purchases under the periodic and the perpetual inventory systems.
5. Define *internal control* and identify the three elements of the internal control structure, including seven examples of control procedures.
6. Describe the inherent limitations of internal control.
7. Apply control procedures to certain trading transactions.

SUPPLEMENTAL OBJECTIVE

8. Apply sales and purchases discounts to trading transactions.

DECISION POINT
MARKS & SPENCER

The management of trading companies has two key decisions to make: the price at which goods are sold and the level of service the company provides. For instance, a department store can set the price of its goods at a relatively high level and provide a great deal of service. A discount store, on the other hand, may price its goods at a relatively low level and provide limited service. Marks & Spencer is a U.K.-based department store which aims to provide "Quality, Value, and Service Worldwide". The company brings together a unique combination of clothing, footwear, home furnishings, foods, and financial services in a way that differentiates itself from other department stores.

Marks & Spencer emphasises quality but at a very competitive price. With stores in 628 locations including 350 outside the U.K., the company is going global with further expansion planned, especially in Europe and the Asia Pacific region. In North America, Marks & Spencer owns Brooks Brothers and Kings Super Markets, both of which are performing well. In 1995, Marks & Spencer earned a net profit, after interest and tax, of 653.8 million pounds on sales of 7,231.6 million pounds.[1]

OBJECTIVE 1

Identify the management issues related to trading businesses

MANAGEMENT ISSUES IN TRADING BUSINESSES

Up to this point you have studied business and accounting issues related to the simplest type of business—the service business. **Service businesses**, such as advertising agencies and law firms, perform services for fees or commissions. **Trading businesses**, on the other hand, earn a profit by buying and selling products or goods. These companies, whether wholesale or retail, use the same basic accounting methods as do service companies, but the buying and selling of goods adds to the complexity of the process. As a foundation for discussing the accounting issues of trading businesses, we must first identify the management issues involved in running a trading business.

Cash Flow Management

Trading businesses differ from service businesses in that they have goods available for sale to customers, or **inventory**, and engage in a series of transactions called the **operating cycle**, as shown in Figure 4-1. The transactions in the operating cycle consist of (1) purchases of inventory, (2) sales of inventory for cash or on credit, and (3) collection of the cash from the sales. In the case of sales of goods for cash, or cash sales, this cash is collected immediately. In the case of sales of goods on credit, or credit sales, the company must wait a period of time before receiving the cash. Some very small retail stores may have mostly cash sales and very few credit sales, whereas large wholesale enterprises may have almost all credit sales. Most trading enterprises, however, have a combination of cash and credit sales.

Regardless of the proportions of cash and credit sales, the operators of a trading business must carefully manage cash flow, or liquidity. Such **cash flow management** involves planning the company's receipts and payments of cash. If the company is not able to pay its bills when they are due, it may be forced out of business. Often goods that are purchased must be paid for before they are sold and the cash from their sale is collected. For example, if a retail business must pay for its purchases in thirty days, it must have cash available or arrange for borrowing if it cannot sell and collect cash for the goods in thirty days.

FIGURE 4-1 *The Operating Cycle of Trading Enterprises*

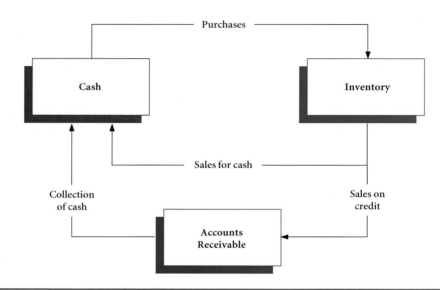

Profitability Management

In addition to managing its cash flow, management must endeavour to sell its goods at a price that exceeds their cost by a sufficient margin to pay operating expenses, such as wages, electricity, advertising, and taxes, and have enough left over to provide sufficient profit. **Profitability management** is a complex activity that includes setting appropriate prices on the goods, purchasing goods at favourable prices and terms, and maintaining acceptable levels of expenses.

Choice of Inventory System

A third issue management of trading businesses must address is the choice of inventory system. There are two basic systems of accounting for the many items in the inventory of a trading business. Under the **periodic inventory system**, the inventory available is counted periodically, usually at the end of the accounting period. No detailed records of the actual inventory available are maintained during the accounting period. Under the **perpetual inventory system**, continuous records are kept of the quantity and, usually, the cost of individual items as they are bought and sold. The periodic inventory system is less costly to maintain than the perpetual inventory system, but it gives management less information about the current status of inventory. Given the number and diversity of items contained in the inventory of most businesses, the perpetual inventory system is usually more effective for keeping track of quantities and ensuring optimal customer service. Management must choose the system or combination of systems that is best for achieving the company's goals.

Control of Trading Operations

The principal transactions of trading businesses, which involve buying and selling, are covered by asset accounts—Cash, Accounts Receivable, and Inventory—that are vulnerable to theft and embezzlement. One reason for this vulnerability is that cash and inventory are fairly easy to steal. Another is that these asset accounts usually are involved in a large number of transactions, such as cash receipts, receipts on account, payments for purchases, and receipts and shipments of inventory, which can become difficult to monitor. If a trading company does not take steps to protect its assets, it can have high losses of cash and inventory. Management's responsibility is to establish an environment, accounting systems, and control procedures that will protect these assets. These systems and procedures are called the **internal control structure.**

OBJECTIVE 2   INCOME STATEMENT FOR A TRADING ENTERPRISE

Compare the income statements for service and trading enterprises and define the components of the trading income statement

Service companies, as illustrated thus far in this book, require only a simple income statement. For those companies, as shown in Figure 4-2, net profit represents the difference between revenues and expenses. But trading companies, because they buy and sell inventory, require a more complex income statement. As shown in Figure 4-2, the income statement for a trader has four major parts: (1) net sales, (2) cost of goods sold, (3) operating expenses, and (4) income taxes. There are also subtotals for (1)

FIGURE 4-2   *The Components of Income Statements for Service and Trading Companies*

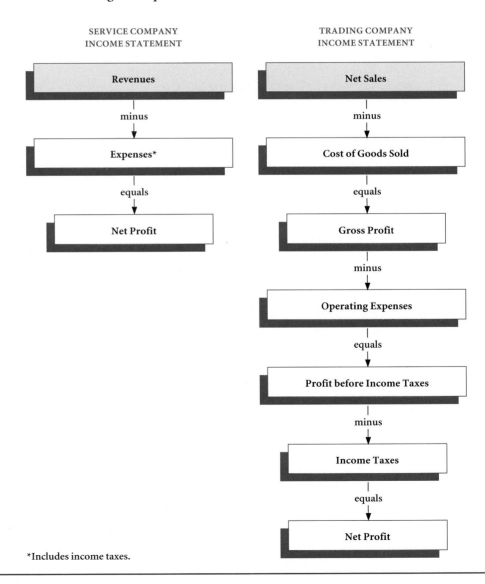

*Includes income taxes.

EXHIBIT 4-1 *Trading Income Statement*

Fenwick Fashions Corporation
Income Statement
For the Year Ended December 31, 20x2

Net Sales			
Gross Sales			246,350
Less Sales Returns and Allowances			7,025
Net Sales			239,325
Cost of Goods Sold			
Inventory, December 31, 20x1		52,800	
Purchases	126,400		
Less Purchases Returns and Allowances	7,776		
Net Purchases	118,624		
Freight In	8,236		
Net Cost of Purchases		126,860	
Goods Available for Sale		179,660	
Less Inventory, December 31, 20x2		48,300	
Cost of Goods Sold			131,360
Gross Profit			107,965
Operating Expenses			
Selling Expenses			
Sales Salaries Expense	22,500		
Freight Out Expense	5,740		
Advertising Expense	10,000		
Insurance Expense, Selling	1,600		
Store Supplies Expense	1,540		
Total Selling Expenses		41,380	
General and Administrative Expenses			
Office Salaries Expense	26,900		
Insurance Expense, General	4,200		
Office Supplies Expense	1,204		
Depreciation Expense, Building	2,600		
Depreciation Expense, Office Equipment	2,200		
Total General and Administrative Expenses		37,104	
Total Operating Expenses			78,484
Profit before Income Taxes			29,481
Income Taxes			5,000
Net Profit			24,481

gross profit, (2) profit before income taxes, and (3) net profit. The main difference between a trader's income statement and that of a service business is that the trader must calculate gross profit before operating expenses and income taxes are deducted. In the following discussion, the income statement for Fenwick Fashions Corporation, presented in Exhibit 4-1, will serve as an example of a trading income statement.

Net Sales

The first major part of the trading income statement is **net sales**, or often simply *sales*. Net sales consist of the gross proceeds from sales of goods, or gross sales, less sales returns and allowances and any discounts allowed. **Gross sales** consist of total cash sales and total credit sales during a given accounting period. Even though the cash may not be collected until the following accounting period, revenue is recognised, under the revenue recognition rule, as being earned when title for the goods passes from seller to buyer at the time of sale. **Sales returns and allowances** are cash refunds, credits on account, and allowances off selling prices made to customers who have received defective or otherwise unsatisfactory products. If other discounts or allowances are given to customers (see supplemental objective 8, for instance), they also should be deducted from gross sales.

Management, investors, and others often use the amount of sales and trends suggested by sales as indicators of a firm's future progress. Increasing sales suggest growth; decreasing sales indicate the possibility of decreased future earnings and other financial problems. To detect trends, comparisons are frequently made between the net sales of different accounting periods.

Cost of Goods Sold

Cost of goods sold, or often simply *cost of sales*, which is the amount a trader paid for the goods that were sold during an accounting period, is the second major part of the trading income statement. The method of calculating cost of goods sold is sometimes confusing because it must take into account both inventory available at the beginning of the accounting period, or **beginning inventory**, and inventory available at the end of the accounting period, or **ending inventory**. The ending inventory appears on the balance sheet at the end of the accounting period and becomes the beginning inventory for the next accounting period.

The calculation of cost of goods sold for Fenwick Fashions based on the income statement in Exhibit 4-1 is illustrated in Figure 4-3. The **goods available for sale** during the year is the sum of two factors, beginning inventory and the net cost of purchases during the year. In this case, the goods available for sale is 179,660 (52,800 + 126,860).

If a company sold all the goods available for sale during a given accounting period, the cost of goods sold would equal the cost of goods available for sale. In most businesses, however, some goods will remain unsold and available at the end of the

FIGURE 4-3 *Components of Cost of Goods Sold*

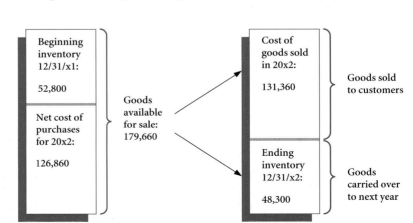

year. These goods, or ending inventory, must be deducted from the cost of goods available for sale to determine cost of goods sold. In the case of Fenwick Fashions, the ending inventory on December 31, 20x2, is 48,300. Thus, cost of goods sold is 131,360 (179,660 − 48,300).

An important component of the cost of goods sold section is **net cost of purchases**, which consists of net purchases plus any freight charges on the purchases. **Net purchases** equals total purchases less any deductions, such as purchases returns and allowances or any discounts allowed by suppliers for early payment (see supplemental objective 8). Because freight charges, or **freight in** (or *transportation in*), are a necessary cost to receive goods for sale, they are added to net purchases to arrive at the net cost of purchases.

Gross Profit

While gross profit information is very important for profitability management, in many countries this information is not required to be disclosed to investors and other external users. However, a growing number of companies, including Roche from Switzerland, are recognising the value to users of making such disclosures on a voluntary basis.

Another major component of the trading income statement is **gross profit**, or *gross margin*, which is the difference between net sales and cost of goods sold. To be successful, traders must sell goods for an amount greater than cost—that is, gross profit must be great enough to pay operating expenses and provide an adequate profit after income taxes have been paid. Management is interested in both the amount and the percentage of gross profit. The percentage of gross profit is calculated by dividing the amount of gross profit by net sales. In the case of Fenwick Fashions, the amount of gross profit is 107,965 and the percentage of gross profit is 45.1 per cent (107,965 ÷ 239,325). This information is helpful in planning business operations. For instance, management may try to increase the value of total sales by reducing the selling price. This strategy reduces the percentage of gross profit, but it will work only if the total items sold increase enough to raise the absolute amount of gross profit. On the other hand, management may decide to keep a high gross profit from sales and attempt to increase sales and the absolute amount of gross profit by increasing operating expenses such as advertising. Other strategies to increase gross profit from sales, such as reducing cost of goods sold by better purchasing methods, can also be explored.

Operating Expenses

The third major area of the trading income statement consists of **operating expenses**, which are the expenses other than cost of goods sold that are incurred in running a business. They are similar to the expenses of a service company. It is customary to group operating expenses into categories, such as selling expenses and general and administrative expenses. Selling expenses include the costs of storing and preparing goods for sale; displaying, advertising, and otherwise promoting sales; making sales; and delivering goods to the buyer, if the seller pays the cost of delivery. The latter cost is often called **freight out expense**, or *delivery expense*. Among general and administrative expenses are general office expense, which includes expenses that apply to the overall operation. Although general occupancy expenses, such as rent expense, insurance expense, and electricity expense, are often classified as general and administrative expenses, they may also be allocated between both the selling and the general and administrative categories. Careful planning and control of operating expenses can improve a company's profitability.

Profit before Income Taxes

Profit before income taxes—that is, the difference between gross profit and operating expenses—is an important measure of profitability because it tells how much profit a business has earned from operations. Profit before income taxes is also referred to as *operating profit* or *profit from operations* because it represents the profit from a company's normal, or main, business. Because companies may be subject to different tax rates, profit before income taxes is often used to compare the profitability of two or more companies or divisions within a company.

Income Taxes

The fourth major area of the trading income statement is income taxes. They are stated separately on the income statement because they are determined by law and are therefore less subject to management control than other items.

Net Profit

Net profit, the final figure, or "bottom line", of the income statement is what remains after operating expenses and income taxes are deducted from the gross profit. It is an important performance measure because it represents the amount of business earnings that accrue to shareholders. It is the amount that is transferred to retained earnings from all the profit-generating activities during the year. Both management and investors often use net profit to measure whether a business has been operating successfully during the past accounting period.

OBJECTIVE 3

Distinguish between the perpetual and the periodic inventory systems and explain the importance of taking a physical inventory

INVENTORY SYSTEMS

As we have seen, inventory is a key factor in determining the cost of goods sold. Consequently, every trader needs a useful and reliable system for determining both the quantity and the cost of the goods available. The two basic systems of accounting for the number of items in the inventory are the periodic inventory system and the perpetual inventory system.

Periodic Inventory System

As discussed earlier, under the periodic inventory system, the inventory available is counted periodically, usually at the end of the accounting period. No detailed records of the actual inventory available are maintained during the period. Cost of goods sold under the periodic inventory system is determined according to the format followed by Fenwick Fashions in Exhibit 4-1 and Figure 4-3. In the simplest case, the cost of inventory purchased is accumulated in a Purchases account. At the end of the accounting period, the cost of the physical inventory, based on an actual count, is deducted from the cost of goods available for sale to arrive at cost of goods sold. Entries are made at the end of the accounting period to remove the beginning inventory (the last period's ending inventory) and to enter the ending inventory of the current period. These are the only entries that will be made to the Inventory account during the period. Consequently, the figure for inventory available is accurate only on the balance sheet date. As soon as any purchases or sales are made, the figure becomes a historical amount and remains so until the new ending inventory is entered at the end of the next accounting period.

Many retail and wholesale businesses use periodic inventory systems because they do not require much clerical work. If a business is fairly small, management can maintain control over inventory simply by observation or by use of an off-line system of cards or computer records. On the other hand, for larger businesses, the lack of detailed records may cause inefficiencies that lead either to lost sales or to high operating costs.

Perpetual Inventory System

Under the perpetual inventory system, records are kept of the quantity and, usually, the cost of individual items as they are bought or sold. The detailed data available under the perpetual inventory system enable management to respond to customers' inquiries about product availability, to order inventory more effectively and thus avoid running out of stock, and to control financial costs associated with investments in the inventory. Under this system, the cost of each item is recorded in the Inventory account when it is purchased. As goods are sold, their cost is transferred from the

Around the world, and especially in countries such as Australia, France, Germany, Japan, and the United States, use of the perpetual inventory system is growing rapidly, as is increased access to computers by businesses small and large.

> ## BUSINESS BULLETIN Technology in Practice
>
> Many grocery stores, which traditionally used the periodic inventory system, now employ bar coding. Electronic markings on each product, called bar codes or universal product codes (UPC), are used to update the physical inventory as items are sold by running them through cash registers linked to a computer. Bar coding has become common in all types of retail companies, as well as in manufacturing firms and hospitals. Some retail businesses commonly use the perpetual system for keeping track of the physical flow of inventory and the periodic system for preparing the financial statements.

Inventory account to the Cost of Goods Sold account. Thus, at all times the balance of the Inventory account equals the cost of goods available, and the balance in Cost of Goods Sold equals the cost of goods sold to customers. The Purchases account is not used in a perpetual inventory system.

Traditionally, the periodic inventory system has been used by companies that sell items of low value in high volume because of the difficulty and expense of accounting for the purchase and sale of each item. Examples of such companies are pharmacies, car parts stores, department stores, discount stores, and grain companies. In contrast, companies that sell items of high unit value, such as appliances or cars, tended to use the perpetual inventory system. This distinction between high and low unit value for inventory systems has blurred considerably in recent years because of the widespread use of the computer. Although the periodic inventory system is still widely used, the use of the perpetual inventory system has increased greatly.

Taking Physical Inventory

Actually counting all goods available is called taking a **physical inventory**. It can be a difficult task because it is easy to omit items or to count them twice. A physical inventory must be taken under both the periodic and the perpetual inventory systems.

Inventory includes all saleable goods owned by the enterprise, regardless of where they are located—on shelves, in storerooms, in warehouses, in trucks en route between warehouses and stores. It includes goods in transit from suppliers if title to the goods has passed to the trader. Ending inventory includes neither goods sold but not yet delivered to customers nor goods that cannot be sold because they are damaged or obsolete. If the damaged or obsolete goods can be sold at a reduced price, however, they should be included in ending inventory at their reduced value.

The actual count usually is taken after the close of business on the last day of the accounting year. To facilitate taking the physical inventory, many companies end their accounting year in a slow season, when inventories are at relatively low levels. Retail department stores often end their accounting year in January or February, for example. After hours, at night or on the weekend, employees count and record all items on numbered inventory tickets or sheets, following procedures to make sure that no items are missed. Sometimes a store closes for all or part of a day for inventory taking. The use of bar coding to take inventory electronically has greatly facilitated the taking of a physical inventory in many companies.

OBJECTIVE 4

Contrast and record transactions related to sales and purchases under the periodic and the perpetual inventory systems

TRADING TRANSACTIONS

Trading transactions can be divided into the two broad categories of sales transactions and purchases transactions. The ways in which these transactions are recorded differ somewhat under the periodic inventory system and the perpetual inventory system. Before we discuss these transactions, some terms related to sales of goods need to be introduced.

Sales Terms

When goods are sold on credit, both parties should understand the amount and timing of payment as well as other terms of the purchase, such as who pays delivery or freight charges and what warranties or rights of return apply. Sellers quote prices in different ways. Many traders quote the price at which they expect to sell their goods. Others, particularly manufacturers and wholesalers, provide a price list or catalogue and quote prices as a percentage (usually 30 per cent or more) off the list or catalogue prices. These discounts are called **trade discounts**. For example, if an article was listed at 1,000 with a trade discount of 40 per cent, or 400, the seller would record the sale at 600 and the buyer would record the purchase at 600. If the seller wishes to change the selling price, the trade discount can be raised or lowered. At times the trade discount may vary depending on the quantity purchased. The list price and related trade discounts are used only to arrive at the agreed-on price; they do not appear in the accounting records.

The terms of sale are usually printed on the sales invoice and thus constitute part of the sales agreement. Customary terms differ from industry to industry. In some industries payment is expected in a short period of time, such as ten or thirty days. In these cases, the invoice is marked "n/10" or "n/30" (read as "net ten" or "net thirty"), meaning that the amount of the invoice is due either ten days or thirty days after the invoice date. If the invoice is due ten days after the end of the month, it is marked "n/10 eom".

In some industries it is customary to give discounts for early payments. These discounts, called **sales discounts**, are intended to increase the seller's liquidity by reducing the amount of money tied up in accounts receivable. An invoice that offers a sales discount might be labelled "2/10, n/30", which means that the buyer either can pay the invoice within ten days of the invoice date and take a 2 per cent discount off of the price, which does not include freight charges, or can wait thirty days and then pay the full amount of the invoice. It is almost always advantageous for a buyer to take the discount because the saving of 2 per cent over a period of 20 days (from the eleventh day to the thirtieth day) represents an effective annual rate of 36 per cent (360 days ÷ 20 days × 2% = 36%). Most companies would be better off borrowing money to take the discount. The practice of giving sales discounts has been declining because it is costly to the seller and because, from the buyers' viewpoint, the amount of the discount is usually very small in relation to the price of the purchase. Accounting for sales discounts is covered as a supplemental objective at the end of this chapter.

In some industries, it is customary for the seller to pay transportation costs and to charge a price that includes those costs. In other industries, it is customary for the purchaser to pay transportation charges on the goods. Special terms designate whether the supplier or the purchaser pays the freight charges. **FOB shipping point** means that the supplier places the goods "free on board" at the point of origin, and the buyer pays the shipping costs. The title to the goods passes to the buyer at that point as well. For example, when the sales agreement for the purchase of a car says "FOB factory", the buyer must pay the freight from where the car was made to wherever he or she is located, and the buyer owns the car from the time it leaves the factory. **FOB destination** means that the supplier pays the transportation costs to the place where the goods are delivered. The supplier retains title until the goods reach their destination and usually prepays the shipping costs, in which case the buyer makes no accounting entry for freight. The effects of these special shipping terms are summarised below:

Shipping Term	Where Title Passes	Who Pays the Cost of Transportation
FOB shipping point	At origin	Buyer
FOB destination	At destination	Seller

Transactions Related to Purchases of Goods

The primary difference in accounting between the perpetual and the periodic inventory systems is that under the perpetual inventory system, the Inventory account is continuously adjusted because purchases, sales, and other inventory transactions are entered in this account as they occur. Purchases increase Inventory, and purchases returns decrease it. As sales of goods occur, the cost of these goods is transferred from Inventory to the Cost of Goods Sold account. Under the periodic inventory system, the Inventory account stays at the beginning level until the physical inventory is recorded at the end of the period. A Purchases account is used to accumulate the purchases of goods during the accounting period, and a Purchases Returns and Allowances account is used to accumulate returns and allowances of purchases. To illustrate these differences, purchase transactions made by Fenwick Fashions are shown below. Differences in the two systems are shown in bold print.

Purchases of goods on credit

Oct. 3   Purchased goods on credit from Neebok Company, invoice dated October 1, terms n/10, FOB shipping point, 4,890.

	Periodic Inventory System			Perpetual Inventory System	
Oct. 3	**Purchases**	4,890		**Inventory**	4,890	
	Accounts Payable		4,890	Accounts Payable		4,890
	Purchase of goods			Purchase of goods		
	from Neebok Company,			from Neebok Company,		
	terms n/10, FOB shipping			terms n/10, FOB shipping		
	point, invoice dated Oct. 1			point, invoice dated Oct. 1		

Under the periodic inventory system, **Purchases** is a temporary account. Its sole purpose is to accumulate the total cost of goods purchased for resale during an accounting period. (Purchases of other assets, such as equipment, should be recorded in the appropriate asset account, not in the Purchases account.) The Purchases account does not indicate whether goods have been sold or are still available. Under the perpetual inventory system, the Purchases account is not necessary, because purchases are recorded directly in the Inventory account.

Transportation costs on purchases

Oct. 4   Received bill from Transfer Freight Company for transportation costs on October 3 shipment, invoice dated October 1, terms n/10, 160.

	Periodic Inventory System			Perpetual Inventory System	
Oct. 4	Freight In	160		Freight In	160	
	Accounts Payable		160	Accounts Payable		160
	Transportation charges on			Transportation charges on		
	Oct. 3 purchase, Transfer			Oct. 3 purchase, Transfer		
	Freight Co., terms n/10,			Freight Co., terms n/10,		
	invoice dated Oct. 1			invoice dated Oct. 1		

In this example, transportation costs, even though billed separately by the freight company, are part of the costs to acquire the goods and should be included in the Purchases or Inventory accounts. However, since most shipments contain many different items of goods, it is usually not practical to identify the specific cost of shipping each item. As a result, transportation costs on purchases are usually accumulated, under both the periodic and perpetual inventory systems, in a Freight In account.

In some cases, the seller pays the freight charges and bills them to the buyer as a separate item on the invoice. When this occurs, the entries are the same as in the October 3 example above, except that an additional debit is made to Freight In for the amount of the freight charges and Accounts Payable is increased by a like amount.

Purchases returns and allowances

Oct. 6   Returned goods received from Neebok Company on October 3 for credit, 480.

	Periodic Inventory System				Perpetual Inventory System		
Oct. 6	Accounts Payable	480			Accounts Payable	480	
	Purchases Returns and Allowances		480		**Inventory**		480
	Goods returned to				Goods returned to		
	Neebok Company for full				Neebok Company for full		
	credit on purchase of Oct. 3				credit on purchase of Oct. 3		

If a seller sends the wrong product or one that is otherwise unsatisfactory, the buyer may be allowed to return the item for a cash refund or credit on account, or the buyer may be given an allowance off the sales price. Under the periodic inventory system, the amount of the return or allowance is recorded in the **Purchases Returns and Allowances** account. This account is a contra-purchases account with a normal credit balance and is deducted from purchases on the income statement. Under the perpetual inventory system, the returned goods are removed from the Inventory account.

Payments on account

Oct. 10   Paid in full the amount due to Neebok Company for the purchase of October 3, part of which was returned on October 6.

	Periodic Inventory System				Perpetual Inventory System		
Oct. 10	Accounts Payable	4,410			Accounts Payable	4,410	
	Cash		4,410		Cash		4,410
	Made payment on account				Made payment on account		
	to Neebok Company				to Neebok Company		
	4,890 − 480 = 4,410				4,890 − 480 = 4,410		

Payments for goods purchased are the same under both systems.

Transactions Related to Sales of Goods

The primary difference in accounting for transactions related to sales under the perpetual and the periodic inventory systems pertains to the Cost of Goods Sold account. Under the perpetual inventory system, at the time of the sale, the cost of the goods is transferred from the Inventory account to the Cost of Goods Sold account. In the case of a return, it is transferred back from Cost of Goods Sold to Inventory. Under the periodic inventory system, the Cost of Goods Sold account is not used because the Inventory account is not updated until the end of the accounting period. To illustrate these differences, transactions related to sales made by Fenwick Fashions are shown below. Differences in the two systems are indicated in bold print.

Sales of goods on credit

Oct. 7   Sold goods on credit to Gonzales Distributors, terms n/30, FOB destination, 1,200; the cost of the goods was 720.

	Periodic Inventory System				Perpetual Inventory System		
Oct. 7	Accounts Receivable	1,200			Accounts Receivable	1,200	
	Sales		1,200		Sales		1,200
	Sale of goods to				Sale of goods to		
	Gonzales Distributors, terms				Gonzales Distributors, terms		
	n/30, FOB destination				n/30, FOB destination		
					Cost of Goods Sold	720	
					Inventory		720
					To transfer cost of inventory sold		
					to Cost of Goods Sold account		

Sales of goods are handled in the same way under both inventory systems, except that under the perpetual inventory system, Cost of Goods Sold is updated by a transfer from Inventory. In the case of cash sales, Cash rather than Accounts Receivable is debited for the amount of the sale.

Payment of delivery costs

Oct. 8   Payment of transportation costs for sales on October 7, 78.

Periodic Inventory System			Perpetual Inventory System		
Oct. 8 Freight Out Expense	78		Freight Out Expense	78	
Cash		78	Cash		78
Delivery costs on			Delivery costs on		
Oct. 7 sale			Oct. 7 sale		

A seller will often absorb delivery or freight out costs in the belief that doing so will facilitate the sale of its products. These costs are accumulated in an account called Delivery Expense or Freight Out Expense, which is shown as a selling expense on the income statement.

Returns of goods sold

Oct. 9   Goods sold on October 7 accepted back from Gonzales Distributors for full credit and returned to inventory, 300; the cost of the goods was 180.

Periodic Inventory System			Perpetual Inventory System		
Oct. 9 Sales Returns and Allowances	300		Sales Returns and Allowances	300	
Accounts Receivable		300	Accounts Receivable		300
Return of goods from			Return of goods from		
Gonzales Distributors			Gonzales Distributors		
			Inventory	180	
			Cost of Goods Sold		180
			To transfer cost of		
			goods returned to		
			Inventory account		

Because returns and allowances to customers for wrong or unsatisfactory goods are often an indicator of customer dissatisfaction, such amounts are accumulated, under both methods, in a Sales Returns and Allowances account. This account is a contra-sales account with a normal debit balance and is deducted from sales on the income statement. In addition, under the perpetual inventory system, the cost of the goods must be transferred from the Cost of Goods Sold account into the Inventory account. If an allowance is made instead of accepting a return, or if goods cannot be returned to inventory and resold, this transfer is not made.

Receipts on account

Nov. 5   Received payment in full from Gonzales Distributors for sale of goods on Oct. 7, less the return on Oct. 9.

Periodic Inventory System			Perpetual Inventory System		
Nov. 5 Cash	900		Cash	900	
Accounts Receivable		900	Accounts Receivable		900
Receipt on account from			Receipt on account from		
Gonzales Distributors			Gonzales Distributors		
1,200 − 300 = 900			1,200 − 300 = 900		

Receipts on account are recorded in the same way under both systems.

EXHIBIT 4-2 *Partial Income Statement under the Perpetual Inventory System*

Fenwick Fashions Corporation
Partial Income Statement
For the Year Ended December 31, 20xx

Net Sales	
Gross Sales	246,350
Less Sales Returns and Allowances	7,025
Net Sales	239,325
Cost of Goods Sold*	131,360
Gross Profit	107,965

*Freight In has been included in Cost of Goods Sold.

Perpetual Inventory System's Effect on the Income Statement

The trading income statement illustrated in Exhibit 4-1 uses the periodic inventory method. This may be determined by the presence of the calculation of net cost of purchases and the figures for beginning and ending inventory. Under the perpetual inventory system, the Cost of Goods Sold account replaces these items. The gross profit for Fenwick Fashions would be presented as shown in Exhibit 4-2. In this example, Freight In is included in Cost of Goods Sold. Theoretically, freight in should be allocated between ending inventory and cost of goods sold, but most companies do not disclose it on the income statement because it is a relatively small amount.

Inventory Losses

Most companies experience losses in inventory from spoilage, shoplifting, and employee pilferage. When such losses occur, the periodic inventory system provides no means of tracking them because the costs are automatically included in the cost of goods sold. For example, assume that a company has lost 1,250 in stolen goods during an accounting period. When the physical inventory is taken, the missing items are not in stock, so they cannot be counted. Because the ending inventory does not contain these items, the amount subtracted from cost of goods available for sale is less than it would be if the goods were in stock. The cost of goods sold, then, is overstated by 1,250. In a sense, the cost of goods sold is inflated by the amount of goods lost.

BUSINESS BULLETIN   Business Practice

In some industries a high percentage of sales returns is an accepted business practice. A book publisher such as HarperCollins will produce and ship more copies of a best seller than it expects to sell because, to gain the attention of potential buyers, copies must be distributed to a wide variety of outlets, such as bookstores, department stores, and discount stores. As a result, returns of unsold books may run as high as 30 to 50 per cent of books shipped. The same sales principles apply to magazines sold on newsstands, like *Fortune*, and to popular recordings produced by companies like Virgin. In all these businesses, management scrutinises the Sales Returns account for ways to reduce returns and increase profitability.

The perpetual inventory system makes it easier to identify such losses. Because the Inventory account is continuously updated for sales, purchases, and returns, the loss will show up as the difference between the inventory records and the physical inventory taken at the end of the accounting period. Once the amount of the loss has been identified, the ending inventory needs to be updated by crediting the Inventory account. The offsetting debit is usually listed as an increase in Cost of Goods Sold because the loss is considered a cost that reduces the company's gross profit.

INTERNAL CONTROL STRUCTURE: BASIC ELEMENTS AND PROCEDURES

A trading company can have high losses of cash and inventory if it does not take steps to protect its assets. The best way to do this is to set up and maintain a good internal control structure.

OBJECTIVE 5

Define internal control and identify the three elements of the internal control structure, including seven examples of control procedures

Internal Control Defined

Internal control has traditionally been defined as all the policies and procedures management uses to protect a firm's assets and to ensure the accuracy and reliability of the accounting records. It also includes controls that deal with operating efficiency and adherence to management's policies. In other words, management wants not only to safeguard assets and have reliable records, but also to maintain an efficient operation that follows its policies. To this end, it establishes an internal control structure that consists of three elements: the control environment, the accounting system, and control procedures.

The **control environment** is created by the overall attitude, awareness, and actions of management. It includes management's philosophy and operating style, organisational structure, methods of assigning authority and responsibility, and personnel policies and practices. Personnel should be qualified to handle responsibilities, which means that employees must be trained and informed. For example, the manager of a retail store should train employees to follow prescribed procedures for handling cash sales, credit card sales, and returns and refunds. It is clear that an accounting system, no matter how well designed, is only as good as the people who run it. The control environment also includes regular reviews for compliance with procedures. For example, large companies often have a staff of internal auditors who review the company's system of internal control to see that it is working properly and that procedures are being followed. In smaller businesses, owners and managers should conduct these reviews.

The **accounting system** consists of all the methods and records established by management to identify, assemble, analyse, classify, record, and report a company's transactions, as well as to make certain that the goals of internal control are being met.

Finally, management uses **control procedures** to safeguard the company's assets and to ensure the reliability of the accounting records. These control procedures include the following:

1. **Authorisation** All transactions and activities should be properly authorised by management. In a retail store, for example, some transactions, such as normal cash sales, are authorised routinely; others, such as issuing a refund, may require the manager's approval.
2. **Recording transactions** To facilitate preparation of financial statements and to establish accountability for assets, all transactions should be recorded. In a retail store, for example, the cash register records sales, refunds, and other transactions internally on a paper tape or computer disk so that the cashier can be held respon-

sible for the cash that has been received and the goods that have been removed during his or her shift.

3. **Documents and records** The design and use of adequate documents help ensure the proper recording of transactions. For example, to ensure that all transactions are recorded, invoices and other documents should be prenumbered and all numbers should be accounted for.

4. **Limited access** Access to assets should be permitted only with management's authorisation. For example, retail stores should use cash registers, and only the cashier responsible for the cash in the register should have access to it. Other employees should not be able to open the cash drawer if the cashier is not present. Likewise, warehouses and storerooms should be accessible only to authorised personnel. Access to accounting records, including company computers, should also be controlled.

5. **Periodic independent verification** The records should be checked against the assets by someone other than the persons responsible for the records and the assets. For example, at the end of each shift or day, the owner or store manager should count the cash in the cash drawer and compare the amount to the amounts recorded on the tape or computer disk in the cash register. Other examples of independent verification are the monthly bank reconciliation and periodic counts of physical inventory.

6. **Separation of duties** The organisational plan should separate functional responsibilities. Within a department, no one person should be in charge of authorising transactions, operating the department, handling assets, and keeping records of assets. For example, in a stereo store, each employee should oversee only a single part of a transaction. A sales employee takes the order and writes out an invoice. A cashier receives the customer's cash or credit card payment and issues a receipt. Once the customer has a paid receipt, and only then, another employee obtains the item from the warehouse and gives it to the customer. A person in the accounting department subsequently records the sales from the tape in the cash register, comparing them with the sales invoices and updating the inventory in the records. The separation of duties means that a mistake or intentional falsification cannot be made without being seen by at least one other person.

7. **Sound personnel procedures** Sound practices should be followed in managing the people who carry out the functions of each department. Among these practices are supervision, rotation of key people among different jobs, insistence that employees take vacations, and bonding of personnel who handle cash or inventories. **Bonding** is the process of carefully checking an employee's background and commercially insuring the company against any theft by that person. Bonding does not guarantee the prevention of theft, but it does prevent or reduce economic loss if theft occurs. Prudent personnel procedures help ensure that employees know their jobs, are honest, and will find it difficult to carry out and conceal embezzlement over time.

OBJECTIVE 6

Describe the inherent limitations of internal control

Limitations of Internal Control

No system of internal control is without weaknesses. As long as control procedures are performed by people, the internal control system is vulnerable to human error. Errors may arise from misunderstandings, mistakes in judgement, carelessness, distraction, or fatigue. Separation of duties can be defeated through collusion by employees who secretly agree to deceive the company. Also, established procedures may be ineffective against employees' errors or dishonesty. Or, controls that may have been effective at first may later become ineffective because conditions have changed. In some cases, the costs of establishing and maintaining elaborate systems may exceed the benefits. In a small business, for example, active involvement by the owner can be a practical substitute for separation of some duties.

INTERNAL CONTROL OVER TRADING TRANSACTIONS

Sound internal control procedures are needed in all aspects of a business, but particularly when assets are involved. Assets are especially vulnerable when they enter or leave the business. When sales are made, for example, cash or other assets enter the business, and goods or services leave the business. Procedures must be set up to prevent theft during these transactions. Likewise, purchases of assets and payments of liabilities must be controlled. The majority of these transactions can be safeguarded by adequate purchasing and payroll systems. In addition, assets available, such as cash, investments, inventory, plant, and equipment, must be protected.

In this section, we apply internal control procedures to such trading transactions as cash sales, receipts, purchases, and cash payments. Internal control for other kinds of transactions is covered later in the book. As mentioned previously, similar procedures are applicable to service and manufacturing businesses.

When a system of internal control is applied effectively to trading transactions, it can achieve important goals for accounting as well as for general management. For example, here are two goals for accounting:

1. To prevent losses of cash or inventory from theft or fraud
2. To provide accurate records of trading transactions and account balances

And here are three broader goals for management:

1. To keep enough inventory available to sell to customers without overstocking
2. To keep enough cash available to pay for purchases in time to receive discounts
3. To keep credit losses as low as possible by making credit sales only to customers who are likely to pay on time

One control used in meeting broad management goals is the cash budget, which projects future cash receipts and disbursements. By maintaining adequate cash balances, the company is able to take advantage of discounts on purchases, prepare to borrow money when necessary, and avoid the damaging effects of being unable to pay bills when they are due. On the other hand, if the company has excess cash, it can be invested, earning interest until it is needed.

A more specific accounting control is the separation of duties involving the handling of cash. This separation means that theft without detection is extremely unlikely except through the collusion of two or more employees. The separation of duties is easier in large businesses than in small ones, because in small businesses one person may have to carry out several duties. The effectiveness of internal control over cash varies, depending on the size and nature of the company. Most firms, however, should use the following procedures:

1. Separate the functions of authorisation, recordkeeping, and custodianship of cash.
2. Limit the number of people who have access to cash.
3. Specifically designate the people who are responsible for handling cash.
4. Use banking facilities as much as possible, and keep the amount of cash available to a minimum.
5. Bond all employees who have access to cash.
6. Physically protect cash available by using cash registers, cashiers' cages, and safes.
7. Have a person who does not handle or record cash make surprise audits of the cash available.
8. Record all cash receipts promptly.
9. Deposit all cash receipts promptly.
10. Make payments by cheque rather than by currency.
11. Have a person who does not authorise, handle, or record cash transactions reconcile the Cash account to the bank statement.

Notice that each of these procedures helps safeguard cash by making it more difficult for any one person who has access to cash to steal or misuse it undetected.

Control of Cash Sales Receipts

Cash receipts for sales of goods and services can be received by mail or over the counter in the form of cheques or currency. Whatever the source, cash should be recorded immediately upon receipt. This usually is done by making an entry in a cash receipts journal. This step establishes a written record of cash receipts that should prevent errors and make theft more difficult.

Control of Cash Received through the Mail

Cash receipts that arrive by mail are vulnerable to theft by the employees who handle them. This way of doing business is increasing, however, because of the expansion of mail order sales. To control these receipts, customers should be urged to pay by cheque instead of currency.

Cash that comes in through the mail should be handled by two or more employees. The employee who opens the mail should make a list in triplicate of the money received. The list should contain each payer's name, the purpose for which the money was sent, and the amount. One copy goes with the cash to the cashier, who deposits the money. The second copy goes to the accounting department for recording. The third copy is kept by the person who opens the mail. Errors can be caught easily because the amount deposited by the cashier must agree with the amount received and the amount recorded in the cash receipts journal.

Control of Cash Received over the Counter

Two common means of controlling cash sales receipts are the use of cash registers and prenumbered sales tickets. The amount of a cash sale should be rung up on a cash register at the time of the sale. The cash register should be placed so that the customer can see the amount recorded. Each cash register should have a locked-in tape on which it prints the day's transactions. At the end of the day, the cashier counts the cash in the cash register and turns it in to the cashier's office. Another employee takes the tape out of the cash register and records the cash receipts for the day in the cash receipts journal. The amount of cash turned in and the amount recorded on the tape should agree; if not, any differences must be accounted for. Large retail chains commonly perform this function by having each cash register tied directly into a computer. In this way, each transaction is recorded as it occurs. This method separates the responsibility for cash receipts, cash deposits, and recordkeeping, thus ensuring good internal control.

In some stores, internal control is strengthened further by the use of prenumbered sales tickets and a central cash register or cashier's office, where all sales are rung up and collected by a person who does not participate in the sale. Under this procedure, the salesperson completes a prenumbered sales ticket at the time of sale, giving one copy to the customer and keeping a copy. At the end of the day, all sales tickets must be accounted for, and the sales total calculated from the sales tickets should equal the total sales recorded on the cash register.

Control of Purchases and Cash Disbursements

Cash disbursements are particularly vulnerable to fraud and embezzlement. To avoid this kind of theft, cash should be paid only on the basis of specific authorisation supported by documents that establish the validity and amount of the claim. In addition,

FIGURE 4-4   *Internal Control for Purchasing and Paying for Goods and Services*

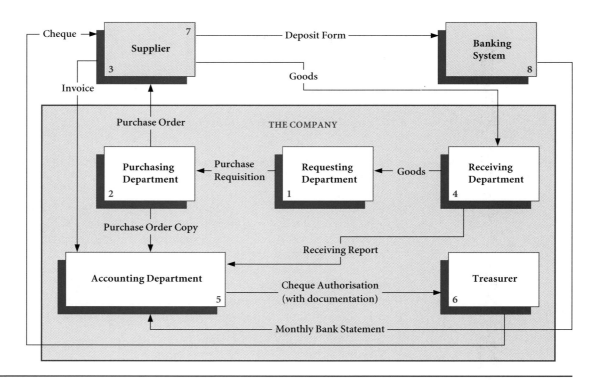

maximum possible use should be made of the principle of separation of duties in the purchase of goods and services and the payment for them. The degree of separation of duties varies, depending on the size of the business. Figure 4-4 shows how this kind of control can be maximised in large companies. In this example, five internal units (the requesting department, the purchasing department, the accounting department, the receiving department, and the treasurer) and two external contacts (the supplier and the banking system) all play a role in the internal control plan. Notice that business documents are also crucial components of the plan.

Under this plan, as summarised in Table 4-1, every action is documented and subject to verification by at least one other person. For instance, the requesting department cannot work out a kickback scheme with the supplier because the receiving department independently records receipts and the accounting department verifies prices. The receiving department cannot steal goods because the receiving report must equal the invoices. For the same reason, the supplier cannot bill for more goods than it ships. The work of the accounting department is verified by the treasurer, and the treasurer ultimately is checked by the accounting department.

Figures 4-5 through 4-9, which show typical documents used in this internal control plan, follow the purchase of twenty boxes of FAX paper rolls. To begin, the credit office (requesting department) of Martin Maintenance Company fills out a formal request for a purchase, or **purchase requisition**, for twenty boxes of FAX paper rolls (Figure 4-5). The department head approves it and forwards it to the purchasing department. The people in the purchasing department prepare a **purchase order**, as shown in Figure 4-6. The purchase order is addressed to the vendor (seller) and con-

TABLE 4-1 *Internal Control Plan for Purchases and Cash Disbursements*

Business Document	Prepared by	Sent to	Verification and Related Procedures
1. Purchase requisition	Requesting department	Purchasing department	Purchasing verifies authorisation.
2. Purchase order	Purchasing department	Supplier	Supplier sends goods or services in accordance with purchase order.
3. Invoice	Supplier	Accounting department	Accounting receives invoice from supplier.
4. Receiving report	Receiving department	Accounting department	Accounting compares invoice, purchase order, and receiving report. Accounting verifies price.
5. Cheque authorisation (or voucher)	Accounting department	Treasurer	Accounting attaches cheque authorisation to invoice, purchase order, and receiving report.
6. Cheque	Treasurer	Supplier	Treasurer verifies all documents before preparing cheque.
7. Deposit form	Supplier	Supplier's bank	Supplier compares cheque with invoice. Bank deducts cheque from buyer's account.
8. Bank statement	Buyer's bank	Accounting department	Accounting compares amount and payee's name on returned cheque with cheque authorisation.

tains a description of the items ordered; the expected price, terms, and shipping date; and other shipping instructions. Martin Maintenance Company does not pay any bill that is not accompanied by a purchase order number.

After receiving the purchase order, the vendor, Henderson Supply Company, ships the goods (in this case, delivers them) and sends an **invoice**, or bill (Figure 4-7), to Martin Maintenance Company. The invoice gives the quantity and description of the goods delivered and the terms of payment. If goods cannot all be shipped immediately, the estimated date for shipment of the remainder is indicated.

When the goods reach the receiving department of Martin Maintenance Company, an employee writes the description, quantity, and condition of the goods on a form called a **receiving report**. The receiving department does not receive a copy of the purchase order or invoice, so its employees do not know what should be received. Thus, they are not tempted to steal any excess that may be delivered.

The receiving report is sent to the accounting department, where it is compared with the purchase order and the invoice. If all is correct, the accounting department

FIGURE 4-5 *Purchase Requisition*

PURCHASE REQUISITION	No. 7077

Martin Maintenance Company

From: Credit Office

To: Purchasing Department

Please purchase the following items:

Date: September 6, 20xx

Suggested Vendor: Henderson Supply Company

Quantity	Number	Description
20 boxes	X 144	FAX paper rolls

Reason for Request

Six months' supply for office

Approved *BM*

To be filled in by Purchasing Department

Date ordered 9/8/xx   P.O. No. J 102

FIGURE 4-6 *Purchase Order*

PURCHASE ORDER	No. J 102

Martin Maintenance Company
XXXX XXXXX XXXXXX
XXXXX XXXX XXXXX

To: Henderson Supply Company
XX XXX XXXXX
XXXX XX XXXXX

Ship to: Martin Maintenance Company
Above Address

Please ship the following:

Date   September 8, 20xx

FOB   Destination

Ship by   September 12, 20xx

Terms   2/10, n/30

Quantity	✓	Number	Description	Price	Per	Amount
20 boxes		X 144	FAX paper rolls	12.00	box	240.00

Purchase order number must appear on all shipments and invoices.

Ordered by
Marsha Owen

FIGURE 4-7   *Invoice*

		INVOICE		No. 0468	

Henderson Supply Company
XX XXX XXXXX
XXXX XX XXXXX

Date   September 12, 20xx

Your Order No.   J 102

Sold to:

Ship to:

Martin Maintenance Company
XXXX XXXXX XXXXXX
XXXXX XXXX XXXXX

Same

Sales Representative: Joe Jacobs

Quantity					
Ordered	Shipped	Description	Price	Per	Amount
20	20	X 144 FAX paper rolls	12.00	box	240.00

FOB Destination	Terms: 2/10, n/30	Date Shipped: 9/12/xx	Via: Self

completes a **cheque authorisation** and attaches it to the three supporting documents. The cheque authorisation form shown in Figure 4-8 has a space for each item to be checked off as it is examined. Notice that the accounting department has all the documentary evidence for the transaction but does not have access to the assets purchased. Nor does it write the cheques for payment. Thus, the people performing the accounting function cannot gain by falsifying documents in an effort to conceal fraud.

FIGURE 4-8   *Cheque Authorisation*

CHEQUE AUTHORISATION

	NO.	CHECK
Requisition	7077	✓
Purchase Order	J 102	✓
Receiving Report	JR 065	✓
INVOICE	0468	
Price		✓
Calculations		✓
Terms		✓

Approved for Payment   *J. Joseph*

FIGURE 4-9 *Cheque with Attached Remittance Advice*

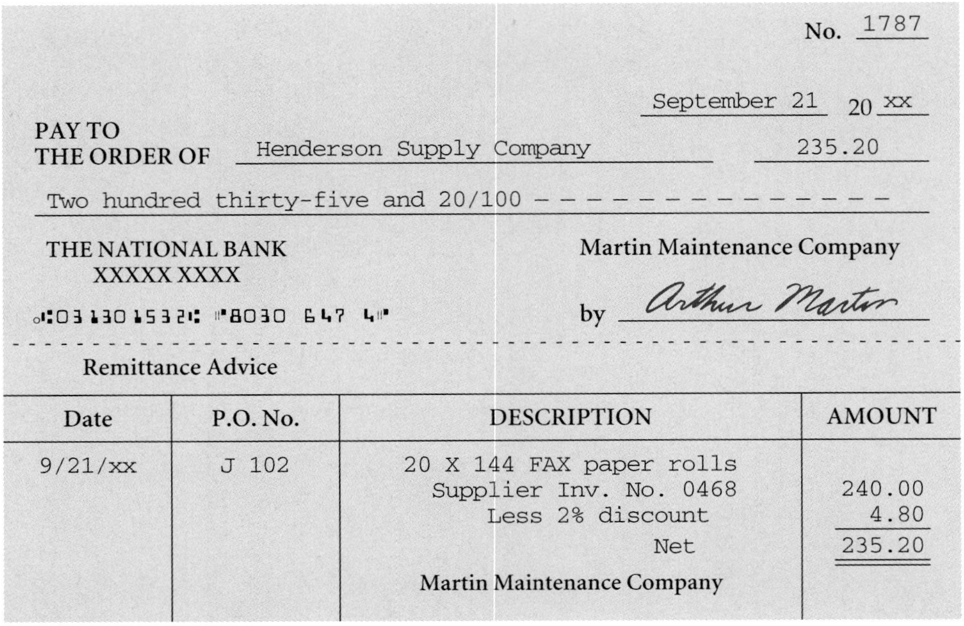

No. 1787

September 21 20 xx

PAY TO
THE ORDER OF   Henderson Supply Company   235.20

Two hundred thirty-five and 20/100 − − − − − − − − − − − − − −

THE NATIONAL BANK   Martin Maintenance Company
XXXXX XXXX

⑆031301532⑆ ⑈8030 647 4⑈   by _Arthur Martin_

- -

Remittance Advice

Date	P.O. No.	DESCRIPTION	AMOUNT
9/21/xx	J 102	20 X 144 FAX paper rolls	
		Supplier Inv. No. 0468	240.00
		Less 2% discount	4.80
		Net	235.20
		Martin Maintenance Company	

Finally, the treasurer examines all the documents and issues an order to the bank for payment, called a **cheque** (Figure 4-9), for the amount of the invoice less any appropriate discount. In some systems, the accounting department fills out the cheque so that all the treasurer has to do is inspect and sign it. The cheque is then sent to the supplier, with a remittance advice that shows what the cheque is for. A supplier who is not paid the proper amount will complain, of course, thus providing a form of outside control over the payment. The supplier deposits the cheque in the bank, which returns the cancelled cheque with Martin Maintenance Company's next bank statement. If the treasurer has made the cheque out for the wrong amount (or altered a prefilled-in cheque), the problem shows up in the bank reconciliation.

There are many variations of the system just described. This example is offered as a simple system that provides adequate internal control.

SUPPLEMENTAL OBJECTIVE 8

Apply sales and purchases discounts to trading transactions

ACCOUNTING FOR DISCOUNTS

Sales Discounts

As mentioned earlier, some industries give sales discounts for early payment. Because it usually is not possible to know at the time of the sale whether the customer will pay in time to take advantage of them, sales discounts are recorded only at the time the customer pays. For example, assume that Fenwick Fashions Corporation sells goods to a customer on September 20 for 300, on terms of 2/10, n/60. This is the entry at the time of the sale:

Sept. 20	Accounts Receivable	300	
	Sales		300
	Sale of goods on credit,		
	Terms 2/10, n/60		

The customer can take advantage of the sales discount any time on or before September 30, ten days after the date of the invoice. For example, if the customer pays on September 29, the entry in Fenwick's records would look like this:

Sept. 29	Cash	294	
	Sales Discounts	6	
	Accounts Receivable		300
	Payment for Sept. 20 sale;		
	discount taken		

If the customer does not take advantage of the sales discount but waits until November 19 to pay for the goods, the entry would be as follows:

Nov. 19	Cash	300	
	Accounts Receivable		300
	Payment for Sept. 20 sale;		
	no discount taken		

At the end of the accounting period, the Sales Discounts account has accumulated all the sales discounts taken during the period. Because sales discounts reduce revenues from sales, Sales Discounts is a contra-revenue account with a normal debit balance that is deducted from gross sales on the income statement.

Purchases Discounts

Purchases of goods are usually made on credit and sometimes involve **purchases discounts** for early payment. Purchases discounts are discounts taken for early payment on goods purchased for resale. They are to the buyer what sales discounts are to the seller. The amount of discounts taken forms a separate account. Assume a credit purchase of goods was made on November 12 for 1,500, terms 2/10, n/30, and a return of 200 in goods was granted on November 14. When payment is made, the journal entry looks like this:

Nov. 22	Accounts Payable		1,300	
	Purchases Discounts			26
	Cash			1,274
	Paid the invoice of Nov. 12			
	Purchase Nov. 12	1,500		
	Less return Nov. 14	200		
	Net purchase	1,300		
	Discount: 2%	26		
	Cash paid	1,274		

If the purchase is not paid for within the discount period, the entry is as follows:

Dec. 12	Accounts Payable	1,300	
	Cash		1,300
	Paid the invoice of Nov. 12		
	on due date; no discount taken		

Like Purchases Returns and Allowances, Purchases Discounts is a contra-purchases account with a normal credit balance that is deducted from Purchases on the income statement. If a company makes only a partial payment on an invoice, most lenders allow the company to take the discount applicable to the partial payment. The discount usually does not apply to freight, postage, taxes, or other charges that might appear on the invoice.

CHAPTER REVIEW

Review of Learning Objectives

1. **Identify the management issues related to trading businesses.** Trading companies differ from service companies in that they earn a profit by buying and selling products or goods. The buying and selling of goods adds to the complexity of the business and raises four issues that management must address. First, the series of transactions that trading companies engage in (the operating cycle) requires careful cash flow management. Second, profitability management requires pricing goods and controlling costs and expenses to ensure that the company earns an adequate profit after operating expenses and income taxes are paid. Third, the company must choose between using the periodic or perpetual inventory system. Fourth, an internal control structure must be established to protect the assets of cash, inventory, and accounts receivable.

2. **Compare the income statements for service and trading enterprises and define the components of the trading income statement.** In the simplest case, the income statement for a service company consists only of revenues and expenses. The income statement for a trading company has four major parts: (1) net sales, (2) cost of goods sold, (3) operating expenses, and (4) income taxes. Gross profit is the difference between revenues from net sales and the cost of goods sold. Profit before income taxes is the difference between gross profit and operating expenses. Net profit is the "bottom line" after income taxes. Some important relationships associated with the calculation of cost of goods sold are as follows:

$$\begin{array}{c} \text{Gross} \\ \text{purchases} \end{array} - \begin{array}{c} \text{purchases returns} \\ \text{and allowances} \end{array} + \begin{array}{c} \text{freight} \\ \text{in} \end{array} = \begin{array}{c} \text{net cost of} \\ \text{purchases} \end{array}$$

$$\begin{array}{c} \text{Beginning} \\ \text{inventory} \end{array} + \begin{array}{c} \text{net cost of} \\ \text{purchases} \end{array} = \begin{array}{c} \text{goods} \\ \text{available for sale} \end{array}$$

$$\begin{array}{c} \text{Goods} \\ \text{available for sale} \end{array} - \begin{array}{c} \text{ending} \\ \text{inventory} \end{array} = \begin{array}{c} \text{cost of} \\ \text{goods sold} \end{array}$$

3. **Distinguish between the perpetual and the periodic inventory systems and explain the importance of taking a physical inventory.** Inventory includes all saleable goods owned, regardless of where they are located. Inventory can be determined by one of two systems. Under the *periodic inventory system*, the company usually waits until the end of an accounting period to take a physical inventory; it does not maintain detailed records of physical inventory available during the period. Under the *perpetual inventory system*, records are kept of the quantity and, usually, the cost of individual items of inventory throughout the year. The cost of goods sold is recorded as goods are transferred to customers, and the inventory balance is kept current throughout the year. Under both systems, a physical inventory, or physical count, is taken at the end of the accounting period—to determine cost of goods sold under the periodic inventory system and to detect inventory losses under the perpetual inventory system.

4. **Contrast and record transactions related to sales and purchases under the periodic and the perpetual inventory systems.** Sales terms define the amount and timing of payment, who pays delivery or freight charges, and what warranties or rights of return apply. Under the perpetual inventory system, the Inventory account is continuously adjusted by entering purchases, sales, and other inventory transactions as they occur. Purchases increase the Inventory account, and purchases returns decrease it. As sales of goods occur, their cost is transferred from the Inventory account to the Cost of Goods Sold account. Under the periodic inventory system, in contrast, the Inventory account stays at the beginning level until the physical inventory is recorded at the end of the period. A Purchases account is used to accumulate the purchases of goods during the accounting period, and a Purchases Returns and Allowances account is used to accumulate returns and allowances of purchases. Under both systems, transportation costs on purchases are accumulated in the Freight In account and transportation costs on sales are recorded as delivery expense or freight out expense.

5. **Define *internal control* and identify the three elements of the internal control structure, including seven examples of control procedures.** Internal control is all the policies and procedures management uses to protect the organisation's assets and to ensure the accuracy and reliability of accounting records. It also works to maintain efficient operations and compliance with management's policies. The internal control structure consists of the control environment, the accounting system, and control procedures. Examples of control procedures are proper authorisation of transactions; recording transactions to facilitate preparation of financial statements and to establish accountability for assets; use of well-designed documents and records; limited access to assets; periodic independent comparison of records and assets; separation of duties into the functions of authorisation, operations, custody of assets, and recordkeeping; and use of sound personnel policies.

6. **Describe the inherent limitations of internal control.** A system of internal control relies on the people who implement it. Thus, the effectiveness of internal control is limited by the people involved. Human error, collusion, the interference of management, and failure to recognise changed conditions all can contribute to a system's failure.

7. **Apply control procedures to certain trading transactions.** Certain procedures strengthen internal control over sales, cash receipts, purchases, and cash disbursements. First, the functions of authorisation, recordkeeping, and custody should be kept separate. Second, the accounting system should provide for physical protection of assets (especially cash and inventory), use of banking services, prompt recording and deposit of cash receipts, and payment by cheque. Third, the people who have access to cash and inventory should be specifically designated and their number limited. Fourth, employees who have access to cash or inventory should be bonded. Fifth, the Cash account should be reconciled each month, and surprise audits of cash available should be made by an individual who does not authorise, handle, or record cash transactions.

Supplemental Objective

8. **Apply sales and purchases discounts to trading transactions.** Sales discounts are discounts for early payment. Terms of 2/10, n/30 mean that the buyer can take a 2 per cent discount if the invoice is paid within ten days of the invoice date. Otherwise, the buyer is obligated to pay the full amount in thirty days. Discounts on sales are recorded in the Sales Discounts account, and discounts on purchases are recorded in the Purchases Discounts account.

Review of Concepts and Terminology

The following concepts and terms were introduced in this chapter.

LO 5 **Accounting system:** The methods and records established to identify, assemble, analyse, classify, record, and report a company's transactions, and to ensure that the goals of internal control are being met.

LO 2 **Beginning inventory:** Goods available at the beginning of an accounting period.

LO 5 **Bonding:** The process of carefully checking an employee's background and commercially insuring the company against theft by that person.

LO 1 **Cash flow management:** The planning of a company's receipts and payments of cash.

LO 7 **Cheque:** A written order to a bank to pay the amount specified from money on deposit.

LO 7 **Cheque authorisation:** A form prepared by the accounting department after it has compared the receiving report for goods received with the purchase order and the invoice.

LO 5 **Control environment:** The overall attitude, awareness, and actions of the management of a business, as reflected in philosophy and operating style, organisational structure, methods of assigning authority and responsibility, and personnel policies and practices.

LO 5 **Control procedures:** Procedures and policies established by management to safeguard the company's assets and ensure the reliability of the accounting records.

LO 2 **Cost of goods sold:** The amount paid for the goods sold during an accounting period. Also called *cost of sales*.

LO 2 **Ending inventory:** Goods available at the end of an accounting period.

LO 4 **FOB destination:** A shipping term that means that the seller pays transportation costs to the destination. The supplier retains title to the goods until they reach the destination.

LO 4 **FOB shipping point:** A shipping term that means that the buyer pays transportation costs from the point of origin. The title to the goods also passes to the buyer at that point.

LO 2 **Freight in:** Transportation charges on goods purchased for resale. Also called *transportation in*.

LO 2 **Freight out expenses:** Transportation charges on goods sold; an operating expense. Also called *delivery expense*.

LO 2 **Goods available for sale:** The sum of beginning inventory and the net cost of purchases during the year; the total goods available for sale to customers during an accounting period.

LO 2 **Gross profit:** The difference between net sales and cost of goods sold. Also called *gross margin*.

LO 2 **Gross sales:** Total sales for cash and on credit during an accounting period.

LO 5 **Internal control:** All the policies and procedures management uses to protect a firm's assets, ensure the accuracy and reliability of its accounting data, promote operational efficiency, and encourage adherence to its policies.

LO 1 **Internal control structure:** A structure established to safeguard the assets of a business and provide reliable accounting records; consists of the control environment, the accounting system, and the control procedures.

LO 1 **Inventory:** The goods available at any one time that are on hand for sale to customers.

LO 7 **Invoice:** A form sent to the purchaser by the vendor that describes the quantity and price of the goods or services delivered and the terms of payment.

LO 2 **Net cost of purchases:** Net purchases plus any freight charges on the purchases.

LO 2 **Net profit:** For trading companies, what is left after deducting operating expenses and income taxes from the gross profit.

LO 2 **Net purchases:** Total purchases less any deductions, such as purchases returns and allowances and purchases discounts.

LO 2 **Net sales:** The gross proceeds from sales of goods less sales returns and allowances and any discounts. Also called *sales* on income statements.

LO 1 **Operating cycle:** A series of transactions that includes purchases of inventory, sales of inventory for cash or on credit, and collection of the cash from the sales.

LO 2 **Operating expenses:** The expenses other than the cost of goods sold that are incurred in running a business.

LO 1 **Periodic inventory system:** A system for determining ending inventory by a physical count at the end of an accounting period.

LO 1 **Perpetual inventory system:** A system for determining inventory by keeping continuous records of the physical inventory as goods are bought and sold.

LO 3 **Physical inventory:** An actual count of all of the goods available at the end of an accounting period.

LO 2 **Profit before income taxes:** Gross profit less operating expenses. Also called *operating profit* or *profit from operations*.

LO 1 **Profitability management:** The process of setting the appropriate prices on goods, purchasing goods at favourable prices and terms, and maintaining acceptable levels of expenses.

LO 7 **Purchase order:** A form prepared by a company's purchasing department and sent to a vendor that describes the items ordered; their expected price, terms, and shipping date; and other shipping instructions.

LO 7 **Purchase requisition:** A formal written request for a purchase, prepared by a department in a company and sent to its purchasing department.

LO 4 **Purchases:** A temporary account used to accumulate the total cost of all of the goods purchased for resale during an accounting period.

SO 8 **Purchases discounts:** Discounts taken for prompt payment for goods purchased for resale; the Purchases Discounts account is a contra-purchases account.

LO 4 **Purchases Returns and Allowances:** A contra-purchases account used to accumulate cash refunds, credits on account, or other allowances made by suppliers on goods originally purchased for resale.

LO 7 **Receiving report:** A form prepared by the receiving department of a company that describes the quantity and condition of goods received.

LO 4 **Sales discounts:** Discounts given to buyers for early payment for sales made on credit; the Sales Discounts account is a contra-revenue account.

LO 2 **Sales Returns and Allowances:** A contra-revenue account used to accumulate cash refunds, credits on account, and other allowances made to customers who have received defective or otherwise unsatisfactory products.

LO 1 **Service businesses:** Businesses that earn a profit by performing a service for fees or commissions.

LO 4 **Trade discounts:** Deductions (usually 30 per cent or more) off list or catalogue prices.

LO 1 **Trading businesses:** Businesses that earn a profit by buying and selling products or goods.

Review Problem

Trading Transactions: Periodic and Perpetual Inventory Systems

LO 4   Dawkins Company engaged in the following transactions:

Oct. 1   Sold goods to Ernie Devlin on credit, terms n/30, FOB shipping point, 1,050 (cost, 630).
      2   Purchased goods on credit from Ruland Company, terms n/30, FOB shipping point, 1,900.
      2   Paid Custom Freight 145 for freight charges on goods received.
      6   Purchased store supplies on credit from Arizin Supply House, terms n/30, 318.
      9   Purchased goods on credit from LNP Company, terms n/30, FOB shipping point, 1,800, including 100 freight costs paid by LNP Company.
     11   Accepted from Ernie Devlin a return of goods, which was returned to inventory, 150 (cost, 90).
     14   Returned for credit 300 of goods received on October 2.
     15   Returned for credit 100 of store supplies purchased on October 6.
     16   Sold goods for cash, 500 (cost, 300).
     22   Paid Ruland Company for purchase of October 2 less return of October 14.
     23   Received full payment from Ernie Devlin for his October 1 purchase, less return on October 11.

REQUIRED   1. Prepare general journal entries to record the transactions, assuming the periodic inventory system is used.
            2. Prepare general journal entries to record the transactions, assuming the perpetual inventory system is used.

Answer to Review Problem

1. Periodic Inventory System			2. Perpetual Inventory System		
20xx					
Oct. 1 Accounts Receivable	1,050		Accounts Receivable	1,050	
Sales		1,050	Sales		1,050
Sales on account to Ernie Devlin, terms n/30, FOB shipping point			Sales on account to Ernie Devlin, terms n/30, FOB shipping point		
			Cost of Goods Sold	630	
			Inventory		630
			To transfer cost of goods sold to Cost of Goods Sold account and to reduce Inventory account		
2 Purchases	1,900		Inventory	1,900	
Accounts Payable		1,900	Accounts Payable		1,900
Purchase on account from Ruland Company, terms n/30			Purchase on account from Ruland Company, terms n/30		
2 Freight In	145		Freight In	145	
Cash		145	Cash		145
Freight on previous purchase			Freight on previous purchase		
6 Store Supplies	318		Store Supplies	318	
Accounts Payable		318	Accounts Payable		318
Purchased store supplies from Arizin Supply House, terms n/30			Purchased store supplies from Arizin Supply House, terms n/30		
9 Purchases	1,700		Inventory	1,700	
Freight In	100		Freight In	100	
Accounts Payable		1,800	Accounts Payable		1,800
Purchase on account from LNP Company, terms n/30, FOB shipping point, freight paid by supplier			Purchase on account from LNP Company, terms n/30, FOB shipping point, freight paid by supplier		

Oct. 11	Sales Returns and Allowances	150			Sales Returns and Allowances	150	
	Accounts Receivable		150		Accounts Receivable		150
	Accepted return of goods from Ernie Devlin				Accepted return of goods from Ernie Devlin		
					Inventory	90	
					Cost of Goods Sold		90
					To transfer cost of goods returned to Inventory		
14	Accounts Payable	300			Accounts Payable	300	
	Purchases Returns and Allowances		300		Inventory		300
	Returned portion of goods purchased from Ruland Company				Returned portion of goods purchased from Ruland Company		
15	Accounts Payable	100			Accounts Payable	100	
	Store Supplies		100		Store Supplies		100
	Returned store supplies (not goods) purchased on October 6 for credit				Returned store supplies (not goods) purchased on October 6 for credit		
16	Cash	500			Cash	500	
	Sales		500		Sales		500
	Sold goods for cash				Sold goods for cash		
					Cost of Goods Sold	300	
					Inventory		300
					To transfer cost of goods sold to Cost of Goods Sold account		
22	Accounts Payable	1,600			Accounts Payable	1,600	
	Cash		1,600		Cash		1,600
	Payment on account to Ruland Company 1,900 − 300 = 1,600				Payment on account to Ruland Company 1,900 − 300 = 1,600		
23	Cash	900			Cash	900	
	Accounts Receivable		900		Accounts Receivable		900
	Receipt on account of Ernie Devlin 1,050 − 150 = 900				Receipt on account of Ernie Devlin 1,050 − 150 = 900		

CHAPTER ASSIGNMENTS

Knowledge and Understanding

Questions

1. What four issues must managers of trading businesses face?
2. What is the operating cycle of a trading business and why is it important?
3. What is the primary difference between the operations of a trading business and those of a service business and how is it reflected on the income statement?
4. Is freight in an operating expense? Explain your answer.
5. Define gross profit. Why is it important?
6. During its first year in operation, Kumler Nursery had a cost of goods sold of 64,000 and a gross profit equal to 40 per cent of sales. What was the monetary amount of the company's sales?

7. Could Kumler Nursery (in Question 6) have a net loss for the year? Explain your answer.
8. What is the difference between the periodic inventory system and the perpetual inventory system?
9. Under the periodic inventory system, how must the amount of inventory at the end of the year be determined?
10. What are the principal differences in the handling of inventory in the accounting records under the periodic inventory system and the perpetual inventory system?
11. Discuss this statement: "The perpetual inventory system is the best system because management always needs to know how much inventory it has."
12. How do a trade discount and a sales discount differ?

13. The following prices and terms on 50 units of product were quoted by two companies:

	Price	Terms
Supplier A	20 per unit	FOB shipping point
Supplier B	21 per unit	FOB destination

Which supplier is quoting the better deal? Explain your answer.

14. What is the principal difference in accounting for the purchase and sale of goods under the perpetual inventory system and the periodic inventory system?

15. Hornberger Hardware purchased the following items: (a) a delivery truck, (b) two dozen hammers, (c) supplies for its office workers, and (d) a broom for the janitor. Which items should be debited to the Purchases account under the periodic inventory system?

16. Is a Cost of Goods Sold account maintained under the perpetual inventory system or the periodic inventory system? Why?

17. Why is it advisable for a company to maintain a Sales Returns and Allowances account when the same result could be obtained by debiting each return or allowance to the Sales account?

18. Most people think of internal control as a means of making fraud harder to commit and easier to detect. Can you think of some other important purposes of internal control?

19. What are the three elements of the internal control structure?

20. What are some examples of control procedures?

21. Why is the separation of duties necessary to ensure sound internal control? What does this principle assume about the relationships of employees in a company and the possibility of two or more of them stealing from the company?

22. In a small business, it is sometimes impossible to separate duties completely. What are three other practices that a small business can follow to achieve the objectives of internal control over cash?

23. At Thrifty Variety Store, each sales clerk counts the cash in his or her cash drawer at the end of the day, then removes the cash register tape and prepares a daily cash form, noting any discrepancies. This information is checked by an employee in the cashier's office, who counts the cash, compares the total with the form, and then gives the cash to the cashier. What is the weakness in this system of internal control?

24. How does a movie theatre control cash receipts?

25. What is the normal balance of the Sales Discounts account? Is it an asset, liability, expense, or contra-revenue account?

Application

Exercises

E 4-1.

LO 1 *Management Issues and Decisions*

The decisions and actions below were undertaken by the management of Banerjee Shoe Company. Indicate whether each action pertains primarily to (a) cash flow management, (b) profitability management, (c) choice of inventory systems, or (d) control of trading operations.

1. Decided to place on each item of inventory a magnetic tag that sets off an alarm if the tag is removed from the store before being deactivated.
2. Decided to reduce the credit terms offered to customers from thirty days to twenty days in order to speed up collection of accounts.
3. Decided that the benefits of keeping track of each item of inventory as it is bought and sold would exceed the costs of such a system and acted to implement the decision.
4. Decided to raise the price of each item of inventory to achieve a higher gross profit to offset an increase in rent expense.
5. Decided to purchase a new type of cash register that can be operated only by a person who knows a predetermined code.
6. Decided to switch to a new cleaning service that will provide the same service at a lower cost.

E 4-2.

LO 2 *Parts of the Income Statement: Missing Data*

Calculate the amount of each item indicated by a letter in the table below. Treat each horizontal row of numbers as a separate problem.

Sales	Beginning Inventory	Net Cost of Purchases	Ending Inventory	Cost of Goods Sold	Gross Profit	Operating Expenses	Profit (Loss)
250,000	a	70,000	20,000	b	80,000	c	24,000
d	24,000	e	36,000	216,000	120,000	80,000	40,000
460,000	44,000	334,000	f	g	100,000	h	(2,000)
780,000	80,000	i	120,000	j	k	240,000	80,000

E 4-3.

LO 2 *Gross Profit from Sales Calculation: Missing Data*

Determine the amount of gross purchases by preparing a partial income statement under the periodic inventory system, showing the calculation of gross profit from sales from the following data: freight in, 13,000; cost of goods sold, 185,000; sales, 275,000; beginning inventory, 25,000; purchases returns and allowances, 7,500; ending inventory, 12,000.

E 4-4.

LO 2 *Preparation of Income Statement: Periodic Inventory System*

Using the selected year-end account balances at December 31, 20x2 for the Mill Pond General Store shown at the top of the following page, prepare a 20x2 income statement. The Mill Pond General Store uses the periodic inventory system. The company's beginning inventory was 26,000; its ending inventory is 22,000.

Account Name	Debit	Credit
Sales		297,000
Sales Returns and Allowances	15,200	
Purchases	114,800	
Purchases Returns and Allowances		4,000
Freight In	5,600	
Selling Expenses	48,500	
General and Administrative Expenses	37,200	
Income Taxes	15,000	

E 4-5.

LO 4 *Preparation of Income Statement: Perpetual Inventory System*

Using the selected account balances at December 31, 20xx for Nature's Adventure Store below, prepare an income statement for the year ended December 31, 20xx. The company uses the perpetual inventory system, and Freight In has not been included in Cost of Goods Sold.

Account Name	Debit	Credit
Sales		475,000
Sales Returns and Allowances	23,500	
Cost of Goods Sold	280,000	
Freight In	13,500	
Selling Expenses	43,000	
General and Administrative Expenses	87,000	
Income Taxes	12,000	

E 4-6.

LO 2 *Trading Income Statement: Missing Data, Multiple Years*

Determine the missing data for each letter in the three income statements below for Lopata Office Supplies Company (in thousands):

	20x3	20x2	20x1
Gross Sales	p	h	572
Sales Returns and Allowances	48	38	a
Net Sales	q	634	b
Inventory, Jan. 1	r	i	76
Purchases	384	338	c
Purchases Returns and Allowances	62	j	34
Freight In	s	58	44
Net Cost of Purchases	378	k	d
Goods Available for Sale	444	424	364
Inventory, Dec. 31	78	l	84
Cost of Goods Sold	t	358	e
Gross Profit	284	m	252
Selling Expenses	u	156	f
General and Administrative Expenses	78	n	66
Total Operating Expenses	260	256	g
Profit before Income Taxes	v	o	54
Income Taxes	6	4	10
Net Profit	w	16	44

E 4-7.

LO 4 *Recording Purchases: Periodic and Perpetual Inventory Systems*

Give the entries to record each of the following transactions (1) under the periodic inventory system and (2) under the perpetual inventory system:

a. Purchased goods on credit, terms n/30, FOB shipping point, 7,500.
b. Paid freight on the shipment in transaction **a**, 405.
c. Purchased goods on credit, terms n/30, FOB destination, 4,200.
d. Purchased goods on credit, terms n/30, FOB shipping point, 7,800, which includes freight paid by the supplier of 600.
e. Returned part of the goods purchased in transaction **c**, 1,500.
f. Paid the amount owed on the purchase in transaction **a**.
g. Paid the amount owed on the purchase in transaction **d**.
h. Paid the amount owed on the purchase in transaction **c** less the return in transaction **e**.

E 4-8.

LO 4 *Recording Sales: Periodic and Perpetual Inventory Systems*

On June 15, the Jackson Company sold goods for 2,600 on terms of n/30 to Clement Company. On June 20, Clement returned some of the goods for a credit of 600, and on June 25 paid the balance owed. Give Jackson's entries to record the sale, return, and receipt of payment (1) under the periodic inventory system and (2) under the perpetual inventory system. The cost of the goods sold on June 15 was 1,500 and the cost of the goods returned to inventory on June 20 was 350.

E 4-9.

LO 5 *Use of Accounting Records in Internal Control*

Careful scrutiny of accounting records and financial statements can lead to the discovery of fraud or embezzlement. Each situation below may indicate a breakdown in internal control. Indicate what the possible fraud or embezzlement is in each situation.

1. Wages expense for a branch office was 30 per cent higher in 20x2 than in 20x1, even though the office employed only the same four employees and raises were only 5 per cent in 20x1.
2. Sales returns and allowances increased from 5 per cent to 20 per cent of sales in the first two months of 20x2, after record sales in 20x1 resulted in large bonuses being paid to the sales staff.
3. Gross profit decreased from 40 per cent of net sales in 20x1 to 30 per cent in 20x2, even though there was no change in pricing. Ending inventory was 50 per cent less at the end of 20x2 than it was at the beginning of the year. There is no immediate explanation for the decrease in inventory.
4. A review of daily cash register receipts records shows that one cashier consistently accepts more discount coupons for purchases than do the other cashiers.

E 4-10.

LO 5 *Control Procedures*

Sean O'Mara, who operates a small grocery store, has established the following policies with regard to the check-out cashiers:

1. Each cashier has his or her own cash drawer, to which no one else has access.
2. Each cashier may accept cheques for purchases under 50 with proper identification. Cheques over 50 must be approved by O'Mara before they are accepted.
3. Every sale must be rung up on the cash register and a receipt given to the customer. Each sale is recorded on a tape inside the cash register.
4. At the end of each day O'Mara counts the cash in the drawer and compares it to the amount on the tape inside the cash register.

Identify by letter which conditions for internal control apply to each of the above policies:

a. Transactions are executed in accordance with management's general or specific authorisation.
b. Transactions are recorded as necessary to (1) permit preparation of financial statements and (2) maintain accountability for assets.
c. Access to assets is permitted only as allowed by management.
d. The recorded accountability for assets is compared with the existing assets at reasonable intervals.

E 4-11.

LO 5 *Internal Control Procedures*

Ruth's Video Store maintains the following policies with regard to purchases of new videotapes at each of its branch stores:

1. Employees are required to take vacations, and duties of employees are rotated periodically.
2. Once each month a person from the home office visits each branch to examine the receiving records and to compare the inventory of video tapes with the accounting records.
3. Purchases of new tapes must be authorised by purchase order in the home office and paid for by the treasurer in the home office. Receiving reports are prepared in each branch and sent to the home office.
4. All new personnel receive a one-hour orientation on receiving and cataloging new video tapes.
5. The company maintains a perpetual inventory system that keeps track of all video tapes purchased, sold, and available.

Indicate by letter which of the following control procedures apply to each of the above policies (some may have several answers):

a. Authorisation
b. Recording transactions
c. Documents and records
d. Limited access
e. Periodic independent verification
f. Separation of duties
g. Sound personnel policies

E 4-12.

LO 5 *Internal Control Evaluation*

Developing a convenient means of providing sales representatives with cash for their incidental expenses, such as entertaining a client at lunch, is a problem many companies face. One company has a plan whereby the sales representatives receive advances in cash from the petty cash fund. Each advance is supported by an authorisation from the sales manager. The representative returns the receipt for the expenditure and any unused cash, which is replaced in the petty cash fund. The cashier of the petty cash fund is responsible for seeing that the receipt and the cash returned equal the advance. At the time that the petty cash fund is reimbursed, the amount of the representative's expenditure is debited to Direct Sales Expense.

What is the weak point in this system? What fundamental principle of internal control is being ignored? What improvement in the procedure can you suggest?

E 4-13.

LO 5 *Internal Control Evaluation*

An accountant is responsible for the following procedures: (1) receiving all cash; (2) maintaining the general ledger; (3) maintaining the accounts receivable subsidiary ledger that includes the individual records of each customer; (4) maintaining the journals for recording sales, purchases, and cash receipts (some companies maintain separate journals to record frequent transactions); and (5) preparing monthly statements to be sent to customers. As a service to customers and employees, the company allows the accountant to cash cheques of up to 50 with money from the cash receipts. When deposits are made, the cheques are included in place of the cash receipts.

What weaknesses in internal control exist in this system?

E 4-14.

SO 8 *Purchases and Sales Involving Discounts*

The Fellini Company purchased 9,200 of goods, terms 2/10, n/30, from the Vance Company and paid for the goods within the discount period. Give the entries (1) by the Fellini Company to record the purchase and payment and (2) by the Vance Company to record the sale and receipt of payment. Both companies use the periodic inventory system.

E 4-15.

SO 8 *Sales Involving Discounts*

Give the entries to record the following transactions engaged in by Westland Corporation, which uses the periodic inventory system:

Mar. 1 Sold goods on credit to Grano Company, terms 2/10, n/30, FOB shipping point, 500.
  3 Accepted a return from Grano Company for full credit, 200.
  10 Received payment from Grano Company for the purchase less the return and discount.
  11 Sold goods on credit to Grano Company, terms 2/10, n/30, FOB destination, 800.
  31 Received payment for amount due from Grano Company for sale of March 11.

E 4-16.

SO 8 *Purchases Involving Discounts*

Give the entries to record the following transactions engaged in by Westland Corporation, which uses the periodic inventory system:

July 2 Purchased goods on credit from Matts Company, terms 2/10, n/30, FOB destination, invoice dated July 1, 800.
  6 Returned goods to Matts Company for full credit, 100.
  11 Paid Matts Company for purchase less return and discount.
  14 Purchased goods on credit from Matts Company, terms 2/10, n/30, FOB destination, invoice dated July 12, 900.
  31 Paid amount owed to Matts Company for purchase of July 14.

Problem Set

P 4-1.

LO 1 *Trading Income Statement:*
LO 2 *Periodic Inventory System*

Selected accounts from the adjusted trial balance for Helen's Toy Shop for the end of the accounting year, March 31, 20x1, are shown below.

The inventory for Helen's Toy Shop was 76,400 at the beginning of the year and 58,800 at the end of the year.

Helen's Toy Shop
Partial Adjusted Trial Balance
March 31, 20x1

Sales		330,000
Sales Returns and Allowances	4,000	
Purchases	140,400	
Purchases Returns and Allowances		5,200
Freight In	4,600	
Store Salaries Expense	65,250	
Office Salaries Expense	25,750	
Advertising Expense	48,600	
Rent Expense	4,800	
Insurance Expense	2,400	
Electricity Expense	3,120	
Store Supplies Expense	5,760	
Office Supplies Expense	2,350	
Depreciation Expense, Store Equipment	2,100	
Depreciation Expense, Office Equipment	1,600	
Income Taxes	2,000	

REQUIRED 1. Using the information given, prepare an income statement for Helen's Toy Shop. Store Salaries Expense; Advertising Expense; Store Supplies Expense; and Depreciation Expense, Store Equipment are selling expenses. The other expenses, except Income Taxes, are general and administrative expenses.

2. Based on your knowledge at this point in the course, how would you use the income statement for Helen's Toy Shop to evaluate the company's profitability?

P 4-2.

LO 2 *Trading Income Statement:*
LO 4 *Perpetual Inventory System*

At the end of the accounting year, August 31, 20x2, selected accounts from the adjusted trial balance for Polly's Fashion Shop appeared as follows:

Polly's Fashion Shop Partial Adjusted Trial Balance August 31, 20x2		
Sales		162,000
Sales Returns and Allowances	2,000	
Cost of Goods Sold	61,400	
Freight In	2,300	
Store Salaries Expense	32,625	
Office Salaries Expense	12,875	
Advertising Expense	24,300	
Rent Expense	2,400	
Insurance Expense	1,200	
Electricity Expense	1,560	
Store Supplies Expense	2,880	
Office Supplies Expense	1,175	
Depreciation Expense, Store Equipment	1,050	
Depreciation Expense, Office Equipment	800	
Income Taxes	4,500	

REQUIRED   Using the information given, prepare an income statement for Polly's Fashion Shop. Freight In should be combined with Cost of Goods Sold. Store Salaries Expense; Advertising Expense; Store Supplies Expense; and Depreciation Expense, Store Equipment are selling expenses. The other expenses, except Income Taxes, are general and administrative expenses.

P 4-3.

LO 4 *Trading Transactions:*
Periodic and Perpetual
Inventory Systems

Heritage Company engaged in the following transactions in October:

Oct. 7 Sold goods on credit to Larry Hill, terms n/30, FOB shipping point, 3,000 (cost, 1,800).
  8 Purchased goods on credit from Tower Company, terms n/30, FOB shipping point, 6,000.
  9 Paid Kendall Company for shipping charges on goods purchased on October 8, 254.
  10 Purchased goods on credit from Centre Company, terms n/30, FOB shipping point, 9,600, which includes 600 freight costs paid by Centre.
  13 Purchased office supplies on credit from Phelan Company, terms n/10, 2,400.
  14 Sold goods on credit to Mary Walton, terms n/30, FOB shipping point, 2,400 (cost, 1,440).
  14 Returned damaged goods received from Tower Company on October 8 for credit, 600.
  17 Received cheque from Larry Hill for his purchase of October 7.
  18 Returned a portion of the office supplies received on October 13 for credit because the wrong items were sent, 400.
  19 Sold goods for cash, 1,800 (cost, 1,080).
  20 Paid Centre Company for purchase of October 10.
  21 Paid Tower Company the balance from the transaction of October 8 and the transaction of October 14.
  24 Accepted from Mary Walton a return of goods, which was put back in inventory, 200 (cost, 120).

REQUIRED   1. Prepare general journal entries to record the transactions, assuming the periodic inventory system is used.

2. Prepare general journal entries to record the transactions, assuming the perpetual inventory system is used.

Critical Thinking and Communication

Conceptual Mini-Case

CMC 4-1.

LO 3 *Periodic versus Perpetual Inventory Systems*

The Book Nook is a well-established chain of bookstores in eastern Michigan, U.S.A. In recent years the company has grown rapidly, adding five new stores in regional shopping malls. Management has relied on the manager of each store to place orders keyed to the market in his or her neighbourhood, selected from a master list of available titles provided by the central office. Every six months, a physical inventory is taken, and financial statements are prepared using the periodic inventory system. At that time, books that have not sold well are placed on sale or, whenever possible, returned to the publisher. As a result of the company's fast growth, management has found that the newer store managers do not have the same ability to judge the market as do managers of the older, established stores. Thus, management is considering a recommendation to implement a perpetual inventory system and carefully monitor sales from the central office. Do you think The Book Nook should switch to the perpetual inventory system or stay with the periodic inventory system? Discuss the advantages and disadvantages of each system.

Cultural Mini-Case

CLMC 4-1.

LO 2 *Presentation of Trading Income Statement*

In the European Union, the income statement can be presented in a number of ways which do not always facilitate the calculation of gross profit or gross margin. The cost of goods sold is sometimes included in the amount given for operating costs in total, and more detailed information has to be looked for in the notes to the accounts.

Data selected from the income statement in the annual report of **Glaxo Wellcome**, one of the world's largest pharmaceutical companies based in the United Kingdom, show the following (in millions of pounds):[2]

Turnover (sales)	10,490
Operating costs	8,108
Trading profit	2,382

In the notes to the financial statements the following additional information is provided about operating costs:

Cost of sales	2,364
Selling, general and administrative expenditures	3,981
Research and development expenditures	1,797
Other operating items	(34)
	8,108

REQUIRED

1. Calculate the gross profit in monetary terms and as a percentage of sales.
2. To what extent is the form of presentation of items in the income statement likely to help or hinder financial analysis?

Ethics Mini-Case

EMC 4-1.

SO 8 *Ethics and Timely Payments*

Files, Folders & Clips, with five branch stores, is the area's largest office supply chain. Francesca Gonzales, a new accountant in charge of accounts payable, is told by her supervisor that many of the company's suppliers allow a 2 per cent discount if payment for a purchase is made within ten days. She is instructed to write all cheques for the net amount after deducting the amount of the discount, and to date them ten days following the invoice date. The cheques are not to be mailed until there is enough money in the bank to pay them. The supervisor says that, although most cheques must be held a week or more after the discount date, suppliers usually allow the discount because they do not want to lose business. He tells Gonzales: "This is business as usual and just good cash management. Last year we got discounts of 30,000." Gonzales wonders if this is true and, more importantly, whether or not the practice is ethical. Is this practice ethical? Would anyone be harmed by it? What other courses of action are available to Gonzales?

Decision-Making Case

DMC 4-1.

LO 2 *Analysis of Trading Income Statement*

In 19x8 Paul Diamond opened a small retail store. Called **Diamond Apparel Company**, the shop sold designer jeans. Paul worked fourteen hours a day and controlled all aspects of the operation. All sales were for cash or bank credit card. The business was such a success that in 19x9 Paul decided to open a second store. Because the new shop needed his attention, he hired a manager to work in the original store with two sales clerks. During 19x9 the new store was successful, but the operations of the original store did not match the first year's performance.

Concerned about this turn of events, Paul compared the two years' results for the original store. The figures are as follows:

	19x9	19x8
Net Sales	650,000	700,000
Cost of Goods Sold	450,000	450,000
Gross Profit	200,000	250,000
Operating Expenses	150,000	100,000
Net Profit before Income Taxes	50,000	150,000

In addition, Paul's analysis revealed that the cost and selling price of jeans were about the same in both years and that the level of operating expenses was roughly the same in both years except for the new manager's 50,000 salary. Sales returns and allowances were insignificant amounts in both years.

Studying the situation further, Paul discovered the following facts about the cost of goods sold:

	19x9	19x8
Gross purchases	400,000	542,000
Total purchases allowances	30,000	40,000
Freight in	38,000	54,000
Physical inventory, end of year	64,000	106,000

Still not satisfied, Paul went through all the individual sales and purchase records for the year. Both sales and purchases were verified. However, the 19x9 ending inventory should have been 114,000, given the unit purchases and sales during the year. After puzzling over all this information, Paul comes to you for accounting help.

REQUIRED

1. Using Paul's new information, recalculate the cost of goods sold for 19x8 and 19x9, and account for the difference in net profit between 19x8 and 19x9.
2. Suggest at least two reasons for the difference. (Assume that the new manager's salary is correct.) How might Paul improve the management of the original store?

Basic Research Activities

RA 4-1.

LO 3   *Inventory Systems*

Identify three retail businesses in your local shopping area or a local shopping mall. Choose three different types of retail enterprises, such as a bookstore, a clothing shop, a gift shop, a grocery, a hardware store, or a car dealership. In each business, ask to speak to someone who is knowledgeable about the store's inventory methods. Find out the answers to the following questions: How is each item of inventory identified? Does the business have a computerised or a manual inventory system? Which inventory system, periodic or perpetual, is used? How often do employees take a physical inventory? What procedures are followed in taking a physical inventory? What kinds of inventory reports are prepared or received? Prepare a table that summarises your findings. In the table, use columns to represent the types of businesses and rows to represent the questions. Be prepared to discuss your findings in class.

RA 4-2.

LO 5   *Internal Control Systems*
LO 6
LO 7

Visit a local outlet of a national retail chain—a fast-food restaurant, a music store, or a jeans or other clothing store. Observe for one hour and record as much as you can about the company's internal control structure. It is usually best to conduct the observation at a busy time of day. How would you go about assessing the control environment? Are any aspects of the company's accounting system apparent? What control procedures, including authorisation, recording transactions, documents and records, limited access, periodic independent verification, separation of duties, and sound personnel policies, can you observe? Be prepared to discuss your observations in class.

Financial Reporting and Analysis

Interpretation Cases from Business

ICB 4-1.

LO 1   *Contrast of Operating*
LO 2   *Philosophies and Income*
        Statements

Wal-Mart Stores and *Kmart*, two of the largest and most successful retailers in the United States, have different approaches to retailing. You can see the difference by analysing their respective income statements and inventories. Selected information from their annual reports for the year ended January 31, 1993, is presented below. (All amounts are in millions of dollars.)

Wal-Mart: Net Sales, 55,484; Cost of Goods Sold, 44,175; Operating Expenses, 8,321; Ending Inventory, 9,268

Kmart: Net Sales, 37,724; Cost of Goods Sold, 28,485; Operating Expenses, 7,781; Ending Inventory, 8,752

REQUIRED 1. Prepare a schedule calculating the gross profit and net profit (ignore income taxes) for both companies as amounts and as percentages of net sales. Also, calculate inventory as a percentage of the cost of goods sold.
2. Assess the different retailing approaches of these two companies from the gross profits and net profits you calculated in item 1. Which company's approach was more successful in 1993? Explain your answer.
3. Both companies have chosen an accounting year that ends on January 31. Why do you suppose they made this choice? How realistic do you think the inventory figures are as indicators of inventory levels during the rest of the year?

ICB 4-2.

LO 1   *Business Objectives and*
LO 2   *Income Statements*

House of Fraser, based in the United Kingdom, has department stores located all over the country trading under names such as Frasers, Army & Navy, Rackhams, Arnotts, and Dickens & Jones. The following selected data are taken from the income statement in House of Fraser's annual report for 1995 (in millions of British pounds):[3]

	Year Ended	
	January 27, 1996	**January 28, 1995**
Turnover (Sales)	748.9	754.7
Cost of Sales	514.9	506.4
Operating Expenses	211.6	205.3

REQUIRED 1. Prepare an income statement for each year.
2. Comment on the company's performance in terms of (a) sales growth, (b) gross profit, (c) cost reductions, and (d) net profit.

Nestlé Case

NC 4-1.

LO 1   *Operating Cycle*

Refer to the consolidated balance sheet in the Annual Report in the appendix on Nestlé. Is inventory or accounts receivable (trade debtors) a more important component of the Nestlé operating cycle? Explain your answer. Over the past few years, Nestlé has been streamlining its manufacturing base, as well as its sales, distribution, and administration organisations. What effects are these actions intended to have on the operating cycle and the future profitability of Nestlé?

ENDNOTES

1. Marks & Spencer, *Annual Report*, 1996.
2. Glaxo Wellcome, *Annual Report*, 1995.
3. House of Fraser, *Annual Report*, 1995.

Chapter 5

FINANCIAL STATEMENT
OBJECTIVES,
PRESENTATION,
AND ANALYSIS

LEARNING OBJECTIVES

1. State the objective of financial statements.
2. State the principal qualitative characteristics of accounting information and describe their interrelationships.
3. Define and describe the constraints on relevant and reliable information.
4. Explain management's responsibility for ethical financial reporting and define *fraudulent financial reporting*.
5. Identify and describe the basic components of a classified balance sheet.
6. Prepare multistep and single-step classified income statements.
7. Use classified financial statements for the simple evaluation of liquidity and profitability.

SUPPLEMENTAL OBJECTIVE

8. Identify the major components of a corporate annual report.

DECISION POINT
NESTLÉ

Corporations issue annual reports in order to distribute their financial statements and communicate other relevant information to shareholders and others outside the business. Because these users have no direct access to the accounting records, they must depend on the information contained in the reports. Beyond the financial statements and accompanying notes and text, management must devise its own methods to help the user understand the data in the statements.

The management of Nestlé, a Swiss company that is one of the most successful beverage, milk products, and chocolate companies in the world, helps users of its annual report by presenting a series of statistics called "Key Figures".[1] Along with such important information as sales, trading profit, net profits, and shareholders' funds, a number of ratios appear, including net profits as a percentage of net sales, and net profits as a percentage of average shareholders' equity. Of course, these ratios are meaningless unless the user understands financial statements and the accounting standards on which the statements are based. Because learning how to read and interpret financial statements is so important, this chapter describes the categories and classifications used in balance sheets and income statements and explains some of the most important ratios for financial statement analysis. The chapter begins by describing the objectives, characteristics, and criteria that underlie the preparation of financial statements. It ends with a discussion of Nestlé's annual report, prepared in accordance with International Accounting Standards.

OBJECTIVE 1

State the objective of financial statements

OBJECTIVE OF FINANCIAL INFORMATION

The users of accounting information and their information needs were reviewed in chapter 1. As stated by the International Accounting Standards Committee (IASC), the objective of financial statements is to provide information about an enterprise "that is useful to a wide range of users in making economic decisions".[2]

These economic decisions generally require an evaluation of the ability of an enterprise to generate future cash flows. Users are better able to make judgements about this ability if they are provided with information that focuses on a company's financial position, its performance and profitability, and changes in its cash flows.

Financial statements are the most effective way of periodically presenting to parties outside the business the information gathered and processed in the accounting system. Thus, these statements—the balance sheet, the income statement, and the cash flow statement—are the accounting system's most important output. They are "general purpose" because of their wide audience. They are "external" because their users are outside the business. Because of a potential conflict of interest between managers, who must prepare the statements, and external users such as investors or lenders, who invest in or lend money to the business, these statements often are audited by outside accountants to increase confidence in their reliability.

OBJECTIVE 2

State the principal qualitative characteristics of accounting information and describe their interrelationships

PRINCIPAL QUALITATIVE CHARACTERISTICS OF ACCOUNTING INFORMATION

It is easy for students in their first accounting course to get the idea that accounting is 100 per cent accurate. This idea is reinforced by the fact that all the problems in this and other introductory books can be solved. The numbers all add up; what is supposed to equal something else does. Accounting seems very much like mathematics in its precision. In this course, the basics of accounting are presented in a simple form at first, to help you understand them. In practice, however, accounting information is neither simple nor precise, and it rarely satisfies all criteria.

The goal of accounting information—to provide the information that different users need to make informed economic decisions—is an ideal. The gap between the ideal and the actual provides much of the interest and controversy in accounting. To facilitate interpretation, the International Accounting Standards Committee (IASC) has described the **qualitative characteristics** of accounting information, which are standards for judging that information.[3] In addition, there are constraints on relevant and reliable information that must be considered. The relationships among these concepts are shown in Figure 5-1.

Understandability

The most important qualitative characteristics are understandability, relevance, reliability, and comparability. **Understandability** is about communicating an intended meaning. This depends on both the accountant and the decision maker. The accountant prepares the financial statements in accordance with accepted practices, generating important information that is believed to be readily understandable to users. But the decision maker must interpret the information and use it in making decisions. The decision maker must judge what information to use, how to use it, and what it means.

FIGURE 5-1   *Qualitative Characteristics of Accounting Information*

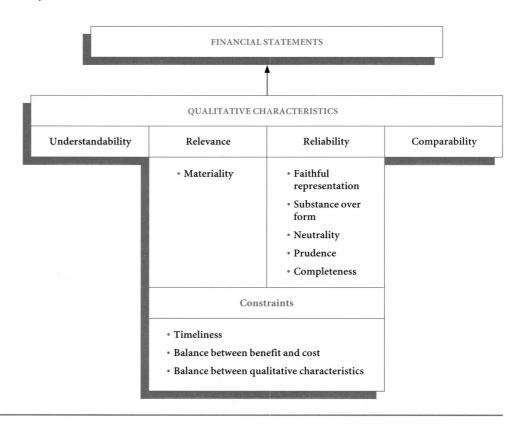

Relevance

Relevance means that the information can make a difference in the outcome of a decision. In other words, another decision would be made if the relevant information were not available. To be relevant, information must provide feedback about past transactions and events and must help predict future conditions. For example, the income statement provides information about how a company performed over the past year (that is, feedback), and it also helps in planning for the next year (that is, prediction).

The relevance of information is affected by its nature and materiality. The term **materiality** refers to the relative importance of an item or event. If an item or event is material, it is probably relevant to the user of financial statements. In other words, an item is material if the user would have done something differently if he or she had not known about the item. The accountant is often faced with decisions about small items or events that make little difference to users no matter how they are handled. For example, a large company may decide that expenditures for durable items of less than 500 should be charged as expenses rather than recorded as long-term assets and depreciated.

In general, an item is material if there is a reasonable expectation that knowing about it would influence the decisions of users of financial statements. The materiality of an item normally is determined by relating its value to an element of the financial statements, such as net profit·or total assets. Some accountants feel that when an item is 5 per cent or more of net profit, it is material. However, materiality also depends on the nature of the item, not just its value. For example, in a multinational company, a mistake in recording an item of 5,000 may not be important, but the discovery of a 5,000 bribe or theft can be very important. Also, many small errors can combine into a material amount. Accountants judge the materiality of many things, and the users of financial statements depend on their judgements being fair and accurate.

Reliability

In addition to being relevant, accounting information must have **reliability.** In other words, the user must be able to depend on the information. It must represent what it is meant to represent. It must be credible and verifiable by independent parties using the same methods of measuring.

In order to be reliable, information must provide a **faithful representation** of transactions and other events. For example, the balance sheet should represent the economic resources, obligations, and shareholders' equity of a business as faithfully as possible in accordance with accounting standards, and this balance sheet should be verifiable by an auditor.

If the information is to faithfully represent transactions and other events, then it is important to maintain **substance over form**. That is, accounting should represent the substance and economic reality of business activities and not just their legal form. For example, the apparent sale of an asset to a third party while agreeing to continue to enjoy the economic benefits of the asset would not represent faithfully the transaction entered into.

If the information is to be reliable, then **neutrality** or freedom from bias is also important. Financial statements are not neutral if they are presented in such a way as to influence the making of a decision or judgement in a particular way.

Accountants try to base their decisions on logic and evidence that lead to the fairest report of what happened. In judging and estimating, however, accountants often are faced with uncertainties. In these cases, they look to the criterion of **prudence,** also called *conservatism.* This criterion means that when accountants face major uncertainties about which accounting method to use, they generally choose the one that is least likely to overstate assets and profit.

One of the most common applications of the prudence criterion is the use of the lower of cost and market method in accounting for inventories (see the chapter on inventories). Under this method, if the market value is greater than cost, the more prudent cost figure is used. If the market value falls below cost, the more prudent market value is used. The latter situation often occurs in the computer industry.

To be reliable, information in financial statements must also be complete. **Completeness** requires that financial statements and their notes present all information that is relevant to the users' understanding of the statements. In other words, accounting information should offer any explanation that is needed to keep it from being misleading. Explanatory notes are considered an integral part of the financial statements. For instance, a change from one accounting method to another should be reported. In general, the form of the financial statements can affect their usefulness in making certain decisions. Also, certain items, such as the amount of depreciation expense on the income statement and the accumulated depreciation on the balance sheet, are essential to the users of financial statements.

Other examples of disclosures are the accounting methods used in preparing the statements, important terms of the company's debt, commitments and contingencies, and important events taking place after the date of the statements. However, there is a point at which the statements become so cluttered that notes impede rather than help understanding. Beyond required disclosures, the application of completeness is based on the judgement of management and of the accountants who prepare the financial statements.

In recent years, the principle of completeness also has been influenced by users of accounting information. To protect investors and lenders, independent auditors, the stock exchanges, and government regulators have made more demands for disclosure by publicly owned companies. So today, more and better information about corporations is available to the public than ever before.

Comparability

Another important characteristic of accounting information is **comparability**, as users must be able to compare the financial statements of a company through time in order to assess trends in performance and financial position. Users must also be able to compare the financial statements of different companies both within a country and across countries if they are going to be able to evaluate relative performance, financial position, and changes in cash flows. So the accounting methods used should be reported and used consistently. Users should be informed of any changes in methods and the effects of such changes. However, comparability does not mean that a uniform approach should always be followed if this becomes inconsistent with the relevance and reliability characteristics of accounting information.

OBJECTIVE 3

Define and describe the constraints on relevant and reliable information

CONSTRAINTS ON RELEVANT AND RELIABLE INFORMATION

There are a number of constraints to consider when endeavouring to provide relevant and reliable information in financial statements.

Timeliness

One constraint is **timeliness,** as reported information may lose its relevance if there is an unreasonable delay. Management needs to balance the advantage of timely reporting against the disadvantage of reporting before all aspects of a transaction are known with consequent limitation as to reliability. However, if the financial reports are delayed, the information may be more reliable but of little use to decision makers who have had to act in the meantime.

Benefit-Cost

The **balance between benefit and cost** is an all-pervasive constraint in financial reporting. While in principle the costs of providing information to users should not exceed the benefits, this is very much a matter of judgement and often controversial, owing to the different perspectives of the parties involved. Of course, minimum levels of relevance and reliability must be reached for accounting information to be useful. Both national and international standard-setting agencies are very much involved in establishing what these minimum levels should be. Beyond these minimum levels, however, it is up to the accountant and the companies who provide the information to judge the costs and benefits in each case. Most of the costs of providing information fall at first on the preparers; the benefits are reaped by both preparers and users. Finally, both the costs and benefits are passed on to society in the form of prices and social benefits from a more efficient allocation of resources.

Balance between Qualitative Characteristics

A trade-off to achieve a **balance between qualitative characteristics** is often necessary in practice. For example, the balancing of relevance versus reliability is a constant issue. In principle, the aim is to achieve a balance which will best meet the objective of financial statements, which is to help users make economic decisions. However, professional judgement is often needed to decide on the relative importance of the qualitative characteristics in a particular case.

In conclusion, the overall application of these qualitative characteristics together with relevant accounting standards is generally described as resulting in financial statements that show a **true and fair view** or **present fairly** the performance, financial position, and changes in cash flows of a business enterprise. Note that the term *true and fair view* tends to be used in Europe and many Asian countries, whereas *present fairly* is preferred, for example, in North America.

<table>
<tr><td>

OBJECTIVE 4

Explain management's responsibility for ethical financial reporting and define fraudulent financial reporting

</td><td>

MANAGEMENT'S RESPONSIBILITY FOR ETHICAL REPORTING

The users of financial statements depend on the good faith of those who prepare these statements. This dependence places a duty on a company's management and its accountants to act ethically in the reporting process. This duty is often expressed in the report of management that accompanies financial statements. For example, the report of the management of Quaker Oats Company in the United States, a company known for strong financial reporting and controls, states:

</td></tr>
</table>

> *Management is responsible for the preparation and integrity of the Company's financial statements. The financial statements have been prepared in accordance with generally accepted accounting principles and necessarily include some amounts that are based on management's estimates and judgment.*[4]

Quaker Oats' management also tells how it meets this responsibility:

> *To fulfill its responsibility, management maintains a strong system of internal controls, supported by formal policies and procedures that are communicated throughout the Company. Management also maintains a staff of internal auditors who evaluate the adequacy of and investigate the adherence to these controls, policies, and procedures.*[5]

The intentional preparation of misleading financial statements is called **fraudulent financial reporting**. It can result from the distortion of records (the manipulation of inventory records), falsified transactions (fictitious sales or orders), or the misapplication of accounting principles (treating as an asset an item that should be expensed). The motivation for fraudulent reporting springs from various sources—for instance, the desire to obtain a higher price in the sale of a company, to meet the expectations of shareholders, or to obtain a loan. Other times, the incentive is personal gain, such as additional compensation, promotion, or avoidance of penalties for poor performance. The personal costs of such actions can be high—individuals who authorise or prepare fraudulent financial statements may face criminal penalties and financial loss. Others, including investors and lenders to the company, employees, and customers, suffer from fraudulent financial reporting as well.

The motivations for fraudulent financial reporting exist to some extent in every company. It is management's responsibility to insist on honest financial reporting, but it is also the company accountants' responsibility to maintain high ethical standards. Ethical reporting demands that accountants apply financial accounting concepts to present a true and fair view of the company's operations and financial position and to avoid misleading users of the financial statements.

OBJECTIVE 5

Identify and describe the basic components of a classified balance sheet

CLASSIFIED BALANCE SHEET

The balance sheets you have seen in the chapters thus far categorise accounts as assets, liabilities, and shareholders' equity. Because even a fairly small company can have hundreds of accounts, simply listing accounts in these broad categories is not particularly helpful to a statement user. Setting up subcategories within the major categories often makes financial statements much more useful. Investors and lenders study and evaluate the relationships among the subcategories. General-purpose external financial statements that are divided into useful subcategories are called **classified financial statements.**

The balance sheet presents the financial position of a company at a particular time. The subdivisions of the classified balance sheet shown in Exhibit 5-1 are typical of most companies in North America. Note that assets are listed in order of liquidity with current assets shown at the top of the list. The subdivisions under owners' or shareholders' equity, of course, depend on the form of business.

In the European Union, in contrast, the balance sheet is often presented somewhat differently, with long-term or noncurrent assets listed at the top and with liabilities shown after shareholders' equity (see Exhibit 5-2). Both of these forms of presentation of the balance sheet are consistent with International Accounting Standards. Indeed, so long as the different components of the balance sheet are clearly presented and do not confuse users, then other variations of these formats are entirely acceptable.

Assets

A company's assets are often divided into four categories: (1) current assets; (2) investments; (3) property, plant, and equipment; and (4) intangible assets. For simplicity, some companies group investments, intangible assets, and other miscellaneous assets into a category called "other assets". These categories are listed in the order of their presumed ease of conversion into cash. For example, current assets are usually more easily converted to cash than are property, plant, and equipment.

Current Assets

Current assets are cash or other assets that are reasonably expected to be realised in cash, sold, or consumed within one year or the normal operating cycle of the business, whichever is longer. A normal operating cycle is the average time needed to go from cash to cash. For example, cash is used to buy inventory, which is sold for cash or for a promise of cash if the sale is made on account. If a sale is made on account, the resulting receivable must be collected before the cycle is completed.

EXHIBIT 5-1 *Classified Balance Sheet for Tang Auto Parts Corporation (North American Version)*

Tang Auto Parts Corporation
Balance Sheet
December 31, 20x1

Assets

Current Assets			
Cash		10,360	
Current Investments		2,000	
Notes Receivable		8,000	
Accounts Receivable		35,300	
Inventory		60,400	
Prepaid Insurance		6,600	
Store Supplies		1,060	
Office Supplies		636	
Total Current Assets			124,356
Investments			
Land held for future use			5,000
Property, Plant, and Equipment			
Land		4,500	
Building	20,650		
Less Accumulated Depreciation	8,640	12,010	
Delivery Equipment	18,400		
Less Accumulated Depreciation	9,450	8,950	
Office Equipment	8,600		
Less Accumulated Depreciation	5,000	3,600	
Total Property, Plant, and Equipment			29,060
Intangible Assets			
Trademark			500
Total Assets			158,916

Liabilities

Current Liabilities			
Notes Payable		15,000	
Accounts Payable		25,683	
Salaries Payable		2,000	
Total Current Liabilities			42,683
Long-Term Liabilities			
Mortgage Payable			17,800
Total Liabilities			60,483

Shareholders' Equity

Share Capital			
5,000 shares authorised, issued and outstanding		50,000	
Share Premium		10,000	
Total Share Capital			60,000
Retained Earnings			38,433
Total Shareholders' Equity			98,433
Total Liabilities and Shareholders' Equity			158,916

EXHIBIT 5-2   *Classified Balance Sheet for Tang Auto Parts Corporation (European Union Version)*

Tang Auto Parts Corporation
Balance Sheet
December 31, 20x1

Assets

Intangible Assets
Trademark			500

Property, Plant, and Equipment
Land		4,500	
Building	20,650		
Less Accumulated Depreciation	8,640	12,010	
Delivery Equipment	18,400		
Less Accumulated Depreciation	9,450	8,950	
Office Equipment	8,600		
Less Accumulated Depreciation	5,000	3,600	
Total Property, Plant, and Equipment			29,060

Investments
Land held for future use			5,000

Current Assets
Cash		10,360	
Current Investments		2,000	
Notes Receivable		8,000	
Accounts Receivable		35,300	
Inventory		60,400	
Prepaid Insurance		6,600	
Store Supplies		1,060	
Office Supplies		636	
Total Current Assets			124,356
Total Assets			158,916

Shareholders' Equity

Share Capital
5,000 shares authorised, issued and outstanding		50,000	
Share Premium		10,000	
Total Share Capital		60,000	
Retained Earnings		38,433	
Total Shareholders' Equity			98,433

Liabilities

Current Liabilities
Notes Payable		15,000	
Accounts Payable		25,683	
Salaries Payable		2,000	
Total Current Liabilities			42,683

Long-Term Liabilities
Mortgage Payable			17,800
Total Liabilities			60,483
Total Shareholders' Equity and Liabilities			158,916

The normal operating cycle for most companies is less than one year, but there are exceptions. Tobacco companies, for example, must cure their tobacco for two or three years before it can be sold. The tobacco inventory is nonetheless considered a current asset because it will be sold within the normal operating cycle. Another example is a company that sells on the instalment basis. The payments for a television set or cooker can be extended over twenty-four or thirty-six months, but these receivables are still considered current assets.

Cash is obviously a current asset. Temporary investments, notes and accounts receivable, and inventory are also current assets because they are expected to be converted to cash within the next year or during the normal operating cycle. Accounting for these short-term assets is presented in the chapter on short-term liquid assets.

Prepaid expenses, such as rent and insurance paid for in advance, and inventories of supplies bought for use rather than for sale also should be classified as current assets. These kinds of assets are current in the sense that if they had not been bought earlier, a current outlay of cash would be needed to obtain them.

In deciding whether an asset is current or noncurrent, the idea of "reasonable expectation" is important. For example, Current Investments is an account used for temporary investments of idle cash, or cash that is not immediately required for operating purposes. Management can reasonably expect to sell these securities as cash needs arise over the next year or operating cycle. Investments in securities that management does not expect to sell within the next year and that do not involve the temporary use of idle cash should be shown in the investments category of a classified balance sheet.

Investments

The **investments** category includes assets, usually long term, that are not used in the normal operation of the business and that management does not plan to convert to cash within the next year. Items in this category are securities held for long-term investment, long-term notes receivable, land held for future use, plant or equipment not used in the business, and special funds established to pay off a debt or buy a building. Also in this category are large permanent investments in another company for the purpose of controlling that company. These topics are covered in the chapter on intercompany investments and consolidated financial statements.

Property, Plant, and Equipment

The **property, plant, and equipment** category includes long-term assets that are used in the continuing operation of the business. They represent a place to operate (land and buildings) and equipment to produce, sell, deliver, and service the company's goods. For this reason, these assets are called *operating assets* or, sometimes, *fixed assets, tangible assets, long-lived assets,* or *plant assets.* Through depreciation, the costs of these assets (except land) are spread over the periods they benefit. Past depreciation is recorded in the Accumulated Depreciation accounts. The exact order in which property, plant, and equipment are listed on the balance sheet is not the same everywhere. In practice, accounts are often combined to make the financial statements less cluttered. For example:

Property, Plant, and Equipment

Land		4,500
Buildings and Equipment	47,650	
Less Accumulated Depreciation	23,090	24,560
Total Property, Plant, and Equipment		29,060

Many companies simply show a single line with a total for property, plant, and equipment and provide the details in a note to the financial statements.

Property, plant, and equipment also includes company-owned natural resources, such as forests, oil and gas properties, and coal mines. Assets not used in the regular course of business are listed in the investments category, as noted above. The chapter on long-term assets is devoted largely to property, plant, and equipment.

Intangible Assets

Intangible assets are long-term assets that have no physical substance but have a value based on the rights or privileges that belong to their owner. Examples are patents, copyrights, goodwill, franchises, and trademarks. These assets are recorded at cost, which is spread over the expected life of the right or privilege. We talk about these assets in detail in the chapter on long-term assets.

Other Assets

Some companies use the category **other assets** to group all owned assets other than current assets and property, plant, and equipment. Other assets can include investments and intangible assets.

Liabilities

Liabilities are divided into two categories: current liabilities and long-term liabilities.

Current Liabilities

The category **current liabilities** consists of obligations due to be paid or performed within a year or within the normal operating cycle of the business, whichever is longer. These liabilities are typically paid from current assets or by incurring new short-term liabilities. Under this heading are notes payable, accounts payable, the current portion of long-term debt, salaries and wages payable, taxes payable, and customer advances (unearned revenues). Current liabilities are discussed in more detail in the chapter on liabilities.

Long-Term Liabilities

The debts of a business that fall due more than one year in the future or beyond the normal operating cycle, or that are to be paid out of noncurrent assets, are **long-term liabilities**. Mortgages payable, long-term notes, bonds payable, employee pension obligations, and long-term lease liabilities generally fall in this category. Deferred income taxes are often disclosed as a separate category in the long-term liability section of the balance sheet of publicly held corporations. This liability arises because the rules for measuring income for tax purposes differ from those for financial reporting. The cumulative annual difference between the income taxes payable to governments and the income taxes expense reported on the income statement is included in the account Deferred Income Taxes.

Shareholders' Equity

The shareholders' equity section of a corporation would appear as shown in the balance sheet for Tang Auto Parts Corporation. As you learned earlier, corporations are separate, legal entities that are owned by their shareholders. The shareholders' equity section of a balance sheet has two parts: contributed or paid-in share capital and retained earnings. Share capital is often shown on corporate balance sheets by two amounts: (1) the nominal value of the issued share capital and (2) the amount paid in or contributed in excess of the nominal value per share, which is often described as the *share premium*.

OBJECTIVE 6

Prepare multistep and single-step classified income statements

FORMS OF THE INCOME STATEMENT

For internal management, a detailed income statement like the one you learned about in the chapter on the trading income statement and internal control is helpful in analysing the company's performance.

For external reporting purposes, however, the income statement usually is presented in condensed form. **Condensed financial statements** present only the major categories of the detailed financial statements. There are two common forms of the condensed income statement, the multistep form and the single-step form. The **multistep form**, illustrated in Exhibit 5-3, derives net profit in the same step-by-step fashion as a detailed income statement would, except that only the totals of significant categories are given. Usually, some breakdown is shown for operating expenses, such as the totals for selling expenses and for general and administrative expenses. In the Tang statement, gross profit less operating expenses is called **profit from operations**, and a new section, **other revenues and expenses**, has been added to include nonoperating revenues and expenses. The latter section includes revenues from investments (such as dividends and interest from shares, bonds, and savings accounts) and interest earned on credit or notes extended to customers. It also includes interest expense and other expenses that result from borrowing money or from credit extended to the company. If the company has other revenues and expenses that are not related to normal business operations, they too are included in this part of the income statement. Thus, an analyst who wants to compare two companies independent of their financing methods—that is, before considering other revenues and expenses—would focus on profit from operations.

The account for **Income Taxes**, also called *provision for income taxes*, represents the expense for income taxes on corporate income and is shown as a separate item on the income statement. Usually the word *expense* is not used. This account would not

EXHIBIT 5-3   *Condensed Multistep Income Statement for Tang Auto Parts Corporation*

Tang Auto Parts Corporation
Income Statement
For the Year Ended December 31, 20x1

Net Sales		289,656
Cost of Goods Sold		181,260
Gross Profit		108,396
Operating Expenses		
Selling Expenses	54,780	
General and Administrative Expenses	34,504	
Total Operating Expenses		89,284
Profit from Operations		19,112
Other Revenues and Expenses		
Interest Income	1,400	
Less Interest Expense	2,631	
Excess of Other Expenses over Other Revenues		1,231
Profit before Income Taxes		17,881
Income Taxes		3,381
Net Profit		14,500
Earnings per share		2.90

BUSINESS BULLETIN   Business Practice

Accounting can be an issue even in the movies. Despite worldwide receipts of $300 million and additional millions in merchandise sales, Warner Bros. in the United States says the original *Batman* has not made a profit and may never do so. However, a lawsuit by two executive producers says that the studio's accounting is fraudulent and unconscionable. At issue is the measurement of "net profits", a percentage of which the producers are to receive. The problem is that the top actors, like Jack Nicholson, the director, and others receive a share of every dollar that the movie generates and, as a result, have earned millions of dollars. Because of these shares, it is impossible for the movie ever to earn a "net profit". Thus, while others are paid handsomely, the two executive producers receive nothing. It pays to know your accounting before signing your movie contract.

appear in the income statements of sole proprietorships and partnerships because they are not tax-paying units. The individuals who own these businesses are the tax-paying units, and they pay income taxes on their share of the business profit. Corporations, however, must report and pay income taxes on earnings. Because income taxes for corporations are substantial, they have a significant effect on business decisions. Most other taxes, such as property taxes, employment taxes, licences, and fees, are shown among the operating expenses.

Earnings per share, often called *net profit per share*, is also unique to corporate reporting. Ownership in corporations is represented by shares, and the net profit per share is often reported immediately below net profit on the income statement. In the simplest case, it is calculated by dividing the net profit by the average number of shares outstanding during the year. For example, Tang's earnings per share of 2.90 was calculated by dividing the net profit of 14,500 by the 5,000 shares outstanding, as reported in the shareholders' equity section of the balance sheet (Exhibit 5-1). Investors find the figure useful as a quick way of assessing both a company's profit-earning success and its earnings in relation to the market price of its share.

The **single-step form** of income statement, illustrated in Exhibit 5-4, derives profit before income taxes in a single step by putting the major categories of revenues in the first part of the statement and the major categories of costs and expenses in the second part. Income taxes are shown as a separate item, as is done on the multistep income statement.

The multistep form and the single-step form each have advantages. The multistep form shows the components used in deriving net profit; the single-step form has the advantage of simplicity.

OBJECTIVE 7

Use classified financial statements for the simple evaluation of liquidity and profitability

USING CLASSIFIED FINANCIAL STATEMENTS

Earlier in this chapter, you learned that financial reporting seeks to provide information that is useful in making economic decisions. These decisions are related to two of the more important goals of management—maintaining adequate liquidity and achieving satisfactory profitability—because investors and lenders base their decisions largely on their assessment of a company's ability to generate future cash flows to ensure survival and growth.

Evaluation of Liquidity

Liquidity means having enough money available to pay bills when they are due and to take care of unexpected needs for cash. Two measures of liquidity are working capital and the current ratio.

EXHIBIT 5-4 *Condensed Single-Step Income Statement for Tang Auto Parts Corporation*

Tang Auto Parts Corporation
Income Statement
For the Year Ended December 31, 20x1

Revenues		
Net Sales		289,656
Interest Income		1,400
Total Revenues		291,056
Costs and Expenses		
Cost of Goods Sold	181,260	
Selling Expenses	54,780	
General and Administrative Expenses	34,504	
Interest Expense	2,631	
Total Costs and Expenses		273,175
Profit before Income Taxes		17,881
Income Taxes		3,381
Net Profit		14,500
Earnings per share		2.90

Working Capital

The first measure, **working capital**, is the amount by which total current assets exceed total current liabilities. This is an important measure of liquidity because current liabilities are debts that must be paid within one year and current assets are assets that will be realised in cash or used up within one year or one operating cycle, whichever is longer. By definition, current liabilities are paid out of current assets. So the excess of current assets over current liabilities is the net current assets available to continue business operations. It is the working capital that can be used to buy inventory, obtain credit, and finance expanded sales. Lack of working capital can lead to a company's failure.

For Tang Auto Parts Corporation, working capital is calculated as follows:

Current assets	124,356
Less current liabilities	42,683
Working capital	81,673

Current Ratio

The second measure of liquidity, the current ratio, is closely related to working capital and is believed by many bankers and other lenders to be a good indicator of a company's ability to pay its bills and to repay outstanding loans. The **current ratio** is the ratio of current assets to current liabilities. For Tang Auto Parts Corporation, it would be calculated like this:

$$\text{Current ratio} = \frac{\text{current assets}}{\text{current liabilities}} = \frac{124,356}{42,683} = 2.9$$

Thus, Tang has 2.90 of current assets for each 1.00 of current liabilities. Is this good or bad? The answer requires the comparison of this year's ratio with those of earlier years and with similar measures for successful companies in the same industry. The average current ratio varies widely from industry to industry. A very low current ratio, of course, can be unfavourable, but so can a very high one. The latter may indicate that a company is not using its assets effectively.

Evaluation of Profitability

Equally as important as paying bills on time is **profitability**—the ability to earn a satisfactory profit. As a goal, profitability competes with liquidity for managerial attention because liquid assets, although important, are not the best profit-producing resources. Cash, for example, means purchasing power, but a satisfactory profit can be made only if purchasing power is used to buy profit-producing (and less liquid) assets, such as inventory and long-term assets.

Among the common measures of a company's ability to earn a profit are (1) profit margin, (2) asset turnover, (3) return on assets, (4) debt to equity, and (5) return on equity. To evaluate a company meaningfully, one must relate its profit performance to its past performance and prospects for the future as well as to the averages for other companies competing in the same industry.

Profit Margin

The **profit margin** shows the percentage of each sales amount that results in net profit. It is calculated by dividing net profit by net sales. It should not be confused with gross profit, which is not a ratio but rather the amount by which revenues exceed the cost of goods sold.

Tang Auto Parts Corporation has a profit margin of 5.0 per cent:

$$\text{Profit margin} = \frac{\text{net profit}}{\text{net sales}} = \frac{14,500}{289,656} = .05 \ (5.0\%)$$

A difference of 1 or 2 per cent in a company's profit margin can mean the difference between a fair year and a very profitable one.

Asset Turnover

Asset turnover measures how efficiently assets are used to produce sales. It is calculated by dividing net sales by average total assets. A company with a higher asset turnover uses its assets more productively than one with a lower asset turnover. Average total assets is calculated by adding total assets at the beginning of the year to total assets at the end of the year and dividing by 2.

Assuming that total assets for Tang Auto Parts Corporation were 148,620 at the beginning of the year, its asset turnover is calculated as follows:

$$\text{Asset turnover} = \frac{\text{net sales}}{\text{average total assets}}$$

$$= \frac{289,656}{(148,620 + 158,916)/2}$$

$$= \frac{289,656}{153,768} = 1.9 \text{ times}$$

Tang Auto Parts Corporation produces 1.90 in sales for each 1.00 invested in average total assets. This ratio shows a meaningful relationship between an income statement figure and a balance sheet figure.

Return on Assets

Both the profit margin and the asset turnover ratios have some limitations. The profit margin ratio does not take into consideration the assets necessary to produce profit, and the asset turnover ratio does not take into account the amount of profit produced. The **return on assets** ratio overcomes these deficiencies by relating net profit to average total assets. It is calculated like this:

$$\text{Return on assets} = \frac{\text{net profit}}{\text{average total assets}}$$

$$= \frac{14{,}500}{(148{,}620 + 158{,}916)/2}$$

$$= \frac{14{,}500}{153{,}768} = .094 \text{ (or 9.4\%)}$$

This ratio indicates the profit-generating strength (that is, profit margin) of the company's resources and how efficiently the company is using all its assets (that is, asset turnover).

Return on assets, then, combines profit margin and asset turnover:

$$\text{Profit margin} \times \text{asset turnover} = \text{return on assets}$$

$$5.0\% \quad \times \quad 1.9 \text{ times} \quad = \quad 9.5\%^*$$

*The slight difference between 9.4 and 9.5 is due to rounding.

Thus, a company's management can improve overall profitability by increasing the profit margin, the asset turnover, or both. Similarly, in evaluating a company's overall profitability, the financial statement user must consider the interaction of both ratios to produce return on assets.

Debt to Equity

Another useful measure is the **debt to equity** ratio, which shows the proportion of the company financed by lenders in comparison to that financed by shareholders. This ratio is calculated by dividing total liabilities by shareholders' equity. The balance sheets of most public companies do not, however, show total liabilities, but a short way of determining total liabilities is to deduct the total of shareholders' equity from total assets. A debt to equity ratio of 1.0 means that total liabilities equal shareholders' equity—that half of the company's assets are financed by lenders. A ratio of .5 would mean that one-third of the assets are financed by lenders. A company with a high debt to equity ratio is more vulnerable in poor economic times because it must continue to repay lenders. Shareholders' investments, on the other hand, do not have to be repaid, and dividends can be deferred if the company is suffering because of weak results.

The Tang Auto Parts debt to equity ratio is calculated as follows:

$$\text{Debt to equity} = \frac{\text{total liabilities}}{\text{shareholders' equity}} = \frac{60{,}483}{98{,}433} = .614 \text{ (or 61.4\%)}$$

Because its ratio of debt to equity is 61.4 per cent, about 38 per cent of Tang Auto Parts Corporation is financed by lenders and roughly 62 per cent is financed by investors.

The debt to equity ratio does not fit neatly into either the liquidity or the profitability category. It is clearly very important to liquidity analysis because it relates to debt and its repayment. However, the debt to equity ratio is also relevant to profitability for two reasons. First, lenders are interested in the proportion of the business that is debt financed because the more debt a company has, the more profit it must earn to protect the payment of interest to its lenders. Second, shareholders are interested in the proportion of the business that is debt financed. The amount of interest that must be paid on the debt affects the amount of profit that is left to provide a return on shareholders' investments. The debt to equity ratio also shows how much expansion is possible by borrowing additional long-term funds.

Return on Equity

Of course, shareholders are interested in how much they have earned on their investment in the business. Their **return on equity** is measured by the ratio of net profit to average shareholders' equity. Taking the ending shareholders' equity from the balance sheet and assuming that beginning shareholders' equity is 100,552, Tang's return on equity is calculated as follows:

$$\text{Return on equity} = \frac{\text{net profit}}{\text{average shareholders' equity}}$$

$$= \frac{14,500}{(100,552 + 98,433)/2}$$

$$= \frac{14,500}{99,492.50} = .146 \text{ (or 14.6\%)}$$

In 20x1, Tang Auto Parts Corporation earned a 14.6 per cent return on equity for its shareholders.

Whether or not this is an acceptable return depends on several factors, such as how much the company earned in prior years and how much other companies in the same industry earned.

SUPPLEMENTAL OBJECTIVE 8

Identify the major components of a corporate annual report

COMPONENTS OF AN ANNUAL REPORT

So far, simple financial statements have been presented. Financial statements for major corporations can be quite complicated, however, and have many additional features. The management of a corporation has a responsibility each year to report to shareholders on the company's performance. This report, called the **annual report**, contains the annual financial statements, the notes related to those financial statements, and other information about the company. In addition to the financial statements and related notes, the annual report usually contains a letter to the shareholders, a summary of financial highlights, a description and review of the business, management's discussion of operating results and financial position, a directors' report including a statement of management's responsibility, the auditors' report, and a list of directors and officers of the company.

To illustrate the annual report of a major corporation, excerpts from the 1996 annual report of Nestlé, presented in an appendix at the end of this book, will be used in the following sections.

Letter to the Shareholders

Traditionally, at the beginning of the annual report, there is a letter in which the top officers of a corporation tell shareholders about the performance of and prospects for the company. The Chairman of the Board and Chief Executive Officer of Nestlé wrote to the shareholders about the highlights of the past year and the outlook for the new year, human resources, and expansion plans.

Financial Highlights

The financial highlights section of the annual report presents key financial statistics and is often accompanied by graphs. The Nestlé annual report, for example, gives "key figures" and ratios relating to operations and financial position. Nestlé also uses graphs to illustrate sales, trading profit, net profit, and market capitalisation for the last five years. A ten-year review of financials is shown later in the report. Other key figures are also shown graphically at appropriate points in the report. Note that these often include nonfinancial data, such as number of factories around the world.

As users, especially investors, are interested in a corporation's future prospects, directors tend to disclose some information about future prospects. This is usually in the form of narrative commentary, as might be expected given the sensitive nature of quantitative forecasts of sales and profits. Disclosures tend to be higher in countries with relatively well-developed stock markets, as in France, Germany, the Netherlands, the U.K., and the U.S.

In addition to financial highlights, an annual report will contain a detailed description of the products and divisions of the company. Some analysts tend to be sceptical of this section of the annual report because it often contains glossy photographs and other image-building material, but it should be looked at carefully because it may provide useful information about past results and future plans.

Financial Statements

All companies present three basic financial statements. Nestlé presents an income statement, a balance sheet, and cash flow statement for the Nestlé Group and an income statement and a balance sheet for the parent company, Nestlé S.A. Refer to the group statements in the Nestlé appendix during the following discussion.

Nestlé's financial statements for the group are preceded by the word *consolidated*. A corporation issues **consolidated financial statements** when it consists of a parent company and subsidiaries and has combined their data for reporting purposes.

Nestlé also provides two years of data for each financial statement. Financial statements presented in this fashion are called **comparative financial statements**. Such statements are in accordance with international accounting standards and help users to assess the company's performance from year to year.

Consolidated Income Statement

Nestlé uses a single-step form of the income statement and so includes all costs and expenses as a deduction from sales to arrive at trading profit before financing costs and taxes on income.

Consolidated Balance Sheet

Nestlé has a typical balance sheet. Several items in the shareholders' equity section need further explanation. Share capital represents the number of shares outstanding at nominal value. Share premium and reserves includes amounts invested by shareholders in excess of the nominal value of shares.

Consolidated Cash Flow Statement

The preparation of the consolidated cash flow statement is presented in the chapter on cash flow statements. Whereas the income statement reflects a company's profitability, the cash flow statement reflects its liquidity. The statement provides information about a company's cash receipts, cash payments, and investing and financing activities during an accounting period.

Refer to the consolidated cash flow statement in the Nestlé appendix. The first section shows cash flows from operating activities. It begins with the net profit from the consolidated income statement and adjusts that figure, which is based on accrual accounting, to a figure that represents the net cash flows provided by operating activities. Among the adjustments are increases for depreciation and amortisation, which are expenses that do not require the use of cash, and increases and decreases for the changes in the working capital accounts.

The second major section of the consolidated cash flow statement is cash flows from investing activities. The main item in this category is capital expenditures. This shows that Nestlé is a growing company.

The third major section of the consolidated cash flow statement consists of cash flows from financing activities. You can see here the sources of cash from financing activities.

At the bottom of the consolidated cash flow statement, the net effect of the operating, investing, and financing activities on the balance of cash and cash equivalents, such as highly liquid current investments, can be seen.

Notes to Consolidated Financial Statements

To meet the requirements of completeness, the company must provide **notes to the financial statements** to aid users in their interpretation. The notes are considered an integral part of the financial statements. In recent years, the need for explanation and further details has become so great that the notes often take more space than the statements themselves. The notes to the financial statements can be put into three broad groups: accounting policies notes, explanatory notes, and supplementary information notes.

Accounting Policies Notes

The International Accounting Standards Committee (IASC) requires that the financial statements include the disclosure of all significant **accounting policies**.[6] This disclosure should be presented in notes to the financial statements. In these notes, the company states which accounting standards it has followed in preparing the statements. For example, in the Nestlé report the company includes the statement:

> ***Accounting convention and accounting standards***
>
> *The Group accounts are prepared in accordance with International Accounting Standards (IAS) issued by the International Accounting Standards Committee (IASC).*
>
> *The accounts have been prepared under the historical cost convention, modified by the inclusion of the revaluation of tangible fixed assets to net replacement value. The accounts are prepared on the accruals basis. All significant consolidated and associated companies have a 31st December accounting year end. All disclosures required by the 4th and 7th European Union company law directives are provided.*

Other important accounting policies listed by Nestlé deal with principles of consolidation, foreign currencies, research and development costs, taxation, inventories, leased assets, tangible fixed assets, financial assets, intangible assets, and provisions.

Explanatory Notes

Other notes explain some of the items in the financial statements. For example, Nestlé shows the details of its Tangible Fixed Assets, including land and buildings; plant and machinery; tools, furniture, and other equipment; and vehicles. Additional notes have to do with intangible assets, long-term debt, **statement of shareholders' equity**, and so on.

Supplementary Information Notes

In recent years, in some countries, notably the United States, certain supplemental information must be presented with the financial statements. Examples are the quarterly or half-yearly reports that most companies present to their shareholders. These reports, which are called **interim financial statements**, are in most cases reviewed but not audited by the company's independent accountants.

Another important item of supplementary information is a **segment report** about the performance of the different lines of business where companies are engaged in more than one type of business operation. Segment information also extends to a geographical analysis of business operations. Nestlé's segment information, which is reported in accordance with International Accounting Standards,[7] is disclosed in a note to the financial statements (see Figure 5-2), but additional information about expenditure on property, plant, and equipment is given in management's review of the business.

While segment information about sales and profits by line of business and geographical market is increasingly perceived as important by users, not all countries currently have requirements to disclose this kind of information. In the European Union, for example, only sales information is required to be disclosed. However, in some member countries, such as the U.K., the disclosure requirements are more comprehensive and consistent with International Accounting Standards.

FIGURE 5-2 *Notes to the Group Accounts of Nestlé S.A.'s Annual Report*

1. Segmental information

In millions of Swiss francs	1996	1995
Sales		
By geographic area:		
Europe	**27 630**	26 104
North and South America	**21 110**	19 797
Other regions of the world	**11 750**	10 583
	60 490	56 484
By major business:		
Beverages	**16 348**	16 215
Milk products, dietetics and ice cream	**16 697**	15 239
Prepared dishes and cooking aids	**15 960**	14 655
Chocolate and confectionery	**9 034**	8 217
Pharmaceutical products	**2 451**	2 158
	60 490	56 484

The analysis of sales by geographic area is stated by customer destination. Inter-segment sales are not significant.

Trading profit	1996	1995
By geographic area:		
Europe	**2 284**	2 202
North and South America	**2 285**	2 083
Other regions of the world	**1 293**	1 213
	5 862	5 498
By major business:		
Beverages	**2 352**	2 151
Milk products, dietetics and ice cream	**1 206**	1 264
Prepared dishes and cooking aids	**984**	904
Chocolate and confectionery	**765**	743
Pharmaceutical products	**555**	436
	5 862	5 498

Directors' Report of Management's Responsibilities

A directors' report, including a statement of management's responsibility for the financial statements and the internal control structure, typically accompanies the financial statements. The report acknowledges management's responsibility for the integrity and objectivity of the financial information and for the system of internal controls. It mentions the company's internal audit programme and its distribution of policies to employees. It also states that the financial statements have been audited.

Management's Discussion and Analysis

Management also presents a discussion and analysis of the operations and financial position of the business. In this section, management explains the difference from one

FIGURE 5-3   *Auditors' Report for Nestlé S.A.*

Report of the Group auditors
to the General Meeting of Nestlé S.A.

As Group auditors we have audited the Group accounts (balance sheet, income statement, cash flow statement and annex) of the Nestlé Group on pages 46 to 66 for the year ended 31st December 1996.

These Group accounts are the responsibility of the Board of Directors. Our responsibility is to express an opinion on these Group accounts based on our audit. We confirm that we meet the legal requirements concerning professional qualification and independence.

Our audit was conducted in accordance with auditing standards promulgated by the profession, and with International Standards on Auditing issued by the International Federation of Accountants (IFAC), which require that an audit be planned and performed to obtain reasonable assurance about whether the Group accounts are free from material misstatement. We have examined on a test basis evidence supporting the amounts and disclosures in the Group accounts. We have also assessed the accounting principles used, significant estimates made and the overall Group accounts presentation. We believe that our audit provides a reasonable basis for our opinion.

In our opinion, the Group accounts give a true and fair view of the financial position, the result of operations and the cash flows in accordance with International Accounting Standard (IAS) and comply with the law.

We recommend that the Group accounts submitted to you be approved.

KPMG Klynveld Peat Marwick Goerdeler SA

W. M. Tannett	B. A. Mathers
Chartered accountant	Chartered accountant

Auditors in charge

London	Zurich

26th March 1997

year to the next. For example, the management of Nestlé discusses the company's sales performance, trading profit, net profit, capital expenditures, acquisitions and disinvestments, cash flows, debt, and intangible assets.

Business Review

An overall review of business operations is generally provided by management which may include many of the performance-related issues referred to earlier, but often goes beyond these to discuss the company's strategy, its research and development activities, the nature of its products and product development, and personnel or human resources issues. A more detailed review by business and/or geographical segment is also frequently provided. Nestlé's annual report is typical in providing wide-ranging comment while taking the opportunity to emphasise its products and brands, which include Nescafé, Milo, Perrier, Carnation Coffee-Mate, Findus, Maggi, Buitoni, La Cremeria, Gloria, Polo, Smarties, KitKat, and After Eight.

Report of Independent Accountants

The **independent auditors' report** describes the nature of the audit and states an opinion about whether the financial statements have been presented fairly or are true and fair. Using financial statements prepared by managers without an independent audit would be like having a judge hear a case in which he or she was personally involved. Management, through its internal accounting system, is logically responsible for recordkeeping because it needs similar information for its own use in operating the business. The auditors, acting independently, add the necessary credibility to management's figures for interested third parties. They report to the board of directors and the shareholders rather than to management.

In form and language, most auditors' reports are similar to Nestlé's report shown in Figure 5-3. Usually such a report is short, but its language is very important. Nestlé's audit report comprises four elements:

1. The first paragraph identifies the financial statements subject to the auditors' report.
2. The second paragraph identifies responsibilities. Company management is responsible for the financial statements, and the auditor is responsible for expressing an opinion on the financial statements based on the audit.
3. The third paragraph states that the audit was made in accordance with International Standards on Auditing and describes the examinations and the assessments carried out in the course of the audit.
4. The fourth paragraph, or **opinion**, states the results of the auditors' examination. The use of the word *opinion* is very important because the auditor does not certify or guarantee that the statements are absolutely correct. To do so would go too far, since many items, such as depreciation, are based on estimates. Instead, the auditors simply give an opinion about whether, overall, the financial statements give a "true and fair view", in all material respects, of the financial position, the results of operations, and cash flows. This means that the statements are prepared in accordance with accounting standards. If, in the auditors' opinion, the statements do not meet accounting standards, the auditors must explain why and to what extent.

Chapter Review

Review of Learning Objectives

1. **State the objective of financial statements.** The objective of financial statements is to provide information about an enterprise that is useful to a wide range of users in making economic decisions.

2. **State the principal qualitative characteristics of accounting information and describe their interrelationships.** The principal qualitative characteristics are understandability, relevance, reliability, and comparability. Understandability depends on the knowledge of the user and the ability of the accountant to provide useful information. Information is relevant when it affects the outcome of a decision. Information that is relevant has feedback value and predictive value. However, the relevance of information is affected by its materiality. To be reliable, information must provide a faithful representation of transactions and other events. The information should maintain substance over form and be neutral or free from bias. In the face of uncertainties, a prudent approach should be followed. The information must also be complete. Comparability means that users must be able to compare financial statements through time with those of other companies both within and across countries so that they can evaluate relative performance, financial position, and changes in cash flows.

3. **Define and describe the constraints on relevant and reliable information.** The constraints to consider when providing relevant and reliable information are timeliness, benefit-cost, and the relationship between the qualitative characteristics. The balance between benefit and cost is important in that the costs of providing information should not exceed the benefits. A trade-off or balancing between qualitative characteristics is often necessary in practice which requires professional judgement to ensure the provision of information which is useful in making economic decisions.

4. **Explain management's responsibility for ethical financial reporting and define** *fraudulent financial reporting.* Management is responsible for the preparation of financial statements in accordance with accounting standards and for the internal controls that provide assurance that this objective is achieved. Fraudulent financial reporting is the intentional preparation of misleading financial statements.

5. **Identify and describe the basic components of a classified balance sheet.** The classified balance sheet is subdivided into assets, liabilities, and shareholders' equity. While the form of presentation may vary, assets generally include current assets; investments; property, plant, and equipment; and intangible assets. Liabilities include current liabilities and long-term liabilities, and shareholders' equity includes share capital and retained earnings. A current asset is an asset that can reasonably be expected to be realised in cash or consumed within one year or the normal operating cycle, whichever is longer. Investments are long-term assets that are not usually used in the normal operation of a business. Property, plant, and equipment are long-term assets that are used in day-to-day operations. Intangible assets are long-term assets whose value stems from the rights or privileges they extend to shareholders. A current liability is a liability that can reasonably be expected to be paid or performed within one year or the normal operating cycle, whichever is longer. Long-term liabilities are debts that fall due more than one year in the future or beyond the normal operating cycle. The equity section for a corporation differs from that of a proprietorship in that it has subdivisions of share capital (the value of assets invested by shareholders) and retained earnings (shareholders' claim to assets earned from operations and reinvested in operations).

6. **Prepare multistep and single-step classified income statements.** Condensed income statements for external reporting can be in multistep or single-step form. The multistep form arrives at net profit through a series of steps; the single-step form arrives at profit before income taxes in a single step. There is usually a separate section in the multistep form for other revenues and expenses.

7. **Use classified financial statements for the simple evaluation of liquidity and profitability.** One major use of classified financial statements is to evaluate a company's liquidity and profitability. Two simple measures of liquidity are working capital and the current ratio. Five simple measures relevant to profitability are profit margin, asset turnover, return on assets, debt to equity, and return on equity.

Supplemental Objective

8. **Identify the major components of a corporate annual report.** In its annual report, a corporation's management reports to shareholders on the company's financial results for the year. The annual report typically has the following principal components: letter to the shareholders, financial highlights, directors' report including a statement of management's responsibilities, management's discussion of operating results and financial position, a review of business operations, the financial statements, notes to the financial statements, and the report of the independent accountants or auditors.

Review of Concepts and Terminology

The following concepts and terms were introduced in this chapter.

SO 8 **Accounting policies:** Accounting standards that the company has followed in preparing the financial statements; usually disclosed in a note to the financial statements or in a separate section of the annual report.

SO 8 **Annual report:** The medium in which the general-purpose external financial statements of a business are communicated once a year to shareholders and other interested parties.

LO 7 **Asset turnover:** A measure of profitability that shows how efficiently a business is using assets to produce sales; net sales divided by average total assets.

LO 3 **Balance between benefit and cost:** The constraint on financial reporting that holds that benefits gained from providing accounting information should be greater than the costs of providing that information. Also called *benefit-cost.*

LO 3   **Balance between qualitative characteristics:** The constraint on financial reporting that results in a trade-off between qualitative characteristics such as relevance versus reliability.

LO 5   **Classified financial statements:** General-purpose external financial statements that are divided into subcategories.

LO 2   **Comparability:** The principal qualitative characteristic of presenting information in a way that enables decision makers to recognise similarities, differences, and trends over different time periods or between different companies both within and across countries.

SO 8   **Comparative financial statements:** Financial statements in which data for two or more years are presented in adjacent columns.

LO 2   **Completeness:** The qualitative characteristic that requires that, to be reliable, financial statements and their notes present all information that is relevant to the users' understanding of the company's performance and financial position.

LO 6   **Condensed financial statements:** Financial statements for external reporting purposes that present only the major categories of information.

SO 8   **Consolidated financial statements:** The combined financial statements of a parent company and its subsidiaries.

LO 5   **Current assets:** Cash or other assets that are reasonably expected to be realised in cash, sold, or consumed within one year or within a normal operating cycle, whichever is longer.

LO 5   **Current liabilities:** Obligations due to be paid or performed within one year or within the normal operating cycle, whichever is longer.

LO 7   **Current ratio:** A measure of liquidity; current assets divided by current liabilities.

LO 7   **Debt to equity:** A ratio that measures the relationship of assets provided by lenders to those provided by shareholders; total liabilities divided by shareholders' equity.

LO 6   **Earnings per share:** Net profit earned on each share; net profit divided by the average number of equity shares outstanding. Also called *net profit per share.*

LO 2   **Faithful representation:** The qualitative characteristic that requires that information should represent what it purports to represent.

LO 4   **Fraudulent financial reporting:** The intentional preparation of misleading financial statements.

LO 6   **Income Taxes:** An account that represents the expense for income taxes on corporate income; this account appears only on income statements of corporations. Also called *provision for income taxes.*

SO 8   **Independent auditors' report:** The section of an annual report in which the independent accountants describe the nature of the audit and state an opinion about whether the financial statements have been presented fairly or are true and fair.

LO 5   **Intangible assets:** Long-term assets that have no physical substance but have a value based on rights or privileges that belong to their owner.

SO 8   **Interim financial statements:** Financial statements prepared for an accounting period of less than one year.

LO 5   **Investments:** Assets, usually long-term, not used in the normal operation of a business and that management does not intend to convert to cash within the next year.

LO 7   **Liquidity:** Having enough money available to pay bills when they are due and to take care of unexpected needs for cash.

LO 5   **Long-term liabilities:** Debts that fall due more than one year in the future or beyond the normal operating cycle; debts to be paid out of noncurrent assets.

LO 2   **Materiality:** The qualitative characteristic that requires that an item or event in a financial statement be important if it is to be relevant to the users of financial statements.

LO 6   **Multistep form:** A form of income statement that arrives at net profit in steps.

LO 2   **Neutrality:** The qualitative characteristic that requires that information should be free from bias.

SO 8   **Notes to the financial statements:** Section of a corporate annual report containing information that aids users in interpreting the financial statements.

SO 8   **Opinion:** Part of the auditors' report that states the results of the auditors' examination.

LO 5   **Other assets:** The balance sheet category that may include various types of assets other than current assets and property, plant, and equipment.

LO 6   **Other revenues and expenses:** The section of a classified income statement that includes nonoperating revenues and expenses.

LO 3   **Present fairly:** Financial statements resulting from the overall application of the qualitative characteristics are said to present fairly the information about an enterprise.

LO 7   **Profitability:** The ability of a business to earn a satisfactory profit.

LO 6   **Profit from operations:** Gross profit less operating expenses.

LO 7   **Profit margin:** A measure of profitability that shows the percentage of sales that results in net profit; net profit divided by net sales.

LO 5   **Property, plant, and equipment:** Tangible long-term assets that are used in the continuing operation of a business. Also called *operating assets, fixed assets, tangible assets, long-lived assets,* or *plant assets.*

LO 2   **Prudence:** The qualitative characteristic that indicates that, when faced with two equally acceptable alternative methods, the accountant must choose the one less likely to overstate assets and profit. Also called *conservatism.*

LO 2   **Qualitative characteristics:** Standards for judging the information that accountants give to decision makers.

LO 2   **Relevance:** The principal qualitative characteristic of bearing directly on the outcome of a decision.

LO 2   **Reliability:** The principal qualitative characteristic of being dependable, credible, and verifiable.

LO 7   **Return on assets:** A measure of profitability that shows how efficiently a company uses its assets to produce a profit; net profit divided by average total assets.

LO 7   **Return on equity:** A measure of profitability that relates the amount earned by a business to the shareholders' investments in the business; net profit divided by average shareholders' equity.

SO 8   **Segment report:** A report of the performance of the different lines of business of a company and of its geographical spread of operations.

LO 6   **Single-step form:** A form of income statement that arrives at profit before income taxes in a single step.

SO 8   **Statement of shareholders' equity:** Financial statement that shows the changes in all shareholders' equity accounts including retained earnings.

LO 2   **Substance over form:** The qualitative characteristic that requires that information should represent the economic substance of transactions and other events.

LO 3   **Timeliness:** A constraint on financial reporting in that the information may lose its relevance if there is an unreasonable delay.

LO 3   **True and fair view:** Financial statements resulting from

the overall application of the qualitative characteristics are said to show a true and fair view.

LO 2   **Understandability:** The qualitative characteristic of communicating an intended meaning.

LO 7   **Working capital:** A measure of liquidity that shows the current assets available (after subtraction of current liabilities) to continue business operations.

Review Problem

Analysing Liquidity and Profitability Using Ratios

LO 7   Flavin Shirt Company has faced increased competition from overseas shirtmakers in recent years. Presented below is summary information for the last two years:

	20x2	20x1
Current Assets	200,000	170,000
Total Assets	880,000	710,000
Current Liabilities	90,000	50,000
Long-Term Liabilities	150,000	50,000
Shareholders' Equity	640,000	610,000
Sales	1,200,000	1,050,000
Net Profit	60,000	80,000

Total assets and shareholders' equity at the start of 20x1 were 690,000 and 590,000, respectively.

REQUIRED   Use (1) liquidity analysis and (2) profitability analysis to document the declining financial position of Flavin Shirt Company.

Answer to Review Problem

1. Liquidity analysis

	Current Assets	Current Liabilities	Working Capital	Current Ratio
20x1	170,000	50,000	120,000	3.40
20x2	200,000	90,000	110,000	2.22
Increase (decrease) in working capital			(10,000)	
Decrease in current ratio				1.18

Both working capital and the current ratio declined because, although current assets increased by 30,000 (200,000 − 170,000), current liabilities increased by a greater amount, 40,000 (90,000 − 50,000), from 20x1 to 20x2.

2. Profitability analysis

	Net Profit	Sales	Profit Margin	Average Total Assets	Asset Turnover	Return on Assets	Average Share-holders' Equity	Return on Equity
20x1	80,000	1,050,000	7.6%	700,000[1]	1.50	11.4%	600,000[3]	13.3%
20x2	60,000	1,200,000	5.0%	795,000[2]	1.51	7.5%	625,000[4]	9.6%
Increase (decrease)	(20,000)	150,000	(2.6)%	95,000	0.01	(3.9)%	25,000	(3.7)%

[1](690,000 + 710,000) ÷ 2   [3](590,000 + 610,000) ÷ 2
[2](710,000 + 880,000) ÷ 2   [4](610,000 + 640,000) ÷ 2

Net profit decreased by 20,000 despite an increase in sales of 150,000, and an increase in average total assets of 95,000. The results were decreases in profit margin from 7.6 per cent to 5.0 per cent and in return on assets from 11.4 per cent to 7.5 per cent. Asset turnover showed almost no change, and so did not contribute to the decline in profitability. The decrease in return on equity from 13.3 per cent to 9.6 per cent was not as great as the decrease in return on assets because the growth in total assets was financed by debt instead of shareholders' equity, as shown by the capital structure analysis below.

	Total Liabilities	Shareholders' Equity	Debt to Equity Ratio
20x1	100,000	610,000	16.4%
20x2	240,000	640,000	37.5%
Increase	140,000	30,000	21.1%

Total liabilities increased by 140,000, while shareholders' equity increased by 30,000. As a result, the amount of the business financed by debt in relation to the amount of the business financed by shareholders' equity increased from 16.4 per cent to 37.5 per cent.

CHAPTER ASSIGNMENTS

Knowledge and Understanding

Questions

1. What is the objective of financial statements?
2. What are the principal qualitative characteristics of accounting information, and what is their significance?
3. What are the constraints on providing relevant and reliable information?
4. Who is responsible for the preparation of reliable financial statements, and what is a principal way of achieving this objective?
5. What is the purpose of classified financial statements?
6. What are four common categories of assets?
7. What criteria must an asset meet to be classified as current? Under what condition is an asset considered current even though it will not be realised as cash within a year? What are two examples of assets that fall into this category?
8. In what order should current assets be listed?
9. What is the difference between a current investment in the current assets section and a security in the investments section of the balance sheet?
10. What is an intangible asset? Give at least three examples.
11. Name the two major categories of liabilities.

12. Explain how the multistep form of income statement differs from the single-step form. What are the relative merits of each?
13. Why are other revenues and expenses separated from operating revenues and expenses in the multistep income statement?
14. Explain earnings per share and how this figure appears on the income statement.
15. Define *liquidity* and name two measures of liquidity.
16. How is the current ratio calculated and why is it important?
17. Which is the more important goal—liquidity or profitability? Explain your answer.
18. Name five measures relevant to profitability.
19. "Return on assets is a better measure of profitability than profit margin." Evaluate this statement.
20. Explain the difference between share capital and retained earnings.
21. Why are notes to financial statements necessary?
22. Why is the disclosure of accounting policies important?
23. What additional information is provided by a segment report?
24. What is the purpose of the independent auditors' report?

Application

Exercises

E 5-1.
LO 2 *Qualitative Characteristics*
LO 3 *and Constraints*

Each of the statements below violates a criterion in accounting. State which of the following qualitative characteristics or constraints is violated: comparability, materiality, prudence, completeness, or benefit-cost.

1. A series of reports that are time-consuming and expensive to prepare is presented to the board of directors each month even though the reports are never used.
2. A company changes its method of accounting for depreciation.
3. The company in 2 does not indicate in the financial statements that the method of depreciation was changed, nor does it specify the effect of the change on net profit.

4. A new office building next to the factory is debited to the Factory account because it represents a fairly small monetary amount in relation to the factory.
5. The asset account for a pickup truck that is still used in the business is written down to what it could be sold for even though the carrying amount under conventional depreciation methods is higher.

E 5-2.

LO 1
LO 2
LO 3

Accounting Concepts

The lettered items below represent a classification scheme for the concepts of financial accounting. Match each numbered term with the letter of the category in which it belongs.

a. Decision makers (users of accounting information)
b. Business activities or entities relevant to accounting measurement
c. Objectives of accounting information
d. Accounting measurement considerations
e. Accounting processing considerations
f. Qualitative characteristics
g. Accounting constraints
h. Financial statements

1. Prudence
2. Reliability
3. Cash flow statement
4. Materiality
5. Faithful representation
6. Recognition
7. Benefit-cost
8. Understandability
9. Business transactions
10. Comparability
11. Completeness
12. Providing information useful to investors and lenders
13. Specific business entities
14. Classification
15. Management
16. Neutrality
17. Internal accounting control
18. Valuation
19. Investors
20. Timeliness
21. Relevance
22. Providing information useful in assessing cash flow prospects

E 5-3.

LO 5 *Classification of Accounts: Balance Sheet*

The lettered items below represent a classification scheme for a balance sheet, and the numbered items are account titles. Match each of the account titles with the letter of the category in which it belongs.

a. Current assets
b. Investments
c. Property, plant, and equipment
d. Intangible assets
e. Current liabilities
f. Long-term liabilities
g. Shareholders' equity
h. Not on balance sheet

1. Patent
2. Building Held for Sale
3. Prepaid Rent
4. Wages Payable
5. Note Payable in Five Years
6. Building Used in Operations
7. Fund Held to Pay Off Long-Term Debt
8. Inventory
9. Prepaid Insurance
10. Depreciation Expense
11. Accounts Receivable
12. Interest Expense
13. Unearned Revenue
14. Current Investments
15. Accumulated Depreciation
16. Retained Earnings

E 5-4.

LO 5 *Classified Balance Sheet Preparation*

The following data pertain to Kyoto Corporation: Accounts Payable, 51,000; Accounts Receivable, 38,000; Accumulated Depreciation, Building, 14,000; Accumulated Depreciation, Equipment, 17,000; Bonds Payable, 60,000; Building, 70,000; Cash, 31,200; Share Capital—10,000 shares authorised, issued, and outstanding, 100,000; Copyright, 6,200; Equipment, 152,000; Inventory, 40,000; Investment in Corporate Securities (long-term), 20,000; Investment in Six-Month Government Securities, 16,400; Land, 8,000; Share Premium, 50,000; Prepaid Rent, 1,200; Retained Earnings, 88,200; and Revenue Received in Advance, 2,800.

Prepare a classified balance sheet at December 31, 20xx.

E 5-5.

LO 6 *Classification of Accounts: Income Statement*

Using the classification scheme below for a multistep income statement, match each account with the letter of the category in which it belongs.

a. Revenues from sales
b. Cost of goods sold
c. Selling expenses
d. General and administrative expenses
e. Other revenues and expenses
f. Not on income statement

<table>
<tr><td>1. Purchases</td><td>9. Electricity Expense</td></tr>
<tr><td>2. Sales Discounts</td><td>10. Sales Salaries Expense</td></tr>
<tr><td>3. Inventory (beginning)</td><td>11. Rent Expense</td></tr>
<tr><td>4. Dividend Income</td><td>12. Purchases Returns and Allowances</td></tr>
<tr><td>5. Advertising Expense</td><td>13. Freight In</td></tr>
<tr><td>6. Office Salaries Expense</td><td>14. Depreciation Expense, Delivery Equipment</td></tr>
<tr><td>7. Freight Out Expense</td><td>15. Taxes Payable</td></tr>
<tr><td>8. Prepaid Insurance</td><td>16. Interest Expense</td></tr>
</table>

E 5-6.

LO 6 *Preparation of Income Statements*

These data pertain to Palm Beach Corporation: Net Sales, 405,000; Cost of Goods Sold, 220,000; Selling Expenses, 90,000; General and Administrative Expenses, 60,000; Income Taxes, 7,500; Interest Expense, 4,000; Interest Income, 3,000; and Share Capital Outstanding, 100,000 shares.

1. Prepare a condensed single-step income statement.
2. Prepare a condensed multistep income statement.

E 5-7.

LO 6 *Condensed Multistep Income Statement*

A condensed single-step income statement appears below. Present this information in a condensed multistep income statement, and state what insights can be obtained from the multistep form as opposed to the single-step form.

Narajan Furniture Corporation
Income Statement
For the Year Ended June 30, 20xx

Revenues		
Net Sales	1,197,132	
Interest Income	5,720	
Total Revenues		1,202,852
Costs and Expenses		
Cost of Goods Sold	777,080	
Selling Expenses	203,740	
General and Administrative Expenses	100,688	
Interest Expense	13,560	
Total Costs and Expenses		1,095,068
Profit before Income Taxes		107,784
Income Taxes		24,000
Net Profit		83,784
Earnings per share		8.38

E 5-8.

LO 7 *Liquidity Ratios*

The following accounts and balances are taken from the general ledger of Mount Fuji Corporation:

Accounts Payable	49,800
Accounts Receivable	30,600
Cash	4,500
Current Portion of Long-Term Debt	30,000
Long-Term Investments	31,200
Marketable Securities	37,800
Inventory	76,200
Notes Payable, 90 days	45,000
Notes Payable, 2 years	60,000
Notes Receivable, 90 days	78,000
Notes Receivable, 2 years	30,000
Prepaid Insurance	1,200
Property, Plant, and Equipment	180,000
Property Taxes Payable	3,750
Retained Earnings	84,900
Salaries Payable	2,550
Supplies	1,050
Unearned Revenue	2,250

Calculate the (1) working capital and (2) current ratio.

E 5-9.

LO 7   *Profitability Ratios*

The following end-of-year amounts are taken from the financial statements of Manakui Corporation: Total Assets, 852,000; Total Liabilities, 344,000; Shareholders' Equity, 508,000; Net Sales, 1,564,000; Cost of Goods Sold, 972,000; Operating Expenses, 357,000; Income Taxes, 47,000; and Dividends, 80,000. During the past year, total assets increased by 150,000. Total shareholders' equity was affected only by net profit and dividends.

Calculate the (1) profit margin, (2) asset turnover, (3) return on assets, (4) debt to equity, and (5) return on equity.

E 5-10.

LO 7   *Calculation of Ratios*

The simplified balance sheet and income statement for Bali Corporation are as follows:

Bali Corporation
Balance Sheet
December 31, 20xx

Assets		Liabilities	
Current Assets	100,000	Current Liabilities	40,000
Investments	20,000	Long-Term Liabilities	60,000
Property, Plant, and		Total Liabilities	100,000
Equipment	293,000		
Intangible Assets	27,000	**Shareholders' Equity**	
Total Assets	440,000		
		Share Capital	200,000
		Retained Earnings	140,000
		Total Shareholders'	
		Equity	340,000
		Total Liabilities and	
		Shareholders' Equity	440,000

Bali Corporation
Income Statement
For the Year Ended December 31, 20xx

Revenues from Sales (net)	820,000
Cost of Goods Sold	500,000
Gross Profit	320,000
Operating Expenses	260,000
Profit before Income Taxes	60,000
Income Taxes	10,000
Net Profit	50,000

Total assets and shareholders' equity at the start of 20xx were 360,000 and 280,000, respectively.

1. Calculate the following liquidity measures: (a) working capital and (b) current ratio.
2. Calculate the following profitability measures: (a) profit margin, (b) asset turnover, (c) return on assets, (d) debt to equity, and (e) return on equity.

E 5-11.

SO 8   *Components of an Annual Report*

State whether the following information that is typically included in an annual report would be found in (a) the letter to the shareholders, (b) the financial highlights, (c) the financial statements, (d) the summary of significant accounting policies, (e) the explanatory notes, (f) the supplementary information notes, (g) directors' report including a statement of management's responsibilities, (h) management's discussion and analysis, (i) the business review, or (j) the report of the independent accountants:

1. A ten-year summary of financial data about operations.
2. Data about cash flows from financing activities.
3. A statement that management is responsible for the company's internal controls.

4. A statement about the company's method of accounting for depreciation.
5. Management's analysis of profit from operations.
6. The company chief executive's description of prospects for next year.
7. Sales and net profit for the last four quarters.
8. Detailed information about the company's long-term liabilities.
9. A statement about whether or not the financial statements are fairly presented or show a true and fair view in accordance with accounting standards.
10. A discussion of new product developments.

Problem Set

P 5-1.

LO 3 *Accounting Criteria*

In each case below, accounting criteria may have been violated.

1. After careful study, Alfa Company has determined that in the future its method of depreciating office furniture should be changed. The new method is adopted for the current year, and the change is noted in the financial statements.
2. In the past, Jafari Corporation has recorded operating expenses in general accounts for each classification (for example, Salaries Expense, Depreciation Expense, and Electricity Expense). Management has determined that in spite of the additional recordkeeping costs, the company's income statement should break down each operating expense into its selling expense and administrative expense components.
3. The auditor of Mendez Corporation discovered that an official of the company may have authorised the payment of a 3,000 bribe to a local official. Management argued that because the item was so small in relation to the size of the company (3,000,000 in sales), the illegal payment should not be disclosed.
4. Brilliant Bookstore built a small addition to its main building to house a new computer games division. Because of uncertainty about whether the computer games division would succeed, the accountant took a prudent approach, recording the addition as an expense.
5. Since its origin ten years ago, Vazquez Company has used the same inventory method. Because there has been no change in the inventory method, the company does not declare in its financial statements what inventory method it uses.

REQUIRED

In each case, state the qualitative characteristic or accounting constraint that is applicable, and state whether or not the treatment is in accord with that characteristic or constraint and with accounting standards. Briefly explain why.

P 5-2.

LO 5 *Classified Balance Sheet*

Accounts from the July 31, 20x2 post-closing trial balance of Kinsella Hardware Corporation follow.

Account Name	Debit	Credit
Cash	31,000	
Current Investments	33,000	
Notes Receivable	10,000	
Accounts Receivable	276,000	
Inventory	145,000	
Prepaid Rent	1,600	
Prepaid Insurance	4,800	
Sales Supplies	1,280	
Office Supplies	440	
Deposit for Future Advertising	3,680	
Building, Not in Use	49,600	
Land	22,400	
Delivery Equipment	41,200	
Accumulated Depreciation, Delivery Equipment		28,400
Franchise Fee	4,000	
Accounts Payable		114,600
Salaries Payable		5,200
Interest Payable		840
Long-Term Notes Payable		80,000
Share Capital		20,000
Share Premium		160,000
Retained Earnings		214,960

REQUIRED   From the information provided, prepare a classified balance sheet.

P 5-3.
LO 7   *Ratio Analysis: Liquidity*
and Profitability

Criss Products Corporation has been disappointed with its operating results for the past two years. As accountant for the company, you have the following information available to you:

	20x2	20x1
Current Assets	45,000	35,000
Total Assets	145,000	110,000
Current Liabilities	20,000	10,000
Long-Term Liabilities	20,000	—
Shareholders' Equity	105,000	100,000
Net Sales	262,000	200,000
Net Profit	16,000	11,000

Total assets and shareholders' equity at the beginning of 20x1 were 90,000 and 80,000, respectively.

REQUIRED   1. Calculate the following measures of liquidity for 20x1 and 20x2: (a) working capital and (b) the current ratio. Comment on the differences between the years.
2. Calculate the following measures of profitability for 20x1 and 20x2: (a) profit margin, (b) asset turnover, (c) return on assets, (d) debt to equity, and (e) return on equity. Comment on the change in performance from 20x1 to 20x2.

Critical Thinking and Communication

Conceptual Mini-Case

CMC 5-1.
LO 7   *Evaluation of Profitability*

Carla Cruz is the principal shareholder and chief executive of *Cruz Tapestries*, which wholesales fine tapestries to retail stores. Because Cruz was not satisfied with the company's earnings in 20x1, she raised prices in 20x2, increasing gross profit from sales from 30 per cent in 20x1 to 35 per cent in 20x2. Cruz is pleased that net profit did go up from 20x1 to 20x2, as shown in the following comparative income statements:

	20x2	20x1
Revenues		
Net Sales	611,300	693,200
Costs and Expenses		
Cost of Goods Sold	397,345	485,240
Selling and Administrative Expenses	154,199	152,504
Total Costs and Expenses	551,544	637,744
Profit before Income Taxes	59,756	55,456
Income Taxes	15,000	14,000
Net Profit	44,756	41,456

Total assets for Cruz Tapestries at year end for 20x0, 20x1, and 20x2 were 623,390, 693,405, and 768,455, respectively. Has Cruz Tapestries profitability really improved? (**Note:** Calculate profit margin and return on assets, and comment.) What factors has Cruz overlooked in evaluating the profitability of the company? (**Note:** Calculate asset turnover and comment on the role it plays in profitability.)

Cultural Mini-Case

CLMC 5-1.
LO 5   *Format of Balance Sheet and*
LO 7   *Analysis of Financial*
Statements

In the European Union, assets on the balance sheet are often presented with long-term assets listed first. This can be contrasted with the North American approach, which is to list current assets before long-term assets. Shareholders' equity is also presented before liabilities by many companies in Continental Europe.

Schering is a leading German pharmaceutical company, founded in 1871, whose major activities are in the areas of diagnostics, fertility control and hormone therapy, therapeutics, and dermatology. In 1995, Schering's foreign sales accounted for 85 per cent of its total sales. Schering's 1995 balance sheet, presented in a typical European format, is shown at the top of the next page.[8]

REQUIRED   1. Reformat Schering's balance sheet to conform with a typical North American format.
2. Given that Schering earned a net profit of 248.4 million Deutsche marks in 1995, calculate the return on assets and return on equity for 1995.

SCHERING
Balance Sheet
(Thousands of DM)

Assets	Notes		31 Dec. 1995		31 Dec. 1994
Intangible assets	(5)		215,866		70,143
Tangible assets	(6)		1,849,234		1,799,686
Shares in related companies		378,857		413,798	
Other long-term investments		172,172		151,841	
Financial assets	(7)		551,029		565,639
Fixed assets			2,616,129		2,435,468
Stocks	(8)		932,733		1,005,333
Trade debtors	(9)	922,101		928,296	
Other debtors	(10)	281,801		313,469	
Trade and other debtors			1,203,902		1,241,765
Liquid funds	(11)		2,357,969		2,094,873
Current assets			4,494,604		4,341,971
Deferred expenses	(12)		55,184		20,300
			7,165,917		6,797,739

Equity and liabilities	Notes		31 Dec. 1995		31 Dec. 1994
Issued capital	(13)	341,710		341,710	
Share premium account		686,191		686,191	
Paid-up capital and capital reserve of Schering AG			1,027,901		1,027,901
Retained earnings of the Group	(14)		2,181,600		2,052,411
Capital and reserves of the Group			3,209,501		3,080,312
Minority interests			5,020		5,014
Capital and reserves			3,214,521		3,085,326
Provisions for pensions and similar obligations	(15)	1,787,083		1,670,144	
Other provisions	(16)	1,156,081		1,026,530	
Provisions			2,943,164		2,696,674
Liabilities to banks		314,742		369,871	
Other liabilities		693,490		645,868	
Liabilities	(17)		1,008,232		1,015,739
			7,165,917		6,797,739

Ethics Mini-Case

EMC 5-1.

LO 4 *Ethics and Financial Reporting*

Champion Microsystems, a manufacturer of microchips for personal computers, has just completed its year-end physical inventory in advance of preparing financial statements. To celebrate, the entire accounting department goes out for a New Year's Eve party at a local establishment. As senior accountant, you join the fun. At the party, you fall into conversation with an employee of one of your main competitors. After a while, the employee reveals that the competitor plans to introduce a new product in sixty days that will make Champion's principal product obsolete.

On Monday morning, you go to the chief financial officer with this information, stating that the inventory may have to be written down and net profit reduced. To your surprise, the chief financial officer says that you were right to come to her, but urges you to say nothing about the problem. She says, "It is probably a rumour, and even if it is true, there will be plenty of time to write down the inventory in sixty days." You wonder if this is the appropriate thing to do. You feel confident that your source knew what he was talking about. You know that the salaries of all top managers, including the chief financial officer, are tied to net profit. What is fraudulent financial reporting? Is this an example of fraudulent financial reporting? What action would you take?

Decision-Making Case

DMC 5-1.

LO 7 *Financial Analysis for Loan Decision*

Steve Sullivan was recently promoted to loan officer at the ***First National Bank***. He has authority to issue loans up to 50,000 without approval from a higher bank official. This week two small companies, Handy Harvey and Sheila's Fashions, have each submitted a proposal for a six-month 50,000 loan. To prepare financial analyses of the two companies, Steve has obtained the information summarised below.

Handy Harvey is a local lumber and home improvement company. Because the company's sales have increased so much during the past two years, Handy Harvey has had to raise additional working capital, especially as represented by receivables and inventory. The 50,000 loan is needed to assure the company of enough working capital for the next year. Handy Harvey began the year with total assets of 740,000 and shareholders' equity of 260,000, and during the past year the company had a net profit of 40,000 on net sales of 760,000. The company's current unclassified balance sheet appears as follows:

Assets		Liabilities and Shareholders' Equity	
Cash	30,000	Accounts Payable	200,000
Accounts Receivable (net)	150,000	Note Payable (short-term)	100,000
Inventory	250,000	Mortgage Payable	200,000
Land	50,000	Share Capital	250,000
Buildings (net)	250,000	Retained Earnings	50,000
Equipment (net)	70,000	Total Liabilities and	
Total Assets	800,000	Shareholders' Equity	800,000

Sheila's Fashions has for three years been a successful clothing store for young professional women. The leased store is located in the downtown financial district. Sheila's loan proposal asks for 50,000 to pay for stocking a new line of professional suits for working women during the coming season. At the beginning of the year, the company had total assets of 200,000 and total shareholders' equity of 114,000. Over the past year, the company earned a net profit of 36,000 on sales of 480,000. The firm's unclassified balance sheet at the current date appears as follows:

Assets		Liabilities and Shareholders' Equity	
Cash	10,000	Accounts Payable	80,000
Accounts Receivable (net)	50,000	Accrued Liabilities	10,000
Inventory	135,000	Share Capital	50,000
Prepaid Expenses	5,000	Retained Earnings	100,000
Equipment (net)	40,000	Total Liabilities and	
Total Assets	240,000	Shareholders' Equity	240,000

REQUIRED

1. Prepare a financial analysis of each company's liquidity before and after receiving the proposed loan. Also, calculate profitability ratios before and after, as appropriate. Write a brief summary of the effect of the proposed loan on each company's financial position.
2. To which company do you suppose Steve would be more willing to make a 50,000 loan? What are the positive and negative factors related to each company's ability to pay back the loan in the next year? What other information of a financial or nonfinancial nature would be helpful for making a final decision?

Basic Research Activity

RA 5-1.

LO 7 *Annual Reports and*
SO 8 *Financial Analysis*

Most university, college, and public libraries file annual reports of major public corporations. In some libraries, these annual reports are on microfiche. Go to the library, obtain the annual report for a company that you recognise, and do the following. (1) In the annual report, identify the three basic financial statements and the notes to the financial statements. Perform a liquidity analysis, including the calculation of working capital and the current ratio. Perform a profitability analysis, calculating profit margin, asset turnover, return on assets, debt to equity, and return on equity. (2) Make a detailed comparison of the content of the annual report you have chosen with the Nestlé annual report in the appendix, noting both similarities and differences. Be prepared to present your findings in class.

Financial Reporting and Analysis

Interpretation Cases from Business

ICB 5-1.

LO 6 *Analysis of a Multistep*
LO 7 *Income Statement*

Toys "R" Us has consistently been one of the best and fastest growing retailers in the United States. Management is proud of its record of cost control, as witnessed by the following quotation from the company's 1987 annual report:

> Toys "R" Us expense levels are among the best controlled in retailing. . . . For example, in 1986 (year ended February 1, 1987) our expenses as a percentage of sales declined by almost 3% from 21.7% to 18.8%. As a result, we were able to operate with lower merchandise margins and still increase our earnings and return on sales.[9]

The company's condensed single-step income statement for 1996 appears below:

Toys "R" Us
Consolidated Statement of Earnings
(In Millions Except per Share Information)

	February 3, 1996	January 28, 1995
Net sales	$9,426.9	$8,745.6
Costs and expenses:		
Cost of sales	6,592.3	6,008.0
Selling, advertising, general and administrative	1,894.8	1,664.2
Restructuring and other charges	396.6	
Depreciation and amortization	191.7	161.4
Interest expenses	103.3	83.9
Interest and other income	(17.4)	(16.0)
	9,161.3	7,901.5
Earnings before taxes on income taxes	265.6	844.1
Taxes on income	117.5	312.3
Net earnings	$148.1	$531.8
Earnings per share	$.53	$1.85

REQUIRED

1. Prepare multistep income statements for Toys "R" Us for 1996 and 1995, and calculate the ratios of gross profit from sales, operating expenses, profit from operations, and net profits to net sales.
2. Comment on whether the trend indicated by management in 1987 continued to be true in 1996. In 1987, gross profit was 31.2 per cent, total operating expenses were 20.0 per cent of net sales, and net profits were 9.9 per cent of sales.

ICB 5-2.

LO 7 *Profitability Analysis*

BMW from Germany and **Volvo** from Sweden are keen competitors in executive and family car markets around the world. In 1995, BMW and Volvo earned net profits of 692 million Deutsche marks and 9,262 million kronor, respectively. Data from the BMW and Volvo 1995 annual reports are presented below to permit a comparative financial analysis of the two companies.[10]

	BMW Millions (marks)	Volvo Millions (kronor)
Sales	46,144	171,511
Ending total assets	40,847	138,699
Beginning total assets	38,693	138,582
Ending total liabilities	32,647	86,894
Beginning total liabilities	30,771	94,412
Ending shareholders' equity	8,200	51,200
Beginning shareholders' equity	7,922	43,332

REQUIRED

1. Calculate the net profit margin, asset turnover, return on assets, debt to equity ratio, and return on equity for the two companies. (**Note:** Calculate percentages to one decimal place.)
2. Comment on the performance and profitability of BMW compared to Volvo in 1995.

Nestlé Case

<table>
<tr><td>NC 5-1.</td></tr>
<tr><td>LO 5</td><td>Reading and Analysing an</td></tr>
<tr><td>LO 6</td><td>Annual Report</td></tr>
<tr><td>LO 7</td><td></td></tr>
<tr><td>SO 8</td><td></td></tr>
</table>

Refer to the Annual Report in the appendix on Nestlé to answer the following questions:

1. Consolidated balance sheet: (a) Did the amount of working capital increase or decrease from 1995 to 1996? By how much? (b) Did the current ratio improve from 1995 to 1996? (c) Does the company have long-term investments or intangible assets? (d) Did the capital structure of Nestlé change from 1995 to 1996? (e) What is the share capital for 1996? How does it compare with the amount of Nestlé's reserves including retained earnings?

2. Consolidated income statement: (a) Did Nestlé use a multistep or a single-step form of income statement? (b) Is it a comparative statement? (c) What is the trend of net profit? (d) How significant are income taxes for Nestlé? (e) What is the trend of net profit per share? (f) Did the profit margin increase from 1995 to 1996? (g) Did asset turnover improve from 1995 to 1996? (h) Did the return on assets increase from 1995 to 1996? (i) Did the return on equity increase from 1995 to 1996?

3. Consolidated cash flow statement: (a) Compare net profit in 1996 with cash provided by operating activities in 1996. Why is there a difference? (b) What are the most important investing activities in 1996? (c) What are the most important financing activities in 1996? (d) How did these investing and financing activities compare with those in prior years? (e) Where did Nestlé get cash to pay for the capital expenditures? (f) How did the change in Cash and Cash Equivalents in 1996 compare to that in the previous year?

4. Auditors' report: (a) What was the name of Nestlé's independent auditor? (b) Who is responsible for the financial statements? (c) What is the auditor's responsibility? (d) Does the auditor examine all the company's records? (e) Did the accountants think that the financial statements presented a true and fair view of the financial situation of the company? (f) Did the company comply with international accounting standards?

ENDNOTES

1. Nestlé, *Annual Report*, 1996.
2. International Accounting Standards Committee, *Framework for the Preparation and Presentation of Financial Statements* (London: IASC, 1996), para. 12.
3. Ibid., paras. 24–46.
4. Quaker Oats Company, *Annual Report*, 1992.
5. Ibid.
6. International Accounting Standard, IAS1, *Presentation of Financial Statements* (London: IASC, revised August 1997), para. 97.
7. International Accounting Standard, IAS14, *Segment Reporting* (London: IASC, revised August 1997).
8. Schering, *Annual Report*, 1995.
9. Toys "R" Us, Inc., *Annual Report*, 1987.
10. BMW, *Annual Report*, 1995; Volvo, *Annual Report*, 1995.

Part Two

The Measurement of Financial Position and Performance: Key Reporting Issues

*A*ccounting, as you have seen, is an information system that measures, processes, and communicates information for decision-making purposes. **Part One** presented the principles and practices of the basic accounting system and financial statements. **Part Two** considers each of the major types of assets, liabilities, and shareholders' equity, with special attention to the effect of their measurement on financial position and performance, to their presentation in the financial statements, and to their importance to the management of the business enterprise.

Chapter 6   Short-Term Liquid Assets focuses on the management of and accounting for four types of short-term assets: cash and cash equivalents, current investments, accounts receivable, and notes receivable.

Chapter 7   Inventories presents a detailed discussion of the management and prices of inventories.

Chapter 8   Long-Term Assets explores the management, acquisition, and disposal of property, plant, equipment, natural resources, and intangible assets, as well as the concepts and methods of depreciation, depletion, and amortisation.

Chapter 9   Liabilities presents the concepts and methods associated with both current and long-term liabilities of corporations, paying special attention to accounting for bond liabilities. It also deals with other long-term liabilities, such as mortgages, instalment notes, and postretirement benefits.

Chapter 10   Share Capital illustrates accounting for the share capital section of shareholders' equity.

Chapter 11   Profit and Retained Earnings focuses on accounting for retained earnings and a number of other transactions that affect the income statement and shareholders' equity.

Chapter 6

SHORT-TERM
LIQUID ASSETS

LEARNING OBJECTIVES

1. Identify and explain the management issues related to short-term liquid assets.
2. Explain cash and cash equivalents and prepare a bank reconciliation.
3. Account for current investments.
4. Define *accounts receivable* and apply the allowance method of accounting for uncollectible accounts, using both the percentage of net sales method and the accounts receivable ageing method.
5. Define and describe a *promissory note*, and make calculations and journal entries involving promissory notes.

SUPPLEMENTAL OBJECTIVE

6. Account for credit card transactions.

DECISION POINT

SONY

A company must use its assets to maximise profit earned while maintaining liquidity. Sony, based in Japan, is one of the world's leading companies in consumer electronics, in industrial electronics, and in music and pictures. Sony manages around 1,375 billion yen in short-term liquid assets. Short-term liquid assets are financial assets that arise from cash transactions, the investment of cash, and the extension of credit. What is the composition of these assets, and why are they important to Sony's management?

As reported on the balance sheet in the company's 1996 annual report, short-term liquid assets (in millions of yen) were:[1]

Cash and Cash Equivalents	*459,339*
Time Deposits	*32,605*
Notes and Accounts Receivable,	
Net Allowances of 68,763	*854,803*
Marketable Securities	*28,420*
Total Short-Term Liquid Assets	*1,375,167*

These assets, which make up about 27 per cent of Sony's total assets, are crucial to the company's strategy for meeting its goals. The asset management methods employed at Sony ensure that these assets remain liquid and usable for operations.

A commonly used ratio for measuring the adequacy of short-term liquid assets is the quick ratio. It is the ratio of short-term liquid assets (defined as quick assets) to current liabilities. Since Sony's current liabilities are 1,707,600 (in millions of yen), its quick ratio is .8, calculated as follows:

$$\text{Quick ratio} = \frac{\text{quick assets}}{\text{current liabilities}} = \frac{1,375,167}{1,707,600} = .8$$

It is also important to look at the trends for a particular company to see if the ratio is improving or deteriorating. When good cash management is practised, a company can get by with fewer funds tied up in quick assets relative to current liabilities. This chapter emphasises management of, and accounting for, short-term liquid assets to achieve the objective of liquidity.

OBJECTIVE 1

Identify and explain the management issues related to short-term liquid assets

MANAGEMENT ISSUES RELATED TO SHORT-TERM LIQUID ASSETS

The management of short-term liquid assets is critical to the goal of providing adequate liquidity. In dealing with short-term liquid assets, management must address three key issues: managing cash needs during seasonal cycles, setting credit policies, and financing receivables.

Managing Cash Needs during Seasonal Cycles

Most companies experience seasonal cycles of business activity during the year. These cycles involve some periods when sales are weak and other periods when sales are strong. There are also periods when expenditures are greater and when expenditures are smaller. In some companies, such as toy companies, textbook publishers, amuse-

185

FIGURE 6-1 *Seasonal Cycles and Cash Requirements for a Home Improvement Company*

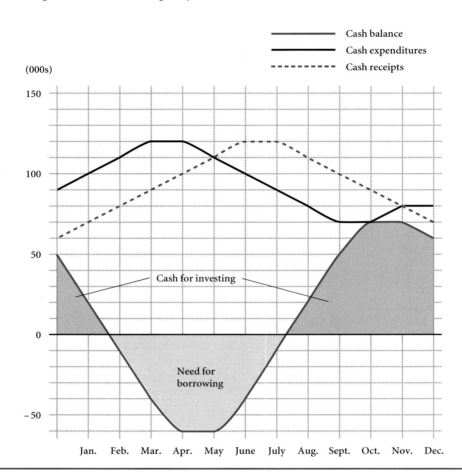

ment parks, construction companies, and sports equipment companies, these cycles are dramatic, but all companies experience them to some degree.

Seasonal cycles require careful planning of cash inflows, outflows, borrowing, and investing. For example, Figure 6-1 might represent the seasonal cycles for a home improvement or do-it-yourself (D-I-Y) company in Europe. As you can see, cash receipts from sales are highest in May through to September because this is the period when most people make home improvements. Sales are relatively low in other months. On the other hand, cash expenditures are highest in November through to April as the company builds up inventory for selling during the peak times. During the later months, the company has excess cash available that it needs to invest in a way that will enable it to earn a return while still giving it access to the cash when it is needed. During February through to July, the company needs to plan for short-term borrowing to tide it over until cash receipts pick up later in the year. The discussion of accounting for cash, cash equivalents, and current investments in this chapter is directly related to managing for the seasonal cycles of a business.

Setting Credit Policies

Companies that sell on credit do so to be competitive and to increase sales. In setting credit terms, the management of these companies must keep in mind both the terms their competitors are offering and the needs of their customers. Obviously, companies that sell on credit want customers who will pay the debts they incur. Therefore, most companies develop control procedures to increase the likelihood of selling only to customers who will pay when they are supposed to. As a result, most companies have a credit department. This department's responsibilities include the examination of each person or company that applies for credit and the approval or rejection of a credit sale to that customer. Typically, the credit department will ask for information on the customer's financial resources and debts. It may also check personal references and established credit bureaus, which may provide additional information about the customer. On the basis of this information, the credit department will decide whether to extend credit to the customer.

Two common measures of the effect of a company's credit policies are **receivable turnover** and **average days' sales uncollected**. The receivable turnover reflects the relative size of a company's accounts receivable and the success of its credit and collection policies. Receivable turnover may also be affected by external factors, such as seasonal conditions and interest rates. It shows how many times, on average, the receivables were turned into cash during the accounting period. The average days' sales uncollected is a related measure that shows, on average, how long it takes to collect accounts receivable.

Turnover ratios usually consist of one balance sheet account and one income statement account. The receivable turnover is calculated by dividing net sales by average net accounts receivable. Theoretically, the numerator should be net credit sales, but the amount of net credit sales is rarely made available in public reports, so total net sales is used. American Greetings is one of the largest producers of greeting cards in the United States. The company's net sales in 1993 were $1,671,692,000, and its net trade accounts receivable in 1992 and 1993 were $264,125,000 and $276,932,000, respectively.[2] Its receivable turnover is calculated as follows:

$$\text{Receivable turnover} = \frac{\text{net sales}}{\text{average net accounts receivable}}$$

$$= \frac{\$1,671,692,000}{(\$264,125,000 + \$276,932,000)/2}$$

$$= \frac{\$1,671,692,000}{\$270,528,500} = 6.2 \text{ times}$$

To find the average days' sales uncollected, the number of days in a year is divided by the receivable turnover, as follows:

$$\text{Average days' sales uncollected} = \frac{365 \text{ days}}{\text{receivable turnover}} = \frac{365 \text{ days}}{6.2} = 58.9 \text{ days}$$

American Greetings turns its receivables 6.2 times a year, or an average of every 58.9 days. While this is a longer period than for many companies, it is not unusual for greeting card companies because their credit terms allow retail outlets to receive and sell cards at various holidays before paying for them. This example demonstrates the need to interpret ratios in light of the specific industry's practice. The receivable turnover ratio varies from industry to industry. Grocery stores, for example, have a high turnover because this type of business has few receivables. Manufacturers' turnover is lower because companies engaged in manufacturing tend to have longer credit terms.

Financing Receivables

Financial flexibility is important to most companies. Companies that have significant amounts of assets tied up in accounts receivable may be unwilling or unable to wait until the receivables are collected to receive the cash they represent. Many companies have set up finance companies to help their customers finance the purchase of their products. For example, Ford of the United States, BMW of Germany, and Toyota of Japan have their own finance company. Some companies borrow funds by pledging their accounts receivable as collateral. If a company does not pay back its loan, the lender can take the collateral, in this case the accounts receivable, and convert it to cash to satisfy the loan.

Companies can also raise funds by selling or transferring accounts receivable to another entity, called a **factor.** This sale or transfer of accounts receivable, called **factoring,** can be done with or without recourse. *Without recourse* means that the factor who buys the accounts receivable bears any losses from uncollectible accounts. A company's acceptance of credit cards like VISA, MasterCard, or American Express is an example of factoring without recourse because the credit card issuers accept the risk of nonpayment.

With recourse means that the seller of the receivables is liable to the purchaser if the receivable is not collected. The factor, of course, charges a fee for its service. The fee for sales with recourse is usually about 1 per cent of the accounts receivable. The fee is higher for sales without recourse because the factor's risk is greater. In accounting terminology, the seller of the receivables with recourse is said to be contingently liable. A **contingent liability** is a potential liability that can develop into a real liability if a possible subsequent event occurs. In this case, the subsequent event would be nonpayment of the receivable by the customer.

Another method of financing receivables is through the **discounting,** or selling, of promissory notes held as notes receivable. Selling notes receivable is called discounting because the bank deducts the interest from the maturity value of the note to determine the proceeds. The holder of the note (usually the payee) endorses the note and delivers it to the bank. The bank expects to collect the maturity value of the note (principal plus interest) on the maturity date but also has recourse against the endorser or seller of the note. If the maker fails to pay, the endorser is liable to the bank for payment. The endorser has a contingent liability in the amount of the discounted notes that must be disclosed in the notes to the financial statements.

| OBJECTIVE 2 | CASH AND CASH EQUIVALENTS |

Explain cash and cash equivalents and prepare a bank reconciliation

The annual report of Nestlé (see appendix) refers to *cash and cash equivalents*. Of these two terms, *cash* is the easier to understand. It is the most liquid of all assets and the most readily available to pay debts. We discussed the control of cash receipts and cash payments in the chapter on the trading income statement and internal control, but we did not deal with the content of the Cash account on the balance sheet. **Cash** normally consists of coin and currency available, cheques and money orders from customers, and deposits in bank cheque accounts that are available on demand. Cash may also include a compensating balance, an amount that is not entirely free to be spent. A **compensating balance** is a minimum amount that a bank requires a company to keep in its bank account as part of a credit-granting arrangement. Such an arrangement restricts cash and may reduce a company's liquidity.

The term *cash equivalents* is a little harder to understand. At times a company may find that it has more cash available than it needs to pay current obligations. This excess cash should not remain idle, especially during periods of high interest rates. Thus, management may periodically invest the idle funds in time deposits or certificates of deposit at banks and other financial institutions, in government securities, or in other securities. These actions are rightfully called investments. However, if these investments are short-term, highly liquid investments that, for example, have a term of less than ninety days when they are purchased, they are called **cash equivalents** because the funds revert to cash so quickly that they are regarded as cash on the balance sheet.[3]

Most companies need to keep some currency and coins available. Currency and coins are needed for cash registers and for paying expenses that are impractical to pay by cheque. A company may need to advance cash to sales representatives for travel expenses, to divisions to cover their payrolls, and to individual employees to cash their paycheques. One way to control a cash fund or cash advances is through the use of an **imprest system**. A common form of imprest system is a **petty cash fund**, which is established at a fixed amount. Each cash payment from the fund is documented by a receipt. Then the fund is periodically reimbursed, based on the documented expenditures, for the exact amount necessary to restore its original cash balance. The person responsible for the petty cash fund must always be able to account for its contents by having cash and receipts whose total equals the originally fixed amount.

Banking and Electronic Funds Transfer

Banks greatly help businesses to control both cash receipts and cash disbursements. Banks serve as safe depositories for cash, negotiable instruments, and other valuable business documents, such as shares and bonds. The cheque accounts that banks provide improve control by minimising the amount of currency a company needs to keep available and by supplying permanent records of all cash payments. Banks can also serve as agents in a variety of transactions, such as the collection and payment of certain kinds of debts and the exchange of foreign currencies.

Many companies commonly conduct transactions through a means of electronic communication called **electronic funds transfer** (EFT). Instead of writing cheques to pay for purchases or to repay loans, cash is transferred electronically from one company's bank to another company's bank. The actual cash, of course, is not transferred. For the banks, an electronic transfer is simply a bookkeeping entry.

In serving customers, banks may also offer automated teller machines (ATMs) for making deposits, withdrawing cash, transferring funds among accounts, and paying bills. Large consumer banks like Citibank in the United States and Barclays in the United Kingdom will process thousands of ATM transactions each week. Many banks also provide customers with the option of paying bills over the telephone and with *debit cards*. When a customer makes a retail purchase using a debit card, the amount of the purchase is deducted directly from the buyer's bank account. The bank usually documents debit card transactions for the retailer, but the retailer must develop new internal controls to ensure that the transactions are recorded properly and that unauthorised transfers are not permitted.

Preparing a Bank Reconciliation

Once a month, the bank sends each depositor a statement. The **bank statement** shows the balance at the beginning of the month, the deposits, the cheques paid, other deb-

BUSINESS BULLETIN   International Practice

Electronic funds transfer has been an important facilitator of international business. Caterpillar of the United States, for example, sells earth-moving equipment throughout the world. To ensure payment and reduce the funds tied up in receivables, Caterpillar uses electronic funds transfer. Under pre-arranged terms, funds are electronically transferred from the customers' accounts to Caterpillar's account at the time orders are shipped. Worldwide, trillions of dollars in business transactions are electronically transferred every day.

FIGURE 6-2   *Bank Statement*

Statement of Account with
THE NATIONAL BANK
XXXXX XXXX

Martin Maintenance Company
XXXX XXXXX XXXXXX
XXXXX XXXX XXXXX

Cheque Acct No
8030-647-4
Period covered
Sept.30-Oct.31,20xx

Previous Balance	Cheques/Debits—No.	Deposits/Credits—No.	S.C.	Current Balance
2,645.78	4,319.33 --15	5,157.12 --7	12.50	3,471.07

CHEQUES/DEBITS			DEPOSITS/CREDITS		DAILY BALANCES	
Posting Date	Check No.	Amount	Posting Date	Amount	Date	Amount
					09/30	2,645.78
10/01	564	100.00	10/01	586.00	10/01	2,881.78
10/01	565	250.00	10/05	1,500.00	10/04	2,825.60
10/04	567	56.18	10/06	300.00	10/05	3,900.46
10/05	566	425.14	10/16	1,845.50	10/06	4,183.34
10/06	568	17.12	10/21	600.00	10/12	2,242.34
10/12	569	1,705.80	10/24	300.00CM	10/16	3,687.84
10/12	570	235.20	10/31	25.62IN	10/17	3,589.09
10/16	571	400.00			10/21	4,189.09
10/17	572	29.75			10/24	3,745.59
10/17	573	69.00			10/25	3,586.09
10/24	574	738.50			10/28	3,457.95
10/24		5.00DM			10/31	3,471.07
10/25	575	7.50				
10/25	577	152.00				
10/28		128.14NSF				
10/31		12.50SC				

Explanation of Symbols:

CM – Credit Memo
DM – Debit Memo
NSF – Non-Sufficient Funds

SC – Service Charge
EC – Error Correction
OD – Overdraft
IN – Interest on Average Balance

The last amount
in this column
is your balance.

Please examine; if no errors are reported within ten (10) days, the account will be considered to be correct.

its and credits during the month, and the balance at the end of the month. A bank statement is illustrated in Figure 6-2.

Rarely will the balance of a company's Cash account exactly equal the cash balance shown on the bank statement. Certain transactions shown in the company's records may not have been recorded by the bank, and certain bank transactions may not appear in the company's records. Therefore, a necessary step in internal control is to prove both the balance shown on the bank statement and the balance of Cash in the accounting records. A **bank reconciliation** is the process of accounting for the differences between the balance appearing on the bank statement and the balance of Cash according to the company's records. This process involves making additions to and subtractions from both balances to arrive at the adjusted cash balance.

The most common examples of transactions shown in the company's records but not entered in the bank's records are the following:

1. **Outstanding cheques**   These are cheques that have been issued and recorded by the company, but do not yet appear on the bank statement.
2. **Deposits in transit**   These are deposits that were mailed or taken to the bank but were not received in time to be recorded on the bank statement.

Transactions that may appear on the bank statement but that have not been recorded by the company include the following:

1. **Service Charges (SC)**   Banks often charge a fee, or service charge, for the use of a cheque account. Many banks base the service charge on a number of factors, such as the average balance of the account during the month or the number of cheques drawn.
2. **NSF (Non-Sufficient Funds) cheques**   An NSF cheque is a cheque deposited by the company that is not paid when the company's bank presents it to the maker's bank. The bank charges the company's account and returns the cheque so that the company can try to collect the amount due. If the bank has deducted the NSF cheque from the bank statement but the company has not deducted it from its book balance, an adjustment must be made in the bank reconciliation. The depositor usually reclassifies the NSF cheque from Cash to Accounts Receivable because the company must now collect from the person or company that wrote the cheque.
3. **Interest income**   It is very common for banks to pay interest on a company's average balance. These accounts are sometimes called money market accounts but can take other forms. Such interest is reported on the bank statement.
4. **Miscellaneous charges and credits**   Banks also charge for other services, such as collection and payment of promissory notes, stopping payment on cheques, and printing cheques. The bank notifies the depositor of each deduction by including a debit memorandum with the monthly statement. A bank will sometimes serve as an agent in collecting on promissory notes for the depositor. In such a case, a credit memorandum will be included.

An error by either the bank or the depositor will, of course, require immediate correction.

Steps in Reconciling the Bank Balance

The steps to be followed in performing a bank reconciliation are as follows:

1. Compare the deposits listed on the bank statement with deposits shown in the accounting records. Any deposits in transit should be added to the bank balance. (Immediately investigate any deposits in transit from the previous month that are still not listed on the bank statement.)
2. Trace paid cheques to the bank statement, making sure that all cheques have been issued by the company and properly charged to the company's account.
3. List cheques issued but not on the bank statement. (Be sure to include any cheques still outstanding from prior months; investigate any cheques outstanding for more than a few months.) Deduct outstanding cheques from the bank balance.
4. Add to the balance per books any interest earned or credit memoranda issued by the bank, such as collection of a promissory note, that are not yet recorded on the company's books.
5. Deduct from the balance per books any debit memoranda issued by the bank, such as NSF cheques and service charges, not yet recorded on the company's records.
6. Make sure the adjusted balance per books and per bank are in agreement.
7. Make journal entries for any items on the bank statement that have not been recorded in the company's books.

Illustration of a Bank Reconciliation

The October bank statement for Martin Maintenance Company, as shown in Figure 6-2, indicates a balance on October 31 of 3,471.07. We shall assume that in its records, Martin Maintenance Company has a cash balance on October 31 of 2,405.91. The purpose of a bank reconciliation is to identify the items that make up the difference between these amounts and to determine the correct cash balance. The bank reconciliation for Martin Maintenance Company is given in Exhibit 6-1. The numbered items in the exhibit refer to the following:

1. A deposit in the amount of 276.00 was mailed to the bank on October 31 and has not been recorded by the bank.
2. Five cheques issued in October or prior months have not yet been paid by the bank, as follows:

Cheque No.	Date	Amount
551	Sept. 14	150.00
576	Oct. 30	40.68
578	Oct. 31	500.00
579	Oct. 31	370.00
580	Oct. 31	130.50

EXHIBIT 6-1 *Bank Reconciliation*

Martin Maintenance Company
Bank Reconciliation
October 31, 20xx

Balance per bank, October 31		3,471.07
① Add deposit of October 31 in transit		276.00
		3,747.07
② Less outstanding cheques:		
No. 551	150.00	
No. 576	40.68	
No. 578	500.00	
No. 579	370.00	
No. 580	130.50	1,191.18
Adjusted bank balance, October 31		**2,555.89** ←
Balance per books, October 31		2,405.91
Add:		
④ Notes receivable collected by bank	280.00	
Interest income on note	20.00	
⑦ Interest income	25.62	325.62
		2,731.53
Less:		
③ Overstatement of deposit of October 6	30.00	
④ Collection fee	5.00	
⑤ NSF cheque of Arthur Clubb	128.14	
⑥ Service charge	12.50	175.64
Adjusted book balance, October 31		**2,555.89** ←

Note: The circled numbers refer to the items listed in the text.

3. The deposit for cash sales of October 6 was incorrectly recorded in Martin Maintenance Company's records as 330.00. The bank correctly recorded the deposit as 300.00.

4. Among the paid cheques was a credit memorandum showing that the bank had collected a promissory note from A. Jacobs in the amount of 280.00, plus 20.00 in interest on the note. A debit memorandum was also enclosed for the 5.00 collection fee. No entry had been made on Martin Maintenance Company's records.

5. Also returned with the bank statement was an NSF cheque for 128.14. This cheque had been received from a customer named Arthur Clubb. The NSF cheque from Clubb was not reflected in the company's accounting records.

6. A debit memorandum was enclosed for the regular monthly service charge of 12.50. This charge was not yet recorded by Martin Maintenance Company.

7. Interest earned by the company on the average balance was reported as 25.62.

Note in Exhibit 6-1 that, starting from their separate balances, both the bank and book amounts are adjusted to the amount of 2,555.89. This adjusted balance is the amount of cash owned by the company on October 31 and thus is the amount that should appear on its October 31 balance sheet.

Recording Transactions after Reconciliation

The adjusted balance of cash differs from both the bank statement and Martin Maintenance Company's records. The bank balance will automatically become correct when outstanding cheques are presented for payment and the deposit in transit is received and recorded by the bank. Entries must be made, however, for the transactions necessary to correct the book balance. All the items reported by the bank but not yet recorded by the company must be recorded in the general journal by means of the following entries:

Oct. 31	Cash	300.00	
	Notes Receivable		280.00
	Interest Income		20.00
	Note receivable of 280.00 and interest of 20.00 collected by bank from A. Jacobs		
31	Cash	25.62	
	Interest Income		25.62
	Interest on average bank account balance		
31	Sales	30.00	
	Cash		30.00
	Correction of error in recording a 300.00 deposit as 330.00		
31	Accounts Receivable	128.14	
	Cash		128.14
	NSF cheque of Arthur Clubb returned by bank		
31	Bank Service Charges Expense	17.50	
	Cash		17.50
	Bank service charge (12.50) and collection fee (5.00) for October		

It is acceptable to record these entries in one or two compound entries to save time and space, as follows:

Oct. 31	Cash	149.98	
	Sales	30.00	
	Accounts Receivable	128.14	
	Bank Service Charges Expense	17.50	
	Notes Receivable		280.00
	Interest Income		45.62
	To record items from bank reconciliation		

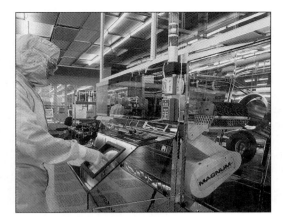

DECISION POINT
CAMPBELL SOUP

During the 1980s, Campbell Soup of the United States was drowning in paperwork. The company had forty locations that processed accounts payable and weekly payroll, which meant that eighty cash accounts had to be maintained and the daily transactions of each tracked manually. Each month, cheques were written to settle more than 1,300 transactions among divisions of the company, and any differences in cash records and cash available in thirty bank accounts had to be explained. What could Campbell Soup do to become more efficient and provide better information to management?

The company developed a system that concentrates its cash management activities in two personal computer networks that perform cash management, reporting, and information management. The system is integrated, and the flow of information is automatic. Cash and general ledger transactions are automatically generated, and a system was developed so that balances among divisions could be netted and cheques would not have to be written to settle accounts. Because banking fees and balances are now closely monitored, the fees the company paid to banks dropped from $5.0 million per year to less than $1.0 million in 1991. And because duplication of effort has been reduced, the staff has been cut in half, which has led to savings of more than $400,000 per year.[4]

OBJECTIVE 3

Account for current investments

CURRENT INVESTMENTS

When investments are readily realisable and are intended to be held for not more than one year, they are called **current investments**.[5] Investments that are intended to be held for more than one year are called long-term investments.

As discussed in the chapter on financial reporting and financial statement analysis, long-term investments are classified in an investments section of the balance sheet, not in the current assets section. Although these investments may be just as marketable as current assets, management intends to hold them for an indefinite period of time.

Marketable Securities

Current investments often take the form of securities, including debt and equity securities. Where these are intended to be held for not more than one year they are classified as current assets on the balance sheet. If there is an active market for these securities they are termed **marketable securities**. These securities may be valued, according to the International Accounting Standards Committee, at either market value or the lower of cost and market value. If the lower of cost and market value basis is used, then the relevant value should be determined either on an aggregate portfolio basis or on an individual investment basis. Although a market value basis, with the recognition of unrealised gains as well as losses, is used in some countries, notably the United States, most countries, including France, Germany, Japan, the Netherlands, Sweden, and the United Kingdom, follow the more prudent lower of cost and market value basis of recognising unrealised losses but not unrealised gains.

For example, assume that Jingles Corporation purchases 10,000 shares of Bells Corporation for 700,000 (70 per share) and 5,000 shares of Whistles Corporation for 300,000 (60 per share) on October 25, 20x1. The purchase is made for trading purposes; that is, management intends to make a gain by holding the shares only for a short period. The entry to record the investment at cost is as follows:

Market value is recognised as a valid basis for valuing current investments in most countries, but usually only where this value is lower than historical cost, thus reflecting a prudent approach to measurement. In the U.S., however, there has been a recent move to value consistently at market value any marketable securities held for trading purposes and to record gains and losses, both realised and unrealised, in the income statement.

20x1
Oct. 25   Current Investments   1,000,000
              Cash   1,000,000
                  Investment in shares for trading
                  700,000 + 300,000 = 1,000,000

Assume that at the end of the year Bells's share price has decreased to 60 per share and Whistles's has risen to 64 per share. Using the portfolio approach, the securities may now be valued at 920,000, as shown below:

Security	Cost	Market Value
Bells (10,000 shares)	700,000	600,000
Whistles (5,000 shares)	300,000	320,000
Totals	1,000,000	920,000

Since the current market value of the portfolio is 80,000 less than the original cost of 1,000,000, an adjusting entry is needed, as follows:

20x1
Dec. 31   Unrealised Loss on Investments   80,000
              Allowance to Adjust Current Investments to Market   80,000
                  Recognition of unrealised loss on portfolio

The unrealised loss will appear on the income statement as a reduction in profit. (The loss is unrealised because the securities have not been sold.) The Allowance to Adjust Current Investments to Market account appears on the balance sheet as a contra-asset, as follows:

Current Investments (at cost)	1,000,000
Less Allowance to Adjust Current Investments to Market	80,000
Current Investments (at market)	920,000

or more simply,

Current Investments (at market value, cost is 1,000,000)	920,000

If Jingles sells its 5,000 shares of Whistles for 70 per share on March 2, 20x2, a realised gain on securities is recorded as follows:

20x2
Mar. 2   Cash   350,000
             Current Investments   300,000
             Realised Gain on Investments   50,000
                 Sale of 5,000 shares of Whistles for 70 per share;
                 cost was 60 per share

The realised gain will appear on the income statement. Note that the realised gain is unaffected by the adjustment for the unrealised loss at the end of 20x1. The two transactions are treated independently. If the shares had been sold for less than cost, a realised loss on investments would have been recorded. Realised losses also appear on the income statement.

Let's now assume that during 20x2 Jingles buys 2,000 shares of Drums Corporation at 64 per share and has no transactions involving Bells. Also, assume that by December 31, 20x2, the price of Bells's shares has risen to 75 per share, or 5 per share more than the original cost, and that Drums's share price has fallen to 58, or 6 less than the original cost. The portfolio now can be analysed as follows:

Security	Cost	Market Value
Bells (10,000 shares)	700,000	750,000
Drums (2,000 shares)	128,000	116,000
Totals	828,000	866,000

The market value of the portfolio now exceeds the cost by 38,000 (866,000 − 828,000). In countries where securities can be stated at market value, this amount represents the targeted ending balance for the Allowance to Adjust Current Investments to Market account. Recall that at the end of 20x1, this account had a credit balance of 80,000, meaning that the market value of the portfolio was less than the cost. This account has no entries during 20x2 and thus retains its balance until adjusting entries are made at the end of the year. The adjustment for 20x2 must be 118,000—enough to result in a debit balance in this account of 38,000:

20x2
Dec. 31   Allowance to Adjust Current
                  Investments to Market   118,000
                      Unrealised Gain on Investments   118,000
                      Recognition of unrealised gain on portfolio
                      80,000 + 38,000 = 118,000

The 20x2 ending balance of the allowance account may be determined this way:

Allowance to Adjust Current Investments to Market

Dec. 31, 20x2 adj.	118,000	Dec. 31, 20x1 bal.	80,000
Dec. 31, 20x2 bal.	38,000		

The balance sheet presentation of current investments at market value is as follows:

Current Investments (at cost)	828,000
Allowance to Adjust Current Investments to Market	38,000
Current Investments (at market)	866,000

or, more simply,

Current Investments (at market value, cost is 828,000)	866,000

Dividend and Interest Income

Dividend and interest income for current investments are shown as income in the Other Income and Expenses section of the income statement.

OBJECTIVE 4

Define accounts receivable *and apply the allowance method of accounting for uncollectible accounts, using both the percentage of net sales method and the accounts receivable ageing method*

ACCOUNTS RECEIVABLE

The other major types of short-term liquid assets are accounts receivable and notes receivable. Both are the result of credit sales being made to customers. Every field of retail trade has expanded by allowing customers to make payments a month or more after the date of sale. Credit has also expanded in the wholesale and manufacturing industries.

Accounts receivable are short-term liquid assets that arise from sales on credit to customers by wholesalers or retailers. This type of credit is often called **trade credit**. Terms on trade credit usually range from five to sixty days, depending on industry practice. For some companies that sell to consumers, **instalment accounts receivable** constitute a significant portion of accounts receivable. Instalment accounts receivable arise from the sale of goods on terms that allow the buyer to make a series of time payments. Department stores, appliance stores, furniture stores, used car companies, and other retail businesses often offer instalment credit. Although the payment period may be twenty-four months or more, instalment accounts receivable are classified as current assets if such credit policies are customary in the industry. The special accounting rules that apply to some instalment sales are usually deferred until a more advanced course.

On the balance sheet, the title Accounts Receivable is reserved for sales made to regular customers in the ordinary course of business. If loans or sales that do not fall into this category are made to employees, officers of the corporation, or owners, they should be shown separately with an asset title such as Receivables from Employees.

Normally, individual customer accounts receivable have debit balances, but sometimes customers overpay their accounts by mistake or in anticipation of future purchases. When individual customer accounts show credit balances, the total of these credits should be shown on the balance sheet as a current liability because the amounts must be refunded if future sales are not made to those customers.

The Accounts Receivable Subsidiary Ledger

In previous chapters, a single Accounts Receivable account has been used. However, this single account does not readily tell how much each customer bought and paid for or how much each customer owes. In practice, all companies that sell to customers on credit keep an individual accounts receivable record for each customer. If the company has 6,000 credit customers, there are 6,000 accounts receivable. To include all these accounts with the other assets, liabilities, and shareholders' equity accounts would make the ledger very bulky. Consequently, most companies take the individual customers' accounts out of the general ledger, which contains the financial statement accounts, and place them in a separate ledger called a **subsidiary ledger**. A subsidiary ledger consists of accounts whose totals tie in with the balance of an account in the general ledger. The customers' accounts are filed alphabetically or by account number in the accounts receivable subsidiary ledger.

When a company puts its individual customers' accounts in an accounts receivable ledger, their balance is maintained in an Accounts Receivable account in the general ledger. This Accounts Receivable account in the general ledger is said to control the subsidiary ledger and is called a **controlling**, or **control, account**. It is a controlling account in the sense that its balance should equal the total of the individual account balances in the subsidiary ledger, as shown in Figure 6-3. When the amounts in the

FIGURE 6-3 *Relationship of Subsidiary Accounts to the Controlling Account*

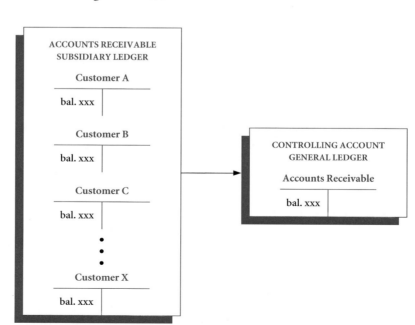

subsidiary ledger and the controlling account do not match, the accountant knows that there is an error and can find and correct it.

Most companies, as you will see, use an accounts payable subsidiary ledger as well. It is possible to use a subsidiary ledger for almost any account in the general ledger for which management wants specific information for individual items, such as Notes Receivable, Current Investments, and Equipment.

Uncollectible Accounts

Regardless of how thorough and efficient its credit control system is, a company will always have some customers who cannot or will not pay. The accounts owed by such customers are called **uncollectible accounts**, or *bad debts*, and are a loss or an expense of selling on credit. Why does a company sell on credit if it expects that some of its accounts will not be paid? The answer is that the company expects to sell much more than it would if it did not sell on credit, thereby increasing its earnings.

Uncollectible Accounts and the Allowance Method

Under the **allowance method** of accounting for uncollectible accounts, bad debt losses are matched against the sales they help to produce. As noted earlier, when management extends credit to increase sales, it knows it will incur some losses from uncollectible accounts. These losses are expenses that occur at the time sales on credit are made and should be matched to the revenues they help to generate. Of course, at the time the sales are made, management cannot identify which customers will not pay their debts or predict the exact amount of money that will be lost. Therefore, to observe the matching rule, losses from uncollectible accounts must be estimated, and this estimate becomes an expense in the accounting year the sales are made.

For example, let us assume that Cottage Sales Company made most of its sales on credit during its first year of operation. At the end of the year, accounts receivable amounted to 100,000. On this date, management reviewed the collectible status of the accounts receivable. Approximately 6,000 of the 100,000 of accounts receivable were estimated to be uncollectible. Therefore, the uncollectible accounts expense for the first year of operation was estimated to be 6,000. The following adjusting entry would be made on December 31 of that year:

Dec. 31	Uncollectible Accounts Expense	6,000	
	Allowance for Uncollectible Accounts		6,000
	To record the estimated uncollectible accounts		
	expense for the year 20x1		

Uncollectible Accounts Expense appears on the income statement as an operating expense. **Allowance for Uncollectible Accounts** appears on the balance sheet as a contra-asset account that is deducted from Accounts Receivable.[6] It reduces the accounts receivable to the amount expected to be realised, or collected in cash, as follows:

Current Assets		
Cash		10,000
Current Investments		15,000
Accounts Receivable	100,000	
Less Allowance for Uncollectible Accounts	6,000	94,000
Inventory		56,000
Total Current Assets		175,000

Accounts receivable may also be shown on the balance sheet as follows:

Accounts Receivable (net of allowance for uncollectible	
accounts of 6,000)	94,000

Or they may be shown at "net" with the amount of the allowance for uncollectible accounts identified in a note to the financial statements. The estimated uncollectible amount cannot be credited to the account of any particular customer. Nor can it be credited to the Accounts Receivable controlling account because that would cause the controlling account to be out of balance with the total customers' accounts in the subsidiary ledger. The estimated uncollectible amount is therefore credited to a separate contra-asset account—Allowance for Uncollectible Accounts.

The allowance account will often have other titles, such as Allowance for Doubtful Accounts or Allowance for Bad Debts. Bad Debts Expense is another title often used for Uncollectible Accounts Expense.

Estimating Uncollectible Accounts Expense

As noted, it is necessary to estimate the expense to cover the expected losses for the year. Of course, estimates can vary widely. If management takes an optimistic view and projects a small loss from uncollectible accounts, the resulting net accounts receivable will be larger than if management takes a pessimistic view. The net profit will also be larger under the optimistic view because the estimated expense will be smaller. The company's accountant makes an estimate based on past experience and current economic conditions. For example, losses from uncollectible accounts are normally expected to be greater in a recession than during a period of economic growth. The final decision, made by management, of what the expense should be will depend on objective information, such as the accountant's analyses, and on certain qualitative factors, such as how investors, bankers, lenders, and others may view the performance of the company. Regardless of the qualitative considerations, the estimated losses from uncollectible accounts should be realistic.

The accountant may choose from two common methods for estimating uncollectible accounts expense for an accounting period: the percentage of net sales method and the accounts receivable ageing method.

Percentage of Net Sales Method

The **percentage of net sales method** asks the question, How much of this year's net sales will not be collected? The answer determines the amount of uncollectible accounts expense for the year.

For example, the following balances represent the ending figures for Hassel Company for the year 20x4:

	Sales				Sales Returns and Allowances	
		Dec. 31	645,000	Dec. 31	40,000	

	Sales Discounts				Allowance for Uncollectible Accounts	
Dec. 31	5,000				Dec. 31	3,600

The actual losses from uncollectible accounts for the past three years have been as follows:

Year	Net Sales	Losses from Uncollectible Accounts	Percentage
20x1	520,000	10,200	1.96
20x2	595,000	13,900	2.34
20x3	585,000	9,900	1.69
Total	1,700,000	34,000	2.00

In many businesses, net sales is understood to approximate net credit sales. If there are substantial cash sales, then net credit sales should be used. Management believes that uncollectible accounts will continue to average about 2 per cent of net sales. The uncollectible accounts expense for the year 20x4 is therefore estimated to be

$$.02 \times (645,000 - 40,000 - 5,000) = .02 \times 600,000 = 12,000$$

The entry to record this estimate is

Dec. 31	Uncollectible Accounts Expense	12,000	
	Allowance for Uncollectible Accounts		12,000
	To record uncollectible accounts expense at 2 per cent of 600,000 net sales		

After the above entry is posted, Allowance for Uncollectible Accounts will have a balance of 15,600, as follows:

Allowance for Uncollectible Accounts

	Dec. 31	3,600
	Dec. 31 adjustment	12,000
	Dec. 31 balance	15,600

The balance consists of the 12,000 estimated uncollectible accounts receivable from 20x4 sales and the 3,600 estimated uncollectible accounts receivable from previous years. The 3,600 is the result of previous adjustments and writeoffs. The amount was not written off in previous years.

Accounts Receivable Ageing Method

In countries where the taxation authorities are a major influence on accounting practice, such as in France, Germany, Italy, Spain, and Portugal, specific rules prescribe the basis for making allowances for uncollectible accounts or bad debts. These rules are usually based on the ageing method.

The **accounts receivable ageing method** asks the question, How much of the year-end balance of accounts receivable will not be collected? Under this method, the year-end balance of Allowance for Uncollectible Accounts is determined directly by an analysis of accounts receivable. The difference between the amount determined to be uncollectible and the actual balance of Allowance for Uncollectible Accounts is the expense for the year. In theory, this method should produce the same result as the percentage of net sales method, but in practice it rarely does.

The **ageing of accounts receivable** is the process of listing each accounts receivable customer according to the due date of the account. If the customer's account is past due, there is a possibility that the account will not be paid. And the further past due an account is, the greater that possibility. The ageing of accounts receivable helps management to evaluate its credit and collection policies and alerts it to possible problems. The ageing of accounts receivable for Meyer Company is shown in Exhibit 6-2. Each account receivable is classified as being not yet due or as 1–30 days, 31–60

BUSINESS BULLETIN   Technology in Practice

Accountants generally believe that the accounts receivable ageing method is the best way to estimate uncollectible accounts because it takes into consideration current conditions, such as payment rates and economic conditions. However, since it is time-consuming to do an ageing of accounts manually, in the past, the percentage of net sales method was generally used for preparing interim financial statements, such as monthly and quarterly reports. Now that most companies' accounts receivable are computerised, the ageing of accounts receivable can be done much more easily and quickly. Indeed, many companies track the collection and ageing of accounts receivables on a weekly or even a daily basis. As a result, the percentage of net sales method is used less often.

EXHIBIT 6-2 *Analysis of Accounts Receivable by Age*

Meyer Company
Analysis of Accounts Receivable by Age
December 31, 20xx

Customer	Total	Not Yet Due	1–30 Days Past Due	31–60 Days Past Due	61–90 Days Past Due	Over 90 Days Past Due
A. Arnold	150		150			
M. Benoit	400			400		
J. Connolly	1,000	900	100			
R. DiCarlo	250				250	
Others	42,600	21,000	14,000	3,800	2,200	1,600
Totals	44,400	21,900	14,250	4,200	2,450	1,600
Estimated Percentage Uncollectible		1.0	2.0	10.0	30.0	50.0
Allowance for Uncollectible Accounts	2,459	219	285	420	735	800

days, 61–90 days, or over 90 days past due. The estimated percentage uncollectible in each category is multiplied by the amount in each category to determine the estimated or target balance of Allowance for Uncollectible Accounts. In total, it is estimated that 2,459 of the 44,400 accounts receivable will not be collected.

Once the target balance for the Allowance for Uncollectible Accounts has been found, it is necessary to determine how much the adjustment needs to be. The amount of the adjustment depends on the current balance of the allowance account. Let us assume two cases for the December 31 balance of Allowance for Uncollectible Accounts for Meyer Company: (1) a credit balance of 800 and (2) a debit balance of 800.

In the first case, an adjustment of 1,659 is needed to bring the balance of the allowance account to 2,459, calculated as follows:

Targeted Balance for Uncollectible Accounts	2,459
Less Credit Balance—Allowance for Uncollectible Accounts	800
Uncollectible Accounts Expense	1,659

The uncollectible accounts expense is recorded as follows:

Dec. 31	Uncollectible Accounts Expense	1,659	
	Allowance for Uncollectible Accounts		1,659
	To record the allowance for uncollectible accounts to the level of estimated losses		

The resulting balance of Allowance for Uncollectible Accounts is 2,459:

Allowance for Uncollectible Accounts

Dec. 31	800
Dec. 31 adjustment	1,659
Dec. 31 balance	2,459

In the second case, since the Allowance for Uncollectible Accounts has a debit balance of 800, the estimated uncollectible accounts expense for the year will have to be 3,259 to reach the targeted balance of 2,459, calculated as follows:

Targeted Balance for Uncollectible Accounts	2,459
Plus Debit Balance—Allowance for Uncollectible Accounts	800
Uncollectible Accounts Expense	3,259

The uncollectible accounts expense will be recorded as follows:

Dec. 31	Uncollectible Accounts Expense	3,259	
	Allowance for Uncollectible Accounts		3,259
	To record the allowance for uncollectible		
	accounts to the level of estimated losses		

After this entry, Allowance for Uncollectible Accounts has a credit balance of 2,459, as follows:

Allowance for Uncollectible Accounts

Dec. 31	800	Dec. 31 adjustment	3,259
		Dec. 31 balance	2,459

Comparison of the Two Methods

Both the percentage of net sales method and the accounts receivable ageing method estimate the uncollectible accounts expense in accordance with the matching rule, but they do so in different ways, as shown in Figure 6-4. The percentage of net sales method is an income statement approach. It assumes that a certain proportion of sales will not be collected, and this proportion is the *amount of Uncollectible Accounts Expense* for the year. The accounts receivable ageing method is a balance sheet approach. It assumes that a certain proportion of accounts receivable outstanding will not be collected. This proportion is the *targeted balance of the Allowance for Uncollectible Accounts account*. The expense for the year is the difference between the targeted balance and the current unadjusted balance of the allowance account.

FIGURE 6-4   *Two Methods of Estimating Uncollectible Accounts*

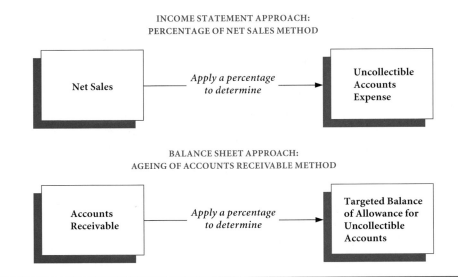

INCOME STATEMENT APPROACH:
PERCENTAGE OF NET SALES METHOD

Net Sales → *Apply a percentage to determine* → Uncollectible Accounts Expense

BALANCE SHEET APPROACH:
AGEING OF ACCOUNTS RECEIVABLE METHOD

Accounts Receivable → *Apply a percentage to determine* → Targeted Balance of Allowance for Uncollectible Accounts

Why Accounts Written Off Will Differ from Estimates

Regardless of which method is used to estimate uncollectible accounts, the total of specific accounts receivable actually written off in any given year will rarely equal the estimated uncollectible accounts. The allowance account will show a credit balance when the specific accounts written off are less than the estimated uncollectible accounts. The allowance account will show a debit balance when the accounts written off are greater than the estimated uncollectible accounts.

Writing Off an Uncollectible Account

When it becomes clear that a specific customer's account receivable will not be collected, the amount should be written off to Allowance for Uncollectible Accounts. Remember that the uncollectible amount was already accounted for as an expense when the allowance was established. For example, assume that R. Deering, who owes Meyer Company 250, is declared bankrupt on January 15 by a court. The entry to *write off* this account is as follows:

Jan. 15	Allowance for Uncollectible Accounts	250	
	Accounts Receivable		250
	To write off receivable from R. Deering as uncollectible; Deering declared bankrupt on January 15		

Although the write-off removes the uncollectible amount from Accounts Receivable, it does not affect the estimated net realisable value of accounts receivable. The write-off simply reduces R. Deering's account to zero and reduces Allowance for Uncollectible Accounts by a similar amount, as the following table shows:

	Balances before Write-off	Balances after Write-off
Accounts Receivable	44,400	44,150
Less Allowance for Uncollectible Accounts	2,459	2,209
Estimated Net Realisable Value of Accounts Receivable	41,941	41,941

Recovery of Accounts Receivable Written Off

Sometimes a customer whose account has been written off as uncollectible will later be able to pay the amount owed in full or in part. When this happens, two journal entries must be made: one to reverse the earlier write-off (which is now incorrect) and another to show the collection of the account.

For example, assume that on September 1, R. Deering, after his bankruptcy on January 15, notified the company that he would be able to pay 100 of his account and sent a cheque for 50. The entries to record this transaction are as follows:

Sept. 1	Accounts Receivable	100	
	Allowance for Uncollectible Accounts		100
	To reinstate the portion of the account of R. Deering now considered collectible; originally written off January 15		
1	Cash	50	
	Accounts Receivable		50
	Collection from R. Deering		

The collectible portion of R. Deering's account must be restored to his account and credited to Allowance for Uncollectible Accounts for two reasons. First, it turned out to be wrong to write off the full 250 on January 15 because only 150 was actually uncollectible. Second, the accounts receivable subsidiary account for R. Deering should reflect his ability to pay a portion of the money he owed in spite of his bankruptcy. Documentation of this action will give a clear picture of his credit record for future credit action.

OBJECTIVE 5

Define and describe a promissory note, and make calculations and journal entries involving promissory notes

NOTES RECEIVABLE

A **promissory note** is an unconditional promise to pay a definite sum of money on demand or at a future date. The entity who signs the note and thereby promises to pay is called the *maker* of the note. The entity to whom payment is to be made is called the *payee*. The promissory note in Figure 6-5 is dated May 20, 20x1, and is an unconditional promise by the maker, Samuel Mason, to pay a definite sum, or principal (1,000), to the payee, County Bank, at the future date of August 18, 20x1. The promissory note bears an interest rate of 8 per cent. The payee regards all promissory notes it holds that are due in less than one year as **notes receivable** in the current assets section of the balance sheet. The makers regard them as notes payable in the current liability section of the balance sheet.

This portion of the chapter is concerned primarily with notes received from customers. The nature of a business generally determines how frequently promissory notes are received from customers. Firms selling durable goods of high value, such as farm machinery and cars, will often accept promissory notes. Among the advantages of promissory notes are that they produce interest income and represent a stronger legal claim against the lender than do accounts receivable. In addition, selling promissory notes to banks is a common financing method. Almost all companies will occasionally receive a note, and many companies obtain notes receivable in settlement of past-due accounts.

FIGURE 6-5   *A Promissory Note*

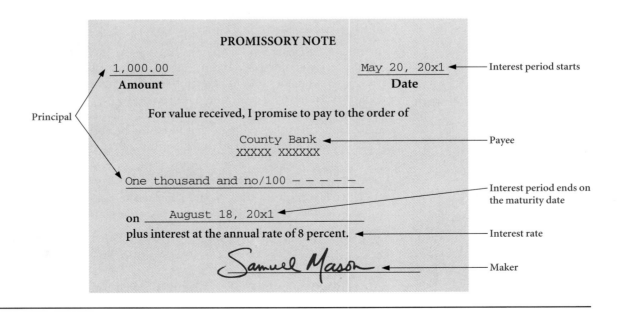

Calculations for Promissory Notes

In accounting for promissory notes, several terms are important to remember. These terms are (1) maturity date, (2) duration of note, (3) interest and interest rate, and (4) maturity value.

Maturity Date

The **maturity date** is the date on which the note must be paid. This date must either be stated on the promissory note or be determinable from the facts stated on the note. Among the most common statements of maturity date are the following:

1. A specific date, such as "November 14, 20xx"
2. A specific number of months after the date of the note, for example, "3 months after date"
3. A specific number of days after the date of the note, for example, "60 days after date"

There is no problem in determining the maturity date when it is stated. When the maturity date is a number of months from the date of the note, one simply uses the same day in the appropriate future month. For example, a note dated January 20 that is due in two months would be due on March 20.

When the maturity date is a specific number of days from the date of the note, it must be based on the exact number of days. In calculating the maturity date, it is important to exclude the date of the note. For example, a note dated May 20 and due in 90 days would be due on August 18, calculated as follows:

Days remaining in May (31 − 20)	11
Days in June	30
Days in July	31
Days in August	18
Total days	90

Duration of Note

Determining the **duration of note**, or its length of time in days, is the opposite problem from determining the maturity date. Knowing the duration of the note is important because interest is calculated for the exact number of days. There is no problem when the maturity date is stated as a specific number of days from the date of the note. However, if the maturity date is a specified date, the exact number of days must be determined. Assume that a note issued on May 10 matures on August 10. The duration of the note is 92 days, determined as follows:

Days remaining in May (31 − 10)	21
Days in June	30
Days in July	31
Days in August	10
Total days	92

Interest and Interest Rate

The **interest** is the cost of borrowing money or the return for lending money, depending on whether one is the borrower or the lender. The amount of interest is based on three factors: the principal (the amount of money borrowed or lent), the rate of interest, and the loan's length of time. The formula used in calculating interest is:

$$\text{Principal} \times \text{rate of interest} \times \text{time} = \text{interest}$$

Interest rates are usually stated on an annual basis. For example, the interest on a 1,000, one-year, 8 per cent note would be 80 ($1,000 \times 8/100 \times 1 = 80$). If the term, or time period, of the note were three months instead of a year, the interest charge would be 20 ($1,000 \times 8/100 \times 3/12 = 20$).

When the term of a note is expressed in days, the exact number of days must be used in calculating the interest. To keep the calculation simple, let us calculate interest on the basis of 360 days per year.[7] Thus, if the term of the above note were 45 days, the interest would be 10, calculated as follows: $1,000 \times 8/100 \times 45/360 = 10$.

Maturity Value

The **maturity value** is the total proceeds of the note at the maturity date. Maturity value is the face value of the note plus interest. The maturity value of a 90-day, 8 per cent, 1,000 note is calculated as follows:

$$
\begin{aligned}
\text{Maturity value} &= \text{principal} + \text{interest} \\
&= 1,000 + (1,000 \times 8/100 \times 90/360) \\
&= 1,000 + 20 \\
&= 1,020
\end{aligned}
$$

There are also non-interest-bearing notes. The maturity value is the face value, or principal amount. In this case, the principal includes an implied interest cost.

Illustrative Accounting Entries

The accounting entries for promissory notes receivable fall into four groups: (1) receipt of a note, (2) collection on a note, (3) recording a dishonoured note, and (4) recording adjusting entries.

Receipt of a Note

Assume that on June 1 a 12 per cent, 30-day note is received from a customer, J. Halsted, in settlement of an existing account receivable of 4,000. The entry for this transaction is as follows:

June 1	Notes Receivable	4,000	
	Accounts Receivable		4,000
	Received 12 per cent, 30-day note in payment of		
	account of J. Halsted		

Collection on a Note

When the note plus interest is collected 30 days later, the entry is as follows:

July 1	Cash	4,040	
	Notes Receivable		4,000
	Interest Income		40
	Collected 12 per cent, 30-day note from J. Halsted		
	$4,000 \times 12/100 \times 30/360 = 40$		

Recording a Dishonoured Note

When the maker of a note does not pay the note at maturity, the note is said to be dishonoured. The holder, or payee, of a **dishonoured note** should make an entry to transfer the total amount due from Notes Receivable to an account receivable from the debtor. If J. Halsted dishonours his note on July 1, the following entry would be made:

July 1	Accounts Receivable	4,040	
	Notes Receivable		4,000
	Interest Income		40
	12 per cent, 30-day note dishonoured		
	by J. Halsted		

The interest earned is recorded because, although J. Halsted did not pay the note, he is still obligated to pay both the principal and the interest.

Two things are accomplished by transferring a dishonoured note receivable into an Accounts Receivable account. First, it leaves the Notes Receivable account with only notes that have not matured and are presumably negotiable and collectible. Second, it establishes a record in the borrower's accounts receivable account that he or she has dishonoured a note receivable. This information may be helpful in deciding whether to extend future credit to this customer.

Recording Adjusting Entries

A promissory note received in one period may not be due until a following accounting period. Because the interest on a note accrues by a small amount each day of the note's duration, it is necessary, according to the matching rule, to apportion the interest earned to the period in which it belongs. For example, assume that on August 31 a 60-day, 8 per cent, 2,000 note was received and that the company prepares financial statements monthly. The following adjusting entry is necessary on September 30 to show how the interest earned for September has accrued:

Sept. 30	Interest Receivable	13.33	
	Interest Income		13.33
	To accrue 30 days' interest earned on a note		
	receivable		
	$2,000 \times 8/100 \times 30/360 = 13.33$		

The account Interest Receivable is a current asset on the balance sheet. Upon receiving payment of the note plus interest on October 30, the following entry is made:[8]

Oct. 30	Cash	2,026.67	
	Notes Receivable		2,000.00
	Interest Receivable		13.33
	Interest Income		13.34
	Receipt of note receivable plus interest		

As seen from these transactions, both September and October receive the benefit of one-half the interest earned.

SUPPLEMENTAL OBJECTIVE 6

Account for credit card transactions

CREDIT CARD SALES

Many retailers allow customers to charge their purchases to a third-party company that the customer will pay later. These transactions are normally handled with credit cards. The most widely used credit cards include American Express, Diners Club, MasterCard, and VISA. The customer establishes credit with the lender (the credit card issuer) and receives a plastic card to use in making charge purchases. If the seller accepts the card, an invoice is prepared and signed by the customer at the time of the sale. The seller then sends the invoice to the lender and receives cash. Because the seller does not have to establish the customer's credit, collect from the customer, or tie money up in accounts receivable, the seller receives an economic benefit that is provided by the lender. For this reason, the lender does not pay 100 per cent of the total amount of the invoices. The lender takes a discount of 2 to 6 per cent on the credit card sales invoices.

One of two procedures is used in accounting for credit card sales, depending on whether the seller must wait for collection from the lender or may deposit the sales invoices in a bank account immediately. The following example illustrates the first procedure. Assume that, at the end of the day, a restaurant has American Express invoices totalling 1,000 and that the discount charged by American Express is 4 per cent. These sales are recorded as follows:

Accounts Receivable	960	
Credit Card Discount Expense	40	
Sales		1,000
Sales made on American Express cards; discount fee is 4 per cent		

The seller sends the invoices to American Express and later receives payment for them at 96 per cent of their face value. When cash is received, the entry is as follows:

Cash	960	
Accounts Receivable		960
Receipt of payment from American Express for invoices at 96 per cent of face value		

The second procedure is typical of sales made through bank credit cards such as VISA and MasterCard. Assume that the restaurant made sales of 1,000 on VISA credit cards and that VISA takes a 4 per cent discount on the sales. Assume also that the sales invoices are deposited in a special VISA bank account in the name of the company, in much the same way that cheques from cash sales are deposited. These sales are recorded as follows:

Cash	960	
Credit Card Discount Expense	40	
Sales		1,000
Sales on VISA cards		

CHAPTER REVIEW

Review of Learning Objectives

1. **Identify and explain the management issues related to short-term liquid assets.** In managing short-term liquid assets, management must (1) consider the effects of seasonal cycles on the need for short-term investing and borrowing as the business's balance of cash fluctuates, (2) establish credit policies that balance the need for sales with the ability to collect, and (3) assess the need for additional cash flows through the financing of receivables.

2. **Explain cash and cash equivalents and prepare a bank reconciliation.** Cash consists of coins and currency available, cheques and money orders received from customers, and deposits in bank accounts that are available on demand. Cash equivalents are short-term, highly liquid investments that are readily convertible to cash. A bank reconciliation accounts for the difference between the balance that appears on the bank statement and the balance in the company's Cash account. It involves adjusting both balances to arrive at the adjusted cash balance. The bank balance is adjusted for outstanding cheques and deposits in transit. The depositor's book balance is adjusted for service charges, NSF cheques, interest earned, and miscellaneous debits and credits.

3. **Account for current investments.** Current investments are readily realisable and are intended to be held for not more than one year. They are classified as current assets on the balance sheet and may be valued at market value or the lower of cost and market value.

4. **Define *accounts receivable* and apply the allowance method of accounting for uncollectible accounts, using both the percentage of net sales method and the accounts receivable ageing method.** Accounts receivable are amounts still to be collected from credit sales to customers. The amounts still owed by individual customers are found in the subsidiary ledger.

   Because credit is offered to increase sales, uncollectible accounts associated with the sales should be charged as expenses in the period in which the sales are made. However, because of the time lag between the sales and the time the accounts are judged to be uncollectible, the accountant must estimate the amount of bad debts in any given period.

   Uncollectible accounts expense is estimated by either the percentage of net sales method or the accounts receivable ageing method. When the first method is used, bad debts are judged to be a certain percentage of sales during the period. When the second method is used, certain percentages are applied to groups of accounts receivable that have been arranged by due dates.

Allowance for Uncollectible Accounts is a contra-asset account to Accounts Receivable. The estimate of uncollectible accounts is debited to Uncollectible Accounts Expense and credited to the allowance account. When an individual account is determined to be uncollectible, it is removed from Accounts Receivable by debiting the allowance account and crediting Accounts Receivable. If the written-off account should later be collected, the earlier entry should be reversed and the collection recorded in the normal way.

5. **Define and describe a *promissory note*, and make calculations and journal entries involving promissory notes.** A promissory note is an unconditional promise to pay a definite sum of money on demand or at a future date. Companies selling durable goods of high value, such as farm machinery and cars, often accept promissory notes, which can be sold to banks as a financing method.

In accounting for promissory notes, it is important to know how to calculate the maturity date, duration of note, interest and interest rate, and maturity value. The accounting entries for promissory notes receivable fall into four groups: receipt of a note, collection on a note, recording a dishonoured note, and recording adjusting entries.

Supplemental Objective

6. **Account for credit card transactions.** The use of third-party credit cards allows a company to sell on credit without incurring the cost of a credit department, keeping records of the account, and absorbing the losses from bad debts. In return, the company pays a fee, which is recorded as an expense at the time of the sale. Some credit card companies allow the business to deposit the credit card receipts in the bank immediately, while others require the business to wait for payment.

Review of Concepts and Terminology

The following concepts and terms were introduced in this chapter.

LO 4 **Accounts receivable:** Short-term liquid assets that arise from sales on credit at the wholesale or retail level.

LO 4 **Accounts receivable ageing method:** A method of estimating uncollectible accounts based on the assumption that a predictable portion of accounts receivable will not be collected.

LO 4 **Ageing of accounts receivable:** The process of listing each accounts receivable customer according to the due date of the account.

LO 4 **Allowance for Uncollectible Accounts:** A contra-asset account that reduces accounts receivable to the amount that is expected to be collected in cash; also called *allowance for bad debts*.

LO 4 **Allowance method:** A method of accounting for uncollectible accounts whereby estimated uncollectible accounts are expensed in the period in which the related sales take place.

LO 1 **Average days' sales uncollected:** A ratio that shows on average how long it takes to collect accounts receivable; 365 days divided by receivable turnover.

LO 2 **Bank reconciliation:** The process of accounting for the difference between the balance appearing on a bank statement and the cash balance in the company records.

LO 2 **Bank statement:** A report sent by a bank to a customer that shows the status of the customer's account.

LO 2 **Cash:** Coins and currency available, cheques and money orders from customers, and deposits in bank cheque accounts that are available on demand.

LO 2 **Cash equivalents:** Short-term, highly liquid investments that are readily convertible to cash.

LO 2 **Compensating balance:** A minimum amount that a bank requires be kept in an account as part of a credit-granting arrangement.

LO 1 **Contingent liability:** A potential liability that can develop into a real liability if a possible subsequent event occurs.

LO 4 **Controlling (or control) account:** An account in the general ledger for which there exists a subsidiary ledger.

LO 3 **Current investments:** Investments, often in the form of securities, that are readily realisable and are intended to be held for not more than one year.

LO 1 **Discounting:** A method of selling notes receivable in which the bank deducts the interest from the maturity value of the note to determine the proceeds.

LO 5 **Dishonoured note:** A promissory note that the maker cannot or will not pay at the maturity date.

LO 5 **Duration of note:** Length of time in days between a promissory note's issue date and its maturity date.

LO 2 **Electronic funds transfer (EFT):** The transfer of funds between banks through electronic communication.

LO 1 **Factor:** An entity that buys accounts receivable.

LO 1 **Factoring:** The selling or transferring of accounts receivable.

LO 2 **Imprest system:** A system for controlling small cash disbursements by establishing a fund at a fixed amount and periodically reimbursing the fund by the amount necessary to restore its original cash balance.

LO 4 **Instalment accounts receivable:** Accounts receivable that are payable in a series of time payments.

LO 5 **Interest:** The cost of borrowing money or the return for lending money, depending on whether one is the borrower or the lender.

LO 3 **Marketable securities:** Securities for which there is an active market.

LO 5 **Maturity date:** The due date of a promissory note.

LO 5 **Maturity value:** The total proceeds of a promissory note, including principal and interest, at the maturity date.

LO 5 **Notes payable:** Collective term for promissory notes owed by the entity (maker) who promises payment to other entities.

LO 5 **Notes receivable:** Collective term for promissory notes held by the entity to whom payment is promised (payee).

LO 4 **Percentage of net sales method:** A method of estimating uncollectible accounts based on the assumption that a predictable portion of sales will not be collected.

LO 2 **Petty cash fund:** A fund established by a business for making small payments of cash.

LO 5 **Promissory note:** An unconditional promise to pay a definite sum of money on demand or at a future date.

LO 1 **Quick ratio:** A ratio for measuring the adequacy of short-term liquid assets; quick or short-term liquid assets divided by current liabilities.

LO 1   **Receivable turnover:** A ratio for measuring the average number of times receivables were turned into cash during an accounting period; net sales divided by average net accounts receivable.

LO 1   **Short-term liquid assets:** Financial assets that arise from cash transactions, the investment of cash, and the extension of credit.

LO 4   **Subsidiary ledger:** A separate ledger consisting of accounts whose total agrees with the balance of an account in the general ledger.

LO 4   **Trade credit:** Credit granted to customers by wholesalers or retailers.

LO 4   **Uncollectible accounts:** Accounts receivable owed by customers who cannot or will not pay. Also called *bad debts*.

Review Problem

Entries for Uncollectible Accounts Expense and Notes Receivable Transactions

LO 4
LO 5
The Farm Equipment Company sells goods on credit and also accepts notes for payment. During the year ended June 30, the company had net sales of 1,200,000, and at the end of the year it had Accounts Receivable of 400,000 and a debit balance in Allowance for Uncollectible Accounts of 2,100. In the past, approximately 1.5 per cent of net sales have proved uncollectible. Also, an ageing analysis of accounts receivable reveals that 17,000 in accounts receivable appears to be uncollectible.

The Farm Equipment Company sold a tractor to R. C. Sims. Payment was received in the form of a 15,000, 9 per cent, 90-day note dated March 16. On June 14, Sims dishonoured the note. On June 29, the company received payment in full from Sims plus additional interest from the date of the dishonoured note.

REQUIRED
1. Prepare journal entries to record uncollectible accounts expense using (a) the percentage of net sales method and (b) the accounts receivable ageing method.
2. Prepare journal entries relating to the note received from R. C. Sims.

Answer to Review Problem

1. Prepare journal entries to record uncollectible accounts expense.
   a. Percentage of net sales method:

June 30	Uncollectible Accounts Expense	18,000	
	Allowance for Uncollectible Accounts		18,000
	To record estimated uncollectible accounts expense at 1.5 per cent of 1,200,000		

   b. Accounts receivable ageing method:

June 30	Uncollectible Accounts Expense	19,100	
	Allowance for Uncollectible Accounts		19,100
	To record estimated uncollectible accounts expense. The debit balance in the allowance account must be added to the estimated uncollectible accounts: 2,100 + 17,000 = 19,100		

2. Prepare journal entries related to note.

Mar. 16	Notes Receivable	15,000.00	
	Sales		15,000.00
	Tractor sold to R. C. Sims; terms of note: 9 per cent, 90 days		
June 14	Accounts Receivable	15,337.50	
	Notes Receivable		15,000.00
	Interest Income		337.50
	The note was dishonoured by R. C. Sims Maturity value: 15,000 + (15,000 × 9/100 × 90/360) = 15,337.50		
29	Cash	15,395.02	
	Accounts Receivable		15,337.50
	Interest Income		57.52
	Received payment in full from R. C. Sims 15,337.50 + (15,337.50 × 9/100 × 15/360) 15,337.50 + 57.52 = 15,395.02		

CHAPTER ASSIGNMENTS

Knowledge and Understanding

Questions

1. Why does a business need short-term liquid assets? What three issues does management face in managing short-term liquid assets?
2. What is a factor, and what do the terms *factoring with recourse* and *factoring without recourse* mean?
3. What items are included in the Cash account? What is a compensating balance?
4. How do cash equivalents differ from cash? From current investments?
5. What are current investments and how are they valued at the balance sheet date?
6. What are unrealised gains and losses on marketable securities? On what statement are they reported?
7. Which of the following lettered items should be in Accounts Receivable? For those that do not belong in Accounts Receivable, state where on the balance sheet they do belong: (a) instalment accounts receivable from regular customers, due monthly for three years; (b) debit balances in customers' accounts; (c) receivables from employees; (d) credit balances in customers' accounts; (e) receivables from officers of the company.
8. What is the function of the accounts receivable subsidiary ledger, and how is this function related to Accounts Receivable?
9. Why does a company sell on credit if it expects that some of the accounts will not be paid? What role does a credit department play in selling on credit?
10. According to accounting standards, at what point in the cycle of selling and collecting does a bad debt loss occur?
11. Are the following terms different in any way: *allowance for bad debts, allowance for doubtful accounts, allowance for uncollectible accounts*?
12. What is the effect on net profit of an optimistic versus a pessimistic view by management of estimated uncollectible accounts?
13. In what ways is Allowance for Uncollectible Accounts similar to Accumulated Depreciation? In what ways is it different?
14. What is the underlying reasoning behind the percentage of net sales method and the accounts receivable ageing method of estimating uncollectible accounts?
15. What procedure for estimating uncollectible accounts also gives management a view of the status of collections and the overall quality of accounts receivable?
16. After adjusting and closing entries at the end of the year, suppose that Accounts Receivable is 176,000 and Allowance for Uncollectible Accounts is 14,500. (a) What is the collectible value of Accounts Receivable? (b) If the 450 account of a bankrupt customer is written off in the first month of the new year, what will be the resulting collectible value of Accounts Receivable?
17. Why should an account written off as uncollectible be reinstated if the amount owed is subsequently collected?
18. What is a promissory note? Who are the maker and payee?
19. What are the maturity dates of the following notes: (a) a 3-month note dated August 16, (b) a 90-day note dated August 16, (c) a 60-day note dated March 25?
20. Why are businesses willing to pay a fee to credit card companies to be able to accept their cards from customers?

Application

Exercises

E 6-1.
LO 1 *Management Issues*

Indicate whether each of the actions below is primarily related to (a) managing cash needs during seasonal cycles, (b) setting credit policies, or (c) financing receivables.

1. Buying a government bond with cash that is not needed for a few months.
2. Comparing receivable turnovers for two years.
3. Setting policy on which customers may buy on credit.
4. Selling notes receivable to a financing company.
5. Borrowing funds for short-term needs during the period of the year when sales are low.
6. Changing terms of sale in an effort to reduce the average days' sales uncollected.
7. Using a factor to provide operating funds.
8. Establishing a department whose responsibility is to approve customers' credit.

E 6-2.
LO 1 *Short-Term Liquidity Ratios*

Using the following information selected from the financial statements of Lee Company, calculate the quick ratio, the receivable turnover, and the average days' sales uncollected:

Current Assets	
Cash	35,000
Current Investments	85,000
Notes Receivable	120,000
Accounts Receivable, net	100,000
Inventory	250,000
Prepaid Assets	25,000
Total Current Assets	615,000

Current Liabilities	
Notes Payable	150,000
Accounts Payable	75,000
Accrued Liabilities	10,000
Total Current Liabilities	235,000
Net Sales	800,000
Last Period's Accounts Receivable, net	90,000

E 6-3.

LO 2 *Bank Reconciliation*

Prepare a bank reconciliation from the following information:

a. Balance per bank statement as of May 31, 4,227.27
b. Balance per books as of May 31, 3,069.02
c. Deposits in transit, 567.21
d. Outstanding cheques, 1,727.96
e. Bank service charge, 2.50

E 6-4.

LO 2 *Bank Reconciliation: Missing Data*

Calculate the correct amount to replace each letter in the following table:

Balance per bank statement	a	8,900	315	1,990
Deposits in transit	600	b	50	125
Outstanding cheques	1,500	1,000	c	75
Balance per books	3,450	9,400	225	d

E 6-5.

LO 3 *Marketable Securities*

Saito Corporation began investing in marketable securities and engaged in these transactions:

Jan. 6   Purchased 7,000 shares of Chemical Bank shares, 30 per share.
Feb. 15   Purchased 9,000 shares of EG&G, 22 per share.

Saito's headquarters is in a country that uses the market value basis at year end.

At June 30 year end, Chemical Bank was trading at 40 per share and EG&G was trading at 18 per share. Record the entries for the purchases. Then record the necessary year-end adjusting entry. (Include a schedule of the portfolio cost and market in the explanation.) Also record the entry for the sale of all the EG&G shares on August 20 for 16 per share. Is the last entry affected by the adjustment made on June 30?

E 6-6.

LO 4 *Percentage of Net Sales Method*

At the end of the year, Lockport Enterprises estimates the uncollectible accounts expense to be .7 per cent of net sales of 30,300,000. The current credit balance of Allowance for Uncollectible Accounts is 51,600. Give the general journal entry to record the uncollectible accounts expense. What is the balance of the Allowance for Uncollectible Accounts after this adjustment?

E 6-7.

LO 4 *Accounts Receivable Ageing Method*

Accounts Receivable of Kinsella Company shows a debit balance of 52,000 at the end of the year. An ageing analysis of the individual accounts indicates estimated uncollectible accounts to be 3,350.

Give the general journal entry to record the uncollectible accounts expense under each of the following independent assumptions: (a) Allowance for Uncollectible Accounts has a credit balance of 400 before adjustment and (b) Allowance for Uncollectible Accounts has a debit balance of 400 before adjustment. What is the balance of Allowance for Uncollectible Accounts after each of these adjustments?

E 6-8.

LO 4 *Ageing Method and Net Sales Method Contrasted*

At the beginning of 20xx, the balances for Accounts Receivable and Allowance for Uncollectible Accounts were 430,000 and 31,400, respectively. During the current year, credit sales were 3,200,000 and collections on account were 2,950,000. In addition, 35,000 in uncollectible accounts were written off. Using T accounts, determine the year-end balances of Accounts Receivable and Allowance for Uncollectible Accounts. Then, make the year-end adjusting entry to record the uncollectible accounts expense, and show the year-end balance sheet presentation of Accounts Receivable and Allowance for Uncollectible Accounts under each of the following conditions:

a. Management estimates the percentage of uncollectible credit sales to be 1.2 per cent of total credit sales.
b. Based on an ageing of accounts receivable, management estimates the end-of-year uncollectible accounts receivable to be 38,700.

Post the results of each entry to the T account for Allowance for Uncollectible Accounts.

E 6-9.

LO 4 *Entries for Uncollectible Accounts Expense*

The Cordero Office Supply Company sells goods on credit. During the accounting year ended July 31, the company had net sales of 4,600,000. At the end of the year, it had Accounts Receivable of 1,200,000 and a debit balance in Allowance for Uncollectible Accounts of 6,800. In the past, approximately 1.4 per cent of net sales have proved uncollectible. Also, an ageing analysis of accounts receivable reveals that 60,000 of the receivables appear to be uncollectible. Prepare journal entries to record uncollectible accounts expense using (a) the percentage of net sales method and (b) the accounts receivable ageing method.

What is the resulting balance of Allowance for Uncollectible Accounts under each method? How would your answers under each method change if Allowance for Uncollectible Accounts had a credit balance of 6,800 instead of a debit balance? Why do the methods result in different balances?

E 6-10.

LO 4 *Accounts Receivable Transactions*

Assuming that the allowance method is being used, prepare journal entries to record the following transactions:

July 12, 20x1 Sold goods to Vera Barnes for 1,800, terms n/10.
Oct. 18, 20x1 Received 600 from Vera Barnes on account.
May 8, 20x2 Wrote off as uncollectible the balance of the Vera Barnes account when she was declared bankrupt.
June 22, 20x2 Unexpectedly received a cheque for 200 from Vera Barnes. No additional amount is expected to be collected from Barnes.

E 6-11.

LO 5 *Interest Calculations*

Determine the interest on the following notes:

a. 22,800 at 10 per cent for 90 days
b. 16,000 at 12 per cent for 60 days
c. 18,000 at 9 per cent for 30 days
d. 30,000 at 15 per cent for 120 days
e. 10,800 at 6 per cent for 60 days

E 6-12.

LO 5 *Notes Receivable Transactions*

Prepare general journal entries to record the following transactions:

Jan. 16 Sold goods to Brighton Corporation on account for 36,000, terms n/30.
Feb. 15 Accepted a 36,000, 10 per cent, 90-day note from Brighton Corporation in lieu of payment on account.
May 16 Brighton Corporation dishonoured the note.
June 15 Received payment in full from Brighton Corporation, including interest at 10 per cent from the date the note was dishonoured.

E 6-13.

SO 6 *Credit Card Sales Transactions*

Prepare journal entries to record the following transactions for Toni's Novelties Store:

Apr. 8 A tabulation of invoices at the end of the day showed 2,200 in American Express invoices and 1,200 in Diners Club invoices. American Express takes a discount of 4 per cent, and Diners Club takes a 5 per cent discount.
     15 Received payment from American Express at 96 per cent of face value and from Diners Club at 95 per cent of face value.
     19 A tabulation of invoices at the end of the day showed 800 in VISA invoices, which are deposited in a special bank account at full value less 5 per cent discount.

Problem Set

P 6-1.

LO 2 *Bank Reconciliation*

The following information is available for Hernandez Company as of November 30, 20xx:

a. Cash on the books as of November 30 amounted to 113,675.28. Cash on the bank statement for the same date was 141,717.08.
b. A deposit of 14,249.84, representing cash receipts of November 30, did not appear on the bank statement.
c. Outstanding cheques totaled 7,293.64.
d. A cheque for 2,420.00 returned with the statement was recorded in the cash payments journal as 2,024.00. The cheque was for advertising.
e. The bank service charge for November amounted to 26.00.
f. The bank collected 36,400.00 for Hernandez Company on a note. The face value of the note was 36,000.00.
g. An NSF cheque for 1,140.00 from a customer, Emma Matthews, was returned with the statement.
h. The bank mistakenly deducted a cheque for 800.00 drawn by Mota Corporation.
i. The bank reported a credit of 960.00 for interest on the average balance.

REQUIRED

1. Prepare a bank reconciliation for Hernandez Company as of November 30, 20xx.
2. Prepare the journal entries necessary from the reconciliation.
3. State the amount of cash that should appear on the balance sheet as of November 30.

P 6-2.

LO 3 *Marketable Securities*

During certain periods, Nicks Company invests its excess cash in marketable securities until it is needed. During 20x1 and 20x2, the company engaged in the following transactions:

20x1

Apr. 15   Purchased 10,000 shares of Goodrich Paper at 40 per share and 5,000 shares of Keuron Power Company at 30 per share.

June 2   Received dividends of 2.00 per share from Goodrich Paper and 1.50 per share from Keuron Power.

June 30   Made year-end adjusting entry for marketable securities. Market price of Goodrich Paper shares is 32 per share; market price of Keuron Power is 35 per share.

Nov. 14   Sold all the shares of Goodrich Paper for 42 per share.

20x2

Feb. 15   Purchased 9,000 shares of Beacon Communications for 50 per share.

June 1   Received dividends of 2.20 per share from Keuron Power.

     30   Made year-end adjusting entry for marketable securities. Market price of Keuron Power shares is 33 per share; market price of Beacon Communications is 60 per share.

REQUIRED

1. Prepare journal entries to record these transactions assuming that Nicks Company's accounting year ends on June 30.
2. Show the balance sheet presentation of current investments on June 30, 20x2.

P 6-3.

LO 4   *Percentage of Net Sales Method*

On December 31 of last year, the balance sheet of Marzano Company had Accounts Receivable of 298,000 and a credit balance in Allowance for Uncollectible Accounts of 20,300. During the current year, the company's records included the following selected activities: sales on account, 1,195,000; sales returns and allowances, 73,000; collections from customers, 1,150,000; accounts written off as worthless, 16,000; and written-off accounts unexpectedly collected, 2,000. In the past, the company had found that 1.6 per cent of net sales would not be collected.

REQUIRED

1. Open ledger accounts for the Accounts Receivable controlling account (112) and Allowance for Uncollectible Accounts (113). Then enter the beginning balances in these accounts.
2. Prepare separate journal entries to record in summary form the five activities listed above.
3. Give the general journal entry on December 31 of the current year to record the estimated uncollectible accounts expense for the year.
4. Post the appropriate parts of the transactions in **2** and **3** to the accounts opened in **1**.

P 6-4.

LO 4   *Accounts Receivable Ageing Method*

Pokorny Company uses the accounts receivable ageing method to estimate uncollectible accounts. The Accounts Receivable controlling account had a debit balance of 88,430 and Allowance for Uncollectible Accounts had a credit balance of 7,200 at the beginning of the year. During the year, the company had sales on account of 473,000, sales returns and allowances of 4,200, worthless accounts written off of 7,900, and collections from customers of 450,730. At the end of the year (December 31), a junior accountant for the company was preparing an ageing analysis of accounts receivable. At the top of page 6 of the report, the following totals appeared:

Customer Account	Total	Not Yet Due	1–30 Days Past Due	31–60 Days Past Due	61–90 Days Past Due	Over 90 Days Past Due
Balance Forward	89,640	49,030	24,110	9,210	3,990	3,300

The following accounts remained to finish the analysis:

Account	Amount	Due Date
K. Foust	930	Jan. 14 (next year)
K. Groth	620	Dec. 24
R. Mejias	1,955	Sept. 28
C. Polk	2,100	Aug. 16
M. Spears	375	Dec. 14
J. Yong	2,685	Jan. 23 (next year)
A. Zorr	295	Nov. 5
	8,960	

The company has found that the following rates are realistic to estimate uncollectible accounts:

Time	Percentage Considered Uncollectible
Not yet due	2
1–30 days past due	4
31–60 days past due	20
61–90 days past due	30
Over 90 days past due	50

REQUIRED
1. Complete the ageing analysis of accounts receivable.
2. Determine the end-of-year balances (before adjustments) of the Accounts Receivable controlling account and Allowance for Uncollectible Accounts.
3. Prepare an analysis calculating the estimated uncollectible accounts.
4. Prepare a general journal entry to record the estimated uncollectible accounts expense for the year. (Round adjustment to the nearest unit.)

Critical Thinking and Communication

Conceptual Mini-Case

CMC 6-1.
LO 1 *Role of Credit Sales*

Mitsubishi Electric, a Japanese corporation, instituted a credit plan, called Three Diamond, for customers who buy its major electronic products, such as large-screen televisions and videotape recorders, from specified retail dealers.[9] Under this plan, which was introduced in 1990, approved customers who make purchases in November do not have to make any payments until April and pay no interest for the intervening months. Mitsubishi pays the dealer the full amount less a small fee, sends the customer a Mitsubishi credit card, and collects from the customer at the specified time. What is Mitsubishi's motivation for establishing these generous credit terms? What costs are involved? What are the accounting implications?

Cultural Mini-Case

CLMC 6-1.
LO 3 *Accounting for Current Investments*

Daimler-Benz, one of Germany's largest industrial companies with interests ranging from cars to microelectronics to aircraft, had current investments of 8,466 million Deutsche marks in 1995. Under German accounting standards these investments are valued at the lower of cost and market value. In the United States, in contrast, statement at market value is required in regard to marketable securities with both unrealised gains and losses recorded in the income statement. In 1995, a gain of 238 million Deutsche marks would have been recognised under U.S. accounting standards.[10] In 1995, Daimler-Benz reported a net loss of 5,734 million Deutsche marks.

REQUIRED
1. Calculate the impact of the valuation at market value as per U.S. accounting standards on the Daimler-Benz reported loss for 1995.
2. Discuss whether the U.S. or German approach to the valuation of current investments is more relevant with regard to reliability and prudence.

Ethics Mini-Case

EMC 6-1.
LO 1 *Ethics, Uncollectible*
LO 4 *Accounts, and Short-Term Objectives*

Fitzsimmons Designs, a successful retail furniture company, is located in an affluent suburb where a major insurance company has just announced a restructuring that will lay off 4,000 employees. Fitzsimmons sells quality furniture, usually on credit. Accounts Receivable represents one of the major assets of the company and, although the company's annual uncollectible accounts losses are not out of line, they represent a sizeable amount. The company depends on bank loans for its financing. Sales and net profit in the past year have declined, and some customers are falling behind in paying their accounts. George Fitzsimmons, the owner of the business, has instructed the controller to underestimate the uncollectible accounts this year in order to show a small growth in earnings. His reason for doing this is that he knows the bank's loan officer likes to see a steady performance. Fitzsimmons believes the short-term action is justified because future successful years will average out the losses, and since the company has a history of success, the adjustments are meaningless accounting measures anyway. Are Fitzsimmons's actions ethical? Would any parties be harmed by his actions? How important is it to try to be accurate in estimating losses from uncollectible accounts?

Decision-Making Case

DMC 6-1.
LO 3 *Accounting for Current Investments*

The **American Christmas Tree Company**'s business—the growing and selling of Christmas trees—is seasonal. By January 1, after a successful season, American Christmas Tree has cash available that will not be needed for several months. The company has minimal expenses from January to October, but during the harvesting and shipping months of November and December, its expenses are heavy. American Christmas Tree's management follows the practice of investing the idle cash in marketable securities, which the company can then sell whenever the funds are needed for operations. The company's accounting year ends on June 30. On January 10 of the current year, the company has cash of $408,300 available. It keeps $20,000 available for operating expenses and invests the rest as follows:

$100,000 3-month Treasury bill	$ 97,800
1,000 shares of Ford Motor Co. ($50 per share)	50,000
2,500 shares of McDonald's ($50 per share)	125,000
2,100 shares of IBM ($55 per share)	115,500
Total current investments	$388,300

On February 10 and May 10, the company receives a quarterly cash dividend from each company: $.40 per share from Ford, $.10 per share from McDonald's, and $1.04 per share from IBM. The Treasury bill is redeemed at face value on April 10. On June 1 management sells 500 shares of McDonald's at $55 per share. On June 30 the market values of the investments are:

Ford Motor Co.	$61 per share
McDonald's	$46 per share
IBM	$50 per share

Another quarterly dividend is received from each company on August 10. All the remaining shares are sold on November 1 at the following prices:

Ford Motor Co.	$55 per share
McDonald's	$44 per share
IBM	$60 per share

REQUIRED

1. Record the investment transactions that occurred on January 10, February 10, April 10, May 10, and June 1. Prepare the required adjusting entry on June 30, and record the investment transactions on August 10 and November 1.
2. Explain how the current investments would be shown on the balance sheet on June 30.
3. After November 1, what is the balance of the account that is called Allowance to Adjust Current Investments to Market Value, and what will happen to this account next June?
4. What is your assessment of American Christmas Tree Company's strategy regarding idle cash?

Basic Research Activity

RA 6-1.

LO 1 *Investments in Marketable Securities*

Find a recent issue of a financial newspaper in your library. Turn to the page with details of shares listed on the Stock Exchange. From the listing of shares, find five companies you have heard of. Copy down the range of the share price for the last year and the current closing price. Also, copy down the dividend, if any, per share. How much did the market values of the shares you picked vary in the last year? Do these data demonstrate the need to value current investments of this type at market? How are dividends received on investments in these shares accounted for? Be prepared to hand in your notes and to discuss the results of your investigation in class.

Financial Reporting and Analysis

Interpretation Cases from Business

ICB 6-1.

LO 3 *Short-Term Liquid Assets in*
LO 4 *Classic Government Bailout*

The car industry, especially **Chrysler** based in the United States, had difficult financial problems in the early 1980s. Chrysler incurred operating losses of over $1 billion in both 1979 and 1980. At that time it received U.S. government loan guarantees of $1 billion and more. Chrysler's short-term liquid assets for 1979 and 1980 were presented in its annual report as follows (in millions of dollars):[11]

	1980	1979
Cash	$101.1	$ 188.2
Time Deposits	2.6	120.8
Marketable Securities—at lower of cost or market	193.6	165.3
Accounts Receivable (less allowance for doubtful accounts: 1980—$40.3 million; 1979—$34.9 million)	476.2	610.3
Total Short-Term Liquid Assets	$773.5	$1,084.6

The company also reported current liabilities of $3,231.6 million in 1979 and $3,029.3 million in 1980. Sales totaled $12,001.9 million in 1979 and $9,225.3 million in 1980. In management's discussion and analysis of financial conditions and results of operations, it was noted that "Chrysler had to defer paying its major suppliers until it received the proceeds from the additional $400 million of government guaranteed debt. Chrysler's liquidity and its long-term viability are predicated on a return to sustained profitable operations".

Epilogue: At the end of 1983, Lee A. Iacocca, chief executive officer of Chrysler, could state in the annual report, "We repaid the $1.2 billion in loans guaranteed by the Federal Government. This action was taken seven years early." At the end of 1983, Chrysler had total short-term liquid assets of $1,360.6 million, consisting of Cash and Time Deposits of $111.6 million; Marketable Securities of $957.8 million; and Accounts Receivable (less allowance for uncollectible accounts of $25.5 million) of $291.2. Current liabilities were $3,453.9 million, and sales for 1983 were $13,240.4 million. By 1990, short-term liquid assets were $3,597 million, consisting of Cash and Time Deposits of $1,491 million, Marketable Securities of $1,473 million, and Accounts Receivable of $633 million. Current liabilities were $7,096 million, and sales for 1990 were $26,965 million. For comparison purposes, 1990 figures are shown for Chrysler operations without the finance and rental subsidiaries included. A separate allowance for uncollectible accounts was not disclosed for Chrysler operations.

REQUIRED

1. Calculate Chrysler's ratio of short-term liquid assets to current liabilities for 1979 and 1980. Did Chrysler's short-term liquidity position improve or deteriorate from 1979 to 1980? What apparent effect did the 1980 government guaranteed loan of $400 million have on the balance sheet and on the liquidity position?

2. It is important to Chrysler's survival that its customers pay their debts, and pay them on time. Calculate for 1979 and 1980 the ratio of the allowance for doubtful accounts to gross accounts receivable and the ratio of net accounts receivable to sales. What can you conclude from these calculations about Chrysler's ability to collect from its customers?

3. Calculate for 1983 the three ratios you calculated in questions 1 and 2 for 1979 and 1980; for 1990, calculate the first and third ratios. Comment on Chrysler's situation in 1983 and 1990 compared to 1979–1980.

ICB 6-2.

LO 1 *Interpretation of Ratios*

Philips and *Heineken* are two of the most famous Dutch companies. Philips is a large, diversified electronics, music, and media company, and Heineken makes a well-known beer. Philips is about six times bigger than Heineken, with 1995 revenues of 64.5 billion guilders versus 10.4 billion guilders. Ratios can help in comparing and understanding the companies. For example, the receivable turnovers for the companies for two recent years are as follows:

	1995	1994
Philips	5.9 times	5.8 times
Heineken	8.4 times	8.7 times

What do these ratios tell you about the credit policies of the two companies? How long does it take each on average to collect a receivable? What do these ratios tell about the companies' relative needs for capital to finance receivables? Can you state which company has a better credit policy? Explain your answers.

Nestlé Case

NC 6-1.

LO 1 *Analysis of Short-Term*
LO 2 *Liquid Assets*
LO 4

Refer to the annual report in the appendix on Nestlé to answer the following questions:

1. How much cash and cash equivalents did Nestlé have in 1996? Do you suppose most of this amount is cash in the bank or cash equivalents?
2. Nestlé does not disclose an allowance for uncollectible accounts. How do you explain this?
3. Calculate the quick ratios for 1995 and 1996 and comment on them.
4. Calculate receivable turnover and average days' sales uncollected for 1996 and comment on Nestlé's credit policies.

ENDNOTES

1. Sony, *Annual Report*, 1996.
2. American Greetings, *Annual Report*, 1993.
3. International Accounting Standard, IAS7, *Cash Flow Statements* (London: IASC, revised 1992).
4. James D. Moss, "Campbell Soup's Cutting Edge Cash Management", *Financial Executive*, September/October 1992.
5. International Accounting Standard, IAS25, *Accounting for Investments* (London: IASC, reformatted 1994).
6. The purpose of Allowance for Uncollectible Accounts is to reduce the gross accounts receivable to the amount estimated to be collectible (net realisable value). The purpose of another contra account, Accumulated Depreciation, is *not* to reduce the gross plant and equipment accounts to realisable value. Rather, its purpose is to show how much of the cost of the plant and equipment has been allocated as an expense to previous accounting periods.
7. Practice varies on the calculation of interest. Most banks use a 365-day year for all loans, but some use a 360-day year for commercial loans. In Europe, use of a 360-day year is common. In this book, we use a 360-day year to keep the calculations simple.
8. Some firms may follow the practice of reversing the September 30 adjusting entry. Here we assume that a reversing entry is not made.
9. Information based on promotional brochures received from Mitsubishi Electric.
10. Daimler-Benz, *Annual Report*, 1995.
11. Chrysler Corporation, *Annual Reports*, 1980, 1983, and 1990.

Chapter 7

INVENTORIES

LEARNING OBJECTIVES

1. Identify and explain the management issues associated with accounting for inventories.
2. Define *inventory cost* and relate it to goods flow and cost flow.
3. Calculate the pricing of inventory, using the cost basis under the periodic inventory system according to the (a) specific identification method; (b) weighted-average-cost method; (c) first-in, first-out (FIFO) method; (d) last-in, first-out (LIFO) method.
4. Apply the perpetual inventory system to the pricing of inventories at cost.
5. State the effects of inventory methods and misstatements of inventory on profit determination and income taxes.
6. Apply the lower of cost and market (LCM) rule to inventory valuation.

SUPPLEMENTAL OBJECTIVE

7. Estimate the cost of ending inventory using the (a) retail inventory method and (b) gross profit method.

DECISION POINT
PHILIPS

The management of inventories for profit is one of management's most complex and challenging tasks. Inventories are often the largest assets of a business.

Philips, a Dutch multinational, is a world leader in lighting, consumer electronics, music and film, multimedia, domestic appliances, semiconductors, medical systems, communications systems, and industrial electronics. While 53 per cent of Philips's sales are in Europe, 21 per cent are in North America and 17 per cent in Asia, its most rapidly growing market.

The current strategy of Philips is to focus on improving the profitability of its existing businesses. The belief that "What gets measured, gets done" has led to a new set of performance processes including a rigorous budgeting system and monthly performance reviews.

The management of inventories around the world presents a major challenge to Philips as these inventories comprise over 23 per cent of a total of 52,242 million guilders invested in company assets.[1]

The amount of money tied up in inventories must be controlled because of the cost of borrowing funds and storing inventories. Important accounting decisions include what assumptions to make about the flow of inventory costs, what prices to put on inventories, what inventory systems to use, and how to protect inventories against loss.

OBJECTIVE 1

Identify and explain the management issues associated with accounting for inventories

MANAGEMENT ISSUES ASSOCIATED WITH ACCOUNTING FOR INVENTORIES

Inventories are considered a current asset because they will normally be sold within a year's time or within a company's operating cycle. For a trading business like Marks & Spencer in Great Britain or Toys "R" Us in the United States, **inventories** encompass all goods purchased and held for sale in the ordinary course of business. Inventories are also very important for manufacturing companies. Since these companies are engaged in the actual making of products, they have three kinds of inventories: raw materials to be used in the production of goods, partially completed products (often called work in process or work in progress), and finished goods ready for sale. For example, in its 1995 annual report, Cadbury Schweppes, the British-based global company in beverages and confectionery, disclosed the following inventories (in millions of pounds):

	1995	1994
Raw materials and consumables	152	134
Work in progress	36	33
Finished goods	247	227
Total inventories	435	394

In manufacturing operations, the cost of work in process and the cost of finished goods inventories include not only the cost of the raw materials that go into the product, but also the cost of the labour used to convert the raw materials to finished goods and the overhead costs that support the production process. Included in this latter category are such costs as indirect materials (for example, paint and lubricants), indirect labour (such as the salaries of supervisors), factory rent, depreciation of plant assets, electricity costs, and insurance costs. The methods for maintaining and pricing inventories explained in this chapter are applicable to manufactured goods, but since the details of accounting for manufacturing companies are usually covered in managerial accounting courses, this chapter focuses on accounting for trading companies.

In the chapter on the trading income statement and internal control, the importance of management's choice of either the periodic or the perpetual inventory system for the processing of accounting information was discussed. The management issues in this chapter relate to the measurement of profit through the allocation of the cost of inventories in accordance with the matching rule; assessing the impact of inventory decisions on such factors as net profit, income taxes, and cash flows; and evaluating the level of inventory.

Applying the Matching Rule to Inventories

The International Accounting Standards Committee (IASC) states that: "When inventories are sold, the carrying amount of those inventories should be recognised as an expense in the period in which the related revenue is recognised."[2] Note that the objective of accounting for inventories is the proper determination of profit through the matching of expenses and revenues, not the determination of the most realistic inventory value. As will be shown, these two objectives are sometimes incompatible, in which case the objective of profit determination takes precedence.

The reason inventory accounting is so important to profit measurement is linked to the way profit is measured on the trading income statement. Recall that gross profit is calculated as the difference between net sales and cost of goods sold and that cost of goods sold is measured by deducting ending inventory from the cost of goods available for sale. Because of these relationships, the higher the cost of ending inventory, the lower the cost of goods sold and the higher the resulting gross profit. Conversely, the lower the value assigned to ending inventory, the higher the cost of goods sold and the lower the gross profit. Since the amount of gross profit has a direct effect on the amount of net profit, the amount assigned to ending inventory directly affects the amount of net profit. *In effect, the value assigned to the ending inventory determines what portion of the cost of goods available for sale is assigned to cost of goods sold and what portion is assigned to the balance sheet as inventory to be carried over into the next accounting period.*

Figure 7-1 shows the management choices related to the application of the matching rule to accounting for inventories. In the context of either the periodic inventory system or the perpetual inventory system, the amount of cost of goods available for sale allocated to cost of goods sold and to ending inventory depends on what assumptions are made about the flow of costs into the company as goods are purchased and out of the company as goods are sold. The methods available to management for assigning costs to these flows are the specific identification method, the weighted-average-cost method, the first-in, first-out (FIFO) method, and the last-in, first-out (LIFO) method. Further, at the end of the accounting period, the market value of the inventory is calculated to determine whether the inventory must be adjusted through the application of the lower of cost and market rule. These choices are described and discussed in this chapter.

Assessing the Impact of Inventory Decisions

Figure 7-1 summarises the management choices with regard to inventory systems and methods. The decisions usually result in different amounts of reported net profit and, as a result, affect both the external evaluation of the company by investors and lenders and internal evaluations such as performance reviews, bonuses, and executive com-

FIGURE 7-1 *Management Choices in Accounting for Inventories*

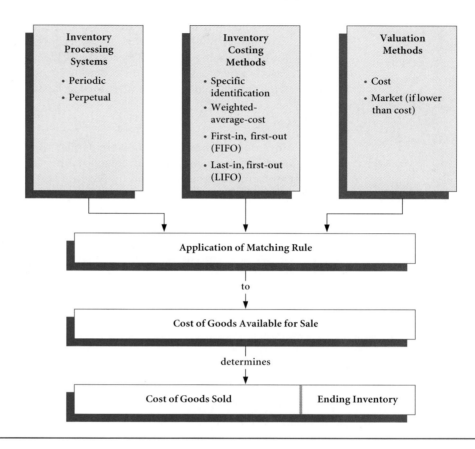

pensation. Further, because profit is affected, the valuation of inventory may also have a considerable effect on the amount of income taxes paid. Income tax authorities have, therefore, been interested in the effects of various inventory valuation methods and have specific regulations about the acceptability of different methods. As a result, management is sometimes faced with the problem of balancing the goal of proper profit determination with that of minimising income taxes. Another consideration is that since the choice of inventory valuation method affects the amount of income taxes paid, it also affects a company's cash flows. The effects of management's decisions are discussed in more detail in this chapter after the inventory methods have been presented.

Evaluating the Level of Inventory

Level of inventory has important economic consequences for a company. Ideally, management wants to have a great variety and quantity available so that customers have a large choice and do not have to wait. Such an inventory policy is not costless, however. The cost of handling and storage and the interest cost of the funds necessary to maintain high inventory levels are usually substantial. On the other hand, the maintenance of low inventory levels may result in lost sales and disgruntled customers. Common measures used in the evaluation of inventory levels are inventory turnover and its related measure, average days' inventory available.

BUSINESS BULLETIN   **Business Practice**

A just-in-time (JIT) inventory system is designed to ensure that goods or
materials arrive at the point of use precisely at the time they are needed.
More and more companies are following the lead taken by Japanese companies such as Toyota and Nissan to reduce inventories and holding costs to the
lowest levels possible. A JIT system works in cases in which managers know
exactly when to order and the orders arrive as scheduled. Sometimes JIT systems are referred to as zero inventory or Japanese *kanban* inventory systems.

Inventory turnover is a measure similar to receivable turnover. It indicates the
number of times a company's average inventory is sold during an accounting period.
Inventory turnover is calculated by dividing cost of goods sold by average inventory.
For example, Marks & Spencer's cost of goods sold was 4,715.6 million pounds in
1996, and its inventory was 377.0 million in 1995 and 422.8 million in 1996. Its
inventory turnover is calculated as follows:

$$\text{Inventory turnover} = \frac{\text{cost of goods sold}}{\text{average inventory}}$$

$$= \frac{4,715,600,000}{(377,000,000 + 422,800,000)/2}$$

$$= \frac{4,715,600,000}{399,900,000} = 11.8 \text{ times}$$

The **average days' inventory available** indicates the average number of days
required to sell the average inventory. To find the average days' inventory available,
the number of days in a year is divided by the inventory turnover, as follows:

$$\text{Average days' inventory available} = \frac{\text{number of days in a year}}{\text{inventory turnover}}$$

$$= \frac{365 \text{ days}}{11.8 \text{ times}} = 30.9 \text{ days}$$

From this information, it may be seen that Marks & Spencer turned its inventory over
11.8 times in 1996, or on average every 30.9 days. These figures are as expected
because Marks & Spencer is in a business that comprises food, clothing, footwear, and
home furnishings. Food, of course, is fast-moving, whereas sales of clothing,
footwear, and home furnishings are more seasonally based.

Many companies, both in trading and in manufacturing, are attempting to
reduce their inventory assets by changing to a **just-in-time operating environment**. In
this environment, rather than stockpiling inventories for later use, companies work
closely with suppliers to coordinate and schedule shipments so that goods arrive just
in time to be used or sold. Less money is thereby tied up in inventories, and the costs
associated with carrying inventories are reduced.

OBJECTIVE 2

*Define inventory cost and
relate it to goods flow and
cost flow*

PRICING INVENTORY UNDER THE PERIODIC INVENTORY SYSTEM

According to the International Accounting Standards Committee (IASC), "The cost
of inventories should comprise all costs of purchase, costs of conversion and other
costs incurred in bringing the inventories to their present location and condition."[3]

This definition of **inventory cost** has generally been interpreted to include the following costs: (1) invoice price less purchases discounts; (2) freight or transportation in, including insurance in transit; and (3) applicable taxes and tariffs. Other costs—for ordering, receiving, and storing—should in principle also be included in inventory cost. In practice, however, it is so difficult to allocate these costs to specific inventory items that they are usually considered an expense of the accounting period instead of an inventory cost.

Goods in Transit

Because inventory includes all items owned by a company and held for sale, the status of any goods in transit, either being sold or being purchased by the inventorying company, must be examined to determine if it should be included in the inventory count. As explained in the chapter on the trading income statement and internal control, the terms of the shipping agreement will indicate whether title has passed. Outgoing goods shipped FOB destination would be included in inventory, whereas those shipped FOB shipping point would not. Conversely, incoming goods shipped FOB shipping point would be included in inventory, but those shipped FOB destination would not.

Goods Available Not Included in Inventory

At the time a physical inventory is taken, there may be goods available to which the company does not hold title. One category of such goods includes goods that have been sold and are awaiting delivery to the buyer. Since the sale has been completed, title to the goods has passed to the buyer, and the goods should not be included in the inventory. A second category is goods held on consignment. A **consignment** is the placing of goods by their owner (known as the *consignor*) on the premises of another company (the *consignee*). Title to consigned goods remains with the consignor until the consignee sells the goods. Thus, consigned goods should not be included in the physical inventory of the consignee because they still belong to the consignor.

Methods of Pricing Inventory at Cost

The prices of most kinds of goods vary during the year. Identical lots of goods may have been purchased at different prices. Also, when identical items are bought and sold, it is often impossible to tell which have been sold and which are still in inventory. For this reason, it is necessary to make an assumption about the order in which items have been sold. Because the assumed order of sale may or may not be the same as the actual order of sale, the assumption is really about the *flow of costs* rather than the *flow of physical inventory*.

Thus, the term **goods flow** refers to the actual physical movement of goods in the operations of a company, and the term **cost flow** refers to the association of costs with their *assumed* flow in the operations of a company. The assumed cost flow may or may not be the same as the actual goods flow. This statement may seem strange at first, but several assumed cost flows are available under accounting standards. In fact, it is sometimes preferable to use an assumed cost flow that bears no relationship to goods flow because it gives a better estimate of profit, which, as stated earlier, is the major goal of inventory valuation.

Accountants usually price inventory by using one of the following methods, each based on a different assumption of cost flow: (1) specific identification method; (2) weighted-average-cost method; (3) first-in, first-out (FIFO) method; and (4) last-in, first-out (LIFO) method. The choice of method depends on the nature of the business, the financial effects of the methods, and the costs of implementing them.

To illustrate the four methods under the periodic inventory system, the following data for the month of June will be used:

Inventory Data, June 30

June 1	Inventory	50 units @ 1.00	50
6	Purchase	50 units @ 1.10	55
13	Purchase	150 units @ 1.20	180
20	Purchase	100 units @ 1.30	130
25	Purchase	150 units @ 1.40	210
Goods Available for Sale		500 units	625
Sales		280 units	
Available June 30		220 units	

Notice that there is a total of 500 units available for sale at a total cost of 625. Stated simply, the problem of inventory pricing is to divide the 625 between the 280 units sold and the 220 units available. Recall that under the periodic inventory system, the inventory is not updated after each purchase and sale. Thus, it is not necessary to know when the individual sales take place.

OBJECTIVE 3a

Calculate the pricing of inventory, using the cost basis under the periodic inventory system according to the specific identification method

Specific Identification Method

If the units in the ending inventory can be identified as coming from specific purchases, the **specific identification method** may be used to price the inventory. For instance, assume that the June 30 inventory consisted of 50 units from the June 1 inventory, 100 units from the purchase of June 13, and 70 units from the purchase of June 25. The cost assigned to the inventory under the specific identification method would be 268, determined as follows:

Periodic Inventory System—Specific Identification Method

50 units @ 1.00	50	Cost of Goods Available	
100 units @ 1.20	120	for Sale	625
70 units @ 1.40	98	Less June 30 Inventory	268
220 units at cost of	268	Cost of Goods Sold	357

The specific identification method might be used in the purchase and sale of high-priced articles, such as cars, heavy equipment, and works of art. Although this method may appear logical, it is rarely used because it has two definite disadvantages. The first disadvantage is that in many cases it is difficult and impractical to keep track of the purchase and sale of individual items. The second disadvantage is that when a company deals in items of an identical nature, deciding which items are sold becomes arbitrary; thus, the company can raise or lower profit by choosing to sell the high- or low-cost items.

OBJECTIVE 3b

Calculate the pricing of inventory, using the cost basis under the periodic inventory system according to the weighted-average-cost method

Weighted-Average-Cost Method

Under the **weighted-average-cost method**, inventory is priced at the average cost of the goods available for sale during the period. Average cost is calculated by dividing the total cost of goods available for sale by the total units available for sale. This gives a weighted-average unit cost that is applied to the units in the ending inventory. In our illustration, the ending inventory would be 275, or 1.25 per unit, determined as follows:

Periodic Inventory System—Weighted-Average-Cost Method

Cost of goods available for sale ÷ units available for sale = Average unit cost

625 ÷ 500 units = 1.25

Ending inventory: 220 units @ 1.25 = 275

Cost of Goods Available for Sale	625
Less June 30 Inventory	275
Cost of Goods Sold	350

The weighted-average-cost method tends to level out the effects of cost increases and decreases because the cost for the ending inventory calculated under this method is influenced by all the prices paid during the year and by the beginning inventory price. Some, however, criticise the weighted-average-cost method because they believe that recent costs are more relevant for profit measurement and decision making.

OBJECTIVE 3c

Calculate the pricing of inventory, using the cost basis under the periodic inventory system according to the first-in, first-out (FIFO) method

First-In, First-Out (FIFO) Method

The **first-in, first-out (FIFO) method** is based on the assumption that the costs of the first items acquired should be assigned to the first items sold. The costs of the goods available at the end of a period are assumed to be from the most recent purchases, and the costs assigned to goods that have been sold are assumed to be from the earliest purchases. The FIFO method of determining inventory cost may be adopted by any business, regardless of the actual physical flow of goods, because the assumption is made regarding the flow of costs and not the flow of goods.

In our illustration, the June 30 inventory would be 301 when the FIFO method is used. It is calculated as follows:

Periodic Inventory System—First-In, First-Out Method

150 units at 1.40 from purchase of June 25	210
70 units at 1.30 from purchase of June 20	91
220 units at a cost of	301
Cost of Goods Available for Sale	625
Less June 30 Inventory	301
Cost of Goods Sold	324

The effect of the FIFO method is to value the ending inventory at the most recent costs and include earlier ones in cost of goods sold. During periods of consistently rising prices, the FIFO method yields the highest possible amount of net profit, since cost of goods sold will show costs closer to the price level at the time the goods were purchased. Another reason for this result is that businesses tend to increase selling prices as costs rise, even though inventories may have been purchased before the price rise. The reverse effect occurs in periods of price decreases. Thus, a major criticism of FIFO is that it magnifies the effects of the business cycle on profit.

OBJECTIVE 3d

Calculate the pricing of inventory, using the cost basis under the periodic inventory system according to the last-in, first-out (LIFO) method

Last-In, First-Out (LIFO) Method

The **last-in, first-out (LIFO) method** of costing inventories is based on the assumption that the costs of the last items purchased should be assigned to the first items used or sold and that the cost of the ending inventory reflects the cost of goods purchased earliest.

Under this method, the June 30 inventory would be 249, calculated in the following manner:

Periodic Inventory System—Last-In, First-Out Method

50 units at 1.00 from June 1 inventory	50
50 units at 1.10 from purchase of June 6	55
120 units at 1.20 from purchase of June 13	144
220 units at a cost of	249
Cost of Goods Available for Sale	625
Less June 30 Inventory	249
Cost of Goods Sold	376

The effect of LIFO is to value inventory at the earliest prices and to include in cost of goods sold the cost of the most recently purchased goods. This assumption, of course, does not agree with the physical movement of goods in most businesses.

However, a strong logical argument supports this method, based on the fact that a certain size inventory is necessary in a going concern. When inventory is sold, it must be replaced with more goods. The supporters of LIFO reason that the fairest determination of profit occurs if the current costs of goods are matched against current sales prices, regardless of which physical units of goods are sold. When prices are moving either up or down, LIFO will mean that the cost of goods sold will show costs closer to the price level at the time the goods were sold. As a result, the LIFO method tends to show a smaller net profit during inflationary times and a larger net profit during deflationary times than other methods of inventory valuation. Thus, the peaks and valleys of the business cycle tend to be smoothed out. The important factor here is that in inventory valuation the flow of costs, and hence profit determination, is more important than the physical movement of goods and balance sheet valuation.

An argument may also be made against the LIFO method. Because the inventory valuation on the balance sheet reflects earlier prices, it often gives an unrealistic picture of the current value of the inventory. Thus, such balance sheet measures as working capital and current ratio may be distorted and must be interpreted carefully.

OBJECTIVE 4

Apply the perpetual inventory system to the pricing of inventories at cost

PRICING INVENTORY UNDER THE PERPETUAL INVENTORY SYSTEM

The pricing of inventories under the perpetual inventory system differs from pricing under the periodic inventory system. This difference occurs because under the perpetual inventory system, a continuous record of quantities and costs of goods is maintained as purchases and sales are made. Under the periodic inventory system, only the ending inventory is counted and priced. Cost of goods sold is determined by deducting the cost of the ending inventory from the cost of goods available for sale. Under the perpetual system, cost of goods sold is accumulated as sales are made and costs are transferred from the Inventory account to Cost of Goods Sold. The cost of the ending inventory is the balance of the Inventory account. In order to illustrate pricing methods under the perpetual inventory system, the same data will be used as before, but specific sales dates and amounts will be added, as follows:

Inventory Data—June 30

June	1	Inventory	50 units @ 1.00
	6	Purchase	50 units @ 1.10
	10	Sale	70 units
	13	Purchase	150 units @ 1.20
	20	Purchase	100 units @ 1.30
	25	Purchase	150 units @ 1.40
	30	Sale	210 units
	30	Inventory	220 units

Pricing the inventory and cost of goods sold using the specific identification method is the same under the perpetual system as it was under the periodic system because cost of goods sold and ending inventory are based on the cost of the identified items sold and available. The perpetual system facilitates the use of the specific identification method because detailed records of purchases and sales are maintained.

Pricing the inventory and cost of goods sold using the weighted-average-cost method differs when the perpetual system is used. Under the periodic system, the average cost is calculated for all goods available for sale during the month. Under the perpetual system, a moving average is calculated after each purchase, as follows:

Perpetual Inventory System—Weighted-Average-Cost Method

June	1	Inventory	50 units @ 1.00	50.00
	6	Purchase	50 units @ 1.10	55.00
	6	Balance	100 units @ 1.05	105.00
	10	Sale	70 units @ 1.05	(73.50)
	10	Balance	30 units @ 1.05	31.50
	13	Purchase	150 units @ 1.20	180.00
	20	Purchase	100 units @ 1.30	130.00
	25	Purchase	150 units @ 1.40	210.00
	25	Balance	430 units @ 1.28*	551.50
	30	Sale	210 units @ 1.28*	(268.80)
	30	Balance	220 units @ 1.29*	282.70
Cost of Goods Sold			73.50 + 268.80	342.30

*Rounded

The sum of the costs applied to sales becomes the cost of goods sold, 342.30. The ending inventory is the balance, or 282.70.

When pricing the inventory using the FIFO and LIFO methods, it is necessary to keep track of the components of inventory at each step of the way because as sales are made, the costs must be assigned in the proper order. To apply the FIFO method, the approach is as follows:

Perpetual Inventory System—FIFO Method

June	1	Inventory	50 units @ 1.00		50.00
	6	Purchase	50 units @ 1.10		55.00
	10	Sale	50 units @ 1.00	(50.00)	
			20 units @ 1.10	(22.00)	(72.00)
	10	Balance	30 units @ 1.10		33.00
	13	Purchase	150 units @ 1.20		180.00
	20	Purchase	100 units @ 1.30		130.00
	25	Purchase	150 units @ 1.40		210.00
	30	Sale	30 units @ 1.10	(33.00)	
			150 units @ 1.20	(180.00)	
			30 units @ 1.30	(39.00)	(252.00)
	30	Balance	70 units @ 1.30	91.00	
			150 units @ 1.40	210.00	301.00
Cost of Goods Sold			72.00 + 252.00		324.00

Note that the ending inventory of 301 and the cost of goods sold of 324 are the same as the figures calculated earlier under the periodic inventory system. This will always occur because the ending inventory under both systems will always consist of the last items purchased—in this case, the entire purchase of June 25 and 70 units from the purchase of June 20.

To apply the LIFO method, the approach is as follows:

Perpetual Inventory System—LIFO Method

June	1	Inventory	50 units @ 1.00		50.00
	6	Purchase	50 units @ 1.10		55.00
	10	Sale	50 units @ 1.10	(55.00)	
			20 units @ 1.00	(20.00)	(75.00)
	10	Balance	30 units @ 1.00		30.00
	13	Purchase	150 units @ 1.20		180.00
	20	Purchase	100 units @ 1.30		130.00
	25	Purchase	150 units @ 1.40		210.00
	30	Sale	150 units @ 1.40	(210.00)	
			60 units @ 1.30	(78.00)	(288.00)
	30	Balance	30 units @ 1.00	30.00	
			150 units @ 1.20	180.00	
			40 units @ 1.30	52.00	262.00
		Cost of Goods Sold	75.00 + 288.00		363.00

Note that the ending inventory of 262 includes 30 units from the beginning inventory, all units from the purchase of June 13, and 40 units from the purchase of June 20.

OBJECTIVE 5

State the effects of inventory methods and misstatements of inventory on profit determination and income taxes

COMPARISON AND IMPACT OF INVENTORY DECISIONS AND MISSTATEMENTS

The specific identification, weighted-average-cost, FIFO, and LIFO methods of pricing inventory under both the periodic and the perpetual inventory systems have now been illustrated. The effects of the four methods on net profit are shown in Exhibit 7-1, using the same data as before and assuming June sales of 500. Because the specific

EXHIBIT 7-1   *Effects of Inventory Systems and Methods Calculated*

	Specific Identification Method	Periodic Inventory System			Perpetual Inventory System[†]		
		Weighted-Average-Cost Method	First-In, First-Out Method	Last-In, First-Out Method	Weighted-Average-Cost Method	First-In, First-Out Method	Last-In, First-Out Method
Sales	500	500	500	500	500	500	500
Cost of Goods Sold							
Beginning Inventory	50	50	50	50			
Purchases	575	575	575	575			
Cost of Goods Available for Sale	625	625	625	625			
Less Ending Inventory	268	275	301	249	283*	301	262
Cost of Goods Sold	357	350	324	376	342*	324	363
Gross Profit	143	150	176	124	158	176	137

*Rounded
†Ending inventory under the perpetual inventory system is provided for comparison only. It is not used in the calculation of cost of goods sold.

identification method is based on actual cost, the effects of this method are the same under both systems.

Keeping in mind that June was a period of rising prices, we can see that LIFO, which charges the most recent and, in this case, the highest prices to cost of goods sold, resulted in the lowest gross profit under both systems.

Conversely, FIFO, which charges the earliest and, in this case, the lowest prices to cost of goods sold, produced the highest gross profit. The gross profit under the weighted-average-cost method is somewhere between those under LIFO and FIFO. Thus, it is clear that the weighted-average-cost method has a less pronounced effect. Note that the results under FIFO are the same under both systems.

During a period of declining prices, the reverse would occur. The LIFO method would produce a higher gross profit than the FIFO method. It is apparent that the method of inventory valuation has the greatest importance during prolonged periods of price changes in one direction, either up or down.

Because the specific identification method depends on the particular items sold, no generalisation can be made about the effect of changing prices.

Effects on the Financial Statements

The LIFO method of inventory cost determination is permitted for tax purposes in a number of countries, including Canada, Germany, Japan, and the U.S. This was instrumental in its acceptance by the IASC as an allowed alternative to the FIFO or weighted-average-cost methods.

Each of these methods of inventory pricing is acceptable, in principle, for use in published financial statements. The FIFO and weighted-average-cost methods are the most widely used in practice and, with the exception of cases in which the specific identification method is appropriate, are the preferred benchmark methods of the International Accounting Standard on inventories.[4] However, LIFO is an allowed alternative and is often used, for example, in the United States. Table 7-1 gives an indication of the diversity of methods used internationally.

TABLE 7-1 *Inventory Pricing Methods*

Country	FIFO or Weighted-Average-Cost	LIFO
Australia	Permitted	Not Permitted
Austria	Permitted	Permitted
Belgium	Permitted	Permitted
Canada	Permitted	Permitted
Denmark	Permitted	Not Permitted
Finland	Permitted	Not Permitted
France	Permitted	Not Permitted
Germany	Permitted	Permitted
Greece	Permitted	Permitted
Italy	Permitted	Permitted
Ireland	Permitted	Not Permitted
Japan	Permitted	Permitted
Netherlands	Permitted	Permitted
Norway	Permitted	Not Permitted
Portugal	Permitted	Permitted
Spain	Permitted	Permitted
Sweden	Permitted	Not Permitted
Switzerland	Permitted	Not Permitted
United Kingdom	Permitted	Not Permitted
United States	Permitted	Permitted

┌───┐

BUSINESS BULLETIN   **International Practice**

In many countries around the world, taxation regulations are a major influence on accounting methods. This is of special significance in respect to inventory valuation. The cost basis used is subject to regulation owing to the significant effects that the different methods—FIFO, weighted-average-cost, and LIFO—have on the measurement of profit and hence on taxation when company accounts are relied upon for tax assessment purposes. Interpretation of the lower of cost and market rule, and the write-downs permitted, is also regulated in view of its impact on profit. In Germany, for example, a very conservative approach to inventory valuation is permitted that includes adjustments to reflect anticipated future price reductions.

Each method has its advantages and disadvantages, and none can be considered best or perfect. The factors that should be considered in choosing an inventory method are the effects of each method on financial statements, income taxes, and management decisions.

A basic problem in determining the best inventory measure for a particular company stems from the fact that inventory affects both the balance sheet and the income statement. As we have seen, the LIFO method is best suited for the income statement because it matches revenues and the current cost of goods sold. But it is not the best measure of the current balance sheet value of inventory, particularly during a prolonged period of price increases or decreases. The FIFO method, on the other hand, is best suited to the balance sheet because the ending inventory is closest to current values and thus gives a more realistic view of the current financial assets of a business. Users of financial statements must be alert to inventory methods and be able to assess their effects.

Effects on Income Taxes

Many accountants believe that the use of the FIFO and weighted-average-cost methods in periods of rising prices causes businesses to report more than their true profit, resulting in the payment of excess income taxes. The profit is overstated because cost of goods sold is understated, relative to current prices. The company must buy replacement inventory at higher prices, but additional funds are also needed to pay income taxes. In some countries, such as Germany and the United States, this effect is recognised and LIFO is permitted for tax purposes.

Effects of Misstatements in Inventory Measurement

The basic problem of separating goods available for sale into two components—goods sold and goods not sold—is that of assigning a cost to the goods not sold, the ending inventory. That portion of the goods available for sale not assigned to the ending inventory is used to determine the cost of goods sold.

For this reason, a misstatement in the inventory figure at the end of the period will cause an equal misstatement in gross profit and net profit in the income statement. The amount of assets and shareholders' equity on the balance sheet will also be misstated by the same amount. The consequences of overstatement and understatement of inventory are illustrated in the three simplified examples that follow. In each case, beginning inventory, net purchases, and cost of goods available for sale have been stated correctly. In the first example, ending inventory has been stated correctly. In the second example, inventory is overstated by 6,000; in the third example, inventory is understated by 6,000.

Example 1. Ending Inventory Correctly Stated at 10,000

Cost of Goods Sold for the Year		Income Statement for the Year	
Beginning Inventory	12,000	Net Sales	100,000
Net Cost of Purchases	58,000	Cost of Goods Sold	60,000
Cost of Goods Available for Sale	70,000	Gross Profit	40,000
Ending Inventory	10,000	Operating Expenses	32,000
Cost of Goods Sold	60,000	Net Profit	8,000

Example 2. Ending Inventory Overstated by 6,000

Cost of Goods Sold for the Year		Income Statement for the Year	
Beginning Inventory	12,000	Net Sales	100,000
Net Cost of Purchases	58,000	Cost of Goods Sold	54,000
Cost of Goods Available for Sale	70,000	Gross Profit	46,000
Ending Inventory	16,000	Operating Expenses	32,000
Cost of Goods Sold	54,000	Net Profit	14,000

Example 3. Ending Inventory Understated by 6,000

Cost of Goods Sold for the Year		Income Statement for the Year	
Beginning Inventory	12,000	Net Sales	100,000
Net Cost of Purchases	58,000	Cost of Goods Sold	66,000
Cost of Goods Available for Sale	70,000	Gross Profit	34,000
Ending Inventory	4,000	Operating Expenses	32,000
Cost of Goods Sold	66,000	Net Profit	2,000

In all three examples, the total cost of goods available for sale was 70,000. The difference in net profit resulted from how this 70,000 was divided between ending inventory and cost of goods sold.

Because the ending inventory in one period becomes the beginning inventory in the next, it is important to recognise that a misstatement in inventory valuation affects not only the current period, but also the following one. Over a two-year period the errors in net profit will offset, or counterbalance, each other. In Example 2, for instance, the overstatement of ending inventory caused a 6,000 overstatement of beginning inventory in the following year, resulting in an understatement of profit by 6,000 in the second year. This offsetting effect is illustrated in Table 7-2.

TABLE 7-2 *Ending Inventory Overstated by 6,000*

		With Inventory at Dec. 31, 20x1 Overstated	
	With Inventory Correctly Stated	Reported Net Profit Will Be	Reported Net Profit Will Be Overstated (Understated)
Net Profit for 20x1	8,000	14,000	6,000
Net Profit for 20x2	15,000	9,000	(6,000)
Total Net Profit for Two Years	23,000	23,000	—

Because the total profit for the two years is the same, there may be a tendency to think that one does not need to worry about inventory misstatements. However, the misstatements violate the matching rule. In addition, management, lenders, and investors make many decisions on an annual basis and depend on the accountant's determination of net profit. The accountant has an obligation to make the net profit figure for each year as useful as possible.

The effects of misstatements in inventory on net profit are as follows:

Year 1	Year 2
Ending inventory overstated	**Beginning inventory overstated**
Cost of goods sold understated	Cost of goods sold overstated
Net profit overstated	Net profit understated
Ending inventory understated	**Beginning inventory understated**
Cost of goods sold overstated	Cost of goods sold understated
Net profit understated	Net profit overstated

If we assume no income tax effects, a misstatement in inventory results in a misstatement in net profit of the same amount. Thus, the measurement of inventory is important.

OBJECTIVE 6

Apply the lower of cost and market (LCM) rule to inventory valuation

Under the lower of cost and market rule, market may be interpreted in Germany, the Netherlands, and the U.S., for example, to mean replacement cost, especially when LIFO has been used. In such cases, the International Accounting Standards Committee requires the disclosure of the difference between the lower of replacement cost and net realisable value.

VALUING THE INVENTORY AT THE LOWER OF COST AND MARKET (LCM)

Although cost is usually the most appropriate basis for valuation of inventory, there are times when inventory may properly be shown in the financial statements at less than its cost. If by reason of physical deterioration, obsolescence, or decline in price level the market value of inventory falls below its cost, a loss has occurred. This loss may be recognised by writing the inventory down to market. The term **market** is used here to mean net realisable value, the amount for which the goods can be sold. The International Accounting Standards Committee states that "Inventories should be measured at the lower of cost and net realisable value."[5] The term **net realisable value** is defined as "estimated selling price in the ordinary course of business less the estimated costs of completion and the estimated costs necessary to make the sale".[6] It may help, therefore, in applying the **lower of cost and market (LCM) rule** to think of it as the "lower of cost and net realisable value" rule.

There are three basic methods of valuing inventories at the lower of cost and net realisable value: (1) the item-by-item method, (2) the major category method, and (3) the total inventory method. For example, an electrical shop could determine lower of cost and market for each kind of television, video, and CD player (item by item); for all televisions, all videos, and all CD players (major categories); or for all televisions, videos, and CD players together (total inventory).

Item-by-Item Method

When the **item-by-item method** is used, cost and market are compared for each item in inventory. The individual items are then valued at their lower price, as shown in Table 7-3.

Major Category Method

Under the **major category method**, the total cost and total market for each category of items are compared. Each category is then valued at its lower amount (see Table 7-4).

TABLE 7-3 *Lower of Cost and Market with Item-by-Item Method*

	Quantity	Per Unit Cost	Per Unit Market	Lower of Cost and Market
Category I				
Item a	200	**1.50**	1.70	300
Item b	100	2.00	**1.80**	180
Item c	100	**2.50**	2.60	250
Category II				
Item d	300	5.00	**4.50**	1,350
Item e	200	**4.00**	4.10	800
Inventory at the lower of cost and market				**2,880**

TABLE 7-4 *Lower of Cost and Market with Major Category Method*

	Quantity	Per Unit Cost	Per Unit Market	Total Cost	Total Market	Lower of Cost and Market
Category I						
Item a	200	1.50	1.70	300	340	
Item b	100	2.00	1.80	200	180	
Item c	100	2.50	2.60	250	260	
Totals				750	780	750
Category II						
Item d	300	5.00	4.50	1,500	1,350	
Item e	200	4.00	4.10	800	820	
Totals				2,300	2,170	2,170
Inventory at the lower of cost and market						**2,920**

VALUING INVENTORY BY ESTIMATION

It is sometimes necessary or desirable to estimate the value of ending inventory. The methods most commonly used for this purpose are the retail method and the gross profit method.

SUPPLEMENTAL OBJECTIVE 7a

Estimate the cost of ending inventory using the retail inventory method

Retail Method of Inventory Estimation

The **retail method** is an inventory estimation method used in retail trading businesses by which inventory at retail value is reduced by the ratio of cost to retail price. There are two principal reasons for its use. First, management usually requires that financial statements be prepared at least once a month and, as taking a physical inventory is time-consuming and expensive, the retail method is used instead to estimate the value

TABLE 7-5   *The Retail Method of Inventory Valuation*

	Cost	Retail
Beginning Inventory	40,000	55,000
Net Purchases for the Period (excluding Freight In)	107,000	145,000
Freight In	3,000	
Goods Available for Sale	150,000	200,000
Ratio of Cost to Retail Price: $\dfrac{150,000}{200,000} = 75\%$		
Net Sales during the Period		160,000
Estimated Ending Inventory at Retail		40,000
Ratio of Cost to Retail	75%	
Estimated Cost of Ending Inventory	30,000	

of inventory available. Second, because items in a retail store normally have a price tag or a universal product code, it is a common practice to take the physical inventory at retail from these price tags and codes and reduce the total value to cost through use of the retail method. The term *at retail* means the amount of the inventory at the marked selling prices of the inventory items.

When the retail method is used to estimate ending inventory, the records must show the beginning inventory at cost and at retail. The records must also show the amount of goods purchased during the period both at cost and at retail. The net sales at retail is, of course, the balance of the Sales account less returns and allowances. A simple example of the retail method is shown in Table 7-5.

Goods available for sale is determined both at cost and at retail by listing beginning inventory and net purchases for the period at cost and at the expected selling price of the goods, adding freight to the cost column, and totalling. The ratio of these two amounts (cost to retail price) provides an estimate of the cost of each monetary unit of retail sales value. The estimated ending inventory at retail is then determined by deducting sales for the period from the retail price of the goods that were available for sale during the period. The inventory at retail is then converted to cost on the basis of the ratio of cost to retail.

The cost of ending inventory may also be estimated by applying the ratio of cost to retail to the total retail value of the physical count of the ending inventory. Applying the retail method in practice is often more difficult than this simple example because of such complications as changes in retail price that take place during the year, different markups on different types of goods, and varying volumes of sales for different types of goods.

SUPPLEMENTAL OBJECTIVE 7b

Estimate the cost of ending inventory using the gross profit method

Gross Profit Method of Inventory Estimation

The **gross profit method** assumes that the ratio of gross profit for a business remains relatively stable from year to year. It is used in place of the retail method when records of the retail prices of beginning inventory and purchases are not kept. The gross profit method is considered acceptable for estimating the cost of inventory for interim reports, but it is not acceptable for valuing inventory in the annual financial statements. This method is also useful in estimating the amount of inventory lost or destroyed by theft, fire, or other hazards. Insurance companies often use this method to verify loss claims.

TABLE 7-6 *The Gross Profit Method of Inventory Valuation*

1. Beginning Inventory at Cost		50,000
Purchases at Cost (including Freight In)		290,000
Cost of Goods Available for Sale		340,000
2. Less Estimated Cost of Goods Sold		
Sales at Selling Price	400,000	
Less Estimated Gross Profit of 30%	120,000	
Estimated Cost of Goods Sold		280,000
3. Estimated Cost of Ending Inventory		60,000

The gross profit method is simple to use. First, calculate the cost of goods available for sale in the usual way (add purchases to beginning inventory). Second, estimate the cost of goods sold by deducting the estimated gross profit from sales. Finally, deduct the estimated cost of goods sold from the goods available for sale to arrive at the estimated cost of ending inventory. This method is shown in Table 7-6.

CHAPTER REVIEW

Review of Learning Objectives

1. **Identify and explain the management issues associated with accounting for inventories.** Included in inventories are goods owned, whether produced or purchased, that are held for sale in the ordinary course of business. Manufacturing companies also include raw materials and work in process. Among the issues management must face in accounting for inventories are allocating the cost of inventories in accordance with the matching rule, assessing the impact of inventory decisions, and evaluating the levels of inventory. The objective of accounting for inventories is the proper determination of profit through the matching of costs and revenues, not the determination of the most realistic inventory value. Because the valuation of inventory has a direct effect on a company's net profit, the choice of inventory systems and methods affects not only the amount of income taxes and cash flows, but also the external and internal evaluation of the company. The level of inventory as measured by the inventory turnover and its related measure, average days' inventory available, is important to managing the amount of investment needed by a company.

2. **Define *inventory cost* and relate it to goods flow and cost flow.** The cost of inventory includes (1) invoice price less purchases discounts, (2) freight or transportation in, including insurance in transit, and (3) applicable taxes and tariffs. Goods flow relates to the actual physical flow of goods, whereas cost flow refers to the assumed flow of costs in the operation of the business.

3. **Calculate the pricing of inventory, using the cost basis under the periodic inventory system according to the (a) specific identification method; (b) weighted-average-cost method; (c) first-in, first-out (FIFO) method; (d) last-in, first-out (LIFO)**

method. The value assigned to ending inventory is the result of two measurements: quantity and price. Quantity is determined by taking a physical inventory. The pricing of inventory is usually based on the assumed cost flow of the goods as they are bought and sold. One of four assumptions is usually made regarding cost flow. These assumptions are represented by four inventory methods. Inventory pricing could be determined by the specific identification method, which associates the actual cost with each item of inventory, but this method is rarely used. The weighted-average-cost method assumes that the cost of inventory is the average cost of goods available for sale during the period. The first-in, first-out (FIFO) method assumes that the costs of the first items acquired should be assigned to the first items sold. The last-in, first-out (LIFO) method assumes that the costs of the last items acquired should be assigned to the first items sold. The inventory method chosen may or may not be equivalent to the actual physical flow of goods.

4. **Apply the perpetual inventory system to the pricing of inventories at cost.** The pricing of inventories under the perpetual inventory system differs from pricing under the periodic system because under the perpetual system a continuous record of quantities and costs of goods is maintained as purchases and sales are made. Cost of goods sold is accumulated as sales are made and costs are transferred from the Inventory account to Cost of Goods Sold. The cost of the ending inventory is the balance of the Inventory account. Under the perpetual inventory system, the specific identification method and the FIFO method will produce the same results as under the periodic method. The results will differ for the weighted-average-cost method because a moving average is calculated prior to each

sale rather than at the end of the accounting period and for the LIFO method because the cost components of inventory change constantly as goods are bought and sold.

5. **State the effects of inventory methods and misstatements of inventory on profit determination and income taxes.** During periods of rising prices, the LIFO method will show the lowest net profit; FIFO, the highest; and weighted-average-cost, in between. The opposite effects occur in periods of falling prices. No generalisation can be made regarding the specific identification method. If the value of ending inventory is understated or overstated, a corresponding error will be made in net profit. Furthermore, because the ending inventory of one period is the beginning inventory of the next, the misstatement affects two accounting periods, although the effects are opposite.

6. **Apply the lower of cost and market (LCM) rule to inventory valuation.** The lower of cost and market rule can be applied to the above methods of determining inventory at cost. This rule states that if the net realisable (market) value of the inventory is lower than the inventory cost, the lower figure should be used.

Supplemental Objective

7. **Estimate the cost of ending inventory using the (a) retail inventory method and (b) gross profit method.** Two methods of estimating the value of inventory are the retail inventory method and the gross profit method. Under the retail inventory method, inventory is determined at retail prices and is then reduced to estimated cost by applying a ratio of cost to retail price. Under the gross profit method, cost of goods sold is estimated by reducing sales by estimated gross profit. The estimated cost of goods sold is then deducted from cost of goods available for sale to estimate the inventory.

Review of Concepts and Terminology

The following concepts and terms were introduced in this chapter.

LO 1 Average days' inventory available: The average number of days required to sell the inventory available; calculated by dividing the number of days in a year by inventory turnover.

LO 2 Consignment: The placing of goods by their owner (the consignor) on the premises of another company (the consignee).

LO 2 Cost flow: The association of costs with their assumed flow within the operations of a company.

LO 3 First-in, first-out (FIFO) method: An inventory cost method based on the assumption that the costs of the first items acquired should be assigned to the first items sold.

LO 2 Goods flow: The actual physical movement of goods in the operation of a company.

SO 7 Gross profit method: A method of inventory estimation based on the assumption that the ratio of gross profit for a business remains relatively stable from year to year.

LO 1 Inventories: All goods purchased or produced and held for sale in the ordinary course of business.

LO 2 Inventory cost: The price paid or consideration given to acquire an asset; includes invoice price less purchases discounts, plus freight or transportation in and applicable taxes or tariffs.

LO 1 Inventory turnover: A ratio indicating the number of times a company's average inventory is sold during an accounting period; cost of goods sold divided by average inventory.

LO 6 Item-by-item method: A lower of cost and market method of valuing inventory in which cost and market are compared for each item in inventory, with each item then valued at its lower price.

LO 1 Just-in-time operating environment: An inventory management system in which companies seek to reduce their levels of inventory by working with suppliers to coordinate and schedule deliveries so that goods arrive just at the time they are needed.

LO 3 Last-in, first-out (LIFO) method: An inventory cost method based on the assumption that the costs of the last items purchased should be assigned to the first items sold.

LO 6 Lower of cost and market (LCM) rule: A method of valuing inventory at an amount below cost if the net realisable (market) value is less than cost.

LO 6 Major category method: A lower of cost and market method for valuing inventory in which the total cost and total market for each category of items are compared, with each category then valued at its lower amount.

LO 6 Market: Net realisable value, the amount for which goods can be sold.

LO 6 Net realisable value: The estimated selling price in the ordinary course of business less the estimated costs of completion and the estimated costs necessary to make the sale.

SO 7 Retail method: A method of inventory estimation used in retail businesses by which inventory at retail value is reduced by the ratio of cost to retail price.

LO 3 Specific identification method: An inventory cost method in which the price of inventory is calculated by identifying the cost of each item in ending inventory as coming from a specific purchase.

LO 3 Weighted-average-cost method: An inventory cost method in which the price of inventory is determined by calculating the weighted average cost of all goods available for sale during the period.

Review Problem

Periodic and Perpetual Inventory Systems

LO 3   The following table summarises the beginning inventory, purchases, and sales of Poon Company's
LO 4   single product during January.

			Beginning Inventory and Purchases			
Date			Units	Cost	Total	Sales Units
Jan.	1	Inventory	1,400	19	26,600	
	4	Sale				300
	8	Purchase	600	20	12,000	
	10	Sale				1,300
	12	Purchase	900	21	18,900	
	15	Sale				150
	18	Purchase	500	22	11,000	
	24	Purchase	800	23	18,400	
	31	Sale				1,350
Totals			4,200		86,900	3,100

REQUIRED

1. Assuming that the company uses the periodic inventory system, calculate the cost that should be assigned to ending inventory and to cost of goods sold using (a) the weighted-average-cost method, (b) the FIFO method, and (c) the LIFO method.
2. Assuming that the company uses the perpetual inventory system, calculate the cost that should be assigned to ending inventory and to cost of goods sold using (a) the weighted-average-cost method, (b) the FIFO method, and (c) the LIFO method.

Answer to Review Problem

	Units	Amount
Beginning Inventory	1,400	26,600
Purchases	2,800	60,300
Available for Sale	4,200	86,900
Sales	3,100	
Ending Inventory	1,100	

1. Periodic inventory system
   a. Weighted-average-cost method

Cost of goods available for sale		86,900
Ending inventory consists of		
1,100 units at 20.69*		22,759
Cost of goods sold		64,141

   *86,900 ÷ 4,200 = 20.69

   b. FIFO method

Cost of goods available for sale		86,900
Ending inventory consists of		
January 24 purchase (800 × 23)	18,400	
January 18 purchase (300 × 22)	6,600	25,000
Cost of goods sold		61,900

   c. LIFO method

Cost of goods available for sale		86,900
Ending inventory consists of		
Beginning inventory (1,100 × 19)		20,900
Cost of goods sold		66,000

2. Perpetual inventory system
   a. Weighted-average-cost method

Date		Units	Cost*	Amount*
Jan. 1	Inventory	1,400	19.00	26,600
4	Sale	(300)	19.00	(5,700)
4	Balance	1,100	19.00	20,900
8	Purchase	600	20.00	12,000
8	Balance	1,700	19.35	32,900
10	Sale	(1,300)	19.35	(25,155)
10	Balance	400	19.36	7,745
12	Purchase	900	21.00	18,900
12	Balance	1,300	20.50	26,645
15	Sale	(150)	20.50	(3,075)
15	Balance	1,150	20.50	23,570
18	Purchase	500	22.00	11,000
18	Balance	1,650	20.95	34,570
24	Purchase	800	23.00	18,400
24	Balance	2,450	21.62	52,970
31	Sale	(1,350)	21.62	(29,187)
31	Inventory	1,100	21.62	23,783

Cost of Goods Sold: 5,700 + 25,155 + 3,075 + 29,187 =   63,117

*Rounded

b. FIFO method

Date		Units	Cost	Amount
Jan. 1	Inventory	1,400	19	26,600
4	Sale	(300)	19	(5,700)
4	Balance	1,100	19	20,900
8	Purchase	600	20	12,000
8	Balance	1,100	19	
		600	20	32,900
10	Sale	(1,100)	19	
		(200)	20	(24,900)
10	Balance	400	20	8,000
12	Purchase	900	21	18,900
12	Balance	400	20	
		900	21	26,900
15	Sale	(150)	20	(3,000)
15	Balance	250	20	
		900	21	23,900
18	Purchase	500	22	11,000
24	Purchase	800	23	18,400
24	Balance	250	20	
		900	21	
		500	22	
		800	23	53,300
31	Sale	(250)	20	
		(900)	21	
		(200)	22	(28,300)
31	Inventory	300	22	
		800	23	25,000

Cost of Goods Sold: 5,700 + 24,900 + 3,000 + 28,300 =   61,900

c. LIFO method

Date		Units	Cost	Amount
Jan. 1	Inventory	1,400	19	26,600
4	Sale	(300)	19	(5,700)
4	Balance	1,100	19	20,900
8	Purchase	600	20	12,000
8	Balance	1,100	19	
		600	20	32,900
10	Sale	(600)	20	
		(700)	19	(25,300)
10	Balance	400	19	7,600
12	Purchase	900	21	18,900
12	Balance	400	19	
		900	21	26,500
15	Sale	(150)	21	(3,150)
15	Balance	400	19	
		750	21	23,350
18	Purchase	500	22	11,000
24	Purchase	800	23	18,400
24	Balance	400	19	
		750	21	
		500	22	
		800	23	52,750
31	Sale	(800)	23	
		(500)	22	
		(50)	21	(30,450)
31	Inventory	400	19	
		700	21	22,300

Cost of Goods Sold: 5,700 + 25,300 + 3,150 + 30,450 =   64,600

CHAPTER ASSIGNMENTS

Knowledge and Understanding

Questions

1. What are inventories, and what is the primary objective of inventory measurement?
2. How does inventory for a manufacturing company differ from that for a trading company?
3. Why is the level of inventory important, and what are two common measures of inventory level?
4. What items are included in the cost of inventory?
5. Fargo Sales Company is very busy at the end of its accounting year on June 30. There is an order for 130 units of product in the warehouse. Although the shipping department tries, it cannot ship the product by June 30, and title has not yet passed. Should the 130 units be included in the year-end count of inventory? Why or why not?
6. What is the difference between goods flow and cost flow?
7. Do the FIFO and LIFO inventory methods result in different quantities of ending inventory?
8. Under which method of cost flow are (a) the earliest costs assigned to inventory, (b) the latest costs assigned to inventory, (c) the average costs assigned to inventory?
9. What are the relative advantages and disadvantages of FIFO and LIFO from management's point of view?

10. In periods of steadily rising prices, which inventory method—weighted-average-cost, FIFO, or LIFO—will give the (a) highest inventory cost, (b) lowest inventory cost, (c) highest net profit, and (d) lowest net profit?
11. How do inventory methods affect income taxes?
12. If the inventory is mistakenly overstated at the end of 20x1, what is the effect on the (a) 20x1 net profit, (b) 20x1 year-end balance sheet value, (c) 20x2 net profit, and (d) 20x2 year-end balance sheet value?
13. Why do you think it is more expensive to maintain a perpetual inventory system?
14. In the phrase *lower of cost and market*, what is meant by the word *market*?
15. What methods can be used to determine lower of cost and market?
16. Does using the retail inventory method mean that inventories are measured at retail value on the balance sheet? Explain.
17. What are some of the reasons that may cause management to use the gross profit method of estimating inventory?
18. Which inventory systems do not require a physical inventory: (a) perpetual, (b) periodic, (c) retail, (d) gross profit?

Application

Exercises

E 7-1.

LO 1 *Management Issues Related to Inventory*

Indicate whether each item listed below is associated with (a) allocating the cost of inventories in accordance with the matching rule, (b) assessing the impact of inventory decisions, or (c) evaluating the level of inventory.

1. Calculating inventory turnover.
2. Application of the just-in-time operating environment.
3. Determining the effects of inventory decisions on cash flows.
4. Apportioning the cost of goods available for sale to ending inventory and cost of goods sold.
5. Determining the assumption about the flow of costs into and out of the company.

E 7-2.

LO 1 *Inventory Ratios*

Costco Discount Stores is assessing its levels of inventory for 20x2 and 20x3 and has gathered the following data:

	20x3	20x2	20x1
Ending inventory	64,000	54,000	46,000
Cost of goods sold	320,000	300,000	

Calculate the inventory turnover and average days' inventory available for 20x2 and 20x3 and comment on the results.

E 7-3.

LO 3 *Inventory Costing Methods*

Helen's Farm Store sells agricultural equipment and supplies. During a recent year, the company had the following purchases and sales of fertiliser:

Jan.	1	Beginning Inventory	250 cases @ 23	5,750
Feb.	25	Purchase	100 cases @ 26	2,600
June	15	Purchase	400 cases @ 28	11,200
Aug.	15	Purchase	100 cases @ 26	2,600
Oct.	15	Purchase	300 cases @ 28	8,400
Dec.	15	Purchase	200 cases @ 30	6,000
		Total Goods Available for Sale	1,350	36,550
		Total Sales	1,000 cases	
Dec.	31	Ending Inventory	350 cases	

Assume that the ending inventory included 50 cases from the beginning inventory, 100 cases from the February 25 purchase, 100 cases from the August 15 purchase, and 100 cases from the October 15 purchase.

Determine the costs that should be assigned to ending inventory and cost of goods sold under each of the following assumptions: (1) costs are assigned by the specific identification method; (2) costs are assigned by the weighted-average-cost method; (3) costs are assigned by the FIFO method; (4) costs are assigned by the LIFO method.

What conclusions can be drawn about the effect of each method on the income statement and the balance sheet of Helen's Farm Store?

E 7-4.

LO 3 *Periodic Inventory System and Inventory Costing Methods*

In chronological order, the inventory, purchases, and sales of a single product of the O'Shaughnessy Company during a recent month are as follows:

			Units	Amount per Unit
June	1	Beginning Inventory	300	10
	4	Purchase	800	11
	8	Sale	400	20
	12	Purchase	1,000	12
	16	Sale	700	20
	20	Sale	500	22
	24	Purchase	1,200	13
	28	Sale	600	22
	29	Sale	400	22

Using the periodic inventory system, calculate the O'Shaughnessy Company's cost of ending inventory, its cost of goods sold, and its gross profit. Use the weighted-average-cost, FIFO, and LIFO inventory costing methods. Explain the differences in gross profit produced by the three methods. Round unit costs and totals.

E 7-5.

LO 3 *Inventory Costing Methods:*
LO 4 *Periodic and Perpetual*
Systems

During July 20x2, Servex sold 250 units of its product Dervex for 2,000. The following units were available:

	Units	Cost
Beginning Inventory	100	1
Purchase 1	40	2
Purchase 2	60	3
Purchase 3	70	4
Purchase 4	80	5
Purchase 5	90	6

A sale of 100 units of Dervex was made after purchase 1, and a sale of 150 units of the product was made after purchase 4. Of the units sold, 100 came from beginning inventory and 150 came from purchases 3 and 4.

Determine cost of goods available for sale and ending inventory in units. Then determine the costs that should be assigned to cost of goods sold and ending inventory under each of the following assumptions: (1) Costs are assigned under the periodic inventory system using (a) the specific identification method, (b) the weighted-average-cost method, (c) the FIFO method, and (d) the LIFO method; (2) Costs are assigned under the perpetual inventory system using (a) the weighted-average-cost method, (b) the FIFO method, and (c) the LIFO method. For each alternative, show the gross profit. Round unit costs and totals.

E 7-6.

LO 5 *Effects of Inventory Methods*
on Cash Flows

Ross Products sold 120,000 cases of glue at 40 per case during 20x1. Its beginning inventory consisted of 20,000 cases at a cost of 24 per case. During 20x1 it purchased 60,000 cases at 28 per case and later 50,000 cases at 30 per case. Operating expenses were 1,100,000, and the applicable income tax rate was 30 per cent.

Using the periodic inventory system, calculate net profit using the FIFO method and the LIFO method for costing inventory. Which alternative produces the larger cash flow? The company is considering a purchase of 10,000 cases at 30 per case just before the year end. What effect on net profit and on cash flow will this proposed purchase have under each method? (**Note:** What are the income tax consequences, assuming LIFO is permitted for tax purposes?)

E 7-7.

LO 3 *Inventory Costing Method*
LO 5 *Characteristics*

The lettered items in the list below represent inventory costing methods. Identify by letter the method that each of the following statements *best* describes.

a. Specific identification
b. Weighted-average-cost
c. First-in, first-out (FIFO)
d. Last-in, first-out (LIFO)

1. Matches recent costs with recent revenues
2. Assumes that each item of inventory is identifiable
3. Results in most realistic balance sheet valuation
4. Results in lowest net profit in periods of deflation
5. Results in lowest net profit in periods of inflation
6. Matches oldest costs with recent revenues
7. Results in highest net profit in periods of inflation
8. Results in highest net profit in periods of deflation
9. Tends to level out the effects of inflation
10. Is unpredictable as to the effects of inflation

E 7-8.

LO 5 *Effects of Inventory Errors*

Condensed income statements for Hamlin Company for two years are shown below.

	20x2	20x1
Sales	126,000	105,000
Cost of Goods Sold	75,000	54,000
Gross Profit	51,000	51,000
Operating Expenses	30,000	30,000
Net Profit	21,000	21,000

After the end of 20x2 it was discovered that an error had resulted in a 9,000 understatement of the 20x1 ending inventory.

Calculate the corrected net profit for 20x1 and 20x2. What effect will the error have on net profit and shareholders' equity for 20x3?

E 7-9.

LO 6 *Lower of Cost and Market Rule*

Mercurio Company values its inventory, shown in the following table, at the lower of cost and market. Calculate Mercurio's inventory value using (1) the item-by-item method and (2) the major category method.

	Quantity	Per Unit Cost	Per Unit Market
Category I			
Item aa	200	2.00	1.80
Item bb	240	4.00	4.40
Item cc	400	8.00	7.50
Category II			
Item dd	300	12.00	13.00
Item ee	400	18.00	18.20

E 7-10.

SO 7 *Retail Method*

Roseanne's Dress Shop had net retail sales of 500,000 during the current year. The following additional information was obtained from the accounting records:

	At Cost	At Retail
Beginning Inventory	80,000	120,000
Net Purchases (excluding Freight In)	280,000	440,000
Freight In	20,800	

1. Estimate the company's ending inventory at cost using the retail method.
2. Assume that a physical inventory taken at year end revealed an inventory available of 36,000 at retail value. What is the estimated amount of inventory shrinkage (loss due to theft, damage, and so forth) at cost?

E 7-11.

SO 7 *Gross Profit Method*

Dale Nolan was at home watching television when he received a call from the fire department. His business was a total loss from fire. The insurance company asked him to prove his inventory loss. For the year, until the date of the fire, Dale's company had sales of 450,000 and purchases of 280,000. Freight in amounted to 13,700, and the beginning inventory was 45,000. It was Dale's custom to price goods to achieve a gross profit of 40 per cent.

Calculate Dale's estimated inventory loss.

Problem Set

P 7-1.

LO 3 *Periodic Inventory System and Inventory Methods*

The inventory, purchases, and sales of Jamboree Products for the months of May and June are presented below. The company closes its books at the end of each month and uses a periodic inventory system.

May	1	Inventory	60 units @ 147
	9	Sale	20 units
	12	Purchase	100 units @ 156
	25	Sale	70 units
	31	Inventory	70 units
June	5	Purchase	120 units @ 159
	9	Sale	110 units
	14	Purchase	50 units @ 162
	19	Sale	80 units
	24	Purchase	100 units @ 165
	28	Sale	100 units
	30	Inventory	50 units

REQUIRED
1. Calculate the cost of the ending inventory on May 31 and June 30 using the weighted-average-cost method. In addition, determine cost of goods sold for May and June. Round unit costs and totals.
2. Calculate the cost of the ending inventory on May 31 and June 30 using the FIFO method. In addition, determine cost of goods sold for May and June.
3. Calculate the cost of the ending inventory on May 31 and June 30 using the LIFO method. In addition, determine cost of goods sold for May and June.

P 7-2.

LO 4   *Perpetual Inventory System and Inventory Methods*

Use the data provided in **P 7-1,** but assume that the company uses the perpetual inventory system. (**Note:** In preparing the solutions below, it is helpful to determine the balance of inventory after each transaction, as shown in this chapter's Review Problem.)

REQUIRED
1. Determine the cost of ending inventory and cost of goods sold for May and June using the weighted-average-cost method. Round unit costs and totals.
2. Determine the cost of ending inventory and cost of goods sold for May and June using the FIFO method.
3. Determine the cost of ending inventory and cost of goods sold for May and June using the LIFO method.

P 7-3.

LO 6   *Lower of Cost and Market Rule*

The employees of Kuberski's Shoes completed their physical inventory as follows:

		Per Unit	
	Pairs of Shoes	**Cost**	**Market**
Men			
Black	400	44	48
Brown	325	42	42
Blue	100	50	46
Tan	200	38	20
Women			
White	300	52	64
Red	150	46	40
Yellow	100	60	50
Blue	250	50	66
Brown	100	40	60
Black	150	40	50

REQUIRED   Determine the value of inventory at lower of cost and market using (1) the item-by-item method and (2) the major category method.

P 7-4.

SO 7   *Retail Inventory Method*

Overland Company switched recently to the retail inventory method to estimate the cost of ending inventory. To test this method, the company took a physical inventory one month after its implementation. Cost, retail, and the physical inventory data are as follows:

	At Cost	At Retail
July 1 Beginning Inventory	472,132	622,800
Purchases	750,000	1,008,400
Purchases Returns and Allowances	(25,200)	(34,800)
Freight In	8,350	
Sales		1,060,000
Sales Returns and Allowances		(28,000)
July 31 Physical Inventory		508,200

REQUIRED
1. Prepare a schedule to estimate the amount of Overland's July 31 inventory using the retail method.
2. Use Overland's cost ratio to reduce the retail value of the physical inventory to cost.
3. Calculate the estimated amount of inventory shortage at cost and at retail.

Critical Thinking and Communication

Conceptual Mini-Case

CMC 7-1.
LO 5 *Inventory Methods, Income Taxes, and Cash Flows*

The **Kyoto Trading Company** began business in 20x1 for the purpose of importing and marketing an electronics component used widely in digital appliances. It is now December 20, 20x1, and management is considering its options. Among its considerations is which inventory method to choose. It has decided to choose either the FIFO or the LIFO method. Under the periodic inventory system, the effects on net profit of using the two methods are as follows:

	FIFO Method	LIFO Method
Sales: 500,000 units × 6	3,000,000	3,000,000
Cost of Goods Sold		
Purchases		
200,000 × 2	400,000	400,000
400,000 × 3	1,200,000	1,200,000
Total Purchases	1,600,000	1,600,000
Less Ending Inventory		
FIFO: 100,000 × 3	(300,000)	
LIFO: 100,000 × 2		(200,000)
Cost of Goods Sold	1,300,000	1,400,000
Gross Profit	1,700,000	1,600,000
Operating Expenses	1,200,000	1,200,000
Profit before Income Taxes	500,000	400,000
Income Taxes	150,000	120,000
Net Profit	350,000	280,000

Also, management has an option to purchase an additional 100,000 units of inventory before year end at a price of 4 per unit, the price that is expected to prevail during 20x2. The income tax rate applicable to the company in 20x1 is 30 per cent. (**Note:** Assume that LIFO is permitted for tax purposes.)

Business conditions are expected to be favourable in 20x2, as they were in 20x1. Management has asked you for advice. Analyse the effects of making the additional purchase. Then prepare a memorandum to management that compares cash outcomes under the four alternatives and advise management on which inventory method to choose and whether to order the additional inventory. Be prepared to discuss your recommendations.

Cultural Mini-Case

CLMC 7-1.
LO 1 *Inventory Methods*
LO 2
LO 3
LO 5

BOC Group, based in the United Kingdom, is a leading global industrial company with interests in industrial and special gases, health care, vacuum technology, and distribution. The company has manufacturing operations in more than 60 countries. BOC's profit before tax in 1995 was £402.2 million and inventories were £328.1 million and £363.5 million in 1994 and 1995, respectively.[7] BOC values inventories at the lower of cost and net realisable value. Cost is determined on a weighted-average-cost or FIFO basis. The use of LIFO is not acceptable practice in the U.K. and is not permitted for tax purposes.

REQUIRED
1. Explain the likely effect of LIFO compared to weighted-average-cost and FIFO on BOC's income statement and balance sheet.
2. Under what circumstances could LIFO be beneficial in terms of lower income taxes, assuming that this method is permitted for tax purposes?
3. What would be the effect on profit before tax if inventories were determined on a LIFO basis with the result that inventories were 10 per cent lower than the amounts stated on the balance sheets for 1994 and 1995?

Ethics Mini-Case

EMC 7-1.
LO 1 *Inventories, Profit Determination, and Ethics*

Flare Corporation, which has a December 31 year end, designs and sells fashions for young professional women. Sandra Mason, chief executive of the company, feared that the forecasted 20x1 profitability goals would not be reached. She was pleased when Flare received a large order on December

30 from The Executive Woman, a retail chain of upscale stores for business women. Mason immediately directed the controller to record the sale, which represented 13 per cent of Flare's annual sales, but directed the inventory control department not to separate the goods for shipment until after January 1. Separated goods are not included in inventory because they have been sold. On December 31 the company's auditors arrived to observe the year-end taking of the physical inventory under the periodic inventory system.

What will be the effect of Mason's action on Flare's 20x1 profitability? What will be the effect on 20x2 profitability? Is Mason's action ethical?

Decision-Making Case

DMC 7-1.
LO 3   *FIFO versus LIFO Analysis*
LO 5

Bell Refrigerated Trucks Company (BRT Company) buys large refrigerated trucks from the manufacturer and sells them to companies and independent truckers who haul perishable goods for long distances. BRT has been successful in this specialised niche of the industry because it provides a unique product and service. Because of the high cost of the trucks and of financing inventory, BRT tries to maintain as small an inventory as possible. In fact, at the beginning of July the company had no inventory or liabilities, as shown by the balance sheet below.

On July 9, BRT takes delivery of a truck at a price of 300,000. On July 19, an identical truck is delivered to the company at a price of 320,000. On July 28, the company sells one of the trucks for 390,000. During July expenses totaled 30,000. All transactions were paid in cash.

BRT Company
Balance Sheet
July 1, 20xx

Assets		**Shareholders' Equity**	
Cash	800,000	Share Capital	800,000
Total Assets	800,000	Total Shareholders' Equity	800,000

REQUIRED

1. Prepare income statements and balance sheets for BRT on July 31 using (a) the FIFO method of inventory valuation and (b) the LIFO method of inventory valuation. Assume an income tax rate of 40 per cent and that LIFO is permitted for tax purposes. Explain the effects that each method has on the financial statements.
2. Assume that Larry Bell, the owner of BRT Company, follows the policy of declaring a cash dividend each period that is exactly equal to net profit. What effects does this action have on each balance sheet prepared in **1**, and how do they compare with the balance sheet at the beginning of the month? Which inventory method, if either, do you feel is more realistic in representing BRT's profit?
3. Assume that BRT receives notice of another price increase of 20,000 on refrigerated trucks, to take effect on August 1. How does this information relate to the owner's dividend policy, and how will it affect next month's operations?

Basic Research Activity

RA 7-1.
LO 2   *Retail Business Inventories*
LO 4

Make an appointment to visit a local retail business—a grocery, clothing, book, music, or appliance store, for example—and interview the manager for thirty minutes about the company's inventory accounting system. The store may be a branch of a larger company. Find out answers to the following questions, summarise your findings in a paper to be handed in, and be prepared to discuss your results in class.

What is the physical flow of goods into the store, and what documents are used in connection with this flow?

What documents are prepared when goods are sold?

Does the store keep perpetual inventory records? If so, does it keep the records in units only or does it keep track of cost as well? If not, what system does the store use?

How often does the company take a physical inventory?

How are financial statements generated for the store?

What method does the company use to price its inventory for financial statements?

Financial Reporting and Analysis

Interpretation Cases from Business

ICB 7-1.
LO 2 *LIFO, FIFO, and Income*
LO 5 *Taxes*

A portion of the income statements for 1992 and 1991 for **Hershey Foods** of the United States, a company that is famous for its chocolate and confectionery products, follows (in thousands of dollars).[8]

	1992	1991
Net Sales	3,219,805	2,899,165
Cost of Goods Sold	1,833,388	1,694,404
Gross Profit	1,386,417	1,204,761
Selling, General and Administrative Expense	958,189	814,459
Profit from Operations	428,228	390,302
Interest Expense, Net	27,240	26,845
Profit before Income Taxes	400,988	363,457
Provision for Income Taxes	158,390	143,929
Net Profit	242,598	219,528

In a note on supplemental balance sheet information, Hershey Foods indicated that most of its inventories are maintained using the last-in, first-out (LIFO) method, which is permitted for tax purposes in the United States. The company also reported that inventories using the LIFO method were $436,917 in 1991 and $457,179 in 1992. In addition, the company reported that if valued using the first-in, first-out (FIFO) method, inventories would have been $494,290 in 1991 and $505,521 in 1992.

REQUIRED

1. Prepare a schedule comparing net profit for 1992 using the LIFO method with what it would have been under FIFO. Use a corporate income tax rate of 39 per cent (Hershey's average tax rate in 1992).
2. Why do you suppose Hershey's management chooses to use the LIFO inventory method? On what economic conditions, if any, do these reasons depend? Given your calculations in 1 above, do you believe the economic conditions relevant to Hershey were advantageous for using LIFO in 1992? Explain your answer.

ICB 7-2.
LO 1 *Inventory Levels and*
LO 5 *Methods*

Two large Japanese diversified electronics companies are **Pioneer Electronic** and **Yamaha.** Both companies use the weighted-average-cost method and the lower of cost and market rule to account for inventories. The following data are for 1992 (in millions of yen):

	Pioneer	Yamaha
Beginning Inventory	76,324	123,768
Ending Inventory	93,148	113,766
Cost of Goods Sold	376,739	506,863

Compare the inventory efficiency of Pioneer and Yamaha by calculating the inventory turnover and average days' inventory available for both companies in 1992. Comment on the results.

Nestlé Case

NC 7-1.
LO 3 *Inventory Method and*
LO 6 *Inventory Ratios*
SO 7

Refer to the note related to inventories in the appendix on Nestlé to answer the following questions: What inventory method(s) does Nestlé use? Do you think many of the company's inventories are valued at market? Calculate and compare the inventory turnover and average days' inventory available for Nestlé for 1995 and 1996. Comment on Nestlé's performance in terms of inventory efficiency in 1996 compared to 1995.

ENDNOTES

1. Philips, *Annual Report*, 1995.
2. International Accounting Standard, IAS2, *Inventories* (London: IASC, revised 1993), para. 31.
3. Ibid., para. 7.
4. Ibid., paras. 21 and 23.
5. Ibid., para. 6.
6. Ibid., para 4.
7. BOC Group, *Annual Report*, 1995.
8. Hershey Foods Corp., *Annual Report*, 1992.

Chapter 8

LONG-TERM ASSETS

LEARNING OBJECTIVES

1. Identify the types of long-term assets and explain the management issues related to accounting for them.
2. Distinguish between capital and revenue expenditures, and account for the cost of property, plant, and equipment.
3. Define *depreciation*, state the factors that affect its calculation, and show how to record it.
4. Calculate periodic depreciation under the (a) straight-line method, (b) production method, and (c) declining-balance method.
5. Account for disposal of depreciable assets.
6. Identify natural resource accounting issues and calculate depletion.
7. Apply the matching rule to intangible assets, including research and development costs and goodwill.

SUPPLEMENTAL OBJECTIVE

8. Apply depreciation methods to problems of partial years, revised rates, groups of similar items, and cost recovery.

DECISION POINT

DANONE

The effects of management's decisions regarding long-term assets are most apparent in the areas of total assets and reported profit. How does one learn of the significance of these items to a company? An idea of the extent and importance of the company's assets can be gained from the financial statements. For example, the following list of assets (in millions of French francs) is taken from the 1995 annual report of the French company Danone, which is one of Europe's largest multiproduct food groups with interests in dairy products, sauces and condiments, biscuits, breweries (including Kronenbourg and San Miguel), mineral water (including Evian, Volvic, and Badoit), and glass containers:[1]

	1995	1994
Capital Assets:		
Property, plant, and equipment		
Land	*1,556*	*1,482*
Buildings and rental property	*12,394*	*11,803*
Machinery and equipment	*31,637*	*29,375*
Consigned containers	*2,078*	*2,011*
Machinery and equipment	*2,765*	*2,723*
Capital assets in progress	*1,591*	*1,210*
	52,021	*48,604*
Less accumulated depreciation	*(30,021)*	*(27,429)*
Total capital assets	*22,000*	*21,175*
Intangible Assets:		
Goodwill	*18,651*	*17,541*
Brand names	*11,491*	*10,425*
Other intangible assets, net	*1,211*	*1,209*
Total intangible assets	*31,353*	*29,175*

Of the company's almost FF93 billion in total assets, about one-fourth consists of property, plant, and equipment. At the same time, about one-third of the company's assets are intangible and include goodwill and brand names. Further, on the income statement, depreciation and amortisation associated with these assets are a significant element of costs, just as new capital expenditures are a significant element of cash outflows recorded on the cash flow statement. This chapter deals with the long-term assets of property, plant, and equipment and intangible assets. Long-term investments are dealt with in the chapter on intercompany investments, consolidated financial statements, and foreign currency accounting.

OBJECTIVE 1

Identify the types of long-term assets and explain the management issues related to accounting for them

MANAGEMENT ISSUES RELATED TO ACCOUNTING FOR LONG-TERM ASSETS

Long-term assets are assets that (1) have a useful life of more than one year, (2) are acquired for use in the operation of the business, and (3) are not intended for resale to customers. For many years, it was common to refer to long-term assets as *fixed assets*, but use of this term is declining because the word *fixed* implies that they last forever.

Although there is no strict minimum useful life for an asset to be classified as long term, the most common criterion is that the asset must be capable of repeated use for a period of at least a year. Included in this category is equipment that is used only in peak or emergency periods, such as an electricity generator.

Assets not used in the ordinary course of business should not be included in this category. Thus, land held for speculative reasons or buildings that are no longer used in ordinary business operations should not be included in the property, plant, and equipment category. Instead, they should be classified as long-term investments.

Finally, if an item is held for sale to customers, it should be classified as inventory —not plant and equipment—no matter how durable it is. For example, a printing press held for sale by a printing press manufacturer would be considered inventory, whereas the same printing press would be plant and equipment for a printing company that buys the press to use in its operations.

Long-term assets are customarily divided into the categories that are shown in Figure 8-1.

FIGURE 8-1 *Classification of Long-Term Assets and Corresponding Expenses*

BALANCE SHEET
Long-term Assets

INCOME STATEMENT
Expenses

Tangible Assets: long-term assets with physical substance

Land

Plant, Buildings, Equipment (plant assets)

Land is *not expensed* because it has an unlimited life

Depreciation: periodic allocation of plant assets cost over its estimated useful life

Natural Resources: land purchased for the economic value of ore, lumber, oil and gas or other resources contained therein

Mines

Timberland

Oil and gas fields

Depletion: exhaustion of a natural resource through mining, cutting, pumping, or other extraction; allocation of the cost of natural resources to expense

Intangible Assets: long-term assets with no physical substance but which usually convey legal rights or advantages

Patents, Copyrights, Trademarks

Franchises, Organisational costs, Goodwill

Amortisation: periodic allocation of intangible asset cost to the periods it benefits

Investments:

Land held for future use

Buildings not currently in use

Reviewed for Asset Impairment

Tangible assets have physical substance. Land is a tangible asset, and because it has an unlimited life it is the only tangible asset not subject to depreciation. Plant, buildings, and equipment (referred to hereafter as plant assets) are subject to depreciation. **Depreciation** is the allocation of the cost or amount, if subsequently revalued, of a tangible long-lived asset (other than land and natural resources) over its estimated useful life. The term applies to manufactured assets only.

Natural resources, or *wasting assets*, differ from land in that they are purchased for the substances that can be taken from the land and used up rather than for the value of their location. Among natural resources are ore from mines, oil and gas from oil and gas fields, and lumber from forests. Natural resources are subject to **depletion** rather than to depreciation. The term depletion refers to the exhaustion of a natural resource through mining, cutting, pumping, or other extraction and to the way in which the cost is allocated.

Intangible assets are long-term assets that do not have physical substance and in most cases relate to legal rights or advantages held from which future economic benefits are expected to flow to the enterprise. Intangible assets include patents, copyrights, trademarks, franchises, organisation costs, and goodwill. The allocation of the cost of intangible assets to the periods they benefit is called **amortisation**. Although the current assets accounts receivable and prepaid expenses do not have physical substance, they are not intangible assets because they are not long term.

The unexpired part of the cost or amount of an asset is generally called its *book value*, or **carrying amount**. The latter term is used in this book when referring to long-term assets. The carrying amount of plant assets, for instance, is cost less accumulated depreciation.

Long-term assets differ from current assets in that they support the operating cycle instead of being a part of it. They are also expected to benefit the business for a longer period than do current assets. Current assets are expected to be realised within one year or during the operating cycle, whichever is longer. Long-term assets are expected to last beyond that period. The management issues related to accounting for long-term assets revolve around the means of financing the assets and the methods of accounting for the assets.

Financing Long-Term Assets

After deciding whether or not to acquire a long-term asset, management must decide how to finance the asset if it is acquired. Some companies are profitable enough to pay for long-term assets out of cash flows from operations, but when financing is needed, some form of long-term financing related to the life of the asset usually is most appropriate. For example, a car loan is generally four or five years, whereas a mortgage loan on a house may be thirty years. For a major long-term acquisition, a company may issue shares and long-term notes or bonds. A good place to study a company's long-term financing is in the financing activities section of the cash flow statement. Another option a company may have is to lease long-term assets instead of buying them. All of these options related to long-term financing are discussed in the chapters on liabilities and share capital.

Applying the Matching Rule to Long-Term Assets

As with inventories and prepaid expenses, accounting for long-term assets requires the proper application of the matching rule through the resolution of two important issues. The first is how much of the total cost should be allocated to expense in the current accounting period. The second and related issue is how much should remain on the balance sheet as an asset to benefit future periods. To resolve these issues, four important questions about the acquisition, use, and disposal of each long-term asset, as illustrated in Figure 8-2, must be answered:

1. How is the cost of the long-term asset determined?
2. How should the cost of the long-term asset be allocated against revenues over time?
3. How should subsequent expenditures, such as repairs, maintenance, and additions, be treated?
4. How should disposal of the long-term asset be recorded?

Because of the long life of long-term assets and the complexity of the transactions involving them, management is faced with a great many choices and estimates. For example, acquisition cost may be complicated by group purchases, trade-ins, or construction costs. In addition, to allocate the cost of the asset to future periods effectively, management must estimate how long the asset will last and what it will be worth at the end of its use. In making these estimates, it is helpful to think of a long-term asset as a bundle of services to be used in the operation of the business over a period of years. A delivery truck may provide 100,000 miles of service over its life. A piece of equipment may have the potential to produce 500,000 parts. A building may provide shelter for fifty years. As each of these assets is purchased, the company is paying in advance for 100,000 miles, the capacity to produce 500,000 parts, or fifty years of service. In essence, each of these assets is a type of long-term prepaid expense. The accounting problem is to spread the cost of these services over the useful life of the asset. As the services benefit the company over the years, the cost becomes an expense rather than an asset.

The remainder of this chapter will address the issues raised in Figure 8-2 as they relate to property, plant, and equipment, natural resources, and intangible assets.

FIGURE 8-2   *Issues of Accounting for Long-Term Assets*

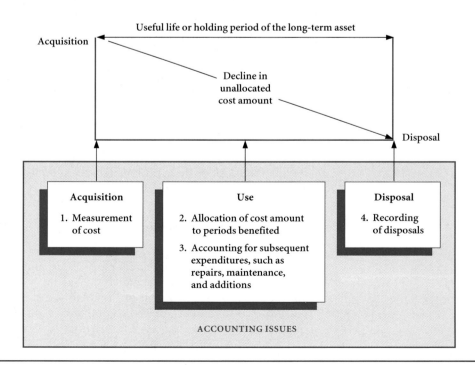

OBJECTIVE 2

Distinguish between capital and revenue expenditures, and account for the cost of property, plant, and equipment

ACQUISITION COST OF PROPERTY, PLANT, AND EQUIPMENT

The term **expenditure** refers to a payment for an asset, such as a truck, or a service received, such as a repair. Expenditures may be classified as capital expenditures or revenue expenditures. A **capital expenditure** is an expenditure for the purchase or expansion of a long-term asset. Capital expenditures are recorded in the asset accounts because they benefit several future accounting periods. A **revenue expenditure** is an expenditure related to the maintenance and operation of long-term assets. Revenue expenditures are recorded in the expense accounts because the benefits from them are realised in the current period.

Careful distinction between capital and revenue expenditures is important to the proper application of the matching rule. For example, if the purchase of a car is mistakenly recorded as a revenue expenditure, the expense for the current period is overstated on the income statement. As a result, current net profit is understated, and in future periods net profit will be overstated. If, on the other hand, a revenue expenditure such as the painting of a building were charged to an asset account, the expense of the current period would be understated. Current net profit would be overstated by the same amount, and net profit of future periods would be understated.

Determining when a payment is an expense and when it is an asset is a matter of judgement in which management takes a leading role. Such latitude, however, does not permit distortion of the financial results.

General Approach to Acquisition Cost

The acquisition cost of property, plant, and equipment includes all expenditures reasonable and necessary to get it in place and ready for use. For example, the cost of installing and testing a machine is a legitimate cost of the machine. However, if the machine is damaged while it is being installed, the cost of repairing the machine is an operating expense and not an acquisition cost.

Cost is easiest to determine when a transaction is made for cash. In this case, the cost of the asset is equal to the cash paid for the asset plus expenditures for freight, insurance while in transit, installation, and other necessary related costs. If a debt is incurred in the purchase of the asset, the interest charges are not a cost of the asset but a cost of borrowing the money to buy the asset. They are therefore an operating expense. An exception to this principle is that interest costs directly attributable to the construction of an asset may be included as a cost of the asset.[2]

Expenditures such as freight, insurance while in transit, and installation are included in the cost of the asset because they are necessary if the asset is to function. Following the matching rule, they are allocated to the useful life of the asset rather than charged as expenses in the current period.

For practical purposes many companies establish policies defining when an expenditure should be recorded as an expense or an asset. For example, small expenditures for items that normally would be treated as assets may be treated as expenses because the amounts involved are not material in relation to net profit. Thus, a wastebasket, which might last for years, would be recorded as a supplies expense rather than as a depreciable asset.

Some of the problems of determining the cost of a long-lived asset are demonstrated in the illustrations for land, buildings, equipment, land improvements, and group purchases presented in the next few sections.

Land

There are often expenditures in addition to the purchase price of land that should be debited to the Land account. Some examples are commissions to property agents;

lawyers' fees; accrued taxes paid by the purchaser; cost of preparing the land to build on, such as drainage, tearing down old buildings, clearing, and levelling; and assessments for local improvements, such as streets and sewage systems. The cost of landscaping is usually debited to the Land account because these improvements are relatively permanent. Land is not subject to depreciation because land does not have a limited useful life.

Let us assume that a company buys land for a new retail operation. It pays a net purchase price of 170,000, pays brokerage fees of 6,000 and legal fees of 2,000, pays 10,000 to have an old building on the site torn down, receives 4,000 salvage from the old building, and pays 1,000 to have the site levelled. The cost of the land will be 185,000, determined as follows:

Net purchase price		170,000
Brokerage fees		6,000
Legal fees		2,000
Tearing down old building	10,000	
Less salvage	4,000	6,000
Levelling		1,000
Total cost		185,000

Land Improvements

Improvements to property, such as driveways, car parks, and fences, have a limited life and thus are subject to depreciation. They should be recorded in an account called Land Improvements rather than in the Land account.

Buildings

When an existing building is purchased, its cost includes the purchase price plus all repairs and other expenses required to put it in usable condition. Buildings are subject to depreciation because they have a limited useful life. When a business constructs its own building, the cost includes all reasonable and necessary expenditures, such as those for materials, labour, part of the overhead and other indirect costs, the architects' fees, insurance during construction, lawyers' fees, and building permits. If outside contractors are used in the construction, the net contract price plus other expenditures necessary to put the building in usable condition are included.

Equipment

The cost of equipment includes all expenditures connected with purchasing the equipment and preparing it for use. These expenditures include invoice price less cash discounts; freight or transportation, including insurance; excise taxes and tariffs; buying expenses; installation costs; and test runs to ready the equipment for operation. Equipment is subject to depreciation.

Group Purchases

Sometimes land and other assets are purchased for a lump sum. Because land is a nondepreciable asset that has an unlimited life, it must have a separate ledger account, and the lump-sum purchase price must be apportioned between the land and the other assets. For example, assume that a building and the land on which it is situated are purchased for a lump-sum payment of 85,000. The apportionment can be made by determining the price of each if purchased separately and applying the appropriate percentages to the lump-sum price. Assume that appraisals yield estimates of 10,000 for the land and 90,000 for the building, if purchased separately. In that case, 10 per cent of the lump-sum price, or 8,500, would be allocated to the land and 90 per cent, or 76,500, would be allocated to the building, as shown below:

	Appraisal	Percentage	Apportionment
Land	10,000	10 (10,000/100,000)	8,500 (85,000 × 10%)
Building	90,000	90 (90,000/100,000)	76,500 (85,000 × 90%)
Totals	100,000	100	85,000

OBJECTIVE 3

Define depreciation, state the factors that affect its calculation, and show how to record it

ACCOUNTING FOR DEPRECIATION

Depreciation is described by the International Accounting Standards Committee as "the allocation of the depreciable amount of an asset over its estimated useful life".[3]

This description contains several important points. First, all tangible assets except land have a limited useful life. Because of this limited useful life, the costs or depreciable amount of these assets must be distributed as expenses over the years they benefit. Physical deterioration and obsolescence are the major causes of the limited useful life of a depreciable asset. The **physical deterioration** of tangible assets results from use and from exposure to the elements, such as wind and sun. Periodic repairs and a sound maintenance policy may keep buildings and equipment in good operating order and extract the maximum useful life from them, but every machine or building at some point must be discarded. The need for depreciation is not eliminated by repairs. **Obsolescence** is the process of becoming out of date. With fast-changing technology as well as fast-changing demands, machinery and even buildings often become obsolete before they wear out. Accountants do not distinguish between physical deterioration and obsolescence because they are interested in the length of the useful life of the asset regardless of what limits that useful life.

Second, the term *depreciation*, as used in accounting, does not refer to the physical deterioration of an asset or the decrease in market value of an asset over time. Depreciation means the allocation of the cost or depreciable amount of a plant asset to the periods that benefit from the services of the asset. The term is used to describe the gradual conversion of the cost of the asset into an expense.

Third, depreciation is not a process of valuation. Accounting records are normally kept in accordance with the historical cost principle, and thus they are not indicators of changing price levels. It is possible that, through an advantageous buy and specific market conditions, the market value of a building may rise. Nevertheless, depreciation must continue to be recorded because it is the result of an allocation, not a valuation, process. Eventually the building will wear out or become obsolete regardless of interim fluctuations in market value. However, in situations where assets are revalued, then the revalued amount becomes the basis for the depreciation expense.

In countries where revaluations are permitted, such as in Australia, Denmark, the Netherlands, Switzerland, and the U.K., the depreciation of buildings and plant and machinery is based on the revaluation amount less the residual value. Depreciation methods and the useful lives of assets may also need to be reviewed at the time such revaluations are carried out.

Factors That Affect the Calculation of Depreciation

Four factors affect the calculation of depreciation. They are (1) cost, (2) residual value, (3) depreciable amount, and (4) estimated useful life.

Cost

As explained earlier in the chapter, cost is the net purchase price plus all reasonable and necessary expenditures to get the asset in place and ready for use.

Residual Value

An asset's **residual value**—also called *salvage value* or *disposal value*—is its estimated net scrap, salvage, or trade-in value as of the estimated date of disposal.

Depreciable Amount

The **depreciable amount** of an asset is its cost less its residual value. For example, a truck that costs 12,000 and has a residual value of 3,000 would have a depreciable amount of 9,000. Depreciable amount must be allocated over the useful life of the asset.

Estimated Useful Life

The **estimated useful life** of an asset is the total number of service units expected from the asset. Service units may be measured in terms of years the asset is expected to be used, units expected to be produced, miles expected to be driven, or similar measures. In calculating the estimated useful life of an asset, the accountant should consider all relevant information, including (1) past experience with similar assets, (2) the asset's present condition, (3) the company's repair and maintenance policy, (4) current technological and industry trends, and (5) local conditions such as weather.

As introduced in the chapter on measuring business profit, depreciation is recorded at the end of the accounting period by an adjusting entry that takes the following form:

Depreciation Expense, Asset Name   xxx
   Accumulated Depreciation, Asset Name   xxx
      To record depreciation for the period

Methods of Calculating Depreciation

Many methods are used to allocate the cost of plant assets to accounting periods through depreciation. Each of them is proper for certain circumstances. The most common methods are (1) the straight-line method, (2) the production method, and (3) an accelerated method known as the declining-balance method.

OBJECTIVE 4a

Calculate periodic depreciation under the straight-line method

Straight-Line Method

When the **straight-line method** is used to allocate depreciation, the depreciable amount of the asset is spread evenly over the estimated useful life of the asset. The straight-line method is based on the assumption that depreciation depends only on the passage of time. The depreciation expense for each period is calculated by dividing the depreciable amount (amount of the depreciating asset less its estimated residual value) by the number of accounting periods in the asset's estimated useful life. The rate of depreciation is the same in each year. Suppose, for example, that a delivery truck costs 10,000 and has an estimated residual value of 1,000 at the end of its estimated useful life of five years. The annual depreciation would be 1,800 under the straight-line method, calculated as follows:

$$\frac{\text{Cost } - \text{ residual value}}{\text{Estimated useful life}} = \frac{10,000 - 1,000}{5} = 1,800$$

The depreciation for the five years would be as follows:

Depreciation Schedule, Straight-Line Method

	Cost	Yearly Depreciation	Accumulated Depreciation	Carrying Amount
Date of purchase	10,000	—	—	10,000
End of first year	10,000	1,800	1,800	8,200
End of second year	10,000	1,800	3,600	6,400
End of third year	10,000	1,800	5,400	4,600
End of fourth year	10,000	1,800	7,200	2,800
End of fifth year	10,000	1,800	9,000	1,000

There are three important points to note from the depreciation schedule for the straight-line depreciation method. First, the depreciation is the same each year. Second, the accumulated depreciation increases uniformly. Third, the carrying amount decreases uniformly until it reaches the estimated residual value.

OBJECTIVE 4b

Calculate periodic depreciation under the production method

Production Method

The **production method** of depreciation is based on the assumption that depreciation is solely the result of use and that the passage of time plays no role in the depreciation process. If we assume that the delivery truck from the previous example has an estimated useful life of 90,000 miles, the depreciation cost per mile would be determined as follows:

$$\frac{\text{Cost} \; - \; \text{residual value}}{\text{Estimated units of useful life}} = \frac{10,000 \; - \; 1,000}{90,000 \text{ miles}} = .10 \text{ per mile}$$

If we assume that the use of the truck was 20,000 miles for the first year, 30,000 miles for the second, 10,000 miles for the third, 20,000 miles for the fourth, and 10,000 miles for the fifth, the depreciation schedule for the delivery truck would appear as follows:

Depreciation Schedule, Production Method

	Cost	Miles	Yearly Depreciation	Accumulated Depreciation	Carrying Amount
Date of purchase	10,000	—	—	—	10,000
End of first year	10,000	20,000	2,000	2,000	8,000
End of second year	10,000	30,000	3,000	5,000	5,000
End of third year	10,000	10,000	1,000	6,000	4,000
End of fourth year	10,000	20,000	2,000	8,000	2,000
End of fifth year	10,000	10,000	1,000	9,000	1,000

There is a direct relation between the amount of depreciation each year and the units of output or use. Also, the accumulated depreciation increases each year in direct relation to units of output or use. Finally, the carrying amount decreases each year in direct relation to units of output or use until it reaches the estimated residual value.

Under the production method, the unit of output or use that is used to measure estimated useful life for each asset should be appropriate for that asset. For example, number of items produced may be an appropriate measure for one machine, but number of hours of use may be a better measure for another. The production method should be used only when the output of an asset over its useful life can be estimated with reasonable accuracy.

OBJECTIVE 4c

Calculate periodic depreciation under the declining-balance method

Declining-Balance Method

An **accelerated method** of depreciation results in relatively large amounts of depreciation in the early years of an asset's life and smaller amounts in later years. Such a method, which is based on the passage of time, assumes that many kinds of plant assets are most efficient when new, and so they provide more and better service in the early years of useful life. It is consistent with the matching rule to allocate more depreciation to the early years than to later years if the benefits or services received in the early years are greater.

An accelerated method also recognises that changing technologies make some equipment lose service value rapidly. Thus, it is realistic to allocate more to depreciation in the early years than in later years. New inventions and products result in obsolescence of equipment bought earlier, making it necessary to replace equipment sooner than if technology changed more slowly.

Another argument in favour of an accelerated method is that repair expense is likely to be greater in later years than in early years. Thus, the total of repair and depreciation expense remains fairly constant over a period of years. This result naturally assumes that the services received from the asset are roughly equal from year to year.

The **declining-balance method** is the most common accelerated method of depreciation. Under this method, depreciation is calculated by applying a fixed rate to the carrying amount (the declining balance) of a long-lived asset, resulting in higher depreciation charges during the early years of the asset's life. The most common rate is a percentage equal to twice the straight-line percentage. When twice the straight-line rate is used, the method is usually called the **double-declining-balance method**.

In our earlier example, the delivery truck had an estimated useful life of five years. Consequently, under the straight-line method, the depreciation rate for each year was 20 per cent (100 per cent ÷ 5 years).

Under the double-declining-balance method, the fixed rate is 40 per cent (2 × 20 per cent). This fixed rate of 40 per cent is applied to the *remaining carrying amount* at the end of each year. Estimated residual value is not taken into account in calculating depreciation except in the last year of an asset's useful life, when depreciation is limited to the amount necessary to bring the carrying amount down to the estimated residual value. The depreciation schedule for this method is as follows:

Depreciation Schedule, Double-Declining-Balance Method

	Cost	Yearly Depreciation		Accumulated Depreciation	Carrying Amount
Date of purchase	10,000	—		—	10,000
End of first year	10,000	(40% × 10,000)	4,000	4,000	6,000
End of second year	10,000	(40% × 6,000)	2,400	6,400	3,600
End of third year	10,000	(40% × 3,600)	1,440	7,840	2,160
End of fourth year	10,000	(40% × 2,160)	864	8,704	1,296
End of fifth year	10,000		296*	9,000	1,000

*Depreciation limited to amount necessary to reduce carrying amount to residual value:
296 = 1,296 (previous carrying amount) − 1,000 (residual value)

Note that the fixed rate is always applied to the carrying amount at the end of the previous year. The depreciation is greatest in the first year and declines each year after that. Finally, the depreciation in the last year is limited to the amount necessary to reduce carrying amount to residual value.

Comparing the Three Methods

A visual comparison may provide a better understanding of the three depreciation methods described above. Figure 8-3 compares yearly depreciation and carrying amount under the three methods. In the graph that shows yearly depreciation, straight-line depreciation is uniform at 1,800 per year over the five-year period. However, the declining-balance method begins at an amount greater than straight-line (4,000) and decreases each year to amounts that are less than straight-line (ultimately, 296). The production method does not generate a regular pattern because of the random fluctuation of the depreciation from year to year. The three yearly depreciation patterns are reflected in the graph of carrying amount. In that graph, each method starts in the same place (cost of 10,000) and ends at the same place (residual value of 1,000). It is the patterns during the useful life of the asset that differ for each method. For instance, the carrying amount under the straight-line method is always greater than that under the double-declining-balance method, except at the beginning and the end of useful life.

FIGURE 8-3 *Graphical Comparison of Three Methods of Determining Depreciation*

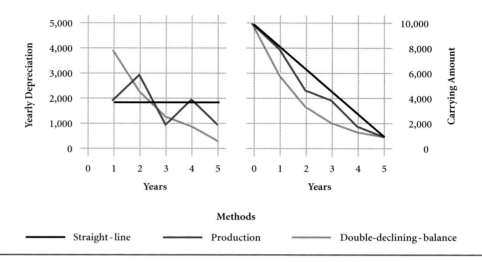

Methods

Straight-line ——— Production ——— Double-declining-balance

OBJECTIVE 5

Account for disposal of depreciable assets

DISPOSAL OF DEPRECIABLE ASSETS

When plant assets are no longer useful because they are worn out or obsolete, they may be discarded, sold, or traded in on the purchase of new plant and equipment. A comprehensive illustration will be used to show how these disposals are recorded in the accounting records.

Assumptions for the Comprehensive Illustration

For accounting purposes, a plant asset may be disposed of in three ways: it may be (1) discarded, (2) sold for cash, or (3) exchanged for another asset. To illustrate how each of these cases is recorded, assume that MGC Corporation purchased a machine on January 1, 20x0 for 6,500 and depreciated it on a straight-line basis over an estimated useful life of ten years. The residual value at the end of ten years was estimated to be 500. On January 1, 20x7, the balances of the relevant accounts in the plant asset ledger appear as follows:

Machinery		Accumulated Depreciation, Machinery	
6,500			4,200

On September 30, 20x7, management disposes of the asset. The next few sections illustrate the accounting treatment to record depreciation for the partial year and the disposal under several assumptions.

Depreciation for Partial Year Prior to Disposal

When a plant asset is discarded or disposed of in some other way, it is first necessary to record depreciation expense for the partial year up to the date of disposal. The reason this step is required is that the asset was used until that date and, under the matching rule, the accounting period should receive the proper allocation of depreciation expense.

In this comprehensive illustration, MGC Corporation disposes of the machinery on September 30. The entry to record the depreciation for the first nine months of 20x7 (nine-twelfths of a year) is as follows:

Sept. 30	Depreciation Expense, Machinery	450	
	Accumulated Depreciation, Machinery		450
	To record depreciation up to date of disposal		

$$\frac{6,500 - 500}{10} \times \frac{9}{12} = 450$$

The relevant accounts in the plant asset ledger appear as follows after the entry is posted:

Machinery		Accumulated Depreciation, Machinery	
6,500			4,650

Recording Discarded Plant Assets

A plant asset rarely lasts exactly as long as its estimated life. If it lasts longer than its estimated life, it is not depreciated past the point at which its carrying amount equals its residual value. The purpose of depreciation is to spread the depreciable amount of the asset over the life of the asset. Thus, the total accumulated depreciation should never exceed the total depreciable amount. If the asset is still used in the business beyond the end of its estimated life, its cost and accumulated depreciation remain in the ledger accounts. Proper records will thus be available for maintaining control over plant assets. If the residual value is zero, the carrying amount of a fully depreciated asset is zero until the asset is disposed of. If such an asset is discarded, no gain or loss results.

In the comprehensive illustration, however, the discarded equipment has a carrying amount of 1,850 at the time of disposal. The carrying amount from the ledger account above is calculated as machinery of 6,500 less accumulated depreciation of 4,650. A loss equal to the carrying amount should be recorded when the machine is discarded:

Sept. 30	Accumulated Depreciation, Machinery	4,650	
	Loss on Disposal of Machinery	1,850	
	Machinery		6,500
	Discarded machine no longer used in the business		

Gains and losses on disposals of long-term assets are classified as other revenues and expenses on the income statement.

Recording Plant Assets Sold for Cash

The entry to record an asset sold for cash is similar to the one illustrated above except that the receipt of cash should also be recorded. The following entries show how to record the sale of a machine under three assumptions about the selling price. In the first case, the 1,850 cash received is exactly equal to the 1,850 carrying amount of the machine; therefore, no gain or loss results.

Sept. 30	Cash	1,850	
	Accumulated Depreciation, Machinery	4,650	
	Machinery		6,500
	Sale of machine for carrying amount; no gain or loss		

In the second case, the 1,000 cash received is less than the carrying amount of 1,850, so a loss of 850 is recorded.

Sept. 30	Cash	1,000	
	Accumulated Depreciation, Machinery	4,650	
	Loss on Sale of Machinery	850	
	Machinery		6,500
	Sale of machine at less than carrying		
	amount; loss of 850 (1,850 − 1,000)		
	recorded		

In the third case, the 2,000 cash received exceeds the carrying amount of 1,850, so a gain of 150 is recorded.

Sept. 30	Cash	2,000	
	Accumulated Depreciation, Machinery	4,650	
	Gain on Sale of Machinery		150
	Machinery		6,500
	Sale of machine at more than the		
	carrying amount; gain of 150		
	(2,000 − 1,850) recorded		

Recording Exchanges of Plant Assets

Businesses also dispose of plant assets by trading them in on the purchase of other plant assets. Exchanges may involve similar assets, such as an old machine traded in on a newer model, or dissimilar assets, such as a machine traded in on a truck. In either case, the purchase price is reduced by the amount of the trade-in allowance.

The basic accounting for exchanges of plant assets is similar to accounting for sales of plant assets for cash. If the trade-in allowance received is greater than the carrying amount of the asset surrendered, there has been a gain. If the allowance is less, there has been a loss.

OBJECTIVE 6

Identify natural resource accounting issues and calculate depletion

ACCOUNTING FOR NATURAL RESOURCES

Natural resources are also known as wasting assets. Examples of natural resources are standing timber, oil and gas fields, and mineral deposits. The distinguishing characteristic of these wasting assets is that they are converted into inventory by cutting, pumping, or mining. For example, an oil field is a reservoir of unpumped oil, and a coal mine is a deposit of unmined coal.

Natural resources are shown on the balance sheet as long-term assets with such descriptive titles as Timber Lands, Oil and Gas Reserves, and Mineral Deposits. When the timber is cut, the oil is pumped, or the coal is mined, it becomes an inventory of the product to be sold. Natural resources are recorded at acquisition cost, which may also include some costs of development. As the resource is converted through the process of cutting, pumping, or mining, the asset account must be proportionally reduced. The carrying amount of oil reserves on the balance sheet, for example, is reduced by a small amount for each barrel of oil pumped. As a result, the original cost of the oil reserves is gradually reduced, and depletion is recognised by the amount of the decrease.

Depletion

The term *depletion* is used to describe not only the exhaustion of a natural resource but also the proportional allocation of the cost of a natural resource to the units extracted. The costs are allocated in a way that is much like the production method used to calculate depreciation. When a natural resource is purchased or developed, there must be an estimate of the total units that will be available, such as barrels of oil, tons of coal, or board-feet of lumber. The depletion cost per unit is determined by dividing the cost (less residual value, if any) of the natural resource by the estimated number of units available. The amount of the depletion cost for each accounting period is then calculated by multiplying the depletion cost per unit by the number of units pumped, mined, or cut. For example, for a mine having an estimated 1,500,000 tons of coal, a cost of 1,800,000, and an estimated residual value of 300,000, the depletion charge per ton of coal is 1. Thus, if 115,000 tons of coal are mined and sold during the first year, the depletion charge for the year is 115,000. This charge is recorded as follows:

Dec. 31   Depletion Expense, Coal Deposits   115,000
                Accumulated Depletion, Coal Deposits   115,000
                   To record depletion of coal mine:
                   1 per ton for 115,000 tons mined
                   and sold

On the balance sheet, the mine would be presented as follows:

Coal Deposits   1,800,000
Less Accumulated Depletion   115,000   1,685,000

Sometimes a natural resource that is extracted in one year is not sold until a later year. It is important to note that it would then be recorded as a depletion *expense* in the year it is *sold*. The part not sold is considered inventory.

Depreciation of Closely Related Plant Assets

Natural resources often require special on-site buildings and equipment, such as conveyors, roads, tracks, and drilling and pumping devices that are necessary to extract the resource. If the useful life of these assets is longer than the estimated time it will take to deplete the resource, a special problem arises. Because these long-term assets are often abandoned and have no useful purpose once all the resources have been extracted, they should be depreciated on the same basis as the depletion is calculated. For example, if machinery with a useful life of ten years is installed on an oil field that is expected to be depleted in eight years, the machinery should be depreciated over the eight-year period using the production method. In other words, each year's depreciation should be proportional to the year's depletion. If one-sixth of the oil field's total reserves is pumped in one year, then the depreciation should be one-sixth of the machinery's cost minus the scrap value. If the useful life of a long-term asset is less than the expected life of the depleting asset, the shorter life should be used to calculate depreciation. In this case or when an asset is not to be abandoned when the reserves are fully depleted, other depreciation methods, such as the straight-line method or the declining-balance method, are appropriate.

Development and Exploration Costs in the Oil and Gas Industry

The costs of exploration and development of oil and gas resources can be accounted for under either of two methods. Under **successful efforts accounting**, successful exploration—for example, the cost of a producing oil well—is a cost of the resource. This cost should be recorded as an asset and depleted over the estimated life of the resource. An unsuccessful exploration—such as the cost of a dry well—is written off immediately as a loss. Because of these immediate write-offs, successful efforts accounting is considered the more prudent method and is used by most large oil companies.

Exploration-minded independent oil companies, on the other hand, argue that the cost of the dry wells is part of the overall cost of the systematic development of the oil field and thus a part of the cost of producing wells. Under this **full-costing** method, all costs, including the cost of dry wells, are recorded as assets and depleted over the estimated life of the producing resources. This method tends to improve earnings performance in the early years for companies using it. Either method is permitted by the International Accounting Standards Committee.

OBJECTIVE 7

Apply the matching rule to intangible assets, including research and development costs and goodwill

ACCOUNTING FOR INTANGIBLE ASSETS

The purchase of an intangible asset is a special kind of capital expenditure. An intangible asset is long term, but has no physical substance. Its value comes from the long-term rights or advantages that it offers to the owner. Among the most common examples are **patents, copyrights, trademarks** and **brand names, franchises, licences,** formulas, processes, and **goodwill.** Some current assets, such as accounts receivable and certain prepaid expenses, have no physical nature, but they are not classified as intangible assets because they are short term. Intangible assets are both long term and nonphysical.

Intangible assets are accounted for at acquisition cost, that is, the amount paid for them. Some intangible assets, such as goodwill and trademarks, may be acquired at little or no cost. Even though they may have great value and be needed for profitable operations, they should not appear on the balance sheet unless they have been purchased from another party at a price established in the marketplace.

The accounting issues connected with intangible assets are the same as those connected with other long-lived assets. These are:

1. Determining an initial carrying amount
2. Accounting for that amount after acquisition under normal business conditions—that is, through periodic write-off or amortisation—in a manner similar to depreciation
3. Accounting for that amount if the value declines substantially and permanently

Besides these three problems, an intangible asset has no physical qualities and so in some cases may be impossible to identify. For these reasons, its value and its useful life may be quite hard to estimate.

The International Accounting Standards Committee has decided that a company should record as assets the costs of intangible assets acquired from others. However, the company should record as expenses the costs of developing intangible assets unless such costs meet the criteria for asset recognition. An intangible asset should be recognised as an asset if it is probable that future economic benefits specifically attributable to the asset will flow to the enterprise and the cost of the asset can be measured reliably.[4] It is considered probable that there will be economic benefits when the role that the intangible asset plays, its effectiveness, and the ability and intention of the enterprise to use the asset can be demonstrated. The existence of adequate technical, financial, and other resources, or their availability, to derive the future economic benefits also needs to be demonstrated.

Further, intangible assets that have a determinable useful life, such as patents and copyrights, should be written off through periodic amortisation over that useful life in much the same way that plant assets are depreciated. Even though some intangible assets, such as goodwill and trademarks, have no measurable limit on their lives, they should also be amortised over a reasonable length of time.

To illustrate these procedures, assume that Soda Bottling Company purchases a patent on a unique bottle cap for 18,000. The entry to record the patent would be as follows:

Patent	18,000	
Cash		18,000
Purchase of bottle cap patent		

Note that if Soda Bottling Company had developed the bottle cap internally instead of purchasing it from a third party, the costs of developing the cap, such as salaries of researchers, supplies used in testing, and costs of equipment, would have been expensed as incurred unless the criteria for asset recognition had been met.

Assume now that Soda's management determines that, although the patent for the bottle cap will last for seventeen years, the product using the cap will be sold only for the next six years. The entry to record the annual amortisation would be as follows:

Amortisation Expense	3,000	
Patent		3,000
Annual amortisation of patent		
18,000 ÷ 6 years = 3,000		

Note that the Patent account is reduced directly by the amount of the amortisation expense. This is in contrast to other long-term asset accounts in which depreciation or depletion is accumulated in a separate contra account.

If the patent becomes worthless before it is fully amortised, the remaining carrying amount is written off as a loss. For instance, assume that after the first year Soda Bottling Company's chief competitor offers a bottle with a new type of cap that makes Soda's cap obsolete. The entry to record the loss would be as follows:

Loss on Patent	15,000	
Patent		15,000
Loss resulting from patent's		
becoming worthless		

Accounting for several different types of intangible assets is outlined in Table 8-1.

TABLE 8-1 *Accounting for Intangible Assets*

Type	Description	Special Accounting Problems
Patent	An exclusive right granted by the government to make a particular product or use a specific process.	The cost of successfully defending a patent in a patent infringement suit is added to the acquisition cost of the patent. Amortise over the useful life.
Copyright	An exclusive right granted by the government to the possessor to publish and sell literary, musical, and other artistic materials for a period of the author's life plus fifty years; includes computer programs.	Record at acquisition cost and amortise over the useful life, which is often much shorter than the legal life. For example, the cost of paperback rights to a popular novel would typically be amortised over a useful life of two to four years.
Trademark, brand name	A registered symbol or name that can be used only by its owner to identify a product or service.	Debit the trademark or brand name for the acquisition cost, and amortise it over a reasonable life.
Franchise, licence	A right to an exclusive territory or to exclusive use of a formula, technique, process, or design.	Debit the franchise or licence for the acquisition cost, and amortise it over a reasonable life.
Goodwill	The excess of the cost of a group of assets (usually a business) over the fair market value of the net assets if purchased individually.	Debit Goodwill for the acquisition cost, and amortise it over a reasonable life, normally not to exceed twenty years.

BUSINESS BULLETIN **Business Practice**

Research and development expenditures can be substantial for many companies. For example, Fujitsu of Japan and Philips of the Netherlands spent ¥346 billion and NLG3,851, respectively, on research and development in 1995. Those amounts are 9 and 7 per cent, respectively, of the companies' revenues. Research and development can be even costlier in high-tech fields like biotechnology. The pharmaceutical industry also invests heavily in research and development. It is estimated that a new drug can cost from US$125 million to US$500 million before taxes to bring to market.[6] Which of these costs are capitalised and amortised and which must be expensed immediately are obviously important questions for both the management and the shareholders of these companies.

Research and Development Costs

Most successful companies carry out activities, possibly within a separate department, involving research and development. Among these activities are development of new products, testing of existing and proposed products, and pure research. Companies should record as an asset those costs that can be directly traced to the development of specific patents, formulas, or other rights provided that such development costs meet the criteria for asset recognition. If they do not meet these criteria, then they should be treated as expenses. Other costs, such as those for testing and pure research, are treated as expenses of the accounting period and deducted from profit.[5]

Computer Software Costs

Many companies develop computer programs or software to be sold or leased to individuals and companies. The costs incurred in creating a computer software product are considered research and development costs until the product has been proved to be technologically feasible. As a result, costs incurred to that point in the process should be charged to expense as incurred. A product is deemed to be technologically feasible when a detailed working program has been designed. After the working program has been developed, all software production costs are recorded as assets and amortised over the estimated economic life of the product. If at any time the company cannot expect to realise from a software product the amount of its unamortised costs on the balance sheet, the asset should be written down to the amount expected to be realised.

Goodwill

The treatment of goodwill is controversial and has been the subject of debate around the world for many years. Where goodwill is deducted directly from shareholders' equity, as has been standard practice in the U.K. until recently, the effect is to boost profits and return on equity as there is no goodwill amortisation to be charged against profits while at the same time shareholders' equity is reduced by the total amount of goodwill written off.

The term goodwill is widely used by business people, lawyers, and the public to mean different things. In most cases goodwill is taken to mean the good reputation of a company. From an accounting standpoint, goodwill exists when a purchaser pays more for a business than the fair market value of the net assets if purchased separately. Because the purchaser has paid more than the fair market value of the physical assets, there must be intangible assets. If the company being purchased does not have patents, copyrights, trademarks, or other identifiable intangible assets of value, the excess payment is assumed to be for goodwill. Goodwill exists because most businesses are worth more as going concerns than as collections of assets. Goodwill reflects all the factors that give rise to future economic benefits, including customer satisfaction, good management, manufacturing efficiency, good brand names, good locations, and good employee relations. The payment above and beyond the fair market value of the tangible assets and other specific intangible assets is thus properly recorded in the Goodwill account.

The International Accounting Standards Committee states that the benefits aris-ing from purchased goodwill will in time disappear. It is hard for a company to keep having above-average earnings unless new factors of goodwill replace the old ones. For this reason, goodwill should be amortised or written off by systematic charges to profit over a reasonable number of future time periods. The total time period should not exceed twenty years, unless a longer period can be justified.[7] Currently, national regulations governing the treatment of goodwill still vary around the world, and the period of amortisation required can range from up to a maximum of forty years in the United States and Canada to a maximum of five years in Japan. In a number of countries, including the Netherlands and Singapore, goodwill is permitted to be writ-ten off immediately as a deduction from shareholders' equity.

Goodwill, as stated, should not be recorded unless it is paid for in connection with the purchase of a whole business. (For more detail on this issue, see the chapter on intercom-pany investments, consolidated financial statements and foreign currency accounting.) The amount to be recorded as goodwill can be determined by writing the identifiable net assets up to their fair market values at the time of purchase and subtracting the total from the purchase price. For example, assume that the owners of Company A agree to sell the company for 11,400,000. If the net assets (total assets − total liabilities) are fairly valued at 10,000,000, then the amount of the goodwill is 1,400,000 (11,400,000 − 10,000,000).

SUPPLEMENTAL OBJECTIVE 8

Apply depreciation methods to problems of partial years, revised rates, groups of similar items, and cost recovery

SPECIAL PROBLEMS OF DEPRECIATING PLANT ASSETS

The illustrations used so far in this chapter have been simplified to explain the con-cepts and methods of depreciation. In real business practice, there is often a need to (1) calculate depreciation for partial years, (2) revise depreciation rates on the basis of new estimates of the useful life or residual value, (3) group together items that are alike in order to calculate depreciation, and (4) use an accelerated cost recovery method for tax purposes. The next sections discuss these four cases.

Depreciation for Partial Years

In practice, businesses do not often buy assets exactly at the beginning or end of the accounting period. In most cases, they buy the assets when they are needed and sell or discard them when they are no longer useful or needed. The time of year is normally not a factor in the decision. Consequently, it is often necessary to calculate deprecia-tion for partial years.

For example, assume that a piece of equipment is purchased for 3,500 and that it has an estimated useful life of six years, and an estimated residual value of 500. Assume also that it is purchased on September 5 and that the yearly accounting period ends on December 31. Depreciation must be recorded for four months, September through December, or four-twelfths of the year. This factor is applied to the calculated depreciation for the entire year. The four months' depreciation under the straight-line method is calculated as follows:

$$\frac{3,500 - 500}{6 \text{ years}} \times \frac{4}{12} = 167$$

For the other depreciation methods, most companies will calculate the first year's depreciation and then multiply by the partial year factor. For example, if the company used the double-declining-balance method on the above equipment, the depreciation on the asset would be calculated as follows:

$$3,500 \times .33 \times 4/12 = 385$$

Typically, the depreciation calculation is rounded off to the nearest whole month because a partial month's depreciation is not usually material and the calculation is easier. In this case, depreciation was recorded from the beginning of September even though the purchase was made on September 5. If the equipment had been purchased on September 16 or thereafter, depreciation would be charged beginning October 1, as if the equipment were purchased on that date. Some companies round off all partial years to the nearest one-half year for ease of calculation (half-year convention).

Revision of Depreciation Rates

Because a depreciation rate is based on an estimate of an asset's useful life, the periodic depreciation charge is seldom precisely accurate. Sometimes it is very inadequate or excessive. This situation may result from an underestimate or overestimate of the asset's useful life or from a wrong estimate of the residual value. What action should be taken when it is found, after several years of use, that a piece of equipment will not last as long as—or will last longer than—originally thought? Sometimes it is necessary to revise the estimate of useful life, so that the periodic depreciation expense increases or decreases. Then, to correct the situation, the remaining depreciable amount of the asset is spread over the remaining years of useful life.

With this method, the annual depreciation expense is increased or decreased to reduce the asset's carrying amount to its residual value at the end of its remaining useful life. To illustrate, assume that a delivery truck was purchased for a price of 7,000, with a residual value of 1,000. At the time of the purchase, the truck was expected to last six years, and it was depreciated on the straight-line basis. However, after two years of intensive use, it is determined that the delivery truck will last only two more years, but that the estimated residual value at the end of the two years will still be 1,000. In other words, at the end of the second year, the estimated useful life is reduced from six years to four years. At that time, the asset account and its related accumulated depreciation account would appear as follows:

Delivery Truck		Accumulated Depreciation, Delivery Truck	
Cost 7,000		Depreciation, year 1	1,000
		Depreciation, year 2	1,000

The remaining depreciable amount is calculated as follows:

cost	minus	depreciation already taken	minus	residual value	
7,000	−	2,000	−	1,000	= 4,000

The new annual periodic depreciation charge is calculated by dividing the remaining depreciable amount of 4,000 by the remaining useful life of two years. Therefore, the new periodic depreciation charge is 2,000. The annual adjusting entry for depreciation for the next two years would be as follows:

Dec. 31	Depreciation Expense, Delivery Truck	2,000	
	Accumulated Depreciation, Delivery Truck		2,000
	To record depreciation expense for the year		

Group Depreciation

To say that the estimated useful life of an asset, such as a piece of equipment, is six years means that the average piece of equipment of that type is expected to last six years. In reality, some equipment may last only two or three years, and other equipment may last eight or nine years, or longer. For this reason, and for reasons of convenience, large companies will group similar items, such as trucks, power lines, office equipment, or transformers, for purposes of calculating depreciation. This method is called **group depreciation**. Group depreciation is used widely in all fields of industry and business.

Cost Recovery for Income Tax Purposes

Tax methods of depreciation are not usually acceptable for financial reporting because the recovery periods are shorter than the depreciable assets' estimated useful lives. Accounting for the differences between tax and book depreciation is discussed in the chapter on profit and retained earnings.

Chapter Review

Review of Learning Objectives

1. **Identify the types of long-term assets and explain the management issues related to accounting for them.** Long-term assets are assets that are used in the operation of a business, are not intended for resale, and have a useful life of more than one year. Long-term assets are either tangible or intangible. In the former category are land, plant assets, and natural resources. In the latter are trademarks, patents, franchises, goodwill, and other rights. The issues associated with accounting for long-term assets relate to the means of financing the assets, and the methods of accounting for the assets.

2. **Distinguish between capital and revenue expenditures, and account for the cost of property, plant, and equipment.** It is important to distinguish between capital expenditures, which are recorded as assets, and revenue expenditures, which are recorded as expenses. The error of classifying one as the other will have an important effect on net profit. The acquisition cost of property, plant, and equipment includes all expenditures that are reasonable and necessary to get the asset in place and ready for use. These expenditures include such payments as purchase price, installation cost, freight charges, and insurance.

3. **Define *depreciation*, state the factors that affect its calculation, and show how to record it.** Depreciation is the allocation of the depreciable amount of an asset over its estimated useful life. It is recorded by debiting Depreciation Expense and crediting a related contra-asset account called Accumulated Depreciation. Factors that affect the calculation of depreciation are cost, residual value, depreciable amount, and estimated useful life.

4. **Calculate periodic depreciation under the (a) straight-line method, (b) production method, and (c) declining-balance method.** Depreciation is commonly calculated by the straight-line method, the production method, or an accelerated method. The straight-line method is related directly to the passage of time, whereas the production method is related directly to use. An accelerated method, which results in relatively large amounts of depreciation in the early years and reduced amounts in later years, is based on the assumption that plant assets provide greater economic benefit in their early years than in later years. The most common accelerated method is the declining-balance method.

5. **Account for disposal of depreciable assets.** Long-term assets may be disposed of by being discarded, sold, or exchanged. When long-term assets are disposed of, it is necessary to record the depreciation up to the date of disposal and to remove the carrying amount from the accounts by removing the cost from the asset account and the depreciation to date from the accumulated depreciation account. If a long-term asset is sold at a price that differs from its carrying amount, there is a gain or loss that should be recorded and reported on the income statement.

6. **Identify natural resource accounting issues and calculate depletion.** Natural resources are wasting assets that are converted to inventory by cutting, pumping, mining, or other forms of extraction. Natural resources are recorded at cost as long-term assets. They are allocated as expenses through depletion charges as the resources are sold. The depletion charge is based on the ratio of the resource extracted to the total estimated resource. A major issue related to this subject is accounting for oil and gas reserves.

7. **Apply the matching rule to intangible assets, including research and development costs and goodwill.** The purchase of an intangible asset should be treated as a capital expenditure and recorded at acquisition cost, which in turn should be amortised over the useful life of the asset (limited by the type of intangible asset). Research costs must be treated as revenue expenditures and charged as expenses in the periods of the expenditures. Development costs should also be expensed unless they meet the criteria for asset recognition, in which case they should be capitalised and amortised on a systematic basis. Software costs are treated as research costs and expensed until a feasible working program is developed, after which time the costs may be capitalised and amortised over a reasonable estimated life. Goodwill is the excess of the amount paid over the fair market value of the net assets in the purchase of a business and is usually related to the superior earning potential of the business. It should be recorded only if paid for in connection with the purchase of a business, and it should be amortised over a period normally not to exceed twenty years.

Supplemental Objective

8. **Apply depreciation methods to problems of partial years, revised rates, groups of similar items, and cost recovery.** In practice, many factors affect depreciation calculations. It may be necessary to calculate depreciation for partial years because assets are bought and sold throughout the year, or to revise depreciation rates because of changed conditions. Because it is often difficult to estimate the useful life of a single item, and because it is more convenient, many large businesses group similar items for purposes of depreciation. For income tax purposes, rapid write-offs of depreciable assets may be allowed. Such rapid write-offs are not usually acceptable for financial accounting because the shortened recovery periods violate the matching rule.

Review of Concepts and Terminology

The following concepts and terms were introduced in this chapter.

LO 4   **Accelerated method:** A method of depreciation that allocates relatively large amounts of the depreciable amount of an asset to earlier years and reduced amounts to later years.

LO 1   **Amortisation:** The allocation of the cost of an intangible asset over its useful life.

LO 7   **Brand names:** Registered names that can be used only by their owners to identify a product or service.

LO 2   **Capital expenditure:** An expenditure for the purchase or expansion of a long-term asset, recorded in the asset accounts.

LO 1   **Carrying amount:** The unexpired part of the cost or amount of an asset. Also called *book value*.

LO 7   **Copyrights:** Exclusive rights granted by the government to the possessor to publish and sell literary, musical, and other artistic materials for a period of the author's life plus fifty years; includes computer programs.

LO 4   **Declining-balance method:** An accelerated method of depreciation in which depreciation is calculated by applying a fixed rate to the carrying amount (the declining balance) of a tangible long-lived asset.

LO 1   **Depletion:** The exhaustion of a natural resource through mining, cutting, pumping, or other extraction, and the way in which the cost is allocated.

LO 3   **Depreciable amount:** The cost or amount of an asset less its residual value.

LO 1   **Depreciation:** The allocation of the cost or amount of a tangible long-lived asset (other than land and natural resources) over its estimated useful life.

LO 4   **Double-declining-balance method:** An accelerated method of depreciation in which a fixed rate percentage equal to twice the straight-line percentage is applied to the carrying amount of a tangible long-term asset.

LO 3   **Estimated useful life:** The total number of service units expected from a long-term asset.

LO 2   **Expenditure:** A payment or an obligation to make future payment for an asset or a service received.

LO 7   **Franchises:** Rights to an exclusive territory or market.

LO 6   **Full-costing:** A method of accounting for the costs of exploration and development of oil and gas resources in which all costs are recorded as assets and depleted over the estimated life of the producing resources.

LO 7   **Goodwill:** The excess of the cost of a group of assets (usually a business) over the fair market value of the net assets if purchased individually.

SO 8   **Group depreciation:** The grouping of similar items for purposes of calculating depreciation.

LO 1   **Intangible assets:** Long-term assets that have no physical substance but have a value based on rights or advantages accruing to the owner.

LO 7   **Licences:** An exclusive right to a formula, technique, process, or design.

LO 1   **Long-term assets:** Assets that (1) have a useful life of more than one year, (2) are acquired for use in the operation of a business, and (3) are not intended for resale to customers. Less commonly called *fixed assets*.

LO 1   **Natural resources:** Long-term assets purchased for the physical substances that can be taken from the land and used up rather than for the value of their location. Also called *wasting assets*.

LO 3   **Obsolescence:** The process of becoming out of date; a contributor, together with physical deterioration, to the limited useful life of tangible assets.

LO 7   **Patents:** Exclusive rights granted by the government for a period of several years to make a particular product or use a specific process.

LO 3   **Physical deterioration:** Limitations on the useful life of a depreciable asset resulting from use and from exposure to the elements.

LO 4   **Production method:** A method of depreciation that bases the depreciation charge for a period of time solely on the amount of the asset's use during the period of time.

LO 3   **Residual value:** The estimated net scrap, salvage, or trade-in value of a tangible asset at the estimated date of disposal. Also called *salvage value* or *disposal value*.

LO 2   **Revenue expenditure:** An expenditure for repairs, maintenance, or other services needed to maintain or operate plant assets, recorded by a debit to an expense account.

LO 4   **Straight-line method:** A method of depreciation that assumes that depreciation depends only on the passage of time and that allocates an equal amount of depreciation to each period of time.

LO 6   **Successful efforts accounting:** A method of accounting for oil and gas resources in which successful exploration is recorded as an asset and depleted over the estimated life of the resource and all unsuccessful efforts are immediately written off as a loss.

LO 1   **Tangible assets:** Long-term assets that have physical substance.

LO 7   **Trademarks:** Registered symbols that can be used only by their owners to identify a product or service.

Review Problem

Comparison of Depreciation Methods

LO 3
LO 4   Norton Construction Company purchased a cement mixer on January 1, 20x1 for 14,500. The mixer is expected to have a useful life of five years and a residual value of 1,000. The company engineers estimate that the mixer will have a useful life of 7,500 hours. It was used 1,500 hours in 20x1, 2,625 hours in 20x2, 2,250 hours in 20x3, 750 hours in 20x4, and 375 hours in 20x5. The company's year end is December 31.

REQUIRED   1. Calculate the depreciation expense and carrying amount for 20x1 to 20x5, using the following three methods: (a) straight-line, (b) production, and (c) double-declining-balance.

2. Prepare the adjusting entry to record the depreciation for 20x1 calculated in **1 (a).**
3. Show the balance sheet presentation for the cement mixer after the entry in **2** on December 31, 20x1.
4. What conclusions can you draw from the patterns of yearly depreciation?

Answer to Review Problem

1. Depreciation calculated:

Depreciation Method	Year	Calculation	Depreciation	Carrying Amount
a. Straight-line	20x1	13,500 × 1/5	2,700	11,800
	20x2	13,500 × 1/5	2,700	9,100
	20x3	13,500 × 1/5	2,700	6,400
	20x4	13,500 × 1/5	2,700	3,700
	20x5	13,500 × 1/5	2,700	1,000
b. Production	20x1	$13,500 \times \frac{1,500}{7,500}$	2,700	11,800
	20x2	$13,500 \times \frac{2,625}{7,500}$	4,725	7,075
	20x3	$13,500 \times \frac{2,250}{7,500}$	4,050	3,025
	20x4	$13,500 \times \frac{750}{7,500}$	1,350	1,675
	20x5	$13,500 \times \frac{375}{7,500}$	675	1,000
c. Double-declining-balance	20x1	14,500 × .4	5,800	8,700
	20x2	8,700 × .4	3,480	5,220
	20x3	5,220 × .4	2,088	3,132
	20x4	3,132 × .4	1,253*	1,879
	20x5		879*†	1,000

*Rounded
†Remaining depreciation to reduce carrying amount to residual value (1,879 − 1,000 = 879)

2. Adjusting entry prepared—straight-line method:

20x1
Dec. 31 Depreciation Expense, Cement Mixer   2,700
            Accumulated Depreciation, Cement Mixer   2,700
               To record depreciation expense,
               straight-line method

3. Balance sheet presentation for 20x1 shown:

Cement Mixer   14,500
Less Accumulated Depreciation   2,700
                                           11,800

4. Conclusions drawn from depreciation patterns:

The pattern of depreciation for the straight-line method differs significantly from that for the double-declining-balance method. In the early years, the depreciation using the double-declining-balance method is significantly more than that using the straight-line method. In the later years, the opposite is true. The carrying amount under the straight-line method is greater than that under the double-declining-balance method in all years except at the end of the fifth year. Depreciation under the production method differs from that under the other methods in that it follows no regular pattern. It varies with the amount of use. Consequently, depreciation is greatest in 20x2 and 20x3, which are the years of greatest use. Use declined significantly in the last two years.

CHAPTER ASSIGNMENTS

Knowledge and Understanding

Questions

1. What are the characteristics of long-term assets?
2. Which items would be classified as plant assets on the balance sheet? (a) A truck held for sale by a truck dealer, (b) an office building that was once the company headquarters but is now to be sold, (c) a typewriter used by a secretary of the company, (d) a machine that is used in manufacturing operations but is now fully depreciated, (e) pollution-control equipment that does not reduce the cost or improve the efficiency of a factory, (f) a car park for company employees.
3. Why is land different from other long-term assets?
4. What do accountants mean by the term *depreciation*, and what is its relationship to depletion and amortisation?
5. How do cash flows relate to the decisions on acquiring long-term assets and how does the useful life of the assets relate to the means of financing them?
6. Why is it useful to think of a plant asset as a bundle of services?
7. What is the distinction between revenue expenditures and capital expenditures, and what in general is included in the cost of a long-term asset?
8. Which expenditures incurred in connection with the purchase of a computer system would be charged to the asset account? (a) The purchase price of the equipment, (b) interest on the debt incurred to purchase the equipment, (c) freight charges, (d) installation charges, (e) the cost of special communications outlets at the computer site, (f) the cost of repairing a door that was damaged during installation, (g) the cost of adjustments to the system during the first month of operation.
9. Hale's Grocery obtained bids on the construction of a dock for receiving goods at the back of its store. The lowest bid was 22,000. The company decided to build the dock itself, however, and was able to do it for 20,000, which it borrowed. The activity was recorded as a debit to Buildings for 22,000 and credits to Notes Payable for 20,000 and Gain on Construction for 2,000. Do you agree with the entry?
10. A firm buys a piece of technical equipment that is expected to last twelve years. Why might the equipment have to be depreciated over a shorter period of time?
11. A company purchased a building five years ago. The market value of the building is now greater than it was when the building was purchased. Explain why the company should continue depreciating the building.
12. Evaluate the following statement: "A car park should not be depreciated because adequate repairs will make it last forever."
13. Is the purpose of depreciation to determine the value of equipment? Explain your answer.
14. Contrast the assumptions underlying the straight-line depreciation method with the assumptions underlying the production depreciation method.
15. What is the principal argument supporting an accelerated depreciation method?
16. If a plant asset is sold during the year, why should depreciation be calculated for the partial year prior to the date of the sale?
17. If a plant asset is discarded before the end of its useful life, how is the amount of loss measured?
18. Old Stake Mining Company calculates the depletion rate of ore to be 2 per ton. During 20xx the company mined 400,000 tons of ore and sold 370,000 tons. What is the total depletion for the year?
19. Under what circumstances can a mining company depreciate its plant assets over a period of time that is less than their useful lives?
20. Because accounts receivable have no physical substance, can they be classified as intangible assets?
21. Under what circumstances can a company have intangible assets that do not appear on the balance sheet?
22. When it is stated that accounting for intangible assets involves the same issues as accounting for tangible assets, what issues are being referred to?
23. How does the International Accounting Standards Committee recommend that research and development costs be treated?
24. Archi Draw Company spent three years developing a new software program for designing office buildings and recently completed the detailed working program. How does accounting for the costs of software development differ before and after the completion of a successful working program?
25. How is accounting for software development costs similar to and different from accounting for research and development costs?
26. Under what conditions should goodwill be recorded? Should it remain in the records permanently once it is recorded?
27. What basic procedure should be followed in revising a depreciation rate?
28. On what basis can depreciation be taken on a group of assets rather than on individual items?
29. What is the difference between depreciation for accounting purposes and cost recovery for income tax purposes?

Application

Exercises

E 8-1.

LO 1 *Management Issues*

Indicate whether each of the following actions is primarily related to (a) acquisition of long-term assets, (b) financing of long-term assets, or (c) choosing methods and estimates related to long-term assets.

1. Deciding to use the production method of depreciation.
2. Allocating costs on a group purchase.
3. Determining the total units a machine will produce.

4. Deciding to borrow funds to purchase equipment.
5. Estimating the savings a new machine will produce and comparing the amount to cost.
6. Deciding whether to rent or buy a piece of equipment.

E 8-2.

LO 2   *Determining Cost of Long-Term Assets*

Pavlenko Manufacturing purchased land next to its factory to be used as a car park. Expenditures incurred by the company were as follows: purchase price, 150,000; broker's fees, 12,000; title search and other fees, 1,100; demolition of a shack on the property, 4,000; general levelling of property, 2,100; paving car park, 20,000; lighting for car park, 16,000; and signs for car park, 3,200. Determine the amount that should be debited to the Land account and to the Land Improvements account.

E 8-3.

LO 2   *Group Purchase*

Linda Regalado went into business by purchasing a car wash for 480,000. The car wash assets included land, building, and equipment. If purchased separately, the land would have cost 120,000, the building 270,000, and the equipment 210,000. Determine the amount that should be recorded in the new business's records for land, building, and equipment.

E 8-4.

LO 2   *Cost of Long-Term Asset*
LO 4   *and Depreciation*

Myron Walker purchased a used tractor for 35,000. Before the tractor could be used, it required new tyres, which cost 2,200, and an overhaul, which cost 2,800. Its first tank of fuel cost 150. The tractor is expected to last six years and have a residual value of 4,000. Determine the cost and depreciable amount of the tractor and calculate the first year's depreciation under the straight-line method.

E 8-5.

LO 3   *Depreciation Methods*
LO 4

Findlay Oil Corporation purchased a drilling truck for 90,000. The company expected the truck to last five years or 200,000 miles, with an estimated residual value of 15,000 at the end of that time. During 20x2, the truck was driven 48,000 miles. The company's year end is December 31.

Calculate the depreciation for 20x2 under each of the following methods, assuming that the truck was purchased on January 13, 20x1: (1) straight-line, (2) production, and (3) double-declining-balance. Using the amount calculated in **3**, prepare the general journal entry to record depreciation expense for the second year and show how drilling trucks would appear on the balance sheet.

E 8-6.

LO 4   *Declining-Balance Method*

Schwab Burglar Alarm Systems Company purchased a word processor for 2,240. It has an estimated useful life of four years and an estimated residual value of 240. Calculate the depreciation charge for each of the four years using the double-declining-balance method.

E 8-7.

LO 5   *Disposal of Plant Assets*

A piece of equipment that cost 32,400 and on which 18,000 of accumulated depreciation had been recorded was disposed of on January 2, the first day of business of the current year. Give general journal entries to record the disposal under each of the following assumptions:

1. It was discarded as having no value.
2. It was sold for 6,000 cash.
3. It was sold for 16,000 cash.

E 8-8.

LO 6   *Natural Resource Depletion and Depreciation of Related Plant Assets*

Church Mining Corporation purchased land containing an estimated 10 million tons of ore for a cost of 8,800,000. The land without the ore is estimated to be worth 1,600,000. The company expects that all the usable ore can be mined in ten years. Buildings costing 800,000 with an estimated useful life of thirty years were erected on the site. Equipment costing 960,000 with an estimated useful life of ten years was installed. Because of the remote location, neither the buildings nor the equipment has an estimated residual value. During its first year of operation, the company mined and sold 800,000 tons of ore.

1. Calculate the depletion charge per ton.
2. Calculate the depletion expense that Church Mining Corporation should record for the year.
3. Determine the annual depreciation expense for the buildings, making it proportional to the depletion.
4. Determine the annual depreciation expense for the equipment under two alternatives: (a) using the straight-line method and (b) making the expense proportional to the depletion.

E 8-9.

LO 7   *Amortisation of Copyrights and Trademarks*

1. Fortunato Publishing Company purchased the copyright to a basic computer textbook for 20,000. The usual life of a textbook is about four years. However, the copyright will remain in effect for at least another fifty years. Calculate the annual amortisation of the copyright.
2. Guzman Company purchased a trademark from a well-known supermarket for 160,000. The management of the company argued that because the trademark value would last forever and might even increase, no amortisation should be charged. Calculate the minimum amount of annual amortisation that should be charged assuming that the rules for goodwill apply to trademarks also.

E 8-10.

SO 8   *Depreciation Methods: Partial Years*

Using the same data given for Findlay Oil Corporation in **E 8-5**, calculate the depreciation for calendar year 20x2 under each of the following methods, assuming that the truck was purchased on July 1, 20x1: (1) straight-line, (2) production, and (3) double-declining-balance.

E 8-11.

SO 8 *Straight-Line Method: Partial Years*

Idriss Manufacturing Corporation purchased three machines during the year:

February 10	Machine 1	3,600
July 26	Machine 2	24,000
October 11	Machine 3	43,200

Each machine is expected to last six years and have no estimated residual value. The company's accounting year corresponds to the calendar year. Using the straight-line method, calculate the depreciation charge for each machine for the year.

E 8-12.

SO 8 *Revision of Depreciation Rates*

Tasman Hospital purchased a special X-ray machine for its operating room. The machine, which cost 311,560, was expected to last ten years, with an estimated residual value of 31,560. After two years of operation (and depreciation charges using the straight-line rate), it became evident that the X-ray machine would last a total of only seven years. The estimated residual value, however, would remain the same. Given this information, determine the new depreciation charge for the third year on the basis of the revised estimated useful life.

Problem Set

P 8-1.

LO 2 *Determining Cost of Assets*

Muraskas Computers constructed a new training centre in 20x2. You have been hired to manage the training centre. A review of the accounting records lists the following expenditures debited to the Training Centre account:

Lawyer's fee, land acquisition	34,900
Cost of land	598,000
Architect's fee, building design	102,000
Contractor's cost, building	1,020,000
Contractor's cost, car park	135,600
Contractor's cost, electrical (for building)	164,000
Landscaping	55,000
Costs of surveying land	9,200
Training equipment, tables, and chairs	136,400
Contractor's cost, installing training equipment	68,000
Cost of levelling the land	14,000
Cost of changes in building to soundproof rooms	59,200
Total account balance	2,396,300

During the centre's construction, someone from Muraskas Computers worked full time on the project. She spent two months on the purchase and preparation of the site, six months on the construction, one month on land improvements, and one month on equipment installation and training room furniture purchase and set-up. Her salary of 64,000 during this ten-month period was charged to Administrative Expense. The training centre was placed in operation on November 1.

REQUIRED

1. Prepare a schedule with the following four column (Account) headings: Land, Land Improvements, Building, and Equipment. Place each of the expenditures above in the appropriate column. Total the columns.
2. Prepare an entry on December 31 to correct the accounts associated with the training centre, assuming that the company's accounts have not been closed at the end of the year.

P 8-2.

LO 3 *Comparison of*
LO 4 *Depreciation Methods*

Larson Manufacturing Company purchased a robot for its manufacturing operations at a cost of 1,440,000 at the beginning of year 1. The robot has an estimated useful life of four years and an estimated residual value of 120,000. The robot is expected to last 20,000 hours. The robot was operated 6,000 hours in year 1; 8,000 hours in year 2; 4,000 hours in year 3; and 2,000 hours in year 4.

REQUIRED

1. Calculate the annual depreciation and carrying amount for the robot for each year, assuming the following depreciation methods: (a) straight-line, (b) production, and (c) double-declining-balance.
2. Prepare the adjusting entry that would be made each year to record the depreciation calculated under the straight-line method.
3. Show the balance sheet presentation for the robot after the adjusting entry in year 2 using the straight-line method.
4. What conclusions can you draw from the patterns of yearly depreciation and carrying amount in 1?

P 8-3.

LO 5 *Recording Disposals*

Langan Designs purchased a computer that will assist it in designing factory layouts. The cost of the computer was 23,500. Its expected useful life is six years. The company can probably sell the computer for 2,500 at the end of six years.

REQUIRED   Prepare journal entries to record the disposal of the computer at the end of the third year, after the depreciation is recorded, assuming that it was depreciated using the straight-line method and making the following assumptions:

a. The computer is sold for 19,000.
b. It is sold for 10,000.

P 8-4.

LO 4   *Depreciation Methods and*
SO 8   *Partial Years*

Isabel Lim purchased a laundry company that caters for university students. In addition to the washing machines, Lim installed a tanning machine and a refreshment centre. Because each type of asset performs a different function, she has decided to use different depreciation methods. Data on each type of asset are summarised in the table below.

The tanning machine was operated 2,100 hours in 20x1, 3,000 hours in 20x2, and 2,400 hours in 20x3.

Asset	Date Purchased	Cost	Installation Cost	Residual Value	Estimated Life	Depreciation Method
Washing machines	3/5/x1	30,000	4,000	5,200	4 years	Straight-line
Tanning machine	4/1/x1	68,000	6,000	2,000	7,500 hours	Production
Refreshment centre	10/1/x1	6,800	1,200	1,200	10 years	Double-declining-balance

REQUIRED   Assuming that the accounting year ends December 31, calculate the depreciation charges for each item and in total for 20x1, 20x2, and 20x3. Round your answers to the nearest whole number and present them by filling in a table with the headings shown below.

			Depreciation		
Asset	Year	Calculations	20x1	20x2	20x3

Critical Thinking and Communication

Conceptual Mini-Case

CMC 8-1.

LO 3   *Choice of Depreciation*
LO4   *Methods*

Ford, one of the world's largest manufacturers of cars, does not use the straight-line depreciation method for financial reporting purposes even though most companies do choose this depreciation method. As noted in Ford's 1990 annual report:

> Depreciation is calculated using an accelerated method that results in accumulated depreciation of approximately two-thirds of asset cost during the first half of the asset's estimated useful life.

What reasons can you give for Ford's choosing this method of depreciation over the straight-line method? Discuss which of these two methods is the more prudent.

Cultural Mini-Case

CLMC 8-1.

LO 7   *Accounting for Trademarks*
        and Goodwill: U.S. and
        British Rules

When the British company *Grand Metropolitan* (Grand Met) purchased *Pillsbury* of the U.S. in 1989, it adopted British accounting policies with regard to intangibles. Many analysts feel this gives British companies advantages over U.S. companies, especially in takeover situations. There are two major differences in accounting for intangibles between U.S. accounting standards and British accounting standards. First, under the U.S. rules, intangible assets such as trademarks and brand names are recorded at their acquisition cost, which is often nominal, and the cost is amortised over a reasonable life. Under British accounting standards, on the other hand, firms are able to record the value of trademarks for the purpose of increasing the total assets on their balance sheets. Further, they do not have to amortise the value if management can show that the value can be preserved through extensive brand support. Grand Met, therefore, elected to record such famous Pillsbury trademarks as the Pillsbury Doughboy, Green Giant vegetables, Haagen Daaz ice cream, and Van de Kamp fish at an estimated value and not to amortise them. Second, when one company purchases another company for more than the market value of the assets if purchased individually, under U.S. rules the excess is recorded as the asset goodwill, which must be amortised over a period not to exceed forty years. Under British accounting rules, until recently, any goodwill resulting from a purchase was permitted to reduce shareholders' equity directly, rather than being recorded as an asset and reducing net profit through amortisation over a number of years. Analysts say that these two rules made Pillsbury more valuable to Grand Met than to Pillsbury shareholders and thus led to Pillsbury's being bought by the British firm. Write a one- or two-page paper that addresses the following questions: What is the rationale behind the argument that the British company has an advantage because of the differences between U.S. and British accounting principles? Do you agree with the U.S. or British accounting rules with regard to intangibles and goodwill? Give reasons for your answers.

Ethics Mini-Case

EMC 8-1.

LO 2   *Ethics of Aggressive*
LO 8   *Accounting Policies*

Is it ethical to choose aggressive accounting practices to advance a company's business? *America Online* (AOL), the largest Internet service provider in the U.S. and one of the hottest shares on Wall Street, has been one of the most aggressive companies in its choice of accounting principles. From its initial share offering in 1992, the share price was up over 2,000 per cent by 1996. Accounting is very important to AOL because healthy earnings enable it to sell shares and raise more cash to fund its phenomenal growth. AOL's strategy calls for building the largest customer base in the industry. Consequently, it spends many millions of dollars each year marketing its services to new customers. These costs are usually recognised as operating expenses in the year in which they are incurred. However, AOL treats these costs as long-term assets, called "deferred subscriber acquisition costs", which are expensed over several years; AOL's argument is that the average customer is going to stay with the company for three years or more. The company also records research and development costs as "product development costs" and amortises them over five years. Both of these practices are justifiable theoretically, but they are not common practice. If the standard or more prudent practice had been followed, the company would have had a net loss in every year that it has been in business.[8] This result could have limited AOL's ability to raise money and, subsequently, its growth. Explain management's rationale in adopting the accounting policies that it did. What could go wrong with management's plan? How would you evaluate the ethics of AOL's actions? Who benefits from them? Who is harmed by them?

Decision-Making Case

DMC 8-1.

LO 4   *Natural Resource Accounting*
LO 6

Billy Daniels is in the gravel business and has engaged you to assist in evaluating his company, *Daniels Gravel Company*. Your first step is to collect the facts about the company's operations. On January 3, 20x2, Billy purchased a piece of property with gravel deposits for 6,310,000. He estimated that the gravel deposits contained 4,700,000 cubic yards of gravel. The gravel is used for making roads. After the gravel is gone, the land will be worth only about 200,000.

The equipment required to extract the gravel cost 1,452,000. In addition, Billy had to build a small frame building to house the mine office and a small dining hall for the workers. The building cost 152,000 and will have no residual value after its estimated useful life of ten years. It cannot be moved from the mine site. The equipment has an estimated useful life of six years (with no residual value) and also cannot be moved from the mine site.

Trucks for the project cost 308,000 (estimated life, six years; residual value, 20,000). The trucks, of course, can be used at a different site.

Billy estimated that in five years all the gravel would be mined and the mine would be shut down. During 20x2, 1,175,000 cubic yards of gravel were mined. The average selling price during the year was 2.66 per cubic yard, and at the end of the year 125,000 cubic yards remained unsold. Operating expenses were 852,000 for labour and 232,000 for other expenses.

REQUIRED

1. Prepare general journal entries to record the purchase of the property and the building and equipment associated with the mine. Assume purchases are made with cash on January 3.
2. Prepare adjusting entries to record depletion and depreciation for the first year of operation (20x2). Assume that the depreciation rate is equal to the percentage of the total gravel mined during the year, unless the asset is moveable. For moveable assets, use the straight-line method.
3. Prepare an income statement for 20x2 for Daniels Gravel Company.
4. What is your evaluation of the company's operations? What are the reasons for your evaluation? Ignore income tax effects.

Basic Research Activity

RA 8-1.

LO 7   *Intangible Assets*

In the library, find the annual reports of three companies, preferably including two from countries other than your own. Assess the existence of intangible assets from the balance sheets and the notes to the accounts. Identify the accounting treatment of these assets, especially goodwill. To what extent do these companies follow International Accounting Standards? How do the accounting policies of these companies differ from those shown in Nestlé's annual report in the appendix? Be prepared to discuss your findings in class.

Financial Reporting and Analysis

Interpretation Cases from Business

ICB 8-1.

LO 3   *Effects of Change in*
LO 4   *Accounting Method*
SO 8

Depreciation expense is a significant expense for companies in industries where plant assets are a high proportion of assets. The amount of depreciation expense in a given year is affected by estimates of useful life and choice of depreciation method. In 1993, *Century Steelworks Company*, a major integrated steel producer in the U.S., changed the estimated useful lives for its major production assets. It also changed the method of depreciation for other steel-making assets from straight-line to the production method.

The company's 1993 annual report states, "A recent study conducted by management shows that actual years-in-service figures for our major production equipment and machinery are, in most cases, higher than the estimated useful lives assigned to these assets. We have recast the depreciable lives of such assets so that equipment previously assigned a useful life of 8 to 26 years now has an extended depreciable life of 10 to 32 years." The report goes on to explain that the new production method of depreciation "recognizes that depreciation of production equipment and machinery correlates directly to both physical wear and tear and the passage of time. The production method of depreciation, which we have now initiated, more closely allocates the cost of these assets to the periods in which products are manufactured".

The report summarised the effects of both actions on the year 1993 as follows:

Incremental Increase in Net Profit	In Millions	Per Share
Lengthened lives	$11.0	$ .80
Production method		
Current year	7.3	.53
Prior years	2.8	.20
Total increase	$21.1	$1.53

During 1993, Century Steelworks reported a net loss of $83,156,500 ($6.03 per share). Depreciation expense for 1993 was $87,707,200.

In explaining the changes, the controller of Century Steelworks was quoted in an article in *Business Journal* as follows: "There is no reason why Century Steelworks should continue to depreciate our assets more conservatively than our competitors do." But the article quotes an industry analyst who argues that, by slowing its method of depreciation, Century Steelworks could be viewed as reporting lower-quality earnings.

REQUIRED

1. Explain the accounting treatment when there is a change in the estimated lives of depreciable assets. What circumstances must exist for the production method to produce the effect it did in relation to the straight-line method? What would have been Century Steelworks' net profit or loss if the changes had not been made? What may have motivated management to make the changes?
2. What does the controller of Century Steelworks mean when he says that Century had been depreciating "more conservatively than our competitors"? Why might the changes at Century Steelworks indicate, as the analyst asserts, "lower-quality earnings"? What risks might Century face as a result of its decision to use the production method of depreciation?

ICB 8-2.

LO 7   *Treatment of Goodwill*

Electrolux, based in Sweden, is one of the world's leading manufacturers of household appliances, operating in more than ninety countries. The group is the European market leader in white goods with famous brand names such as Electrolux, Zanussi, AEG, Tricity Bendix, Frigidaire, Westinghouse, and Kelvinator. As corporate acquisitions are an important element of the group's expansion, acquisitions are often made in competition with other firms whose accounting differs from the Swedish approach. Electrolux has decided, therefore, to amortise goodwill over forty years for its acquisitions of Zanussi, White, and American Yard products. Supplementary information is also provided in the notes regarding the effects of amortisation over twenty years as required by the International Accounting Standards Committee.

Electrolux's net profit for 1995 and 1994 was 2,748 and 4,830 million kronor, respectively. The goodwill charge for 1995 and 1994 on a forty-year basis was 282 and 305 million kronor, whereas on a 20-year basis, it would have been 365 and 406 million kronor, respectively.

REQUIRED

1. What would be the impact on net profit in 1995 and 1994 of adopting a twenty-year amortisation policy?
2. What are the reasons for amortising goodwill against profit?
3. Discuss the arguments for a twenty-year maximum period of amortisation compared to a forty-year maximum period.

Nestlé Case

NC 8-1.

LO 2   *Long-Term Assets*
LO 3
LO 4

1. Refer to the consolidated balance sheets and to the note on tangible fixed assets in the notes to consolidated financial statements in the appendix on Nestlé to answer the following questions: What percentage of total assets in 1996 was tangible fixed assets? What is the most significant type of asset? Does Nestlé have a significant investment in land and buildings?

2. Refer to the summary of significant accounting policies and to the note on tangible fixed assets in the appendix on Nestlé. What method of valuation does Nestlé use? What method of depreciation is used? How long does management estimate its buildings to last as compared to tools, furniture, and equipment?

3. Refer to the cash flow statement in the appendix on Nestlé. How much did Nestlé spend on tangible fixed assets during 1996? Is this an increase or a decrease from prior years?

4. How does Nestlé treat goodwill arising from acquisitions?

ENDNOTES

1. Danone, *Annual Report*, 1995.
2. International Accounting Standard, IAS23, *Borrowing Costs* (London: IASC, revised 1993), para. 11.
3. International Accounting Standard, IAS4, *Depreciation Accounting* (London: IASC, reformatted 1994), para. 4.
4. International Accounting Standard, IAS38, *Intangible Assets* (London: IASC, 1998).
5. Ibid.
6. George Anders, "Vital Statistic: Disputed Cost of Creating a Drug", *Wall Street Journal*, November 9, 1993.
7. International Accounting Standard, IAS22, *Business Combinations* (London: IASC, revised 1998), para. 42.
8. "Stock Gives Case the Funds He Needs to Buy New Technology", *Business Week*, April 15, 1996.

Chapter 9

LIABILITIES

LEARNING OBJECTIVES

1. Identify the management issues related to accounting for *current liabilities*.
2. Identify, calculate, and record definitely determinable and estimated current liabilities.
3. Define *contingent liability*.
4. Define *interest* and distinguish between simple and compound interest.
5. Identify the management issues related to accounting for *long-term liabilities*.
6. Identify and contrast the major characteristics of bonds.
7. Record the issuance of bonds at face value and at a discount or premium.
8. Amortise bond discounts (and bond premiums) using the effective interest method.
9. Account for year-end adjustments to bonds.
10. Account for the conversion of bonds into shares.
11. Explain the basic features of mortgages payable, instalment notes payable, long-term leases, and pensions as long-term liabilities.

DECISION POINT

TSINGTAO BREWERY

Liabilities *are one of the three major parts of the balance sheet. They are present obligations for the future payment of assets or the future performance of services that result from past transactions. For example, the current and long-term liabilities of the Tsingtao Brewery of China, which has total assets of almost 2.8 billion Renminbi, are as follows (in thousands):*[1]

	1995	1994
Current Liabilities		
Short-term loans	*282,257*	*194,185*
Accounts payable	*128,779*	*81,654*
Bills payable	*20,000*	*—*
Advances from customers	*12,931*	*27,351*
Staff welfare payable	*1,637*	*208*
Dividends payable	*77,805*	*80,866*
Tax payable	*62,047*	*33,825*
Other payables	*19,608*	*25,483*
Accruals	*34,974*	*21,143*
Current portion of long-term loans	*20,570*	*54,939*
	660,608	*519,654*
Long-term Liabilities		
Long-term loans	*83,027*	*65,917*
Other long-term liabilities	*111,418*	*147,734*
	194,445	*213,651*
Total Liabilities	*855,053*	*733,305*

Liabilities are important because they are closely related to the goals of profitability and liquidity. Liabilities are sources of cash for operating, investing, and financing activities when they are incurred, but they are also obligations that use cash when they are paid as required. Achieving the appropriate level of liabilities is critical to business success. A company that has too few liabilities may not be earning up to its potential. A company that has too many liabilities may be incurring excessive risks. This chapter focuses on the management and accounting issues involving current liabilities, contingent liabilities, and long-term liabilities.

OBJECTIVE 1

Identify the management issues related to accounting for current liabilities

MANAGEMENT ISSUES RELATED TO ACCOUNTING FOR CURRENT LIABILITIES

The primary reason for incurring current liabilities is to meet needs for cash during the operating cycle. In a previous chapter, the operating cycle was presented as the process of converting cash to purchases, to sales, to accounts receivable, and back to cash. Most current liabilities arise in support of this cycle, as when accounts payable arise from purchases of inventory, accrued expenses arise from operating costs, and unearned revenues arise from customers' advance payments. Short-term debt is used to raise cash during periods of inventory build-up or while waiting for collection of receivables. Sometimes cash is siphoned off to pay current maturities of long-term debt, to make investments in long-term assets, or to pay cash dividends.

Failure to manage the cash flows related to current liabilities can have serious consequences for a business. For instance, if suppliers are not paid in a timely manner, they may withhold shipments that are vital to a company's operations. Continued failure to pay current liabilities can lead to bankruptcy. To evaluate a company's ability to pay its current liabilities, three measures of liquidity presented in previous chapters—working capital, the current ratio, and the quick ratio—are often used. Current liabilities is a key component of each of these measures. To properly identify and manage current liabilities requires an understanding of how they are recognised, valued, classified, and disclosed.

Recognition of Liabilities

Timing is important in the recognition of liabilities. Failure to record a liability in an accounting period very often goes along with failure to record an expense. This leads to an understatement of expense and an overstatement of profit. A liability is recorded when an obligation occurs. This rule is harder to apply than it might appear. When a transaction obligates a company to make future payments, a liability arises and is recognised, as when goods are bought on credit. However, current liabilities are often not represented by direct transactions. One of the major reasons for adjusting entries at the end of an accounting period is to recognise unrecorded liabilities. Among these accrued liabilities are salaries payable and interest payable. Other liabilities that can only be estimated, such as taxes payable, must also be recognised through adjusting entries.

On the other hand, companies often enter into agreements for future transactions. For instance, a company may agree to pay an executive 50,000 a year for a period of three years, or a utility company may agree to buy an unspecified quantity of coal at a certain price over the next five years. These contracts, though they are definite commitments, are not considered liabilities because they are for future—not past—transactions. As there is no current obligation, no liability is recognised.

Valuation of Liabilities

A liability is generally valued on the balance sheet at the amount of money needed to pay the debt or at the fair market value of goods or services to be delivered. For most liabilities the amount is definitely known, but for some it must be estimated. For example, a car dealer who sells a car with a one-year warranty must provide parts and service during the year. The obligation is definite because the sale of the car has occurred, but the amount must be estimated. These estimates are usually based on past experience and anticipated changes in the business environment. Additional disclosures of the fair value of liabilities may be required in the notes to the financial statements, as explained below.

Classification of Liabilities

The classification of liabilities directly matches the classification of assets. **Current liabilities** are debts and obligations that are expected to be liquidated within one year. They are normally paid out of current assets or with cash generated from operations. **Long-term liabilities**, which are liabilities that are due beyond one year, have a different purpose. They are used to finance long-term assets, such as aircraft. These distinctions are important because they affect the evaluation of a company's liquidity.

Disclosure of Liabilities

To explain some accounts, supplemental disclosure may be required in the notes to the financial statements. For example, if a company has a large amount of notes payable, an explanatory note may disclose the balances, maturities, interest rates, and other features of the debts. Any special credit arrangements, such as issues of commercial paper and lines of credit should also be disclosed.

<table>
<tr><td>OBJECTIVE 2</td></tr>
<tr><td>Identify, calculate, and record definitely determinable and estimated current liabilities</td></tr>
</table>

COMMON CATEGORIES OF CURRENT LIABILITIES

Current liabilities fall into two major groups: (1) definitely determinable liabilities and (2) estimated liabilities.

Definitely Determinable Liabilities

Current liabilities that are set by contract or by statute and can be measured exactly are called **definitely determinable liabilities**. The related accounting problems are to determine the existence and amount of each such liability and to see that it is recorded properly. Definitely determinable liabilities include trade accounts payable, bank loans and commercial paper, notes payable, accrued liabilities, dividends payable, sales and excise taxes payable, current portions of long-term debt, payroll liabilities, and unearned revenues.

Accounts Payable

Accounts payable, sometimes called trade accounts payable, are short-term obligations to suppliers for goods and services. The amount in the Accounts Payable account is generally supported by an accounts payable subsidiary ledger, which contains an individual account for each person or company to whom money is owed.

Bank Loans and Commercial Paper

Management will often establish a **line of credit** from a bank; this preapproved arrangement allows the company to borrow funds when they are needed to finance current operations. A promissory note for the full amount of the line of credit is signed when the credit is granted, but the company has great flexibility in using the available funds. The company can increase its borrowing up to the limit when it needs cash and reduce the amount borrowed when it generates enough cash of its own. Both the amount borrowed and the interest rate charged by the bank may change daily. The bank may require the company to meet certain financial goals (such as maintaining certain profit margins, current ratios, or debt to equity ratios) to retain the line of credit. Companies with excellent credit ratings may borrow short-term funds by issuing **commercial paper**, unsecured loans that are sold to the public, usually through professionally managed investment firms. The portion of a line of credit that is currently borrowed and the amount of commercial paper issued are usually combined with notes payable in the current liabilities section of the balance sheet. Details are disclosed in a note to the financial statements.

Notes Payable

Short-term notes payable, which also arise out of the ordinary course of business, are obligations represented by promissory notes. These notes may be used to secure bank loans, to pay suppliers for goods and services, and to secure credit from other sources.

As with notes receivable, presented in the chapter on short-term liquid assets, the interest on notes may be stated separately on the face of the note (Case 1), or it may be deducted in advance by discounting it from the face value of the note (Case 2). The entries to record the note in each case are as follows:

Case 1—Interest stated separately			Case 2—Interest in face amount		
Aug. 31 Cash	5,000		Aug. 31 Cash	4,900	
Notes Payable		5,000	Discount on Notes Payable	100	
To record 60-day,			Notes Payable		5,000
12% promissory note			To record 60-day		
with interest stated			promissory note with		
separately			100 interest included		
			in face amount		

Note that in Case 1 the money borrowed equalled the face value of the note, whereas in Case 2 the money borrowed (4,900) was less than the face value (5,000) of the note. The amount of the discount equals the amount of the interest for sixty days. Although the amount of interest on each of these notes is the same, the effective interest rate is slightly more in Case 2 because the amount borrowed is slightly less (4,900 in Case 2 versus 5,000 in Case 1). Discount on Notes Payable is a contra account to Notes Payable and is deducted from Notes Payable on the balance sheet.

On October 30, when the note is paid, each alternative is recorded as follows:

Case 1—Interest stated separately			Case 2—Interest in face amount		
Oct. 30 Notes Payable	5,000		Oct. 30 Notes Payable	5,000	
Interest Expense	100		Cash		5,000
Cash		5,100	Payment of note with		
Payment of note with			interest included in face		
interest stated separately			amount		
			30 Interest Expense	100	
			Discount on Notes Payable		100
			Interest expense on		
			matured note		

Accrued Liabilities

A key reason for adjusting entries at the end of an accounting period is to recognise and record liabilities that are not already in the accounting records. This practice applies to any type of liability. For example, in the chapter on measuring business profit, adjustments relating to wages payable were made. As you will see, accrued liabilities can also include estimated liabilities.

Here the focus is on interest payable, a definitely determinable liability. Interest accrues daily on interest-bearing notes. At the end of the accounting period, an adjusting entry should be made in accordance with the matching rule to record the interest obligation up to that point in time. Let us again use the example of the two notes presented earlier in this chapter. If we assume that the accounting period ends on September 30, or thirty days after the issuance of the sixty-day notes, the adjusting entries for each case would be as follows:

Case 1—Interest stated separately			Case 2—Interest in face amount		
Sept. 30 Interest Expense	50		Sept. 30 Interest Expense	50	
Interest Payable		50	Discount on Notes Payable		50
To record interest expense			To record interest expense		
for 30 days on note with			for 30 days on note with		
interest stated separately			interest included in face		
			amount		

$$5,000 \times \frac{30}{360} \times .12 = 50$$

$$100 \times \frac{30}{60} = 50$$

In Case 2, Discount on Notes Payable will now have a debit balance of 50, which will become interest expense during the next thirty days.

Dividends Payable

Cash dividends are a distribution of earnings by a corporation. The payment of dividends is solely the decision of the corporation's board of directors. A liability does not exist until the board declares the dividends. There is usually a short time between the date of declaration and the date of payment of dividends. During that short time, the dividends declared are current liabilities of the corporation. Accounting for dividends is treated extensively in the chapter on profit and retained earnings.

Sales and Excise Taxes Payable

In most countries, taxes are levied on retail transactions. A trader who sells goods subject to these taxes must collect the taxes and forward them periodically to the appropriate government agency. The amount of tax collected represents a current liability until it is remitted to the government. For example, assume that a trader makes a 100 sale that is subject to a 15 per cent sales tax. Assuming that the sale takes place on June 1, the correct entry to record the sale is as follows:

June 1	Cash	115	
	Sales		100
	Sales Tax Payable		15
	Sale of goods and collection of sales tax		

The sale is properly recorded at 100, and tax collections are recorded as liabilities to be remitted at the proper time to the appropriate government agency.

Current Portions of Long-Term Debt

The IASC permits the current portion of a long-term liability to be excluded from current liabilities if the enterprise intends to refinance the obligations on a long-term basis and there is a reasonable assurance that the enterprise will be able to do so. While this practice is followed in many countries, there are some exceptions, including Belgium, France, Germany, Greece, and Japan, where this issue is not addressed at the national regulatory level.

If a portion of long-term debt is due within the next year and is to be paid from current assets, then the current portion of long-term debt is properly classified as a current liability. For example, suppose that a 500,000 debt is to be paid in instalments of 100,000 per year for the next five years. The 100,000 instalment due in the current year should be classified as a current liability. The remaining 400,000 should be classified as a long-term liability. Note that no journal entry is necessary. The total debt of 500,000 is simply reclassified when the financial statements are prepared, in the following manner:

Current Liabilities	
Current Portion of Long-Term Debt	100,000
Long-Term Liabilities	
Long-Term Debt	400,000

Payroll Liabilities

For most companies, the cost of labour and related payroll taxes is a major expense. In some industries, such as banking and airlines, payroll costs represent more than half of all operating costs. Payroll accounting is important because complex laws and significant liabilities are involved. The employer is liable to employees for wages and salaries and to various agencies for amounts withheld from wages and salaries and for related taxes. The term **wages** refers to payment for the services of employees at an hourly rate or on a piecework basis. The term **salaries** refers to the compensation of employees who are paid at a monthly or yearly rate.

To illustrate the recording of the payroll, assume that on February 15 gross employee wages are 32,500, with withholdings of 6,600 for income taxes, 2,015 for social security taxes, 471 for health taxes, 900 for medical insurance, and 1,300 for pension contributions. The entry to record this payroll is as follows:

┌───┐

BUSINESS BULLETIN   **Technology in Practice**

The processing of payroll is an ideal application of computers because it is
one of the most routine procedures in accounting and very complex, and it
must be done with absolute accuracy: employees want to be paid exactly
what they are owed and failure to pay the taxes and other costs as required
can result in severe penalties and high interest charges. As a result, many
companies purchase carefully designed and tested computer software for use
in preparing the payroll. Other companies do not process their own payroll
but rely on outside businesses that specialise in providing such services.

Feb. 15	Wages Expense	32,500	
	Employees' Income Taxes Payable		6,600
	Social Security Taxes Payable		2,015
	Health Taxes Payable		471
	Medical Insurance Payable		900
	Pension Contributions Payable		1,300
	Wages Payable		21,214
	To record payroll		

Note that the employees' take-home pay is only 21,214 out of 32,500 earned. Using
the same data, the additional employer taxes and other costs would be recorded as
follows, assuming that the payroll taxes correspond to the discussion above and that
the employer pays 80 per cent of the medical insurance premiums and half of the
pension contributions:

Feb. 15	Payroll Expense	9,401	
	Social Security Taxes Payable		2,015
	Health Taxes Payable		471
	Medical Insurance Payable		3,600
	Pension Contributions Payable		1,300
	Unemployment Taxes Payable		2,015
	To record payroll taxes and other costs		

Note that the payroll taxes and employee benefit costs increase the total cost of the
payroll to 41,901 (9,401 + 32,500), which exceeds by almost 29 per cent the amount
earned by employees. This is a typical situation.

Unearned Revenues

Unearned revenues represent obligations for goods or services that the company
must provide or deliver in a future accounting period in return for an advance payment from a customer. For example, a publisher of a monthly magazine who receives
annual subscriptions totalling 240 would make the following entry:

Cash	240	
Unearned Subscriptions		240
Receipt of annual subscriptions		
in advance		

The publisher now has a liability of 240 that will be reduced gradually as monthly
issues of the magazine are mailed, as follows:

Unearned Subscriptions	20	
Subscription Revenues		20
Delivery of monthly magazine issues		

Many businesses, such as repair companies, construction companies, and special-order firms, ask for a deposit or advance from a customer before they will begin work. These advances are also current liabilities until the goods or services are delivered.

Estimated Liabilities

Estimated liabilities are debts or obligations of a company for which the exact amount cannot be known until a later date. Since there is no doubt about the existence of the legal obligation, the primary accounting problem is to estimate and record the amount of the liability. Examples of estimated liabilities are income taxes, property taxes, product warranties, and vacation pay.

Income Taxes Payable

The profit of a corporation is taxed by the government. The amount of income tax liability depends on the results of operations. Often that is not certain until after the end of the year. However, because income taxes are an expense in the year in which profit is earned, an adjusting entry is necessary to record the estimated tax liability. An example of this entry follows:

Dec. 31	Income Tax Expense	53,000	
	Income Tax Payable		53,000
	To record estimated income tax		

Remember that sole proprietorships and partnerships do *not* pay income taxes. Their owners must report their share of the firm's profit on their individual tax returns.

Property Taxes Payable

Property taxes are taxes levied on real property, such as land and buildings, and on personal property, such as inventory and equipment. Property taxes are often a main source of revenue for local governments. Usually they are assessed annually against the property involved. Because the accounting years of local governments and their assessment dates rarely correspond to a firm's accounting year, it is necessary to estimate the amount of property taxes that applies to each month of the year. Assume, for instance, that a local government has an accounting year of July 1 to June 30, that its assessment date is November 1 for the current year that began on July 1, and that its payment date is December 15. Assume also that on July 1, Janis Corporation estimates that its property tax assessment for the coming year will be 24,000. The adjusting entry to be made on July 31, which would be repeated on August 31, September 30, and October 31, would be as follows:

July 31	Property Taxes Expense	2,000	
	Estimated Property Taxes Payable		2,000
	To record estimated property taxes		
	expense for the month		
	24,000 ÷ 12 months = 2,000		

On November 1, the firm receives a property tax bill for 24,720. The estimate made in July was too low. The charge should have been 2,060 per month. Because the difference between the actual assessment and the estimate is small, the company decides to absorb in November the amount undercharged in the previous four months. Therefore, the property tax expense for November is 2,300 [2,060 + 4(60)] and is recorded as follows:

Nov. 30	Property Taxes Expense	2,300	
	Estimated Property Taxes Payable		2,300
	To record estimated property taxes		

The Estimated Property Taxes Payable account now has a balance of 10,300. The entry to record payment on December 15 would be as follows:

Dec. 15	Estimated Property Taxes Payable	10,300	
	Prepaid Property Taxes	14,420	
	Cash		24,720
	Payment of property taxes		

Beginning December 31 and each month afterwards until June 30, property tax expense is recorded by a debit to Property Taxes Expense and a credit to Prepaid Property Taxes in the amount of 2,060. The total of these seven entries will reduce the Prepaid Property Taxes account to zero on June 30.

Product Warranty Liability

When a firm places a warranty or guarantee on its product at the time of sale, a liability exists for the length of the warranty. The cost of the warranty is properly debited to an expense account in the period of sale because it is a feature of the product or service sold and thus is included in the price paid by the customer for the product. On the basis of experience, it should be possible to estimate the amount the warranty will cost in the future. Some products or services will require little warranty service; others may require much. Thus, there will be an average cost per product or service.

For example, assume that a car battery company guarantees that it will replace any battery free of charge if it fails during the time you own your car. The company charges a small service fee for replacing the battery. This guarantee is an important selling feature for the firm's batteries. In the past, 6 per cent of the batteries sold have been returned for replacement under the guarantee. The average cost of a battery is 25. Assume that during July, 350 batteries were sold. This accrued liability would be recorded as an adjustment at the end of July as follows:

July 31	Product Warranty Expense	525	
	Estimated Product Warranty Liability		525
	To record estimated product		
	warranty expense:		
	Number of units sold	350	
	Rate of replacement under warranty	× .06	
	Estimated units to be replaced	21	
	Estimated cost per unit	× 25	
	Estimated liability for product warranty	525	

When a battery is returned for replacement under the product warranty, the cost of the battery is charged against the Estimated Product Warranty Liability account.

BUSINESS BULLETIN   Business Practice

Many companies promote their products by issuing coupons that offer price deductions or other enticements for purchasers. Since four out of five shoppers use coupons, companies are forced by competition to use them. The total value of these coupons, each of which represents a potential liability for the issuing company, is truly staggering. NCH Promotional Services, a company owned by Dun & Bradstreet of the United States, estimates that more than 300 billion coupons were issued in 1993. Of course, the liability depends on how many of the coupons will actually be redeemed. NCH estimates that approximately 7 billion, or about 2.3 per cent, will be redeemed. This is not a large percentage, but the value of the redeemed coupons is estimated to be more than $4 billion.[2]

For example, assume that a customer returns on December 5 with a defective battery and pays a 10 service fee to have the battery replaced. Assume that this particular battery cost 20. The entry is as follows:

Dec. 5	Cash	10	
	Estimated Product Warranty Liability	20	
	Service Revenue		10
	Inventory		20
	Replacement of battery under warranty		

Vacation Pay Liability

In most companies, employees earn the right to paid vacation days or weeks as they work during the year. For example, an employee may earn two weeks of paid vacation for each fifty weeks of work. Therefore, she or he is paid fifty-two weeks' salary for fifty weeks' work. Theoretically, the cost of the two weeks' vacation should be allocated as an expense over the whole year so that month-to-month costs will not be distorted. The vacation pay represents 4 per cent (two weeks' vacation divided by fifty weeks) of a worker's pay. Every week worked earns the employee a small fraction (4 per cent) of his or her vacation pay. Vacation pay liability can amount to a substantial amount of money.

Suppose that a company with this vacation policy has a payroll of 21,000, of which 1,000 was paid to employees on vacation for the week ended April 20. Since not all employees in every company will collect vacation pay because of turnover and rules regarding term of employment, it is assumed that 75 per cent of employees will ultimately collect vacation pay. The calculation of vacation pay expense based on the payroll of employees not on vacation (21,000 − 1,000) is as follows: 20,000 × 4 per cent × 75 per cent = 600. The entry to record vacation pay expense for the week ended April 20 is as follows:

Apr. 20	Vacation Pay Expense	600	
	Estimated Liability for Vacation Pay		600
	Estimated vacation pay expense		

At the time employees receive their vacation pay, an entry is made debiting Estimated Liability for Vacation Pay and crediting Cash or Wages Payable. For example, the entry to record the 1,000 paid to employees on vacation is as follows:

Aug. 31	Estimated Liability for Vacation Pay	1,000	
	Cash (or Wages Payable)		1,000
	Wages of employees on vacation		

The treatment presented in this example for vacation pay may also be applied to other payroll costs, such as bonus plans and contributions to pension plans.

OBJECTIVE 3

Define contingent liability

CONTINGENT LIABILITIES

A **contingent liability** is not an existing liability. Rather, it is a potential liability because it depends on a future event arising out of a past transaction or event. For instance, a construction company that built a bridge may have been sued for using poor materials. The past transaction is the building of the bridge under contract. The future event is the outcome of the lawsuit, which is not yet known.

The International Accounting Standards Committee has determined that a contingency should be entered in the accounting records when (1) the liability is probable and (2) a reasonable estimate of the amount can be made.[3] Estimated liabilities such as the estimated income taxes liability, product warranty liability, and vacation pay liability that were described earlier in this chapter meet these conditions.

Therefore, they are accrued in the accounting records. Potential liabilities that do not meet both conditions (probable and reasonably estimated) are reported in the notes to the financial statements.

THE TIME VALUE OF MONEY

Interest is the cost associated with the use of money for a specific period of time. It is an important cost to the debtor and an important revenue to the lender. Because it is a cost associated with time, and "time is money", it is also an important consideration in any business decision. For example, an individual who holds 100 for one year without putting it in a savings account has forgone the interest that could have been earned. Thus, there is a cost associated with holding this money equal to the interest that could have been earned. Similarly, a businessperson who accepts a non-interest-bearing note instead of cash for the sale of goods is not forgoing the interest that could have been earned on that money but is including the interest implicitly in the price of the goods. These examples illustrate the point that the timing of the receipt and payment of cash must be considered in making business decisions.

Simple Interest and Compound Interest

Simple interest is the interest cost for one or more periods if we assume that the amount on which the interest is calculated stays the same from period to period. **Compound interest** is the interest cost for two or more periods if we assume that after each period the interest of that period is added to the amount on which interest is calculated in future periods. In other words, compound interest is interest earned on a principal sum that is increased at the end of each period by the interest of that period.

Example: Simple Interest

Joe Sanchez accepts an 8 per cent, 30,000 note due in ninety days. How much will he receive in total at that time? Remember the formula for calculating simple interest, which was presented in Chapter 6 as part of the discussion of notes receivable:

$$
\begin{aligned}
\text{Interest} &= \text{principal} \times \text{rate} \times \text{time} \\
&= 30{,}000 \times 8/100 \times 90/360 \\
&= 600
\end{aligned}
$$

The total that Sanchez will receive is calculated as follows:

$$
\begin{aligned}
\text{Total} &= \text{principal} + \text{interest} \\
&= 30{,}000 + 600 \\
&= 30{,}600
\end{aligned}
$$

Example: Compound Interest

Ann Clary deposits 5,000 in a savings account that pays 6 per cent interest. If she leaves the principal and accumulated interest in the account for three years, how much will her account total at the end of that time? Assume that the interest is paid at the end of the year, that it is added to the principal at that time, and that this total in turn earns interest. The amount at the end of three years may be calculated as follows:

(1) Year	(2) Principal Amount at Beginning of Year	(3) Annual Amount of Interest (col. 2 × .06)	(4) Accumulated Amount at End of Year (col. 2 + col. 3)
1	5,000.00	300.00	5,300.00
2	5,300.00	318.00	5,618.00
3	5,618.00	337.08	5,955.08

At the end of three years, Clary will have 5,955.08 in her savings account. Note that the annual amount of interest increases each year by the interest rate times the interest of the previous year. For example, between year 1 and year 2, the interest increased by 18 (318 − 300), which exactly equals .06 times 300.

OBJECTIVE 5

Identify the management issues related to accounting for long-term liabilities

MANAGEMENT ISSUES RELATED TO ACCOUNTING FOR LONG-TERM LIABILITIES

Profitable operations and short-term credit are seldom sufficient for a growing business that must invest in long-term assets, research and development, and other assets or activities that will produce profit in future years. For such assets and activities, the company requires funds that will be available for longer periods of time. Two key sources of long-term funds are the issuance of share capital and the issuance of long-term debt in the form of bonds, notes, mortgages, and leases. The management issues related to issuing long-term debt are (1) whether or not to have long-term debt, (2) how much long-term debt to have, and (3) what types of long-term debt to have.

The Decision to Issue Long-Term Debt

A key decision faced by management is whether to rely solely on shareholders' equity—share capital issues and retained earnings—for long-term funds for the business or to rely partially on long-term debt for these funds.

Since long-term debts represent financial commitments that must be paid at maturity and interest or other payments that must be paid periodically, shares would seem to have two advantages over long-term debt: the money does not have to be paid back, and dividends on shares are usually paid only if the company earns sufficient profit. There are, however, some advantages of long-term debt over shares.

Shareholder control   Since bondholders or other lenders do not have voting rights, shareholders do not relinquish any control of the company.

Tax effects   The interest on debt is tax deductible, whereas dividends on shares are not. For example, if a corporation pays 100,000 in interest and the income tax rate is 30 per cent, the net cost to the corporation is 70,000 because it will save 30,000 on its income taxes. To pay 100,000 in dividends, the company would have to earn 142,857 before taxes (100,000 ÷ .70).

Financial leverage   If a corporation is able to earn more on its assets than it pays in interest on debt, all of the excess will increase its earnings for shareholders. This concept is called **financial leverage** or trading on the equity. For example, if a company is able to earn 12 per cent or 120,000 on a 1,000,000 investment financed by long-term 10 per cent notes, it will earn 20,000 before taxes (120,000 − 100,000). Financial leverage makes heavily debt-financed investments in office buildings and shopping centres attractive to investors: they hope to earn a higher return than the interest cost. The debt to equity ratio is considered an overall measure of the financial leverage of a company.

In spite of these advantages, using debt financing is not always in a company's best interest. First, since cash is required to make periodic interest payments and to pay back the principal amount of the debt at the maturity date, a company whose plans for earnings are not realised, whose operations are subject to ups and downs, or whose cash flow is weak can be in danger; if it fails to meet its obligations, it can be forced into bankruptcy by lenders. In other words, a company may become overcommitted. Consider, for example, the heavily debt-financed airline industry in recent years. Companies such as TWA and Continental Airlines in the United States became bankrupt because they could not make payments on their long-term debt and other liabilities. Second, financial leverage can reverse direction and work against a company if the investments do not earn more than the interest payments.

OBJECTIVE 6

Identify and contrast the major characteristics of bonds

THE NATURE OF BONDS

A **bond** is a security, usually long term, representing money borrowed by a corporation from the investing public. Bonds must be repaid at a certain time and require periodic payments of interest. Interest usually is paid semiannually (twice a year). Bonds must not be confused with shares. Shareholders are owners. Bondholders are lenders. Bonds are promises to repay the amount borrowed, called the *principal*, and interest at a certain rate on specified future dates.

The bondholder receives a **bond certificate** as evidence of the company's debt. A **bond issue** is the total amount of bonds issued at one time. For example, a 1,000,000 bond issue could consist of a thousand 1,000 bonds. Because a bond issue can be bought and held by many investors, the corporation usually enters into a supplementary agreement, called a **bond covenant**. The bond covenant defines the rights, privileges, and limitations of the bondholders. It generally describes such things as the maturity date of the bonds, interest payment dates, interest rate, and other characteristics of the bonds such as call features. In addition, repayment plans and restrictions may be covered.

The prices of bonds are stated in terms of a percentage of face value. A bond issue quoted at 103½ means that a 1,000 bond costs 1,035 (1,000 × 1.035). When a bond sells at exactly 100, it is said to sell at face or nominal value. When it sells above 100, it is said to sell at a premium; below 100, at a discount. For example, a 1,000 bond quoted at 87.62 would be selling at a discount and would cost the buyer 876.20.

A bond covenant can be written to fit the financing needs of an individual company. As a result, the bonds being issued by corporations in today's financial markets have many different features. Several of the more important ones are described here.

Secured or Unsecured Bonds

Bonds can be either secured or unsecured. If issued on the general credit of the company, they are **unsecured bonds** (also called *debenture bonds*). **Secured bonds** give the bondholders a pledge of certain assets of the company as a guarantee of repayment. The security identified by a secured bond can be any specific asset of the company or a general category of asset, such as property, plant, or equipment.

Term or Serial Bonds

When all the bonds of an issue mature at the same time, they are called **term bonds**. For instance, a company may issue 1,000,000 worth of bonds, all due twenty years from the date of issue. If the bonds in an issue mature on several different dates, the bonds are **serial bonds**. An example of serial bonds would be a 1,000,000 issue that calls for retiring 200,000 of the principal every five years. This arrangement means that after the first 200,000 payment is made, 800,000 of the bonds would remain outstanding for the next five years. In other words, 1,000,000 is outstanding for the first five years, 800,000 for the second five years, and so on. A company may issue serial bonds to ease the task of retiring its debt.

Registered or Coupon Bonds

Most bonds that are issued today are **registered bonds**. The names and addresses of the owners of these bonds must be recorded with the issuing company. The company keeps a register of the owners and pays interest by cheque to the bondholders of record on the interest payment date. **Coupon bonds** generally are not registered with the corporation; instead, they bear interest coupons stating the amount of interest due and the payment date. The bondholder removes the coupons from the bonds on the interest payment dates and presents them at a bank for collection.

OBJECTIVE 7

Record the issuance of bonds at face value and at a discount or premium

ACCOUNTING FOR BONDS PAYABLE

When the board of directors decides to issue bonds, it generally presents the proposal to the shareholders. If the shareholders agree to the issue, the company prints the certificates and draws up an appropriate legal document. The bonds then are authorised for issuance. It is not necessary to make a journal entry for the authorisation, but most companies prepare a memorandum in the Bonds Payable account describing the issue. This note lists the number and value of bonds authorised, the interest rate, the interest payment dates, and the life of the bonds.

Once the bonds are issued, the corporation must pay interest to the bondholders over the life of the bonds (in most cases, semiannually) and the principal (face value) of the bonds at maturity.

Balance Sheet Disclosure of Bonds

Bonds payable and either unamortised discounts or premiums (which we explain later) generally are shown on a company's balance sheet as long-term liabilities. However, if the maturity date of the bond issue is one year or less and the bonds will be retired using current assets, bonds payable should be listed as a current liability. If the issue is to be paid with segregated assets or replaced by another bond issue, the bonds still should be shown as a long-term liability.

Important provisions of the bond covenant are reported in the notes to the financial statements. Often reported with them is a list of all bond issues, the kinds of bonds, interest rates, any securities connected with the bonds, interest payment dates, maturity dates, and effective interest rates.

Bonds Issued at Face Value

Suppose that the Jason Corporation has authorised the issuance of 100,000 of 9 per cent, five-year bonds on January 1, 20x1. According to the bond covenant, interest is to be paid on January 1 and July 1 of each year. Assume that the bonds are sold on January 1, 20x1 for their face value. The entry to record the issuance is as follows:

20x1
Jan. 1 Cash   100,000
            Bonds Payable   100,000
                Sold 100,000 of 9%, 5-year
                bonds at face value

As stated above, interest is paid on January 1 and July 1 of each year. Therefore, the corporation would owe the bondholders 4,500 interest on July 1, 20x1:

$$\begin{aligned} \text{Interest} &= \text{principal} \times \text{rate} \times \text{time} \\ &= 100{,}000 \times .09 \times \tfrac{1}{2}\,\text{year} \\ &= 4{,}500 \end{aligned}$$

The interest paid to the bondholders on each semiannual interest payment date (January 1 or July 1) would be recorded as follows:

Bond Interest Expense   4,500
    Cash   4,500
        Paid semiannual interest to bondholders
        of 9%, 5-year bonds

Face Interest Rate and Market Interest Rate

When issuing bonds, most companies try to set the face interest rate as close as possible to the market interest rate. The **face interest rate** is the rate of interest paid to bondholders based on the face value or principal of the bonds. The rate and amount are fixed over the life of the bond. The **market interest rate** is the rate of interest paid in the market on bonds of similar risk. It is also referred to as the *effective interest rate.* The market interest rate fluctuates daily. However, a company must decide in advance what the face interest rate will be to allow time to file with regulatory bodies, publicise the issue, and print the certificates. Because the company has no control over the market interest rate, there is often a difference between the market or effective interest rate and the face interest rate on the issue date. The result is that the issue price of the bonds does not always equal the principal or face value of the bonds. If the market rate of interest is greater than the face interest rate, the issue price will be less than the face value and the bonds are said to be issued at a **discount**. The discount equals the excess of the face value over the issue price. On the other hand, if the market rate of interest is less than the face interest rate, the issue price will be more than the face value and the bonds are said to be issued at a **premium**. The premium equals the excess of the issue price over the face value.

Bonds Issued at a Discount

Suppose that the Jason Corporation issues its 100,000 of 9 per cent, five-year bonds at 96.149 on January 1, 20x1, when the market rate of interest is 10 per cent. In this case, the bonds are being issued at a discount because the market rate of interest exceeds the face interest rate. This entry records the issuance of the bonds at a discount:

20x1				
Jan. 1	Cash		96,149	
	Unamortised Bond Discount		3,851	
	Bonds Payable			100,000
	Sold 100,000 of 9%, 5-year			
	bonds at 96.149			
	Face amount of bonds	100,000		
	Less purchase price of bonds			
	(100,000 × .96149)	96,149		
	Unamortised bond discount	3,851		

As shown, Cash is debited for the amount received (96,149), Bonds Payable is credited for the face amount (100,000) of the bond liability, and the difference (3,851) is debited to Unamortised Bond Discount. If a balance sheet is prepared right after the bonds are issued at a discount, the liability for bonds payable is as follows:

Long-Term Liabilities		
9% Bonds Payable, due 1/1/x6	100,000	
Less Unamortised Bond Discount	3,851	96,149

BUSINESS BULLETIN   **Business Practice**

In 1993, interest rates on long-term debt were at historically low levels, and this induced some companies to attempt to lock in these low costs for long periods. One of the most aggressive companies in this regard was The Walt Disney Company of the United States, which issued $150 million of 100-year bonds at a yield of only 7.5 per cent. This was the first time since 1954 that 100-year bonds had been issued. Some analysts wondered if even Mickey Mouse could survive 100 years. Investors who purchase these bonds are taking a financial risk because if interest rates rise, the value of the bonds on the market will decrease.[4]

Unamortised Bond Discount is a contra-liability account: Its balance is deducted from the face amount of the bonds to arrive at the carrying amount or present value of the bonds. The bond discount is described as unamortised because it will be amortised (written off) over the life of the bonds.

Bonds Issued at a Premium

When bonds have a face interest rate above the market rate for similar investments, they are issued at a price above the face value, or at a premium. For example, assume that the Jason Corporation issues 100,000 of 9 per cent, five-year bonds for 104,100 on January 1, 20x1, when the market rate of interest is 8 per cent. This means that investors will purchase the bonds at 104.1 per cent of their face value. The issuance would be recorded as follows:

```
20x1
Jan. 1   Cash                                   104,100
              Unamortised Bond Premium                         4,100
              Bonds Payable                                  100,000
                  Sold 100,000 of 9%, 5-year
                  bonds at 104.1
                  (100,000  ×  1.041)
```

Right after this entry is made, bonds payable would be presented on the balance sheet as follows:

Long-Term Liabilities		
9% Bonds Payable, due 1/1/x6	100,000	
Unamortised Bond Premium	4,100	104,100

The carrying amount of the bonds payable is 104,100, which equals the face value of the bonds plus the unamortised bond premium. The cash received from the bond issue is also 104,100. This means that the purchasers were willing to pay a premium of 4,100 to buy these bonds because the face interest on them was greater than the market rate.

Bond Issue Costs

Most bonds are sold through underwriters, who receive a fee for taking care of the details of marketing the issue or for taking a chance on getting the selling price. These costs are connected with the issuance of bonds. Because bond issue costs benefit the whole life of a bond issue, it makes sense to spread the costs over that period. It is generally accepted practice to establish a separate account for bond issue costs and to amortise them over the life of the bonds. However, issue costs decrease the amount of money received by the company through the bond issue. They have the effect, then, of raising the discount or lowering the premium on the issue. As a result, bond issue costs can be spread over the life of the bonds through the amortisation of a discount or premium. Because this method simplifies the recordkeeping, we assume in the text and problems of this book that all bond issue costs increase the discounts or decrease the premiums of bond issues.

OBJECTIVE 8

Amortise bond discounts (and bond premiums) using the effective interest method

AMORTISING A BOND DISCOUNT

In the earlier example, Jason Corporation issued 100,000 of five-year bonds at a discount because the market interest rate of 10 per cent exceeded the face interest rate of 9 per cent. The bonds were sold for 96,149, resulting in an unamortised bond discount of 3,851. Because this discount, as you will see, affects interest expense in each year of the bond issue, the bond discount should be amortised (reduced gradually) over the life of the issue. This means that the unamortised bond discount will decrease gradually over time, and that the carrying amount of the bond issue (face value less unamortised discount) will increase gradually. By the maturity date of the bond, the carrying amount of the issue will equal its face value, and the unamortised bond discount will be zero.

Calculation of Total Interest Cost

When bonds are issued at a discount, the effective interest rate paid by the company is greater than the face interest rate on the bonds. The reason is that the interest cost to the company is the stated interest payments *plus* the amount of the bond discount. That is, although the company does not receive the full face value of the bonds on issue, it still must pay back the full face value at maturity. The difference between the issue price and the face value must be added to the total interest payments to arrive at the actual interest expense. The full cost to the corporation of issuing the bonds at a discount is as follows:

Cash to be paid to bondholders	
Face value at maturity	100,000
Interest payments (100,000 × .09 × 5 years)	45,000
Total cash paid to bondholders	145,000
Less cash received from bondholders	96,149
Total interest cost	48,851
Or, alternatively:	
Interest payments (100,000 × .09 × 5 years)	45,000
Bond discount	3,851
Total interest cost	48,851

The total interest cost of 48,851 is made up of 45,000 in interest payments and the 3,851 bond discount. So, the bond discount increases the interest paid on the bonds from the stated to the effective interest rate. The *effective interest rate* is the real interest cost of the bond over its life.

In order for each year's interest expense to reflect the effective interest rate, the discount must be allocated over the remaining life of the bonds as an increase in the interest expense each period. The process of allocating this expense is called *amortisation of the bond discount*. Thus, interest expense for each period will exceed the actual payment of interest by the amount of the bond discount amortised over the period.

Effective Interest Method of Amortising a Bond Discount

To calculate the interest and amortisation of a bond discount for each interest period under the **effective interest method**, we have to apply a constant interest rate to the carrying amount of the bonds at the beginning of each interest period. This constant rate equals the market rate or effective rate at the time the bonds are issued. The amount of Unamortised Bond Discount to be amortised each period is the difference between the interest calculated by using the effective rate and the actual interest paid to bondholders.

As an example, we use the same facts presented earlier—a 100,000 bond issue at 9 per cent, with a five-year maturity, interest to be paid twice a year. The market or effective rate of interest at the time the bonds were issued was 10 per cent. The bonds

TABLE 9-1 *Interest and Amortisation of Bond Discount: Effective Interest Method*

	A	B	C	D	E	F
Semiannual Interest Period	Carrying Amount at Beginning of Period	Semiannual Interest Expense at 10% to Be Recorded* (5% × A)	Semiannual Interest to Be Paid to Bondholders (4½% × 100,000)	Amortisation of Discount (B − C)	Unamortised Bond Discount at End of Period	Carrying Amount at End of Period (A + D)
0					3,851	96,149
1	96,149	4,807	4,500	307	3,544	96,456
2	96,456	4,823	4,500	323	3,221	96,779
3	96,779	4,839	4,500	339	2,882	97,118
4	97,118	4,856	4,500	356	2,526	97,474
5	97,474	4,874	4,500	374	2,152	97,848
6	97,848	4,892	4,500	392	1,760	98,240
7	98,240	4,912	4,500	412	1,348	98,652
8	98,652	4,933	4,500	433	915	99,085
9	99,085	4,954	4,500	454	461	99,539
10	99,539	4,961†	4,500	461	—	100,000

*Rounded
†Difference due to rounding

were sold for 96,149, a discount of 3,851. The interest and amortisation of the bond discount are shown in Table 9-1.

Here are explanations of how the amounts in the table are calculated:

Column A   The carrying amount of the bonds is the face value of the bonds less the unamortised bond discount at the beginning of the period (100,000 − 3,851 = 96,149).

Column B   The interest expense to be recorded is the effective interest. It is found by multiplying the carrying amount of the bonds by the effective interest rate for one-half year (96,149 × .10 × 6/12 = 4,807).

Column C   The interest paid in the period is a constant amount that is calculated by multiplying the face value of the bonds by the face interest rate for the bonds by the interest time period (100,000 × .09 × 6/12 = 4,500).

Column D   The discount amortised is the difference between the effective interest expense to be recorded and the interest to be paid on the interest payment date (4,807 − 4,500 = 307).

Column E   The unamortised bond discount is the balance of the bond discount at the beginning of the period less the current period amortisation of the discount (3,851 − 307 = 3,544). The unamortised discount decreases each interest payment period because it is amortised as a portion of interest expense.

Column F   The carrying amount of the bonds at the end of the period is the carrying amount at the beginning of the period plus the amortisation during the period (96,149 + 307 = 96,456). Notice that the sum of the carrying amount and the unamortised discount (Column F + Column E) always equals the face value of the bonds (96,456 + 3,544 = 100,000).

Using the effective interest method, the entry for July 1, 20x1 would be recorded as follows:

20x1
July1   Bond Interest Expense   4,807
              Unamortised Bond Discount   307
              Cash   4,500
                 Paid semiannual interest to
                 bondholders and amortised
                 the discount on 9%, 5-year
                 bonds

Notice that it is not necessary to prepare an interest and amortisation table to determine the amortisation of a discount for any one interest payment period. It is necessary only to multiply the carrying amount by the effective interest rate and subtract the interest payment from the result. For example, the amount of discount to be amortised in the seventh interest payment period equals 412 [(98,240 × .05) − 4,500].

The interest and amortisation of bond premiums are calculated in the same way as bond discounts, the difference being that the amortisation of a bond premium decreases the amount of effective interest payable.

OBJECTIVE 9

Account for year-end adjustments to bonds

OTHER BONDS PAYABLE ISSUES

Several other issues arise in accounting for bonds payable. Among them are the year-end accrual of bond interest expense and the conversion of bonds into shares.

Year-End Accrual for Bond Interest Expense

It is not often that bond interest payment dates correspond with a company's accounting year. Therefore, an adjustment must be made at the end of the accounting period to accrue the interest expense on the bonds from the last payment date to the end of the accounting year. Further, if there is any discount or premium on the bonds, it also must be amortised for the fractional period.

Remember that in an earlier example, Jason Corporation issued 100,000 in bonds on January 1, 20x1 at 96,149. Suppose the company's accounting year ends on September 30, 20x1. In the period since the interest payment and amortisation of the discount on July 1, three months' worth of interest has accrued, and the following adjusting entry under the effective interest method must be made:

20x1
Sept. 30   Bond Interest Expense   2,411.50
                 Unamortised Bond Discount   161.50
                 Interest Payable   2,250.00
                    To record accrual of interest on 9% bonds
                    payable for 3 months and amortisation
                    of one-half of the discount for the
                    second interest payment period

This entry covers one-half of the second interest period. Unamortised Bond Discount is credited for 161.50, which is one-half of 323, the amortisation of the discount for the second period from Table 9-1. Interest Payable is credited for 2,250, which is three months' interest on the face value of the bonds (100,000 × .09 × 3/12). The net debit figure of 2,411.50 (2,250 + 161.50) is the bond interest expense for the three-month period.

When the January 1, 20x2 payment date arrives, the entry to pay the bondholders and amortise the discount is as follows:

```
20x2
Jan.   1   Bond Interest Expense                       2,411.50
           Interest Payable                            2,250.00
               Unamortised Bond Discount                              161.50
               Cash                                                 4,500.00
                   Paid semiannual interest including
                   interest previously accrued, and
                   amortised the discount for the
                   period since the end of the year
```

One-half (2,250) the amount paid (4,500) was accrued on September 30. Unamortised Bond Discount is credited for 161.50, the remaining amount to be amortised for the period (323.00 − 161.50). The resulting bond interest expense is the amount that applies to the three-month period from October 1 to December 31.

Bond premiums are recorded at year end in the same way as bond discounts. The difference is that the amortisation of a bond premium decreases interest expense instead of increasing it, as a discount does.

OBJECTIVE 10

Account for the conversion of bonds into shares

Conversion of Bonds into Shares

Convertible bonds can be exchanged for other securities of the corporation (in most cases, shares). The conversion feature allows the investor to make more money because if the market price of the shares rises, the value of the bonds rises. However, if the price of the shares does not rise, the investor still holds the bonds and receives the periodic interest payment as well as the principal at the maturity date.

When a bondholder wishes to convert bonds into shares, the rule is that the shares are recorded at the carrying amount of the bonds. Because the bond liability and the associated unamortised discount or premium are written off the books, no gain or loss is recorded on the transaction. For example, suppose that Jason Corporation's bonds are not called on July 1, 20x4. Instead, the corporation's bondholders decide to convert all the bonds to shares at a nominal value of 8 each under a convertible provision of 40 shares for each 1,000 bond. The entry would be as follows:

```
20x4
July   1   Bonds Payable                              100,000
               Unamortised Bond Discount                            1,348
               Shares                                              32,000
               Share Premium                                       66,652
                   Converted 9% bonds payable into
                   8 nominal value shares at a rate
                   of 40 shares for each 1,000 bond
```

The unamortised bond discount is found in Column E of Table 9-1. At a rate of 40 shares for each 1,000 bond, 4,000 shares will be issued at a total nominal value of 32,000 (4,000 × 8). The Share Capital account is credited for the amount of the nominal value of the shares issued. The Share Premium account is credited for the difference between the carrying amount of the bonds and the nominal value of the shares issued (98,652 − 32,000 = 66,652). No gain or loss is recorded.

OBJECTIVE 11

Explain the basic features of mortgages payable, instalment notes payable, long-term leases, and pensions as long-term liabilities

OTHER LONG-TERM LIABILITIES

A company can have other long-term liabilities besides bonds. The most common are mortgages payable, instalment notes payable, long-term leases, and pensions.

Mortgages Payable

A **mortgage** is a long-term debt secured by real property. It usually is paid in equal monthly instalments. Each monthly payment includes interest on the debt and a

TABLE 9-2   *Monthly Payment Schedule on 50,000, 12 Per Cent Mortgage*

Payment Date	A Unpaid Balance at Beginning of Period	B Monthly Payment	C Interest for 1 Month at 1% on Unpaid Balance* (1% × A)	D Reduction in Debt (B − C)	E Unpaid Balance at End of Period (A − D)
June 1					50,000
July 1	50,000	800	500	300	49,700
Aug. 1	49,700	800	497	303	49,397
Sept. 1	49,397	800	494	306	49,091

*Rounded

reduction in the principal. Table 9-2 shows the first three monthly payments on a 50,000, 12 per cent mortgage. The mortgage was obtained on June 1, and the monthly payments are 800. According to the table, the entry to record the July 1 payment would be as follows:

July 1	Mortgage Payable	300	
	Mortgage Interest Expense	500	
	Cash		800
	Made monthly mortgage payment		

Notice from the entry and from Table 9-2 that the July 1 payment represents interest expense of 500 (50,000 × .12 × $\frac{1}{12}$) and a reduction in the debt of 300 (800 − 500). Therefore, the unpaid balance is reduced by the July payment to 49,700. The interest expense for August is slightly less than July's because of the decrease in the debt.

Instalment Notes Payable

Long-term notes or bills can be paid at the maturity date by making a lump-sum payment that includes the amount borrowed plus the interest. Often, however, the terms of the note will call for a series of periodic payments. When this situation occurs, the notes payable are called **instalment notes payable** because each payment includes the interest from the previous payment to date plus a repayment of part of the amount which was borrowed. For example, let's assume that on December 31, 20x1, 100,000 is borrowed on a 15 per cent instalment note, to be paid annually over five years. The entry to record the note is as follows:

20x1			
Dec. 31	Cash	100,000	
	Notes Payable		100,000
	Borrowed 100,000 at 15% on a 5-year instalment note		

Payments of Accrued Interest Plus Equal Amounts of Principal

Installment notes most often call for payments consisting of accrued interest plus equal amounts of principal repayment. The amount of each instalment decreases because the amount of principal on which the accrued interest is calculated decreases by the amount of the principal repaid. Banks use instalment notes to finance equipment purchases by businesses; these notes are also common for other kinds of purchases when payment is spread over several years. They can be set up on a revolving basis whereby the borrower can borrow additional funds as the instalments are paid. Moreover, the interest rate charged on instalment notes can be adjusted periodically by the bank as market rates of interest change.

Under this method of payment, the principal declines by an equal amount each year for five years, or by 20,000 per year (100,000 ÷ 5 years). The interest is calculated on the balance of the note that remains each year. Because the balance of the note declines each year, the amount of interest also declines. For example, the entries for the first two payments of the instalment note are as follows:

20x2			
Dec. 31	Notes Payable	20,000	
	Interest Expense	15,000	
	Cash		35,000
	First instalment payment		
	on note		
	100,000 × .15 = 15,000		

20x3			
Dec. 31	Notes Payable	20,000	
	Interest Expense	12,000	
	Cash		32,000
	Second instalment payment		
	on note		
	80,000 × .15 = 12,000		

Notice that the amount of the payment decreases from 35,000 to 32,000 because the amount owed on the note has decreased from 100,000 to 80,000. The difference of 3,000 is the interest on the 20,000 that was repaid in 20x2. Each subsequent payment decreases by 3,000, as the note itself decreases by 20,000 each year until it is fully paid. This example assumes that the repayment of principal and the interest rate remain the same from year to year.

Long-Term Leases

There are several ways for a company to obtain new operating assets. One way is to borrow money and buy the asset. Another is to rent the equipment on a short-term lease. A third way is to obtain the equipment on a long-term lease. The first two methods do not create accounting problems. In the first case, the asset and liability are recorded at the amount paid, and the asset is subject to periodic depreciation. In the second case, the lease is short term or cancellable, and the risks of ownership lie with the lessor. This type of lease is called an **operating lease**. It is proper accounting to treat operating lease payments as an expense and to debit the amount of each monthly payment to Rent Expense.

The third case, a long-term lease, is one of the fastest-growing ways of financing operating equipment today. It has several advantages. For instance, a long-term lease requires no immediate cash payment, the rental payment may be fully deductible for tax purposes, and it costs less than a short-term lease. Acquiring the use of plant assets under long-term leases does cause several accounting problems, however. Often, these leases cannot be cancelled. Also, their duration may be about the same as the useful life of the asset. Finally, they may provide for the lessee to buy the asset at a nominal price at the end of the lease. The lease is much like an instalment purchase because the risks of ownership lie with the lessee. Both the lessee's available assets and its legal obligations (liabilities) increase because it must make a number of payments over the life of the asset.

TABLE 9-3   *Payment Schedule on 16 Per Cent Finance Lease**

Year	A Lease Payment	B Interest (16%) on Unpaid Obligation (D × 16%)	C Reduction of Lease Obligation (A − B)	D Balance of Lease Obligation (D − C)
Beginning				14,740
1	4,000	2,358	1,642	13,098
2	4,000	2,096	1,904	11,194
3	4,000	1,791	2,209	8,985
4	4,000	1,438	2,562	6,423
5	4,000	1,028	2,972	3,451
6	4,000	549	3,451	—
	24,000	9,260	14,740	

*Calculations are rounded.

Noting this problem, the International Accounting Standards Committee has described this kind of long-term lease as a **finance lease**. The term reflects the provisions of the lease, which make the transaction more like a purchase or sale on instalment. The IASC has stated that in the case of a finance lease, the lessee must recognise an asset and a liability equal to the fair value of the leased property or, if lower, at the present value of the lease payments.[5] In much the same way as mortgage payments are treated, each lease payment becomes partly interest expense and partly a repayment of debt. Further, depreciation expense is figured on the asset and entered on the records of the lessee.

Suppose, for example, that Isaacs Company enters into a long-term lease for a machine used in its manufacturing operations. The lease terms call for an annual payment of 4,000 for six years, which approximates the useful life of the machine (see Table 9-3). At the end of the lease period, the title to the machine passes to Isaacs. This lease is clearly a finance lease.

A lease is a periodic payment for the right to use an asset or assets. Present value techniques can be used to place a value on the asset and on the corresponding liability associated with a finance lease. If Isaacs's interest cost is 16 per cent, the present value of the lease payments is calculated as 14,740.

The entry to record the lease contract is as follows:

Equipment under Finance Lease	14,740	
Obligations under Finance Lease		14,740

Equipment under finance lease is classified as a long-term asset; obligations under finance lease are classified as a long-term liability. Each year, Isaacs must record depreciation on the leased asset. If we assume straight-line depreciation, a six-year life, and no salvage value, this entry would record the depreciation:

Depreciation Expense	2,457	
Accumulated Depreciation, Leased Equipment under Finance Lease		2,457

The interest expense for each year is calculated by multiplying the interest rate (16 per cent) by the amount of the remaining lease obligation. Table 9-3 shows these calculations. Using the data in the table, the first lease payment would be recorded as follows:

Interest Expense (Column B)	2,358	
Obligations under Finance Lease (Column C)	1,642	
Cash		4,000

Pensions

While pensions are of increasing concern to international and national standard setters, countries such as China, Korea, and New Zealand have yet to issue regulations on the subject.

Most employees who work for medium-sized and large companies are covered by some sort of pension plan. A **pension plan** is a contract between the company and its employees in which the company agrees to pay benefits to the employees after they retire. Most companies contribute the full cost of the pension, but sometimes the employees also pay part of their salary or wages towards their pension. The contributions from both parties generally are paid into a **pension fund**, from which benefits are paid out to retirees. In most cases, pension benefits consist of monthly payments to employees after retirement and other payments on disability or death.

There are two kinds of pension plans. Under *defined contribution plans*, the employer is required to contribute an annual amount determined in the current year on the basis of agreements between the company and its employees or a resolution of the board of directors. Retirement payments depend on the amount of pension payments the accumulated contributions can support. Under *defined benefit plans*, the employer's required annual contribution is the amount required to fund pension liabilities that arise as a result of employment in the current year but whose amount will not be determined finally until the retirement and death of the persons currently employed. Here, the amount of the contribution required in the current year depends on agreed future benefits but uncertain current contributions; under a defined contribution plan, the uncertain future amount of pension liabilities depends on the cumulative amounts of fixed current contributions.[6]

Accounting for annual pension expense under defined contribution plans is straightforward. After the contribution required is determined, Pension Expense is debited and a liability (or Cash) is credited.

Accounting for annual expense under defined benefit plans is one of the most complex topics in accounting; thus, the intricacies are reserved for advanced courses. In concept, however, the procedure is simple. First, the amount of pension expense is determined. Then, if the amount of cash contributed to the fund is less than the pension expense, a liability results, which is reported on the balance sheet. If the amount of cash paid to the pension plan exceeds the pension expense, a prepaid expense arises and appears on the asset side of the balance sheet.

CHAPTER REVIEW

Review of Learning Objectives

1. **Identify the management issues related to accounting for** *current liabilities*. Liabilities represent present legal obligations for future payment of assets or future performance of services. They result from past transactions and should be recognised when there is a transaction that obligates the company to make future payments. Liabilities are valued at the amount of money necessary to liquidate the obligation or the fair value of goods or services that must be delivered. Liabilities are classified as current or long term. Supplemental disclosure is required when the nature or details of the obligations would help in understanding the liability.

2. **Identify, calculate, and record definitely determinable and estimated current liabilities.** Two principal categories of current liabilities are definitely determinable liabilities and estimated liabilities. Although definitely determinable liabilities,

such as accounts payable, notes payable, dividends payable, accrued liabilities, and the current portion of long-term debt, can be measured exactly, the accountant must still be careful not to overlook existing liabilities in these categories. Estimated liabilities, such as liabilities for income taxes, property taxes, and product warranties, definitely exist, but the amounts must be estimated and recorded properly.

3. **Define** *contingent liability*. A contingent liability is a potential liability arising from a past transaction and dependent on a future event. Examples are lawsuits, income tax disputes, discounted notes receivable, guarantees of debt, and the potential cost of changes in government regulations.

4. **Define** *interest* **and distinguish between simple and compound interest.** Interest is the cost of using money for a period of time. In calculating simple interest, the amount on

which the interest is calculated stays the same from period to period. However, in calculating compound interest, the interest for a period is added to the principal amount before the interest for the next period is calculated.

5. **Identify the management issues related to accounting for *long-term liabilities*.** Long-term debt is used to finance long-term assets and business activities such as research and development that have long-run earnings potential for the business. Among the advantages of long-term debt financing are (1) shareholders do not relinquish any control, (2) interest on debt is tax deductible, and (3) financial leverage may increase a company's earnings. Disadvantages of long-term financing are (1) interest and principal must be repaid on schedule, and (2) financial leverage can reverse direction and work against a company if a project is not successful.

6. **Identify and contrast the major characteristics of bonds.** A bond is a security that represents money borrowed from the investing public. When it issues bonds, the corporation enters into a contract, called a bond covenant, with the bondholders. The bond covenant identifies the major conditions of the bonds. A corporation can issue several types of bonds, each having different characteristics. For example, a bond issue may or may not require security (secured versus unsecured). It may be payable at a single time (term) or at several times (serial). And the holder may receive interest automatically (registered bond) or may have to return coupons to receive the interest (coupon bond).

7. **Record the issuance of bonds at face value and at a discount or premium.** When bonds are issued, the bondholders pay an amount equal to, less than, or greater than the face value of the bond. Bondholders pay face value for bonds when the interest rate on the bonds approximates the market rate for similar investments. The issuing corporation records the bond issue as a long-term liability, in the Bonds Payable account, equal to the face value of the bonds.

   Bonds are issued at an amount less than face value when the bond interest rate is below the market rate for similar investments. The difference between the face value and the issue price is called a discount and is debited to Unamortised Bond Discount.

   When the interest rate on bonds is greater than the market rate on similar investments, investors are willing to pay more than face value for the bonds. The difference between the issue price and the face value is called a premium and is credited to Unamortised Bond Premium.

8. **Amortise bond discounts (and bond premiums) using the**

effective interest method. When bonds are sold at a discount or a premium, the result is an adjustment of the interest rate on the bonds from the face rate to an effective rate that is close to the market rate when the bonds were issued. Therefore, bond discounts or premiums have the effect of increasing or decreasing the interest paid on the bonds over their life. Under these conditions, it is necessary to amortise the discount or premium over the life of the bonds by the effective interest method.

   The effective interest method results in a constant rate of interest on the carrying amount of the bonds. To find interest and the amortisation of discounts or premiums, we apply the effective interest rate to the carrying amount (face value minus the discount or plus the premium) of the bonds at the beginning of the interest period. The amount of the discount or premium to be amortised is the difference between the interest calculated by using the effective rate and that obtained by using the stated or face rate.

9. **Account for year-end adjustments to bonds.** When the end of a corporation's accounting year does not fall on an interest payment date, the corporation must accrue bond interest expense from the last interest payment date to the end of the company's accounting year. This accrual results in the inclusion of the interest expense in the year incurred.

10. **Account for the conversion of bonds into shares.** Convertible bonds allow the bondholder to convert bonds to shares in the issuing corporation. In this case, the shares issued are recorded at the carrying amount of the bonds being converted. No gain or loss is recognised.

11. **Explain the basic features of mortgages payable, instalment notes payable, long-term leases, and pensions as long-term liabilities.** A mortgage is a long-term debt secured by real property. It usually is paid in equal monthly instalments. Each payment is partly interest expense and partly debt repayment. Instalment notes payable are long-term notes that are paid in a series of payments. Part of each payment is interest, and part is repayment of principal. If a long-term lease is a finance lease, the risks of ownership lie with the lessee. Like a mortgage payment, each lease payment is partly interest and partly a reduction of debt. For a finance lease, both an asset and a long-term liability should be recorded. The liability should be equal to the present value at the beginning of the lease of the total lease payments over the lease term. The recorded asset is subject to depreciation. Pension expense must be recorded in the current period.

Review of Concepts and Terminology

The following concepts and terms were introduced in this chapter.

LO 6 **Bond:** A security, usually long term, representing money borrowed by a corporation from the investing public.

LO 6 **Bond certificate:** Evidence of a company's debt to the bondholder.

LO 6 **Bond covenant:** A supplementary agreement to a bond issue that defines the rights, privileges, and limitations of bondholders.

LO 6 **Bond issue:** The total amount of bonds issued at one time.

LO 2 **Commercial paper:** A means of borrowing funds by unsecured loans that are sold directly to the public, usually through professionally managed investment firms.

LO 4 **Compound interest:** The interest cost for two or more periods if we assume that after each period the interest of that period is added to the amount on which interest is calculated in future periods.

LO 3 **Contingent liability:** A potential liability that depends on a future event arising out of a past transaction or event.

LO 10 **Convertible bonds:** Bonds that can be exchanged for other securities of the corporation, usually its shares.

LO 6 **Coupon bonds:** Bonds that generally are not registered with the issuing corporation but instead bear interest coupons stating the amount of interest due and the payment date.

LO 1 **Current liabilities:** Debts and obligations that are expected to be liquidated within one year.

LO 2 **Definitely determinable liabilities:** Current liabilities that are set by contract or by statute and can be measured exactly.

LO 7 **Discount:** The amount by which the face value of a bond exceeds the issue price; applies to bonds issued when the market rate of interest is greater than the face interest rate.

LO 8 **Effective interest method:** A method of amortising bond discounts or premiums that applies a constant interest rate, the market rate at the time the bonds were issued, to the carrying amount of the bonds at the beginning of each interest period.

LO 2 **Estimated liabilities:** Definite debts or obligations for which the exact amounts cannot be known until a later date.

LO 7 **Face interest rate:** The rate of interest paid to bondholders based on the face value or principal of the bonds.

LO 11 **Finance lease:** A long-term lease in which the risk of ownership lies with the lessee and whose terms resemble a purchase or sale on instalment.

LO 5 **Financial leverage:** The ability to increase earnings for shareholders by earning more on an investment than is paid in interest on debt incurred to finance the investment. Also called *trading on the equity.*

LO 11 **Instalment notes payable:** Long-term notes payable in a series of payments, of which part is interest and part is repayment of principal.

LO 4 **Interest:** The cost associated with the use of money for a specific period of time.

LO 1 **Liabilities:** Present obligations arising from past events, the settlement of which is expected to result in an outflow of economic resources.

LO 2 **Line of credit:** A preapproved arrangement with a commercial bank that allows a company to borrow funds as needed.

LO 1 **Long-term liabilities:** Debts or obligations that are due beyond one year.

LO 7 **Market interest rate:** The rate of interest paid in the market on bonds of similar risk. Also called *effective interest rate.*

LO 11 **Mortgage:** A long-term debt secured by real property; usually paid in equal monthly instalments.

LO 11 **Operating lease:** A short-term or cancellable lease in which the risks of ownership lie with the lessor, and whose payments are recorded as a rent expense.

LO 11 **Pension fund:** A fund established through contributions from an employer and sometimes employees that pays pension benefits to employees after retirement or on their disability or death.

LO 11 **Pension plan:** A contract between a company and its employees under which the company agrees to pay benefits to the employees after they retire.

LO 7 **Premium:** The amount by which the issue price of a bond exceeds its face value; for bonds issued when the market rate of interest is less than the face interest rate.

LO 6 **Registered bonds:** Bonds for which the names and addresses of bondholders are recorded with the issuing company.

LO 2 **Salaries:** Compensation to employees who are paid at a monthly or yearly rate.

LO 6 **Secured bonds:** Bonds that give the bondholders a pledge of certain assets of the company as a guarantee of repayment.

LO 6 **Serial bonds:** A bond issue with several different maturity dates.

LO 4 **Simple interest:** The interest cost for one or more periods if we assume that the amount on which the interest is calculated stays the same from period to period.

LO 6 **Term bonds:** Bonds of a bond issue that all mature at the same time.

LO 2 **Unearned revenues:** Revenues received in advance for which the goods will not be delivered or the services not performed during the current accounting period.

LO 6 **Unsecured bonds:** Bonds issued on the general credit of a company. Also called *debenture bonds.*

LO 2 **Wages:** Payment for services of employees at an hourly rate or on a piecework basis.

Review Problem

Interest and Amortisation of a Bond Discount

LO 7
LO 8
LO 10

When the Koliver Manufacturing Company was expanding its metal window division, the company did not have enough capital to finance the expansion. So, management sought and received approval from the board of directors to issue bonds. The company planned to issue 5,000,000 of 8 per cent, five-year bonds in 20x1. Interest would be paid on June 30 and December 31 of each year. The bonds would be convertible into 30 shares of 10 nominal value.

The bonds were sold at 96 on January 1, 20x1 because the market rate for similar investments was 9 per cent. The company decided to amortise the bond discount by using the effective interest method.

REQUIRED

1. Prepare an interest and amortisation schedule for the first five interest payment dates.
2. Prepare the journal entries to record the sale of the bonds and the first two interest payments.

Answer to Review Problem

1. Prepare a schedule for the first five interest periods.

Interest and Amortisation of Bond Discount

Semiannual Interest Payment Date	Carrying Amount at Beginning of Period	Semiannual Interest Expense* (9% × ½ × carrying amount)	Semiannual Interest Paid per Period (8% × ½ × 5,000,000)	Amortisation of Discount	Unamortised Bond Discount at End of Period	Carrying Amount at End of Period
Jan. 1, 20x1					200,000	4,800,000
June 30, 20x1	4,800,000	216,000	200,000	16,000	184,000	4,816,000
Dec. 31, 20x1	4,816,000	216,720	200,000	16,720	167,280	4,832,720
June 30, 20x2	4,832,720	217,472	200,000	17,472	149,808	4,850,192
Dec. 31, 20x2	4,850,192	218,259	200,000	18,259	131,549	4,868,451
June 30, 20x3	4,868,451	219,080	200,000	19,080	112,469	4,887,531

*Rounded

2. Prepare the journal entries.

20x1

Jan.	1	Cash	4,800,000	
		Unamortised Bond Discount	200,000	
		Bonds Payable		5,000,000
		Sold 5,000,000 of 8%,		
		5-year bonds at 96		
June 30		Bond Interest Expense	216,000	
		Unamortised Bond Discount		16,000
		Cash		200,000
		Paid semiannual interest and		
		amortised the discount on 8%,		
		5-year bonds		
Dec. 31		Bond Interest Expense	216,720	
		Unamortised Bond Discount		16,720
		Cash		200,000
		Paid semiannual interest and		
		amortised the discount on 8%,		
		5-year bonds		

CHAPTER ASSIGNMENTS

Knowledge and Understanding

Questions

1. What are liabilities?
2. Why is the timing of liability recognition important in accounting?
3. At the end of the accounting period, Janson Company had a legal obligation to accept delivery and pay for a truckload of hospital supplies the following week. Is this legal obligation a liability?
4. Ned Johnson, a star basketball player, received a contract to play professional basketball. The contract calls for a salary of 300,000 a year for four years, dependent on his making the team in each of those years. Should this contract be considered a liability and recorded on the books of the basketball team?
5. What is the rule for classifying a liability as current?
6. What are a line of credit and commercial paper? Where do they appear on the balance sheet?

7. Where should the Discount on Notes Payable account appear on the balance sheet?
8. When can a portion of long-term debt be classified as a current liability?
9. Why are unearned revenues classified as liabilities?
10. What is definite about an estimated liability?
11. Why are income taxes payable considered to be estimated liabilities?
12. When does a company incur a liability for a product warranty?
13. What is a contingent liability, and how does it differ from an estimated liability?
14. What are some examples of contingent liabilities? For what reason is each a contingent liability?
15. What are the advantages and disadvantages of issuing long-term debt?

16. What is the difference amongst a bond certificate, a bond issue, and a bond covenant? What are some examples of items found in a bond covenant?

17. What are the essential differences between (a) secured and debenture bonds, (b) term and serial bonds, and (c) registered and coupon bonds?

18. Napier Corporation sold 500,000 of 5 per cent 1,000 bonds on the interest payment date. What would the proceeds from the sale be if the bonds were issued at 95, at 100, and at 102?

19. If you were buying bonds on which the face interest rate was less than the market interest rate, would you expect to pay more or less than nominal value for the bonds? Why?

20. Why does the amortisation of a bond discount increase interest expense to an amount greater than interest paid? Why does the amortisation of a premium have the opposite effect?

21. When the effective interest method of amortising a bond discount or premium is used, why does the amount of interest expense change from period to period?

22. What are the advantages of convertible bonds to the company issuing them and to the investor?

23. What are the two components of a uniform monthly mortgage payment?

24. When is a long-term lease called a finance lease? Why should the accountant record both an asset and a liability in connection with this type of lease? What items should appear on the income statement as the result of a finance lease?

25. What is a pension plan? What assumptions must be made to account for the expenses of such a plan?

26. What is the difference between a defined contribution plan and a defined benefit plan?

Application

Exercises

E 9-1.
LO 2 *Interest Expense: Interest Not Included in Face Value of Note*

On the last day of October, Bayview Company borrows 30,000 on a bank note for sixty days at 12 per cent interest. Assume that interest is not included in the face amount. Prepare the following general journal entries: (1) October 31, recording of note; (2) November 30, accrual of interest expense; (3) December 30, payment of note plus interest.

E 9-2.
LO 2 *Payroll Transactions*

Clarence Henry earns a salary of 70,000 per year. Social security taxes are 6.20 per cent up to 60,600 and health taxes are 1.45 per cent. Unemployment insurance taxes are 6.2 per cent of the first 9,000. During the year, 18,000 was withheld for income taxes, and 1,500 for medical insurance.

1. Prepare a general journal entry summarising the payment of 70,000 to Henry during the year.
2. Prepare a general journal entry summarising the employer payroll taxes and other costs on Henry's salary for the year. Assume the company pays 80 per cent of the total premiums for medical insurance.
3. Determine the total cost paid by Clarence Henry's employer to employ Henry for the year.

E 9-3.
LO 2 *Product Warranty Liability*

Keystone Company manufactures and sells electronic games. Each game costs 25 to produce and sells for 45. In addition, each game carries a warranty that provides for free replacement if it fails for any reason during the two years following the sale. In the past, 7 per cent of the games sold had to be replaced under the warranty. During July, Keystone sold 26,000 games and 2,800 games were replaced under the warranty.

1. Prepare a general journal entry to record the estimated liability for product warranties in July.
2. Prepare a general journal entry to record the games replaced under warranty during the month.

E 9-4.
LO 7 *Journal Entries for Interest*
LO 8 *Using the Effective Interest*
LO 9 *Method*

On March 1, 20x1, the Sperlazzo Corporation issued 1,200,000 of 10 per cent, five-year bonds. The semiannual interest payment dates are March 1 and September 1. Because the market rate for similar investments was 11 per cent, the bonds had to be issued at a discount. The discount on the issuance of the bonds was 48,670. The company's accounting year ends February 28.

Prepare journal entries to record the bond issue on March 1, 20x1; the payment of interest and the amortisation of the discount on September 1, 20x1; the accrual of interest and the amortisation of the discount on February 28, 20x2; and the payment of interest on March 1, 20x2. Use the effective interest method. (Round answers to the nearest whole number.)

E 9-5.
LO 5 *Journal Entries for Interest Payments Using the Effective Interest Method*

The long-term debt section of the Fleming Corporation's balance sheet at the end of its accounting year, December 31, 20x1, was as follows:

Long-Term Liabilities
Bonds Payable—8%, interest payable
1/1 and 7/1, due 12/31/21x3   1,000,000
Less Unamortised Bond Discount   80,000   920,000

Prepare the journal entries relevant to the interest payments on July 1, 20x2, December 31, 20x2, and January 1, 20x3, using the effective interest method of amortisation. Assume an effective interest rate of 10 per cent.

E 9-6.
LO 3 *Bond Issue Entries*
LO 6

Graphic World is authorised to issue 1,800,000 in bonds on June 1. The bonds carry a face interest rate of 9 per cent, which is to be paid on June 1 and December 1.

Prepare journal entries for the issue of the bonds by Graphic World under the assumptions that (a) the bonds are issued on September 1 at 100 and (b) the bonds are issued on June 1 at 105.

E 9-7.
LO 7 *Year-End Accrual of Bond*
LO 8 *Interest*
LO 9

Swoboda Corporation issued 1,000,000 of 9 per cent bonds on October 1, 20x1, at 96. The bonds are dated October 1 and pay interest semiannually. The market rate of interest is 10 per cent, and the company's accounting year ends on December 31.

Prepare the entries to record the issuance of the bonds, the accrual of the interest on December 31, 20x1, and the first semiannual interest payment on April 1, 20x2. Assume the company does not use reversing entries and uses the effective interest method to amortise the bond discount.

E 9-8.
LO 10 *Bond Conversion*

The Gallery Corporation has 400,000 of 6 per cent bonds outstanding. There is 20,000 of unamortised discount remaining on these bonds after the July 1, 20x2 semiannual interest payment. The bonds are convertible at the rate of 40 shares at a nominal value of 5 for each 1,000 bond. On July 1, 20x2, bondholders presented 300,000 of the bonds for conversion.

Prepare the journal entry to record the conversion of the bonds.

E 9-9.
LO 11 *Mortgage Payable*

Inland Corporation purchased a building by signing a 150,000 long-term mortgage with monthly payments of 2,000. The mortgage carries an interest rate of 12 per cent.

1. For the first three months, prepare a monthly payment schedule showing the monthly payment, the interest for the month, the reduction in debt, and the unpaid balance. (Round to the nearest unit.)
2. Prepare journal entries to record the purchase and the first two monthly payments.

E 9-10.
LO 11 *Recording Lease Obligations*

Ramos Corporation has leased a piece of equipment that has a useful life of twelve years. The terms of the lease are 43,000 per year for twelve years. Ramos currently is able to borrow money at a long-term interest rate of 15 per cent. The value of the lease is 233,103.

1. Prepare the journal entry to record the lease agreement.
2. Prepare the entry to record depreciation of the equipment for the first year using the straight-line method.
3. Prepare the entries to record the lease payments for the first two years.

E 9-11.
LO 11 *Instalment Notes Payable:*
Unequal Payments

On December 31, 20x1, 40,000 is borrowed on a 12 per cent instalment note, to be paid annually over four years. Prepare the entry to record the note and the first two annual payments, assuming the principal is paid in equal annual instalments and interest on the unpaid balance accrues annually. How would your answer change if the interest rate rose to 13 per cent in the second year?

Problem Set

P 9-1.
LO 2 *Notes Payable Transactions*
and End-of-Period Entries

Landover Corporation, whose accounting year ends June 30, 20x1, completed the following transactions involving notes payable:

May 11   Signed a 90-day, 66,000 note payable to Village Bank for a working capital loan. The face value included interest of 1,980. Proceeds received were 64,020.
    21   Obtained a sixty-day extension on an 18,000 trade account payable owed to a supplier by signing a 60-day, 18,000 note. Interest, at 14 per cent, is in addition to the face value.
June 30   Made end-of-year adjusting entry to accrue interest expense.
    30   Made end-of-year adjusting entry to recognise interest expired on the note.
July 20   Paid off the note plus interest due the supplier.
Aug. 9   Paid the amount due to the bank on the 90-day note.

REQUIRED

Prepare general journal entries for the notes payable transactions.

P 9-2.
LO 2 *Product Warranty Liability*

Marrero Company is engaged in the retail sale of washing machines. Each machine has a twenty-four-month warranty on parts. If a repair under warranty is required, a charge for the labour is made. Management has found that 20 per cent of the machines sold require some work before the warranty expires. Furthermore, the average cost of replacement parts has been 120 per repair. At the beginning of June, the account for the estimated liability for product warranties had a credit balance of 28,600. During June, 112 machines were returned under the warranty. The cost of the parts used in repairing the machines was 17,530, and 18,884 was collected as service revenue for the labour involved. During the month, Marrero Company sold 450 new machines.

REQUIRED

1. Prepare general journal entries to record each of the following: (a) the warranty work completed during the month, including related revenue, and (b) the estimated liability for product warranties for machines sold during the month.
2. Calculate the balance of the Estimated Product Warranty Liability account at the end of the month.

P 9-3.

LO 7 *Bonds Issued at a Discount*
LO 8 *and a Premium*
LO 9

Bannchi Corporation issued bonds twice during 20x1. The transactions were as follows:

20x1

Jan. 1 Issued 2,000,000 of 9¹⁄₅ per cent, ten-year bonds dated January 1, 20x1, with interest payable on June 30 and December 31. The bonds were sold at 98.1, resulting in an effective interest rate of 9.5 per cent.

Apr. 1 Issued 4,000,000 of 9⁴⁄₅ per cent, ten-year bonds dated April 1, 20x1, with interest payable on March 31 and September 30. The bonds were sold at 102, resulting in an effective interest rate of 9.5 per cent.

June 30 Paid semiannual interest on the January 1 issue and amortised the discount, using the effective interest method.

Sept. 30 Paid semiannual interest on the April 1 issue and amortised the premium, using the effective interest method.

Dec. 31 Paid semiannual interest on the January 1 issue and amortised the discount, using the effective interest method.

     31 Made an end-of-year adjusting entry to accrue interest on the April 1 issue and to amortise half the premium applicable to the interest period.

20x2

Mar. 31 Paid semiannual interest on the April 1 issue and amortised the premium applicable to the second half of the interest period.

REQUIRED Prepare general journal entries to record the bond transactions. (Round amounts to the nearest whole number.)

Critical Thinking and Communication

Conceptual Mini-Case

CMC 9-1.

LO 11 *Lease Financing*

Federal Express, based in the United States and known for overnight delivery and distribution of high-priority goods and documents throughout the world, has an extensive fleet of aircraft and vehicles. Under lease commitments in its 1993 annual report, the company stated that it "utilizes certain aircraft, land, facilities, and equipment under capital and operating leases which expire at various dates through 2021. In addition, supplemental aircraft are leased under agreements which generally provide for cancellation upon 60 days' notice". The annual report further stated that the minimum commitments for capital (finance) leases and noncancellable operating leases for 1994 are $18,635,000 and $458,112,000, respectively.[7] What is the difference between a finance lease and an operating lease? How does the accounting treatment for the two types of leases differ? How do you interpret management's reasoning in placing some aircraft under finance leases and others under operating leases? Why do you think the management of Federal Express leases most of its aircraft instead of buying them?

Cultural Mini-Case

CLMC 9-1.

LO 1 *Classification and Disclosure*
LO 2 *of Current Liabilities and*
LO 3 *Contingent Liabilities*

Daimler-Benz, one of Germany's major manufacturers of cars, trucks, rail systems, microelectronics, diesel engines, aircraft systems, and defence systems, does not distinguish between current and long-term liabilities on the face of the balance sheet as follows:[8]

Liabilities (Deutsche marks, millions)	1995	1994
Liabilities for Leasing including Sales Financing	15,933	14,543
Accounts Payable, Trade	7,222	7,718
Other Liabilities	17,618	14,159
	40,733	37,220

However, the notes to the accounts provide a breakdown between those liabilities due within one year and others, with further information on liabilities due in more than five years. Another note lists "Commitments and Contingencies" that do not appear on the balance sheet, comprising for 1995: guarantees of DM 3,515 million, notes payable of DM 255 million, contractual guarantees of DM 616 million, and pledges for indebtedness of others of DM 393 million.

REQUIRED 1. Does it matter if short-term and long-term liabilities are not identified separately on the balance sheet?

2. Do you think any of the contingent liabilities should be recorded and shown on the balance sheet?

Ethics Mini-Case

LO 2 *Ethical Dilemma*

EMC 9-1. Last summer, Joe Murray, an accounting student at the local university, secured a full-time accounting job at the popular *Tower Restaurant.* Joe felt fortunate to have a good job that accommodated his class schedule because the local economy was very bad. After a few weeks on the job, Joe realised that his boss, the owner of the business, was paying the kitchen workers in cash and was not withholding income taxes or social security and health taxes. Joe understands that the law requires that these taxes be withheld and paid in a timely manner to the appropriate agency. Joe also realises that if he raises this issue, he may lose his job. What alternatives are available to Joe? What action would you take if you were in Joe's position? Why did you make this choice?

Decision-Making Case

LO 10 *Pros and Cons of Convertible Bonds*

DMC 9-1. *Sumitomo Corporation*, a Japanese company that is one of the world's leading traders of commodities, industrial goods, and consumer goods, has a number of issues of long-term debt. Amongst them are almost ¥20,000 million of 1⅗ per cent convertible bonds payable in Japanese yen in the year 2002.[9] (The interest rate illustrates the historically low rates in Japan.) The bonds are unsecured and are convertible into ordinary shares at ¥1,193 per share.

REQUIRED

1. What reasons can you suggest for the company's decision to issue bonds that are convertible into ordinary shares rather than simply issuing nonconvertible bonds or ordinary shares directly?
2. Are there any disadvantages to this approach?

Basic Research Activity

LO 2
LO 3 *Basic Research Skills*

RA 9-1. Your library has indexes for business periodicals in which you can look up articles on topics of interest. Using one or more of these indexes, locate and photocopy two articles related to bank financing, commercial paper, product warranties, airline frequent flyer plans, or contingent liabilities. You may have to look under related topics to find an article. For example, to find articles about contingent liabilities, you might look under litigation, debt guarantees, environmental losses, or other topics. For each of the two articles, write a short summary of the situation and state how it relates to accounting for the topic as described in the text. Be prepared to discuss your results in class.

Financial Reporting and Analysis

Interpretation Cases from Business

LO 1
LO 2 *Analysis of Current Liabilities for a Bankrupt Company*

ICB 9-1. *Trans World Airlines* is an American airline that experienced financial difficulties in 1988 and 1989. TWA's 1989 annual report refers to the company's deteriorating liquidity situation as follows:[10]

> TWA's net working capital deficit was $55.5 million at December 31, 1989, representing a reduction of $82.6 million from net working capital of $27.1 million at December 31, 1988. Working capital deficits are not unusual in the airline industry because of the large advance ticket sales current liability account.

In 1991, the company declared bankruptcy. By 1993, the company had reorganised and was planning to come out of bankruptcy. The company's current liabilities and current assets at December 31 for 1989 and 1992 are as follows (in thousands):

	1992	1989
Current liabilities:		
Short-term notes payable	$ 75,000	—
Current maturities of long-term debt	252,023	$ 127,301
Current obligations under finance leases	228	93,194
Advance ticket sales	151,221	276,549
Accounts payable, principally trade	114,467	387,256
Accounts payable to affiliated companies	22,815	8,828
Securities sold, not yet purchased	—	82,302
Accrued expenses:		
Employee compensation and vacations earned	100,013	148,175
Contributions to retirement and pension trusts	4,583	14,711
Interest on debt and finance leases	6,543	86,761
Taxes	17,069	33,388
Other accrued expenses	148,714	122,295
Total	$892,676	$1,380,760

	1992	1989
Current assets:		
Cash and cash equivalents	$ 42,389	$ 454,415
Marketable securities	—	10,355
Receivables, less allowance for doubtful		
accounts, $13,432 in 1989 and $10,361 in 1992	311,915	435,061
Receivables from affiliated companies	2,925	15,506
Due from brokers	—	70,636
Spare parts, materials, and supplies, less		
allowance for obsolescence, $38,423 in 1989		
and $47,872 in 1992	175,235	227,098
Prepaid expenses and other	44,047	112,232
Total	$576,511	$1,325,303

REQUIRED

1. Identify any current liabilities that do not require a current outlay of cash and identify any current estimated liabilities for 1989 and 1992. Why is management not worried about the cash flow consequences of advance ticket sales?
2. For 1989 and 1992, which current assets will not generate cash, and which will most likely be available to pay for the remaining current liabilities? Compare the amount of these current assets to the amount of current liabilities other than those identified in 1 as not requiring a cash outlay.
3. In light of the calculations in 2, comment on TWA's liquidity position for 1989 and 1992 and its ability to operate successfully after bankruptcy. Identify alternative sources of additional cash.

ICB 9-2.

LO 11 *Lease Financing*

UAL Corporation, owner of United Airlines, states in its 1992 annual report that it leased 271 of its aircraft, 43 of which were finance leases.[11] United has leased many of these planes for terms of ten to twenty-two years. Some leases carry the right of first refusal to purchase the aircraft at fair market value at the end of the lease term and others at fair market value or a percentage of cost.

On United's December 31, 1992 balance sheet, the following accounts appear (in thousands):

Owned—Flight Equipment	$7,790,100
Finance Leases—Flight Equipment	959,200
Current Obligations under Finance Leases	53,700
Long-Term Obligations under Finance Leases	812,400

Expected payments in 1993 for operating leases are $1,106,600 and for finance leases, $135,900.

REQUIRED

1. Why did UAL characterise some of the aircraft leases described in the first sentence as operating leases and others as finance leases? Explain your answer.
2. Explain in general the difference in accounting (a) for operating and finance leases and (b) for Owned—Flight Equipment and Finance Leases—Flight Equipment.

Nestlé Case

NC 9-1.

LO 5 *Business Practice, Long-Term*
LO 11 *Debt, and Leases*

Refer to the Management's Discussion, Financial Statements, and Notes to Consolidated Financial Statements in the appendix on Nestlé to answer the following questions.

1. Is it the practice of Nestlé to own or lease most of its long-term assets?
2. What proportion of total assets is financed with long-term debt? What proportion of long-term debt is classified as current obligations due within the next year?
3. In what countries has Nestlé incurred long-term debt? When is the last maturity date?
4. Does Nestlé lease property predominantly under finance leases or operating leases? What is the accounting treatment of finance leases?

ENDNOTES

1. Tsingtao Brewery, *Annual Report*, 1995.
2. "Coupons Show Less Redeeming Value", *Chicago Tribune*, July 16, 1993.
3. International Accounting Standard, IAS10, *Contingencies and Events Occurring after the Balance Sheet Date* (London: IASC, reformatted 1994), para. 8.
4. Thomas T. Vogel, Jr., "Disney Amazes Investors with Sale of 100-Year Bonds", *Wall Street Journal*, July 21, 1993.
5. International Accounting Standard, IAS17, *Leases* (London: IASC, revised 1997), para. 2.
6. International Accounting Standard, IAS19, *Employee Benefits* (London: IASC, revised 1998), para. 7.
7. Federal Express Corporation, *Annual Report*, 1993.
8. Daimler-Benz, *Annual Report*, 1995.
9. Sumitomo Corporation, *Annual Report*, 1992.
10. Trans World Airlines, Inc., *Annual Reports*, 1989 and 1992.
11. UAL Corporation, *Annual Report*, 1992.

Chapter 10   # SHARE CAPITAL

LEARNING OBJECTIVES

1. State the advantages and disadvantages of the corporate form of business.
2. Account for organisation costs.
3. Identify the components of shareholders' equity.
4. Account for cash dividends.
5. Identify the characteristics of preference shares, including the effect on division of dividends.
6. Account for the issuance of shares for cash and other assets.
7. Account for the purchase of treasury stock.
8. Account for the exercise of share options.

DECISION POINT

DAIMLER-BENZ

In the chapter on liabilities, bonds were presented as a popular way for corporations to raise new capital because of such factors as income tax advantages, flexibility, and leverage. Although much less prevalent than bonds, share issues are still favoured by many corporations. Daimler-Benz, one of Germany's largest industrial companies with manufacturing interests in cars, trucks, rail systems, microelectronics, diesel engines, aircraft, space systems, and financial services, was the first German company to be listed on the New York Stock Exchange. This event took place in October 1993, and in June 1994 Daimler-Benz raised about U.S. $2 billion in new equity from a global share issue, the largest ever issue of shares by a German company.[1]

As a means of financing, shares have disadvantages. Unlike the interest expense on bonds, dividends paid on shares are not tax deductible under most corporation tax systems. Also, by issuing more shares, the corporation may dilute its ownership. This means that the current shareholders must yield some control to the new shareholders. On the other hand, there are definite advantages to financing with shares. First, financing with share issues is less risky than financing with bonds, because dividends on shares are discretionary and subject to a decision by the board of directors and the shareholders. In contrast, if the interest on bonds is not paid, a company can be forced into bankruptcy. Second, when a company does not pay a cash dividend, the cash generated by profitable operations can be invested in the company's operations. Third, a company may need the proceeds of a share issue to improve the balance between liabilities and shareholders' equity. It is important to understand the nature and characteristics of corporations as well as the process of accounting for a share issue and other share transactions.

OBJECTIVE 1

State the advantages and disadvantages of the corporate form of business

THE CORPORATION

A **corporation** is defined as "a body made up of more than one person that is formed and authorised by law to act as a single person with a legal identity separate from that of its members and that is legally given various rights and duties including the capacity to continue in existence after the death or withdrawal of individual members".[2] In other words, the corporation is a legal entity separate and distinct from its owners. Although there are fewer corporations than sole proprietorships and partnerships in most countries, the corporate form of business dominates the economy in terms of total assets and output of goods and services. Corporations are well suited to today's trends towards large organisations, international trade, and professional management. However, the choice of the corporate form of business is not automatic. The advantages and disadvantages of the corporate form must be considered.

The Advantages of a Corporation

The corporate form of business organisation has several advantages. Among them are separate legal entity, limited liability, ease of capital generation, ease of transfer of ownership, lack of mutual agency, continuous existence, centralised authority and responsibility, and professional management.

Separate Legal Entity

A corporation is a separate legal entity that has most of the rights of a person except those of voting and marrying. As such, it can buy, sell, or own property; sue and be sued; enter into contracts; hire and fire employees; and be taxed.

Limited Liability

Because a corporation is a separate legal entity, it is responsible for its own actions and liabilities. This means that a corporation's lenders can satisfy their claims only against the assets of the corporation, not against the personal property of the owners of the company. Because the owners of a corporation are not responsible for the company's debts, their liability is limited to the amount of their investment. The personal property of sole proprietors and partners, however, generally is available to lenders.

Ease of Capital Generation

It is fairly easy for a corporation to raise capital because shares of ownership in the business are widely available to potential investors for a small amount of money. As a result, a single corporation can be owned by many people.

The development and growth of stock exchanges around the world—especially in emerging economies where deregulation and the privatisation of government-owned enterprises has been the spur for change—has enhanced the popularity of the corporate form of organisation and the capacity of its owners to buy and sell shares without affecting the activities of the business. In China, for example, many new corporations have been formed and listed on stock exchanges, including Tsingtao Brewery which is listed on the New York Stock Exchange.

Ease of Transfer of Ownership

The ownership of a corporation is represented by a transferable unit, a share. An owner of shares, or a shareholder, normally can buy and sell shares without affecting the activities of the corporation or needing the approval of other owners.

Lack of Mutual Agency

There is no mutual agency in the corporate form of business. If a shareholder, acting as an owner, tries to enter into a contract for the corporation, the corporation is not bound by the contract. But in a partnership, because of mutual agency, all the partners can be bound by one partner's actions.

Continuous Existence

Another advantage of the corporation's being a separate legal entity is that an owner's death, incapacity, or withdrawal does not affect the life of the corporation. The life of a corporation is set by its charter and regulated by law.

Centralised Authority and Responsibility

The board of directors represents the shareholders and delegates the responsibility and authority for the day-to-day operation of the corporation to a single person, usually the chief executive of the organisation. This power is not divided among the many owners of the business. The chief executive may delegate authority for certain segments of the business to others, but he or she is held accountable to the board of directors for the business. If the board is dissatisfied with the performance of the chief executive, he or she can be replaced.

Professional Management

Large corporations are owned by many people who probably do not have the time or training to make timely decisions about the business's operations. So, in most cases, management and ownership are separate. This allows the corporation to hire the best talent available to manage the business.

The Disadvantages of a Corporation

The corporate form of business also has disadvantages. Among the more important ones are government regulation, taxation, limited liability, and separation of ownership and control.

Government Regulation

Corporations must meet the requirements of the law. These "creatures of the state" are subject to greater control and regulation by the government than are other forms of business. Corporations must typically file many reports in the country in which they are established. Also, corporations that are traded publicly must file reports with the government securities agencies and with the stock exchanges. Meeting these requirements can be very costly.

Taxation

A major disadvantage of the corporation relates to taxation. Because the corporation is a separate legal entity, its earnings are subject to income taxes. If any of the corporation's after-tax earnings then are paid out to its shareholders as dividends, the earnings are taxed again as income to the shareholders, though in many countries such as the United Kingdom relief is given for tax already paid by the corporation. Taxation is different for the sole proprietorship and the partnership, whose earnings are taxed only as personal income to the owners.

Limited Liability

Above, we listed limited liability as an advantage of a corporation; it also can be a disadvantage. Limited liability restricts the ability of a small corporation to borrow money. Because lenders can lay claim only to the assets of the corporation, they limit their loans to the level secured by those assets or ask shareholders to guarantee the loans personally.

Separation of Ownership and Control

Just as limited liability can be a drawback, so can the separation of ownership and control. Sometimes management makes decisions that are not good for the corporation as a whole. Poor communication also can make it hard for shareholders to exercise control over the corporation or even to recognise that management's decisions are harmful.

BUSINESS BULLETIN   International Practice

The location of corporations as separate legal entities involves corresponding legal obligations to file accounts and a variety of other reports required by governments. Where corporations issue their shares to the public, accounting requirements tend in general to be more rigorous for the protection of investors. In Japan, for example, the Securities and Exchange Law first introduced in 1948 now requires consolidated financial statements to be prepared for approval by shareholders. This is additional to the requirements of the Commercial Code and Corporate Income Tax Law. Further important sources of accounting standards in Japan are the Business Accounting Deliberation Council (BADC), an advisory body of the Ministry of Finance, and the Japanese Institute of Certified Public Accountants.

Costs

There are significant costs involved in the formation, organisation, and operation of a corporation.

OBJECTIVE 2

Account for organisation costs

Organisation Costs

The costs of forming a corporation are called **organisation costs.** These costs, which are incurred before the corporation begins operation, include incorporation fees and lawyers' fees for drawing up the articles of incorporation. They also include the cost of printing share certificates, accountants' fees for services rendered in registering the firm's initial share capital, and other expenditures necessary for forming the corporation.

Theoretically, organisation costs benefit the entire life of the corporation. For this reason, a case can be made for recording organisation costs as intangible assets and amortising them over the years of the life of the corporation. However, the life of a corporation normally is not known, so accountants amortise these costs over the early years of a corporation's life. Organisation costs normally appear as other assets or as intangible assets on the balance sheet.

To show how organisation costs are accounted for, we assume that a corporation pays a lawyer 5,000 for services rendered on July 1, 20x0 to prepare the application for a charter. The entry to record this cost would be as follows:

20x0			
July 1	Organisation Costs	5,000	
	Cash		5,000
	Lawyer's fee for services rendered in corporate organisation		

If the corporation amortises the organisation costs over a five-year period, the entry to record the amortisation at the end of the accounting year, June 30, 20x1, would look like this:

20x1			
June 30	Amortisation Expense, Organisation Costs	1,000	
	Organisation Costs		1,000
	To amortise organisation costs for one year		
	5,000 ÷ 5 years = 1,000		

OBJECTIVE 3

Identify the components of shareholders' equity

THE COMPONENTS OF SHAREHOLDERS' EQUITY

In a corporation's balance sheet, the owners' claims to the business are called shareholders' equity, as shown below.

Shareholders' Equity

Share Capital		
Ordinary Shares—5 nominal value, 30,000 shares authorised, 20,000 shares issued and outstanding	100,000	
Share Premium	50,000	150,000
Preference Shares—50 nominal value, 1,000 shares authorised, issued, and outstanding		50,000
Total Share Capital		200,000
Retained Earnings		60,000
Total Shareholders' Equity		260,000

Notice that the equity section of the corporate balance sheet is divided into two parts: (1) share capital and (2) retained earnings. Share capital represents the initial investment made by the shareholders in the corporation. Retained earnings are the earnings of the corporation since its inception less any losses, dividends, or transfers to share capital. Retained earnings in many countries represent the basis of the calculation for the maximum distribution of past profits that can be made to shareholders. Retained earnings are not a pool of funds to be distributed to the shareholders; they represent, instead, earnings reinvested in the corporation.

The share capital part of shareholders' equity on the balance sheet, in keeping with the criterion of completeness, gives a great deal of information about the corporation's share capital: the kinds of share capital; their nominal value; and the number of shares authorised, issued, and outstanding. The information in the share capital part of shareholders' equity is the subject of the rest of this chapter. We explain retained earnings fully in the chapter on profit and retained earnings.

Share Capital

A share is a unit of ownership in a corporation. A **share certificate** is issued to the owner. It shows the number of shares of the corporation owned by the shareholder. Shareholders can transfer their ownership at will. When they do, they must sign their share certificate and send it to the corporation's secretary. In large corporations, those listed on the organised stock exchanges, it is hard to maintain shareholders' records. These companies can have millions of shares, several thousand of which change ownership every day. Therefore, they often appoint independent registrars and transfer agents (usually banks and trust companies) to help perform the secretary's duties. They are responsible for transferring the corporation's shares, maintaining shareholders' records, preparing a list of shareholders for shareholders' meetings, and paying dividends. To help with the initial issue of capital, corporations often use an **underwriter**—an intermediary between the corporation and the investing public. For a fee—usually less than 1 per cent of the selling price—the underwriter guarantees the sale of the shares. The corporation records the amount of the net proceeds of the offering—what the public paid less the underwriter's fee, legal and printing expenses, and any other direct costs of the offering—in its share capital and share premium accounts.

Authorised Capital

When a corporation applies for a charter, the articles of incorporation in most countries indicate the maximum number of shares the corporation is allowed to issue. This number represents **authorised capital**. Most corporations are authorised to issue more shares than are necessary at the time of organisation, enabling them to issue shares in the future to raise additional capital. For example, if a corporation is planning to expand later, a possible source of capital would be the unissued shares that were authorised in its charter. If all authorised capital is issued immediately, before it can issue more, the corporation must change its charter by applying to the government to increase its shares of authorised capital.

The charter also shows the nominal or par value of the shares that have been authorised. **Nominal or par value** is an arbitrary amount, often determined by law, that is printed on each share. It must be recorded in the Share Capital accounts and constitutes the legal capital of a corporation. **Legal capital** equals the number of shares issued times the nominal or par value; it is the minimum amount that can be reported as share capital. Nominal or par value usually bears little if any relationship to the market value or book value of the shares. When the corporation is formed, a memorandum entry can be made in the general journal giving the number and description of authorised shares.

Issued and Outstanding Capital

The **issued capital** of a corporation are the shares sold or otherwise transferred to shareholders. For example, a corporation can be authorised to issue 500,000 shares but may choose to issue only 300,000 shares when the company is organised. The holders of those 300,000 shares own 100 per cent of the corporation. The remaining 200,000 shares are unissued shares. No rights or privileges are associated with them until they are issued.

Outstanding capital are the shares that have been issued and are still in circulation. A share is not outstanding if it has been repurchased by the issuing corporation or given back to the company that issued it by a shareholder. So, a company can have more shares issued than are currently outstanding. Issued shares that are bought back and held by the corporation are called treasury stock, which we discuss in detail later in this chapter.

Ordinary Shares

A corporation can issue two basic types of shares: ordinary shares and preference shares. If only one kind of share is issued by the corporation, such shares are called **ordinary shares**. Ordinary shares are the company's **residual equity**. This means that all other lenders' and preferred shareholders' claims to the company's assets rank ahead of those of the ordinary shareholders in case of liquidation. Because ordinary shares are generally the only shares that carry voting rights, they represent the means of controlling the corporation.

OBJECTIVE 4

Account for cash dividends

Dividends

A **dividend** is the distribution of a corporation's profits to its shareholders. Each shareholder receives assets, usually cash, in proportion to the number of shares held. The board of directors has sole authority to declare dividends.

Dividends can be paid quarterly, semiannually, annually, or at other times decided on by the board. Most countries do not allow the board to declare a dividend that exceeds retained earnings. When this kind of dividend is declared, the corporation essentially is returning to the shareholders part of their share capital. This is called a **liquidating dividend** and normally is paid when a company is going out of business or is reducing its operations. Having sufficient retained earnings in itself does not justify the distribution of a dividend. If cash or other readily distributed assets are not available for distribution, the company might have to borrow money in order to pay a dividend—an action most boards of directors want to avoid.

There are three important dates associated with dividends. In order of occurrence, they are (1) the date of declaration, (2) the date of record, and (3) the date of payment. The *date of declaration* is the date the board of directors formally declares that a dividend is going to be paid. The *date of record* is the date on which ownership of the share of a company, and therefore of the right to receive a dividend, is determined. Those individuals who own the share on the date of record will receive the dividend. After that date, the share is said to be **ex-dividend**: If one person sells the shares to another, the right to the cash dividend remains with the first person; it does not transfer with the shares to the second person. The *date of payment* is the date on which the dividend is paid to the shareholders of record.

To illustrate the accounting for cash dividends, we assume that the board of directors has decided that sufficient cash is available to pay a 56,000 cash dividend to the ordinary shareholders. The process has two steps. First, the board declares the dividend to be given as of a certain date. Second, the dividend is paid. Assume that the dividend is declared on February 21, 20xx, for shareholders of record on March 1, 20xx, to be paid on March 11, 20xx. Here are the entries to record the declaration and payment of the cash dividend:

Date of Declaration

Feb. 21	Cash Dividends Declared	56,000	
	Cash Dividends Payable		56,000
	Declaration of a cash dividend		
	to ordinary shareholders		

Date of Record

Mar. 1 No entry is required. This date is used simply to determine the owners of the shares who will receive the dividends. After this date (starting March 2), the shares are ex-dividend.

Date of Payment

Mar. 11	Cash Dividends Payable	56,000	
	Cash		56,000
	Payment of cash dividends		
	declared February 21		

Notice that the liability for the dividend is recorded on the date of declaration because the legal obligation to pay the dividend is established on that date. No entry is required on the date of record. The liability is liquidated, or settled, on the date of payment. The Cash Dividends Declared account is a temporary shareholders' equity account that is closed at the end of the accounting period by debiting Retained Earnings and crediting Cash Dividends Declared. Retained earnings are thereby reduced by the total dividends declared during the period.

Some companies do not pay dividends very often. A company may not have any earnings. Or, a corporation may need the assets generated by the earnings kept in the company for business purposes, perhaps expansion of the plant. Investors in growth companies expect a return on their investment in the form of an increase in the market value of their shares. Share dividends or bonus issues, another kind of return, are discussed in the chapter on profit and retained earnings.

OBJECTIVE 5

Identify the characteristics of preference shares, including the effect on division of dividends

Preference Shares

The second kind of shares a company can issue is called **preference shares**. Both ordinary shares and preference shares are sold to raise money. But investors in preference shares have different investment goals from investors in ordinary shares. Preference shares have preference over ordinary shares in one or more areas. There can be several different classes of preference shares, each with distinctive characteristics to attract different investors. Most preference shares have one or more of the following characteristics: preference as to dividends, preference as to assets of the business in liquidation, convertibility, and a redemption option.

Preference as to Dividends

Preference shares normally have a *preference* over ordinary shares in the receipt of dividends; that is, the holders of preference shares must receive a certain amount of dividends before the holders of ordinary shares can receive dividends. The amount that preference shareholders must be paid before ordinary shareholders can be paid usually is stated in amounts per share or as a percentage of the face value of the preference shares. For example, a corporation can issue preference shares and pay a dividend of 4 per share, or it might issue preference shares at 50 nominal value and pay a yearly dividend of 8 per cent of nominal value, 4 annually per share.

DECISION POINT

J.C. PENNEY COMPANY

Preference share issues can be used strategically to accomplish manage-ment's objectives. For instance, an article in the Wall Street Journal *reported that J.C. Penney Company, the large U.S. retailer, planned to sell an issue of preference shares to its newly created Employee Share Ownership Plan (ESOP) and use the $700 million in proceeds to buy back up to 11 per cent of its outstanding ordinary shares. The plan would result in the employees owning about 24 per cent of the company. The new preference shares would pay a dividend of 7.9 per cent and would be convertible into ordinary shares at $60 per ordinary share. The stock market reacted positively to the plan; the company's shares rose almost $2 per share to $48 on the date of the announcement. What benefits to the company does management see from this elaborate plan?*

As reported by the Wall Street Journal, *"Analysts said the move should make the company less attractive as a takeover candidate by increasing its share price and per share earnings as well as by putting more shares in employees' hands."[3] Further, the company feels that its shares are undervalued and that because there will be fewer ordinary shares outstanding after the plan is put into effect, the market value of the company's shares will be enhanced.*

Preference shareholders have no guarantee of receiving dividends: The company must have earnings and the board of directors must declare dividends on preference shares before any liability to pay them arises. The consequences of not declaring a div-idend to preference shareholders in the current year vary according to the exact terms under which the shares were issued. In the case of **noncumulative preference shares**, if there is failure to declare a dividend to preference shareholders in a given year, there is no obligation to make up the missed dividend in future years. In the case of **cumu-lative preference shares**, however, the fixed dividend amount per share accumulates from year to year, and the whole amount must be paid before any ordinary dividends can be paid. Dividends that are not paid in the year they are due are called **dividends in arrears**.

Assume that a corporation has been authorised to issue 10,000 shares of 100 nominal value, 5 per cent cumulative preference shares, and that the shares have been issued and are outstanding. If no dividends were paid in 20x1, at the end of the year there would be preferred dividends of 50,000 (10,000 shares × 100 × .05 = 50,000) in arrears. If dividends are paid in 20x2, the preference shareholders' divi-dends in arrears plus the 20x2 preferred dividends must be paid before any dividends on ordinary shares can be paid.

Dividends in arrears are not recognised as liabilities of a corporation because there is no liability until the board declares a dividend that is subsequently approved by the shareholders. A corporation cannot be sure it is going to make a profit. So, of course, it cannot promise dividends to shareholders. However, if a company has divi-dends in arrears, they should be reported either in the body of the financial state-ments or in a footnote.

Suppose that on January 1, 20x1, a corporation issued 10,000 shares of 10 nomi-nal value, 6 per cent cumulative preference shares and 50,000 shares of ordinary shares. The first year's operations resulted in income of only 4,000. The corporation's board of directors declared a 3,000 cash dividend to the preference shareholders. The dividend picture at the end of 20x1 looked like this:

Just as financial instruments have become more complex, so have the problems of distinguishing shares from liabilities. The International Accounting Standards Committee has developed requirements to deal with this issue, but in many countries, including China and Korea, regulators are only just beginning to consider the problems involved.

20x1 dividends due preference shareholders (100,000 × .06)	6,000	
Less 20x1 dividends declared to preference shareholders	3,000	
20x1 preference share dividends in arrears	3,000	

Now, suppose that in 20x2 the company earned a profit of 30,000 and wanted to pay dividends to both the preference and the ordinary shareholders. But the preference shares are cumulative. So the corporation must pay the 3,000 in arrears on the preference shares, plus the current year's dividends on its preference shares, before it can distribute a dividend to the ordinary shareholders. For example, assume that the corporation's board of directors declared a 12,000 dividend to be distributed to preference and ordinary shareholders. The dividend would be distributed as follows:

20x2 declaration of dividends	12,000	
Less 20x1 preference share dividends in arrears	3,000	
Available for 20x2 dividends		9,000
Less 20x2 dividends due preference shareholders (100,000 × .06)		6,000
Remainder available to ordinary shareholders		3,000

And this is the journal entry when the dividend is declared:

Dec. 31 Cash Dividends Declared	12,000	
Cash Dividends Payable		12,000
Declaration of a 9,000 cash dividend to preference shareholders and a 3,000 cash dividend to ordinary shareholders		

Preference as to Assets

Some preference shares have preference in terms of the assets of the corporation in the case of liquidation. So, when the business is ended, the preference shareholders have a right to receive the nominal value of their shares or a larger stated liquidation value per share before the ordinary shareholders receive any share of the company's assets. This preference also can include any dividends in arrears owed to the preference shareholders.

Convertible Preference Shares

A corporation can make its preference shares more attractive to investors by adding a convertibility feature. People who hold **convertible preference shares** can exchange their preference shares for the company's ordinary shares at a ratio stated in the preference share contract. Convertibility appeals to investors for two reasons. First, like all preference shareholders, owners of convertible shares are more likely to receive regular dividends than are ordinary shareholders. Second, if the market value of a company's ordinary shares rises, the conversion feature allows the preference shareholders to share in the increase. The rise in value would come either through equal increases in the value of the preference shares or through conversion to ordinary shares.

For example, suppose that a company issues 1,000 shares of 8 per cent, 100 nominal value convertible preference capital for 100 per share. Each share can be converted into five shares of the company's ordinary capital at any time. The market value of the ordinary shares is now 15 per share. In the past, dividends on the ordinary shares have been about 1 per share per year. The shareholder owning one share of preference capital, on the other hand, now holds an investment that is approaching a worth of 100 on the market and is more likely to receive dividends than is the owner of ordinary shares.

Assume that in the next several years, the corporation's earnings increase, and the dividends paid to ordinary shareholders also increase, to 3 per share. In addition, the market value of a share goes up from 15 to 30. Preference shareholders can convert each of their preference shares into five ordinary shares and increase their dividends from 8 on each preference share to the equivalent of 15 (3 on each of five ordinary shares). Furthermore, the market value of each share of preference capital will be close to the 150 value of the five shares of ordinary capital because each share can be converted into five shares of ordinary capital.

Redeemable Preference Shares

Most preference shares are **redeemable preference shares**. That is, they can be redeemed or retired at the option of the issuing corporation at a price stated in the preference share contract. The shareholder must surrender a nonconvertible preference share to the corporation when asked to do so. If the preference shares are convertible, the shareholder can either surrender the shares to the corporation or convert them into ordinary shares when the corporation redeems the shares. The redemption price is usually higher than the nominal value of the shares. For example, a 100 nominal value preference share might be redeemable at 103 per share. When preference shares are redeemed and surrendered, the shareholder is entitled to (1) the nominal value of the share, (2) the premium on redemption, (3) any dividends in arrears, and (4) a prorated (by the proportion of the year to the redemption date) portion of the current period's dividend.

There are several reasons why a corporation would redeem its preference shares. First, the company may want to force conversion of the preference shares to ordinary shares because the cash dividend being paid on the equivalent ordinary shares is less than the dividend being paid on the preference shares. Second, it may be possible to replace the outstanding preference shares on the current market with preference shares at a lower dividend rate or with long-term debt, which can have a lower after-tax cost. Third, the company may simply be profitable enough to retire the preference capital.

Retained Earnings

Retained earnings, the other component of shareholders' equity, represent shareholders' claims to the assets of the company resulting from profitable operations. The chapter on profit and retained earnings explains in detail the retained earnings section of the balance sheet.

BUSINESS BULLETIN   Business Practice

The shares of corporations are increasingly being listed on stock exchanges around the world. While the price at which such shares are initially issued may be clearly determined and accounted for, the price at which shares are likely to start trading on a stock exchange is uncertain and difficult to predict. In Australia, for example, the newly listed AMP shares started trading on the Sydney Stock Exchange at $35.99 on June 15, 1998, well in excess of what had been expected, i.e. around $20. Deutsche Bank's aggressive bidding on behalf of its clients had apparently been responsible for this rise. But by July 6, AMP shares had settled at $19.92, leaving Deutsche Bank and its clients with significant losses.[4]

OBJECTIVE 6

Account for the issuance of shares for cash and other assets

ACCOUNTING FOR SHARE ISSUES

A share of capital is either nominal (par) or no-par capital. If the capital is nominal (or par) capital, the corporation charter states the nominal (or par) value, and this value must be printed on each share. Nominal or par value can be 10, 1, 5, 100, or any other amount worked out by the organisers of the corporation. The nominal or par values of ordinary shares tend to be lower than those of preference shares.

In most countries, nominal or par value is the amount per share that is entered into the corporation's Share Capital accounts and that makes up the legal capital of the corporation. A corporation cannot declare a dividend that would cause shareholders' equity to fall below the legal capital of the firm. Therefore, the nominal or par value is a minimum cushion of capital that protects lenders. Any amount in excess of nominal or par value received from the issuance of shares is termed **share premium** and represents a portion of the company's share capital.

No-par shares are shares that do not have a nominal or par value. There are several reasons for issuing shares without a nominal or par value. One is that some investors confuse nominal or par value with the market value of shares instead of recognising it as an arbitrary figure. Another reason is that most countries do not allow an original capital issue below nominal or par value and thereby limit a corporation's flexibility in obtaining capital.

No-par shares can be issued with or without a stated value. The board of directors of the corporation issuing the no-par shares can be required by law to place a **stated value** on each share or may choose to do so as a matter of convenience. The stated value can be any value set by the board, although some countries do indicate a minimum stated value per share. The stated value can be set before or after the shares are issued if the law does not specify this point.

If a company issues no-par shares without a stated value, all proceeds of the issue are recorded in the Share Capital account. This amount becomes the corporation's legal capital unless the amount is specified by law. Because additional shares can be issued at different prices, the credit to the Share Capital account per share will not be uniform. In this way, it differs from nominal or par value shares and no-par shares with a stated value.

When no-par shares with a stated value are issued, the shares are recorded in the Share Capital account at the stated value. Any amount received in excess of the stated value is recorded in a Share Premium account. The excess of the stated value is a part of the corporation's share capital. However, the stated value normally is considered to be the legal capital of the corporation.

Nominal or Par Value Shares

When nominal or par value shares are issued, the appropriate share capital account (usually Ordinary Shares or Preference Shares) is credited for the nominal value (legal capital) regardless of whether the proceeds are more or less than the nominal value. For example, assume that Bradley Corporation is authorised to issue 20,000 shares of 10 par value ordinary shares and actually issues 10,000 shares at 10 per share on January 1, 20xx. The entry to record the share issue at nominal value would be:

Jan. 1	Cash	100,000	
	Ordinary Shares		100,000
	Issued 10,000 ordinary shares of 10 nominal value for 10 per share		

Cash is debited 100,000 (10,000 shares × 10), and Ordinary Shares is credited an equal amount because the shares were sold for nominal or par value (legal capital).

If the shares had been issued for a price greater than nominal value, the proceeds in excess of nominal value would be credited to a capital account called Share

Premium account. For example, assume that the 10,000 shares of Bradley sold for 12 per share on January 1, 20xx. The entry to record the issuance of the shares at the price in excess of nominal value would be as follows:

Jan. 1	Cash	120,000	
	Ordinary Shares		100,000
	Share Premium		20,000
	Issued 10,000 ordinary shares		
	of 10 nominal value for		
	12 per share		

Cash is debited for the proceeds of 120,000 (10,000 shares × 12), and Ordinary Shares is credited for the total nominal value of 100,000 (10,000 shares × 10). Shares Premium account is credited for the difference of 20,000 (10,000 shares × 2). This amount is part of the corporation's share capital and will be included in the shareholders' equity section of the balance sheet. The shareholders' equity section for Bradley Corporation immediately following the share issue would appear as follows:

Share Capital	
Ordinary Shares—10 nominal value, 20,000 shares	
authorised, 10,000 shares issued and outstanding	100,000
Share Premium	20,000
Total Share Capital	120,000
Retained Earnings	—
Total Shareholders' Equity	120,000

No-Par Shares

As mentioned earlier, shares can be issued without a nominal or par value. However, most countries require that all or part of the proceeds from the issuance of what are called no-par shares be designated as legal capital, which cannot be withdrawn except in liquidation. The purpose of this requirement is to protect the corporation's assets for lenders. Assume that the Bradley Corporation's share capital is no-par ordinary shares and that 10,000 shares are issued on January 1, 20xx at 15 per share. The 150,000 (10,000 shares × 15) in proceeds would be recorded as shown in the following entry:

Jan. 1	Cash	150,000	
	Ordinary Shares		150,000
	Issued 10,000 no-par ordinary		
	shares for 15 per share		

Because the shares do not have a stated or nominal value, all proceeds of the issue are credited to Ordinary Shares and are part of the company's legal capital.

Most countries allow the board of directors to put a stated value on no-par shares, and this value represents the corporation's legal capital. Assume that Bradley's board puts a 10 stated value on its no-par shares. The entry to record the issue of 10,000 shares of no-par ordinary shares with a 10 stated value for 15 per share would appear as follows:

Jan. 1	Cash	150,000	
	Ordinary Shares		100,000
	Share Premium		50,000
	Issued 10,000 no-par ordinary shares		
	of 10 stated value for 15 per share		

Notice that the legal capital credited to Ordinary Shares is the stated value decided by the board of directors. Notice also that the account Share Premium is credited for

50,000. The 50,000 is the difference between the proceeds (150,000) and the total stated value (100,000).

Issuance of Shares for Noncash Assets

Shares can be issued for assets or services other than cash. The problem here is the amount that should be recorded for the exchange. The generally preferred rule is to record the transaction at the fair market value of what the corporation is giving up— in this case, the shares. If the fair market value of the shares cannot be determined, the fair market value of the assets or services received can be used to record the transaction. Transactions of this kind usually involve the use of shares to pay for land or buildings or for the services of lawyers and others who helped organise the company.

Where there is an exchange of shares for noncash assets, the board of directors has the right to determine the fair market value of the property. Suppose that when the Bradley Corporation was formed on January 1, 20xx, its lawyer agreed to accept 100 shares of its 10 nominal value ordinary shares for services rendered. At the time the shares were issued, their market value could not be determined. However, for similar services the lawyer would have billed the company 1,500. This is the entry to record the noncash transaction:

Jan. 1	Organisation Costs	1,500	
	Ordinary Shares		1,000
	Share Premium		500
	Issued 100 ordinary shares of		
	10 nominal value for lawyer's		
	services		

Now suppose that two years later the Bradley Corporation exchanged 1,000 shares of its 10 nominal value ordinary shares for a piece of land. At the time of the exchange, the shares were selling on the market for 16 per share. The entry to record this exchange would be as follows:

Jan. 1	Land	16,000	
	Ordinary Shares		10,000
	Share Premium		6,000
	Issued 1,000 ordinary shares of 10 nominal		
	value with a market value of 16 per share		
	for a piece of land		

OBJECTIVE 7

Account for the purchase of treasury stock

Treasury Stock

Treasury stock consists of shares, either ordinary or preference, that have been issued and reacquired by the issuing company but have not been sold or retired. The company normally gets its own shares back by purchasing them on the market.

It is common in a number of countries for companies to buy back and hold their own shares. There are several reasons why a company purchases its own shares:

1. It may want to have shares available to distribute to employees through share option plans.
2. It may be trying to maintain a favourable market for the company's shares.
3. It may want to increase the company's earnings per share.
4. It may want to have additional shares available for such activities as purchasing other companies.
5. It may want to prevent a hostile takeover.

The effect of an own share or treasury stock purchase is to reduce the assets and shareholders' equity of the company. It is not considered a purchase of assets, as the purchase of shares in another company would be. Treasury stock is share capital that has been issued but is no longer outstanding. Treasury stock can be held for an indefinite period of time, reissued, or retired. Like unissued shares, treasury stock has no rights until reissued. Treasury stock does not have voting rights, rights to cash dividends or share dividends, or rights to share in assets during liquidation of the company, and is not considered to be outstanding in the calculation of book value. However, there is one major difference between unissued shares and treasury stock: A share that originally was issued at nominal value or greater and fully paid for, and that then was reacquired as treasury stock, can be reissued at less than nominal value without negative consequences attaching to it.

The Purchase of Treasury Stock

When treasury stock is purchased, it normally is recorded at cost. The transaction reduces both the assets and the shareholders' equity of the firm. For example, assume that on September 15 the Caprock Corporation purchases 1,000 of its own shares on the market at a price of 50 per share. The purchase would be recorded as follows:

Sept. 15	Treasury Stock, Ordinary	50,000	
	Cash		50,000
	Acquired 1,000 of the company's ordinary shares for 50 per share		

Notice that the treasury stock is recorded at cost. The nominal value, stated value, or original issue price of the shares is ignored. It should also be noted here that in some countries, such as New Zealand, treasury stock is required to be cancelled.

The shareholders' equity section of Caprock's balance sheet shows the cost of the treasury stock as a deduction from the total of share capital and retained earnings:

Share Capital	
Ordinary Shares—5 nominal value, 100,000 shares authorised,	
30,000 shares issued, 29,000 shares outstanding	150,000
Share Premium	30,000
Total Share Capital	180,000
Retained Earnings	900,000
Total Share Capital and Retained Earnings	1,080,000
Less Treasury Stock, Ordinary (1,000 shares at cost)	50,000
Total Shareholders' Equity	1,030,000

Notice that the number of shares issued, and thus the legal capital, has not changed, although the number of outstanding shares has decreased as a result of the transaction.

The Sale of Treasury Stock

Treasury stock can be sold at cost, above cost, or below cost. For example, assume that on November 15 the 1,000 own shares of the Caprock Corporation are sold for 50 per share. This entry records the transaction:

Nov. 15	Cash	50,000	
	Treasury Stock, Ordinary		50,000
	Reissued 1,000 shares of treasury stock for 50 per share		

When shares of treasury stock are sold for an amount greater than their cost, the excess of the sales price over cost should be credited to Share Premium, Treasury Stock. No gain should be recorded. For example, suppose that on November 15 the 1,000 shares of treasury stock of the Caprock Corporation are sold for 60 per share. The entry for the reissue would be as follows:

Nov. 15	Cash	60,000	
	Treasury Stock, Ordinary		50,000
	Share Premium, Treasury Stock		10,000
	Sale of 1,000 shares of treasury stock for 60 per share; cost was 50 per share		

If shares of treasury stock are sold below their cost, the difference is deducted from Share Premium, Treasury Stock. When this account does not exist or is insufficient to cover the excess of cost over the reissue price, Retained Earnings absorbs the excess. No loss is recorded. For example, suppose that on September 15, the Caprock Corporation bought 1,000 of its ordinary shares on the market at a price of 50 per share. The company sold 400 shares on October 15 for 60 per share and the remaining 600 shares on December 15 for 42 per share. The entries to record these transactions are as follows:

Sept. 15	Treasury Stock, Ordinary	50,000	
	Cash		50,000
	Purchase of 1,000 shares of treasury stock at 50 per share		

Oct. 15	Cash	24,000	
	Treasury Stock, Ordinary		20,000
	Share Premium, Treasury Stock		4,000
	Sale of 400 shares of treasury stock for 60 per share; cost was 50 per share		

Dec. 15	Cash	25,200	
	Share Premium, Treasury Stock	4,000	
	Retained Earnings	800	
	Treasury Stock, Ordinary		30,000
	Sale of 600 shares of treasury stock for 42 per share; cost was 50 per share		

In the entry for the December 15 transaction, Retained Earnings is debited 800 because the 600 shares were sold for 4,800 less than cost. That amount is 800 greater than the 4,000 of share capital generated by the sale of the 400 shares on October 15.

OBJECTIVE 8

Account for the exercise of share options

EXERCISING SHARE OPTIONS

Many companies encourage the ownership of the company's ordinary shares through a **share option plan**, which is an agreement to issue shares to employees according to the terms of the plan. Under some plans, the option to purchase shares applies to all employees equally, and the purchase of shares is made at a price close to the market value at the time of purchase. In this situation, the share issue is recorded in the same way any share issue to an outsider is recorded. If, for example, we assume that on March 30 the employees of a company purchased 2,000 shares of 10 nominal value at the current market value of 25 per share, the entry would be as follows:

Mar. 30	Cash	50,000	
	Ordinary Shares		20,000
	Share Premium		30,000
	Issued 2,000 ordinary shares of 10 nominal value under employee share option plan		

In other cases, the share option plan gives the employee the right to purchase shares in the future at a fixed price. This type of plan, which usually is offered only to management personnel, both compensates and motivates the employee because the market value of a company's shares is tied to its performance. As the market value of the share goes up, the difference between the option price and the market price increases, increasing the employee's compensation. When an option eventually is exercised and the share is issued, the entry is similar to the one above. For example, assume that on July 1, 20x1, a company grants its key management personnel the option to purchase 50,000 shares of 10 nominal value at the market value (as of that date) of 15 per share. Suppose that one of the firm's executives exercises the option to purchase 2,000 shares on March 30, 20x2, when the market price is 25 per share. This entry would record the issue:

20x2			
Mar. 30	Cash	30,000	
	Ordinary Shares		20,000
	Share Premium		10,000
	Issued 2,000 ordinary shares of 10 nominal value under the employee share option plan		

Although the executive has a gain of 20,000 (the 50,000 market value less the 30,000 option price), no compensation expense is recorded. Compensation expense would be recorded only if the option price is less than the 15 market price on July 1, 20x1, the date of grant. Methods of handling compensation in this situation are covered in more advanced courses. Information pertaining to employee share option plans should be discussed in the notes to the financial statements.

CHAPTER REVIEW

Review of Learning Objectives

1. **State the advantages and disadvantages of the corporate form of business.** A corporation is a separate legal entity that has its own rights and duties distinct from its owners. Among the advantages of the corporate form of business are that (a) a corporation is a separate legal entity, (b) shareholders have limited liability, (c) it is easy to generate capital for a corporation, (d) shareholders can buy and sell shares easily, (e) there is a lack of mutual agency, (f) the corporation has a continuous existence, (g) authority and responsibility are centralised, and (h) it is run by a professional management team. The disadvantages of corporations include (a) a large amount of government regulation, (b) potential incidence of double taxation, (c) difficulty of raising funds because of limited liability, (d) separation of ownership and control, and (e) formation, organisation, and operating costs.

2. **Account for organisation costs.** The costs of organising a corporation are recorded as an asset and are usually amortised over the early years of a corporation's life.

3. **Identify the components of shareholders' equity.** Shareholders' equity consists of share capital and retained earnings. Share capital includes two basic types of shares: ordinary shares and preference shares. When only one kind of share is issued, it is ordinary shares. Ordinary shareholders have voting rights; they also share in the earnings of the corporation and in its assets in case of liquidation.

    Retained earnings, the other component of shareholders' equity, represents the claim of shareholders to the assets of the company resulting from profitable operations. These are earnings that have been reinvested in the corporation.

4. **Account for cash dividends.** The liability for payment of cash dividends arises on the date of declaration by the board of directors. The declaration is recorded with a debit to Cash Dividends Declared and a credit to Cash Dividends Payable. The date of record, on which no entry is required, establishes the shareholders who will receive the cash dividend on the date of payment. Payment is recorded with a debit to Cash Dividends Payable and a credit to Cash.

5. **Identify the characteristics of preference shares, including the effect on division of dividends.** Preference shares, like ordinary shares, are sold to raise capital. But the investors have different objectives. To attract these investors, corporations usually give them a preference—in terms of receiving dividends and assets—over ordinary shareholders. The dividend on preference shares is generally calculated first; then the remainder goes to the ordinary shares. If the preference shares are cumulative and in arrears, the amount in arrears also has to be allocated to preference shareholders before any allocation is made to ordinary shareholders. In addition, certain preference shares are convertible. Preference shares are often redeemable at the option of the corporation.

6. **Account for the issuance of shares for cash and other assets.** A corporation's shares normally are issued for cash and other assets. The majority of countries require that shares be issued at a minimum value called legal capital. Legal capital is represented by the nominal or stated value of the share.

    When shares are issued for cash at nominal or stated value, Cash is debited and Ordinary Shares or Preference Shares is credited. When shares are sold at an amount greater than nominal or stated value, the excess is recorded in the Share Premium account.

Sometimes shares are issued for noncash assets. Here, the accountant must decide how to value the shares. The generally preferred rule is to record the shares at their fair market value. If this value cannot be determined, then the accountant uses the fair market value of the asset received to record the transaction.

7. **Account for the purchase of treasury stock.** The treasury stock of a company is shares that have been issued and reacquired but not resold or retired. A company acquires its own shares to create share option plans, maintain a favourable market for

the shares, increase earnings per share, or to purchase other companies. Treasury stock is similar to unissued shares in that it does not have rights until reissued. However, treasury stock can be resold at less than nominal value without incurring a discount liability.

8. **Account for the exercise of share options.** Companywide share option plans are used to encourage employees to own a part of the company. Other plans are offered only to management personnel, both to compensate and to motivate them. Usually, the issue of shares to employees under share option plans is recorded in a manner similar to the issue of shares to any outsider.

Review of Concepts and Terminology

The following concepts and terms were introduced in this chapter.

LO 3 **Authorised capital:** The maximum number of shares a corporation is allowed to issue without changing its charter.

LO 5 **Convertible preference shares:** Preference shares that can be exchanged for ordinary shares at the option of the holder.

LO 1 **Corporation:** A legal entity separate and distinct from its owners.

LO 5 **Cumulative preference shares:** Preference shares on which unpaid dividends accumulate over time and must be satisfied in any given year before a dividend can be paid to ordinary shareholders.

LO 4 **Dividend:** The distribution of a corporation's assets (usually cash) to its shareholders.

LO 5 **Dividends in arrears:** Dividends on cumulative preference shares that are not paid in the year they are due.

LO 4 **Ex-dividend:** A description of share capital between the date of record and the date of payment when the right to a dividend already declared on the shares remains with the person who sells the shares and does not transfer to the person who buys it.

LO 3 **Issued capital:** The shares sold or otherwise transferred to shareholders.

LO 3 **Legal capital:** The number of shares issued times the nominal value; the minimum amount that can be reported as share capital.

LO 4 **Liquidating dividend:** A dividend that exceeds retained earnings; usually paid when a corporation goes out of business or reduces its operations.

LO 3 **Nominal or par value:** The arbitrary amount printed on each share; used to determine the legal capital of a corporation.

LO 5 **Noncumulative preference shares:** Preference shares that do not carry an obligation to pay missed or undeclared dividends in future years.

LO 6 **No-par shares:** Share capital that does not have a nominal or par value.

LO 3 **Ordinary shares:** Shares that carry voting rights but that rank below preference shares in terms of dividends and the distribution of assets in the event of liquidation.

LO 2 **Organisation costs:** The costs of forming a corporation.

LO 3 **Outstanding capital:** Shares that have been issued and are still in circulation.

LO 5 **Preference shares:** Shares that have preference over ordinary shares in terms of dividends and the distribution of assets in the event of liquidation.

LO 5 **Redeemable preference shares:** Preference shares that can be redeemed and retired at the option of the corporation.

LO 3 **Residual equity:** The ordinary shares of a corporation plus retained earnings and reserves.

LO 3 **Share certificate:** A document issued to a shareholder indicating the number of shares the shareholder owns.

LO 8 **Share option plan:** An agreement to issue shares to employees according to the terms of a plan.

LO 6 **Share premium:** The amount received in excess of the nominal or par value of shares issued.

LO 6 **Stated value:** A value assigned by the board of directors of a corporation to shares that do not have a nominal or par value.

LO 7 **Treasury stock:** Shares, either ordinary or preference, that have been issued and reacquired by the issuing company but that have not been sold or retired.

LO 3 **Underwriter:** An intermediary between the corporation and the public who facilitates an issue of shares or other securities for a fee.

Review Problem

Share Journal Entries and Shareholders' Equity

LO 2
LO 3
LO 4
LO 5
LO 6
LO 7

The Beta Corporation was organised in 20xx. Its charter authorised the corporation to issue 1,000,000 shares of 1 nominal value ordinary shares and an additional 25,000 shares of 4 per cent, 20 nominal value cumulative convertible preference shares. Here are the transactions that related to the company's shares during 20xx:

Feb. 12 Issued 100,000 ordinary shares for 125,000.

20 Issued 3,000 ordinary shares for accounting and legal services. The services were billed to the company at 3,600.

Mar. 15 Issued 120,000 ordinary shares to Edward Jackson in exchange for a building and land that had an appraised value of 100,000 and 25,000, respectively.

Apr. 2 Purchased 20,000 own shares at 1.25 per share from an individual who changed his mind about being an investor in the company.

July 1 Issued 25,000 preference shares for 500,000.

Sept. 30 Sold 10,000 of shares in the treasury for 1.50 per share.

Dec. 31 The company reported net profit of 40,000 for 20xx, and the board declared dividends of 25,000, payable on January 15 to shareholders of record on January 8. Dividends included preference shares cash dividends for one-half year.

REQUIRED   1. Prepare the journal entries necessary to record these transactions. Then close the Profit Summary and Cash Dividends Declared accounts to Retained Earnings. Following the December 31 entry to record dividends, show dividends payable for each class of share.

2. Prepare the shareholders' equity section of Beta's balance sheet as of December 31, 20xx.

Answer to Review Problem

1. Prepare the journal entries.

20xx

Feb. 12	Cash		125,000	
	Ordinary Shares			100,000
	Share Premium			25,000
	Sale of 100,000 ordinary shares of 1 nominal value for 1.25 per share			
20	Organisation Costs		3,600	
	Ordinary Shares			3,000
	Share Premium			600
	Issue of 3,000 ordinary shares of 1 nominal value for billed accounting and legal services of 3,600			
Mar. 15	Building		100,000	
	Land		25,000	
	Ordinary Shares			120,000
	Share Premium			5,000
	Issue of 120,000 ordinary shares of 1 nominal value for a building and land valued at 100,000 and 25,000, respectively			
Apr. 2	Treasury Stock, Ordinary		25,000	
	Cash			25,000
	Purchase of 20,000 ordinary shares for the treasury at 1.25 per share			
July 1	Cash		500,000	
	Preference Shares			500,000
	Sale of 25,000 preference shares of 20 nominal value for 20 per share			
Sept. 30	Cash		15,000	
	Treasury Stock, Ordinary			12,500
	Share Premium, Treasury Stock			2,500
	Sale of 10,000 shares of treasury stock at 1.50 per share; original cost was 1.25 per share			
Dec. 31	Cash Dividends Declared		25,000	
	Cash Dividends Payable			25,000
	Declaration of a 25,000 cash dividend to preference and ordinary shareholders			
	Total dividend	25,000		
	Less preference share cash dividend:			
	500,000 × .04 × 6/12	10,000		
	Ordinary shares cash dividend	15,000		

	Dec. 31	Profit Summary	40,000	
		Retained Earnings		40,000
		To close the Profit Summary account to Retained Earnings		
	31	Retained Earnings	25,000	
		Cash Dividends Declared		25,000
		To close the Cash Dividends Declared account to Retained Earnings		

2. Prepare the shareholders' equity section of the balance sheet.

Beta Corporation
Shareholders' Equity
December 31, 20xx

Share Capital		
Ordinary Shares—1 nominal value, 1,000,000 shares authorised, 223,000 shares issued, and 213,000 shares outstanding	223,000	
Share Premium, Ordinary Shares	30,600	
Share Premium, Treasury Stock	2,500	256,100
Preference Shares—4% cumulative convertible, 20 nominal value, 25,000 shares authorised, issued, and outstanding		500,000
Total Share Capital		756,100
Retained Earnings		15,000
Total Share Capital and Retained Earnings		771,100
Less Treasury Stock, Ordinary (10,000 shares, at cost)		12,500
Total Shareholders' Equity		758,600

CHAPTER ASSIGNMENTS

Knowledge and Understanding

Questions

1. What is a corporation, and how is it formed?
2. Identify and explain several advantages of the corporate form of business.
3. Identify and explain several disadvantages of the corporate form of business.
4. What are the organisation costs of a corporation?
5. What is the proper accounting treatment of organisation costs?
6. What is the legal capital of a corporation, and what is its significance?
7. How is the value of shares determined when shares are issued for noncash assets?
8. Describe the significance of the following dates as they relate to dividends: (a) date of declaration, (b) date of record, and (c) date of payment.

9. Explain the accounting treatment of cash dividends.
10. Define the terms *cumulative, convertible,* and *redeemable* as they apply to preference shares.
11. What are dividends in arrears, and how should they be disclosed in the financial statements?
12. What is the proper classification of the following accounts on the balance sheet? For shareholders' equity accounts, indicate whether they are share capital, retained earnings, or contra shareholders' equity: (a) Organisation Costs; (b) Ordinary Shares; (c) Treasury Stock; (d) Share Premium; and (e) Retained Earnings.
13. Define treasury stock and explain why a company would purchase its own shares.
14. What is a share option plan and why does a company have one?

Application

Exercises

LO 2 *Journal Entries for*
LO 6 *Organisation Costs*

E 10-1. The Wong Corporation was organised during 20x1. At the beginning of the accounting year, the company incurred the following organisation costs: (1) Lawyer's fees, market value of services, 6,000; paid with 2,000 ordinary shares of 2 nominal value. (2) Incorporation fees, 5,000. (3) Accountant's services that normally would be billed at 3,000; paid with 1,100 ordinary shares of 2 nominal value.

Prepare the separate journal entries necessary to record these transactions and to amortise organisation costs for the first year, assuming that the company elects to write off organisation costs over five years.

LO 3 *Shareholders' Equity*
LO 7

E 10-2. The accounts and balances below were taken from the records of Jamil Corporation on December 31, 20xx.

		Balance	
Account		Debit	Credit
Ordinary Shares—12 nominal value, 90,000 shares authorised, 60,000 shares issued, and 55,000 shares outstanding			720,000
Share Premium			340,000
Preference Shares—100 nominal value, 9% cumulative, 20,000 shares authorised, 12,000 shares issued and outstanding			1,200,000
Retained Earnings			46,000
Treasury Stock, Ordinary (5,000 shares)		110,000	

Prepare a shareholders' equity section for Jamil Corporation's balance sheet.

LO 3 *Characteristics of Ordinary*
LO 5 *and Preference Shares*

E 10-3. For each of the characteristics listed below, indicate whether it is more closely associated with ordinary shares (O) or with preference shares (P).

1. Often receives dividends at a set rate
2. Is known as the residual equity of a company
3. Can be redeemable
4. Can be convertible
5. Amount of dividend more likely to vary from year to year
6. Can be entitled to receive dividends not paid in past years
7. Likely to have full voting rights
8. Receives assets first in liquidation
9. Generally receives dividends before other classes of shares

LO 3 *Journal Entries and*
LO 6 *Shareholders' Equity*

E 10-4. The Winkler Hospital Supply Corporation was organised in 20xx. The company was authorised to issue 100,000 ordinary shares with a stated value of 5 per share, and 20,000 preference shares of 100 nominal value, 6 per cent noncumulative. On March 1 the company sold 60,000 ordinary shares for 15 per share and 8,000 preference shares for 100 per share.

1. Prepare the journal entries to record the sale of the shares.
2. Prepare the company's shareholders' equity section of the balance sheet immediately after the ordinary and preference shares were issued.

LO 4 *Cash Dividends*

E 10-5. Downey Corporation has secured authorisation for 200,000 ordinary shares of 10 nominal value. There are 160,000 shares issued and 140,000 shares outstanding. On June 5, the corporation declared a .50 per share cash dividend to be paid on June 25 to shareholders of record on June 15. Prepare the journal entries necessary to record these events.

LO 4 *Cash Dividends with*
LO 5 *Dividends in Arrears*

E 10-6. The Matsuta Corporation has 10,000 preference shares of 100 nominal value, 7 per cent cumulative outstanding, and 50,000 ordinary shares of 1 nominal value outstanding. In its first four years of operation, the board of directors of Matsuta Corporation paid cash dividends as follows: 20x1, none; 20x2, 120,000; 20x3, 140,000; 20x4, 140,000.

Determine the dividends per share and total cash dividends paid to the preference and ordinary shareholders during each of the four years.

E 10-7.

LO 4 *Preference and Ordinary*
LO 5 *Cash Dividends*

The Levinson Corporation pays dividends at the end of each year. The dividends paid for 20x1, 20x2, and 20x3 were 80,000, 60,000, and 180,000, respectively.

Calculate the total amount of dividends paid each year to the ordinary and preference shareholders if each of the following capital structures is assumed: (1) 20,000 preference shares of 100 nominal value, 6 per cent noncumulative, and 60,000 ordinary shares of 10 nominal value. (2) 10,000 preference shares of 100 nominal value, 7 per cent cumulative, and 60,000 ordinary shares of 10 nominal value. There were no dividends in arrears at the beginning of 20x1 and all shares were outstanding.

E 10-8.

LO 6 *Issuance of Shares for*
Noncash Assets

The Yang Corporation issued 2,000 ordinary shares of 20 nominal value for some land. The land had a fair market value of 60,000.

Prepare the journal entries necessary to record the share issue for the land under each of the following conditions: (1) The shares were selling for 28 per share on the day of the transaction; and (2) management attempted to place a market value on the shares but could not do so.

E 10-9.

LO 7 *Treasury Stock Transactions*

Prepare the journal entries necessary to record the following share transactions of the Henderson Company during 20xx:

May   5   Purchased 400 of its own 1 nominal value ordinary shares for 10 per share, the current market price.
17   Sold 150 shares of treasury stock purchased on May 5 for 11 per share.
21   Sold 100 shares of treasury stock purchased on May 5 for 10 per share.
28   Sold the remaining 150 shares of treasury stock purchased on May 5 for 9.50 per share.

E 10-10.

LO 8 *Exercise of Share Options*

Record the following equity transaction of the Evans Company in 20xx:

May 5   Walter Evans exercised his option to purchase 10,000 ordinary shares of 1 nominal value at an option price of 12. The market price per share was 12 on the grant date and 25 on the exercise date.

Problem Set

P 10-1.

LO 2 *Organisation Costs, Share*
LO 3 *and Dividend Journal*
LO 4 *Entries, and Shareholders'*
LO 6 *Equity*

Lasser Corporation began operations on September 1, 20xx. The corporation's charter authorised 300,000 ordinary shares of 8 nominal value. Lasser Corporation engaged in the following transactions during its first quarter:

Sept. 1   Issued 50,000 ordinary shares, 500,000.
1   Paid a lawyer 32,000 to help organise the corporation and obtain the corporate charter.
Oct.   2   Issued 80,000 ordinary shares, 960,000.
24   Issued 24,000 ordinary shares for land and a warehouse. The land and warehouse had a fair market value of 50,000 and 200,000, respectively.
Nov. 30   The corporation declared a cash dividend of .40 per share to be paid on December 15 to shareholders of record on December 10.
Nov. 30   Closed the Profit Summary and Cash Dividends Declared accounts for the first quarter. Revenues were 420,000 and expenses 340,000. (Assume revenues and expenses already have been closed to Profit Summary.)

REQUIRED

1. Prepare general journal entries to record the first quarter transactions and the closing entries.
2. Prepare the shareholders' equity section of Lasser Corporation's November 30, 20xx balance sheet.
3. Assuming that the payment to the lawyer on September 1 was going to be amortised over five years, what adjusting entry was made on November 30?
4. How does the adjusting entry in **3** affect the balance sheet, including the resulting amount of organisation costs?

P 10-2.

LO 5 *Preference and Ordinary*
Share Dividends

The Rayner Corporation had both ordinary shares and preference shares outstanding from 20x1 through 20x3. Information about each share for the three years is as follows:

Type	Nominal Value	Shares Outstanding	Other
Preference	100	40,000	7% cumulative
Ordinary	20	600,000	

The company paid 140,000, 800,000, and 1,100,000 in dividends for 20x1 through 20x3, respectively.

REQUIRED
1. Determine the dividend per share paid to the ordinary and preference shareholders each year.
2. Repeat the calculation performed in **1**, with the assumption that the preference shares were noncumulative.

P 10-3.

LO 2
LO 3 *Comprehensive Shareholders'*
Equity Transactions
LO 4
LO 5
LO 6
LO 7

The Loomis Plastics Corporation was authorised to issue 20,000 preference shares of 100 nominal value, 6 per cent, and 100,000 ordinary shares. The ordinary shares have a 2 nominal value. The share-related transactions for March and April 20xx were as follows:

Mar. 30 Issued 10,000 shares of share capital for 120,000 worth of services rendered in organising and chartering the corporation.

15 Issued 16,000 ordinary shares for land, which had an asking price of 200,000. The shares had a market value of 12 per share.

22 Issued 10,000 shares of preference shares for 1,000,000.

31 Closed the Profit Summary account. Net profit for March was 18,000.

Apr. 4 Issued 10,000 ordinary shares for 120,000.

10 Purchased 5,000 own shares for 13,000.

15 Declared a cash dividend for one month on the outstanding preference shares and .10 per share dividend on ordinary shares outstanding, payable on April 30 to shareholders of record on April 25.

25 Date of record for cash dividends.

30 Paid cash dividends.

30 Closed the Profit Summary and Cash Dividends Declared accounts. Net profit for April was 28,000.

REQUIRED
1. Prepare general journal entries for March and April.
2. Prepare the shareholders' equity section of the company's balance sheet as of April 30, 20xx.

Critical Thinking and Communication

Conceptual Mini-Case

CMC 10-1.

LO 3 *Reasons for Issuing Ordinary Shares*

For decades *Allstate Corporation,* one of the United States' largest car, home, and life insurance companies, was a division of *Sears, Roebuck.* In June 1993, the company had an initial public offering that raised $2.5 billion, as the public bought 19.9 per cent of Allstate ordinary shares for $27 per share. Sears retained 80.1 per cent of the shares. Coming off a year in which the company had paid an estimated $2.5 billion in claims as a result of Hurricane Andrew in Florida, the company expected to return to profitable operations in 1993 and 1994. Allstate's chief executive officer is quoted as saying, "Going public really focused us."[5] What advantages are there to Sears and to Allstate in raising money by issuing shares rather than bonds? Why would the chief executive officer say that going public "really focused us"?

Cultural Mini-Case

CLMC 10-1.

LO 3 *Reasons for Issuing Ordinary*
LO 6 *Shares*

In July 1993, *Tsingtao Brewery Company* was the first government-owned enterprise from the People's Republic of China (PRC) to be listed on the Hong Kong Stock Exchange. The company's shares were also later listed in Shanghai. The shares listed in Hong Kong are designated H shares and are held by foreign investors. The shares listed in Shanghai are designated A shares and are held by PRC investors. Tsingtao Brewery details its listed shares as follows:[6]

Listed Shares ('000 of nominal value, RMB 1), 1995

Renminbi Ordinary Shares of PRC investors (A shares)	100,000
Foreign Currency Shares of non-PRC investors (H shares)	346,850
	446,850

What was the purpose of issuing two classes of shares? Is it likely that more H shares will be issued in the future?

Ethics Mini-Case

EMC 10-1.

LO 1 *The Corporate Form of Business and Ethical Considerations for the Accounting Profession*

Traditionally, accounting firms have organised as partnerships. In recent years, some accounting firms have suffered large judgements as a result of lawsuits by investors who lost money when they invested in companies that went bankrupt. In one case, a large international accounting firm went bankrupt mainly because of liabilities that were anticipated to arise from problems in the savings and loan industry. The partners dissolved the firm rather than put up the additional capital needed to keep it going. Because of the increased risk of large losses from malpractice suits, there is a movement to allow accounting firms to incorporate as long as they maintain a minimum level of partners' capital and carry malpractice insurance. Some accounting practitioners feel that incorporating would be a violation of their responsibility to the public. What features of the corporate form of business would be most advantageous to the partners of an accounting firm? Do you think it would be a violation of the public trust for an accounting firm to incorporate?

Decision-Making Case

DMC 10-1.

LO 3 *Analysis of Alternative*
LO 4 *Financing Methods*
LO 5

Companies offering services to the computer technology industry are growing quickly. Participating in this growth, Infinite Systems Corporation has expanded rapidly in recent years. Because of its profitability, the company has been able to grow without obtaining external financing. This fact is reflected in its current balance sheet, which contains no long-term debt. The liability and shareholders' equity sections of the balance sheet are shown below.

The company is now faced with the possibility of doubling its size by purchasing the operations of a rival company for 8,000,000. If the purchase goes through, Infinite Systems will become the top company in its specialised industry in the northeastern part of the country. The problem for management is how to finance the purchase. After much study and discussion with bankers and underwriters, management has prepared three financing alternatives to present to the board of directors, which must authorise the purchase and the financing.

Alternative A: The company could issue 8,000,000 of long-term debt. Given the company's financial rating and the current market rates, management believes the company will have to pay an interest rate of 12 per cent on the debt.

Alternative B: The company could issue 80,000 preference shares of 10 per cent, 100 nominal value.

Alternative C: The company could issue 100,000 ordinary shares of 20 nominal value at 80 per share.

Management explains to the board that the interest on the long-term debt is tax deductible and that the applicable income tax rate is 40 per cent. The board members know that a dividend of 1.60 per ordinary share was paid last year, up from 1.20 and .80 per share in the two previous years. The board has had a policy of regular increases in dividends of .40 per share. The board feels that each of the three financing alternatives is feasible, and the board now wants to study the financial effects of each alternative.

Infinite Systems Corporation
Partial Balance Sheet

Liabilities

Current Liabilities		1,000,000

Shareholders' Equity

Ordinary Shares—20 nominal value, 500,000 shares authorised, 100,000 shares issued and outstanding	2,000,000	
Share Premium	3,600,000	
Retained Earnings	3,400,000	
Total Shareholders' Equity		9,000,000
Total Liabilities and Shareholders' Equity		10,000,000

REQUIRED

1. Prepare a schedule to show how the liabilities and shareholders' equity side of Infinite Systems' balance sheet would look under each alternative, and calculate the debt to equity ratio (total liabilities ÷ total shareholders' equity) for each.
2. Calculate and compare the cash needed to pay the interest or dividends for each kind of new financing net of income taxes in the first year.
3. How might the cash needed to pay for the financing change in future years?
4. Evaluate the alternatives, giving arguments for and against each one.

Basic Research Activity

RA 10-1.
LO 3   *Reading Corporate Annual*
LO 4   *Reports*
LO 5
LO 6
LO 8

In your library, select the annual reports of three corporations. You can choose them from the same industry, from different countries, or at the direction of your teacher. (**Note:** You will use these companies again in the Basic Research Activities in later chapters.) Prepare a table with a column for each corporation. Then answer the following questions for each corporation: Does the corporation have preference shares? If so, what are the nominal value and the indicated dividend, and is the preference share cumulative or convertible? Are the ordinary shares nominal value or no-par? What is the nominal value or stated value? What cash dividends, if any, were paid in the past year? From the notes to the financial statements, determine whether the company has an employee share option plan. What are some of its provisions? Be prepared to discuss the characteristics of the shares and dividends for your selected companies in class.

Financial Reporting and Analysis

Interpretation Cases from Business

ICB 10-1.
LO 7   *Analysis of Effects of Treasury*
       Stock Transactions

In November 1987, **Ford Motor Company** announced a plan to buy up to $2 billion of its own shares in the open market, constituting the company's second large-scale share repurchase since 1984. At the then current market price of $71.75, Ford estimated that it could purchase more than 27 million shares, which would effectively reduce the number of outstanding shares by more than 11 per cent.

The plan represented management's belief that Ford shares were undervalued and would be an exceptional investment for both the company and its shareholders. It was an action that demonstrated management's confidence in Ford's future in the highly competitive car market.

Another interpretation of the action might be that Ford had generated a tremendous amount of cash for which the company had limited investment opportunities other than its own shares. By the close of 1987, it was estimated that the company would have $8 billion in cash revenues.

On October 8, eleven days before the stock market crash of October 19, Ford proposed to shareholders a 2 for 1 share split; the new shares were expected to be issued January 12. The calculations for the buyback move were based on presplit figures. October 8 was also the day of Ford's ninth dividend increase in the past seventeen quarters; the company's quarterly dividend rose from .75 to 1.00 a share on a presplit basis.

The condensed balance sheet for Ford Motor Company on December 31, 1986 is shown below.[7]

Ford Motor Company
Condensed Balance Sheet
December 31, 1986
(in billions)

Current Assets	$18.5	Current Liabilities	$15.6
Long-Term Assets	19.4	Long-Term Liabilities	7.5
	$37.9	Shareholders' Equity	.5
		Ordinary Shares ($2 nominal value)	
		Share Premium	.6
		Retained Earnings	13.7
		Total Liabilities and Shareholders' Equity	$37.9

REQUIRED

1. Assuming that the buyback was completed as planned (before December 31, 1987), prepare the journal entry to record the purchase of treasury stock (use the total dollar amount and date given above).
2. Prepare the condensed balance sheet after the buyback in **1** was recorded, assuming that the balance immediately before the buyback was the same as the balance sheet on December 31, 1986.
3. State whether the buyback would have increased or decreased the following ratios: current ratio, debt to equity, return on assets, return on equity, and earnings per share. Also indicate whether the increase or decrease was favourable or unfavourable.

ICB 10-2.

LO 3   *Shareholders' Equity*

LO 4   *Transactions*

LO 6

LO 8

Peugeot S.A. is France's largest car maker. Its brands are Peugeot and Citroen. The company's shareholders' equity section of the balance sheet appears as follows:

	1992	1991
Shareholders' Equity (in millions of French francs)		
Ordinary shares (nominal value FF35 a share, 49,992,620 shares authorised and 49,964,000 shares issued and outstanding)	1,750	1,749
Share premium	5,214	5,203
Reserves	46,180	44,766
Total shareholders' equity	53,144	51,718

Reserves are similar to retained earnings. During 1992, the company paid FF648 million in dividends. The changes in ordinary shares and share premium represent shares issued to employees in connection with the exercise of employee share options. Prepare the journal entries to record the declaration and payment of dividends in 1992 and the issue of shares in connection with the employee share options. Assuming that dividends and net profit were the only factors that affected reserves during 1992, how much did Peugeot earn in 1992?

Nestlé Case

NC 10-1.

LO 3   *Shareholders' Equity*

LO 4

LO 7

Refer to the Annual Report in the appendix on Nestlé to answer the following questions:

1. What type of share capital does Nestlé have? What is the nominal value? How many shares are issued and outstanding at the end of 1996?
2. What is the policy of Nestlé with regard to dividends? Does the company rely mostly on shares or earnings for its shareholders' equity?

ENDNOTES

1. Lee H. Radebaugh, Günter Gebhardt, and Sidney J. Gray, "Foreign Stock Exchange Listings: A Case Study of Daimler-Benz", *Journal of International Financial Management and Accounting*, Summer 1995.
2. From *Longman Dictionary of the English Language*. Copyright© 1984. Reprinted by permission of Addison Wesley Longmen Ltd.
3. Karen Blumenthal, "J.C. Penney Plans to Buy Back Stock with ESOP Gains", *Wall Street Journal*, August 31, 1988.
4. *Sydney Morning Herald*, July 7, 1998, p. 21.
5. Hillary Durgin, "A New Hand Dealt to 1990s Allstate", *Crain's Chicago Business*, December 20, 1993.
6. Tsingtao Brewery Company, *Annual Report*, 1995.
7. Ford Motor Company, *Annual Report*, 1986.

Chapter 11

PROFIT AND RETAINED
EARNINGS

LEARNING OBJECTIVES

1. Prepare an income statement for the corporation.
2. Show the relationships among income taxes expense, deferred income taxes, and net of taxes.
3. Describe the disclosure on the income statement of discontinuing operations and extraordinary items.
4. Calculate earnings per share.
5. Define *retained earnings* and prepare a statement of retained earnings.
6. Account for share dividends and share splits.
7. Describe the disclosure of restrictions on retained earnings.
8. Prepare a statement of shareholders' equity.
9. Calculate book value per share and distinguish it from market value.

DECISION POINT

SOUTH AFRICAN BREWERIES

South African Breweries (SAB) is a company based in South Africa serving mainly the Southern African region but with growing international involvement in central Europe and China. As well as beer, SAB has interests in complementary beverages, including the bottling and distribution of Coca-Cola and Schweppes, retailing, hotels, and the manufacture and supply of selected consumer goods and services. SAB states that "The Group is committed to active participation in the setting of and regular revision of accounting standards and to the development of new and improved accounting practices. This is to ensure that the information reported to the management and the stakeholders of the Group continues to be internationally comparable, relevant and reliable."[1]

SAB provides some innovative disclosures. While earnings per share is presented on the face of the income statement consistent with International Accounting Standards, additional per share information is provided on a cash basis. Inflation adjusted (on a current replacement cost basis) per share information is also provided in a supplementary statement. Dividends and shareholders' equity per share are also presented in a seven-year financial review. This chapter examines components of the income statement, the calculation and presentation of earnings per share, and transactions impacting on retained earnings.

OBJECTIVE 1

Prepare an income statement for the corporation

The recently revised International Accounting Standard, Presentation of Financial Statements, requires a statement of shareholders' equity, including nonowner movements in equity, or a separate statement of recognised gains and losses not included in the income statement. The former is now a requirement in the United States and the latter in the United Kingdom. But in many countries, including China, Japan, Malaysia, and New Zealand, this information is not currently required to be disclosed.

PROFIT AND THE INCOME STATEMENT

This chapter briefly describes some important features of the corporate income statement and shows how certain transactions are reflected in the shareholders' equity section of the corporate balance sheet.

The International Accounting Standards Committee has not specified the format of the income statement because some flexibility has been considered more important than a standard format. Expenses may be analysed using a classification based on either the nature of the expenses (see Exhibit 11-1) or their function within the enterprise (see Exhibit 11-2). The classification of expenses by nature is often used in Europe, including France and Germany, whereas the classification by function is preferred in Australia, the United Kingdom, and the United States. Further, either the single-step or the multistep form may be used (see the chapter on financial statement objectives, presentation, and analysis).

At the same time, however, profit for a period should be all-inclusive or **comprehensive profit**. This means that the profit or loss for a period should include all revenues, expenses, gains, and losses for the accounting period. This approach to the measurement of profit has resulted in several items being added to the income statement, among them discontinuing operations and extraordinary items. A recently revised International Accounting Standard requires that there should also be a statement showing those gains and losses not currently presented in the income statement, such as revaluation and foreign currency translation adjustments, but taken directly to shareholders' equity.[2] This should be presented as a reconciliation of shareholders' equity in the statement of shareholders' equity (see discussion later in the chapter) or as a statement of performance in its own right. In addition, earnings per share figures must be disclosed on the face of the income statement.

EXHIBIT 11-1   *Illustrating the Classification of Expenses by Nature*

ABC Corporation
Income Statement
For the Year Ended December 31, 20xx

Revenues	X
Changes in Inventories of Finished Goods and Work in Progress	(X)
Work Performed by the Enterprise and Capitalised	X
Raw Material and Consumables Used	(X)
Staff Costs	(X)
Depreciation and Amortisation Expense	(X)
Other Operating Expenses	(X)
Profit from Operations	X
Finance Costs	(X)
Profit before Taxes	X
Income Taxes Expense	(X)
Profit after Taxes from Ordinary Activities	X
Extraordinary Items	X
Net Profit for the Period	X

The following sections discuss some important components of the income statement, including income taxes expense, discontinuing operations, and extraordinary items. These components are illustrated in the income statement of Jumanji Corporation (see Exhibit 11-3).

EXHIBIT 11-2   *Illustrating the Classification of Expenses by Function*

ABC Corporation
Income Statement
For the Year Ended December 31, 20xx

Revenues	X
Costs of Sales	(X)
Gross Profit	X
Distribution Costs	(X)
Administrative Expenses	(X)
Other Operating Expenses	(X)
Profit from Operations	X
Finance Costs	(X)
Profit before Taxes	X
Income Taxes Expense	(X)
Profit after Taxes from Ordinary Activities	X
Extraordinary Items	X
Net Profit for the Period	X

EXHIBIT 11-3 *A Corporate Income Statement*

Jumanji Corporation
Income Statement
For the Year Ended December 31, 20xx

Revenues		925,000
Costs of Sales		350,000
Gross Profit		575,000
Distribution Costs		(50,000)
Administrative Expenses		(80,000)
Other Operating Expenses		(20,000)
Profit from Continuing Operations before Taxes		425,000
Income Taxes Expense		119,000
Profit from Continuing Operations after Taxes		306,000
Discontinuing Operations		
Pretax Profit from Operations of Discontinuing		
Segment	125,000	
Income Taxes Expense	35,000	
	90,000	
Pretax Loss on Disposal of Segment	(115,000)	
Income Taxes Expense	42,000	
	(73,000)	17,000
Profit from Ordinary Activities		323,000
Extraordinary Gain (net of taxes, 17,000)		43,000
Net Profit		366,000
Earnings per Share		3.66

OBJECTIVE 2

Show the relationships among income taxes expense, deferred income taxes, and net of taxes

Income Taxes Expense

Corporations determine their taxable profit (the amount on which taxes are paid) by subtracting allowable business deductions from taxable gross income. The tax laws determine what business deductions are allowed and what must be included in taxable gross income.

Income taxes expense is the expense recognised in the accounting records on an accrual basis to be applicable to profit from continuing operations. This expense may or may not equal the amount of taxes actually paid by the corporation and recorded as income taxes payable in the current period. The amount payable is determined from taxable profit, which is measured according to the rules and regulations of the income tax code. For convenience, most small businesses keep accounting records on the same basis as tax records so that the income taxes expense on the income statement equals the income taxes liability to be paid to the taxation authorities. This practice is acceptable when there is no material difference between the profit on an accounting basis and the profit on an income tax basis. However, the purpose of accounting is to determine net profit in accordance with accounting standards, not to determine taxable profit and tax liability.

Management has an incentive to use methods that minimise the firm's tax liability, but accountants, who are bound by accrual accounting and the materiality concept, cannot let tax procedures dictate their method of preparing financial statements if the result would be misleading to investors. As a consequence, there can be a material difference between accounting and taxable profit, especially in larger businesses. This difference between accounting and taxable profit can result from differences in the timing of the recognition of revenues and expenses because of different methods used. Some possible alternatives are shown below.

Topic	Accounting Method	Tax Method
Expense recognition	Accrual or deferral	At time of expenditure
Accounts receivable	Allowance	Direct charge-off
Inventories	Weighted-average-cost	FIFO
Depreciation	Straight-line	Accelerated cost recovery

Deferred Income Taxes

Accounting for the difference between income taxes expense based on accounting profit and the actual income taxes payable based on taxable profit is accomplished by a method called **tax effect accounting**.[3] The amount by which income taxes expense differs from income taxes payable is reconciled in an account called **Deferred Income Taxes**. For example, suppose Jumanji Corporation shows income taxes expense of 119,000 on its income statement but has actual income taxes payable of 92,000. The entry to record the estimated income taxes expense applicable to profit from continuing operations using the tax effect accounting procedure would be as follows:

Dec. 31	Income Taxes Expense	119,000	
	Income Taxes Payable		92,000
	Deferred Income Taxes		27,000
	To record estimated current and deferred income taxes		

In other years, Income Taxes Payable may exceed Income Taxes Expense, in which case the same entry is made except that Deferred Income Taxes is debited.

When the Deferred Income Taxes account has a credit balance, which is its normal balance, it is classified as a liability on the balance sheet. Whether it is classified as a current or long-term (noncurrent) liability depends on when the timing difference is expected to reverse (to have the opposite effect). For instance, if an income tax deferral is caused by an expenditure that is deducted for income tax purposes in one year but is not an expense for accounting purposes until the next year, the deferral that is present in the first year will reverse in the second year. In this case, the income tax deferral in the first year is classified as a current liability. On the other hand, if the deferral is not expected to reverse for more than one year, the deferred income taxes are classified as a long-term liability. This situation can occur when the income tax deferral is caused by a difference in depreciation methods for items of plant and equipment that have useful lives of more than one year. In other words, an income tax liability is classified as short term or long term based on the nature of the transactions that gave rise to the deferral and the expected date of reversal.

The Deferred Income Taxes account can have a debit balance, in which case it should be classified as an asset. In this situation, the company has prepaid its income taxes because total income taxes paid exceed income taxes expensed. Classification of the debit balance as a current asset or as a long-term asset is the same as for liabilities, but the amount of the asset is subject to certain limitations, which are covered in more advanced courses.

Each year, the balance of the Deferred Income Taxes account is evaluated to determine whether it still accurately represents the expected asset or liability in light of changes in income tax laws and regulations in the current year. If changes have occurred in the income tax laws, an adjusting entry is required to bring the account balance into line with the current laws. For example, a decrease in corporate income tax rates means that a company with deferred income tax liabilities will pay less taxes in future years than indicated by the credit balance of its Deferred Income Taxes account. As a result, it would debit Deferred Income Taxes to reduce the liability and credit Gain from Reduction in Income Tax Rates. This credit increases the reported profit on the income statement. If the tax rate increases in future years, a loss would be recorded and the deferred income tax liability increased.

In any given year, the amount a company pays in income taxes is determined by subtracting (or adding, as the case may be) the deferred income taxes for that year (as reported in the notes to the financial statements) from (or to) income taxes expense, which also is reported in the notes to the financial statements. In subsequent years, the amount of deferred income taxes can vary based on changes in tax laws and rates.

Net of Taxes

The phrase **net of taxes**, as used in Exhibit 11-3 and in the discussion below, means that the effect of applicable taxes (usually income taxes) has been considered in determining the overall effect of the item on the financial statements. The phrase is used on the corporate income statement when a company has extraordinary items (such as those explained below) that must be disclosed in a separate section of the income statement. Each of these items should be reported net of the income taxes applicable to that item to avoid distorting the net operating profit figure.

For example, assume that a corporation with 120,000 operating profit before taxes has a total tax liability of 66,000 based on taxable profit, which is high because it includes a capital gain of 100,000 on which a tax of 30,000 is due. Assume also that the gain is an extraordinary item (see Extraordinary Items below) and must be disclosed as such. This is how the tax liability would be reported on the income statement:

Profit from Continuing Operations before Taxes	120,000
Income Taxes Expense (actual taxes are 66,000, of which 30,000 is applicable to extraordinary gain)	36,000
Profit before Extraordinary Item	84,000
Extraordinary Gain (net of taxes) (100,000 − 30,000)	70,000
Net Profit	154,000

If all the taxes payable were deducted from operating profit before taxes, both the profit before extraordinary items and the extraordinary gain would be distorted.

A company follows the same procedure in the case of an extraordinary loss. For example, assume the same facts as before except that total tax liability is only 6,000 because of a 100,000 extraordinary loss, which results in a 30,000 tax saving, as shown below.

Operating Profit before Taxes	120,000
Income Taxes Expense (actual taxes of 6,000 as a result of an extraordinary loss)	36,000
Profit before Extraordinary Item	84,000
Extraordinary Loss (net of taxes) (100,000 − 30,000)	(70,000)
Net Profit	14,000

In Exhibit 11-3, the total of the income tax items is 129,000. This amount is allocated among four statement components, as follows:

Income taxes expense on profit from continuing operations	119,000
Income tax on profit from a discontinuing segment	35,000
Income tax saving on the loss on disposal of the segment	(42,000)
Income tax on the extraordinary gain	17,000
Total income taxes expense	129,000

Because of the complexity of the corporate income statement, analysts have learned not to look at just the bottom line but to study carefully the components of the income statement to discover the long-term outlook for the company.

OBJECTIVE 3

Describe the disclosure on the income statement of discontinuing operations and extraordinary items

Discontinuing Operations

Large companies usually have many **segments**. A segment of a business can be a separate major line of business or serve a separate class of customer. For example, a company that makes heavy drilling equipment may also have another line of business, such as the manufacture of mobile homes. These large companies may discontinue or otherwise dispose of certain segments of their business that do not fit in with the company's future plans or are not profitable. **Discontinuing operations** are segments of a business that are no longer part of its ongoing operations. The International Accounting Standards Committee requires that the pretax gains and losses from discontinuing operations be reported separately in the income statement.[4] The reason for this requirement is that the income statement is more useful for evaluating the ongoing activities of the business if results from continuing operations are reported separately from those of discontinuing operations.

In Exhibit 11-3, the disclosure of discontinuing operations has two parts. One part shows that the profit during the year from operations of the segment of the business that has been disposed of (or will be disposed of) after the date of the decision to discontinue was 90,000 (net of 35,000 taxes). Therefore the original pretax profit was 125,000, the 90,000 net after tax profit plus the 35,000 taxes paid. The other part shows that the loss from the disposal of the segment was 73,000 (net of 42,000 tax savings). Therefore the original pretax loss was 115,000, the 73,000 net after tax loss plus the 42,000 tax saving. Discontinuing operations should not be presented as an extraordinary item. Calculation of the gains or losses is covered in more advanced accounting courses. The disclosure has been described, however, to give a complete view of the corporate income statement.

Extraordinary Items

The International Accounting Standards Committee defines **extraordinary items** as "income or expenses that arise from events or transactions that are clearly distinct from the ordinary activities of the enterprise and therefore are not expected to recur frequently or regularly".[5] As stated in the definition, the major criteria for extraordinary items are that they must be unusual and must not happen very often. If an item is both unusual and infrequent (and material in amount), it should be reported separately from continuing operations on the income statement. This disclosure allows the user of the statement to identify gains or losses shown in the calculation of profit that would not be expected to happen again soon. Items that usually are treated as extraordinary include (1) an uninsured loss from flood, earthquake, fire, or theft; (2) a gain or loss resulting from the passage of a new law; (3) the expropriation (taking) of property by a foreign government; and (4) a gain or loss from early retirement of debt. Gains or losses from extraordinary items should be reported on the income statement after discontinuing operations. They should be shown net of applicable taxes. In Exhibit 11-3, the extraordinary gain was 43,000 after applicable taxes of 17,000.

OBJECTIVE 4

Calculate earnings per share

EARNINGS PER SHARE

Users of financial statements use earnings per share information to judge a company's performance and to compare that performance over time. The International Accounting Standards Committee recognises the importance of this information and has concluded that earnings per share should be presented on the face of the income statement.[6] As shown in Exhibit 11-3, the information generally is disclosed just below the net profit figure.

While earnings per share is recognised as an important disclosure item in countries with highly developed stock markets such as Japan and the United States, many countries, including China, Germany, and New Zealand, do not have requirements as yet.

An earnings per share amount may also be shown for (1) profit from continuing operations, (2) profit from ordinary activities, and (3) net profit. If the statement shows a gain or loss from discontinuing operations or a gain or loss on extraordinary items, earnings per share amounts also can be presented for these items.

A basic earnings per share amount is found when a company has only ordinary shares and has the same number of shares outstanding throughout the year. For example, Exhibit 11-3 tells us that Jumanji Corporation, with a net profit of 366,000, had 100,000 ordinary shares outstanding for the entire year. The earnings per share were calculated as follows:

$$\text{Earnings per share} = \frac{\text{net profit}}{\text{shares outstanding}}$$

$$= \frac{366,000}{100,000 \text{ shares}}$$

$$= 3.66 \text{ per share}$$

If the number of shares outstanding changes during the year, it is necessary to calculate a weighted-average number of shares outstanding for the year. Suppose that Jumanji Corporation had the following numbers of shares outstanding during various periods of the year: January–March, 100,000 shares; April–September, 120,000 shares; and October–December, 130,000 shares. The weighted-average number of ordinary shares outstanding and earnings per share would be found this way:

100,000 shares × ¼ year	25,000
120,000 shares × ½ year	60,000
130,000 shares × ¼ year	32,500
Weighted-average shares outstanding	117,500

$$\text{Earnings per share} = \frac{366,000}{117,500 \text{ shares}}$$

$$= 3.11 \text{ per share}$$

If a company has nonconvertible preference shares outstanding, the dividend for the shares must be subtracted from net profit before earnings per share are calculated. Suppose that Jumanji Corporation has preference shares on which the annual dividend is 23,500. Earnings per share on the ordinary shares would be 2.91 [(366,000 − 23,500) ÷ 117,500 shares].

Companies with a capital structure in which there are no bonds, preference shares, or share options that could be converted into ordinary shares are said to have a

BUSINESS BULLETIN   **Business Practice**

Earnings per share is probably the most widely used performance statistic for listed companies. The calculation and disclosure of earnings per share are important because users of financial statements rely on this information to evaluate the earnings performance of a company relative to the market value of the shares, which embodies an assessment of future earnings. This relationship is known as the price/earnings (P/E) ratio. Financial analysts often use a multiple of earnings as a means of approximating market value, so any change in reported earnings per share is likely to indicate a change in future earnings and hence market value. In general, the P/E ratio may be viewed as a summary indicator of the stockmarket's perception of the earnings generating power of a company.

simple capital structure. The earnings per share for these companies are calculated as shown previously. Some companies, however, have a complex capital structure, which includes convertible shares and bonds. These convertible securities have the potential of diluting the earnings per share of ordinary shares. *Potential dilution* means that a person's proportionate share of ownership in a company could be reduced through a conversion of preference shares or bonds or the exercise of share options, which would increase the total shares outstanding.

For example, suppose that a person owns 10,000 shares of a company, which equals 2 per cent of the outstanding shares of 500,000. Now, suppose that holders of convertible bonds convert the bonds into 100,000 shares. The person's 10,000 shares then would be only 1.67 per cent (10,000 ÷ 600,000) of the outstanding shares. And the added shares outstanding would lower earnings per share and most likely would lower market price per share.

Because share options and convertible preference shares or bonds have the potential to dilute earnings per share, they are referred to as **potential ordinary shares.**

When a company has a complex capital structure, it must report two earnings per share figures: basic earnings per share and diluted earnings per share. **Basic earnings per share** are calculated by including in the denominator the total of weighted-average ordinary shares outstanding. **Diluted earnings per share** are calculated by including in the denominator the additional potential ordinary shares. The latter figure shows shareholders the maximum potential effect of dilution of their ownership in the company. The calculation of these figures is a complex process reserved for more advanced courses.

OBJECTIVE 5

Define retained earnings *and prepare a statement of retained earnings*

RETAINED EARNINGS TRANSACTIONS

Shareholders' equity, as presented earlier, has two parts: share capital and retained earnings. The **retained earnings** of a company are the part of shareholders' equity that represents claims to assets arising from the earnings of the business. Retained earnings equal a company's profits since the date of its inception, less any losses, dividends to shareholders, or transfers to share capital. Exhibit 11-4 shows a statement of retained earnings for Blackrock Corporation for 20x2. The beginning balance of retained earnings of 854,000 is increased by net profit of 76,000 and decreased by cash dividends of 30,000. The ending balance is 900,000. The statement of retained earnings also can disclose other transactions that are explained in this chapter.

It is important to remember that retained earnings are not the assets themselves. The existence of retained earnings means that assets generated by profitable operations have been kept in the company to help it grow or to meet other business needs.

EXHIBIT 11-4 *A Statement of Retained Earnings*

Blackrock Corporation
Statement of Retained Earnings
For the Year Ended December 31, 20x2

Retained Earnings, December 31, 20x1	854,000
Net Profit, 20x2	76,000
Subtotal	930,000
Less Cash Dividends	30,000
Retained Earnings, December 31, 20x2	900,000

A credit balance in Retained Earnings does not mean that cash or any designated set of assets is associated directly with retained earnings. The fact that earnings have been retained means that assets as a whole have been increased.

Retained Earnings can carry a debit balance. Generally, this happens when a company's dividends and subsequent losses are greater than its accumulated profits from operations. In such a case, the firm is said to have a deficit (debit balance) in Retained Earnings. A deficit is shown in the shareholders' equity section of the balance sheet as a deduction from share capital.

Fundamental errors are errors that relate to prior periods and are of such significance that the financial statements of one or more prior periods can no longer be considered to have been reliable. When they become known, corrections are shown on the statement of retained earnings as an adjustment to the beginning balance or, alternatively, are shown in the current year's income statement.

OBJECTIVE 6

Account for share dividends and share splits

Share Dividends

A **share dividend**, or bonus issue, is a proportional distribution of the corporation's shares to its shareholders. The distribution of shares does not change the assets or liabilities of the firm because there is no distribution of assets as there is when a cash dividend is distributed.

The board of directors may declare a share dividend for several reasons:

1. It may want to give shareholders some evidence of the success of the company without paying a cash dividend, which would affect the firm's working capital position.
2. It may seek to reduce the market price of the shares by increasing the number of shares outstanding, although this goal more often is met by share splits.
3. It may want to make a nontaxable distribution to shareholders. Share dividends that meet certain conditions are not considered profit and so are not taxed.
4. It communicates that the permanent capital of the company has increased by transferring an amount from retained earnings to share capital.

The total shareholders' equity is not affected by a share dividend. The effect of a share dividend is to transfer an amount from retained earnings to the share capital section on the date of declaration. The amount transferred is the fair market value (usually, the market price) of the additional shares to be issued. The laws of most countries specify the minimum value of each share transferred under a share dividend, which is normally the minimum legal capital (nominal or stated value). However, market value reflects the economic effect of small share distributions (less than 20 to 25 per cent of a company's outstanding ordinary shares) better than nominal or stated value does. For this reason, market price should be used to account for small share dividends.

To illustrate the accounting for a share dividend, we assume that Blackrock Corporation has the following shareholders' equity structure:

Share Capital	
Ordinary Shares—5 nominal value, 100,000 shares authorised, 30,000 shares issued and outstanding	150,000
Share Premium	30,000
Total Share Capital	180,000
Retained Earnings	900,000
Total Shareholders' Equity	1,080,000

Suppose that the corporation's board of directors declares a 10 per cent share dividend on February 24, distributable on March 31 to shareholders of record on March 15, and that the market price of the shares on February 24 is 20 per share. The entries to record the share dividend declaration and distribution are as follows:

Date of Declaration

Feb. 24	Share Dividends Declared	60,000	
	Ordinary Shares Distributable		15,000
	Share Premium		45,000

                Declared a 10% share dividend
                on ordinary shares, distributable on
                March 31 to shareholders of record
                on March 15:

                30,000 shares $\times$ .10   = 3,000 shares
                 3,000 shares $\times$ 20/share = 60,000
                 3,000 shares $\times$ 5/share = 15,000

The Share Dividends Declared account is used to record share dividends; the Cash Dividends Declared account is used for cash dividends, as shown in the chapter on share capital. Retained Earnings is reduced by the amount of the share dividend by closing the Share Dividends Declared account to Retained Earnings at the end of the accounting period in the same way that Cash Dividends Declared is closed.

Date of Record

Mar. 15	No entry required

Date of Distribution

Mar. 31	Ordinary Shares Distributable	15,000	
	Ordinary Shares		15,000
	Distributed a share dividend of		
	3,000 shares		

    The effect of this share dividend is to transfer permanently the market value of the shares, 60,000, from retained earnings to share capital and to increase the number of shares outstanding by 3,000. Ordinary Shares Distributable is credited for the nominal value of the shares to be distributed (3,000 $\times$ 5 = 15,000). In addition, when the market value is greater than the nominal value of the shares, Share Premium must be credited for the amount by which the market value exceeds the nominal value. In this case, the total market value of the share dividend (60,000) exceeds the total nominal value (15,000) by 45,000. No entry is required on the date of record. On the distribution date, the ordinary shares are issued by debiting Ordinary Shares Distributable and crediting Ordinary Shares for the nominal value of the shares (15,000).

    Ordinary Shares Distributable is not a liability because there is no obligation to distribute cash or other assets. The obligation is to distribute additional shares. If financial statements are prepared between the date of declaration and the distribution of shares, Ordinary Shares Distributable should be reported as part of share capital.

Share Capital	
Ordinary Shares—5 nominal value, 100,000 shares	
authorised, 30,000 shares issued and outstanding	150,000
Ordinary Shares Distributable, 3,000 shares	15,000
Share Premium	75,000
Total Share Capital	240,000
Retained Earnings	840,000
Total Shareholders' Equity	1,080,000

    Three points can be made from this example. First, the total shareholders' equity is the same before and after the share dividend. Second, the assets of the corporation are not reduced as in the case of a cash dividend. Third, the proportionate ownership in the corporation of any individual shareholder is the same before and after the share dividend. To illustrate these points, assume that a shareholder owns 1,000 shares before the share dividend. After the 10 per cent share dividend is distributed, this shareholder would own 1,100 shares.

Shareholders' Equity	Before Dividend	After Dividend
Ordinary Shares	150,000	165,000
Share Premium	30,000	75,000
Total Share Capital	180,000	240,000
Retained Earnings	900,000	840,000
Total Shareholders' Equity	1,080,000	1,080,000
Shares Outstanding	30,000	33,000
Shareholders' Equity per share	36.00	32.73
Shareholders' Investment		
Shares owned	1,000	1,100
Shares outstanding	30,000	33,000
Percentage of ownership	3⅓%	3⅓%
Proportionate investment (1,080,000 × .03⅓)	36,000	36,000

Both before and after the share dividend, the shareholders' equity totals 1,080,000 and the shareholder owns 3⅓ per cent of the company. The proportionate investment (shareholders' equity times percentage ownership) stays at 36,000.

All share dividends have an effect on the market price of a company's shares. But some share dividends are so large that they have a material effect on the price per share. For example, a 50 per cent share dividend would cause the market price of the shares to drop about 33 per cent because there is a one-third increase in the number of shares outstanding.

Share Splits

A **share split** occurs when a corporation increases the number of issued shares and reduces the nominal or stated value proportionally. A company may plan a share split when it wants to lower the market value per share of its shares and increase the liquidity of the shares. This action may be necessary if the market value per share has become so high that it hinders the trading of the company's shares.

To illustrate a share split, suppose that Blackrock Corporation has 30,000 5.00 nominal value shares outstanding. The market value is 70.00 per share. The corporation plans a 2 for 1 split. This split will lower the nominal value to 2.50 and increase the number of shares outstanding to 60,000. A shareholder who previously owned 400 shares of the 5.00 nominal value shares would own 800 shares of the 2.50 nominal value shares after the split. When a share split occurs, the market value tends to fall in proportion to the increase in outstanding shares. For example, a 2 for 1 share split would cause the price of the shares to drop by approximately 50 per cent, to about 35.00. It would also halve earnings per share and cash dividends per share (if the board does not increase the dividend). The lower price plus the increase in shares tend to promote the buying and selling of shares.

A share split does not increase the number of shares authorised. Nor does it change the balances in the shareholders' equity section of the balance sheet. It simply changes the nominal value and the number of shares issued, both those that are outstanding and those that are held as treasury stock. Therefore, an entry is not necessary. However, it is appropriate to document the change by making a memorandum entry in the general journal:

July 15   The 30,000 ordinary shares of 5 nominal value that are issued and outstanding were split 2 for 1, resulting in 60,000 ordinary shares of 2.50 nominal value issued and outstanding.

Although the amount of shareholders' equity per share would be half as much, each shareholder's proportionate interest in the company would remain the same.

| OBJECTIVE 7 | RESTRICTIONS ON RETAINED EARNINGS |

Describe the disclosure of restrictions on retained earnings

A corporation may be required or want to restrict all or a portion of retained earnings. A **restriction on retained earnings** means that dividends can be declared only to the extent of the *unrestricted* retained earnings. The following are several reasons a company might restrict retained earnings:

1. A *contractual agreement*. For example, bond covenants may place a limitation on the dividends the company can pay.
2. *Company law*. Many countries do not allow a corporation to distribute dividends or purchase treasury stock if doing so impairs the legal capital of the company.
3. *Voluntary action by the board of directors*. Many times a board decides to retain assets in the business for future needs. For example, the company may be planning to build a new plant and may want to show that dividends will be limited to save enough money for the building. A company also might restrict retained earnings to prepare for a possible future loss of assets resulting from a lawsuit.

There are two ways of reporting restrictions on retained earnings to the users of financial statements: a restriction can be shown in the shareholders' equity section of the balance sheet, or it can be disclosed in a note to the financial statements.

A restriction on retained earnings does not change the total retained earnings or shareholders' equity of the company. It simply divides retained earnings into two parts, restricted and unrestricted. Assets in the restricted part cannot be used to pay dividends. The unrestricted amount represents earnings kept in the business that the company can use for dividends and other purposes.

Assuming that Blackrock's board of directors has decided to restrict 300,000 in retained earnings because of plans for plant expansion, the disclosure in Blackrock's shareholders' equity section would be as follows:

Share Capital		
Ordinary Shares—5 nominal value, 100,000 shares authorised, 30,000 shares issued and outstanding		150,000
Share Premium		30,000
Total Share Capital		180,000
Retained Earnings		
Restricted for Plant Expansion	300,000	
Unrestricted	600,000	
Total Retained Earnings		900,000
Total Shareholders' Equity		1,080,000

The same facts about restricted retained earnings also could be presented by reference to a note to the financial statements. For example:

Retained Earnings (Note 15)	900,000

Note 15: Because of plans to expand the capacity of the clothing division, the board of directors has restricted retained earnings available for dividends by 300,000.

Notice that the restriction of retained earnings does not restrict cash or other assets in any way. It simply explains to the users of the financial statements that a certain amount of assets generated by earnings will remain in the business for the purpose stated. It is still management's job to make sure that there is enough cash or assets available to fulfil the purpose. Also, the removal of a restriction does not necessarily mean that the board of directors is now able to declare a dividend.

| OBJECTIVE 8 | THE STATEMENT OF SHAREHOLDERS' EQUITY |

Prepare a statement of shareholders' equity

The **statement of shareholders' equity**, also called the statement of changes in shareholders' equity, summarises the changes in the components of the shareholders' equity section of the balance sheet. The International Accounting Standards Committee requires this statement because it reveals much about the year's shareholders' equity transactions. In Exhibit 11-5, for example, the first line of the Tucci Corporation's statement of shareholders' equity contains the beginning balance (the last period's ending balance) of each account in the shareholders' equity section. Each additional line in the statement discloses the effects of transactions that affect the accounts. It is possible to determine from this statement that during 20x2 Tucci Corporation issued 5,000 ordinary shares for 250,000, had a conversion of 100,000 of preference shares into ordinary shares, declared and issued a 10 per cent share dividend on ordinary shares, had a net purchase of treasury stock of 24,000, earned net profit of 270,000, and paid cash dividends on both preference and ordinary shares. The ending balances of the accounts are presented at the bottom of the statement. These accounts and balances make up the shareholders' equity section of Tucci's balance sheet on December 31, 20x2, as shown in Exhibit 11-5.

EXHIBIT 11-5 *A Statement of Shareholders' Equity*

Tucci Corporation
Statement of Shareholders' Equity
For the Year Ended December 31, 20x2

	Preference Shares 100 Nominal Value 8% Convertible	Ordinary Shares 10 Nominal Value	Share Premium	Retained Earnings	Treasury Stock	Total
Balance, December 31, 20x1	400,000	300,000	300,000	600,000	—	1,600,000
Issuance of 5,000 Ordinary Shares		50,000	200,000			250,000
Conversion of 1,000 Preference Shares into 3,000 Ordinary Shares	(100,000)	30,000	70,000			—
10% Share Dividend on 3,800 Ordinary Shares		38,000	152,000	(190,000)		—
Purchase of 500 Shares of Treasury Stock					(24,000)	(24,000)
Net Profit				270,000		270,000
Cash Dividends						
Preference Shares				(24,000)		(24,000)
Ordinary Shares				(47,600)		(47,600)
Balance, December 31, 20x2	300,000	418,000	722,000	608,400	(24,000)	2,024,400

Share Values

The word *value* is associated with shares in several ways. As noted earlier, both *nominal or par value* and *stated value* are values per share that establish the legal capital of a company. Nominal value or stated value is set arbitrarily when the shares are authorised. Neither has any relationship to a share's book or market value.

OBJECTIVE 9

Calculate book value per share and distinguish it from market value

Book Value of Shares

A company's **book value of shares** represents the total assets of the company less its liabilities. It is simply the shareholders' equity of the company or, to look at it another way, the company's net assets. The book value per share, therefore, represents the equity of the owner of one share in the net assets of the corporation. This value, of course, does not necessarily equal the amount the shareholder would receive if the company were sold or liquidated. It is probably different because most assets are recorded at historical cost, not at the current value at which they could be sold.

To determine the book value per share when the company has only ordinary shares outstanding, divide the total shareholders' equity by the total ordinary shares outstanding. In calculating the shares outstanding, ordinary shares distributable are included, but treasury stock (shares previously issued and now held by the company) is not included. For example, suppose that Blackrock Corporation has total shareholders' equity of 1,030,000 and 29,000 shares outstanding after recording the purchase of treasury stock. The book value per share of Blackrock's ordinary shares is 35.52 (1,030,000 ÷ 29,000 shares).

If a company has both preference and ordinary shares, the determination of book value per share is not so simple. The general rule is that the redeemable value of the preference shares plus any dividends in arrears is subtracted from total shareholders' equity to calculate the equity pertaining to the ordinary shares. As an illustration, refer to the shareholders' equity section of Tucci Corporation's balance sheet in Exhibit 11-6. Assuming that there are no dividends in arrears and the preference shares are redeemable at 105, the equity pertaining to ordinary shares is calculated as shown below.

Total shareholders' equity	2,024,400
Less equity allocated to preference shareholders (3,000 shares × 105)	315,000
Equity pertaining to ordinary shareholders	1,709,400

There are 41,300 ordinary shares outstanding (41,800 shares issued less 500 shares of treasury stock). The book values per share are as follows:

Preference Shares: 315,000 ÷ 3,000 shares = 105 per share
Ordinary Shares: 1,709,400 ÷ 41,300 shares = 41.39 per share

BUSINESS BULLETIN   Business Practice

In a dramatic demonstration that investor expectations of earnings per share drive the market value of a company's shares, Eastman Kodak's share price plunged nearly 12 per cent in one day, from $63 to $55.50 per share, after George Fisher, then the new chairman, warned financial analysts that their 1994 earnings estimates were too high. Fisher said that cost cutting alone would not overcome Kodak's poor showing in recent years and the company would have to build a foundation for growth. Analysts had thought Fisher would move faster to improve earnings. They revised their earnings estimates downward, which would negatively affect the share price over the next year.[7]

EXHIBIT 11-6 *Shareholders' Equity Section of a Balance Sheet*

Tucci Corporation
Shareholders' Equity
December 31, 20x2

Share Capital		
Ordinary Shares—10 nominal value, 100,000 shares authorised, 41,800 shares issued, 41,300 shares outstanding	418,000	
Share Premium	722,000	1,140,000
Preference Shares—100 nominal value, 8% convertible, 10,000 shares authorised, 3,000 shares issued and outstanding		300,000
Total Share Capital		1,440,000
Retained Earnings		608,400
Total Share Capital and Retained Earnings		2,048,400
Less Treasury Stock, Ordinary (500 shares, at cost)		24,000
Total Shareholders' Equity		2,024,400

If we assume the same facts except that the preference shares are 8 per cent cumulative and that one year of dividends is in arrears, the shareholders' equity would be allocated as follows:

Total shareholders' equity		2,024,400
Less: Redeemable value of outstanding preference shares	315,000	
Dividends in arrears (300,000 × .08)	24,000	
Equity allocated to preference shareholders		339,000
Equity pertaining to ordinary shareholders		1,685,400

The book values per share here are as follows:

Preference Shares: 339,000 ÷ 3,000 shares = 113 per share
Ordinary Shares: 1,685,400 ÷ 41,300 shares = 40.81 per share

Market Value of Shares

Market value of shares is the price that investors are willing to pay for a share on the open market. Whereas book value is based on historical cost, market value is usually determined by investors' expectations for the particular company and general economic conditions. That is, people's expectations about the company's future profitability and dividends per share, their perceptions of the risk attached to the company and of its current financial condition, and the state of the money market all play a part in determining the market value of a corporation's shares. Although book value per share often bears little relationship to market value per share, some investors use the relationship between the two measures as a rough indicator of the value added by management to the book value of a company's assets. For example, in early 1991, a large U.S. car company, Chrysler Corporation, had a market value per share of $14 and a book value per share of $31. By early 1994, the book value per share had dropped to $26 because of losses, but the market value of the shares in New York had climbed to $54. Other factors being equal, investors were more optimistic about Chrysler's prospects of earnings generation in 1994 than they were in 1991.

CHAPTER REVIEW

Review of Learning Objectives

1. **Prepare an income statement for the corporation.** The corporate income statement shows comprehensive profit—all revenues, expenses, gains, and losses for the accounting period. The top part of the corporate income statement includes all revenues, costs and expenses, and income taxes that apply to continuing operations. The bottom part of the statement may contain information about discontinuing operations and extraordinary items. Earnings per share data should be shown at the bottom of the statement, below net profit.

2. **Show the relationships among income taxes expense, deferred income taxes, and net of taxes.** Income taxes expense is the taxes applicable to profit from operations on an accrual basis. Tax effect accounting is necessary when differences between accrual-based accounting profit and taxable profit cause a material difference between income taxes expense as shown on the income statement and actual income tax liability. The difference between income taxes expense and income taxes payable is debited or credited to an account called Deferred Income Taxes. Net of taxes is a phrase used to indicate that the effect of taxes has been considered when showing an item on the income statement after profit from continuing operations.

3. **Describe the disclosure on the income statement of discontinuing operations and extraordinary items.** There are several accounting items that must be disclosed separately from continuing operations and net of income taxes on the income statement because of their unusual nature. These items include a gain or loss on discontinuing operations and on extraordinary gains or losses.

4. **Calculate earnings per share.** Shareholders and other users of financial statements use earnings per share data to evaluate a company's performance and to compare that performance with the performance of other companies. Therefore, earnings per share data are presented on the face of the income statement. The amounts are calculated by dividing the profit applicable to ordinary shares by the ordinary shares outstanding for the year. If the number of shares outstanding has varied during the year, then the weighted-average shares outstanding should be used in the calculation. When the company has a complex capital structure, both basic and diluted earnings per share data must be disclosed on the face of the income statement.

5. **Define *retained earnings* and prepare a statement of retained earnings.** Retained earnings are the part of shareholders' equity that comes from retaining assets earned in business operations. They represent the claims of the shareholders against the assets of the company that arise from profitable operations. Retained earnings are different from share capital, which represents the claims against assets brought about by the initial and subsequent investments by the shareholders. Both are claims against the general assets of the company, not against any specific assets that have been set aside. It is important not to confuse the assets themselves with the claims against the assets. The statement of retained earnings always shows the beginning and ending balance of retained earnings, net profit or loss, and cash dividends. It also can show other transactions that affect retained earnings.

6. **Account for share dividends and share splits.** A share dividend is a proportional distribution of shares by a corporation to its shareholders. Here is a summary of the key dates and accounting treatment of share dividends:

Key Date	Share Dividend
Date of declaration	Debit Share Dividends Declared for the market value of the shares to be distributed (if it is a small share dividend), and credit Ordinary Shares Distributable for the share's nominal value and Share Premium for the excess of the market value over the share's nominal value.
Date of record	No entry.
Date of distribution	Debit Ordinary Shares Distributable and credit Ordinary Shares for the nominal value of the shares that have been distributed.

A share split usually is undertaken to reduce the market value and improve the liquidity of a company's shares. Because there is normally a decrease in the nominal value of the shares in proportion to the number of additional shares issued, a share split has no effect on the amounts in the shareholders' equity accounts. The split should be recorded in the general journal by a memorandum entry only.

7. **Describe the disclosure of restrictions on retained earnings.** A restriction on retained earnings means that dividends can be declared only to the extent of unrestricted retained earnings. A corporation may be bound by contractual agreement or the company law of accounting to restrict retained earnings, or it may do so voluntarily, to retain assets in the business for a plant expansion or a possible loss in a lawsuit. A restriction on retained earnings can be disclosed in two ways: in the shareholders' equity section of the balance sheet or, more commonly, as a note to the financial statements. Once a restriction is removed, its disclosure can be removed from the financial statements.

8. **Prepare a statement of shareholders' equity.** A statement of shareholders' equity shows changes over the period in each component (account) of the shareholders' equity section of the balance sheet. This statement reveals much about the transactions that adjust shareholders' equity.

9. **Calculate book value per share and distinguish it from market value.** Book value per share is the shareholders' equity per share. It is calculated by dividing shareholders' equity by the number of ordinary shares outstanding plus shares distributable. When a company has both preference and ordinary shares, the redeemable or nominal value of the preference shares plus any dividends in arrears is deducted from total shareholders' equity before dividing by the ordinary shares outstanding. Market value per share is the price investors are willing to pay based on their expectations about the future earning ability of the company and general economic conditions.

Review of Concepts and Terminology

The following concepts and terms were introduced in this chapter.

LO 4 **Basic earnings per share:** The net profit applicable to ordinary shares divided by the sum of the weighted average of ordinary shares outstanding.

LO 9 **Book value of shares:** The total assets of a company less its liabilities, i.e. the shareholders' equity or net assets per share as recorded in the accounts.

LO 4 **Complex capital structure:** A capital structure that includes securities (convertible preference shares and bonds) that can be converted into ordinary shares.

LO 1 **Comprehensive profit:** Profit or loss for a period that includes all revenues, expenses, gains, and losses.

LO 2 **Deferred Income Taxes:** The account used to record the difference between the Income Taxes Expense and the Income Taxes Payable accounts.

LO 4 **Diluted earnings per share:** The net profit applicable to ordinary shares divided by the sum of the weighted average of ordinary shares outstanding and potential ordinary shares.

LO 3 **Discontinuing operations:** Segments of a business that are no longer part of the ongoing operations of the company.

LO 3 **Extraordinary items:** Events or transactions clearly distinct from ordinary activities of the enterprise and therefore not expected to recur frequently or regularly.

LO 5 **Fundamental errors:** Errors that relate to earlier accounting periods and are of such significance that the financial statements of earlier periods are no longer considered reliable.

LO 9 **Market value of shares:** The price investors are willing to pay for a share on the open market.

LO 2 **Net of taxes:** Taking into account the effect of applicable taxes (usually income taxes) on an item to determine the overall effect of the item on the financial statements.

LO 4 **Potential ordinary shares:** Share options and convertible preference shares or bonds, which have the potential to dilute earnings per share.

LO 7 **Restriction on retained earnings:** The required or voluntary restriction of a portion of retained earnings that cannot be used to pay dividends.

LO 5 **Retained earnings:** Shareholders' claims to assets arising from the earnings of the business; the accumulated earnings of a corporation from its inception, minus any losses, dividends, or transfers to share capital.

LO 3 **Segments:** Distinct parts of business operations, such as lines of business or classes of customer.

LO 6 **Share dividend:** A proportional distribution of a corporation's shares to its shareholders; also called *bonus issue*.

LO 6 **Share split:** An increase in the number of outstanding shares accompanied by a proportionate reduction in the nominal or stated value.

LO 4 **Simple capital structure:** A capital structure with no other securities (shares or bonds) or share options that can be converted into ordinary shares.

LO 8 **Statement of shareholders' equity:** A financial statement that summarises changes in the components of the shareholders' equity section of the balance sheet; also called *statement of changes in shareholders' equity*.

LO 2 **Tax effect accounting:** An accounting method used to accrue income taxes expense on the basis of accounting profit whenever accounting and taxable profit differ.

Review Problem

Comprehensive Shareholders' Equity Transactions

LO 5
LO 6
LO 7
LO 8
LO 9

The shareholders' equity of the Szatkowski Company on June 30, 20x1 is shown below.

Share Capital	
Ordinary Shares—no-par value, 6 stated value, 1,000,000 shares authorised, 250,000 shares issued and outstanding	1,500,000
Share Premium	820,000
Total Share Capital	2,320,000
Retained Earnings	970,000
Total Shareholders' Equity	3,290,000

Shareholders' equity transactions for the next accounting year were as follows:

a. The board of directors declared a 2 for 1 split.

b. The board of directors obtained authorisation to issue 50,000 preference shares of 100 nominal value, 6 per cent noncumulative, redeemable at 104.

c. Issued 12,000 ordinary shares for a building valued at 96,000.

d. Purchased 8,000 of the company's ordinary shares for 64,000.

e. Issued 20,000 preference shares of 100 nominal value for 100 per share.

f. Sold 5,000 shares of the treasury stock for 35,000.

g. Declared cash dividends of 6 per share on preference shares and .20 on ordinary shares.

h. Date of record.

i. Paid the preference and ordinary shares cash dividends.

j. Declared a 10 per cent share dividend on the ordinary shares. The market value was 10 per share. The share dividend is distributable after the end of the accounting year.

k. Net profit for the year was 340,000.

l. Closed the Cash Dividends Declared and Share Dividends Declared accounts to Retained Earnings.

Because of a loan agreement, the company is not allowed to reduce retained earnings below 100,000. The board of directors determined that this restriction should be disclosed in the notes to the financial statements.

REQUIRED   1. Make the general journal entries to record the transactions above.

2. Prepare the company's statement of retained earnings for the year ended June 30, 20x2.

3. Prepare the shareholders' equity section of the company's balance sheet on June 30, 20x2, including appropriate disclosure of the restriction on retained earnings.

4. Calculate the book values of ordinary shares on June 30, 20x1 and 20x2, and of preference shares on June 30, 20x2.

Answer to Review Problem

1. Prepare the journal entries.

a. Memorandum entry: 2 for 1 share split, ordinary, resulting in 500,000 shares issued and outstanding of no-par value ordinary shares with a stated value of 3

b. No entry required

c. Building	96,000	
Ordinary Shares		36,000
Share Premium		60,000
Issue of 12,000 ordinary shares for a building valued at 96,000		

d. Treasury Stock, Ordinary	64,000	
Cash		64,000
Purchase of 8,000 ordinary shares for the treasury for 8 per share		

e. Cash	2,000,000	
Preference Shares		2,000,000
Sale of 20,000 preference shares of 100 nominal value at 100 per share		

f. Cash	35,000	
Retained Earnings	5,000	
Treasury Stock, Ordinary		40,000
Sale of 5,000 shares of treasury stock for 35,000, originally purchased for 8 per share		

g. Cash Dividends Declared	221,800	
Cash Dividends Payable		221,800
Declaration of cash dividends of 6 per share on 20,000 preference shares and .20 per share on 509,000 ordinary shares:		

$$20,000 \times 6 \quad = \quad 120,000$$
$$509,000 \times .20 = \quad \underline{101,800}$$
$$\quad\quad\quad\quad\quad\quad \overline{\overline{221,800}}$$

h. No entry required

i. Cash Dividends Payable	221,800	
Cash		221,800
Paid cash dividend to preference and ordinary shareholders		

j. Share Dividends Declared	509,000	
Ordinary Shares Distributable		152,700
Share Premium		356,300
Declaration of a 50,900-share dividend (509,000 × .10) on 3 stated value ordinary shares at a market value of 509,000 (50,900 × 10)		

k. Profit Summary	340,000	
Retained Earnings		340,000
To close the Profit Summary account to Retained Earnings		

l. Retained Earnings   730,800

   Cash Dividends Declared   221,800

   Share Dividends Declared   509,000

    To close the Cash Dividends Declared and Share

    Dividends Declared accounts to Retained Earnings

2. Prepare a statement of retained earnings.

Szatkowski Company
Statement of Retained Earnings
For the Year Ended June 30, 20x2

Retained Earnings, June 30, 20x1		970,000
Net Profit, 20x2		340,000
Subtotal		1,310,000
Less: Cash Dividends		
Preference	120,000	
Ordinary	101,800	
Share Dividends	509,000	
Treasury Stock Transaction	5,000	735,800
Retained Earnings, June 30, 20x2 (Note x)		574,200

3. Prepare the shareholders' equity section of the balance sheet.

Szatkowski Company
Shareholders' Equity
June 30, 20x2

Share Capital		
Ordinary Shares—no-par value, 3 stated value,		
1,000,000 shares authorised, 512,000 shares		
issued, 509,000 shares outstanding	1,536,000	
Ordinary Shares Distributable, 50,900 shares	152,700	
Share Premium	1,236,300	2,925,000
Preference Shares—100 nominal value, 6%		
noncumulative, 50,000 shares authorised,		
20,000 shares issued and outstanding		2,000,000
Total Share Capital		4,925,000
Retained Earnings (Note x)		574,200
Total Share Capital and Retained Earnings		5,499,200
Less Treasury Stock, Ordinary (3,000 shares at cost)		24,000
Total Shareholders' Equity		5,475,200

Note x: The board of directors has restricted retained earnings available for dividends by the amount of 100,000 as required under a loan agreement.

4. Calculate the book values.

  June 30, 20x1

   Ordinary Shares: 3,290,000 ÷ 250,000 shares = 13.16 per share

  June 30, 20x2

   Preference Shares:

    Redeemable price of 104 per share equals book value per share

   Ordinary Shares:

    (5,475,200 − 2,080,000) ÷ (509,000 shares + 50,900 shares) =

    3,395,200 ÷ 559,900 shares = 6.06 per share

CHAPTER ASSIGNMENTS

Knowledge and Understanding

Questions

1. How does the classification of expenses by nature differ from classification by function?
2. "Accounting profit should be geared to the concept of taxable profit because the public understands the concept of taxable profit." Comment on this statement, and state why tax effect accounting is necessary.
3. Exxon Corporation of the U.S. had about $11.1 billion of deferred income taxes in 1992, equal to about 20 per cent of total liabilities. This percentage has risen or remained steady for many years. Given management's desire to put off the payment of taxes as long as possible, the long-term growth of the economy and inflation, and the definition of a liability (probable future sacrifices of future benefits arising from present obligations), make an argument for not accounting for deferred income taxes.
4. Why should a gain or loss on discontinuing operations be disclosed separately on the income statement?
5. Explain the two major criteria for extraordinary items. How should extraordinary items be disclosed in the financial statements?

6. How are earnings per share disclosed in financial statements?
7. When does a company have a simple capital structure? A complex capital structure?
8. What is the difference between basic and diluted earnings per share?
9. What are retained earnings, and how do they relate to the assets of a corporation?
10. When does a company have a deficit in retained earnings?
11. Explain how the accounting treatment of share dividends differs from that of cash dividends.
12. What is the difference between a share dividend and a share split? What is the effect of each on the capital structure of a corporation?
13. What is the purpose of restricting retained earnings?
14. What is the difference between the statement of shareholders' equity and the shareholders' equity section of the balance sheet?
15. Would you expect a corporation's book value per share to equal its market value per share? Why or why not?

Application

Exercises

E 11-1.
LO 1 *Corporate Income Statement*

Assume that the Shortall Furniture Company's chief financial officer gave you the following information: Net Sales, 1,900,000; Cost of Goods Sold, 1,050,000; Extraordinary Gain (net of income taxes of 3,500), 12,500; Loss from Discontinuing Operations (net of income tax benefit of 30,000), 50,000; Loss on Disposal of Discontinuing Operations (net of income tax benefit of 13,000), 35,000; Selling Expenses, 50,000; Administrative Expenses, 40,000; Income Taxes Expense on Continuing Operations, 300,000.

From this information, prepare the company's income statement for the year ended June 30, 20xx. (Ignore earnings per share information.)

E 11-2.
LO 2 *Tax Effect Accounting*

The Delcampo Corporation reported the following accounting profit before income taxes, income taxes expense, and net profit for 20x2 and 20x3:

	20x3	20x2
Accounting profit before taxes	280,000	280,000
Income taxes expense	88,300	88,300
Net profit	191,700	191,700

Also, on the balance sheet, deferred income taxes liability increased by 38,400 in 20x2 and decreased by 18,800 in 20x3.

1. How much did Delcampo Corporation actually pay in income taxes for 20x2 and 20x3?
2. Prepare journal entries to record income taxes expense for 20x2 and 20x3.

E 11-3.
LO 4 *Earnings per Share*

During 20x1, the Heath Corporation reported a net profit of 1,529,500. On January 1, 20x1, the Heath Corporation had 700,000 ordinary shares outstanding. The corporation issued an additional 420,000 ordinary shares on October 1. In 20x1, the corporation had a simple capital structure. During 20x2, there were no transactions involving ordinary shares, and the corporation reported net profit of 2,016,000.

1. Determine the weighted-average number of ordinary shares outstanding each year.
2. Calculate earnings per share for each year.

<table>
<tr><td>E 11-4.
LO 1 *Corporate Income Statement*
LO 2
LO 3
LO 4</td><td></td></tr>
</table>

E 11-4.

LO 1 *Corporate Income Statement*
LO 2
LO 3
LO 4

The following items are components in the income statement of Cohen Corporation for the year ended December 31, 20x1:

Sales	500,000
Cost of Goods Sold	(275,000)
Operating Expenses	(112,500)
Total Income Taxes Expense for Period	(82,350)
Profit from Operations of a Discontinuing Segment	80,000
Gain on Disposal of Segment	70,000
Extraordinary Gain on Retirement of Bonds	36,000
Net Profit	216,150
Earnings per share	1.08

Recast the 20x1 income statement in proper multistep form, including allocating income taxes to appropriate items (assume a 30 per cent income tax rate) and showing earnings per share figures (200,000 shares outstanding).

E 11-5.

LO 5 *Retained Earnings*

The Drennan Corporation had a balance in Retained Earnings on December 31, 20x1 of 520,000. During 20x2, the company reported a profit of 224,000 after taxes. In addition, the company located an 88,000 (net of taxes) error that resulted in an overstatement of prior years' profit and meets the criteria for adjustment. During 20x2, the company declared cash dividends totalling 32,000.

Prepare the company's statement of retained earnings for the year ended December 31, 20x2.

E 11-6.

LO 6 *Journal Entries: Share Dividends*

The Geyer Company has 30,000 ordinary shares of 1 nominal value outstanding. Record the following transactions as they relate to the company's ordinary shares:

July 17 Declared a 10 per cent share dividend on ordinary shares to be distributed on August 10 to shareholders of record on July 31. Market value was 5 per share on this date.

  31 Record date.

Aug. 10 Distributed the share dividend declared on July 17.

Sept. 1 Declared a .50 per share cash dividend on ordinary shares to be paid on September 16 to shareholders of record on September 10.

E 11-7.

LO 6 *Share Split*

The Colson Company currently has 200,000 ordinary shares of 1 nominal value outstanding. There are 500,000 shares authorised. The board of directors declared a 2 for 1 split on May 15, when the market value of the shares was 2.50 per share. The Retained Earnings balance on May 15 was 700,000. Share Premium on this date was 20,000.

Prepare the shareholders' equity section of the company's balance sheet before and after the share split. What journal entry, if any, would be necessary to record the share split?

E 11-8.

LO 7 *Restriction of Retained Earnings*

The board of directors of the Geroulis Company has approved plans to acquire another company during the coming year. The acquisition will cost approximately 1,100,000. The board took action to restrict retained earnings of the company in the amount of 1,100,000 on July 17, 20x1. On July 31, the company had retained earnings of 1,950,000.

1. Show two ways the restriction on retained earnings can be disclosed.
2. What effect will the purchase have on retained earnings and future disclosures?

E 11-9.

LO 8 *Statement of Shareholders' Equity*

The shareholders' equity section of Kolb Corporation's balance sheet on December 31, 20x2 appears as follows:

Share Capital	
Ordinary Shares—2 nominal value, 500,000 shares	
authorised, 400,000 issued and outstanding	800,000
Share Premium	1,200,000
Total Share Capital	2,000,000
Retained Earnings	4,200,000
Total Shareholders' Equity	6,200,000

Prepare a statement of shareholders' equity for the year ended December 31, 20x3, assuming the following transactions occurred in sequence during 20x3:

a. Issued 10,000 preference shares of 100 nominal value, 9 per cent cumulative, after obtaining authorisation.

b. Issued 40,000 ordinary shares in connection with the conversion of bonds having a carrying amount of 600,000.

c. Declared and issued a 2 per cent ordinary share dividend. The market value on the date of declaration was 14 per share.
d. Purchased 10,000 ordinary shares for the treasury at a cost of 16 per share.
e. Earned net profit of 460,000.
f. Declared and paid the full year's dividend on preference shares and a dividend of .40 per share on ordinary shares outstanding at the end of the year.

E 11-10.

LO 9 *Book Value for Preference and Ordinary Shares*

The shareholders' equity section of the Colombus Corporation's balance sheet is shown below.

Share Capital		
Ordinary Shares—5 nominal value, 100,000 shares authorised, 10,000 shares issued, 9,000 shares outstanding	50,000	
Share Premium	28,000	78,000
Preference Shares—100 nominal value, 6% cumulative, 10,000 shares authorised, 200 shares issued and outstanding*		20,000
Total Share Capital		98,000
Retained Earnings		95,000
Total Share Capital and Retained Earnings		193,000
Less Treasury Stock, Ordinary (1,000 shares, at cost)		15,000
Total Shareholders' Equity		178,000

*The preference shares are redeemable at 105 per share, and one year's dividends are in arrears.

Determine the book value per share for both the preference and the ordinary shares.

Problem Set

P 11-1.

LO 1
LO 2
LO 3
LO 4

Corporate Income Statement

Income statement information for the Shah Corporation during 20x1 is as follows:

a. Administrative expenses, 220,000.
b. Cost of goods sold, 880,000.
c. Extraordinary loss from a storm (net of taxes, 20,000), 40,000.
d. Income taxes expense, continuing operations, 84,000.
e. Net sales, 1,780,000.
f. Selling expenses, 380,000.

REQUIRED

Prepare Shah Corporation's income statement for the year ended December 31, 20x1, including earnings per share information assuming a weighted average of 200,000 ordinary shares outstanding for 20x1.

P 11-2.

LO 5
LO 6
LO 7
LO 9

Comprehensive Shareholders' Equity Transactions

The shareholders' equity on June 30, 20x1 of the Gagliano Company is shown below:

Share Capital	
Ordinary Shares—no-par value, 4 stated value, 500,000 shares authorised, 200,000 shares issued and outstanding	800,000
Share Premium	1,280,000
Total Share Capital	2,080,000
Retained Earnings	840,000
Total Shareholders' Equity	2,920,000

Shareholders' equity transactions for the next accounting year are as follows:

a. The board of directors declared a 2 for 1 split.
b. The board of directors obtained authorisation to issue 200,000 preference shares, 100 nominal value, 4 per cent noncumulative, redeemable at 105.
c. Issued 10,000 ordinary shares for a building valued at 44,000.
d. Purchased 6,000 of the company's ordinary shares for 30,000.
e. Issued 30,000 preference shares, 100 nominal value, for 100 per share.
f. Sold 4,000 shares of treasury stock for 18,000.
g. Declared cash dividends of 4 per share on the preference shares and .20 per share on the ordinary shares.
h. Date of record.
i. Paid the preference and ordinary shares cash dividends.

j. Declared a 5 per cent share dividend on the ordinary shares. The market value was 18 per share. The share dividend was distributable after the end of the accounting year.

k. Net profit for the year was 420,000.

l. Closed the Cash Dividends Declared and Share Dividends Declared accounts to Retained Earnings.

Because of a loan agreement, the company is not allowed to reduce retained earnings below 200,000. The board of directors determined that this restriction should be disclosed in the notes to the financial statements.

REQUIRED

1. Make the appropriate general journal entries to record the transactions.
2. Prepare the company's statement of retained earnings for the year ended June 30, 20x2, including disclosure of the restriction.
3. Prepare the shareholders' equity section of the company's balance sheet on June 30, 20x2, including an appropriate disclosure of the restriction on retained earnings. (**Note:** Use T accounts to keep track of transactions.)
4. Calculate the book values per share of preference and ordinary shares (including ordinary shares distributable) on June 30, 20x1 and 20x2.

P 11-3.

LO 6 *Share Dividend and Share Split Transactions*

The shareholders' equity section of the balance sheet of Borkowski Corporation as of December 31, 20x1 was as follows:

Share Capital	
Ordinary Shares—4 nominal value, 500,000 shares authorised, 200,000 shares issued and outstanding	800,000
Share Premium	1,000,000
Total Share Capital	1,800,000
Retained Earnings	1,200,000
Total Shareholders' Equity	3,000,000

The following transactions occurred in 20x2 for Borkowski Corporation:

Feb. 28 The board of directors declared a 10 per cent share dividend to shareholders of record on March 25 to be distributed on April 5. The market value on this date is 16.

Mar. 25 Date of record for share dividend.

Apr. 5 Issued share dividend.

Aug. 3 Declared a 2 for 1 share split.

Dec. 31 Declared a 5 per cent share dividend to shareholders of record on January 25 to be distributed on February 5. The market value per share was 9.

Dec. 31 Closed Share Dividends Declared to Retained Earnings.

REQUIRED

1. Record the transactions for Borkowski Corporation in general journal form.
2. Prepare the shareholders' equity section of the company's balance sheet as of December 31, 20x2. Assume net profit for 20x2 is 108,000. (**Note:** Use T accounts to keep track of transactions.)

Critical Thinking and Communication

Conceptual Mini-Case

CMC 11-1.

LO 1 *Interpretation of Corporate*
LO 3 *Income Statement*
LO 4

Westinghouse Electric is a major technology company whose main businesses are power systems, electronic systems, environmental services, transport temperature control, and broadcasting. In recent years, the company has faced difficult restructurings, including the sale of several of its businesses, and changes in accounting principles, indicated as follows in this excerpt from the report of the company's independent auditors, Price Waterhouse:[8]

As discussed in Note 1 to these financial statements, the Corporation adopted Statement of Financial Accounting Standards (SFAS) No. 106, "Employers' Accounting for Postretirement Benefits Other Than Pensions," and SFAS No. 109, "Accounting for Income Taxes," in 1992. As discussed in Note 2 to these financial statements, the Corporation adopted a comprehensive plan in November 1992 that entails exiting the financial services business and certain other non-strategic businesses. These businesses have been accounted for as discontinued operations.

These changes are reflected in the company's 1991 and 1992 income statements, a portion of which follows (amounts in millions except per share data):

	1992	1991
Income from Continuing Operations	$ 348	$ 265
Discontinued Operations, net of income taxes (note 2):		
Loss from operations	(21)	(1,351)
Estimated loss on disposal of Discontinued Operations	(1,280)	—
Loss from Discontinued Operations	(1,301)	(1,351)
Income (loss) before cumulative effect of changes in		
accounting principles	(953)	(1,086)
Cumulative effect of changes in accounting principles:		
Postretirement benefits other than pensions (notes 1 and 4)	(742)	
Income taxes (notes 1 and 5)	404	—
Net income (loss)	($1,291)	($1,086)
Earnings (loss) per ordinary share (note 15):		
From Continuing Operations	$ .93	$ .84
From Discontinued Operations	(3.76)	(4.30)
From cumulative effect of changes in accounting principles	(.98)	—
Earnings (loss) per ordinary share	($3.81)	($3.46)
Cash dividends per ordinary share (note 15)	$ .72	$ 1.40

(1) Identify the amounts in the partial income statement for each item mentioned in the independent auditors' report. (2) Define discontinuing operations and explain the difference between loss from operations and estimated loss on disposal of discontinuing operations. Why are discontinuing operations shown separately on the income statement? (3) Why are several figures given for earnings per ordinary share? Which earnings (loss) per ordinary share figure would you say is most relevant to future operations? Why is this the most relevant?

Cultural Mini-Case

CLMC 11-1.

LO 3 *Restriction of Retained Earnings*

Some countries restrict the availability of retained earnings for the payment of dividends. The following is from the annual report of *Mazda Motor Corporation*, the Japanese car maker:[9]

> Under the Commercial Code of Japan, the Company is required to appropriate to legal reserve an amount equal to at least 10% of cash dividends paid in each period through March 31, 1991, and at least 10% of the total amount of cash dividends paid and bonuses to directors and statutory auditors in the period ended March 31, 1992, until the reserve equals 25% of common shares [ordinary share capital].
>
> This reserve is not available for dividends but may be used to reduce a deficit by resolution of the shareholders or may be capitalized by resolution of the Board of Directors.

For Mazda, this legal reserve amounted to a substantial sum, ¥14 billion. How does this practice differ from that in your own country? Why is it government policy in Japan? Is it a good idea?

Ethics Mini-Case

EMC 11-1.

LO 6 *Ethics and Share Dividends*

Publicly owned *Bass Products Corporation* for twenty years has paid a cash dividend every quarter and promoted itself to investors as a stable, reliable company. Recent competition from Asian companies has negatively affected its earnings and cash flows. As a result, chief executive Sandra Bass is proposing that the board of directors declare a share dividend of 5 per cent this year instead of a cash dividend. She says, "This will maintain our consecutive dividend record and will not require any cash outflow." What is the difference between a cash dividend and a share dividend? Why does a corporation usually issue them, and how does each affect the financial statements? Is the action proposed by Bass ethical?

Decision-Making Case

DMC 11-1.

LO 6 *Analysing Effects of*
LO 9 *Shareholders' Equity Transactions*

Borders Steel Corporation (BSC), a small U.S. speciality steel manufacturer, has been owned by the Borders family for several generations. Myron Borders is a major shareholder, having inherited 200,000 shares in the company. Myron has not shown much interest in the business because of his enthusiasm for archaeology, which takes him to far parts of the world. However, when he received minutes of the last board of directors meeting, he questioned a number of transactions involving the shareholders' equity of BSC. He asks you, as a person with a knowledge of accounting, to help him interpret the effect of these transactions on his interest in BSC. You begin by examining the shareholders' equity section of BSC's January 1, 20xx balance sheet.

Borders Steel Corporation
Shareholders' Equity
January 1, 20xx

Share Capital	
Ordinary Shares—20 nominal value, 5,000,000 shares	
authorised, 1,000,000 shares issued and outstanding	20,000,000
Share Premium	50,000,000
Total Share Capital	70,000,000
Retained Earnings	40,000,000
Total Shareholders' Equity	110,000,000

Then you read the relevant parts of the minutes of the last board of directors meeting:

Item A: The chief executive reported these share transactions during the last quarter:

October 15. Sold 500,000 authorised ordinary shares through the investment banking firm of T. R. Kendall at a net price of 100 per share.

November 1. Purchased 100,000 own shares for the corporate treasury from Lucy Borders at a price of 110 per share.

Item B: The board declared a 2 for 1 share split (accomplished by halving the nominal value, doubling each shareholder's shares, and increasing authorised shares to 10,000,000), followed by a 10 per cent share dividend. The board then declared a cash dividend of 4 per share on the resulting shares. All of these transactions are applicable to shareholders of record on December 20 and are payable on January 10. The market value of Borders shares on the board meeting date after the share split was estimated to be 60.

Item C: The chief financial officer predicted a net profit for the year of 8,000,000.

REQUIRED
1. Prepare a shareholders' equity section of BSC's balance sheet as of December 31, 20xx that reflects the transactions above. (**Note:** Use T accounts to analyse the transactions. Also, use a T account to keep track of the ordinary shares outstanding.)
2. Calculate book value per share and Myron's percentage of ownership at the beginning and end of the year. Explain the differences. Has Myron's position improved? Why or why not?

Basic Research Activity

RA 11-1.
LO 1 *Shareholders' Equity and*
LO 2 *Book Value Versus Market*
LO 3 *Price*
LO 6
LO 8
LO 9

Select the annual reports of three corporations. (If you did the basic research activity in Chapter 10, use the same three companies.) Prepare a table with a column for each corporation. Then, for any year covered by the balance sheet, the statement of shareholders' equity, and the income statement, answer the following: Does the company own treasury stock? Did it buy or retire any treasury stock? Did it declare a share dividend or a share split? What other transactions appear in its statement of shareholders' equity? Has it deferred any income taxes? Were there any discontinuing operations or extraordinary items? Calculate book value per ordinary share. Find the current market price of each company's shares in a daily newspaper and compare it to the book value you calculated. Should there be a relationship between the two values? Be prepared to discuss your answers to these questions in class.

Financial Reporting and Analysis

Interpretation Cases from Business

ICB 11-1.
LO 1 *Interpretation of Earnings*
LO 3 *Report in Financial Press*

Below are excerpts from an article in the February 2, 1982, *Wall Street Journal* entitled "Lockheed Had Loss in 4th Quarter, Year; $396 Million TriStar Write-Off Is Cited".

As expected, **Lockheed Corp.** took a $396 million write-off to cover expenses of its production phase-out of L-1011 TriStar commercial jets, resulting in a net loss of … $289 million for the year. … Roy A. Anderson, Lockheed Chairman, said he believed the company had "recognised all costs, including those yet to be incurred, that are associated with the phase-out of the TriStar program." He said he thinks the company now is in a sound position to embark on a program of future growth and earnings improvement.

Included in the $396 million net write-off are remaining deferred production start-up costs, adjustments for redundant inventories, and provisions for losses and other costs expected to be incurred while TriStar production is completed. In addition to the write-off, discontinued operations include a $70 million after-tax loss associated with 1981 L-1011 operations. The comparable 1980 L-1011 loss was $108 million.

The $289 million net loss in 1981 consists of the TriStar losses, reduced by the [extraordinary after-tax] gain of $23 million from the exchange of debentures.

For the year, Lockheed had earnings from continuing operations of $154 million, a 14% gain from $135 million in 1980. In 1981 the company had a $466 million loss from discontinued operations, resulting in a net loss of $289 million. A year earlier, the concern had a $108 million loss from discontinued operations, resulting in a net profit of $28 million.[10]

REQUIRED

1. Interpret the financial information from the *Wall Street Journal* by preparing a partial income statement for Lockheed for 1981, beginning with "profit from continuing operations". Be prepared to explain the nature of each item on the income statement.
2. How do you explain the fact that on the New York Stock Exchange, Lockheed shares closed at $50 per share, up $.75 on the day after the quoted announcement of a net loss of $289 million and up from $41 per share two months earlier?

ICB 11-2.
LO 2 *Analysis of Income Taxes from Annual Report*

In its 1993 annual report, **Sara Lee Corporation**, an international food and packaged products company based in the United States, provided the following data about its current and deferred income tax provisions (in millions):

	1993	
	Current	Deferred
Federal	$175	($ 7)
Foreign	159	17
State	33	1
	$367	$11

REQUIRED

1. How much in income taxes was paid in 1993? What was the income tax expense? Prepare a journal entry to record the overall income tax liability for 1993, using tax effect accounting.
2. In the long-term liability section of the balance sheet, Sara Lee shows deferred income taxes of $512 million in 1993 versus $488 million in 1992. This shows the amount of deferred income taxes to have grown. How do such deferred income taxes arise? Give an example of this process. Given the definition of a liability, do you see a potential problem with the company's classifying deferred income taxes as a liability while it is continuing to grow?

Nestlé Case

NC 11-1.
LO 1 *Corporate Income Statement,*
LO 3 *Statement of Shareholders'*
LO 8 *Equity, and Book Value per*
LO 9 *Share*

Refer to the Annual Report in the appendix on Nestlé. Consult the financial statements and notes to answer the following questions:

1. Does Nestlé have discontinuing operations or extraordinary items? Would you say the income statement for Nestlé is relatively simple or relatively complex?
2. What transactions most affect the shareholders' equity section of Nestlé's balance sheet?
3. Compare the book value of Nestlé shares in 1996 and 1995 and compare it to the market price. What interpretation do you place on these relationships?

ENDNOTES

1. South African Breweries, *Annual Report*, 1996.
2. International Accounting Standard, IAS1, *Presentation of Financial Statements* (London: IASC, revised 1997), para. 86.
3. International Accounting Standard, IAS12, *Income Taxes* (London: IASC, revised 1996).
4. International Accounting Standard, IAS35, *Discontinuing Operations* (London: IASC, 1998), para. 39.
5. International Accounting Standard, IAS8, *Net Profit or Loss for the Period, Fundamental Errors and Changes in Accounting Policies* (London: IASC, revised 1993), para. 6.
6. International Accounting Standard, IAS33, *Earnings per Share* (London: IASC, 1997), para. 47.
7. Joan E. Rigdon, "Kodak's Stock Plunges, Chairman Says Analysts' 1994 Forecasts Are High", *Wall Street Journal*, December 16, 1993.
8. Westinghouse Electric Company, *Annual Report*, 1992.
9. Mazda Motor Corporation, *Annual Report*, 1992.
10. "Lockheed Had Loss in 4th Quarter, Year; $396 Million TriStar Write-Off Is Cited", *Wall Street Journal*, February 2, 1982. Reprinted by permission of *Wall Street Journal*, © 1982 Dow Jones & Company, Inc. All Rights Reserved Worldwide.

Part Three

Special Topics in Financial Accounting and Analysis

*B*ecause business organisations are so complex today, special reports are needed to present important information about their activities. Furthermore, to understand and evaluate financial statements, it is necessary to learn how to analyse them. Part Three deals with the cash flow statement; intercompany investments, consolidated financial statements, and foreign currency accounting; and the analysis of financial statements.

Chapter 12   Cash Flow Statements presents a detailed analysis of the cash flow statement, which explains the major operating, financing, and investing activities of a business. The chapter discusses this statement using both the direct approach and the indirect approach.

Chapter 13   Intercompany Investments, Consolidated Financial Statements, and Foreign Currency Accounting addresses three areas of relevance to most corporations in today's complex and global environment. The first is accounting for long-term investments by one company in the share capital of another. The second is consolidated financial statements. The third is the effects of changing rates of exchange for foreign currencies on the interpretation of financial statements.

Chapter 14   Financial Statement Analysis explains the objectives and methods of financial statement analysis from the standpoint of the financial analyst. As an extended illustration, the financial statements of Volvo are analysed.

Chapter 12

CASH FLOW
STATEMENTS

LEARNING OBJECTIVES

1. Describe the cash flow statement, and define *cash, cash equivalents,* and *cash flows.*
2. State the principal purposes and uses of the cash flow statement.
3. Identify the principal components of the classifications of cash flows, and state the significance of noncash investing and financing transactions.
4. Determine cash flows from operating activities using the (a) direct and (b) indirect methods.
5. Determine cash flows from (a) investing activities and (b) financing activities.
6. Prepare a cash flow statement using the (a) direct and (b) indirect methods.
7. Analyse the cash flow statement.

SUPPLEMENTAL OBJECTIVE

8. Prepare a work sheet for the cash flow statement.

DECISION POINT

THE BROKEN HILL PROPRIETARY COMPANY

The Broken Hill Proprietary Company (BHP), an Australian company, is one of the world's largest diversified resource companies. BHP has interests in minerals that include coal and iron ore, copper, steel, and petroleum. Around 40 per cent of sales and assets are now international, and the company has operations, plants, or assets in fifty-nine countries. In 1996, BHP's revenues amounted to 19.124 billion Australian dollars, while assets totalled 35.230 billion Australian dollars.[1]

While the income statement and balance sheet are essential to the evaluation of a company, some information that they do not cover is presented in a third statement, the cash flow statement. This statement shows how much cash was generated by the company's operations during the year and how much was used or came from investing and financing activities. BHP's view is that maintaining adequate cash flow is important to the future of the company.

A strong cash flow is essential to management's key goal of liquidity. If cash flow exceeds what is needed for operations and for expansion, the company will not have to borrow additional funds for expansion. The excess cash flow will be available to reduce the company's debt and improve its financial position by lowering its debt to equity ratio.

The cash flow statement demonstrates management's commitments for the company in ways that are not readily apparent in the other financial statements. For example, the cash flow statement can show whether management's focus is on the short term or the long term. This statement is required by the International Accounting Standards Committee[2] and satisfies the view that a primary objective of financial statements is to provide investors and lenders with information on a company's cash flows.[3]

In this chapter, we provide a detailed analysis of the cash flow statement and the alternative approaches to its preparation and presentation.

PURPOSES, USES, AND COMPONENTS OF THE CASH FLOW STATEMENT

OBJECTIVE 1

Describe the cash flow statement, and define cash, cash equivalents, and cash flows

The **cash flow statement** is a basic financial statement that shows the effect on cash of a company's operating, investing, and financing activities for an accounting period. It explains the net increase (or decrease) in cash during the accounting period. For purposes of preparing this statement, **cash** is defined to comprise cash available and demand deposits. **Cash equivalents** are defined as short-term, highly liquid investments, including money market accounts, commercial paper, and government bonds that are readily convertible to cash. **Cash flows** are inflows and outflows of cash and cash equivalents. A company maintains cash equivalents in order to earn interest on cash that otherwise would temporarily lie idle. Suppose, for example, that a company has 1,000,000 that it will not need for thirty days. To earn a return on this sum, the company may place the cash in an account that earns interest (for example, a money market account); it may loan the cash to another corporation by purchasing that corporation's short-term notes (commercial paper); or it might purchase a short-term obligation of the government (a bond). In this context, short-term is defined as original maturities of ninety days or less. Since cash and cash equivalents are considered as cash flows, transfers between the cash account and cash equivalents are not treated as cash receipts or cash payments. In effect, cash equivalents are combined with the cash account on the cash flow statement.

Cash equivalents should not be confused with current investments or marketable securities, which are not combined with the cash account on the cash flow statement. Purchases of marketable securities are treated as cash outflows and sales of marketable securities as cash inflows on the cash flow statement.

<table>
<tr><td>OBJECTIVE 2</td></tr>
<tr><td>State the principal purposes and uses of the cash flow statement</td></tr>
</table>

Purposes of the Cash Flow Statement

The primary purpose of the cash flow statement is to provide information about cash flows that is "useful in providing users of financial statements with a basis to assess the ability of the enterprise to generate cash and cash equivalents and the needs of the enterprise to utilise those cash flows".[4] This objective is achieved by providing information about the historical changes in cash and cash equivalents that classifies a company's operating, investing, and financing activities during the accounting period. Some of the information on these activities may be inferred by examining other financial statements, but it is on the cash flow statement that all of the transactions affecting cash are summarised.

Internal and External Uses of the Cash Flow Statement

The cash flow statement is useful internally to management and externally to investors and lenders. Management uses the statement to assess the liquidity of the business, to determine dividend policy, and to evaluate the effects of major policy decisions involving investments and financing. In other words, management may use the statement to determine if short-term financing is needed to pay current liabilities, to decide whether to raise or lower dividends, and to plan for investing and financing needs.

Investors and lenders will find the statement useful in assessing the company's ability to manage cash flows, to generate positive future cash flows, to pay its liabilities, to pay dividends and interest, and to anticipate its need for additional financing. Also, they may use the statement to explain the differences between net profit on the income statement and the net cash flows generated from operations. In addition, the statement shows both the cash and noncash effects of investing and financing activities during the accounting period.

<table>
<tr><td>OBJECTIVE 3</td></tr>
<tr><td>Identify the principal components of the classifications of cash flows, and state the significance of noncash investing and financing transactions</td></tr>
</table>

Classification of Cash Flows

The cash flow statement classifies cash receipts and cash payments into the categories of operating, investing, and financing activities. The components of these activities are shown in Figure 12-1 and summarised as follows:

1. **Operating activities** include the cash effects of transactions and other events that enter into the determination of net profit. Included in this category as cash inflows are cash receipts from customers for goods and services, interest and dividends received on loans and investments, and sales of marketable securities. Included as cash outflows are cash payments for wages, goods and services, interest, taxes, and purchases of marketable securities. In effect, the income statement is changed from an accrual to a cash basis.
2. **Investing activities** include the acquiring and selling of long-term assets, the acquiring and selling of marketable securities other than cash equivalents, and the making and collecting of loans. Cash inflows include the cash received from selling long-term assets and marketable securities and from collecting loans. Cash outflows include the cash expended for purchases of long-term assets and marketable securities and the cash loaned to borrowers.

FIGURE 12-1 *Classification of Cash Inflows and Cash Outflows*

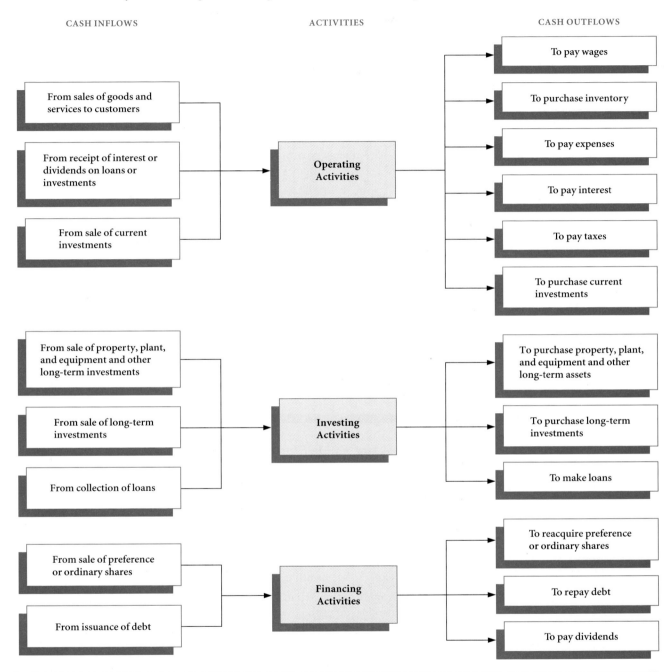

3. **Financing activities** include (1) obtaining or returning resources from or to owners and providing them with a return on their investment and (2) obtaining resources from lenders and repaying the amounts borrowed or otherwise settling the obligations. Cash inflows include the proceeds from issues of shares and from short-term and long-term borrowing. Cash outflows include the repayments of loans and payments to owners, including cash dividends. Treasury stock transactions are also considered financing activities. Repayments of accounts payable or

accrued liabilities are not considered repayments of loans under financing activities, but are classified as cash outflows under operating activities.

A company will occasionally engage in significant **noncash investing and financing transactions** involving only long-term assets, long-term liabilities, or shareholders' equity, such as the exchange of a long-term asset for a long-term liability or the settlement of a debt by issuing share capital. For instance, a company might take out a long-term mortgage for the purchase of land and a building. Or it might convert long-term bonds into ordinary shares. These transactions represent significant investing and financing activities, but they would not be reflected on the cash flow statement because they do not involve either cash inflows or cash outflows. However, since one purpose of the cash flow statement is to show investing and financing activities, and since transactions like these will affect future cash flows, they should be disclosed in a separate schedule as part of the cash flow statement. In this way, the user of the statement will see the company's investing and financing activities clearly.

Format of the Cash Flow Statement

The cash flow statement, shown in Exhibit 12-1, is divided into three sections corresponding to the three categories of activities just discussed. The cash flows from operating activities are followed by cash flows from investing activities and cash flows from financing activities. The individual inflows and outflows from investing and financing activities are usually shown separately in their respective categories. For instance, cash inflows from the sale of property, plant, and equipment are shown separately from cash outflows for the purchase of property, plant, and equipment. Similarly, cash inflows from borrowing are shown separately from cash outflows to retire loans. A reconciliation of the beginning and ending balances of cash is shown at the end of the statement. A list of noncash transactions appears in the schedule at the bottom of the statement.

EXHIBIT 12-1   *Format for the Cash Flow Statement*

Company Name
Cash Flow Statement
Period Covered

Cash Flows from Operating Activities		
(List of individual inflows and outflows)	xxx	
Net Cash Flows from Operating Activities		xxx
Cash Flows from Investing Activities		
(List of individual inflows and outflows)	xxx	
Net Cash Flows from Investing Activities		xxx
Cash Flows from Financing Activities		
(List of individual inflows and outflows)	xxx	
Net Cash Flows from Financing Activities		xxx
Net Increase (Decrease) in Cash		xx
Cash at Beginning of Year		xx
Cash at End of Year		xx

Schedule of Noncash Investing and Financing Transactions

(List of individual transactions)	xxx

PREPARING THE CASH FLOW STATEMENT

To demonstrate the preparation of the cash flow statement, we will work through an example step by step. The data for this example are presented in Exhibits 12-2 and 12-3. These two exhibits present Lee Corporation's balance sheets for December 31, 20x1 and 20x2, and its 20x2 income statement, with additional data about transactions affecting noncurrent accounts during 20x2. Since the changes in the balance sheet accounts will be used for analysis, those changes are shown in Exhibit 12-2.

EXHIBIT 12-2   *Comparative Balance Sheets with Changes in Accounts Indicated for Lee Corporation*

Lee Corporation
Comparative Balance Sheets
December 31, 20x2 and 20x1

	20x2	20x1	Change	Increase or Decrease
Assets				
Current Assets				
Cash	46,000	15,000	31,000	Increase
Accounts Receivable (net)	47,000	55,000	(8,000)	Decrease
Inventory	144,000	110,000	34,000	Increase
Prepaid Expenses	1,000	5,000	(4,000)	Decrease
Total Current Assets	238,000	185,000	53,000	
Investments	115,000	127,000	(12,000)	Decrease
Plant Assets				
Plant Assets	715,000	505,000	210,000	Increase
Accumulated Depreciation	(103,000)	(68,000)	(35,000)	Increase
Total Plant Assets	612,000	437,000	175,000	
Total Assets	965,000	749,000	216,000	
Liabilities				
Current Liabilities				
Accounts Payable	50,000	43,000	7,000	Increase
Accrued Liabilities	12,000	9,000	3,000	Increase
Income Taxes Payable	3,000	5,000	(2,000)	Decrease
Total Current Liabilities	65,000	57,000	8,000	
Long-Term Liabilities				
Bonds Payable	295,000	245,000	50,000	Increase
Total Liabilities	360,000	302,000	58,000	
Shareholders' Equity				
Ordinary Shares, 5 nominal value	276,000	200,000	76,000	Increase
Share Premium	189,000	115,000	74,000	Increase
Retained Earnings	140,000	132,000	8,000	Increase
Total Shareholders' Equity	605,000	447,000	158,000	
Total Liabilities and Shareholders' Equity	965,000	749,000	216,000	

EXHIBIT 12-3   *Income Statement and Other Information on Noncurrent Accounts for Lee Corporation*

Lee Corporation
Income Statement
For the Year Ended December 31, 20x2

Sales		698,000
Cost of Goods Sold		520,000
Gross Profit		178,000
Operating Expenses (including Depreciation		
Expense of 37,000)		147,000
Operating Profit		31,000
Other Income (Expenses)		
Interest Expense	(23,000)	
Interest Income	6,000	
Gain on Sale of Investments	12,000	
Loss on Sale of Plant Assets	(3,000)	(8,000)
Profit before Taxes		23,000
Income Taxes		7,000
Net Profit		16,000

Other transactions affecting noncurrent accounts during 20x2:

1. Purchased investments in the amount of 78,000.
2. Sold investments classified as long-term for 102,000. These investments cost 90,000.
3. Purchased plant assets in the amount of 120,000.
4. Sold plant assets that cost 10,000 with accumulated depreciation of 2,000 for 5,000.
5. Issued 100,000 of bonds at face value in a noncash exchange for plant assets.
6. Repaid 50,000 of bonds at face value at maturity.
7. Issued 15,200 ordinary shares of 5 nominal value for 150,000.
8. Paid cash dividends in the amount of 8,000.

Whether the change in each account is an increase or a decrease is also shown. In addition, Exhibit 12-3 contains data about transactions that affected noncurrent accounts. These transactions would be identified by the company's accountants from the records.

There are four steps in preparing the cash flow statement:

1. Determine cash flows from operating activities.
2. Determine cash flows from investing activities.
3. Determine cash flows from financing activities.
4. Present the information obtained in the first three steps in the form of the cash flow statement.

Determining Cash Flows from Operating Activities

The first step in preparing the cash flow statement is to determine cash flows from operating activities. The income statement indicates a business's success or failure in earning a profit from its operating activities, but it does not reflect the inflow and outflow of cash from those activities. The reason for this is that the income statement

The presentation of a cash flow statement is still relatively new and not required in all countries, including, for example, China and Japan. In some countries, such as Korea, New Zealand, and the United Kingdom, there is an exemption for "small" companies.

FIGURE 12-2 *Relationship of Accrual and Cash Bases of Accounting*

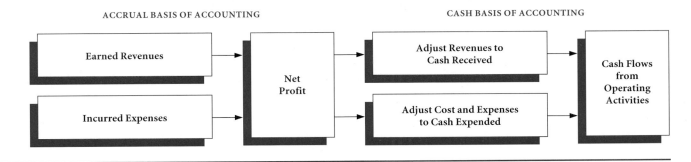

is prepared on an accrual basis. Revenues are recorded even though the cash for them may not have been received, and expenses are recorded even though the cash for them may not have been expended. As a result, to arrive at cash flows from operations, the figures on the income statement must be converted from an accrual basis to a cash basis by adjusting earned revenues to cash received from sales and incurred costs and expenses to cash expended, as shown in Figure 12-2.

OBJECTIVE 4a

Determine cash flows from operating activities using the direct method

There are two methods of converting the income statement from an accrual basis to a cash basis: the direct method and the indirect method. Under the **direct method**, each item in the income statement is adjusted from the accrual basis to the cash basis. The result is a statement that begins with cash receipts from sales and deducts cash payments for purchases, operating expenses, interest payments, and income taxes to arrive at net cash flows from operating activities:

Cash Flows from Operating Activities		
Cash Receipts from		
Sales	xxx	
Interest and Dividends Received	xxx	xxx
Cash Payments for		
Purchases	xxx	
Operating Expenses	xxx	
Interest Payments	xxx	
Income Taxes	xxx	xxx
Net Cash Flows from Operating Activities		xxx

OBJECTIVE 4b

Determine cash flows from operating activities using the indirect method

The **indirect method**, on the other hand, does not require the individual adjustment of each item in the income statement, but lists only those adjustments necessary to convert net profit to cash flows from operations, as follows:

Cash Flows from Operating Activities		
Net Profit		xxx
Adjustments to Reconcile Net Profit to Net		
Cash Flows from Operating Activities		
(List of individual items)	xxx	xxx
Net Cash Flows from Operating Activities		xxx

Both methods, however, analyse certain income statement items and changes in certain current assets and current liabilities. In the sections that follow, the direct method will be used to illustrate the conversion of the income statement to a cash basis, and the indirect method will be used to summarise the process.

Cash Receipts from Sales

Sales result in a positive cash flow for a company. Cash sales are direct cash inflows. Credit sales are not, because they are recorded originally as accounts receivable. When they are collected, they become cash inflows. You cannot, however, assume that credit sales are automatically inflows of cash, because the collections of accounts receivable in any one accounting period are not likely to equal credit sales. Receivables may be uncollectible, sales from a prior period may be collected in the current period, or sales from the current period may be collected next period. For example, if accounts receivable increases from one accounting period to the next, cash receipts from sales will not be as great as sales. On the other hand, if accounts receivable decreases from one accounting period to the next, cash receipts from sales will exceed sales.

The relationships among sales, changes in accounts receivable, and cash receipts from sales are reflected in the following formula:

$$\begin{matrix} \text{Cash Receipts} \\ \text{from Sales} \end{matrix} = \text{Sales} \begin{cases} + \text{ Decrease in Accounts Receivable} \\ \quad\quad\quad\quad or \\ - \text{ Increase in Accounts Receivable} \end{cases}$$

Refer to the balance sheets and income statement for Lee Corporation in Exhibits 12-2 and 12-3. Note that sales were 698,000 in 20x2, and accounts receivable decreased by 8,000. Thus, cash received from sales is 706,000:

$$706,000 = 698,000 + 8,000$$

Lee Corporation collected 8,000 more from sales than it sold during the year. This relationship may be illustrated as follows:

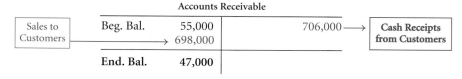

If Lee Corporation had unearned revenues or advances from customers, an adjustment would be made for changes in those items as well.

A knowledge of the direct method helps the manager and the user of financial statements perceive the underlying causes for the difference between reported net profit and cash flows from operations. The indirect method is a practical way of presenting the differences. Both methods have merit.

Cash Receipts from Interest and Dividends Received

Although interest and dividends received are most closely associated with investment activity and are often called investment income, the International Accounting Standards Committee has decided to classify the cash received from these items as operating activities. To simplify the examples in this text, it is assumed that interest income equals interest received and that dividend income equals dividends received. Thus, from Exhibit 12-3, interest received by Lee Corporation is assumed to equal 6,000, which is the amount of interest income.

Cash Payments for Purchases

Cost of goods sold (from the income statement) must be adjusted for changes in two balance sheet accounts to arrive at cash payments for purchases. First, cost of goods sold must be adjusted for changes in inventory to arrive at net purchases. Then, net purchases must be adjusted for the change in accounts payable to arrive at cash payments for purchases. If inventory has increased from one accounting period to another, net purchases will be greater than cost of goods sold because net purchases during the period have exceeded the monetary amount of the items sold during the period. If inventory has decreased, net purchases will be less than cost of goods sold. Conversely, if accounts payable has increased, cash payments for purchases will be less than net purchases; if accounts payable has decreased, cash payments for purchases will be greater than net purchases.

These relationships may be stated in equation form as follows:

$$\text{Cash Payments for Purchases} = \text{Cost of Goods Sold} \left\{ \begin{array}{c} + \text{ Increase in Inventory} \\ \text{or} \\ - \text{ Decrease in Inventory} \end{array} \right\} \left\{ \begin{array}{c} + \text{ Decrease in Accounts Payable} \\ \text{or} \\ - \text{ Increase in Accounts Payable} \end{array} \right.$$

From Exhibits 12-2 and 12-3, cost of goods sold is 520,000, inventory increased by 34,000, and accounts payable increased by 7,000. Thus, cash payments for purchases is 547,000, as the following calculation shows:

$$547,000 = 520,000 + 34,000 - 7,000$$

In this example, Lee Corporation purchased 34,000 more inventory than it sold and paid out 7,000 less in cash than it purchased. The net result is that cash payments for purchases exceeded cost of goods sold by 27,000 (547,000 − 520,000). These relationships can be visualised as follows:

Accounts Payable			Inventory		
Cash Payments to Suppliers ← 547,000	Beg. Bal. 43,000	Pur-chases	Beg. Bal. 110,000	520,000 →	Cost of Goods Sold
	554,000 ←		→ 554,000		
	End. Bal. 50,000		End. Bal. 144,000		

Cash Payments for Operating Expenses

Just as cost of goods sold does not represent the amount of cash paid for purchases during an accounting period, operating expenses do not match the amount of cash paid to employees, suppliers, and others for goods and services. Three adjustments must be made to operating expenses to arrive at the cash outflows. The first adjustment is for changes in prepaid expenses, such as prepaid insurance or prepaid rent. If prepaid assets increase during the accounting period, more cash will have been paid out than appears on the income statement as expenses. If prepaid assets decrease, the expenses shown on the income statement will exceed the cash spent.

The second adjustment is for changes in liabilities resulting from accrued expenses, such as wages payable and payroll taxes payable. If accrued liabilities increase during the accounting period, operating expenses on the income statement will exceed the cash spent. And if accrued liabilities decrease, operating expenses will fall short of cash spent.

The third adjustment is made because certain expenses do not require a current outlay of cash; these expenses must be subtracted from operating expenses to arrive at cash payments for operating expenses. The most common expenses in this category are depreciation expense, amortisation expense, and depletion expense. Expenditures for plant assets, intangibles, and natural resources occur when these assets are purchased and are classified as an investing activity at that time. Depreciation expense, amortisation expense, and depletion expense are simply allocations of the costs of those original purchases to the current accounting period; they do not affect cash flows in the current period. For example, Lee Corporation recorded 20x2 depreciation expense as follows:

Depreciation Expense	37,000	
Accumulated Depreciation		37,000
To record depreciation on plant assets		

No cash payment was made in this transaction. Therefore, to the extent that operating expenses include depreciation and similar items, an adjustment is needed in order to reduce operating expenses to the amount of cash expended.

The three adjustments to operating expenses are summarised in the following equation.

$$
\begin{array}{l}
\text{Cash Payments} \\
\text{for Operating} \\
\text{Expenses}
\end{array}
=
\begin{array}{l}
\text{Operating} \\
\text{Expenses}
\end{array}
\left\{
\begin{array}{l}
+ \text{ Increase in} \\
\quad \text{Prepaid} \\
\quad \text{Expenses} \\
\quad\quad \text{or} \\
- \text{ Decrease in} \\
\quad \text{Prepaid} \\
\quad \text{Expenses}
\end{array}
\right.
\left\{
\begin{array}{l}
+ \text{ Decrease in} \\
\quad \text{Accrued} \\
\quad \text{Liabilities} \\
\quad\quad \text{or} \\
- \text{ Increase in} \\
\quad \text{Accrued} \\
\quad \text{Liabilities}
\end{array}
\right.
\left\{
\begin{array}{l}
- \text{ Depreciation} \\
\quad \text{and Other} \\
\quad \text{Noncash} \\
\quad \text{Expenses}
\end{array}
\right.
$$

From Exhibits 12-2 and 12-3, Lee's operating expenses (including depreciation of 37,000) were 147,000; prepaid expenses decreased by 4,000; and accrued liabilities increased by 3,000. As a result, Lee Corporation's cash payments for operating expenses are 103,000, calculated as follows:

$$103,000 = 147,000 - 4,000 - 3,000 - 37,000$$

If prepaid expenses and accrued liabilities that are *not* related to specific operating expenses exist, they are not included in these calculations. One example is income taxes payable, which is the accrued liability related to income taxes expense. The cash payment for income taxes is discussed in a later section of this chapter.

Cash Payments for Interest

The International Accounting Standards Committee (IASC) classifies cash payments for interest as operating activities, although some authorities argue that they should be considered financing activities because of their association with loans incurred to finance the business. The IASC feels that interest expense is a cost of operating a business. We follow the IASC position in this text. Also, for the sake of simplicity, all examples in this text assume that interest payments are equal to interest expense on the income statement. Thus, from Exhibit 12-3, Lee Corporation's interest payments are assumed to be 23,000 in 20x2.

Cash Payments for Income Taxes

The amount of income taxes expense that appears on the income statement rarely equals the amount of income taxes actually paid during the year. One reason for this difference is that the final payments for the income taxes of one year are not due until some time in the following year. A second reason is that there may be differences between what is deducted from or included in profit for accounting purposes and what is deducted from or included in profit for tax purposes. The latter reason often results in a deferred income tax liability. Its effects were discussed in the chapter on profit and retained earnings. Here, we deal only with the changes that result from increases or decreases in income taxes payable.

To determine cash payments for income taxes, income taxes expense (from the income statement) is adjusted by the change in income taxes payable. If income taxes payable increased during the accounting period, cash payments for taxes will be less than the expense shown on the income statement. If income taxes payable decreased, cash payments for taxes will exceed income taxes on the income statement. In other words, the following equation is applicable:

$$
\begin{array}{l}
\text{Cash Payments for} \\
\text{Income Taxes}
\end{array}
=
\begin{array}{l}
\text{Income} \\
\text{Taxes}
\end{array}
\left\{
\begin{array}{l}
+ \text{ Decrease in Income Taxes Payable} \\
\quad\quad\quad\quad\quad \text{or} \\
- \text{ Increase in Income Taxes Payable}
\end{array}
\right.
$$

In 20x2, Lee Corporation showed income taxes of 7,000 on its income statement and a decrease of 2,000 in income taxes payable on its balance sheets (see Exhibits 12-2 and 12-3). As a result, cash payments for income taxes during 20x2 were 9,000, calculated as follows:

$$9,000 \ = \ 7,000 \ + \ 2,000$$

Other Income and Expenses

In calculating cash flows from operations, some items classified on the income statement as other income and expenses are not considered operating items because they are more closely related to financing and investing activities. Items must be analysed individually to determine their proper classification on the cash flow statement. For instance, we have already dealt with interest income and interest expense as operating activities. Unlike interest, however, the effects of gains and losses are considered with the item that gave rise to the gain or loss. The effects of gains or losses on the sale of assets are considered with investing activities, and the effects of gains or losses related to liabilities are considered with financing activities. Consequently, the effects of the gain on sale of investments and of the loss on sale of plant assets reported on Lee Corporation's income statement (Exhibit 12-3) are considered under cash flows from investing activities.

Schedule of Cash Flows from Operating Activities—Direct Method

It is now possible to prepare a schedule of cash flows from operations using the direct method and the calculations made in the preceding paragraphs. As illustrated in Exhibit 12-4, Lee Corporation had cash receipts from sales and interest received of 712,000 and cash payments for purchases, operating expenses, interest payments, and income taxes of 682,000, resulting in net cash flows from operating activities of 30,000 in 20x2.

Schedule of Cash Flows from Operating Activities—Indirect Method

It is also possible to calculate net cash flows from operations using the indirect method, as demonstrated in Exhibit 12-5. Notice that the amount for net cash flows from operating activities is the same as it was under the direct method (see Exhibit 12-4).

First, the indirect method is based on the fact that cash flows from operations will not equal net profit (or net loss). Under this method, net profit is adjusted for expenses such as depreciation expense, amortisation expense, depletion expense, and other income and expenses, such as gains and losses. These are items included on the income statement that do not affect cash flows. As a result, they are added or deducted as follows:

**Adjustments to Convert Net Profit to
Net Cash Flows from Operating Activities**

	Add to (Deduct from) Net Profit
Depreciation Expense	Add
Amortisation Expense	Add
Depletion Expense	Add
Losses	Add
Gains	Deduct

EXHIBIT 12-4   *Schedule of Cash Flows from Operating Activities—*
Direct Method

Lee Corporation
Schedule of Cash Flows from Operating Activities
For the Year Ended December 31, 20x2

Cash Flows from Operating Activities		
Cash Receipts from		
Sales	706,000	
Interest Received	6,000	712,000
Cash Payments for		
Purchases	547,000	
Operating Expenses	103,000	
Interest	23,000	
Income Taxes	9,000	682,000
Net Cash Flows from Operating Activities		30,000

EXHIBIT 12-5   *Schedule of Cash Flows from Operating Activities—*
Indirect Method

Lee Corporation
Schedule of Cash Flows from Operating Activities
For the Year Ended December 31, 20x2

Cash Flows from Operating Activities		
Net Profit		16,000
Adjustments to Reconcile Net Profit to Net		
Cash Flows from Operating Activities		
Depreciation	37,000	
Gain on Sale of Investments	(12,000)	
Loss on Sale of Plant Assets	3,000	
Changes in Current Assets and Current Liabilities		
Decrease in Accounts Receivable	8,000	
Increase in Inventory	(34,000)	
Decrease in Prepaid Expenses	4,000	
Increase in Accounts Payable	7,000	
Increase in Accrued Liabilities	3,000	
Decrease in Income Taxes Payable	(2,000)	14,000
Net Cash Flows from Operating Activities		30,000

Note that these adjustments to net profit are made for several reasons. For example, depreciation expense is added because it is a noncash expense that was deducted in the income statement to arrive at net profit. Adjustments are made for gains and losses for reasons that will become clear when investing activities and financing activities are discussed in the next two sections.

Second, the same adjustments for the changes in current assets and current liabilities are made as under the direct method, except that they are made as additions to or subtractions from net profit instead of as adjustments to the individual income statement items. For instance, under the direct method, the decrease in accounts receivable was added to sales to adjust sales from an accrual basis to a cash basis. Since sales is included in the calculation of net profit, the same effect is achieved by adding the decrease in accounts receivable to net profit. The same logic applies to adjustments to cost of goods sold, operating expenses, and income taxes, except that the signs will be opposite for these adjustments for the reason that the adjustments are to net profit, not to the individual expense items. In general, in arriving at cash flows, the effects on net profit of increases and decreases in current liabilities will be in the same direction and the effects of increases and decreases in current assets will be in the opposite direction, as summarised in the following table:

**Adjustments to Convert Net Profit to
Net Cash Flows from Operating Activities**

	Add to Net Profit	Deduct from Net Profit
Current Assets		
Accounts Receivable (net)	Decrease	Increase
Inventory	Decrease	Increase
Prepaid Expenses	Decrease	Increase
Current Liabilities		
Accounts Payable	Increase	Decrease
Accrued Liabilities	Increase	Decrease
Income Taxes Payable	Increase	Decrease

OBJECTIVE 5a

Determine cash flows from investing activities

Determining Cash Flows from Investing Activities

The second step in preparing the cash flow statement is to determine cash flows from investing activities. Each account that involves cash receipts and cash payments from investing activities is examined individually. The objective is to explain the change in each account balance from one year to the next.

Investing activities centre on the long-term assets shown on the balance sheet, but they also include transactions affecting current investments from the current asset section of the balance sheet and investment income from the income statement. From the balance sheet in Exhibit 12-2, we can see that Lee Corporation has long-term assets of investments and plant assets, but no current investments. From the income statement in Exhibit 12-3, we see that Lee Corporation has investment income in the form of interest income, a gain on sale of investments, and a loss on sale of plant assets. Also, from the schedule at the bottom of Exhibit 12-3, we find the following five items pertaining to investing activities in 20x2:

1. Purchased investments in the amount of 78,000.
2. Sold long-term investments that cost 90,000 for 102,000.
3. Purchased plant assets in the amount of 120,000.
4. Sold plant assets that cost 10,000 with accumulated depreciation of 2,000 for 5,000, resulting in a loss of 3,000.
5. Issued 100,000 of bonds at face value in a noncash exchange for plant assets.

The following paragraphs analyse the accounts related to investing activities to determine their effects on Lee Corporation's cash flows.

Investments

The objective here is to explain the corporation's 12,000 decrease in investments, all of which are classified as available-for-sale securities, by analysing the increases and decreases in the Investments account to determine the effects on the Cash account. Purchases increase investments and sales decrease investments. Item **1** in the list of Lee's investing activities shows purchases of 78,000 during 20x2. The transaction is recorded as follows:

Investments	78,000	
Cash		78,000
Purchase of investments		

As we can see from the entry, the effect of this transaction is a 78,000 decrease in cash flows.

Item **2** in the list shows a sale of investments at a gain. This transaction is recorded as follows:

Cash	102,000	
Investments		90,000
Gain on Sale of Investments		12,000
Sale of investments for a gain		

The effect of this transaction is a 102,000 increase in cash flows. Note that the gain on sale of investments is included in the 102,000. This is the reason it was excluded earlier in calculating cash flows from operations. If it had been included in that section, it would have been counted twice.

The 12,000 decrease in the Investments account during 20x2 has now been explained, as may be seen in the following T account:

Investments			
Beg. Bal.	127,000	Sales	90,000
Purchases	78,000		
End. Bal.	**115,000**		

The cash flow effects from these transactions are shown under the Cash Flows from Investing Activities section on the cash flow statement as follows:

Purchase of Investments	(78,000)
Sale of Investments	102,000

Notice that purchases and sales are disclosed separately as cash outflows and cash inflows. They are not netted against each other into a single figure. This disclosure gives the user of the statement a more complete view of investing activity.

If Lee Corporation had current investments or marketable securities, the analysis of cash flows would be the same.

Plant Assets

In the case of plant assets, it is necessary to explain the changes in both the asset account and the related accumulated depreciation account. According to Exhibit 12-2, plant assets increased by 210,000 and accumulated depreciation increased by 35,000. Purchases increase plant assets and sales decrease plant assets. Accumulated depreciation is increased by the amount of depreciation expense and decreased by the removal of the accumulated depreciation associated with plant assets that are sold. Three items listed in Exhibit 12-3 affect plant assets. Item **3** in the list indicates that Lee Corporation purchased plant assets totalling 120,000 during 20x2, as shown by this entry:

Plant Assets	120,000	
Cash		120,000
Purchase of plant assets		

This transaction results in a cash outflow of 120,000.

Item **4** states that Lee Corporation sold plant assets for 5,000 that had cost 10,000 and had accumulated depreciation of 2,000. The entry to record this transaction is shown below:

Cash	5,000	
Accumulated Depreciation	2,000	
Loss on Sale of Plant Assets	3,000	
Plant Assets		10,000
Sale of plant assets at a loss		

Note that in this transaction the positive cash flow is equal to the amount of cash received, or 5,000. The loss on sale of plant assets is considered here rather than in the operating activities section. The amount of a loss or gain on the sale of an asset is determined by the amount of cash received and does not represent a cash outflow or inflow.

The disclosure of these two transactions in the investing activities section of the cash flow statement is as follows:

Purchase of Plant Assets	(120,000)
Sale of Plant Assets	5,000

As with investments, cash outflows and cash inflows are not netted, but are presented separately to give full information to the statement user.

Item **5** on the list of Lee's investing activities is a noncash exchange that affects two long-term accounts, Plant Assets and Bonds Payable. It is recorded as follows:

Plant Assets	100,000	
Bonds Payable		100,000
Issued bonds at face value for plant assets		

Although this transaction is not an inflow or outflow of cash, it is a significant transaction involving both an investing activity (the purchase of plant assets) and a financing activity (the issue of bonds payable). Because one purpose of the cash flow statement is to show important investing and financing activities, the noncash transaction should be listed in a separate schedule, either at the bottom of the cash flow statement or accompanying the statement, as follows:

Schedule of Noncash Investing and Financing Transactions

Issue of Bonds Payable for Plant Assets	100,000

Through our analysis of these transactions and the depreciation expense for plant assets of 37,000, all the changes in the plant assets accounts have now been accounted for, as shown in these T accounts:

Plant Assets

Beg. Bal.	505,000	Sale	10,000
Purchase	120,000		
Noncash Purchase	100,000		
End. Bal.	**715,000**		

Accumulated Depreciation

Sale	2,000	Beg. Bal.	68,000
		Dep. Exp.	37,000
		End. Bal.	**103,000**

If the balance sheet had included specific plant asset accounts, such as Buildings and Equipment and related accumulated depreciation accounts, or other long-term asset accounts, like intangibles or natural resources, the analysis would be the same.

Determining Cash Flows from Financing Activities

The third step in preparing the cash flow statement is to determine cash flows from financing activities. The procedure followed in this step is the same as that applied to the analysis of investing activities, including treatment of related gains or losses. The only difference between the two is that the accounts to be analysed are the short-term borrowings, long-term liabilities, and shareholders' equity accounts. Cash dividends from the statement of shareholders' equity must also be considered. Since Lee Corporation does not have short-term borrowings, only long-term liabilities and shareholders' equity accounts are considered here. The following items from Exhibit 12-3 pertain to Lee Corporation's financing activities in 20x2:

5. Issued 100,000 of bonds at face value in a noncash exchange for plant assets.
6. Repaid 50,000 of bonds at face value at maturity.
7. Issued 15,200 ordinary shares of 5 nominal value for 150,000.
8. Paid cash dividends in the amount of 8,000.

Bonds Payable

Exhibit 12-2 shows that bonds payable increased by 50,000 in 20x2. This account is affected by items **5** and **6**. Item **5** was analysed in connection with plant assets. It is reported on the schedule of noncash investing and financing transactions (see Exhibit 12-6 on p. 382). It must be remembered here in preparing the T account for bonds payable. Item **6** results in a cash outflow, as can be seen in the following transaction:

Bonds Payable	50,000	
Cash		50,000
Repayment of bonds at face value at maturity		

This cash outflow is shown in the financing activities section of the cash flow statement as follows:

Repayment of Bonds	(50,000)

From these transactions, the change in the Bonds Payable account can be explained as follows:

Bonds Payable

Repayment	50,000	Beg. Bal.	245,000
		Noncash Issue	100,000
		End. Bal.	**295,000**

If Lee Corporation had notes payable, either short-term or long-term, the analysis would be the same.

Ordinary Shares

As with plant assets, related shareholders' equity accounts should be analysed together. For example, Share Premium should be examined together with Ordinary Shares. In 20x2 Lee Corporation's Ordinary Shares account increased by 76,000 and Share Premium increased by 74,000. These increases are explained by item **7**, which states that Lee Corporation issued 15,200 shares for 150,000. The entry to record this cash inflow is as follows:

Cash	150,000	
Ordinary Shares		76,000
Share Premium		74,000
Issue of 15,200 ordinary shares of		
5 nominal value		

BUSINESS BULLETIN   **International Practice**

A change in accounting standards in the United Kingdom caused consterna-tion on the part of Saatchi & Saatchi (now Cordiant), a British company that is one of the largest advertising agencies in the world. The chief executive announced that in 1992 the company had had the highest pretax loss— £595.1 million—in its history. According to the chief executive, the 1992 fig-ures were caused by a £600 million writedown of assets, reflecting the fall in value of a large group of companies purchased by Saatchi & Saatchi during the 1980s. He explained that it was entirely a paper item that did not affect cash flows and described the new accounting standard as "a typical account-ing trick which I do not understand".[5]

In fact, the new rule is understandable as good accounting practice. The writedowns are not a cash outflow in the *current* year because the companies were purchased in *prior* years; however, they are appropriately deducted in determining net profit because if the values of the purchased companies have declined, as all agree they have, *future* cash flows will be negatively affected. A purpose of net profit is to provide information about future cash flows. The net loss reported by Saatchi & Saatchi reflects reduced future cash flows.

This cash inflow is shown in the financing activities section of the cash flow statement as follows:

Issue of Ordinary Shares   150,000

The analysis of this transaction is all that is needed to explain the changes in the two accounts during 20x2, as follows:

Ordinary Shares				Share Premium		
	Beg. Bal.	200,000			Beg. Bal.	115,000
	Issue	76,000			Issue	74,000
	End. Bal.	**276,000**			**End. Bal.**	**189,000**

Retained Earnings

At this point in the analysis, several items that affect Retained Earnings have already been dealt with. For instance, in the case of Lee Corporation, net profit was used as part of the analysis of cash flows from operating activities. The only other item affect-ing the Retained Earnings of Lee Corporation is the payment of 8,000 in cash divi-dends (item **8** on the list above), as reflected by the following transaction:

Retained Earnings   8,000
   Cash   8,000
     Cash dividends for 20x2

Lee Corporation would have declared the dividend before paying it and debited the Dividends Declared account instead of Retained Earnings, but after paying the divi-dend and closing the Dividends Declared account to Retained Earnings, the effect is as shown. Cash dividends are displayed in the financing activities section of the cash flow statement as follows:

Dividends Paid   (8,000)

The change in the Retained Earnings account is explained in the T account that follows:

Retained Earnings			
Dividends	8,000	Beg. Bal.	132,000
		Net Profit	16,000
		End. Bal.	**140,000**

OBJECTIVE 6

Prepare a cash flow statement using the (a) direct and (b) indirect methods

Presenting the Information in the Form of the Cash Flow Statement

At this point in the analysis, all income statement items have been analysed, all balance sheet changes have been explained, and all additional information has been taken into account. The resulting information may now be assembled into a cash flow statement for Lee Corporation. The statement in Exhibit 12-6 was prepared using the direct method and contains the operating activities section from Exhibit 12-4. The statement is just as easily prepared using the indirect approach and the data in Exhibit

EXHIBIT 12-6   *Cash Flow Statement—Direct Method*

Lee Corporation
Cash Flow Statement
For the Year Ended December 31, 20x2

Cash Flows from Operating Activities		
Cash Receipts from		
Sales	706,000	
Interest Received	6,000	712,000
Cash Payments for		
Purchases	547,000	
Operating Expenses	103,000	
Interest	23,000	
Income Taxes	9,000	682,000
Net Cash Flows from Operating Activities		30,000
Cash Flows from Investing Activities		
Purchase of Investments	(78,000)	
Sale of Investments	102,000	
Purchase of Plant Assets	(120,000)	
Sale of Plant Assets	5,000	
Net Cash Flows from Investing Activities		(91,000)
Cash Flows from Financing Activities		
Repayment of Bonds	(50,000)	
Issue of Ordinary Shares	150,000	
Dividends Paid	(8,000)	
Net Cash Flows from Financing Activities		92,000
Net Increase (Decrease) in Cash		31,000
Cash at Beginning of Year		15,000
Cash at End of Year		46,000

Schedule of Noncash Investing and Financing Transactions

Issue of Bonds Payable for Plant Assets	100,000

EXHIBIT 12-7 *Cash Flow Statement—Indirect Method*

Lee Corporation
Cash Flow Statement
For the Year Ended December 31, 20x2

Cash Flows from Operating Activities		
Net Profit		16,000
Adjustments to Reconcile Net Profit to Net		
Cash Flows from Operating Activities		
Depreciation	37,000	
Gain on Sale of Investments	(12,000)	
Loss on Sale of Plant Assets	3,000	
Changes in Current Assets and Current Liabilities		
Decrease in Accounts Receivable	8,000	
Increase in Inventory	(34,000)	
Decrease in Prepaid Expenses	4,000	
Increase in Accounts Payable	7,000	
Increase in Accrued Liabilities	3,000	
Decrease in Income Taxes Payable	(2,000)	14,000
Net Cash Flows from Operating Activities		30,000
Cash Flows from Investing Activities		
Purchase of Investments	(78,000)	
Sale of Investments	102,000	
Purchase of Plant Assets	(120,000)	
Sale of Plant Assets	5,000	
Net Cash Flows from Investing Activities		(91,000)
Cash Flows from Financing Activities		
Repayment of Bonds	(50,000)	
Issue of Ordinary Shares	150,000	
Dividends Paid	(8,000)	
Net Cash Flows from Financing Activities		92,000
Net Increase (Decrease) in Cash		31,000
Cash at Beginning of Year		15,000
Cash at End of Year		46,000

Schedule of Noncash Investing and Financing Transactions

Issue of Bonds Payable for Plant Assets	100,000

12-5, as presented in Exhibit 12-7. The Schedule of Noncash Investing and Financing Transactions is presented at the bottom of each statement.

OBJECTIVE 7

Analyse the cash flow statement

ANALYSIS OF THE CASH FLOW STATEMENT

Now that the statement is prepared, it is important to know how to interpret it. What can you learn about Lee Corporation and its management by reading its cash flow statement? As with the other financial statements, analysis can be used to show significant relationships. Two areas that analysts look at in analysing a company are its cash-generating efficiency and its free cash flow.

Cash-Generating Efficiency

Analysts tend to focus first on the cash flows from operating activities in assessing the cash-generating efficiency of a company. **Cash-generating efficiency** is the ability of a company to generate cash from its current or continuing operations. Three ratios that are helpful in measuring cash-generating efficiency are the cash flow yield, cash flows to sales, and cash flows to assets. These ratios are calculated and discussed below for Lee Corporation. Data for the calculations are obtained from Exhibits 12-2, 12-3, and 12-6.

Cash flow yield is the ratio of net cash flows from operating activities to net profit, as follows:

$$\text{Cash flow yield} = \frac{\text{net cash flows from operating activities}}{\text{net profit}}$$

$$= \frac{30,000}{16,000}$$

$$= 1.9 \text{ times}$$

Lee Corporation provides a good cash flow yield of 1.9 times. This means that operating activities are generating almost twice as much cash flow as net profit. If the company has material special items on the income statement, such as discontinuing operations, income from continuing operations should be used as the denominator.

Cash flows to sales is the ratio of net cash flows from operating activities to net sales, as follows:

$$\text{Cash flows to sales} = \frac{\text{net cash flows from operating activities}}{\text{net sales}}$$

$$= \frac{30,000}{698,000}$$

$$= 4.3\%$$

Lee Corporation generates cash flows to sales of only 4.3 per cent. This means that the company is not generating a high level of cash from sales.

Cash flows to assets is the ratio of net cash flows from operating activities to average total assets, as follows:

$$\text{Cash flows to assets} = \frac{\text{net cash flows from operating activities}}{\text{average total assets}}$$

$$= \frac{30,000}{(749,000 + 965,000)/2}$$

$$= 3.5\%$$

The cash flows to assets is even lower than cash flows to sales because Lee Corporation has a poor asset turnover ratio (net sales ÷ average total assets) of less than 1.0 times. Cash flows to sales and cash flows to assets are closely related to the profitability measures profit margin and return on assets. They equal those measures times the amount of the cash flow yield ratio because cash flow yield is the ratio of net cash flows from operating activities to net profit.

Although Lee Corporation's cash flow yield is relatively strong, the latter two ratios show its efficiency at generating cash flows from operating activities to be low.

Free Cash Flow

It would be logical to move along in the analysis to investing and financing activities. Since there is a net cash outflow of 91,000 in the investing activities section, it is apparent that the company is expanding. However, this figure mixes net capital expenditures for plant assets, which reflect management's expansion of operations, with purchases and sales of investments. Also, cash flows from financing activities were a positive 92,000, but this figure combines financing activities associated with bonds and shares with dividends paid to shareholders. While something can be learned by looking at these broad categories, many analysts find it more fruitful to go beyond them and focus on a new calculation called free cash flow.

Free cash flow is the cash generated or cash deficiency after providing for commitments that must be made if a company is to continue operating at its planned level. These commitments are for current or continuing operations, interest, income taxes, dividends, and net capital expenditures. Cash requirements for current or continuing operations, interest, and income taxes must be paid or the company's lenders and the government can bring action against the company. Although the payment of dividends is not strictly required, dividends normally represent a commitment to shareholders. If they are reduced or eliminated, shareholders will be unhappy and the price of the company's shares will suffer. Net capital expenditures represent management's plans for the future.

If free cash flow is positive, it means that the company has met all of its planned cash commitments and has cash available to reduce debt or expand further. On the other hand, if free cash flow is negative, it means that the company will have to sell investments, borrow money, or issue shares in the short term to continue at its planned levels. If a negative situation continues for several years, a company may run out of sources of cash from selling investments or issuing shares or bonds.

Since cash commitments for current or continuing operations, interest, and income taxes are incorporated in cash flows from current operations, free cash flow for Lee Corporation is calculated as follows:

$$\text{Free cash flow} = \text{net cash flows from operating activities} - \text{dividends} - \text{purchases of plant assets} + \text{sales of plant assets}$$

$$= 30,000 - 8,000 - 120,000 + 5,000$$

$$= (93,000)$$

Purchases and sales of plant assets appear in the investing activities section of the cash flow statement. Many companies provide this number as a "net" amount, using terms such as "net capital expenditures". Dividends are found in the financing activities section. Lee Corporation has negative free cash flow of 93,000 and thus must make up the difference from sales of investments and from financing activities. Net sales of investments provided 24,000 (102,000 − 78,000). Looking at the financing activities section, it may be seen that the company repaid debt of 50,000, while issuing ordinary shares in the amount of 150,000, providing more than enough cash to over-

While the concept of "free cash flow" has a number of interpretations, its use is primarily a feature of highly developed capital markets, such as in the United Kingdom and the United States where financial analysts often use valuation approaches based on an assessment of the future cash flows arising from an enterprise's activities.

BUSINESS BULLETIN   Business Practice

Because the cash flow statement has not been around long, no generally accepted analyses have yet been developed. For example, the term *free cash flow* is used commonly in the business press, but there is no agreement on its definition. In the *Wall Street Journal*, free cash flow was defined as "operating income less maintenance-level capital expenditures".[6] However, the definition we feel is best is the one used in *Business Week*, which is net cash flows from operating activities less net capital expenditures and dividends. This "measures truly discretionary funds—company money that an owner could pocket without harming the business".[7]

come the negative free cash flow. In addition, reducing debt while increasing equity is a wise action on management's part in light of the negative free cash flow. Unless the company improves its free cash flow, it may have difficulty meeting future debt repayments.

Because cash flows can vary from year to year, it is best to look at trends over several years when analysing a company's cash flows.

SUPPLEMENTAL
OBJECTIVE 8

*Prepare a work sheet for the
cash flow statement*

PREPARING THE WORK SHEET

Previous sections illustrated the preparation of the cash flow statement for Lee Corporation, a relatively simple company. To assist in preparing the cash flow statement in more complex companies, accountants developed a work sheet approach. The work sheet approach employs a special format that allows for the systematic analysis of all the changes in the balance sheet accounts to arrive at the cash flow statement. In this section, the work sheet approach is demonstrated using the cash flow statement for Lee Corporation. The work sheet approach uses the indirect method of determining cash flows from operating activities because of its basis in changes in the balance sheet accounts.

Procedures in Preparing the Work Sheet

The work sheet for Lee Corporation is presented in Exhibit 12-8. The work sheet has four columns, labelled as follows:

Column A Description
Column B Account balances for the end of the prior year (20x1)
Column C Analysis of transactions for the current year
Column D Account balances for the end of the current year (20x2)

Five steps are followed in the preparation of the work sheet. As you read each one, refer to Exhibit 12-8.

1. Enter the account names from the balance sheet (Exhibit 12-2) in column A. Note that all accounts with debit balances are listed first, followed by all accounts with credit balances.
2. Enter the account balances for 20x1 in column B and the account balances for 20x2 in column D. In each column, total the debits and the credits. The total debits should equal the total credits in each column. (This is a check of whether all accounts were transferred from the balance sheet correctly.)
3. Below the data entered in step **2**, insert the captions Cash Flows from Operating Activities, Cash Flows from Investing Activities, and Cash Flows from Financing Activities, leaving several lines of space between each one. As you do the analysis in step **4**, write the results in the appropriate categories.
4. Analyse the changes in each balance sheet account using information from both the income statement (see Exhibit 12-3) and other transactions affecting noncurrent accounts during 20x2. (The procedures for this analysis are presented in the next section.) Enter the results in the debit and credit columns. Identify each item with a letter. On the first line, identify the change in cash with an (x). In a complex situation, these letters will reference a list of explanations on another working paper.
5. When all the changes in the balance sheet accounts have been explained, add the debit and credit columns in both the top and bottom portions of column C. The debit and credit columns in the top portion should equal each other. They should *not* be equal in the bottom portion. If no errors have been made, the difference between columns in the bottom portion should equal the increase or decrease in the Cash account, identified with an (x) on the first line of the work sheet. Add

EXHIBIT 12-8 *Work Sheet for the Cash Flow Statement*

Lee Corporation
Work Sheet for Cash Flow Statement
For the Year Ended December 31, 20x2

Description	Account Balances 12/31/x1	Analysis of Transactions Debit		Analysis of Transactions Credit		Account Balances 12/31/x2
Debits						
Cash	15,000	(x)	31,000			46,000
Accounts Receivable (net)	55,000			(b)	8,000	47,000
Inventory	110,000	(c)	34,000			144,000
Prepaid Expenses	5,000			(d)	4,000	1,000
Investments	127,000	(h)	78,000	(i)	90,000	115,000
Plant Assets	505,000	(j)	120,000	(k)	10,000	715,000
		(l)	100,000			
Total Debits	817,000					1,068,000
Credits						
Accumulated Depreciation	68,000	(k)	2,000	(m)	37,000	103,000
Accounts Payable	43,000			(e)	7,000	50,000
Accrued Liabilities	9,000			(f)	3,000	12,000
Income Taxes Payable	5,000	(g)	2,000			3,000
Bonds Payable	245,000	(n)	50,000	(l)	100,000	295,000
Ordinary Shares	200,000			(o)	76,000	276,000
Share Premium	115,000			(o)	74,000	189,000
Retained Earnings	132,000	(p)	8,000	(a)	16,000	140,000
Total Credits	817,000		425,000		425,000	1,068,000
Cash Flows from Operating Activities						
Net Profit		(a)	16,000			
Decrease in Accounts Receivable		(b)	8,000			
Increase in Inventory				(c)	34,000	
Decrease in Prepaid Expenses		(d)	4,000			
Increase in Accounts Payable		(e)	7,000			
Increase in Accrued Liabilities		(f)	3,000			
Decrease in Income Taxes Payable				(g)	2,000	
Gain on Sale of Investments				(i)	12,000	
Loss on Sale of Plant Assets		(k)	3,000			
Depreciation Expense		(m)	37,000			
Cash Flows from Investing Activities						
Purchase of Investments				(h)	78,000	
Sale of Investments		(i)	102,000			
Purchase of Plant Assets				(j)	120,000	
Sale of Plant Assets		(k)	5,000			
Cash Flows from Financing Activities						
Repayment of Bonds				(n)	50,000	
Issue of Ordinary Shares		(o)	150,000			
Dividends Paid				(p)	8,000	
			335,000		304,000	
Net Increase in Cash				(x)	31,000	
			335,000		335,000	

this difference to the lesser of the two columns, and identify it as either an increase or a decrease in cash. Label the change with an (x) and then compare it with the change in cash on the first line of the work sheet, which is also labelled (x). The amounts should be equal, just as they are in Exhibit 12-8, where the net increase in cash is 31,000.

When the work sheet is complete, the cash flow statement may be prepared using the information in the lower half of the work sheet.

Analysing the Changes in Balance Sheet Accounts

The most important step in the preparation of the work sheet is the analysis of the changes in the balance sheet accounts (step **4**). Although there are a number of transactions and reclassifications to analyse and record, the overall procedure is systematic and not overly complicated. It is as follows:

1. Record net profit.
2. Account for changes in current assets and current liabilities.
3. Account for changes in noncurrent accounts using the information about other transactions.
4. Reclassify any other income and expense items not already dealt with. In the following explanations, the identification letters refer to the corresponding transactions and reclassifications in the work sheet.

a. *Net Profit*

Net profit results in an increase in Retained Earnings. It is also the starting point under the indirect method for determining cash flows from operating activities. Under this method, additions and deductions are made to net profit to arrive at cash flows from operating activities. Work sheet entry **a** is as follows:

(a) Cash Flows from Operations:
    Net Profit   16,000
        Retained Earnings   16,000

b–g. *Changes in Current Assets and Current Liabilities*

Entries **b** to **g** record the effects of the changes in current assets and current liabilities on cash flows. In each case, there is a debit or credit to the current asset or current liability to account for the change in the year and a corresponding debit or credit in the operating activities section of the work sheet. Recall that in the prior analysis, each item on the accrual-based income statement was adjusted for the change in the related current assets or current liabilities to arrive at the cash-based figure. The same reasoning applies in recording these changes in accounts as debits or credits in the operating activities section. For example, work sheet entry **b** records the decrease in Accounts Receivable as a credit (decrease) to Accounts Receivable and as a debit in the operating activities section because the decrease has a positive effect on cash flows, as follows:

(b) Cash Flows from Operating Activities:
    Decrease in Accounts Receivable   8,000
        Accounts Receivable   8,000

Work sheet entries **c–g** reflect the effects of the changes in the other current assets and current liabilities on cash flows from operating activities. As you study these entries, note how the effects of each entry on cash flows are automatically determined by debits or credits reflecting changes in the balance sheet accounts.

(c)	Inventory	34,000	
	Cash Flows from Operating Activities:		
	Increase in Inventory		34,000
(d)	Cash Flows from Operating Activities:		
	Decrease in Prepaid Expenses	4,000	
	Prepaid Expenses		4,000
(e)	Cash Flows from Operating Activities:		
	Increase in Accounts Payable	7,000	
	Accounts Payable		7,000
(f)	Cash Flows from Operating Activities:		
	Increase in Accrued Liabilities	3,000	
	Accrued Liabilities		3,000
(g)	Income Taxes Payable	2,000	
	Cash Flows from Operating Activities:		
	Decrease in Income Taxes Payable		2,000

h–i. *Investments*

Among the other transactions affecting noncurrent accounts during 20x2 (see Exhibit 12-3), two items pertain to investments. One is the purchase for 78,000 and the other is the sale at 102,000. The purchase is recorded on the work sheet as a cash flow in the investing activities section, as follows:

(h)	Investments	78,000	
	Cash Flows from Investing Activities:		
	Purchase of Investments		78,000

Instead of crediting Cash, a credit entry with the appropriate designation is made in the appropriate section in the lower half of the work sheet. The sale transaction is more complicated because it involves a gain that appears on the income statement and is included in net profit. The work sheet entry accounts for this gain as follows:

(i)	Cash Flows from Investing Activities:		
	Sale of Investments	102,000	
	Investments		90,000
	Cash Flows from Operating Activities:		
	Gain on Sale of Investments		12,000

This entry records the cash inflow in the investing activities section, accounts for the remaining difference in the Investments account, and removes the gain on sale of investments from net profit.

j–m. *Plant Assets and Accumulated Depreciation*

Four transactions affect plant assets and the related accumulated depreciation. These are the purchase of plant assets, the sale of plant assets at a loss, the noncash exchange of bonds for plant assets, and the depreciation expense for the year. Because these transactions may appear complicated, it is important to work through them systematically when preparing the work sheet. First, the purchase of plant assets for 120,000 is entered (entry **j**) in the same way the purchase of investments was entered in entry **h**:

(j)	Plant Assets	120,000	
	Cash Flows from Investing Activities:		
	Purchase of Plant Assets		120,000

Second, the sale of plant assets is similar to the sale of investments, except that a loss is involved, as follows:

(k) Cash Flows from Investing Activities:
    Sale of Plant Assets   5,000
Cash Flows from Operating Activities:
    Loss on Sale of Plant Assets   3,000
Accumulated Depreciation   2,000
    Plant Assets   10,000

The cash inflow from this transaction is 5,000. The rest of the entry is necessary to add the loss back into net profit in the operating activities section of the cash flow statement (since it was deducted to arrive at net profit and no cash outflow resulted) and to record the effects on plant assets and accumulated depreciation.

The third transaction (entry l) is the noncash issue of bonds for the purchase of plant assets, as follows:

(l) Plant Assets   100,000
    Bonds Payable   100,000

This transaction does not affect cash but must be recorded to account for all changes in the balance sheet accounts. It is listed at the end of the cash flow statement (Exhibit 12-7) in the schedule of noncash investing and financing transactions.

At this point the increase of 210,000 (715,000 − 505,000) in plant assets has been explained by the two purchases less the sale (120,000 + 100,000 − 10,000 = 210,000), but the change in Accumulated Depreciation has not been completely explained. The depreciation expense for the year needs to be entered, as follows:

(m) Cash Flows from Operating Activities:
    Depreciation Expense   37,000
       Accumulated Depreciation   37,000

The debit is to the operating activities section of the work sheet because, as explained earlier in the chapter, no current cash outflow is required for depreciation expense. The effect of this debit is to add the amount for depreciation expense back into net profit. The 35,000 increase in Accumulated Depreciation has now been explained by the sale transaction and the depreciation expense (−2,000 + 37,000 = 35,000).

n. Bonds Payable

Part of the change in Bonds Payable was explained in entry l when a noncash transaction, a 100,000 issue of bonds in exchange for plant assets, was entered. All that remains is to enter the repayment, as follows:

(n) Bonds Payable   50,000
    Cash Flows from Financing Activities:
       Repayment of Bonds   50,000

o. Ordinary Shares and Share Premium

One transaction affects both these accounts. It is an issue of 15,200 ordinary shares of 5 nominal value for a total of 150,000. The work sheet entry is

(o) Cash Flows from Financing Activities:
    Issue of Ordinary Shares   150,000
       Ordinary Shares   76,000
       Share Premium   74,000

p. Retained Earnings

Part of the change in Retained Earnings was recognised when net profit was entered (entry a). The only remaining effect to be recognised is the 8,000 in cash dividends paid during the year, as follows:

(p) Retained Earnings	8,000	
Cash Flows from Financing Activities:		
Dividends Paid		8,000

x. *Cash*

The final step is to total the debit and credit columns in the top and bottom portions of the work sheet and then to enter the net change in cash at the bottom of the work sheet. The columns in the upper half equal 425,000. In the lower half, the debit column totals 335,000 and the credit column totals 304,000. The credit difference of 31,000 (entry **x**) equals the debit change in cash on the first line of the work sheet.

CHAPTER REVIEW

Review of Learning Objectives

1. **Describe the cash flow statement, and define *cash, cash equivalents,* and *cash flows*.** The cash flow statement explains the changes in cash and cash equivalents from one accounting period to the next by showing cash inflows and cash outflows from the operating, investing, and financing activities of a company for an accounting period. For purposes of preparing the cash flow statement, *cash* is defined to comprise cash available and demand deposits. *Cash equivalents* are short-term (ninety days or less), highly liquid investments, including money market accounts, commercial paper, and government bonds. *Cash flows* are inflows and outflows of cash and cash equivalents.

2. **State the principal purposes and uses of the cash flow statement.** The primary purpose of the cash flow statement is to provide information about cash flows that is useful to users in making economic decisions. This objective is achieved by providing information about the historical changes in cash and cash equivalents that classifies a company's operating, investing, and financing activities. It is useful to management as well as to investors and lenders in assessing the liquidity of a business, including the ability of the business to generate future cash flows and to pay its debts and dividends.

3. **Identify the principal components of the classifications of cash flows, and state the significance of noncash investing and financing transactions.** Cash flows may be classified as (1) operating activities, which include the cash effects of transactions and other events that enter into the determination of net profit; (2) investing activities, which include the acquiring and selling of long- and short-term marketable securities, property, plant, and equipment, and the making and collecting of loans, excluding interest; or (3) financing activities, which include the obtaining and returning or repaying of resources, excluding interest, to owners and lenders. Noncash investing and financing transactions are particularly important because they are exchanges of assets and/or liabilities that are of interest to investors and lenders when evaluating the financing and investing activities of a business.

4. **Determine cash flows from operating activities using the (a) direct and (b) indirect methods.** The direct method of determining cash flows from operating activities is accomplished by adjusting each item in the income statement from an accrual basis to a cash basis, in the following form:

Cash Flows from Operating Activities		
Cash Receipts from		
Sales	xxx	
Interest and Dividends Received	xxx	xxx
Cash Payments for		
Purchases	xxx	
Operating Expenses	xxx	
Interest	xxx	
Income Taxes	xxx	xxx
Net Cash Flows from Operating Activities		xxx

In the indirect method, net profit is adjusted for all noncash effects to arrive at a cash flow basis, as follows:

Cash Flows from Operating Activities		
Net Profit		xxx
Adjustments to Reconcile Net Profit to		
Net Cash Flows from Operating Activities		
(List of individual items)	xxx	xxx
Net Cash Flows from Operating Activities		xxx

5. **Determine cash flows from (a) investing activities and (b) financing activities.** Cash flows from investing activities are determined by identifying the cash flow effects of the transactions that affect each account relevant to investing activities. These accounts include all long-term assets and short-term marketable securities. The same procedure is followed for financing activities, except that the accounts involved are short-term notes payable, long-term liabilities, and shareholders' equity accounts. The effects on related accounts of gains and losses reported on the income statement must also be considered. When the change in a balance sheet account from one accounting period to the next has been explained, all the cash flow effects should have been identified.

6. **Prepare a cash flow statement using the (a) direct and (b) indirect methods.** The cash flow statement lists cash flows from operating activities, investing activities, and financing activities, in that order. The section on operating activities may be prepared using either the direct method or the indirect method of determining cash flows from operating activities. The sections on investing activities and financing activities are prepared by examining individual accounts involving cash

receipts and cash payments in order to explain year-to-year changes in the account balances. Significant noncash transactions are included in a schedule of noncash investing and financing transactions that accompanies the cash flow statement.

7. **Analyse the cash flow statement.** In analysing a company's cash flow statement, analysts tend to focus on the company's cash-generating efficiency and free cash flow. Cash-generating efficiency is a company's ability to generate cash from its current or continuing operations. Three ratios used in measuring cash-generating efficiency are cash flow yield, cash flows to sales, and cash flows to assets. Free cash flow is the cash generated or cash deficiency after providing for commitments that must be made if a company is to continue operating at its planned level. These commitments are for current or continuing operations, interest, income taxes, dividends, and net capital expenditures.

Supplemental Objective

8. **Prepare a work sheet for the cash flow statement.** A work sheet is useful in preparing complex cash flow statements. The basic procedures are to analyse the changes in the balance sheet accounts for their effects on cash flows (in the top portion of the work sheet) and to classify those effects according to the format of the cash flow statement (in the lower portion of the work sheet). When all changes in the balance sheet accounts have been explained and entered on the work sheet, the change in the cash account will be explained, and the information will be available to prepare the cash flow statement. This approach lends itself to the indirect method of preparing the cash flow statement.

Review of Concepts and Terminology

The following concepts and terms were introduced in this chapter.

LO 1   Cash: For purposes of the cash flow statement, both cash available and demand deposits.

LO 1   Cash equivalents: Short-term (ninety days or less), highly liquid investments, including money market accounts, commercial paper, and government bonds.

LO 1   Cash flow statement: A basic financial statement that shows the effect on cash of a company's operating, investing, and financing activities for an accounting period.

LO 1   Cash flows: Inflows and outflows of cash and cash equivalents.

LO 7   Cash flows to assets: The ratio of net cash flows from operating activities to average total assets.

LO 7   Cash flows to sales: The ratio of net cash flows from operating activities to sales.

LO 7   Cash flow yield: The ratio of net cash flows from operating activities to net profit.

LO 7   Cash-generating efficiency: The ability of a company to generate cash from its current or continuing operations.

LO 4   Direct method: The procedure for converting the income statement from an accrual basis to a cash basis by adjusting each item in the income statement separately.

LO 3   Financing activities: Business activities that involve obtaining or returning resources from or to owners and providing them with a return on their investment, and obtaining resources from lenders and repaying the amounts borrowed or otherwise settling the obligations.

LO 7   Free cash flow: The cash generated or cash deficiency after providing for commitments that must be made if a company is to continue operating at its planned level; net cash flows from operating activities minus dividends minus net capital expenditures.

LO 4   Indirect method: The procedure for converting the income statement from an accrual basis to a cash basis by adjusting net profit for items that do not affect cash flows, including depreciation, amortisation, depletion, gains, losses, and changes in current assets and current liabilities.

LO 3   Investing activities: Business activities that include the acquiring and selling of long-term assets, the acquiring and selling of marketable securities other than cash equivalents, and the making and collecting of loans.

LO 3   Noncash investing and financing transactions: Significant investing and financing transactions involving no actual cash inflow or outflow but only long-term assets and liabilities or shareholders' equity, such as the exchange of a long-term asset for a long-term liability or the settlement of a debt by the issue of share capital.

LO 3   Operating activities: Business activities that include the cash effects of transactions and other events that enter into the determination of net profit.

Review Problem

The Cash Flow Statement

LO 4
LO 5
LO 6

The comparative balance sheets for Northwest Corporation for the years 20x2 and 20x1 appear on the opposite page, along with the 20x2 income statement.

The following additional information was taken from the company's records:

a. Long-term investments (available-for-sale securities) that cost 70,000 were sold at a gain of 12,500; additional long-term investments were made in the amount of 20,000.

b. Five acres of land were purchased for 25,000 for a car park.

c. Equipment that cost 37,500 with accumulated depreciation of 25,300 was sold at a loss of 2,300; new equipment costing 30,000 was purchased.

d. Notes payable in the amount of 100,000 were repaid; an additional 30,000 was borrowed by signing notes payable.

e. Bonds payable in the amount of 100,000 were converted into 6,000 ordinary shares.

Northwest Corporation
Comparative Balance Sheets
December 31, 20x2 and 20x1

	20x2	20x1	Change	Increase or Decrease
Assets				
Cash	115,850	121,850	(6,000)	Decrease
Accounts Receivable (net)	296,000	314,500	(18,500)	Decrease
Inventory	322,000	301,000	21,000	Increase
Prepaid Expenses	7,800	5,800	2,000	Increase
Long-Term Investments	36,000	86,000	(50,000)	Decrease
Land	150,000	125,000	25,000	Increase
Building	462,000	462,000	—	—
Accumulated Depreciation, Building	(91,000)	(79,000)	(12,000)	Increase
Equipment	159,730	167,230	(7,500)	Decrease
Accumulated Depreciation, Equipment	(43,400)	(45,600)	2,200	Decrease
Intangible Assets	19,200	24,000	(4,800)	Decrease
Total Assets	1,434,180	1,482,780	(48,600)	
Liabilities and Shareholders' Equity				
Accounts Payable	133,750	233,750	(100,000)	Decrease
Notes Payable (current)	75,700	145,700	(70,000)	Decrease
Accrued Liabilities	5,000	—	5,000	Increase
Income Taxes Payable	20,000	—	20,000	Increase
Bonds Payable	210,000	310,000	(100,000)	Decrease
Mortgage Payable	330,000	350,000	(20,000)	Decrease
Ordinary Shares—10 nominal value	360,000	300,000	60,000	Increase
Share Premium	90,000	50,000	40,000	Increase
Retained Earnings	209,730	93,330	116,400	Increase
Total Liabilities and Shareholders' Equity	1,434,180	1,482,780	(48,600)	

Northwest Corporation
Income Statement
For the Year Ended December 31, 20x2

Sales		1,650,000
Cost of Goods Sold		920,000
Gross Profit from Sales		730,000
Operating Expenses (including Depreciation Expense of 12,000 on Buildings and 23,100 on Equipment and Amortisation Expense of 4,800)		470,000
Operating Profit		260,000
Other Income (Expense)		
Interest Expense	(55,000)	
Dividend Income	3,400	
Gain on Sale of Investments	12,500	
Loss on Disposal of Equipment	(2,300)	(41,400)
Profit before Taxes		218,600
Income Taxes		52,200
Net Profit		166,400

f. The Mortgage Payable account was reduced by 20,000 during the year.

g. Cash dividends declared and paid were 50,000.

REQUIRED   1. Prepare a schedule of cash flows from operating activities using the (a) direct method and (b) indirect method.

2. Prepare a cash flow statement using the indirect method.

Answer to Review Problem

1. (a) Prepare a schedule of cash flows from operating activities—direct method.

Northwest Corporation
Schedule of Cash Flows from Operating Activities
For the Year Ended December 31, 20x2

Cash Flows from Operating Activities		
Cash Receipts from		
Sales	1,668,500[1]	
Dividends Received	3,400	1,671,900
Cash Payments for		
Purchases	1,041,000[2]	
Operating Expenses	427,100[3]	
Interest	55,000	
Income Taxes	32,200[4]	1,555,300
Net Cash Flows from Operating Activities		116,600

---

1. 1,650,000 + 18,500 = 1,668,500
2. 920,000 + 100,000 + 21,000 = 1,041,000
3. 470,000 + 2,000 − 5,000 − (12,000 + 23,100 + 4,800) = 427,100
4. 52,200 − 20,000 = 32,200

1. (b) Prepare a schedule of cash flows from operating activities—indirect method.

Northwest Corporation
Schedule of Cash Flows from Operating Activities
For the Year Ended December 31, 20x2

Cash Flows from Operating Activities		
Net Profit		166,400
Adjustments to Reconcile Net Profit to		
Net Cash Flows from Operating Activities		
Depreciation Expense, Buildings	12,000	
Depreciation Expense, Equipment	23,100	
Amortisation Expense, Intangible Assets	4,800	
Gain on Sale of Investments	(12,500)	
Loss on Disposal of Equipment	2,300	
Changes in Current Assets		
and Current Liabilities		
Decrease in Accounts Receivable	18,500	
Increase in Inventory	(21,000)	
Increase in Prepaid Expenses	(2,000)	
Decrease in Accounts Payable	(100,000)	
Increase in Accrued Liabilities	5,000	
Increase in Income Taxes Payable	20,000	(49,800)
Net Cash Flows from Operating Activities		116,600

---

2. Prepare a cash flow statement—indirect method.

Northwest Corporation
Cash Flow Statement
For the Year Ended December 31, 20x2

Cash Flows from Operating Activities		
Net Profit		166,400
Adjustments to Reconcile Net Profit to		
Net Cash Flows from Operating Activities		
Depreciation Expense, Buildings	12,000	
Depreciation Expense, Equipment	23,100	
Amortisation Expense, Intangible Assets	4,800	
Gain on Sale of Investments	(12,500)	
Loss on Disposal of Equipment	2,300	
Changes in Current Assets and		
Current Liabilities		
Decrease in Accounts Receivable	18,500	
Increase in Inventory	(21,000)	
Increase in Prepaid Expenses	(2,000)	
Decrease in Accounts Payable	(100,000)	
Increase in Accrued Liabilities	5,000	
Increase in Income Taxes Payable	20,000	(49,800)
Net Cash Flows from Operating Activities		116,600
Cash Flows from Investing Activities		
Sale of Long-Term Investments	82,500[1]	
Purchase of Long-Term Investments	(20,000)	
Purchase of Land	(25,000)	
Sale of Equipment	9,900[2]	
Purchase of Equipment	(30,000)	
Net Cash Flows from Investing Activities		17,400
Cash Flows from Financing Activities		
Repayment of Notes Payable	(100,000)	
Issuance of Notes Payable	30,000	
Reduction in Mortgage	(20,000)	
Dividends Paid	(50,000)	
Net Cash Flows from Financing Activities		(140,000)
Net Increase (Decrease) in Cash		(6,000)
Cash at Beginning of Year		121,850
Cash at End of Year		115,850

Schedule of Noncash Investing and Financing Transactions

Conversion of Bonds Payable into Ordinary Shares	100,000

1. $70,000 + 12,500 \text{ (gain)} = 82,500$
2. $37,500 - 25,300 = 12,200 \text{ (book value)} - 2,300 \text{ (loss)} = 9,900$

CHAPTER ASSIGNMENTS

Knowledge and Understanding

Questions

1. What is the term *cash flows* in the cash flow statement understood to include?
2. In order to earn a return on cash available during 20x1, Sallas Corporation transferred 45,000 from its cheque account to a money market account, purchased a 25,000 government

bond, and bought 35,000 in ordinary shares. How will each of these transactions affect the cash flow statement?
3. What are the purposes of the cash flow statement?
4. Most of the information in the cash flow statement is available from a company's comparative balance sheets and the

income statement. Why, then, is the cash flow statement needed?

5. What are the three classifications of cash flows? Give some examples of each.

6. Why is it important to disclose certain noncash transactions? How should they be disclosed?

7. How do the direct and indirect methods of determining cash flows from operations essentially differ?

8. Are these items shown as increases or decreases in cash flows from operations (assuming the direct method is used): (a) increase in accounts receivable, (b) decrease in inventory, (c) increase in accounts payable, (d) decrease in wages payable, (e) depreciation expense, and (f) amortisation of patents?

9. Glen Corporation has these other income and expense items: interest expense, 12,000; interest income, 3,000; dividend income, 5,000; and loss on retirement of bonds, 6,000. How does each of these items appear on or affect the cash flow statement (assuming the direct method is used)?

10. Cell-Borne Corporation has a net loss of 12,000 in 20x1 but has positive cash flows from operations of 9,000. What conditions may have caused this situation?

11. What is the proper treatment on the cash flow statement of a transaction in which a building that cost 50,000 with accumulated depreciation of 32,000 is sold for a loss of 5,000?

12. What is the proper treatment on the cash flow statement of (a) a transaction in which buildings and land are purchased by the issuance of a mortgage for 234,000 and (b) a conversion of 50,000 in bonds payable into 2,500 ordinary shares of 6 nominal value?

13. Define *cash-generating efficiency* and identify three ratios that measure cash-generating efficiency.

14. Define *free cash flow* and identify its components. What does it mean to have a positive or a negative free cash flow?

15. Why is the work sheet approach considered to be more compatible with the indirect method of determining cash flows from operations than with the direct method of determining such flows?

16. Assuming in each of the following independent cases that only one transaction occurred, what transactions would be likely to cause (a) a decrease in investments and (b) an increase in ordinary shares? How would each case be treated on the work sheet for the cash flow statement?

Application

Exercises

E 12-1.

LO 3   *Classification of Cash Flow Transactions*

Identify each of the following transactions as (a) an operating activity, (b) an investing activity, (c) a financing activity, (d) a noncash transaction, or (e) none of the above.

1. Declared and paid a cash dividend.
2. Purchased a long-term investment.
3. Received cash from customers.
4. Paid interest.
5. Sold equipment at a loss.
6. Issued long-term bonds for plant assets.
7. Received dividends on securities held.
8. Issued ordinary shares.
9. Declared and issued a share dividend.
10. Repaid notes payable.
11. Paid employees their wages.
12. Purchased a 60-day government bond.
13. Purchased land.

E 12-2.

LO 4   *Cash Receipts from Sales*

During 20x2, Union Chemical Company, a distributor of farm fertilisers and herbicides, had sales of 6,500,000. The ending balance of Accounts Receivable was 850,000 in 20x1 and 1,200,000 in 20x2. Calculate cash receipts from sales in 20x2.

E 12-3.

LO 4   *Cash Payments for Purchases*

During 20x2, Union Chemical Company had cost of goods sold of 3,800,000. The ending balance of Inventory was 510,000 in 20x1 and 420,000 in 20x2. The ending balance of Accounts Payable was 360,000 in 20x1 and 480,000 in 20x2. Calculate cash payments for purchases in 20x2.

E 12-4.

LO 4   *Cash Payments for Operating Expenses and Income Taxes*

During 20x2, Union Chemical Company had operating expenses of 1,900,000 and income taxes expense of 200,000. Depreciation expense of 410,000 for 20x2 was included in operating expenses. The ending balance of Prepaid Expenses was 90,000 in 20x1 and 130,000 in 20x2. The ending balance of Accrued Liabilities (excluding Income Taxes Payable) was 50,000 in 20x1 and 30,000 in 20x2. The ending balance of Income Taxes Payable was 60,000 in 20x1 and 70,000 in 20x2. Calculate cash payments for operating expenses and income taxes in 20x2.

E 12-5.

LO 4   *Cash Flows from Operating Activities—Direct Method*

Using the calculations you made in E 12-2, 12-3, and 12-4, prepare in good form a schedule of cash flows from operating activities for 20x2, using the direct method. The company has a December 31 year end.

E 12-6.

LO 4   *Cash Flows from Operating Activities—Indirect Method*

The condensed single-step income statement of Union Chemical Company, a distributor of farm fertilisers and herbicides, appears as follows:

Sales		6,500,000
Less: Cost of Goods Sold	3,800,000	
Operating Expenses (including depreciation of 410,000)	1,900,000	
Income Taxes	200,000	5,900,000
Net Profit		600,000

Selected accounts from the company's balance sheets for 20x1 and 20x2 appear as shown below:

	20x2	20x1
Accounts Receivable	1,200,000	850,000
Inventory	420,000	510,000
Prepaid Expenses	130,000	90,000
Accounts Payable	480,000	360,000
Accrued Liabilities	30,000	50,000
Income Taxes Payable	70,000	60,000

Present a schedule of cash flows from operating activities for 20x2 using the indirect method.

E 12-7.

LO 4 *Calculating Cash Flows from Operating Activities—Direct Method*

Europa Corporation engaged in the following transactions in 20x2. Using the direct method, calculate the various cash flows from operating activities as required.

a. During 20x2, Europa Corporation had cash sales of 41,300 and sales on credit of 123,000. During the same year, accounts receivable decreased by 18,000. Determine the cash received from sales during 20x2.

b. During 20x2, Europa Corporation's cost of goods sold was 119,000. During the same year, inventory increased by 12,500 and accounts payable decreased by 4,300. Determine the cash payments for purchases during 20x2.

c. During 20x2, Europa Corporation had operating expenses of 45,000, including depreciation of 15,600. Also during 20x2, related prepaid expenses decreased by 3,100 and relevant accrued liabilities increased by 1,200. Determine the cash payments for operating expenses to suppliers of goods and services during 20x2.

d. Europa Corporation's income taxes expense for 20x2 was 4,300. Income taxes payable decreased by 230 that year. Determine the cash payment for income taxes during 20x2.

E 12-8.

LO 4 *Calculating Cash Flows from Operating Activities— Indirect Method*

During 20x1, Mayfair Corporation had a net profit of 41,000. Included on the income statement was depreciation expense of 2,300 and amortisation expense of 300. During the year, accounts receivable increased by 3,400, inventories decreased by 1,900, prepaid expenses decreased by 200, accounts payable increased by 5,000, and accrued liabilities decreased by 450. Determine cash flows from operating activities using the indirect method.

E 12-9.

LO 4 *Preparing a Schedule of Cash Flows from Operating Activities—Direct Method*

The income statement for the Karsko Corporation appears below. The following is additional information: (a) All sales were on credit, and accounts receivable increased by 4,400 during the year; (b) all goods purchased were on credit; inventories increased by 7,000, and accounts payable increased by 14,000 during the year; (c) prepaid rent decreased by 1,400, while salaries payable increased by 1,000; and (d) income taxes payable decreased by 600 during the year. Prepare a schedule of cash flows from operating activities using the direct method.

Karsko Corporation
Income Statement
For the Year Ended June 30, 20xx

Sales		122,000
Cost of Goods Sold		60,000
Gross Profit		62,000
Operating Expenses		
Salaries Expense	32,000	
Rent Expense	16,800	
Depreciation Expense	2,000	50,800
Profit before Income Taxes		11,200
Income Taxes		2,400
Net Profit		8,800

E 12-10.

LO 4 *Preparing a Schedule of Cash Flows from Operating Activities—Indirect Method*

Using the data provided in E 12-9, prepare a schedule of cash flows from operating activities using the indirect method.

E 12-11.

LO 5 *Calculating Cash Flows from Investing Activities— Investments*

Krieger Company's T account for long-term available-for-sale investments at the end of 20x3 is shown below.

Investments			
Beg. Bal.	38,500	Sales	39,000
Purchases	58,000		
End. Bal.	57,500		

In addition, Krieger's income statement shows a loss on the sale of investments of 6,500. Calculate the amounts to be shown as cash flows from investing activities and show how they are to appear on the cash flow statement.

E 12-12.

LO 5 *Calculating Cash Flows from Investing Activities—Plant Assets*

The T accounts for the Plant Assets and Accumulated Depreciation accounts for Krieger Company at the end of 20x3 are as follows:

Plant Assets			
Beg. Bal.	65,000	Disposals	23,000
Purchases	33,600		
End. Bal.	75,600		

Accumulated Depreciation			
Disposals	14,700	Beg. Bal.	34,500
		20x3	
		Depreciation	10,200
		End. Bal.	30,000

In addition, Krieger Company's income statement shows a gain on sale of plant assets of 4,400. Calculate the amounts to be shown as cash flows from investing activities and show how they are to appear on the cash flow statement.

E 12-13.

LO 5 *Determining Cash Flows from Investing and Financing Activities*

All transactions involving Notes Payable and related accounts engaged in by Krieger Company during 20x3 are as follows:

Cash	18,000	
Notes Payable		18,000
Bank loan		
Patent	30,000	
Notes Payable		30,000
Purchase of patent by issuing note payable		
Notes Payable	5,000	
Interest Expense	500	
Cash		5,500
Repayment of note payable at maturity		

Determine the amounts and how these transactions are to be shown in the cash flow statement for 20x3.

E 12-14.

LO 6 *Preparing the Cash Flow Statement*

Bradbury Corporation's 20x2 income statement and its comparative balance sheets for June 30, 20x2 and 20x1 appear on the opposite page.

The following information is also available: (a) Issued a 44,000 note payable for the purchase of furniture; (b) sold furniture that cost 54,000 with accumulated depreciation of 30,600 at carrying amount; (c) recorded depreciation on the furniture during the year, 38,600; (d) repaid a note in the amount of 40,000 and issued 50,000 of ordinary shares at nominal value; and (e) declared and paid dividends of 8,600. Without using a work sheet, prepare a cash flow statement for 20x2 using the direct method.

E 12-15.

LO 7 *Cash-Generating Efficiency Ratios and Free Cash Flow*

In 20x2, Kenetics Corporation had total assets of 2,400,000, net sales of 3,300,000, net profit of 280,000, net cash from operations of 390,000, dividends of 120,000, and net capital expenditures of 410,000. In 20x1, total assets were 2,100,000. Calculate the cash-generating efficiency ratios of cash flow yield, cash flows to sales, and cash flows to assets. Also calculate free cash flow.

Bradbury Corporation
Income Statement
For the Year Ended June 30, 20x2

Sales	468,000
Cost of Goods Sold	312,000
Gross Profit	156,000
Operating Expenses	90,000
Operating Profit	66,000
Interest Expense	5,600
Profit before Income Taxes	60,400
Income Taxes	24,600
Net Profit	35,800

Bradbury Corporation
Comparative Balance Sheets
June 30, 20x2 and 20x1

	20x2	20x1
Assets		
Cash	139,800	25,000
Accounts Receivable (net)	42,000	52,000
Inventory	86,800	96,800
Prepaid Expenses	6,400	5,200
Furniture	110,000	120,000
Accumulated Depreciation, Furniture	(18,000)	(10,000)
Total Assets	367,000	289,000
Liabilities and Shareholders' Equity		
Accounts Payable	26,000	28,000
Income Taxes Payable	2,400	3,600
Notes Payable (long-term)	74,000	70,000
Ordinary Shares—10 nominal value	230,000	180,000
Retained Earnings	34,600	7,400
Total Liabilities and Shareholders' Equity	367,000	289,000

Problem Set

P 12-1.

LO 6 *The Cash Flow Statement—*
LO 7 *Direct Method*

Gutierrez Corporation's 20x2 income statement and its comparative balance sheets as of June 30, 20x2 and 20x1 appear on the next page.

Additional information about 20x2 is as follows: (a) Equipment that cost 48,000 with accumulated depreciation of 34,000 was sold at a loss of 8,000; (b) land and building were purchased in the amount of 200,000 through an increase of 200,000 in the mortgage payable; (c) a 40,000 payment was made on the mortgage; (d) the notes were repaid, but the company borrowed an additional 60,000 through the issuance of new notes payable; and (e) a 120,000 cash dividend was declared and paid.

REQUIRED

1. Prepare a cash flow statement using the direct method. Include a supporting schedule of noncash investing and financing transactions.

Gutierrez Corporation
Income Statement
For the Year Ended June 30, 20x2

Sales		2,081,800
Cost of Goods Sold		1,312,600
Gross Profit		769,200
Operating Expenses (including Depreciation		
Expense of 120,000)		378,400
Income from Operations		390,800
Other Income (Expenses)		
Loss on Sale of Equipment	(8,000)	
Interest Expense	(75,200)	(83,200)
Profit before Income Taxes		307,600
Income Taxes		68,400
Net Profit		239,200

Gutierrez Corporation
Comparative Balance Sheets
June 30, 20x2 and 20x1

	20x2	20x1
Assets		
Cash	334,000	40,000
Accounts Receivable (net)	200,000	240,000
Finished Goods Inventory	360,000	440,000
Prepaid Expenses	1,200	2,000
Property, Plant, and Equipment	1,256,000	1,104,000
Accumulated Depreciation, Property,		
Plant, and Equipment	(366,000)	(280,000)
Total Assets	1,785,200	1,546,000
Liabilities and Shareholders' Equity		
Accounts Payable	128,000	84,000
Notes Payable (due in 90 days)	60,000	160,000
Income Taxes Payable	52,000	36,000
Mortgage Payable	720,000	560,000
Ordinary Shares—5 nominal value	400,000	400,000
Retained Earnings	425,200	306,000
Total Liabilities and Shareholders' Equity	1,785,200	1,546,000

2. What are the primary reasons for Gutierrez Corporation's large increase in cash from 20x1 to 20x2?

3. Calculate and assess cash flow yield and free cash flow for 20x2.

P 12-2.

LO 6 *The Cash Flow Statement—*
LO 7 *Indirect Method*

Use the information for Gutierrez Corporation given in P 12-1 to answer the requirements below.

REQUIRED Prepare a cash flow statement using the indirect method. Include a supporting schedule of noncash investing and financing transactions.

P 12-3.

LO 3 *Classification of Transactions*

Analyse each transaction in the following schedule and place an X in the appropriate columns to indicate its classification and its effect on cash flows using the direct method.

Transaction	Cash Flow Classification				Effect on Cash		
	Operating Activity	Investing Activity	Financing Activity	Noncash Transaction	Increase	Decrease	No Effect
1. Earned a net profit.							
2. Declared and paid cash dividend.							
3. Issued shares for cash.							
4. Retired long-term debt by issuing shares.							
5. Paid accounts payable.							
6. Purchased inventory for cash.							
7. Purchased a one-year insurance policy for cash.							
8. Purchased a long-term investment with cash.							
9. Sold marketable securities at a gain.							
10. Sold a machine at a loss.							
11. Retired fully depreciated equipment.							
12. Paid interest on debt.							
13. Purchased available-for-sale securities (long-term).							
14. Received dividend income.							
15. Received cash on account.							
16. Converted bonds to ordinary shares.							
17. Purchased ninety-day government bond.							

Critical Thinking and Communication

Conceptual Mini-Case

CMC 12-1.

LO 4 *Direct Versus Indirect Method*

Compaq Computer Corporation, a leading manufacturer of personal computers, uses the direct method of presenting the cash flows from operating activities in its cash flow statement. State clearly the difference between the direct and indirect methods of presenting cash flows from operating activities. Then take either the direct or the indirect method and develop an argument for it as the best way of presenting cash flows from operations. Be prepared to present your opinion in class.

Cultural Mini-Case

CLMC 12-1.

LO 3 *Format and Interpretation of*
LO 7 *the Cash Flow Statement*

The format of the cash flow statement can differ from country to country. One of the more interesting presentations is that of *Guinness*, based in the U.K. and Ireland, which is one of the world's leading drinks companies, producing and marketing brands such as Johnnie Walker Scotch Whisky, Gordon's Gin, and Guinness Stout.[8] Refer to Guinness's consolidated group cash flow statement, which follows, to answer these questions: What unusual features can you identify in this cash flow statement? In what ways do you find the Guinness format to be more useful than the typical format used?

Guinness
Cash Flow Statement
For the Years Ended December 31, 1995 and 1994

	1995 £m	1994 £m
Net Cash Inflow from Operating Activities*	922	970
Interest received	33	35
Interest paid	(153)	(183)
Dividends received from associated undertakings	67	25
Dividends paid to minority shareholders in subsidiary undertakings	(22)	(20)
Dividends paid to ordinary shareholders	(285)	(263)
Net Cash Outflow from Returns on Investments and Servicing of Finance	(360)	(406)
United Kingdom corporation tax paid	(127)	(87)
Overseas tax paid	(81)	(75)
Total Tax Paid	(208)	(162)
Net Cash Inflow before Investing Activities	354	402
Purchase of tangible fixed assets	(179)	(221)
Sale of tangible fixed assets	24	16
Investment in MH	—	(945)
Purchase of subsidiary undertakings	(15)	(17)
Purchase of other long-term investments	(16)	(106)
Disposal of investment in LVMH	—	1,344
Other disposals	90	1
Net Cash Outflow from Investing Activities	(96)	72
Net Cash Inflow/(Outflow) before Financing	258	474
Proceeds of new borrowings	227	106
Borrowings repaid	(301)	(425)
Issue of shares (employee share schemes)	26	24
Net Cash (Outflow)/Inflow from Financing	(48)	(295)
Increase in Cash and Cash Equivalents	210	179
Analysis of Free Cash Flow		
Net cash inflow before investing activities	354	402
Purchase of tangible fixed assets	(179)	221
Sale of tangible fixed assets	24	16
Free Cash Flow (after Dividends)	199	197
Free Cash Flow (before Dividends)	484	460

*The company provides the detail for this item in a note to the financial statements.

Ethics Mini-Case

EMC 12-1.

LO 3   *Ethics and Cash Flow*
        Classifications

Chemical Waste Treatment is a fast-growing company that disposes of chemical wastes. The company has an 800,000 line of credit at its bank. One covenant in the loan agreement stipulates that the ratio of cash flows from operations to interest expense must exceed 3.0. If this ratio falls below 3.0, the company must pay down its line of credit to one-half if the funds borrowed against it currently exceed that amount. After the end of the accounting year, the controller informs the chief executive: "We will not meet our ratio requirements on our line of credit in 20x2 because interest expense was 1.2 million and cash flows from operations were 3.2 million. Also, we have borrowed 100 per cent of our line of credit. We do not have the cash to reduce the credit line by 400,000." The chief executive says, "This is a serious situation. To be able to pay our ongoing bills, we need our bank to increase our line of credit, not decrease it. What can we do?" "Do you recall the 500,000 two-year note payable for equipment?" replies the controller. "It is now classified as 'Proceeds from Notes Payable' in cash flows provided from financing activities in the cash flow statement. If we move it up to cash flows from operations and call it 'Increase in Payables', it would put us over the limit at 3.7 million." "Well, do it", orders the chief executive. "It surely doesn't make any difference where it is on the statement. It is an increase in both places. It would be much worse for our company in the long term if we failed to meet this ratio requirement." What is your opinion of the chief executive's reasoning? Is the chief executive's order ethical? Who benefits and who is harmed if the controller follows the chief executive's order? What are management's alternatives? What would you do if you were in this situation?

Decision-Making Case

DMC 12-1.

LO 6   *Analysis of Cash Flow*
LO 7   *Difficulty*

May Hashimi, chief executive of *Hashimi Print Gallery*, is examining her company's income statement, which has just been handed to her by her accountant, Bill Klein. After looking at the statement, Ms. Hashimi says to Mr. Klein, "Bill, the statement seems to be well done, but what I need to know is why I don't have enough cash to pay my bills this month. You show that I have earned 120,000 in 20x2, but I have only 24,000 in the bank. I know I bought a building on a mortgage and paid a cash dividend of 48,000, but what else is going on?" Mr. Klein replies, "To answer your question, we have to look at comparative balance sheets and prepare another type of statement. Take a look at these balance sheets." The statements handed to Ms. Hashimi follow.

Hashimi Print Gallery
Comparative Balance Sheets
December 31, 20x2 and 20x1

	20x2	20x1
Assets		
Cash	24,000	40,000
Accounts Receivable (net)	178,000	146,000
Inventory	240,000	180,000
Prepaid Expenses	10,000	14,000
Building	400,000	—
Accumulated Depreciation	(20,000)	—
Total Assets	832,000	380,000
Liabilities and Shareholders' Equity		
Accounts Payable	74,000	96,000
Income Taxes Payable	6,000	4,000
Mortgage Payable	400,000	—
Ordinary Shares	200,000	200,000
Retained Earnings	152,000	80,000
Total Liabilities and Shareholders' Equity	832,000	380,000

Hashimi Print Gallery
Income Statement
For the Year Ended December 31, 20x2

Sales	884,000
Cost of Goods Sold	508,000
Gross Profit	376,000
Operating Expenses (including Depreciation Expense of 20,000)	204,000
Operating Profit	172,000
Interest Expense	24,000
Profit before Taxes	148,000
Income Taxes	28,000
Net Profit	120,000

REQUIRED

1. From the information given, prepare a cash flow statement for Hashimi Print Gallery using the direct method.
2. Hashimi Print Gallery has a cash problem despite profitable operations. What are the reasons for this cash problem?

Basic Research Activity

RA 12-1.

LO 7 *Basic Research Skills*

In your library, select the annual reports of three corporations. You may choose them from the same industry or at random, at the direction of your teacher. (If you did a related exercise in a previous chapter, use the same three companies.) Prepare a table with a column for each corporation. Then, for any year covered by the cash flow statement, answer the following questions: (1) Does the company use the direct or the indirect approach? (2) Is net profit more or less than net cash flows from operating activities? (3) What are the major causes of differences between net profit and net cash flows from operating activities? (4) Calculate cash flow efficiency ratios and free cash flow. (5) Does the dividend appear secure? (6) Did the company make significant capital expenditures during the year? (7) How were the expenditures financed? (8) Do you notice anything unusual about the investing and financing activities of your companies? (9) Do the investing and financing activities provide any insights into management's plan for each company? If so, what are they? Be prepared to discuss the answers to these questions in class.

Financial Reporting and Analysis

Interpretation Cases from Business

ICB 12-1.

LO 7 *Analysis of the Cash Flow Statement*

Airborne Freight Corporation, which is known as Airborne Express, is an air express transportation company, providing next-day, morning delivery of small packages and documents throughout the United States. Airborne Express is one of three major participants, along with Federal Express and United Parcel Service, in the air express industry. The following statement appears in "Management's discussion and analysis of results of operations and financial condition" from the company's 1992 annual report: "Capital expenditures and financing associated with those expenditures have been the primary factors affecting the financial condition of the company over the last three years."[9] Airborne Express's consolidated cash flow statements for the years 1992, 1991, and 1990 follow.

The following data (in thousands) are also available:

	1992	1991	1990	1989
Net Sales	$1,484,316	$1,367,047	$1,181,890	$949,896
Total Assets	964,739	823,647	613,534	470,605

Airborne Freight Corporation and Subsidiaries
Consolidated Cash Flow Statements
Year Ended December 31
(in Thousands)

	1992	1991	1990
Operating Activities			
Net earnings	$ 5,157	$ 29,999	$ 33,577
Adjustments to reconcile net earnings to net cash provided by operating activities:			
Depreciation and amortisation	110,206	90,586	69,055
Provision for aircraft engine overhauls	10,426	8,445	6,224
Deferred income taxes	(9,930)	(3,256)	536
Other	5,949	8,125	1,921
Cash Provided by Operations	121,808	133,899	111,313
Change in:			
Receivables	(16,158)	(11,880)	(19,722)
Inventories and prepaid expenses	(5,635)	(7,594)	(6,496)
Accounts payable	16	(3,177)	14,514
Accrued expenses, salaries and taxes payable	5,167	19,229	10,715
Net Cash Provided by Operating Activities	105,198	130,477	110,324
Investing Activities			
Additions to property and equipment	(252,733)	(248,165)	(217,926)
Disposition of property and equipment	1,068	1,674	2,286
Expenditures for engine overhauls	(1,933)	(4,970)	(7,483)
Other	206	1,094	(1,868)
Net Cash Used in Investing Activities	(253,392)	(250,367)	(224,991)
Financing Activities			
Proceeds from bank note borrowings, net	30,700	17,900	(6,800)
Proceeds from debt issuances	132,786	126,479	—
Principal payments on debt	(6,273)	(19,190)	(8,642)
Proceeds from sale-leaseback of aircraft	—	—	28,464
Proceeds from redeemable preference share issuance	—	—	40,000
Proceeds from ordinary share issuance	1,641	2,370	69,461
Dividends paid	(8,503)	(8,442)	(7,609)
Net Cash Provided by Financing Activities	150,351	119,117	114,874
Net Increase (Decrease) in Cash	2,157	(773)	207
Cash at Beginning of Year	8,022	8,795	8,588
Cash at End of Year	$ 10,179	$ 8,022	$ 8,795

REQUIRED
1. Have operations provided Airborne Express with significant cash flows over the past three years? What is the role of net earnings in this provision? Other than net earnings, what is the most significant factor in providing the cash flows? Have changes in working capital accounts been a significant factor?
2. Calculate and assess Airborne Express's cash-generating ability for the three years 1992, 1991, and 1990.
3. Calculate free cash flow for the three years. Is management's statement about capital expenditures and associated financing substantiated by the figures? If your answer is yes, what were Airborne Express's primary means of financing the expansion in 1992?

South African Breweries
Cash Flow Statements
For the Years Ended March 31
(in Millions)

	Notes	Group 1996 Rm	1995 Rm
Cash Retained from Operating Activities			
Trading profit		3,474.4	2,934.0
Depreciation and amortisation	5.3	1,086.4	930.0
Other noncash items and adjustments	10.1	(54.9)	(41.9)
Cash generated from trading		4,505.9	3,822.1
Increase in net working capital	10.2	(357.7)	(420.7)
Dividend income received		112.2	106.0
Cash generated from operating activities		4,260.4	3,507.4
Net financing costs paid	10.3	(587.8)	(463.4)
Taxation paid	10.4	(752.7)	(699.3)
Cash Flow from Operations		2,919.9	2,344.7
Dividends paid	10.5	(174.2)	(398.6)
Net Cash Retained		2,745.7	1,946.1
Cash Utilised in Investment Activities			
Investment to maintain operations	10.7	(1,388.9)	(1,117.4)
Investment to expand operations		(429.6)	(371.3)
Net acquisition of subsidiaries and associates	10.8	(381.9)	(162.9)
Net Cash Invested		(2,200.4)	(1,651.6)
Cash Effects of Financing Activities			
Decrease in interest-bearing debt	10.9	(143.5)	(302.9)
Increase in liquid resources	10.10	(428.7)	(49.9)
Increase in shareholder funding	10.11	26.9	58.3
Decrease in intergroup indebtedness			
Net Financing		(545.3)	(294.5)
Attributable Cash Flow per Ordinary Share (cents)	3.2	793.4	647.2
Cash Realisation Rate	2.2.8		
Cash flow to cash equivalent earnings (%)		95	94

<table>
<tr><td>ICB 12-2.
LO 3   Format and Interpretation of
LO 7   Cash Flow Statements</td></tr>
</table>

ICB 12-2.

LO 3 *Format and Interpretation of*
LO 7 *Cash Flow Statements*

South African Breweries (SAB), based in South Africa, has interests in beer, complementary beverages, retailing, hotels, and the manufacture and supply of selected consumer goods and services. In addition to a cash flow statement, SAB also provides a cash value added statement, which shows the cash generated from operations in excess of external costs and its distribution among the company's stakeholders. The group's cash flow and cash value added statements are presented above and at the top of the next page. (1) What are the main differences between the cash flow statement and the cash value added statement? (2) To what extent does the cash value added statement provide additional useful information?

Nestlé Case

NC 12-1.

LO 7 *Analysis of the Cash Flow Statement*

Refer to the cash flow statement in the appendix on Nestlé to answer the following questions:

1. Does Nestlé use the direct or the indirect method of reporting cash flows from operating activities? Other than net profit, what are the three most important factors affecting cash flows from operating activities? Explain the trend of each.
2. Based on the cash flows from investing activities, would you say that Nestlé is a contracting or an expanding company?
3. Calculate the cash flow yield, cash flows to sales, cash flows to assets, and free cash flow for the last two years for Nestlé. How would you evaluate the company's cash-generating efficiency? Does Nestlé need external financing? If so, where has it come from?

South African Breweries
Cash Value Added Statements
For the Years Ended March 31
(in Millions)

	Group			
	1996		1995	
	Rm	%	Rm	%
Cash Generated				
Cash derived from sales	31,991.2		27,263.6	
Income from investments	112.2		106.0	
Cash value generated	32,103.4		27,369.6	
Cash payments outside the Group to suppliers of materials, facilities, and services	20,138.3		17,128.6	
Cash Value Added	11,965.1	100	10,241.0	100
Cash Utilised to:				
Remunerate employees for their services	5,289.8	44	4,687.7	46
Pay direct and excise taxes to the State	3,167.6	26	2,745.2	27
Provide lenders with a return on borrowings	587.8	5	463.4	4
Provide shareholders with cash dividends	174.2	2	398.6	4
Cash Disbursed among Stakeholders	9,219.4	77	8,294.9	81
Cash Retained in the Business:				
From shareholders in exchange for capitilisation share rewards	603.0	5	353.9	4
Further retentions	2,142.7	18	1,592.2	15
Available to Fund the Replacement of Assets and Facilitate Further Growth	2,745.7	23	1,946.1	19

ENDNOTES

1. Broken Hill Proprietary Company, *Annual Report*, 1996.
2. International Accounting Standard, IAS7, *Cash Flow Statements* (London: IASC, revised 1992).
3. International Accounting Standards Committee, *Framework for the Preparation and Presentation of Financial Statements* (London: IASC, 1996), para. 7.
4. International Accounting Standard, IAS7, *Cash Flow Statements*.
5. Martin Waller, "Writedown Condemns Saatchi to £595m Loss", *The Times*, March 10, 1993.
6. Jonathan Clements, "Yacktman Fund is Bloodied but Unbowed", *Wall Street Journal*, November 8, 1993.
7. Jeffrey Laderman, "Earnings, Schmearnings—Look at the Cash", *Business Week*, July 24, 1989.
8. Guinness, *Annual Report*, 1995.
9. Airborne Freight Corporation, *Annual Report*, 1992.

Chapter 13

INTERCOMPANY INVESTMENTS, CONSOLIDATED FINANCIAL STATEMENTS, AND FOREIGN CURRENCY ACCOUNTING

LEARNING OBJECTIVES

1. Apply the appropriate method to influential and noninfluential situations in accounting for long-term investments.
2. Explain when to prepare consolidated financial statements, and describe their uses.
3. Prepare consolidated balance sheets at acquisition date for purchase at (a) book value and (b) other than book value.
4. Prepare consolidated income statements for intercompany transactions.
5. Define *exchange rate* and record transactions that are affected by changes in foreign exchange rates.
6. Describe the restatement of a foreign subsidiary's financial statements.

DECISION POINT

SIME DARBY

Sime Darby, based in Malaysia, is one of South East Asia's leading multinational corporations. The company is a conglomerate that operates more than three hundred companies in twenty-one countries around the world, employing about thirty-seven thousand people.[1] The company is listed on the Kuala Lumpur and London Stock Exchanges. Sime Darby was founded in 1910 as a rubber plantation company but then widened its involvement in plantations to other areas including general trading and equipment distribution. Sime Darby's core business activities now comprise plantations, tyre manufacturing, heavy equipment and motor vehicle distribution, property development, financial services, and oil and gas. Besides Malaysia, the group has extensive trading and manufacturing interests in Hong Kong, Singapore, the Philippines, and Australia.

Sime Darby's size, diversity of business interests, and geographical spread highlight the need by management and other users for information about the group as an economic entity including its controlled subsidiaries and its influential but noncontrolling investments. Consolidated financial statements give users a clear financial picture of the total economic entity by treating the parent and subsidiaries as if they were one company. Investments that are influential but noncontrolling are also incorporated in a way that reflects the investor's share in the success or failure of the investee companies.

The aim of this chapter is to examine the issues involved in accounting for long-term intercompany investments, in preparing consolidated financial statements, and in foreign currency accounting.

OBJECTIVE 1

Apply the appropriate method to influential and noninfluential situations in accounting for long-term investments

LONG-TERM INTERCOMPANY INVESTMENTS

One corporation may invest in another corporation by purchasing bonds or shares. These investments may be either current or long term. In this section, we are concerned with long-term investments in shares.

All long-term investments in shares are recorded initially at cost. The treatment of the investment in the accounting records after the initial purchase depends on the extent to which the investing company can exercise significant influence or control over the operating and financial policies of the other company.

The International Accounting Standards Committee defined the terms *significant influence* and *control* in its IAS28. **Significant influence** is "the power to participate in the financial and operating policy decisions of the investee but is not control over those policies."[2] Ability to influence a company may be shown by representation on the board of directors, participation in policy making, material transactions between the companies, exchange of managerial personnel, and technological dependency. For practical purposes, the IASC has decided that a holding of 20 per cent of the voting power should be presumed to confer significant influence on the investor corporation.

Control is defined as "the power to govern the financial and operating policies of an enterprise so as to obtain benefits from its activities."[3] Control is usually said to exist when the investing company owns more than 50 per cent of the voting shares of the company in which it has invested.

Thus, in the absence of information to the contrary, a noninfluential and noncontrolling investment would be less than 20 per cent ownership. An influential but noncontrolling investment would be 20 to 50 per cent ownership. And a controlling investment would be more than 50 per cent ownership. The accounting treatment differs for each kind of investment.

Noninfluential and Noncontrolling Investment

Noninfluential and noncontrolling investments are holdings of shares comprising less than 20 per cent of the voting shares. The International Accounting Standards Committee permits the **lower of cost and market method** to be used in accounting for marketable equity securities classified as long-term investments. Under this method, such securities are recorded initially at cost and thereafter adjusted periodically to reflect any decreases in the market value of the securities determined on a portfolio basis.[4] However, the IASC also permits long-term investments to be held at cost or at revalued amounts. If held at cost, then when there is a decline, other than temporary, in value, the carrying amount should be reduced to recognise the decline. In some countries, such as the United States, long-term investments may be revalued to fair market value, and in such cases a consistent policy of regular revaluation should be followed.

In the case of marketable equity securities, at the end of each accounting period, the total cost and the total market value of these long-term investments must be determined. If the total market value is less than the total cost, the difference must be credited to a contra-asset account called Allowance to Adjust Long-Term Investments to Market. The debit part of the entry, which represents a decrease in value below cost, is treated as a loss on the income statement.

When long-term investments in shares are sold, the difference between the sale price and the shares cost is recorded and reported as a gain or loss on the income statement. For example, assume the following facts about the long-term investments of Coleman Corporation:

June 1, 20x0	Paid cash for the following long-term investments: 10,000 ordinary shares of Durbin Corporation (representing 2 per cent of outstanding shares) at 25 per share; 5,000 ordinary shares of Kotes Corporation (representing 3 per cent of outstanding shares) at 15 per share.
Dec. 31, 20x0	Quoted market prices at year end: Durbin, 21; Kotes, 17.
Apr. 1, 20x1	Change in policy required sale of 2,000 ordinary shares of Durbin Corporation at 23.

Entries to record these transactions follow:

Investment

20x0			
June 1	Long-Term Investments	325,000	
	Cash		325,000
	Investments in Durbin ordinary shares (10,000 shares $\times$ 25 = 250,000) and Kotes ordinary shares (5,000 shares $\times$ 15 = 75,000)		

Year-End Adjustment

20x0			
Dec. 31	Loss on Long-Term Investments	30,000	
	Allowance to Adjust Long-Term Investments to Market		30,000
	To record reduction of long-term investments to market		

Company	Shares	Market Price	Total Market	Total Cost
Durbin	10,000	21	210,000	250,000
Kotes	5,000	17	85,000	75,000
			295,000	325,000

$$\text{Cost} - \text{market value} = 325,000 - 295,000 = 30,000$$

Influential but Noncontrolling Investment

As we have seen, ownership of 20 to 50 per cent or more of a company's voting shares is considered sufficient to influence the operations of another corporation. When this is the case, the investment in the shares of the influenced company should be accounted for using the **equity method**. The equity method presumes that an investment of 20 to 50 per cent is more than a passive investment, and that therefore the investing company should share in the success or failure of the investee company. Hence, the investment is adjusted for postacquisition changes in the investor's share of the results of operations of the investee. The following are the three main features of the equity method:

1. The investor records the original purchase of the shares at cost.
2. The investor records its share of the investee's periodic net profit as an increase in the Investment account, with a corresponding credit to a profit account. In like manner, the investor records its share of the investee's periodic loss as a decrease in the Investment account, with a corresponding debit to a loss account.
3. When the investor receives a cash dividend, the asset account Cash is increased and the Investment account decreased.

To illustrate the equity method of accounting, we will assume the following facts about an investment by the Vassor Corporation. On January 1 of the current year, Vassor Corporation acquired 40 per cent of the voting ordinary shares of the Block Corporation for 180,000. With this share of ownership, the Vassor Corporation can exert significant influence over the operations of the Block Corporation. During the year, the Block Corporation reported net profit of 80,000 and paid cash dividends of 20,000. The entries to record these transactions by the Vassor Corporation are

Investment

Investment in Block Corporation	180,000	
Cash		180,000
Investment in Block Corporation ordinary shares		

Recognition of Profit

Investment in Block Corporation	32,000	
Profit, Block Corporation Investment		32,000
Recognition of 40% of profit reported by Block Corporation		
40% × 80,000 = 32,000		

Receipt of Cash Dividend

Cash	8,000	
Investment in Block Corporation		8,000
Cash dividend from Block Corporation		
40% × 20,000 = 8,000		

The balance of the Investment in Block Corporation account after these transactions is 204,000, as follows:

Investment in Block Corporation

Investment	180,000	Dividends received	8,000
Share of profit	32,000		
Balance	204,000		

Controlling Investment

A controlling investment is one in which the investor has the power to govern the financial and operating policies of the investee. In some cases, an investor who owns less than 50 per cent of the voting shares of a company may exercise such powerful influence that for all practical purposes the investor controls the policies of the other company. In any event, control is presumed to exist when the investor owns more than 50 per cent of the voting shares.[5] When there is a controlling interest, a parent-subsidiary relationship is formed. The investing company is known as the **parent company**, the investee company as the **subsidiary**. Because both corporations are separate legal entities, each prepares separate financial statements. However, owing to their special relationship, they are viewed for public financial reporting purposes as a single economic entity or **group** comprising a parent and all its subsidiaries. For this reason, they must combine their financial statements into a single set of statements called **consolidated financial statements**.

Accounting for consolidated financial statements is very complex. It is usually the subject of an advanced accounting course. However, most large public corporations have subsidiaries and must prepare consolidated financial statements. It is therefore important to have some understanding of accounting for consolidations.

The appropriate accounting treatments for long-term investments in shares are summarised in Table 13-1.

TABLE 13-1 *Accounting Treatments of Long-Term Investments in Shares*

Level of Ownership	Percentage of Ownership Voting Power	Accounting Treatment
Noninfluential and noncontrolling	Less than 20%	Cost initially; investment adjusted subsequent to purchase for decreases in market value
Influential but noncontrolling	Between 20% and 50%	Equity method; investment valued subsequently at cost plus investor's share of profit (or minus investor's share of loss) minus dividends received
Controlling	More than 50%	Consolidated financial statements

OBJECTIVE 2

Explain when to prepare consolidated financial statements, and describe their uses

CONSOLIDATED FINANCIAL STATEMENTS

Most major corporations find it convenient for economic, legal, tax, or other reasons to operate in parent-subsidiary relationships. When we speak of a large company such as Ford, ABB, or Sony, we generally think of the parent company, not of its many subsidiaries. When considering investment in one of these firms, however, the investor wants a clear financial picture of the total economic entity or group. The main purpose of consolidated financial statements is to provide such a view of the parent and subsidiary firms by treating them as if they were one company. This has become even more important in recent years as many companies have grown through mergers and acquisitions (M&A) including some significant cross-border deals (see Table 13-2 for 1995 data on deals with a value above U.S. $1 billion). On a consolidated balance sheet, the inventory account includes the inventory held by the parent and all its subsidiaries. Similarly, on the consolidated income statement, the sales account is the total revenue from sales by the parent and all its subsidiaries. This overview helps management and shareholders of the parent company judge the company's progress in meeting its goals. In addition, long-term lenders of the parent find consolidated statements useful because of their interest in the long-range financial health of the company.

In the past, it was acceptable not to consolidate the statements of certain subsidiaries, even though the parent owned a controlling interest, when the business of the subsidiary was not homogeneous with that of the parent. For instance, a retail company or a car manufacturer might have had a wholly-owned finance subsidiary that was not consolidated. However, such practices were criticised because they tended to remove certain assets (accounts and notes receivable) and certain liabilities (borrowing by the finance subsidiary) from the consolidated financial statements. As a result, with few exceptions, the financial statements of all majority-owned subsidiaries must now be consolidated with the parent company's financial statements for external reporting purposes.

In many countries, including France, Greece, Italy, and Japan, the presentation of consolidated financial statements is a relatively recent development. In Japan, for example, these statements are even now not required as primary financial statements but as supplementary information to the financial statements of the parent company. In many European countries there is also an exemption for "small" companies from the consolidation requirements set out in company law.

Methods of Accounting for Business Combinations

Interests in subsidiary companies may be acquired by paying cash; issuing long-term bonds, other debt, or ordinary or preference shares; or working out some combination of these forms of payment, such as exchanging shares of the parent's own unissued capital for the outstanding shares of the subsidiary's share capital. For parent-subsidiary relationships that arise when cash is paid or debt or preference shares are issued, it is mandatory to use the purchase method, which is explained below. For simplicity, our illustrations assume payment in cash. In the special case of establishing a parent-subsidiary relationship through an exchange of shares, the uniting of interests method may be appropriate. This latter method is the subject of more advanced courses.

Consolidated Balance Sheet

In preparing consolidated financial statements under the **purchase method**, similar accounts from the separate statements of the parent and the subsidiaries are combined. Some accounts result from transactions between the parent and the subsidiary. Examples are debt owed by one of the entities to the other and sales and purchases between the two entities. When considering the group of companies as a single business, it is not appropriate to include these accounts in the group financial statements; the purchases and sales are only transfers between different parts of the business, and the payables and receivables do not represent amounts due to or receivable from outside parties. For this reason, it is important that certain **eliminations** be made. These

TABLE 13-2   *Cross-border M&A Deals with a Value of above U.S. $1 billion, 1995*

Acquiring Company	Home Country	Acquired Company	Host Country	Value (Billions of Dollars)	Industry
Hoeschst AG	Germany	Marion Merrel Dow	United States	7.1	Pharmaceutical R&D and manufacturing
The Seagram Co. Ltd.	Canada	MCA Inc.	United States	5.7	Film production
Crown Cork & Seal Co. Inc.	United States	Carnaudmetalbox S.A.	France	5.2	Packaging products
Atlas (a joint venture of France Telecom/ Deutsche Telekom)	Belgium	Sprint	United States	4.2	Telecommunications
United Communication Industry PLC (via Total Access PLC)	Thailand	Intercity Paging Service PTE LTD	Sri Lanka	2.8	Telecommunications
Grand Metropolitan PLC (via Pillsbury)	United Kingdom	Pet Inc. (United States)	United States	2.6	Pet foods
The Broken Hill Proprietary Co. Ltd.	Australia	Magma Copper Company	United States	2.4	Production and refining of copper
Zuerich Versicherungs-Gesellschaft (together with insurance partners)	Switzerland	Kemper Corp.	United States	2.0	Finance (fund management)
Interbrew S.A.	Belgium	John Labatt	Canada	2.0	Brewing
Wolters Kluwer NV	Netherlands	CCH Commerce Clearing House Inc.	United States	1.9	Business services (tax and business law information services)
Central and South-west Corp.	United States	Seeboard PLC	United Kingdom	1.9	Electricity distribution
Softbank Corporation	Japan	Ziff-Davis Publishing Co.	United States	1.7	Publishing of computer magazines
Cadbury Schweppes PLC	United Kingdom	Dr. Pepper/ Seven-Up Co.	United States	1.7	Soft drinks
Southern Company	United States	South Western Electricity PLC	United Kingdom	1.7	Power station and distribution
Texas Utilities Co.	United States	Eastern Energy	Australia	1.6	Electricity distribution
Dresdener Bank AG	Germany	Kleinwort Benson Group PLC	United Kingdom	1.6	Investment bank
Pacificorp	United States	Powercor Ltd.	Australia	1.6	Electricity distribution
National Australia Bank Ltd.	Australia	Michigan National Corporation	United States	1.6	Banking
Veba AG	Germany	Cable & Wireless PLC	United Kingdom	1.5	Telecommunications

(continued)

TABLE 13-2 *Cross-border M&A Deals with a Value of above U.S. $1 billion, 1995 (continued)*

Acquiring Company	Home Country	Acquired Company	Host Country	Value (Billions of Dollars)	Industry
Telsource (consortium led by Koninklijke PTT Nederland NV and Swiss Telecom)	Netherlands	SPT Telecom	Czech Republic	1.5	Telecommunications
Schweizerischer Bankverein (Swiss Bank Corp.)	Switzerland	SG Warburg's Investment Banking Business	United Kingdom	1.4	Investment banking
Utilcorp (consortium including AMP Investments and States Authorities Super-annuation Board)	United States	United Energy	Australia	1.4	Electricity distribution
Energy Corporation	United States	Citipower	Australia	1.3	Electricity distribution
BASF AG	Germany	Boots Pharma-ceuticals	United Kingdom	1.3	Pharmaceuticals
Lyonnaise des Eaux Dumez S. A.	France	Northumbrian Water	United Kingdom	1.2	Water utility
International Property Corporation Ltd.	Canada	Canary Wharf	United Kingdom	1.2	Real estate
Sodexho S. A.	France	Gardner Merchant	United Kingdom	1.2	Catering
International Paper Co.	United States	Carter Holt Harvey Ltd.	New Zealand	1.2	Paper and pulp
Daewoo Corp.	Republic of Korea	FSO Fabryka Samochodow Osobowych	Poland	1.1	Transport equipment
ING Internationale Nederlanden Group NV	Netherlands	Barings Investment Banking, Securities and Asset Management Divisions	United Kingdom	1.1	Banking
Colgate-Palmolive	United States	Kolynos	Brazil	1.0	Chemical and pharmaceuticals/ oral-care products
SEE Corp.	United States	First Hydro	United Kingdom	1.0	Power-generating stations
MCI Communications Corp.	United States	SHE Systemhouse	Canada	1.0	Information technology
Tomkins PLC	United Kingdom	Gates Rubber	United States	1.0	Rubber and plastic products (for cars)
MCI Communications	United States	The News Corp.	Australia	1.0	Media company

Source: *World Investment Report 1996*, United Nations, Geneva, 1996, pp. 12–13.

eliminations avoid the duplication of accounts and reflect the financial position and operations from the standpoint of a single entity. Eliminations appear only on the work sheets used in preparing consolidated financial statements. They are never shown in the accounting records of either the parent or the subsidiary. There are no consolidated journals or ledgers.

Another good example of accounts that result from transactions between the two entities is the Investment in Subsidiary account in the parent's balance sheet and the shareholders' equity section of the subsidiary. When the balance sheets of the two companies are combined, these accounts must be eliminated to avoid duplicating these items in the consolidated financial statements.

To illustrate the preparation of a consolidated balance sheet under the purchase method, we will use the following balance sheets for Parent Company and Subsidiary Company:

Accounts	Parent Company	Subsidiary Company
Cash	100,000	25,000
Other Assets	760,000	60,000
Total Assets	860,000	85,000
Liabilities	60,000	10,000
Ordinary Shares—10 nominal value	600,000	55,000
Retained Earnings	200,000	20,000
Total Liabilities and Shareholders' Equity	860,000	85,000

OBJECTIVE 3a

Prepare consolidated balance sheets at acquisition date for purchase at book value

100 Per Cent Purchase at Book Value

Suppose that Parent Company purchases 100 per cent of the shares of Subsidiary Company for an amount exactly equal to Subsidiary's book value. The book value of Subsidiary Company is 75,000 (85,000 − 10,000). Parent Company would record the purchase as shown below:

Investment in Subsidiary Company	75,000	
Cash		75,000
Purchase of 100 per cent of Subsidiary Company at book value		

It is helpful to use a work sheet like the one shown in Exhibit 13-1 in preparing consolidated financial statements. Note that the balance of Parent Company's Cash account is now 25,000 and that Investment in Subsidiary Company is shown as an asset in Parent Company's balance sheet, reflecting the purchase of the subsidiary. To prepare a consolidated balance sheet, it is necessary to eliminate the investment in the subsidiary. This procedure is shown by elimination entry 1 in Exhibit 13-1. This elimination entry does two things. First, it eliminates the double counting that would take place when the net assets of the two companies are combined. Second, it eliminates the shareholders' equity section of Subsidiary Company.

The theory underlying consolidated financial statements is that parent and subsidiary are a single entity. The shareholders' equity section of the consolidated balance sheet is the same as that of Parent Company. So after eliminating the Investment in Subsidiary Company and the shareholders' equity of the subsidiary, we can take the

EXHIBIT 13-1 *Work Sheet for Preparation of Consolidated Balance Sheet*

Parent and Subsidiary Companies
Work Sheet for Consolidated Balance Sheet
As of Acquisition Date

Accounts	Balance Sheet Parent Company	Balance Sheet Subsidiary Company	Eliminations		Consolidated Balance Sheet
			Debit	Credit	
Cash	25,000	25,000			50,000
Investment in Subsidiary Company	75,000			(1) 75,000	
Other Assets	760,000	60,000			820,000
Total Assets	860,000	85,000			870,000
Liabilities	60,000	10,000			70,000
Ordinary Shares— 10 nominal value	600,000	55,000	(1) 55,000		600,000
Retained Earnings	200,000	20,000	(1) 20,000		200,000
Total Liabilities and Shareholders' Equity	860,000	85,000	75,000	75,000	870,000

(1) Elimination of intercompany investment.

information from the right-hand column in Exhibit 13-1 and present it in the following form:

Parent and Subsidiary Companies
Consolidated Balance Sheet
As of Acquisition Date

Cash	50,000	Liabilities	70,000
Other Assets	820,000	Ordinary Shares	600,000
		Retained Earnings	200,000
		Total Liabilities and	
Total Assets	870,000	Shareholders' Equity	870,000

Less than 100 Per Cent Purchase at Book Value

A parent company does not have to purchase 100 per cent of a subsidiary to control it. If it purchases more than 50 per cent of the voting shares of the subsidiary company, it will have legal control. In the consolidated financial statements, therefore, the total assets and liabilities of the subsidiary are combined with the assets and liabilities of the parent. However, it is still necessary to account for the interests of those shareholders of the subsidiary company who own less than 50 per cent of the voting shares. These are the minority shareholders, and their **minority interest** must appear on the

EXHIBIT 13-2   *Work Sheet Showing Elimination of Less than 100 Per Cent Ownership*

Parent and Subsidiary Companies
Work Sheet for Consolidated Balance Sheet
As of Acquisition Date

Accounts	Balance Sheet Parent Company	Balance Sheet Subsidiary Company	Eliminations		Consolidated Balance Sheet
			Debit	Credit	
Cash	32,500	25,000			57,500
Investment in Subsidiary Company	67,500			(1) 67,500	—
Other Assets	760,000	60,000			820,000
Total Assets	860,000	85,000			877,500
Liabilities	60,000	10,000			70,000
Ordinary Shares— 10 nominal value	— 600,000	— 55,000	(1) 55,000		600,000
Retained Earnings	200,000	20,000	(1) 20,000		200,000
Minority Interest				(1) 7,500	7,500
Total Liabilities and Shareholders' Equity	860,000	85,000	75,000	75,000	877,500

(1) Elimination of intercompany investment. Minority interest equals 10 per cent of subsidiary's shareholders' equity.

consolidated balance sheet as an amount equal to their percentage of ownership times the net assets of the subsidiary.

Suppose that the same Parent Company buys, for 67,500, only 90 per cent of Subsidiary Company's voting shares. In this case, the portion of the company purchased has a book value of 67,500 (90% × 75,000). The work sheet used for preparing the consolidated balance sheet appears in Exhibit 13-2. The elimination is made in the same way as in the case above, except that the minority interest must be accounted for. All of the Investment in Subsidiary Company (67,500) is eliminated against all of Subsidiary Company's shareholders' equity (75,000). The difference (7,500, or 10% × 75,000) is set as minority interest.

There are two ways to classify minority interest on the consolidated balance sheet. One is to place it between long-term liabilities and shareholders' equity. The other is to consider the shareholders' equity section as consisting of (1) minority interest and (2) Parent Company's shareholders' equity, as shown here:

Minority Interest	7,500
Ordinary Shares	600,000
Retained Earnings	200,000
Total Shareholders' Equity	807,500

OBJECTIVE 3b

Prepare consolidated balance sheets at acquisition date for purchase at other than book value

Purchase at More or Less than Book Value

The purchase price of a business depends on many factors, such as the current market price, the relative strength of the buyer's and seller's bargaining positions, and the prospects for future earnings. Thus, it is only by chance that the purchase price of a subsidiary will equal the book value of the subsidiary's equity. Usually, it will not. For example, a parent company may pay more than the book value of a subsidiary to purchase a controlling interest if the assets of the subsidiary are understated. In that case, the recorded historical cost less depreciation of the subsidiary's assets may not reflect current market or fair values. The parent may also pay more than book value if the subsidiary has something that the parent wants, such as an important technical process, a new and different product, or a new market. On the other hand, the parent may pay less than book value for its share of the subsidiary's capital if the subsidiary's assets are not worth their depreciated cost. Or the subsidiary may have suffered heavy losses, causing its shares to sell at rather low prices.

The International Accounting Standards Committee has the following requirements for consolidating a purchased subsidiary and its parent:

(1) The individual assets and liabilities identified should be measured at their fair value at the date of acquisition; (2) any excess of the cost of the acquisition over the fair value of the identifiable assets and liabilities should be described as goodwill and recorded as an asset.[6]

To illustrate the application of these requirements, we will assume that Parent Company purchases 100 per cent of Subsidiary Company's voting shares for 92,500, or 17,500 more than book value. Parent Company considers 10,000 of the 17,500 to be due to the increase in fair value of Subsidiary's other assets and 7,500 of the 17,500 to be due to the overall strength that Subsidiary Company would add to Parent Company's organisation. The work sheet used for preparing the consolidated balance sheet appears in Exhibit 13-3. All of the Investment in Subsidiary Company (92,500) has been eliminated against all of the Subsidiary Company's shareholders' equity (75,000). The excess of cost over book value (17,500) has been debited in the amounts

EXHIBIT 13-3 *Work Sheet Showing Elimination When Purchase Cost Is Greater than Book Value*

Parent and Subsidiary Companies
Work Sheet for Consolidated Balance Sheet
As of Acquisition Date

Accounts	Balance Sheet Parent Company	Balance Sheet Subsidiary Company	Eliminations		Consolidated Balance Sheet
			Debit	Credit	
Cash	7,500	25,000			32,500
Investment in Subsidiary Company	92,500			(1) 92,500	
Other Assets	760,000	60,000	(1) 10,000		830,000
Goodwill			(1) 7,500		7,500
Total Assets	860,000	85,000			870,000
Liabilities	60,000	10,000			70,000
Ordinary Shares— 10 nominal value	600,000	55,000	(1) 55,000		600,000
Retained Earnings	200,000	20,000	(1) 20,000		200,000
Total Liabilities and Shareholders' Equity	860,000	85,000	92,500	92,500	870,000

(1) Elimination of intercompany investment. Excess of cost over book value (92,500 − 75,000 = 17,500) allocated 10,000 to Other Assets and 7,500 to Goodwill.

of 10,000 to Other Long-Term Assets and 7,500 to a new account called **Goodwill**, or **Goodwill from Consolidation**.

The amount of goodwill is determined as follows:

Cost of investment in subsidiary	92,500
Book value of subsidiary	75,000
Excess of cost over book value	17,500
Portion of excess attributable to fair value of long-term assets of subsidiary	10,000
Portion of excess attributable to goodwill	7,500

Goodwill appears as an asset on the consolidated balance sheet representing the excess of the cost of the investment over the fair value of the identifiable assets and liabilities. Other Assets appears on the consolidated balance sheet at the combined total of 830,000 (760,000 + 60,000 + 10,000).

According to the International Accounting Standards Committee, positive goodwill should be amortised over its useful life over a period not normally exceeding twenty years.[7] However, the maximum period of amortisation used in practice still varies quite significantly around the world as can be seen from Exhibit 13-4. In Japan, a maximum period of five years is normally required whereas in Canada and the United States a maximum period of forty years is permitted. In some countries such as Brazil, China, and France, the stated criterion is "useful economic life", leaving the period applicable as a matter of judgement. In the Netherlands, on the other hand, amortisation of goodwill is not required. An alternative approach, the direct write-off against shareholders' equity is still permitted contrary to International Accounting Standards. The outcome of this diversity of treatments is likely to be significantly different measures of net profit across countries.

When the parent pays less than book value for its investment in the subsidiary, and where it is not possible to record a reduction in the fair values of subsidiary assets, then the IASC requires this excess to be described as negative goodwill and recognised as income on a systematic basis.

EXHIBIT 13-4 *Treatment of Consolidation Goodwill*

	Write-off against Shareholders' Equity	Recognition as Asset and Amortisation	Maximum Period of Amortisation
Australia	Not permitted	Required	20 years
Brazil	Not permitted	Required	Useful economic life
Canada	Not permitted	Required	40 years
China	Not permitted	Required	Useful economic life
France	Exceptionally permitted	Normally required	Useful economic life
Germany	Permitted	Permitted	4 years or useful economic life
Italy	Permitted	Preferred	5 years or useful economic life
Japan	Not permitted	Required	5 years
Netherlands	Permitted	Permitted	5–10 years
Spain	Not permitted	Required	5–10 years
Sweden	Not permitted	Required	10–20 years
Switzerland	Permitted	Permitted	Normally 8 years
U.K.	Not permitted	Normally required	Useful economic life
U.S.	Not permitted	Required	40 years

> ## BUSINESS BULLETIN Business Practice
>
> While mergers and acquisitions are nothing new, what has been different about corporate behaviour since the late 1980s has been the growth of cross-border deals (see Table 13-2). Moreover, these deals are often between very large companies, such as the merger between Hoechst of Germany and Marion Merrel Dow of the United States. As these business combinations tend to give rise to large amounts of goodwill, the impact of the accounting treatment on profits can be significant. As shown in Exhibit 13-4, amortisation of goodwill is not always required, but even where it is, the maximum period of amortisation can vary from four to forty years with consequent differential effects on the amount of amortisation charged against profit. This flexibility is considered by some to give an unfair bidding advantage to those companies that can show higher profits following a merger.

Intercompany Receivables and Payables

If either the parent or the subsidiary company owes money to the other, there will be a receivable on the lender company's individual balance sheet and a payable on the debtor company's individual balance sheet. When a consolidated balance sheet is prepared, both the receivable and the payable should be eliminated because, from the viewpoint of the consolidated entity, neither the asset nor the liability exists. In other words, it does not make sense for a company to owe money to itself. The eliminating entry would be made on the work sheet by debiting the payable and crediting the receivable for the amount of the intercompany loan.

OBJECTIVE 4

Prepare consolidated income statements for intercompany transactions

Consolidated Income Statement

The consolidated income statement for a consolidated entity is prepared by combining the revenues and expenses of the parent and subsidiary companies. The procedure is the same as the procedure for preparing a consolidated balance sheet. That is, intercompany transactions are eliminated to prevent double counting of revenues and expenses. Several intercompany transactions affect the consolidated income statement. They are: (1) sales and purchases of goods and services between parent company and subsidiary company (purchases for the buying company and sales for the selling company); (2) income and expenses on loans, receivables, or bond indebtedness between parent and subsidiary; and (3) other income and expenses from intercompany transactions.

To illustrate the eliminating entries, we will assume the following transactions between a parent and its wholly-owned subsidiary. Parent Company made sales of 120,000 in goods to Subsidiary Company, which in turn sold all the goods to others. Subsidiary Company paid Parent Company 2,000 interest on a loan from the parent.

The work sheet in Exhibit 13-5 shows how to prepare a consolidated income statement. The purpose of the eliminating entries is to treat the two companies as a single entity. Thus, it is important to include in Sales only those sales made to outsiders and to include in Cost of Goods Sold only those purchases made from outsiders. This goal is met with the first eliminating entry, which eliminates the 120,000 of intercompany sales and purchases by a debit of that amount to Sales and a credit of that amount to Cost of Goods Sold. As a result, only sales to outsiders (510,000) and purchases from outsiders (240,000) are included in the Consolidated Income Statement column. The intercompany interest income and expense are eliminated by a debit to Other Revenues and a credit to Other Expenses.

EXHIBIT 13-5   *Work Sheet Showing Eliminations for Preparing a Consolidated Income Statement*

Parent and Subsidiary Companies
Work Sheet for Consolidated Income Statement
For the Year Ended December 31, 20xx

Accounts	Income Statement Parent Company	Income Statement Subsidiary Company	Eliminations		Consolidated Income Statement
			Debit	Credit	
Sales	430,000	200,000	(1) 120,000		510,000
Other Revenues	60,000	10,000	(2) 2,000		68,000
Total Revenues	490,000	210,000			578,000
Cost of Goods Sold	210,000	150,000		(1) 120,000	240,000
Other Expenses	140,000	50,000		(2) 2,000	188,000
Total Cost and Expenses	350,000	200,000			428,000
Net Profit	140,000	10,000	122,000	122,000	150,000

(1) Elimination of intercompany sales and purchases.
(2) Elimination of intercompany interest income and interest expense.

Other Consolidated Financial Statements

Public corporations also prepare consolidated cash flow statements. For an example of this statement, see the appendix containing the financial statements of Nestlé.

OBJECTIVE 5

Define exchange rate *and record transactions that are affected by changes in foreign exchange rates*

FOREIGN CURRENCY ACCOUNTING

As businesses grow, they naturally look for new sources of supply and new markets in other countries. Today, it is common for businesses, called **multinational** or **transnational corporations**, to operate in more than one country, and many of them operate throughout the world. The significance of this development is indicated in Table 13-3, which shows the top fifty multinational corporations ranked by foreign assets in 1994.

TABLE 13-3   *The Top Fifty Multinational Corporations Ranked by Foreign Assets, 1994 (Billions of Dollars and Number of Employees)*

Ranking by:					Foreign	Total	Foreign	Total	Foreign	Total	
Foreign Assets	Index[b]	Corporation	Country	Industry[a]	Assets		Sales		Employment		Index[b]
1	27	Royal Dutch Shell[c]	U.K./Netherlands	Petroleum	63.7	102.0	51.1	94.8	79,000	106,000	63.6
2	80	Ford	U.S.	Motor vehicles/parts	60.6	219.4	38.1	128.4	96,726	337,778	28.6
3	26	Exxon	U.S.	Petroleum	56.2	87.9	72.3	113.9	55,000	86,000	63.8
4	85	General Motors	U.S.	Motor vehicles/parts	—[d]	198.6	44.0	152.2	177,730	692,800	25.7
5	38	IBM	U.S.	Computers	43.9	81.1	39.9	64.1	115,555	219,839	56.4
6	30	Volkswagen	Germany	Motor vehicles/parts	—[d]	52.4	29.0	49.3	96,545	242,318	60.4

(continued)

TABLE 13-3 *The Top Fifty Multinational Corporations Ranked by Foreign Assets, 1994 (Billions of Dollars and Number of Employees) (continued)*

Ranking by: Foreign Assets	Index[b]	Corporation	Country	Industry[a]	Foreign Assets	Total Assets	Foreign Sales	Total Sales	Foreign Employment	Total Employment	Index[b]
7	97	General Electric	U.S.	Electronics	33.9	251.5	11.9	59.3	36,169	216,000	16.7
8	82	Toyota	Japan	Motor vehicles/parts	—[d]	116.8	37.2	91.3	27,567	172,675	28.1
9	59	Daimler-Benz	Germany	Transport and communication	27.9	66.5	46.3	74.0	79,297	330,551	42.8
10	37	Elf Aquitaine	France	Petroleum	—[d]	48.9	26.2	38.9	43,950	89,500	56.7
11	32	Mobil	U.S.	Petroleum	26.2	41.5	44.1	66.8	27,400	58,500	58.7
12	74	Mitsubishi	Japan	Diversified	—[d]	109.3	67.0	175.8	11,146	36,000	31.0
13	8	Nestlé	Switzerland	Food	25.4	38.7	47.3	48.7	206,125	212,687	86.5
14	72	Nissan Motor	Japan	Motor vehicles/parts	—[d]	80.8	27.3	65.6	34,464	143,310	32.2
15	6	ABB Asea Brown Boveri Ltd[e]	Switzerland	Electrical equipment	24.8	29.1	25.6	29.7	194,557	207,557	88.4
16	68	Matsushita Electric	Japan	Electronics	—[d]	92.2	39.2	78.1	112,314	265,397	39.8
17	4	Roche Holdings	Switzerland	Pharmaceuticals	23.4	25.9	10.3	10.5	50,869	61,381	90.5
18	31	Alcatel Alsthom	France	Electronics	23.1	51.2	21.9	30.2	117,000	197,000	58.9
19	33	Sony	Japan	Electronics	—[d]	47.6	30.3	43.3	90,000	156,000	58.5
20	51	Fiat	Italy	Motor vehicles/parts	22.5	59.1	26.3	40.6	95,930	251,333	47.0
21	14	Bayer	Germany	Chemicals	22.4	27.4	21.9	26.8	78,300	146,700	72.5
22	83	Hitachi	Japan	Electronics	—[d]	92.5	19.8	56.8	80,000	331,852	27.7
23	10	Unilever[f]	U.K./Netherlands	Food	22.0	28.4	39.1	45.4	276,000	307,000	84.5
24	9	Philips Electronics	Netherlands	Electronics	—[d]	27.8	31.7	33.7	210,000	253,000	85.0
25	49	Siemens	Germany	Electronics	—[d]	50.6	30.1	52.1	158,000	376,000	47.3
26	55	Renault	France	Motor vehicles/parts	—[d]	41.2	16.7	32.5	39,982	138,279	43.7
27	18	British Petroleum	U.K.	Petroleum	19.5	28.8	30.8	50.7	48,650	66,550	67.2
28	67	Philip Morris	U.S.	Food	18.0	52.6	24.2	65.1	85,000	165,000	41.0
29	28	Hanson	U.K.	Building materials	18.0	34.0	10.3	17.7	58,000	74,000	63.3
30	78	Mitsui	Japan	Diversified	—[d]	82.5	64.5	171.5	23,560	80,000	29.5
31	62	Du Pont	U.S.	Chemicals	—[d]	36.9	18.6	39.3	35,000	107,000	42.0
32	79	Nissho Iwai	Japan	Trading	—[d]	55.5	34.3	118.4	2,101	7,245	29.0
33	20	B.A.T. Industries	U.K.	Tobacco	15.8	48.5	25.0	32.8	158,205	173,475	66.7
34	24	Hoechst	Germany	Chemicals	15.7	26.2	23.9	30.6	92,333	165,671	64.6
35	29	Rhône-Poulenc	France	Chemicals	15.6	22.9	9.4	15.5	46,430	81,582	61.8
36	25	Ciba-Geigy	Switzerland	Chemicals	15.5	31.8	15.4	22.0	63,095	83,980	64.6
37	81	ENI	Italy	Petroleum	—[d]	54.3	10.9	31.1	19,527	91,544	28.1
38	87	Sumitomo	Japan	Trading	—[d]	59.0	48.5	167.7	—[g]	22,000	24.2
39	21	Volvo	Sweden	Motor vehicles/parts	14.2	18.6	16.7	20.2	30,664	75,549	66.6
40	76	Chevron	U.S.	Petroleum	13.0	34.4	10.6	35.1	10,636	45,758	30.3
41	92	Toshiba	Japan	Electronics	—[d]	63.2	11.4	56.6	38,000	190,000	20.0
42	5	Sandoz	Switzerland	Pharmaceuticals	—[d]	14.9	11.3	11.6	51,258	60,304	88.8
43	89	Itochu Corporation	Japan	Trading	—[d]	62.5	36.1	162.3	2,706	10,140	22.7
44	54	Texaco	U.S.	Petroleum	11.7	25.5	16.6	32.5	10,640	29,713	44.2
45	41	BASF	Germany	Chemicals	11.3	25.7	19.6	27.0	40,297	106,266	51.5
46	48	VIAG AG	Germany	Diversified	11.2	23.5	8.6	17.8	41,288	86,018	48.0
47	95	Marubeni	Japan	Trading	—[d]	78.8	37.3	153.8	1,915	10,006	19.1
48	52	Dow Chemical	U.S.	Chemicals	10.4	26.5	8.6	16.7	24,165	53,700	45.3
49	70	Xerox	U.S.	Scientific and photo. equipment	10.2	38.6	7.9	16.8	32,150	87,600	36.7
50	3	RTZ	U.K.	Mining	—[d]	11.7	5.6	6.1	43,112	44,499	91.4

Source: *World Investment Report 1996*, United Nations, Geneva, 1996, pp. 30–31.

a Industry classification for companies follows that in the "*Fortune* Global 500" list in *Fortune*, July 25, 1994, and the "*Fortune* Global Service 500" list in *Fortune*, August 22, 1994. *Fortune* classifies companies according to the industry or service that represents the greatest volume of their sales. Industry groups are based on categories established by the United States Office of Management and Budget. Several companies are, however, highly diversified. These companies include Asea Brown Boveri, General Electric, Grand Metropolitan, Hanson, Sandoz, Total, and Veba.

b The index of transnationality is calculated as the average of foreign assets to total assets, foreign sales to total sales, and foreign employment to total employment.

c Foreign sales are outside Europe, whereas foreign employment figures are outside the United Kingdom and the Netherlands.

d Data on foreign assets are either suppressed to avoid disclosure or they are not available. In the case of nonavailability, they are estimated on the basis of the ratio of foreign to total employment, foreign to total sales, and similar ratios for the transnationality index.

e The company's business includes electric power generation, transmission, and distribution, and rail transportation. The company was formed by the merger of a Swedish and a Swiss firm. Data on foreign sales and assets are outside Switzerland.

f Foreign sales, assets, and employment figures are outside the United Kingdom and the Netherlands.

g Data on foreign employment are suppressed to avoid disclosure.

Foreign business transactions have two major effects on accounting. First, most sales or purchases of goods and services in other countries involve different currencies. Thus, one currency needs to be translated into another, using exchange rates. An **exchange rate** is the value of one currency in terms of another. For example, an English person purchasing goods from a U.S. company and paying in U.S. dollars must exchange British pounds for U.S. dollars before making payment. In effect, currencies are goods that can be bought and sold. Like the price of any good or service, these prices change daily according to supply and demand for the currencies. Accounting for these price changes in recording foreign transactions and preparing financial statements for foreign subsidiaries are the subjects of the next two sections.

Accounting for Transactions in Foreign Currencies

Among the first activities of an expanding company in the international market are the buying and selling of goods and services. For example, a U.S. maker of precision tools may expand by selling its product to foreign customers. Or it might lower its product cost by buying a less expensive part from a source in another country.

In the international marketplace, a transaction may take place in U.S. dollars, Japanese yen, British pounds, or some other currency such as the new euro, which will be used in a number of European countries. The values of these currencies rise and fall daily in relation to each other.

Foreign Sales

When a domestic company sells goods abroad, it may bill either in its own country's currency or in the foreign currency. If the billing and the subsequent payment are both in the domestic currency, no accounting problem arises. For example, assume that the U.S. precision toolmaker sells 160,000 worth of tools to a British company and bills the British company in dollars. The entry to record the sale and payment is as follows:

Date of sale

Accounts Receivable, British company	$160,000	
Sales		$160,000

Date of payment

Cash	$160,000	
Accounts Receivable, British company		$160,000

Most countries require the net exchange gain or loss on foreign currency transactions to be reported in the income statement. But there are some, including Canada and Korea, that permit exchange gains or losses relating to long-term monetary items to be deferred.

However, if the U.S. company bills the British company in British pounds and accepts payment in pounds, the U.S. company may incur an **exchange gain or loss**. A gain or loss will occur if the exchange rate of dollars to pounds changes between the date of sale and the date of payment. Since gains and losses tend to offset one another, a single account is used during the year to accumulate the activity. The net exchange gain or loss is reported in the income statement. For example, assume that the sale of $160,000 above was billed as £100,000, reflecting an exchange rate of 1.60 (that is, $1.60 per pound) on the sale date. Now assume that by the date of payment, the exchange rate has fallen to 1.50. The entries to record the transactions follow:

Date of sale

Accounts Receivable, British company	$160,000	
Sales		$160,000
£100,000 × $1.60 = $160,000		

Date of payment

Cash	$150,000	
Exchange Gain or Loss	$ 10,000	
Accounts Receivable, British company		$160,000
£100,000 × $1.50 = $150,000		

BUSINESS BULLETIN International Practice

Since the Asian currency crisis struck in July 1997, the currencies of Thailand, Indonesia, and South Korea have depreciated significantly against most other currencies, especially the U.S. dollar. Depreciation against the dollar for these three nations, in the order listed, has been around 40 per cent, 80 per cent, and 35 per cent as of July 1998.[8] This has caused tremendous problems and often bankruptcy for companies with significant amounts of foreign debt or reliance on imported materials. In order to help stabilise exchange rates, interest rates have gone up, making it expensive for companies to borrow locally. But even if local banks wished to make loans available, they have problems of their own caused by a mounting volume of bad debts from bankruptcies following the currency crisis. Hence, a vicious circle of economic depression has set in.

The U.S. company has incurred an exchange loss of $10,000 because it agreed to accept a fixed number of British pounds in payment, and the value of each pound dropped before the payment was made. Had the value of the pound in relation to the dollar increased, the U.S. company would have made an exchange gain.

Foreign Purchases

Purchases are the opposite of sales. The same logic applies to them, except that the relationship of exchange gains and losses to changes in exchange rates is reversed. For example, assume that the U.S. maker of precision tools purchases $15,000 of a certain part from a Japanese supplier. If the purchase and subsequent payment are made in U.S. dollars, no accounting problem arises.

Date of purchase

Purchases	$15,000	
Accounts Payable, Japanese company		$15,000

Date of payment

Accounts Payable, Japanese company	$15,000	
Cash		$15,000

However, the Japanese company may bill the U.S. company in yen and be paid in yen. If so, the U.S. company will incur an exchange gain or loss if the exchange rate changes between the date of purchase and the date of payment. For example, assume that the transaction is for 2,500,000 yen and the exchange rates on the dates of purchase and payment are $.0060 and $.0055 per yen, respectively. The entries would be recorded as follows:

Date of purchase

Purchases	$15,000	
Accounts Payable, Japanese company		$15,000
¥2,500,000 $\times$ $.0060 = $15,000		

Date of payment

Accounts Payable, Japanese company	$15,000	
Exchange Gain or Loss		$ 1,250
Cash		$13,750
¥2,500,000 $\times$ $.0055 = $13,750		

In this case the U.S. company received an exchange gain of $1,250 because it agreed to pay a fixed ¥2,500,000, and between the dates of purchase and payment the exchange value of the yen decreased in relation to the dollar.

Realised Versus Unrealised Exchange Gains or Losses

The preceding illustration dealt with completed transactions (in the sense that payment was completed). In each case the exchange gain or loss was recognised on the date of payment. If financial statements are prepared between the sale or purchase and the subsequent receipt or payment, and exchange rates have changed, there will be unrealised gains or losses. The International Accounting Standards Committee requires that exchange gains and losses should be recognised as income or expenses in the period in which they arise.[9] This requirement applies whether or not a transaction is complete.

This ruling has caused much debate. Critics charge that it gives too much weight to fleeting changes in exchange rates, causing random changes in earnings that hide long-run trends. Others believe that the use of current exchange rates to value receivables and payables as of the balance sheet date is a major step towards economic reality (current values).

To illustrate, we will use the preceding case, in which a U.S. company buys parts from a Japanese supplier. We will assume that the transaction has not been completed by the balance sheet date, when the exchange rate is $.0051 per yen:

Date		Exchange Rate ($ per Yen)
Date of purchase	Dec. 1	.0060
Balance sheet date	Dec. 31	.0051
Date of payment	Feb. 1	.0055

The accounting effects of the unrealised gain are as follows:

	Dec. 1	Dec. 31	Feb. 1
Purchase recorded in U.S. dollars (billed as ¥2,500,000)	$15,000	$15,000	$15,000
Dollars to be paid to equal ¥2,500,000 (¥2,500,000 × exchange rate)	15,000	12,750	13,750
Unrealised gain (or loss)	—	$ 2,250	
Realised gain (or loss)			$ 1,250

Dec.	1	Purchases		15,000		
		Accounts Payable, Japanese company			15,000	
Dec.	31	Accounts Payable, Japanese company		2,250		
		Exchange Gain or Loss			2,250	
Feb.	1	Accounts Payable, Japanese company		12,750		
		Exchange Gain or Loss		1,000		
		Cash			13,750	

In this case, the original sale was billed in yen by the Japanese company. An exchange gain of $2,250 is recorded on December 31, and an exchange loss of $1,000 is recorded on February 1. Even though these large fluctuations do not affect the net exchange gain of $1,250 for the whole transaction, the effect on each year's income statements may be important.

OBJECTIVE 6

Describe the restatement of a foreign subsidiary's financial statements

Restatement of Foreign Subsidiary Financial Statements

Growing companies often expand by setting up or buying foreign subsidiaries. If a foreign subsidiary is more than 50 per cent owned and the parent company exercises control, then the foreign subsidiary should be included in the consolidated financial statements (see the discussion of parent and subsidiary companies earlier in this chapter). The consolidation procedure is the same as that for domestic subsidiaries, except that the statements of the foreign subsidiary must be restated in the reporting currency before consolidation takes place. The **reporting currency** is the currency in which the consolidated financial statements are presented. Clearly, it makes no sense to combine the assets of a Mexican subsidiary stated in pesos with the assets of a U.S. parent company stated in dollars. Most U.S. companies present their financial statements in U.S. dollars, so the following discussion assumes that the U.S. dollar is the reporting currency used.

Restatement is the stating of one currency in terms of another. The method of restatement depends on the foreign subsidiary's functional currency. The **functional currency** is the currency of the place where the subsidiary carries on most of its business. Generally, it is the currency in which a company earns and spends its cash. The functional currency to be used depends on the kind of foreign operation in which the subsidiary takes part. There are two broad types of foreign operations. Type I includes those that are fairly self-contained and integrated within a certain country or economy. Type II includes those that are mainly a direct and integral part or extension of the parent company's operations. As a general rule, Type I subsidiaries use the currency of the country in which they are located, and Type II subsidiaries use the currency of the parent company. If the parent company is a U.S. company, the functional currency of a Type I subsidiary will be the currency of the country where the subsidiary carries on its business, and the functional currency of a Type II subsidiary will be the U.S. dollar.

CHAPTER REVIEW

Review of Learning Objectives

1. **Apply the appropriate method to influential and noninfluential situations in accounting for long-term investments.** Long-term investments in shares fall into three categories. First are noninfluential and noncontrolling investments, representing less than 20 per cent ownership. To account for these investments, use the lower of cost and market, cost, or revaluation methods. Second are influential but noncontrolling investments, representing 20 per cent to 50 per cent ownership. Use the equity method to account for these investments. Third are controlling interest investments, representing more than 50 per cent ownership. Account for them using consolidated financial statements.

2. **Explain when to prepare consolidated financial statements, and describe their uses.** Consolidated financial statements must be prepared when an investing company has effective control over another company. Control is presumed to exist when the parent company owns more than 50 per cent of the voting shares of the subsidiary company. Consolidated financial statements are useful to investors and others because they treat the parent company and its subsidiaries realistically, as an integrated economic unit.

3. **Prepare consolidated balance sheets at acquisition date for purchase at (a) book value and (b) other than book value.** At the date of acquisition, a work sheet entry is made to eliminate the investment from the parent company's financial statements and the shareholders' equity section of the subsidiary's financial statements. The assets and liabilities of the two companies are combined. If the parent owns less than 100 per cent of the subsidiary, minority interest will appear on the consolidated balance sheet equal to the percentage of the subsidiary owned by minority shareholders multiplied by the shareholders' equity in the subsidiary. If the cost of the parent's invest-

ment in the subsidiary is greater than the subsidiary's book value, an amount equal to the excess of cost over book value will be allocated on the consolidated balance sheet to account for the fair values of subsidiary assets and to goodwill. If the cost of the parent's investment in the subsidiary is less than book value, and where it is not possible to record a reduction in the fair values of subsidiary assets, the excess of book value over cost should be treated as negative goodwill and recognised as income on a systemic basis.

4. **Prepare consolidated income statements for intercompany transactions.** In consolidated income statements for intercompany transactions, intercompany sales, purchases, interest income and expense, and other income and expenses must be eliminated to avoid double counting them.

5. **Define *exchange rate* and record transactions that are affected by changes in foreign exchange rates.** An *exchange rate* is the value of one currency stated in terms of another. A domestic company may make sales or purchases abroad in either its own country's currency or the foreign currency. If a transaction (sale or purchase) and its resolution (receipt and payment) are made in the domestic currency, no accounting problem arises. However, if the transaction and its resolution are made in a foreign currency and the exchange rate changes between the time of the transaction and its resolution, an exchange gain or loss will occur and should be recorded.

6. **Describe the restatement of a foreign subsidiary's financial statements.** Foreign financial statements are converted to the domestic currency by multiplying the appropriate exchange rates by the amounts in the foreign financial statements. In general, the rates that apply depend on whether the subsidiary is separate and self-contained (Type I) or an integral part of the parent company (Type II).

Review of Concepts and Terminology

The following concepts and terms were introduced in this chapter.

LO 1   Consolidated financial statements: Financial statements that reflect the combined operations of parent company and subsidiaries.

LO 1   Control: The power to govern the financial and operating policies of an enterprise so as to obtain benefits from its activities.

LO 2   Eliminations: Entries made on consolidated work sheets to eliminate transactions between parent and subsidiary companies.

LO 1   Equity method: A method of accounting in which investment is initially recorded at cost and adjusted thereafter for postacquisition changes in the investor's share of the results of operations of the investee.

LO 5   Exchange gain or loss: A change due to exchange rate fluctuations that is reported in the income statement.

LO 5   Exchange rate: The value of one currency in terms of another.

LO 6   Functional currency: The currency of the place where a subsidiary carries on most of its business.

LO 3   Goodwill (Goodwill from Consolidation): The amount paid for a subsidiary that exceeds the fair value of the subsidiary's assets less its liabilities.

LO 1   Group: A parent company and all its subsidiaries.

LO 1   Lower of cost and market method: A method of accounting for long-term securities at cost adjusted for reductions in the market value of the securities.

LO 3   Minority interest: The amount recorded on a consolidated balance sheet that represents the holdings of shareholders who own less than 50 per cent of the voting shares of a subsidiary.

LO 5   Multinational (transnational) corporation: A company that operates in more than one country.

LO 1   Parent company: An enterprise that has one or more subsidiaries.

LO 2   Purchase method: A method of accounting for parent/subsidiary relationships in which similar accounts from separate statements are combined. Used when the investing company controls another company.

LO 6   Reporting currency: The currency in which consolidated financial statements are presented.

LO 6   Restatement: The stating of one currency in terms of another.

LO 1   Significant influence: The power of the investing company to participate in the financial and operating policy decisions of the investee company without having control over those policies.

LO 1   Subsidiary: An enterprise controlled by another.

Review Problem

Consolidated Balance Sheet: Less than 100 Per Cent Ownership

LO 3   In a cash transaction, Taylor Company purchased 90 per cent of the outstanding shares of Schumacher Company for 763,200 on June 30, 20xx. Directly after the acquisition, separate balance sheets of the companies appeared as follows:

	Taylor Company	Schumacher Company
Assets		
Cash	400,000	48,000
Accounts Receivable	650,000	240,000
Inventory	1,000,000	520,000
Investment in Schumacher Company	763,200	—
Plant and Equipment (net)	1,500,000	880,000
Other Assets	50,000	160,000
Total Assets	4,363,200	1,848,000
Liabilities and Shareholders' Equity		
Accounts Payable	800,000	400,000
Long-Term Debt	1,000,000	600,000
Ordinary Shares—5 nominal value	2,000,000	800,000
Retained Earnings	563,200	48,000
Total Liabilities and Shareholders' Equity	4,363,200	1,848,000

Additional information: (a) Schumacher Company's other assets represent a long-term investment in Taylor Company's long-term debt. The debt was purchased for an amount equal to Taylor's carrying amount of the debt. (b) Taylor Company owes Schumacher Company 100,000 for services rendered.

REQUIRED   Prepare a work sheet as of the acquisition date for preparing a consolidated balance sheet.

Answer to Review Problem

Taylor and Schumacher Companies
Work Sheet for Consolidated Balance Sheet
June 30, 20xx

Accounts	Balance Sheet Taylor Company	Balance Sheet Schumacher Company	Eliminations Debit	Eliminations Credit	Consolidated Balance Sheet
Cash	400,000	48,000			448,000
Accounts Receivable	650,000	240,000		(3) 100,000	790,000
Inventory	1,000,000	520,000			1,520,000
Investment in					
Schumacher Company	763,200	—		(1) 763,200	—
Plant and Equipment (net)	1,500,000	880,000			2,380,000
Other Assets	50,000	160,000		(2) 160,000	50,000
Total Assets	4,363,200	1,848,000			5,188,000
Accounts Payable	800,000	400,000	(3) 100,000		1,100,000
Long-Term Debt	1,000,000	600,000	(2) 160,000		1,440,000
Ordinary Shares—					
5 nominal value	2,000,000	800,000	(1) 800,000		2,000,000
Retained Earnings	563,200	48,000	(1) 48,000		563,200
Minority Interest				(1) 84,800	84,800
Total Liabilities and					
Shareholders' Equity	4,363,200	1,848,000	1,108,000	1,108,000	5,188,000

(1) Elimination of intercompany investment. Minority interest equals 10 per cent of Schumacher Company shareholders' equity
   (10% × [800,000 + 48,000] = 84,800).
(2) Elimination of intercompany long-term debt.
(3) Elimination of intercompany receivables and payables.

CHAPTER ASSIGNMENTS

Knowledge and Understanding

Questions

1. Why are the concepts of significant influence and control important in accounting for long-term investments?
2. For each of the following categories of long-term investments, briefly describe the applicable percentage of ownership and accounting treatment: (a) noninfluential and noncontrolling investment, (b) influential but noncontrolling investment, and (c) controlling investment.
3. What is meant by a parent-subsidiary relationship?
4. Would the shareholders of Nestlé be more interested in the consolidated financial statements of the overall company than in the statements of its many subsidiaries? Explain.
5. What is the equity method of accounting for investments?

6. Why should intercompany receivables, payables, sales, and purchases be eliminated in the preparation of consolidated financial statements?
7. What is meant by "minority interest"? Explain how it arises and where it appears on the consolidated balance sheet.
8. Why may the price paid to acquire a controlling interest in a subsidiary company exceed the subsidiary's book value?
9. What is meant by "goodwill from consolidation"? Explain how this item arises and where you would expect to find it on the consolidated balance sheet.
10. Subsidiary Corporation has a book value of 100,000, of which Parent Corporation purchases 100 per cent for 115,000. None

of the excess of cost over book value is attributed to the fair value of tangible assets. What is the amount of goodwill from consolidation?

11. Subsidiary Corporation, a wholly-owned subsidiary, has total sales of 500,000, 100,000 of which were made to Parent Corporation. Parent Corporation has total sales of 1,000,000, including sales of all items purchased from Subsidiary Corporation. What is the amount of sales on the consolidated income statement?

12. What does it mean to say that the exchange rate for a Swiss franc in terms of the U.S. dollar is .15? If a bottle of perfume from Switzerland costs 200 francs, how much will it cost in U.S. dollars?

13. If a British firm does business with a Russian firm and all their transactions take place in Russian roubles, which firm may incur exchange gains or losses, and why?

14. What is the difference between a reporting currency and a functional currency?

15. If you as an investor were trying to evaluate the relative performance of General Motors, Volkswagen, and Toyota Motors from their published financial statements, what problems might you encounter (other than a language problem)?

Application

Exercises

E 13-1.
LO 1   *Long-Term Investments*

Peter Corporation has the following portfolio of long-term investments at year end:

Company	Percentage of Voting Shares Held	Cost	Year-End Market Value
N Corporation	4	160,000	190,000
O Corporation	12	750,000	550,000
P Corporation	5	60,000	110,000
Total		970,000	850,000

Prepare the year-end adjustment to reflect the above information.

E 13-2.
LO 1   *Long-Term Investments: Equity Method*

On January 1, 20xx, Romano Corporation acquired 40 per cent of the voting shares of Burke Corporation for 2,400,000 in cash, an amount sufficient to exercise significant influence over Burke Corporation's activities. On December 31, Romano determined that Burke paid dividends of 400,000 but incurred a net loss of 200,000 for 20xx. Prepare journal entries in Romano Corporation's records to reflect this information.

E 13-3.
LO 1   *Methods of Accounting for*
LO 2   *Long-Term Investments*

Diversified Corporation has the following long-term investments:

1. 60 per cent of the ordinary shares of the American company Calcor Corporation
2. 13 per cent of the ordinary shares of the British company Virgin Atlantic
3. 50 per cent of the nonvoting preference shares of the American company Camrad Corporation
4. 100 per cent of the ordinary shares of its financing subsidiary, DCF.
5. 35 per cent of the ordinary shares of the French company Maison de Boutaine
6. 70 per cent of the ordinary shares of the Canadian company Alberta Mining Company

For each of these investments, state which of the following methods should be used for external financial reporting.

a. Lower of cost and market method
b. Equity method
c. Consolidation of parent and subsidiary financial statements

E 13-4.
LO 3   *Elimination Entry for a Purchase at Book Value*

The Lardner Manufacturing Company purchased 100 per cent of the shares of the Gwynn Manufacturing Company for 300,000. Gwynn's shareholders' equity included ordinary shares of 200,000 and retained earnings of 100,000. Prepare the eliminating entry in general journal form that would appear on the work sheet for consolidating the balance sheets of these two entities as of the acquisition date.

E 13-5.
LO 3   *Elimination Entry and Minority Interest*

The shareholders' equity section of the Brandt Corporation's balance sheet appeared as follows on December 31:

Ordinary Shares—10 nominal value, 40,000 shares authorised and issued	400,000
Retained Earnings	48,000
Total Shareholders' Equity	448,000

Assume that Wegner Manufacturing Company owns 80 per cent of the voting shares of Brandt Corporation and paid 11.20 for each share. In general journal form, prepare the entry (including minority interest) to eliminate Wegner's investment and Brandt's shareholders' equity that would appear on the work sheet used in preparing the consolidated balance sheet for the two firms.

E 13-6.

LO 3 *Consolidated Balance Sheet with Goodwill*

On September 1, Y Company purchased 100 per cent of the voting shares of Z Company for 960,000 in cash. The separate condensed balance sheets immediately after the purchase follow:

	Y Company	Z Company
Other Assets	2,206,000	1,089,000
Investment in Z Company	960,000	—
	3,166,000	1,089,000
Liabilities	871,000	189,000
Ordinary Shares—1 nominal value	1,000,000	300,000
Retained Earnings	1,295,000	600,000
	3,166,000	1,089,000

Prepare a work sheet for preparing the consolidated balance sheet immediately after Y Company acquired control of Z Company. Assume that any excess cost of the investment in the subsidiary over book value is attributable to goodwill from consolidation.

E 13-7.

LO 3 *Analysing the Effects of Elimination Entries*

Some of the separate accounts from the balance sheets for A Company and B Company, just after A Company purchased 85 per cent of B Company's voting shares for 1,530,000 in cash, follow:

	A Company	B Company
Accounts Receivable	2,600,000	800,000
Interest Receivable, Bonds of B Company	14,400	—
Investment in B Company	1,530,000	—
Investment in B Company Bonds	360,000	—
Accounts Payable	1,060,000	380,000
Interest Payable, Bonds	64,000	40,000
Bonds Payable	1,600,000	1,000,000
Ordinary Shares	2,000,000	1,200,000
Retained Earnings	1,120,000	600,000

Accounts Receivable and Accounts Payable included the following: B Company owed A Company 100,000 for services rendered, and A Company owed B Company 132,000 for purchases of goods. A bought B Company's bonds for an amount equal to B's carrying amount of the bonds. Determine the amount, including minority interest, that would appear on the consolidated balance sheet for each of the accounts listed.

E 13-8.

LO 4 *Preparation of Consolidated Income Statement*

Polonia Company has owned 100 per cent of Cardwell Company since 20x0. The income statements of these two companies for the year ended December 31, 20x1 appear below. Also assume the following information: (a) Cardwell Company purchased 560,000 of inventory from Polonia Company, which had been sold to Cardwell Company customers by the end of the year. (b) Cardwell Company leased its building from Polonia Company for 120,000 per year. Prepare a consolidated income statement work sheet for the two companies for the year ended December 31, 20x1. Ignore income taxes.

	Polonia Company	Cardwell Company
Net Sales	3,000,000	1,200,000
Cost of Goods Sold	1,500,000	800,000
Gross Profit	1,500,000	400,000
Less: Selling Expenses	500,000	100,000
General and Administrative Expenses	600,000	200,000
Total Operating Expenses	1,100,000	300,000
Profit from Operations	400,000	100,000
Other Income	120,000	—
Net Profit	520,000	100,000

E 13-9.

LO 5 *Recording International Transactions: Fluctuating Exchange Rate*

London Corporation purchased a special-purpose machine from Hamburg Corporation on credit for DM 50,000. At the date of purchase, the exchange rate was GB£.55 per mark. On the date of the payment, which was made in marks, the value of the mark had increased to GB£.60. Prepare journal entries to record the purchase and payment in London Corporation's accounting records.

E 13-10.

LO 5 *Recording International Transactions*

U.S. Corporation made a sale on account to U.K. Company on November 15 in the amount of £300,000. Payment was to be made in British pounds on February 15. U.S. Corporation's accounting year is the same as the calendar year. The British pound was worth $1.70 on November 15, $1.58 on December 31, and $1.78 on February 15. Prepare journal entries to record the sale, year-end adjustment, and collection on U.S. Corporation's books.

Problem Set

Since foreign exchange rates can fluctuate widely, a variety of rates have been used in the Problem Set.

P 13-1.

LO 1 *Long-Term Investments: Equity Method*

The Samir Company owns 40 per cent of the voting shares of the Gorman Company. The Investment account for this company on the Samir Company's balance sheet had a balance of 600,000 on January 1, 20xx. During 20xx, the Gorman Company reported the following quarterly earnings and dividends paid:

Quarter	Earnings	Dividends Paid
1	80,000	40,000
2	60,000	40,000
3	160,000	40,000
4	(40,000)	40,000
	260,000	160,000

The Samir Company exercises a significant influence over the operations of the Gorman Company and therefore uses the equity method to account for its investment.

REQUIRED

1. Prepare the journal entries that the Samir Company must make each quarter in accounting for its investment in the Gorman Company.
2. Prepare a ledger account for the investment in the ordinary shares of the Gorman Company. Enter the beginning balance and post relevant portions of the entries made in 1.

P 13-2.

LO 3 *Consolidated Balance Sheet: Less than 100 Per Cent Ownership*

In a cash transaction, Kamper Company purchased 70 per cent of the outstanding shares of Woolf Company for 593,600 cash on June 30, 20xx. Immediately after the acquisition, the separate balance sheets of the companies appeared as shown below.

	Kamper Company	Woolf Company
Assets		
Cash	320,000	48,000
Accounts Receivable	520,000	240,000
Inventory	800,000	520,000
Investment in Woolf Company	593,600	—
Plant and Equipment (net)	1,200,000	880,000
Other Assets	40,000	160,000
Total Assets	3,473,600	1,848,000
Liabilities and Shareholders' Equity		
Accounts Payable	640,000	400,000
Long-Term Debt	800,000	600,000
Ordinary Shares—10 nominal value	1,600,000	800,000
Retained Earnings	433,600	48,000
Total Liabilities and Shareholders' Equity	3,473,600	1,848,000

Also assume the following additional information: (a) Woolf Company's other assets represent a long-term investment in Kamper Company's long-term debt. The debt was purchased for an amount equal to Kamper's carrying amount of the debt. (b) Kamper Company owes Woolf Company 80,000 for services rendered.

REQUIRED   Prepare a work sheet for preparing a consolidated balance sheet as of the acquisition date, June 30, 20xx.

P 13-3.

LO 3 *Consolidated Balance Sheet: Cost Exceeding Book Value*

The balance sheets of Magreb Company and Nicario Company as of December 31, 20xx are shown below.

	Magreb Company	Nicario Company
Assets		
Cash	120,000	80,000
Accounts Receivable	200,000	60,000
Investment in Nicario Company	700,000	—
Other Assets	200,000	360,000
Total Assets	1,220,000	500,000
Liabilities and Shareholders' Equity		
Liabilities	220,000	60,000
Ordinary Shares—20 nominal value	800,000	400,000
Retained Earnings	200,000	40,000
Total Liabilities and Shareholders' Equity	1,220,000	500,000

REQUIRED   Prepare a consolidated balance sheet work sheet for the Magreb and Nicario Companies. Assume that the Magreb Company purchased 100 per cent of Nicario's ordinary shares for 700,000 immediately before the balance sheet date. Also assume that 160,000 of the excess of cost over book value is attributable to the increase in fair value of Nicario Company's other assets. The rest of the excess is considered by the Magreb Company to be goodwill.

P 13-4.

LO 5 *International Transactions*

Blue Mountain Company, an American company, whose year end is June 30, engaged in the following international transactions (exchange rates in parentheses):

May 15   Purchased goods from a Japanese firm for $110,000; terms n/10 in U.S. dollars (yen = $.0080).

17   Sold goods to a German company for $165,000; terms n/30 in marks (mark = $.55).

21   Purchased goods from a Mexican company for $120,000; terms n/30 in pesos (peso = $.30).

25   Paid for the goods purchased on May 15 (yen = $.0085).

31   Sold goods to an Italian firm for $200,000; terms n/60 in lire (lira = $.0005).

June 5   Sold goods to a British firm for $56,000; terms n/10 in U.S. dollars (pound = $1.30).

7   Purchased goods from a Japanese firm for $221,000; terms n/30 in yen (yen = $.0085).

15   Received payment for the sale made on June 5 (pound = $1.80).

16   Received payment for the sale made on May 17 (mark = $.60).

17   Purchased goods from a French firm for $66,000; terms n/30 in U.S. dollars (franc = $.16).

20   Paid for the goods purchased on May 21 (peso = $.25).

22   Sold goods to a British firm for $108,000; terms n/30 in pounds (pound = $1.80).

30   Made year-end adjusting entries for incomplete foreign exchange transactions (franc = $.17; peso = $.30; mark = $.60; lira = $.0003; pound = $1.70; yen = $.0090).

July 7   Paid for the goods purchased on June 7 (yen = $.0085).

17   Paid for the goods purchased on June 17 (franc = $.15).

22   Received payment for the goods sold on June 22 (pound = $1.60).

30   Received payment for the goods sold on May 31 (lira = $.0004).

REQUIRED   Prepare general journal entries for these transactions.

Critical Thinking and Communication

Conceptual Mini-Case

CMC 13-1.

LO 5 *Effect of Change in Exchange Rate*

Michelin, the famous French maker of Michelin tyres, became the world's largest tyremaker when it purchased the U.S. tyremaker Uniroyal Goodrich in 1990. The *Wall Street Journal* reported that excluding Uniroyal Goodrich sales, sales revenue in 1990 decreased 4.4 per cent to 52.74 billion francs. The decrease was due mainly to the weak dollar in 1990. Michelin executives said, the article reported, that about 25 per cent of Michelin's sales, not counting those of Uniroyal Goodrich, were exports to the United States. Without the dollar's drop, revenue expressed in francs would have increased instead of decreased.[10] Explain why a weak dollar would lead to a decrease in Michelin's sales. Why are sales of Uniroyal Goodrich excluded from this discussion?

Cultural Mini-Case

CLMC 13-1.

LO 3 *Treatment of Consolidation Goodwill and Brands*

Guinness (now *Diageo*), based in the United Kingdom and Ireland, is one of the world's leading drinks companies with international best-selling brands such as Johnnie Walker, Bell's and Dewar's Scotch whiskies, Gordons and Tanqueray gins, and Guinness Stout. Guinness's consolidated balance sheet includes the value of its acquired brands at a cost of £1,395 million pounds. However, the value of goodwill at £1,298 million pounds is deducted from shareholders' equity. The accounting policies for brands and goodwill are stated as follows:[11]

> **Brands**. The fair value of businesses acquired and of interests taken in associated undertakings includes brands, which are recognised where the brand has a value which is substantial and long-term. Acquired brands are only recognised where title is clear, brand earnings are separately identifiable, the brand could be sold from the rest of the business and where the brand achieves earnings in excess of those achieved by unbranded products.
>
> Amortisation is not provided except where the end of the useful economic life of the acquired brand can be foreseen. The useful economic lives of brands and their carrying value are subject to annual review and any amortisation or provision for permanent impairment would be charged against the profit for the period in which they arose.
>
> **Goodwill**. The goodwill arising on the acquisition of businesses and interests in associated undertakings is calculated by reference to the fair value of net assets acquired and is deducted in arriving at shareholders' funds.

REQUIRED

1. What are the likely reasons for Guinness not amortising brand values? What is the effect on consolidated net profit and the consolidated balance sheet? Is an annual review of the value of brands an adequate response to the problem of properly valuing brands on the balance sheet?
2. What is the effect of deducting goodwill from shareholders' equity on consolidated net profit and the consolidated balance sheet? What are the likely reasons for eliminating goodwill from the balance sheet while recognising brands? How does Guinness's treatment of goodwill differ from that required by the International Accounting Standards Committee?

Ethics Mini-Case

EMC 13-1.

LO 1 *Influential and Noninfluential Investments*

The Magnificent Company is a company with influential but noncontrolling long-term investments in a variety of companies around the world. However, Rainbow Enterprises, in which it has a 20 per cent holding of voting shares, is one of the major contributors to Magnificent's profits. In 1997, the finance director of Magnificent was concerned about Rainbow's results for the year as losses had been reported for the last quarter and the year-end loss was expected to be substantial. Under the equity method, Magnificent's share of Rainbow's losses would be reflected in the consolidated income statement and in the value of long-term investments reported in the consolidated balance sheet. However, if Magnificent's holding in Rainbow could be reduced to 19 per cent by selling some shares, then this investment could be treated as noninfluential and the share of losses would not need to be included in Magnificent's income statement. Moreover, because the cost of the Rainbow investment is below its market value, there would be no need to write down the value of the investment in the consolidated balance sheet. How would you advise the finance director to deal with this issue?

Decision-Making Case

DMC 13-1.

LO 1 *Accounting for Investments*

San Antonio Corporation is a successful oil and gas exploration business. At the beginning of 20xx, the company made investments in three companies that perform services in the oil and gas industry. The details of each of these investments are as follows:

San Antonio Corporation purchased 100,000 shares in Bellows Service Corporation at a cost of 8 per share. Bellows Service Corporation has 1.5 million shares outstanding, and during 20xx paid dividends of .40 per share on earnings of .80 per share. At the end of the year, Bellows's shares were selling for 12 per share.

San Antonio also purchased 2 million shares of Sunrise Drilling Company at 4 per share. Sunrise has 10 million shares outstanding. In 20xx, Sunrise paid a dividend of .20 per share on earnings of .40 per share. During the current year the chief executive of San Antonio was appointed to the board of directors of Sunrise. At the end of the year, Sunrise's shares were selling for 6 per share.

In another action, San Antonio purchased 1 million of Blue Sky Oil Field Supplies Company's 5 million outstanding shares at 6 per share. The chief executive of San Antonio sought membership on the board of directors of Blue Sky but was rebuffed by Blue Sky's board when shareholders representing a majority of Blue Sky's outstanding shares stated that they did not want to be associated with San Antonio. Blue Sky paid a dividend of .40 per share and reported a net profit of only .20 per share for the year. By the end of the year, the price of its shares had dropped to 2 per share.

REQUIRED

1. What principal factors must you consider in order to determine how to account for San Antonio's investments? Should they be shown on the balance sheet as current or long-term investments? What factors affect this decision?
2. For each of the three investments, make general journal entries for each of the following: (a) initial investment, (b) receipt of cash dividend, and (c) recognition of profit (if appropriate).
3. What adjusting entry (if any) is required at the end of the year?
4. Assuming that San Antonio's investment in Blue Sky is sold after the first of the year for 3 per share, what general journal entry would be made? Assuming that the market value of the remaining investments held by San Antonio exceeds cost by 1,200,000 at the end of the second year, what adjusting entry (if any) would be required?

Basic Research Activity

RA 13-1.

LO 5 *Reading and Analysing Foreign Currency Markets*

Go to the section of the library where recent issues of the financial daily newspapers are located. From the index find the page number of world markets. Find a table entitled "Exchange Rates". This table shows the exchange rates of the currencies of a number of countries with your own currency. Choose the currency of any country in which you are interested. Write down the value of that currency in local currency equivalents for one day in the first week of each month for the past six months, as reported in the newspaper. Prepare a chart that shows the variation in exchange rate for this currency over this time period. Assuming that you run a company that exports goods to the country you chose, would you find the change in exchange rate over the past six months favourable or unfavourable? Assuming that you run a company that imports goods from the country you chose, would you find the change in exchange rate over the past six months favourable or unfavourable? Explain your answers and state what business practices you would follow to offset any adverse effects of exchange rate fluctuations. Be prepared to discuss your results in class.

Financial Reporting and Analysis

Interpretation Cases from Business

ICB 13-1.

LO 3 *Consolidation of Two Large Companies*

One of the major corporate takeovers in the United States in 1986 was *General Electric Company*'s purchase of *RCA Corporation*. This transaction is described in a note to GE's financial statements in its 1986 annual report as follows:

On June 9, 1986, GE acquired RCA Corporation and its subsidiaries (RCA) in a transaction for which the total consideration to former RCA shareholders was $6.406 billion in cash. RCA businesses include the manufacture and sale of a wide range of electronic products and related research and services for consumer, commercial, military and space applications; the National Broadcasting Company's (NBC) radio and television stations and network broadcasting services; and domestic and international message and data communications services.

The acquisition was accounted for as a purchase, and the operating results of RCA have been consolidated with those of GE since June 1, 1986. In preparing 1986 financial information, the purchase price ($6.426 billion, including an estimated $20 million of related costs) has been allocated to the assets and liabilities of RCA based on estimates of fair market values. The excess of purchase price over the estimate of fair values of net assets acquired (goodwill) was $2.7 billion, which is being amortised on a straight-line basis over 40 years.[12]

REQUIRED

1. Show the entry in GE's records to record the purchase of RCA.
2. Did GE pay more or less than book value for RCA?
3. Show the year-end adjusting entry on GE's records related to the amortisation of goodwill. (GE's year end is December 31.)

ICB 13-2.

LO 3   *Analysis of an Acquisition*

In 1981 two American companies, **USX Corporation** and **Mobil Oil Corporation** fought each other for control of **Marathon Oil Company**. USX won this battle of the giants by reaching an agreement to purchase all of Marathon's shares. The *Chicago Tribune* reported on March 12, 1982 that the $6 billion merger, as approved by the shareholders of Marathon, was the second largest in history and created the twelfth largest industrial corporation in the United States.

In a note to USX's 1981 annual report, the details of the purchase were revealed. USX "purchased 30 million common shares of Marathon Oil Company for $125 per share . . . as the first step in its planned acquisition of the entire equity of Marathon". Additional Marathon shares would be purchased by issuing $100 principal amount of 12½ per cent notes due in 1994 for each share. These notes were estimated by the financial press to have a fair market value of $80 per note. The total number of Marathon shares prior to these two transactions was 59.0 million. On December 31, 1981, just before the merger, the condensed balance sheets of USX and Marathon Oil appeared as shown below (in millions).

	USX	Marathon Oil
Assets		
Current Assets, Excluding Inventories	$ 4,214	$ 907
Inventories	1,198	576
Property, Plant, and Equipment (net)	6,676	4,233
Other Assets	1,228	278
Total Assets	$13,316	$5,994
Liabilities and Shareholders' Equity		
Current Liabilities	$ 2,823	$1,475
Long-Term Debt	2,340	1,368
Deferred Income Taxes	732	588
Other Liabilities	1,161	501
Total Liabilities	$ 7,056	$3,932
Shareholders' Equity	6,260	2,062
Total Liabilities and Shareholders' Equity	$13,316	$5,994

Further information in USX's annual report indicated that when consolidated financial statements were prepared using the purchase method, management would adjust Marathon's assets and liabilities in the following manner. It would (a) increase inventory by $1,244 million; (b) increase current liabilities by $392 million; and (c) decrease deferred income taxes by $588 million. After these adjustments, any remaining excess of the purchase price over book value of Marathon's shares would be attributed to property, plant, and equipment.[13]

REQUIRED

1. Prepare the entry in USX's journals to record the purchase of Marathon Oil.
2. Prepare the eliminating entry, including the adjustments indicated, that would be made to consolidate USX and Marathon.
3. Prepare a consolidated balance sheet for the merged companies.
4. Did USX pay more or less than book value for Marathon? Why would USX take this action? Did the purchase raise or lower USX's book value per share?

Nestlé Case

NC 13-1.

LO 5   *Effects of Foreign Exchange*

LO 6

Refer to the Annual Report in the appendix on Nestlé to answer the following questions. In the Management's Business Review, management states that "After several years in which their impact had been unfavourable, exchange rate variations had a positive effect in 1996, contributing 1.4% to sales growth" (p. 13). It should be remembered that Nestlé's business represents a kind of "currency basket", as a result of the vast geographic spread of the group's activities, which limits its risks and enhances its prospects for growth. Why would a strong U.S. dollar have a *favourable* impact on results? Why would a strong Swiss franc have an *unfavourable* impact on results? Why is the geographic spread of Nestlé's activities a good thing?

ENDNOTES

1. Sime Darby, *Annual Report*, 1995.
2. International Accounting Standard, IAS28, *Accounting for Investments in Associates* (London: IASC, reformatted 1994), para. 3.
3. Ibid.
4. International Accounting Standard, IAS25, *Accounting for Investments* (London: IASC, reformatted 1994), para. 23.
5. International Accounting Standard, IAS27, *Consolidated Financial Statements and Accounting for Investments in Subsidiaries* (London: IASC, reformatted 1994), para. 12.
6. International Accounting Standard, IAS22, *Business Combinations* (London: IASC, revised 1998).
7. Ibid., para. 42.
8. *The Economist*, July 11, 1998, pp. 31–32.
9. International Accounting Standard, IAS21, *The Effects of Changes in Foreign Exchange Rates* (London: IASC, revised 1993), para. 15.
10. E. S. Browning, "Michelin Sees Heavy Net Loss for the Year", *Wall Street Journal*, October 19, 1990.
11. Guinness, *Annual Report*, 1995.
12. General Electric, *Annual Report*, 1986.
13. USX Corporation, *Annual Report*, 1981.

Chapter 14

FINANCIAL STATEMENT
ANALYSIS

LEARNING OBJECTIVES

1. Describe and discuss the objectives of financial statement analysis.
2. Describe and discuss the standards for financial statement analysis.
3. State the sources of information for financial statement analysis.
4. Identify the issues related to evaluating the quality of a company's earnings.
5. Apply horizontal analysis, trend analysis, and vertical analysis to financial statements.
6. Apply ratio analysis to financial statements in a comprehensive analysis of a company's financial situation.

DECISION POINT

UNILEVER

Unilever, an Anglo-Dutch company, is one of the world's largest multi-nationals with operations in more than ninety countries, spanning every continent. Unilever's consumer goods businesses include foods and home and personal products. The foods businesses include ice cream, yellow fats, tea-based beverages, and culinary products with famous brand names such as Magnum, Lipton, Flora, and Batchelors. The home and personal care businesses include laundry; mass skin care; prestige fragrances; and hair, oral, and deodorant products with brand names such as Brut, Calvin Klein, Elizabeth Arden, Vaseline, and Ponds. In addition, Unilever has a group of speciality chemicals companies including National Starch, Crosfield, Quest, and Unichema.

In February 1997, Unilever surprised the stock markets with an announcement that it was going to put up its speciality chemicals businesses for sale with the intention of using the proceeds, estimated at around £5 to £6 billion, to develop its global activities in food and personal products, especially in the emerging economies. Speciality chemicals was one of Unilever's best businesses in 1996, according to Morris Tabaksblat, co-chairman of Unilever, accounting for 13 per cent of its profits and generating an operating profit of 14.1 per cent.[1] However, the problem was that the business was too capital intensive and lacked significant synergy with the food and personal care businesses. This most radical realignment in the company's sixty-seven-year history was well received by analysts and investors, frustrated by the company's sluggish growth in value in recent years, with the shares closing up about 5 per cent.

Unilever is now considering potential investments, including possible acquisition targets such as Heinz and Campbell Soup, with good prospects in rapidly developing markets in Central and Eastern Europe, Asia, and Latin America. This case demonstrates several features of the evaluation of a company's financial prospects. First, the analysis is centred on performance as reported in the financial statements (for example, profits and returns on investment). Second, it is directed towards the future (for example, investment plans and growth). Third, the analysis requires consideration of the global business environment (for example, faster growth opportunities in food and personal care).

OBJECTIVE 1

Describe and discuss the objectives of financial statement analysis

OBJECTIVES OF FINANCIAL STATEMENT ANALYSIS

Financial statement analysis comprises all the techniques employed by users of financial statements to show important relationships in the financial statements. Users of financial statements fall into two broad categories: internal and external. Management is the main internal user. However, because those who run a company have inside information on operations, other techniques are available to them. Since these techniques are covered in managerial accounting courses, the main focus here is on the external use of financial analysis.

Lenders make loans in the form of trade accounts, notes, or bonds, on which they receive interest. They expect a loan to be repaid according to its terms. Investors buy shares, from which they hope to receive dividends and an increase in value. Both groups face risks. The lender faces the risk that the debtor will fail to pay back the loan. The investor faces the risk that dividends will be reduced or not paid or that the market price of the shares will drop. For both groups, the goal is to achieve a return that makes up for the risk. In general, the greater the risk taken, the greater the return required as compensation.

Any one loan or any one investment can turn out badly. As a result, most lenders and investors put their funds into a **portfolio**, or group of loans or investments. The portfolio allows them to average both the returns and the risks. Nevertheless, the portfolio is made up of a number of loans or shares on which individual decisions must be made. It is in making these individual decisions that financial statement analysis is most useful. Lenders and investors use financial statement analysis in two general ways: (1) to judge past performance and current position and (2) to judge future potential and the risk connected with the potential.

Assessment of Past Performance and Current Position

Past performance is often a good indicator of future performance. Therefore, an investor or lender looks at the trend of past sales, expenses, net profit, cash flow, and return on investment not only as a means for judging management's past performance but also as a possible indicator of future performance. In addition, an analysis of current position will tell, for example, what assets the business owns and what liabilities must be paid. It will also tell what the cash position is, how much debt the company has in relation to equity, and how reasonable the inventories and receivables are. Knowing a company's past performance and current position is often important in achieving the second general objective of financial analysis.

Assessment of Future Potential and Related Risk

Information about the past and present is useful only to the extent that it bears on decisions about the future. An investor judges the potential earning ability of a company because that ability will affect the market price of the company's shares and the amount of dividends the company will pay. A lender judges the potential debt-paying ability of the company.

The potentials of some companies are easier to predict than those of others, so there is less risk associated with them. The riskiness of an investment or loan depends on how easy it is to predict future profitability or liquidity. If an investor can predict with confidence that a company's earnings per share will be between 2.50 and 2.60 next year, the investment is less risky than if the earnings per share are expected to fall between 2.00 and 3.00. For example, the potential associated with an investment in an established and stable electric company, or a loan to it, is relatively easy to predict on the basis of the company's past performance and current position. The potential associated with a small microcomputer manufacturer, on the other hand, may be much harder to predict. For this reason, the investment in or loan to the electric company carries less risk than the investment in or loan to the small microcomputer company.

Often, in return for taking a greater risk, an investor in the microcomputer company will demand a higher expected return (increase in market price plus dividends) than will an investor in the electric company. Also, a lender of the microcomputer company will demand a higher interest rate and possibly more assurance of repayment (a secured loan, for instance) than a lender of the electric company. The higher interest rate reimburses the lender for assuming a higher risk.

OBJECTIVE 2	STANDARDS FOR FINANCIAL STATEMENT ANALYSIS

Describe and discuss the standards for financial statement analysis

In using financial statement analysis, decision makers must judge whether the relationships they have found are favourable or unfavourable. Three standards of comparison often used are (1) rule-of-thumb measures, (2) past performance of the company, and (3) industry norms.

Rule-of-Thumb Measures

Many financial analysts, investors, and lenders employ ideal or rule-of-thumb measures for key financial ratios. For example, it has long been thought that a current ratio (current assets divided by current liabilities) of 2:1 is acceptable. The credit rating firm of Dun & Bradstreet in the United States, in its *Key Business Ratios*, offers these guidelines:

> *Current debt to tangible net worth. Ordinarily, a business begins to pile up trouble when this relationship exceeds 80%.*
>
> *Inventory to net working capital. Ordinarily, this relationship should not exceed 80%.*

Although such measures may suggest areas that need further investigation, there is no proof that these levels are the best for any company, especially in an international context. A company with a current ratio higher than 2:1 may have a poor credit policy (resulting in accounts receivable being too large), too much or out-of-date inventory, or poor cash management. Another company may have a ratio lower than 2:1 as a result of excellent management in these three areas. Thus, rule-of-thumb measures must be used with great care.

Past Performance of the Company

An improvement over rule-of-thumb measures is the comparison of financial measures or ratios of the same company over a period of time. This standard will at least give the analyst some basis for judging whether the measure or ratio is getting better or worse. It may also be helpful in showing possible future trends. However, since trends do reverse at times, such projections must be made with care. Another problem with trend analysis is that the past may not be a useful measure of adequacy. In other words, past performance may not be enough to meet present needs. For example, even if return on total investment improved from 3 per cent last year to 4 per cent this year, the 4 per cent return may in fact not be adequate.

Industry Norms

One way of making up for the limitations of using past performance as a standard is to use industry norms. This standard will reveal how the company being analysed compares with other companies in the same industry. For example, suppose that other companies in an industry have an average rate of return on total investment of 8 per cent. In such a case, 3 and 4 per cent returns are probably not adequate. Industry norms can also be used to judge trends. Suppose that, because of a downward turn in the economy, a company's profit margin dropped from 12 to 10 per cent. A finding that other companies in the same industry had experienced an average drop in profit margin from 12 to 4 per cent would indicate that the company being analysed did relatively well.

There are three limitations to using industry norms as standards. First, two companies that seem to be in the same industry may not be strictly comparable. Consider two companies said to be in the oil industry. The main business of one may be marketing oil products it buys from other producers through service stations. The other, an international company, may discover, produce, refine, and market its own oil products. The operations of these two companies cannot be compared because they are different.

Second, most large companies today operate in more than one industry. Some of these **diversified companies**, or *conglomerates*, operate in many unrelated industries. The individual segments of a diversified company generally have different rates of profitability and different degrees of risk. In analysing the consolidated financial statements of these companies, it is often impossible to use industry norms as standards.

There are simply no other companies that are similar enough. A requirement by the International Accounting Standards Committee in IAS14 provides a partial solution to this problem. This requirement states that diversified companies must report revenues, profit from operations, and identifiable assets for each of their operating segments. Depending on specific criteria, segment information may be reported for operations in different industries or foreign markets.[2]

The third limitation of industry norms is that companies in the same industry with similar operations may use different acceptable accounting methods. That is, inventories may be valued using different methods, or different depreciation methods may be used for similar assets. Even so, if little information about a company's prior performance is available, industry norms probably offer the best available standards for judging current performance. But they should be used with care.

OBJECTIVE 3

State the sources of information for financial statement analysis

SOURCES OF INFORMATION

The external analyst is often limited to publicly available information about a company. The major sources of information about publicly held corporations are reports published by the company, reports filed with securities regulators, business periodicals, and credit and investment advisory services.

Reports Published by the Company

The annual report of a publicly held corporation is an important source of financial information. The major parts of this annual report are (1) management's analysis of the past year's operations, (2) the financial statements, (3) the notes to the statements, including the principal accounting methods used by the company, (4) the auditors'

DECISION POINT
CADBURY SCHWEPPES

Most people who know Cadbury Schweppes, voted "Britain's most admired company" in 1995, tend to think of the company as mainly a maker of chocolate and confectionery including such famous brand names as Dairy Milk, Roses, Timeout, and Trebor. However, in recent years the company has been growing rapidly in beverages with the acquisition of Dr. Pepper/Seven-Up to add to its Schweppes, Crush, and Canada Dry brands. Since these beverages businesses are different, the overall success of Cadbury Schweppes as reflected in its financial statements will be affected by the relative amount of investment and earnings in each of its businesses. How should a financial analyst assess the impact of the confectionery and beverages segments on the company's overall financial performance?

Cadbury Schweppes reports the information about its business segments in a note to the financial statements in its annual report (see Exhibit 14-1).[3] The analyst can learn a lot about the company from this information. Sales, trading profit, and operating assets are shown for each segment together with an analysis by geographical area. This information allows the analyst to assess the growth and profitability of each segment and to see where management is investing most for the future. For example, beverages is growing more rapidly than confectionery with trading profit margins in this segment increasing from 12.2 per cent in 1994 to 14.6 per cent in 1995. In contrast, confectionery trading profit margins have fallen from 12.8 per cent to 12.2 per cent.

EXHIBIT 14-1 *Segment Information for Cadbury Schweppes*

| | 1995 | | | | | |
	Total £m	United Kingdom £m	Europe £m	Americas £m	Pacific Rim £m	Africa & Others £m
Sales*						
Beverages	2,809	937	461	1,096	228	87
Confectionery	1,967	893	429	126	347	172
	4,776	1,830	890	1,222	575	259
Trading Profit*†						
Beverages	409	113	29	240	15	12
Confectionery	240	108	36	21	60	15
	649	221	65	261	75	27
Operating Assets						
Beverages	526	183	149	89	88	17
Confectionery	995	353	249	63	229	101
	1,521	536	398	152	317	118
Trading Margin†	%	%	%	%	%	%
Beverages	14.6	12.0	6.3	21.8	6.8	14.1
Confectionery	12.2	12.2	8.4	16.7	17.3	8.6
	13.6	12.1	7.3	21.3	13.1	10.4

*See Note 2 for the impact of acquisitions.
†Excluding acquisition-related restructuring costs of £49m

| | 1994 | | | | | |
	Total £m	United Kingdom £m	Europe £m	Americas £m	Pacific Rim £m	Africa & Others £m
Sales						
Beverages	2,203	833	406	671	215	78
Confectionery	1,827	896	369	96	324	142
	4,030	1,729	775	767	539	220
Trading Profit						
Beverages	269	120	8	113	14	14
Confectionery	235	111	37	19	53	15
	504	231	45	132	67	29
Operating Assets						
Beverages	591	210	155	108	93	16
Confectionery	863	357	191	41	198	76
	1,454	576	346	149	291	92
Trading Margin	%	%	%	%	%	%
Beverages	12.2	14.4	1.9	16.9	6.8	18.3
Confectionery	12.8	12.4	10.1	20.1	16.1	10.5
	12.5	13.4	5.8	17.3	12.4	13.3

> ## BUSINESS BULLETIN Technology in Practice
>
> Performance reports and other financial information, share prices, reference data, and news about companies and markets are available instantaneously to individuals on what is called the information superhighway through such services as CompuServe. The information superhighway is an international web of computer-driven communications systems that links tens of millions of homes and businesses through telephone, cable, and computer networks. Combined with the services of brokers that allow customers to buy and sell shares and other securities using their own computers, individuals have access to resources equivalent to those used by many professional analysts.

In the United States, interim reports have long been required to be published on a quarterly basis. In the European Union, on the other hand, only half-yearly reports are required, though some major listed companies such as Cadbury Schweppes voluntarily publish quarterly reports to keep investors informed on a more frequent basis.

report, and (5) a summary of operations for a five- or ten-year period. Most publicly held companies also publish **interim financial statements** usually quarterly or half-yearly. These reports present limited information in the form of condensed financial statements, which may be subject to a limited review or a full audit by the independent auditor. The interim statements are watched closely by the financial community for early signs of important changes in a company's earnings trend.

Reports to Securities Regulators

In most countries, publicly held corporations must file annual and interim reports with securities regulatory agencies such as the Securities and Exchange Commission (SEC) in the United States. All such reports are available to the public.

Business Periodicals and Credit and Investment Advisory Services

Financial analysts must keep up with current events in the financial world. Probably the best source of financial news is financial newspapers such as the *Wall Street Journal* and the *Financial Times*, which are published every business day. Some helpful magazines, published every week or every two weeks, include *The Economist*, *Business Week*, and *Fortune*.

For further details about the financial history of companies, the publications of such services as Moody's Investors Service, Bloomberg's, Standard & Poor's, and Datastream are useful. Data on industry norms, average ratios and relationships, and credit ratings are available from such agencies as Dun & Bradstreet.

OBJECTIVE 4

Identify the issues related to evaluating the quality of a company's earnings

EVALUATING A COMPANY'S QUALITY OF EARNINGS

It is clear from the preceding sections that current and expected earnings play an important role in the analysis of a company's prospects. Two of the most important economic indicators in evaluating shares are (1) expected changes in earnings per share and (2) expected return on equity. Net profit is a key component of both measures. Because of the importance of net profit, or the "bottom line", in measures of a company's prospects, there is significant interest in evaluating the quality of the net profit figure, or the *quality of earnings*. The quality of a company's earnings may be affected by (1) the accounting methods and estimates the company's management chooses and/or (2) the nature of nonoperating items in the income statement.

Choice of Accounting Methods and Estimates

Two aspects of the choice of accounting methods affect the quality of earnings. First, some accounting methods are by nature more prudent than others because they tend to produce a lower net profit in the current period. Second, there is considerable latitude in the choice of the estimated useful life over which assets are written off and in the amount of estimated residual value. In general, an accounting method or estimated useful life and/or residual value that results in lower current earnings is considered to produce better-quality earnings.

In earlier chapters, various acceptable methods were used in applying the matching rule. These methods are based on allocation procedures, which in turn are based on certain assumptions. Here are some of these methods:

1. For estimating uncollectible accounts expense: percentage of net sales method and accounts receivable ageing method
2. For pricing the ending inventory: weighted average-cost method; first-in, first-out (FIFO) method; and last-in, first-out (LIFO) method
3. For estimating depreciation expense: straight-line method, production method, and declining-balance method
4. For estimating depletion expense: production (extraction) method
5. For estimating amortisation of intangibles: straight-line method

All these methods are designed to allocate the costs of assets to the periods in which those costs contribute to the production of revenue. They are based on a determination of the benefits to the current period (expenses) versus the benefits to future periods (assets). They are estimates, and the period or periods benefited cannot be demonstrated conclusively. They are also subjective, because in practice it is hard to justify one method of estimation over another.

For this reason, it is important for both the accountant and the financial statement user to understand the possible effects of different accounting methods on net profit and financial position. For example, suppose that two companies have similar operations, but that one uses FIFO for inventory pricing and the straight-line (SL) method for calculating depreciation and the other uses LIFO for inventory pricing and the double-declining-balance (DDB) method for calculating depreciation. The income statements of the two companies might appear as follows:

	FIFO and SL	LIFO and DDB
Sales	500,000	500,000
Goods Available for Sale	300,000	300,000
Less Ending Inventory	60,000	50,000
Cost of Goods Sold	240,000	250,000
Gross Profit from Sales	260,000	250,000
Less: Depreciation Expense	40,000	80,000
Other Expenses	170,000	170,000
Total Operating Expenses	210,000	250,000
Net Profit before Income Taxes	50,000	0

This 50,000 difference in profit before income taxes stems only from the differences in accounting methods. Differences in the estimated lives and residual values of the plant assets could lead to an even greater variation. In practice, of course, differences in net profit occur for many reasons, but the user must be aware of the discrepancies that can occur as a result of the methods chosen by management.

The existence of these alternatives could cause problems in the interpretation of financial statements were it not for the criteria of completeness and comparability described in the chapter on financial statement objectives, presentation, and analysis. Completeness requires that management explain the significant accounting policies used in preparing the financial statements in a note to the statements. Comparability requires that the same accounting method be followed from year to year. If a change in method is made, the nature of the change and its monetary effect must be explained in a note.

Accounting methods can differ systematically across countries. For example, in the United Kingdom and the Netherlands profits tend to be significantly higher than in Germany and Japan solely on account of these differences. The major goal of the International Accounting Standards Committee is to harmonise accounting standards around the world.

Nature of Nonoperating Items

As seen in the chapter on profit and retained earnings, the corporate income statement consists of several components. The top of the statement presents earnings from current ongoing operations, called profit from operations. The lower part of the statement can contain such nonoperating items as discontinuing operations and extraordinary gains and losses. These items may drastically affect the bottom line, or net profit, of the company.

For practical reasons, the calculations of trends and ratios are based on the assumption that net profit and other components are comparable from year to year and from company to company. However, in making interpretations the astute analyst will always look beyond the ratios to the quality of the components. In a recent year, AT&T of the United States wrote off $7 billion for retiree health benefits and another $1.3 billion to cover future disability and severance payments. Despite these huge losses, the company's share price has been higher because profit from operations before these charges was up for the year.[4] Although such write-offs reduce a company's net worth, they do not affect current operations or cash flows and are usually ignored by analysts assessing current performance and future prospects.

In some cases, a company may boost profit by selling assets on which it can report a gain. For example, in 1992, Lotus Development Corporation, the American software company, reported a 40 per cent increase in net profit when earnings from operations actually decreased by 66 per cent. Weak sales and earnings were camouflaged by a one-time $33.3 million gain after taxes from the sale of shares that Lotus owned in another company.[5] The quality of Lotus's earnings was lower than might appear on the surface. Unless analysts go beyond the "bottom line" in analysing and interpreting financial reports, they can come to the wrong conclusions.

TOOLS AND TECHNIQUES OF FINANCIAL ANALYSIS

Few numbers by themselves mean very much. It is their relationship to other numbers or their change from one period to another that is important. The tools of financial analysis are intended to show relationships and changes. Among the more widely used of these financial analysis techniques are horizontal analysis, trend analysis, vertical analysis, and ratio analysis.

OBJECTIVE 5

Apply horizontal analysis, trend analysis, and vertical analysis to financial statements

Horizontal Analysis

International accounting standards call for the presentation of comparative financial statements that give the current year's and past year's financial information. A common starting point for studying such statements is **horizontal analysis**, which begins with the calculation of monetary amount changes and percentage changes from the previous to the current year. The percentage change must be calculated to show how the size of the change relates to the size of the amounts involved. A change of 1 million in sales is not so drastic as a change of 1 million in net profit, because sales is a relatively larger amount than net profit.

Exhibits 14-2 and 14-3 present condensed versions of the comparative balance sheets and income statements, respectively, for Volvo, the Swedish car, truck, and bus manufacturer, with the monetary amount and percentage changes shown.[6] The percentage change is calculated as follows:

$$\text{Percentage change} = 100\left(\frac{\text{amount of change}}{\text{previous year amount}}\right)$$

The **base year** in any set of data is always the first year being studied. For example, from 1994 to 1995, Volvo's long-term assets increased by Kr 2,350 million, from Kr

EXHIBIT 14-2   *Comparative Balance Sheets with Horizontal Analysis*

Volvo
Consolidated Balance Sheets
December 31, 1995 and 1994

	(Kronor in Millions)		Increase (Decrease)	
	1995	1994	Amount	Percentage
Assets				
Current assets:				
Liquid funds	23,306	24,449	(1,143)	(4.7)
Receivables	28,906	30,545	(1,639)	(5.4)
Inventories	23,929	23,380	612	2.6
	76,141	78,374	(2,233)	(2.8)
Long-term assets:				
Property, plant, and equipment, net	27,941	28,196	(255)	(0.9)
Investments in shares	18,087	18,548	(461)	(2.5)
Long-term receivables and loans	10,904	8,919	1,985	22.3
Intangible assets	5,626	4,545	1,081	23.8
	62,558	60,208	2,350	3.9
Total assets	138,699	138,582	117	—
Liabilities and Shareholders' Equity				
Current liabilities:				
Accounts payable	12,702	13,075	(373)	(2.9)
Advances from customers	2,627	2,623	4	0.2
Bank and other loans	11,691	21,555	(9,864)	(45.8)
Other current liabilities and provisions	32,749	34,959	(2,210)	(6.3)
	59,769	72,212	(12,443)	(17.2)
Long-term liabilities:				
Bond loans	6,975	4,317	2,658	61.6
Other long-term loans and accruals	16,800	13,776	3,024	22.0
Deferred tax liabilities	3,350	4,107	(757)	(18.4)
	27,125	22,200	4,925	22.2
Minority interests	605	838	233	27.8
Shareholders' equity	2,318	2,220	98	4.4
Share capital				
Reserves and retained earnings	48,882	41,112	7,770	18.9
Total shareholders' equity	51,200	43,332	7,868	18.2
Total liabilities and shareholders' equity	138,699	138,582	117	—

60,208 million to Kr 62,558 million, or by 3.9 per cent. The percentage increase is calculated as follows:

$$\text{Percentage increase} = 100 \left(\frac{2{,}350 \text{ million}}{60{,}208 \text{ million}} \right) = 3.9\%$$

EXHIBIT 14-3   *Comparative Income Statements with Horizontal Analysis*

Volvo
Consolidated Income Statements
December 31, 1995 and 1994

| | (Kronor in Millions) | | Increase (Decrease) | |
	1995	1994	Amount	Percentage
Net sales	171,511	155,866	15,645	10.0
Costs and expenses:				
Cost of sales	132,693	118,876	13,817	11.6
Selling, general, and administrative expenses	24,138	22,512	1,626	7.2
Depreciation and amortisation	5,656	5,107	549	10.7
Total costs and expenses	162,487	146,495	15,992	10.9
Operating profit before nonrecurring items	9,024	9,371	(347)	(3.7)
Nonrecurring items	1,215	—	1,215	NA
Operating profit	10,239	9,371	868	9.3
Equity investment and financial income, net	2,809	7,007	(4,198)	59.9
Profit before taxes and minority interests	13,048	16,378	(3,330)	20.3
Provision for taxes	3,741	2,783	958	34.4
	9,307	13,595	(4,288)	31.5
Minority interests	45	365	(320)	87.7
Net profit	9,262	13,230	(3,968)	30.0

An examination of the comparative balance sheets shows some changes from 1994 to 1995. Inventories increased by 2.6 per cent while intangible assets increased substantially by 23.8 per cent. The percentage decrease in current liabilities of 17.2 per cent was more than six times the percentage decrease in current assets of 2.8 per cent. Bank and other loans showed a large decrease of 45.8 per cent. Total shareholders' equity increased by 18.2 per cent. Overall, Volvo became more liquid and less heavily financed by short-term debt.

Care must be taken in the analysis of percentage changes. For example, in Exhibit 14-2, one might view the 61.6 per cent increase in bond loans as more important than the 22.0 per cent increase in other long-term loans and accruals. However, this is not the proper conclusion because in monetary amounts the increase of Kr 3,024 million in other long-term loans is greater than the increase of Kr 2,658 million in bond loans.

From the income statements in Exhibit 14-3, the increases in cost of sales of 11.6 per cent and in total costs and expenses of 10.9 per cent exceeded the increase in sales of 10.0 per cent, resulting in a decline in operating profit before nonrecurring items of 3.7 per cent. In 1995, Volvo had significant nonrecurring gains from the sale of businesses. Also note that in both years equity investment and financial income is a positive amount, meaning that financial income exceeded interest expense in each year.

EXHIBIT 14-4   *Trend Analysis*

Volvo
International Net Sales
Trend Analysis

	1995	1994	1993	1992	1991
Net Sales					
(in Millions of Kronor)					
Europe	102,843	92,155	60,936	51,585	46,632
North America	40,557	38,917	31,707	19,822	18,284
Other Markets	28,111	24,794	18,512	11,595	12,307
Trend Analysis					
(in Percentages)					
Europe	220.5	197.6	130.7	110.6	100.0
North America	221.8	212.8	173.4	108.4	100.0
Other Markets	228.4	201.5	150.4	94.2	100.0

Trend Analysis

A variation of horizontal analysis is **trend analysis,** in which percentage changes are calculated for several successive years instead of two years. Trend analysis is important because, with its long-run view, it may point to basic changes in the nature of a business. In addition to comparative financial statements, most companies present a summary of operations and data on other key indicators for five or more years. Domestic and international net sales from Volvo's summary of operations together with a trend analysis are presented in Exhibit 14-4.

Trend analysis uses an **index number** to show changes in related items over a period of time. For index numbers, one year, the base year, is equal to 100 per cent. Other years are measured in relation to that amount. For example, the 1995 index for sales in Europe was calculated as follows:

$$\text{Index} \;=\; 100 \left(\frac{\text{index year amount}}{\text{base year amount}} \right) \;=\; 100 \left(\frac{102{,}843}{46{,}632} \right) \;=\; 220.5$$

This index means 1995 sales are 220.5 per cent of, or 2.205 times, 1991 sales.

A study of the trend analysis in Exhibit 14-4 clearly shows that Volvo's sales in Europe rose more rapidly than in North America and Other Markets from 1991 to 1992 but were then overtaken in 1993 by dramatic increases in North America and Other Markets as shown by changes in the indexes to 173.4 and 150.4 respectively. By 1995, European sales had caught up, but Other Markets had outperformed both Europe and North America with growth in the five-year index to 228.4. These contrasting trends are presented graphically in Figure 14-1.

Vertical Analysis

In **vertical analysis,** percentages are used to show the relationship of the different parts to the total in a single statement. The accountant sets a total figure in the statement equal to 100 per cent and calculates each component's percentage of that total. (The figure would be total assets or total liabilities and shareholders' equity on the balance sheet, and revenues or sales on the income statement.) The resulting state-

FIGURE 14-1 *Trend Analysis of Sales for Volvo Presented Graphically*

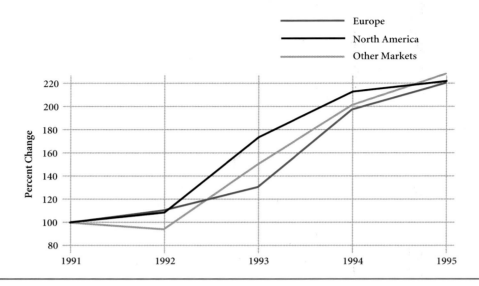

ment of percentages is called a **common-size statement**. Common-size balance sheets and income statements for Volvo are shown in pie-chart form in Figures 14-2 and 14-3, and in financial-statement form in Exhibits 14-5 and 14-6.

FIGURE 14-2 *Common-Size Balance Sheets for Volvo Presented Graphically*

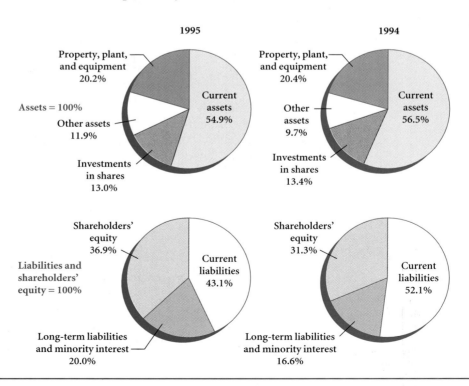

FIGURE 14-3 *Common-Size Income Statements for Volvo Presented Graphically*

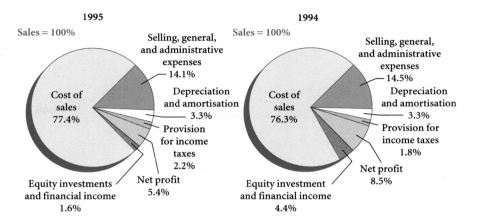

Note: Nonrecurring items and minority interests are not presented.

Equity investment and financial income causes some items not to total to 100%.

Vertical analysis is useful for comparing the importance of certain components in the operation of a business. It is also useful for pointing out important changes in the components from one year to the next in comparative common-size statements. For Volvo, the composition of assets in Exhibit 14-5 did not change significantly from

EXHIBIT 14-5 *Common-Size Balance Sheets*

Volvo
Common-Size Balance Sheets
December 31, 1995 and 1994

	1995*	1994*
Assets		
Current assets	54.9%	56.5%
Property, plant, and equipment, net	20.2	20.4
Investments in shares	13.0	13.4
Other assets	11.9	9.7
Total assets	100.0%	100.0%
Liabilities		
Current liabilities	43.1%	52.1%
Long-term liabilities and minority interest	20.0	16.6
Total liabilities	63.1%	68.7%
Total shareholders' equity	36.9%	31.3%
Total liabilities and shareholders' equity	100.0%	100.0%

*Results are rounded in some cases to equal 100.0%.

EXHIBIT 14-6   *Common-Size Income Statements*

Volvo
Common-Size Income Statements
December 31, 1995 and 1994

	1995*	1994*
Sales	100.0%	100.0%
Costs and expenses		
Cost of sales	77.4%	76.3%
Selling, general and administrative	14.1	14.5
Depreciation and amortisation	3.3	3.3
Total costs and expenses	94.8%	94.1%
Operating profit before nonrecurring and financial items	5.2%	5.9%
Nonrecurring items	0.7	—
Operating profit	5.9	5.9
Equity investment and financial income	1.6	4.4
Profit before taxes and minority interest	7.6%	10.3%
Provision for taxes	2.2%	1.8%
Net profit	5.4%	8.5%

*Rounding causes some additions and subtractions not to total precisely.
Note: Minority interests in net profit are not presented.

1994 to 1995. A slightly larger proportion of assets was in "Other assets" such as long-term receivables and loans (11.9 per cent versus 9.7 per cent), with a corresponding decrease in current assets (54.9 per cent versus 56.5 per cent) between 1995 and 1994. The composition of liabilities shows more change. Current liabilities decreased from 52.1 per cent to 43.1 per cent. Correspondingly, shareholders' equity increased from 31.3 per cent to 36.9 per cent.

The common-size income statements (Exhibit 14-6) show the significance of the increase in costs and expenses from 94.1 to 94.8 per cent of sales. Additional factors in 1995 were the gain from nonrecurring items and the increase in taxes. But most important was the decrease in equity investment and financial income from 4.4 to 1.6 per cent. This factor was the major cause of the decrease in profit from 8.5 to 5.4 per cent. On the other hand, operating profit before nonrecurring items decreased less significantly from 5.9 per cent to 5.2 per cent.

Common-size statements are often used to make comparisons between companies. They allow an analyst to compare the operating and financing characteristics of two companies of different size in the same industry. For example, the analyst may want to compare Volvo to other companies in terms of the percentage of total assets financed by debt or the percentage of selling, general and administrative expenses to sales. Common-size statements would show these and other relationships.

OBJECTIVE 6

Apply ratio analysis to financial statements in a comprehensive analysis of a company's financial situation

Ratio Analysis

Ratio analysis is an important way to state meaningful relationships between two components of a financial statement. To be most useful, the interpretation of ratios must include a study of the underlying data. Ratios are guides or shortcuts that are useful in evaluating a company's financial position and operations and making comparisons with results in previous years or with other companies. The primary purpose of ratios is to point out areas needing further investigation. They should be used in connection with a general understanding of the company and its environment. Ratios for financial analysis were introduced in the chapter on financial statement objectives, presentation, and analysis. The following section briefly reviews the ratios covered in that chapter and expands the analysis to cover new ratios.

Ratios may be expressed in several ways. For example, a ratio of net profit of 100,000 to sales of 1,000,000 may be stated as (1) net profit is 1/10, or 10 per cent of sales; or (2) the ratio of sales to net profit is 10 to 1 (10:1), or 10 times net profit.

COMPREHENSIVE ILLUSTRATION OF RATIO ANALYSIS

In prior chapters, financial ratios have been introduced at appropriate points. The purpose of this section is to show a comprehensive ratio analysis of a real company, Volvo, using the ratios that have been introduced and a few new ones. These ratios are used to compare Volvo's performance for the years 1994 and 1995 in achieving the following objectives: (1) liquidity, (2) profitability, (3) long-term solvency, (4) cash flow adequacy, and (5) market strength. Most data for the analyses come from the financial statements of Volvo presented in Exhibits 14-2 and 14-3. Other data are presented as needed.

Evaluating Liquidity

Liquidity is the ability to pay bills when they are due and to meet unexpected needs for cash. The ratios that relate to this goal all have to do with working capital or some part of it, because it is out of working capital that debts are paid. The objective of liquidity is also closely related to the cash flow ratios discussed in a following section.

The liquidity ratios for Volvo in 1994 and 1995 are presented in Exhibit 14-7. The **current ratio** and the **quick ratio** are measures of short-term debt-paying ability. The major difference between the two ratios is that the current ratio includes inventories in the numerator and the quick ratio does not. Inventories are not included in the quick ratio because they take longer to convert to cash than the other current assets. Both ratios increased from 1994 to 1995. The primary reason for the increases was the large decrease in current liabilities. Overall, Volvo's short-term debt-paying ability increased, and the company is in a stronger liquidity position.

Analysis of two major components of current assets, receivables and inventories, also shows increases in liquidity from 1994 to 1995. The relative size of accounts receivable and the effectiveness of credit policies are measured by the **receivable turnover**, which increased from 5.4 to 5.8 times. The relative size of inventories is measured by **inventory turnover**, which grew from 5.3 to 5.6 times. The related ratios of **average days' sales uncollected** and **average days' inventory available** decreased from 67.6 to 62.9 days and from 68.9 to 65.2 days, respectively. These results mean that Volvo's **operating cycle**, or the time it takes to sell and collect for products sold,

---

BUSINESS BULLETIN **International Practice**

Just because a company lists substantial cash and cash equivalents on its balance sheet does not necessarily mean that this cash is available to pay short-term debt in its home country. For example, although Apple showed almost $.7 billion dollars in cash and cash equivalents at the end of 1993, management warned that continued short-term borrowing would be necessary "because a substantial portion of the company's cash, cash equivalents, and short-term investments is held by foreign subsidiaries. . . . Amounts held by foreign subsidiaries would be subject to U.S. income taxation upon repatriation to the United States".[7]

EXHIBIT 14-7   *Liquidity Ratios of Volvo*

	1995	1994

Current ratio: Measure of short-term debt-paying ability

$$\frac{\text{Current assets}}{\text{Current liabilities}} \qquad \frac{76,141}{59,769} = 1.3 \text{ times} \qquad \frac{78,374}{72,212} = 1.1 \text{ times}$$

Quick ratio: Measure of short-term debt-paying ability

$$\frac{(\text{Cash} + \text{marketable securities}) + \text{receivables}}{\text{Current liabilities}} \qquad \frac{23,306 + 28,906}{59,769} \qquad \frac{24,449 + 30,545}{72,212}$$

$$= \frac{52,212}{59,769} = .9 \text{ times} \qquad = \frac{54,994}{72,212} = 0.8 \text{ times}$$

Receivable turnover: Measure of relative size of accounts receivable balance and effectiveness of credit policies

$$\frac{\text{Net sales}}{\text{Average accounts receivable*}} \qquad \frac{171,511}{(28,906 + 30,545)/2} \qquad \frac{155,866}{(30,545 + 27,424)/2}$$

$$= \frac{117,511}{29,726} = 5.8 \text{ times} \qquad = \frac{155,866}{28,985} = 5.4 \text{ times}$$

Average days' sales uncollected: Measure of average time taken to collect receivables

$$\frac{\text{Days in year}}{\text{Receivable turnover}} \qquad \frac{365 \text{ days}}{5.8 \text{ times}} = 62.9 \text{ days} \qquad \frac{365 \text{ days}}{5.4 \text{ times}} = 67.6 \text{ days}$$

Inventory turnover: Measure of relative size of inventory

$$\frac{\text{Cost of goods sold}}{\text{Average inventory*}} \qquad \frac{132,693}{(23,929 + 23,380)/2} \qquad \frac{118,876}{(23,380 + 21,390)/2}$$

$$= \frac{132,693}{23,655} = 5.6 \text{ times} \qquad = \frac{118,876}{22,385} = 5.3 \text{ times}$$

Average days' inventory available: Measure of average days taken to sell inventory

$$\frac{\text{Days in year}}{\text{Inventory turnover}} \qquad \frac{365 \text{ days}}{5.6 \text{ times}} = 65.2 \text{ days} \qquad \frac{365 \text{ days}}{5.3 \text{ times}} = 68.9 \text{ days}$$

*1993 figures are from Volvo's annual report.

decreased from 136.5 days (67.6 days + 68.9 days) in 1994 to 128.1 days (62.9 days + 65.2 days) in 1995. This significant decrease has a positive effect on Volvo's liquidity because the company has to wait 8.4 fewer days (136.5 days − 128.1 days) to receive cash from sales.

Evaluating Profitability

The objective of profitability relates to a company's ability to earn a satisfactory profit so that investors and shareholders will continue to provide capital to it. A company's profitability is also closely linked to its liquidity because earnings ultimately produce cash flow. For this reason, evaluating profitability is important to both investors and lenders. The profitability ratios and analysis of Volvo are shown in Exhibit 14-8.

EXHIBIT 14-8 *Profitability Ratios of Volvo*

	1995	1994

Profit margin: Measure of net profit produced by each monetary unit of sales

$$\frac{\text{Net profit}^*}{\text{Net sales}} \qquad \frac{9,262}{171,511} = 5.4\% \qquad \frac{13,230}{155,866} = 8.5\%$$

Asset turnover: Measure of how efficiently assets are used to produce sales

$$\frac{\text{Net sales}}{\text{Average total assets}} \qquad \frac{171,511}{(138,699 + 138,582)/2} \qquad \frac{155,866}{(138,582 + 134,516)/2}$$

$$= \frac{171,511}{138,641} \qquad\qquad = \frac{155,866}{136,549}$$

$$= 1.2 \text{ times} \qquad\qquad = 1.1 \text{ times}$$

Return on assets: Measure of overall earning power or profitability

$$\frac{\text{Net profit}}{\text{Average total assets}} \qquad \frac{9,262}{138,641} = 6.7\% \qquad \frac{13,230}{136,549} = 9.7\%$$

Return on equity: Measure of the profitability of shareholders' investments

$$\frac{\text{Net profit}}{\text{Average shareholders' equity}} \qquad \frac{9,262}{(51,200 + 43,332)/2} \qquad \frac{13,230}{(43,332 + 27,088)/2}$$

$$= \frac{9,262}{47,266} \qquad\qquad = \frac{13,230}{35,210}$$

$$= 19.6\% \qquad\qquad = 37.6\%$$

*In comparing companies in an industry, some analysts use net profit before income taxes as the numerator to eliminate the effect of differing tax rates among firms.

Volvo's profitability declined by most measures from 1994 to 1995 primarily because of the large decrease in profit. The reasons for this decrease were discussed previously in the sections on horizontal and vertical analysis. **Profit margin**, which measures the percentage of revenue that contributes to net profit, declined from 8.5 to 5.4 per cent. However, **asset turnover**, which measures how efficiently assets are used to produce sales, increased slightly from 1.1 to 1.2 times. The result is a decline in the **return on assets**, which measures the amount earned on the assets invested, from 9.7 to 6.7 per cent. These relationships may be illustrated as follows:

	Profit Margin	×	**Asset Turnover**	=	**Return on Assets**
	$\dfrac{\text{net profit}}{\text{net sales}}$	×	$\dfrac{\text{net sales}}{\text{average total assets}}$	=	$\dfrac{\text{net profit}}{\text{average total assets}}$
1995	5.4%	×	1.2	=	6.5%
1994	8.5%	×	1.1	=	9.4%

The slight differences in the two sets of return on assets figures result from the rounding of the ratios in the second set of calculations.

Finally, the **return on equity**, which measures how much profit was earned on the amounts invested by shareholders, declined from a generous 37.6 per cent to a more modest 19.6 per cent.

EXHIBIT 14-9   *Long-Term Solvency Ratios of Volvo*

	1995	1994
Debt to equity ratio: Measure of capital structure and leverage		

$$\frac{\text{Total liabilities}}{\text{Shareholders' equity}} \qquad \frac{86,894}{51,200} = 1.7 \text{ times} \qquad \frac{94,412}{43,332} = 2.2 \text{ times}$$

Interest coverage ratio: Measure of lenders' protection from default on interest payments

$$\frac{\text{Net profit before}}{\text{taxes} + \text{interest expense*}} \qquad \frac{13,048 + 3,757}{3,757} \qquad \frac{16,378 + 3,608}{3,608}$$

$$= 4.5 \text{ times} \qquad\qquad = 5.5 \text{ times}$$

*Interest expense was taken from Volvo's full income statement.

Evaluating Long-Term Solvency

Long-term solvency has to do with a company's ability to survive for many years. The aim of long-term solvency analysis is to point out early that a company is on the road to bankruptcy. Studies have shown that accounting ratios can show as much as five years in advance that a company may fail.[8] Declining profitability and liquidity ratios are key signs of possible business failure. Two other ratios that analysts often consider when assessing long-term solvency are debt to equity and interest coverage. These ratios are shown in Exhibit 14-9.

Increasing amounts of debt in a company's capital structure mean that the company is becoming more heavily leveraged or geared. This condition negatively affects long-term solvency because it represents increasing legal obligations to pay interest periodically and the principal at maturity. Failure to make these payments can result in bankruptcy. The **debt to equity ratio** measures the amount of a company's assets financed by lenders in relation to the amount financed by shareholders. This relationship is described as *leverage* or *gearing*. Volvo's capital structure became much less leveraged from 1994 to 1995, during which time the debt to equity ratio decreased significantly, from 2.2 times to 1.7 times. At the latter level, however, Volvo still has more than one-and-a-half times as much debt as equity, which is significant. It is noteworthy to recall from Exhibit 14-2 that the decrease in debt came from short-term financing rather than long-term financing. Long-term financing was in fact increased. The overall effect was nevertheless beneficial as overall debt was reduced, as was pressure on short-term cash flows to repay short-term debt.

If debt is bad, why have any? The answer is that the level of debt is a matter of balance. In spite of its riskiness, debt is a flexible means of financing certain business operations. Volvo is using debt to finance what management plans to be a temporary increase in inventory. The interest paid on this debt is deductible for income tax purposes, whereas dividends on shares are not. Also, because debt usually carries a fixed interest charge, the cost of financing can be limited and leverage, or gearing, can be used to advantage. If the company can earn a return on assets greater than the cost of interest, it makes an overall profit. However, it runs the risk of not earning a return on assets equal to the cost of financing those assets, thus incurring a loss.

The **interest coverage ratio** measures the degree of protection lenders have from a default on interest payments. This ratio declined from 5.5 times in 1994 to 4.5 times in 1995, mainly because of the decrease in net profit. An interest coverage ratio of 4.5 times is normally considered adequate, so unless it declines further in 1996, it is not a problem for Volvo.

Evaluating Cash Flow Adequacy

Because cash flows are needed to pay debts when they are due, cash flow measures are closely related to the objectives of liquidity and long-term solvency. Volvo's cash flow adequacy ratios, using data from the company's cash flow statement, are presented in Exhibit 14-10. Volvo's ability to generate positive operating cash flows generally declined from 1994 to 1995, even though the **cash flow yield**, or the ability to generate operating cash flows in relation to net profit, increased from 0.9 times to 1.2 times. While net cash flows from operating activities showed a decline from 12,236 in 1994 to 11,067 in 1995, net profit declined even further. **Cash flows to sales**, or the ability of sales to generate operating cash flows, declined from 7.9 per cent to 6.5 per cent. **Cash flows to assets**, or the ability of assets to generate operating cash flows, declined from 9.0 per cent to 8.0 per cent. Overall, Volvo's **free cash flow**, or cash generated after providing for commitments, went from a positive 12,945 to a negative 2,590 in 1995. These calculations include dividends and net capital expenditures as presented in the cash flow statement, from which it can be seen that both dividends and capital expenditures increased significantly in 1995. Indeed, in 1994 net capital expenditures were positive, indicating a surplus from asset disposals relative to purchases.

Evaluating Market Ratios

The market price of a company's shares is of interest to the analyst because it represents what investors as a whole think of the company at a point in time. Market price is the price at which people are willing to buy or sell the shares. It provides information about how investors view the potential return and risk connected with owning

---

EXHIBIT 14-10 *Cash Flow Adequacy Ratios of Volvo*

	1995	1994

Cash flow yield: Measure of a company's ability to generate operating cash flows in relation to net profit

$$\frac{\text{Net cash flows from operating activities}}{\text{Net profit}} \qquad \frac{11{,}067}{9{,}262} = 1.2 \text{ times} \qquad \frac{12{,}236}{13{,}230} = 0.9 \text{ times}$$

Cash flows to sales: Measure of the ability of sales to generate operating cash flows

$$\frac{\text{Net cash flows from operating activities}}{\text{Net sales}} \qquad \frac{11{,}067}{171{,}511} = 6.5\% \qquad \frac{12{,}236}{155{,}866} = 7.9\%$$

Cash flows to assets: Measure of the ability of assets to generate operating cash flows

$$\frac{\text{Net cash flows from operating activities}}{\text{Average total assets}} \qquad \frac{11{,}067}{(138{,}699 + 138{,}582)/2} \qquad \frac{12{,}236}{(138{,}582 + 134{,}516)/2}$$

$$= \frac{11{,}067}{138{,}641} = 8.0\% \qquad = \frac{12{,}236}{136{,}549} = 9.0\%$$

Free cash flow: Measure of cash generated or cash deficiency after providing for commitments

Net cash flows from operating activities − dividends − net capital expenditures

$$11{,}067 - 1{,}512 - 12{,}145 = -2{,}590 \qquad 12{,}236 - 601 + 1{,}310 = 12{,}945$$

EXHIBIT 14-11 *Market Strength Ratios of Volvo*

	1995	1994

Price/earnings ratio: Measure of investor confidence in a company

$$\frac{\text{Market price per share}^*}{\text{Earnings per share}} \qquad = \frac{136}{20.20} = 6.7 \text{ times} \qquad = \frac{140}{31.80} = 4.4 \text{ times}$$

Dividends yield: Measure of the current return to an investor in a share

$$\frac{\text{Dividends per share}^*}{\text{Market price per share}} \qquad = \frac{4.00}{136} = 2.9\% \qquad = \frac{3.40}{140} = 2.4\%$$

*Market price and dividends are from Volvo's annual report.

the company's shares. Market price by itself, however, is not very informative for this purpose. Companies differ in number of outstanding shares and amount of underlying earnings and dividends. Thus, market price must be related to earnings by considering the price/earnings ratio and the dividends yield. These ratios for Volvo appear in Exhibit 14-11 and have been calculated using the year-end market price for Volvo's shares during 1994 and 1995.

The **price/earnings (P/E) ratio**, which measures investor confidence in a company, is the ratio of the market price per share to earnings per share. The P/E ratio is useful in comparing the relative values placed on the earnings of different companies and in comparing the value placed on a company's shares in relation to the overall market. Volvo's price/earnings ratio increased from 4.4 times in 1994 to 6.7 times in 1995. Although its net profit dropped significantly, the market price of its shares did not decline as much. This would indicate that investors are confident that Volvo will rebound in profitability in 1996 and beyond. The **dividends yield** measures a share's current return to an investor in the form of dividends. Volvo's dividends yield increased from 2.4 per cent in 1994 to 3.9 per cent in 1995 because the market price of the shares declined and the dividends per share were increased.

Summary of Financial Analysis of Volvo

This ratio analysis clearly shows that while Volvo's profitability and cash flow declined from 1994 to 1995, there has been some improvement in liquidity and long-term solvency. The main problems to be addressed by management are weak profitability and the high level of debt. Based on the market ratios, investors seem confident about Volvo's ability to achieve better results in the future.

CHAPTER REVIEW

Review of Learning Objectives

1. **Describe and discuss the objectives of financial statement analysis.** Lenders and investors, as well as managers, use financial statement analysis to judge the past performance and current position of a company. In this way they also judge its future potential and the risk associated with it. Lenders use the information gained from their analysis to make reliable loans that will be repaid with interest. Investors use the information to make investments that will provide a return that is worth the risk.

2. **Describe and discuss the standards for financial statement analysis.** Three commonly used standards for financial statement analysis are rule-of-thumb measures, past performance of the company, and industry norms. Rule-of-thumb measures are weak because of the lack of evidence that they can be applied widely. The past performance of a company can offer a guideline for measuring improvement but is not helpful in judging performance relative to other companies. Although the use of industry norms overcomes this last problem, its

disadvantage is that firms are not always comparable, even in the same industry.

3. **State the sources of information for financial statement analysis.** The major sources of information about publicly held corporations are company-published reports such as annual reports and interim financial statements, regulatory agency reports, business periodicals, and credit and investment advisory services.

4. **Identify the issues related to evaluating the quality of a company's earnings.** Current and prospective net profit is an important component in many ratios used to evaluate a company. The user should recognise that the quality of reported net profit can be influenced by certain choices made by management. First, management exercises judgement in choosing the accounting methods and estimates used in calculating net profit. Second, discontinuing operations, extraordinary gains or losses, and changes in accounting methods may affect net profit positively or negatively.

5. **Apply horizontal analysis, trend analysis, and vertical analysis to financial statements.** Horizontal analysis involves the calculation of monetary amount changes and percentage changes from year to year. Trend analysis is an extension of horizontal analysis in that percentage changes are calculated for several years. The changes are usually calculated by setting a base year equal to 100 and calculating the results for subsequent years as a percentage of that base year. Vertical analysis uses percentages to show the relationship of the component parts to the total in a single statement. The resulting financial statements, which are expressed entirely in percentages, are called common-size statements.

6. **Apply ratio analysis to financial statements in a comprehensive analysis of a company's financial situation.** A comprehensive ratio analysis includes the evaluation of a company's liquidity, profitability, long-term solvency, cash flow adequacy, and market ratios. The ratios for measuring these characteristics are found in Exhibits 14-7 to 14-11.

Review of Concepts and Terminology

The following concepts and terms were introduced in this chapter.

LO 6   **Asset turnover:** Net sales divided by average total assets. Measures how efficiently assets are used to produce sales.

LO 6   **Average days' inventory available:** Days in year divided by inventory turnover. Shows the average number of days taken to sell inventory.

LO 6   **Average days' sales uncollected:** Days in year divided by receivable turnover. Shows the speed at which receivables are turned over—i.e. number of days, on average, a company must wait to receive payment for credit sales.

LO 5   **Base year:** First year used in analysing financial data.

LO 6   **Cash flows to assets:** Net cash flows from operating activities divided by average total assets. Used to measure the ability of assets to generate operating cash flows.

LO 6   **Cash flows to sales:** Net cash flows from operating activities divided by net sales. Used to measure the ability of sales to generate operating cash flows.

LO 6   **Cash flow yield:** Net cash flows from operating activities divided by net profit. Measures ability to generate operating cash flows in relation to net profit.

LO 5   **Common-size statement:** A financial statement in which the components of a total figure are stated in terms of percentages of the total.

LO 6   **Current ratio:** Current assets divided by current liabilities. Used as an indicator of a company's liquidity and short-term debt-paying ability.

LO 6   **Debt to equity ratio:** Total liabilities divided by shareholders' equity. Used to measure the relationship of debt financing to equity financing, or the extent to which a company is leveraged or geared.

LO 2   **Diversified companies:** Companies that operate in more than one industry. Also called *conglomerates*.

LO 6   **Dividends yield:** Dividends per share divided by market price per share. Used as a measure of the current return to an investor in a share.

LO 1   **Financial statement analysis:** All techniques used to show important relationships among figures in financial statements.

LO 6   **Free cash flow:** Net cash flows from operating activities minus dividends minus net capital expenditures. Used to measure cash generated or cash deficiency after providing for commitments.

LO 5   **Horizontal analysis:** A technique for analysing financial statements that involves the calculation of monetary amount changes and percentage changes from the previous to the current year.

LO 5   **Index number:** In trend analysis, a number against which changes in related items over a period of time are measured. Calculated by setting the base year equal to 100 per cent.

LO 6   **Interest coverage ratio:** Net profit before taxes plus interest expense divided by interest expense. Used as a measure of the degree of protection lenders have from a default on interest payments.

LO 3   **Interim financial statements:** Financial statements issued for a period of less than one year, usually quarterly or half-yearly.

LO 6   **Inventory turnover:** The cost of goods sold divided by average inventory. Used to measure the relative size of inventory.

LO 6   **Operating cycle:** Time it takes to sell and collect for products sold; average days' inventory available plus average days' sales uncollected.

LO 1   **Portfolio:** A group of loans or investments designed to average the returns and risks of a lender or investor.

LO 6   **Price/earnings (P/E) ratio:** Market price per share divided by earnings per share. Used as a measure of investor confidence in a company and as a means of comparison among shares.

LO 6   **Profit margin:** Net profit divided by net sales. Measures the percentage of revenue that contributes to net profit.

LO 6   **Quick ratio:** The more liquid current assets—cash, marketable securities or current investments, and receivables—divided by current liabilities. Used as a measure of short-term liquidity.

LO 6   **Ratio analysis:** A technique of financial analysis in which meaningful relationships are shown between components of financial statements.

LO 6   **Receivable turnover:** Net sales divided by average accounts receivable. Measures the relative size of accounts receivable and the success of credit and collection policies; shows how many times, on average, receivables were turned into cash during the period.

LO 6 **Return on assets:** Net profit divided by average total assets. Measures the amount earned on assets invested. An overall measure of earning power or profitability.

LO 6 **Return on equity:** Net profit divided by average shareholders' equity. Used to measure how much profit was earned on the amounts invested by shareholders.

LO 5 **Trend analysis:** A type of horizontal analysis in which percentage changes are calculated for several successive years instead of two years.

LO 5 **Vertical analysis:** A technique for analysing financial statements that uses percentages to show the relationships of the different parts to the total in a single statement.

Review Problem

Comparative Analysis of Two Companies

LO 6 Maggie Wong is considering an investment in one of two fast-food restaurant chains, Quik Burger and Big Steak, whose balance sheets and income statements follow.

Balance Sheets
(in Thousands)

	Quik Burger	Big Steak
Assets		
Cash	2,000	4,500
Accounts Receivable (net)	2,000	6,500
Inventory	2,000	5,000
Property, Plant, and Equipment (net)	20,000	35,000
Other Assets	4,000	5,000
Total Assets	30,000	56,000
Liabilities and Shareholders' Equity		
Accounts Payable	2,500	3,000
Notes Payable	1,500	4,000
Bonds Payable	10,000	30,000
Ordinary Shares (1 nominal value)	1,000	3,000
Share Premium	9,000	9,000
Retained Earnings	6,000	7,000
Total Liabilities and Shareholders' Equity	30,000	56,000

Income Statements
(in Thousands, except per Share Amounts)

	Quik Burger	Big Steak
Net Sales	53,000	86,000
Cost of Goods Sold (including restaurant operating expenses)	37,000	61,000
Gross Profit	16,000	25,000
General Operating Expenses		
Selling Expenses	7,000	10,000
Administrative Expenses	4,000	5,000
Interest Expense	1,400	3,200
Income Taxes Expense	1,800	3,400
Total Operating Expenses	14,200	21,600
Net Profit	1,800	3,400
Earnings per share	1.80	1.13

From the cash flow statement, net cash flows from operations were 2,200,000 for Quik Burger and 3,000,000 for Big Steak. Net capital expenditures were 2,100,000 for Quik Burger and 1,800,000 for Big Steak. Dividends of 500,000 were paid for Quik Burger and 600,000 for Big Steak. The market prices of the shares for Quik Burger and Big Steak were 30 and 20, respectively. Financial information pertaining to prior years is not readily available to Maggie Wong. Assume that all notes payable are current liabilities and that all bonds payable are long-term liabilities.

REQUIRED   Conduct a comprehensive ratio analysis of Quik Burger and Big Steak and compare the results. In the analysis, perform these steps (round all ratios and percentages to one decimal place):

1. Prepare an analysis of liquidity.
2. Prepare an analysis of profitability.
3. Prepare an analysis of long-term solvency.
4. Prepare an analysis of cash flow adequacy.
5. Prepare an analysis of market strength.
6. Compare the two companies by inserting the ratio calculations from the preceding five steps in a table with the following column headings: Ratio Name, Quik Burger, Big Steak, and More Favourable Ratio. Indicate in the last column the company that apparently had the more favourable ratio in each case. (Consider changes of .1 or less to be neutral.)
7. In what ways would having access to prior years' information aid this analysis?

Answer to Review Problem

Ratio Name	Quik Burger	Big Steak
1. Liquidity analysis		
a. Current ratio	$\dfrac{2,000 + 2,000 + 2,000}{2,500 + 1,500}$	$\dfrac{4,500 + 6,500 + 5,000}{3,000 + 4,000}$
	$= \dfrac{6,000}{4,000} = 1.5$ times	$= \dfrac{16,000}{7,000} = 2.3$ times
b. Quick ratio	$\dfrac{2,000 + 2,000}{2,500 + 1,500}$	$\dfrac{4,500 + 6,500}{3,000 + 4,000}$
	$= \dfrac{4,000}{4,000} = 1.0$ times	$= \dfrac{11,000}{7,000} = 1.6$ times
c. Receivable turnover	$\dfrac{53,000}{2,000} = 26.5$ times	$\dfrac{86,000}{6,500} = 13.2$ times
d. Average days' sales uncollected	$\dfrac{365}{26.5} = 13.8$ days	$\dfrac{365}{13.2} = 27.7$ days
e. Inventory turnover	$\dfrac{37,000}{2,000} = 18.5$ times	$\dfrac{61,000}{5,000} = 12.2$ times
f. Average days' inventory available	$\dfrac{365}{18.5} = 19.7$ days	$\dfrac{365}{12.2} = 29.9$ days
2. Profitability analysis		
a. Profit margin	$\dfrac{1,800}{53,000} = 3.4\%$	$\dfrac{3,400}{86,000} = 4.0\%$
b. Asset turnover	$\dfrac{53,000}{30,000} = 1.8$ times	$\dfrac{86,000}{56,000} = 1.5$ times
c. Return on assets	$\dfrac{1,800}{30,000} = 6.0\%$	$\dfrac{3,400}{56,000} = 6.1\%$
d. Return on equity	$\dfrac{1,800}{1,000 + 9,000 + 6,000}$	$\dfrac{3,400}{3,000 + 9,000 + 7,000}$
	$= \dfrac{1,800}{16,000} = 11.3\%$	$= \dfrac{3,400}{19,000} = 17.9\%$

Ratio Name	Quik Burger	Big Steak

3. Long-term solvency analysis

a. Debt to equity ratio

$$\frac{2,500 + 1,500 + 10,000}{1,000 + 9,000 + 6,000}$$

$$= \frac{14,000}{16,000} = .9 \text{ times}$$

$$\frac{3,000 + 4,000 + 30,000}{3,000 + 9,000 + 7,000}$$

$$= \frac{37,000}{19,000} = 1.9 \text{ times}$$

b. Interest coverage ratio

$$\frac{1,800 + 1,800 + 1,400}{1,400}$$

$$= \frac{5,000}{1,400} = 3.6 \text{ times}$$

$$\frac{3,400 + 3,400 + 3,200}{3,200}$$

$$= \frac{10,000}{3,200} = 3.1 \text{ times}$$

4. Cash flow adequacy analysis

a. Cash flow yield

$$\frac{2,200}{1,800} = 1.2 \text{ times}$$

$$\frac{3,000}{3,400} = .9 \text{ times}$$

b. Cash flows to sales

$$\frac{2,200}{53,000} = 4.2\%$$

$$\frac{3,000}{86,000} = 3.5\%$$

c. Cash flows to assets

$$\frac{2,200}{30,000} = 7.3\%$$

$$\frac{3,000}{56,000} = 5.4\%$$

d. Free cash flow (in thousands)

$$2,200 - 500 - 2,100$$
$$= -400$$

$$3,000 - 600 - 1,800$$
$$= 600$$

5. Market strength analysis

a. Price/earnings ratio

$$\frac{30}{1.80} = 16.7 \text{ times}$$

$$\frac{20}{1.13} = 17.7 \text{ times}$$

b. Dividends yield

$$\frac{500,000 \div 1,000,000}{30} = 1.7\%$$

$$\frac{600,000 \div 3,000,000}{20} = 1.0\%$$

6. Comparative analysis

Ratio Name	Quik Burger	Big Steak	More Favourable Ratio*
1. Liquidity analysis			
a. Current ratio	1.5 times	2.3 times	Big Steak
b. Quick ratio	1.0 times	1.6 times	Big Steak
c. Receivable turnover	26.5 times	13.2 times	Quik Burger
d. Average days' sales uncollected	13.8 days	27.7 days	Quik Burger
e. Inventory turnover	18.5 times	12.2 times	Quik Burger
f. Average days' inventory available	19.7 days	29.9 days	Quik Burger
2. Profitability analysis			
a. Profit margin	3.4%	4.0%	Big Steak
b. Asset turnover	1.8 times	1.5 times	Quik Burger
c. Return on assets	6.0%	6.1%	Neutral
d. Return on equity	11.3%	17.9%	Big Steak
3. Long-term solvency analysis			
a. Debt to equity ratio	0.9 times	1.9 times	Quik Burger
b. Interest coverage ratio	3.6 times	3.1 times	Quik Burger
4. Cash flow adequacy analysis			
a. Cash flow yield	1.2 times	.9 times	Quik Burger
b. Cash flows to sales	4.2%	3.5%	Quik Burger
c. Cash flows to assets	7.3%	5.4%	Quik Burger
d. Free cash flow	−400,000	600,000	Big Steak
5. Market strength analysis			
a. Price/earnings ratio	16.7 times	17.7 times	Big Steak
b. Dividends yield	1.7%	1.0%	Quik Burger

*Class discussion of the company with the apparently more favourable ratio may focus on conditions under which different conclusions may be drawn.

7. **Usefulness of prior years' information**

Prior years' information would be helpful in two ways. First, turnover, return, and cash flows to assets ratios could be based on average amounts. Second, a trend analysis could be performed for each company.

CHAPTER ASSIGNMENTS

Knowledge and Understanding

Questions

1. What are the differences and similarities in the objectives of investors and lenders in using financial statement analysis?
2. What role does risk play in making loans? What role does it play in making investments?
3. What standards are commonly used to evaluate financial statements, and what are their relative merits?
4. Why would a financial analyst compare the ratios of Steelco, a steel company, with the ratios of other companies in the steel industry? What factors might invalidate such a comparison?
5. Where may an investor look to find information about a publicly held company in which he or she is thinking of investing?
6. What is the basis of the statement "Accounting profit is a useless measurement because it is based on so many arbitrary decisions"? Is the statement true?
7. Why would an investor want to see both horizontal and trend analyses of a company's financial statements?
8. What does the following sentence mean: "Based on 1980 equalling 100, net profit increased from 240 in 1996 to 260 in 1997"?

9. What is the difference between horizontal and vertical analysis?
10. What is the purpose of ratio analysis?
11. Under what circumstances would a current ratio of 3:1 be good? Under what circumstances would it be bad?
12. In a period of high interest rates, why are receivable and inventory turnover especially important?
13. Company A and Company B both have net profits of 1,000,000. Is it possible to say that these companies are equally successful? Why or why not?
14. A company has a return on assets of 12 per cent and a debt to equity ratio of .5. Would you expect return on equity to be more or less than 12 per cent?
15. What amount is common to all cash flow adequacy ratios? To what other groups of ratios are the cash flow adequacy ratios most closely related?
16. The market price of Company J's shares are the same as the market price of Company Q's shares. How might you determine whether investors are equally confident about the future of these companies?

Application

Exercises

E 14-1.

LO 4 *Effect of Alternative Accounting Methods*

At the end of its first year of operations, a company could calculate its ending inventory according to three different accounting methods, as follows: FIFO, 95,000; weighted average-cost, 90,000; LIFO, 86,000. If the company uses the weighted average-cost method, net profit for the year would be 34,000.

1. Determine net profit if the FIFO method is used.
2. Determine net profit if the LIFO method is used.
3. Which method is more prudent?
4. Will the comparability criterion be violated if the company chooses to use the LIFO method?
5. Does the completeness criterion require disclosure of the inventory method selected by management in the financial statements?

E 14-2.

LO 4 *Effect of Alternative*
LO 6 *Accounting Methods*

Jeans F' All and Jeans 'R' Us are very similar companies in size and operation. Jeans F' All uses FIFO and straight-line depreciation methods, and Jeans 'R' Us uses LIFO and accelerated depreciation. Prices have been rising during the past several years. Both Jeans F' All and Jeans 'R' Us have paid their taxes in full for the current year, and both companies use the same method for figuring income taxes as for financial reporting. Identify which company will report the greater amount for each of the following ratios:

1. Current ratio
2. Inventory turnover
3. Profit margin
4. Return on assets

If you cannot state which company will report the greater amount, explain why.

E 14-3.

LO 5 *Horizontal Analysis*

Calculate the amount and percentage changes for the Lindquist Company's balance sheets, which follow, and comment on the changes from 20x1 to 20x2. (Round the percentage changes to one decimal place.)

Lindquist Company
Comparative Balance Sheets
December 31, 20x2 and 20x1

	20x2	20x1
Assets		
Current Assets	37,200	25,600
Property, Plant, and Equipment (net)	218,928	194,400
Total Assets	256,128	220,000
Liabilities and Shareholders' Equity		
Current Liabilities	22,400	6,400
Long-Term Liabilities	70,000	80,000
Shareholders' Equity	163,728	133,600
Total Liabilities and Shareholders' Equity	256,128	220,000

E 14-4.

LO 5 *Trend Analysis*

Prepare a trend analysis of the following data using 20x1 as the base year. State whether the trends show a favourable or unfavourable situation. (Round answers to one decimal place.)

	20x5	20x4	20x3	20x2	20x1
Net Sales	25,520	23,980	24,200	22,880	22,000
Cost of Goods Sold	17,220	15,400	15,540	14,700	14,000
General and Administrative Expenses	5,280	5,184	5,088	4,896	4,800
Operating Profit	3,020	3,396	3,572	3,284	3,200

E 14-5.

LO 5 *Vertical Analysis*

Express the comparative income statements that follow as common-size statements, and comment on the changes from 20x1 to 20x2. (Round calculations to one decimal place.)

Lindquist Company
Comparative Income Statements
For the Years Ended December 31, 20x2 and 20x1

	20x2	20x1
Net Sales	424,000	368,000
Cost of Goods Sold	254,400	239,200
Gross Profit	169,600	128,800
Selling Expenses	106,000	73,600
General Expenses	50,880	36,800
Total Operating Expenses	156,880	110,400
Net Operating Profit	12,720	18,400

E 14-6.

LO 6 *Turnover Analysis*

Alberto's Men's Shop has been in business for four years. Because the company has recently had a cash flow problem, management wonders whether there is a problem with receivables or inventories. Here are selected figures from the company's financial statements (in thousands):

	20x4	20x3	20x2	20x1
Net Sales	288	224	192	160
Cost of Goods Sold	180	144	120	96
Accounts Receivable (net)	48	40	32	24
Inventory	56	44	32	20

Calculate receivable turnover and inventory turnover for each of the four years, and comment on the results relative to the cash flow problem that Alberto's Men's Shop has been experiencing. Round calculations to one decimal place.

E 14-7.
LO 6 *Liquidity Analysis*

Partial comparative balance sheet and income statement information for Lam Company follows.

	20x2	20x1
Cash	6,800	5,200
Marketable Securities	3,600	8,600
Accounts Receivable (net)	22,400	17,800
Inventory	27,200	24,800
Total Current Assets	60,000	56,400
Current Liabilities	20,000	14,100
Net Sales	161,280	110,360
Cost of Goods Sold	108,800	101,680
Gross Profit	52,480	8,680

The year-end balances for Accounts Receivable and Inventory in 20x0 were 16,200 and 25,600, respectively. Calculate the current ratio, quick ratio, receivable turnover, average days' sales uncollected, inventory turnover, and average days' inventory available for each year. (Round calculations to one decimal place.) Comment on the change in the company's liquidity position from 20x1 to 20x2.

E 14-8.
LO 6 *Profitability Analysis*

At year end, Canzoneri Company had total assets of 640,000 in 20x0, 680,000 in 20x1, and 760,000 in 20x2. Its debt to equity ratio was .67 in all three years. In 20x1, the company earned a net profit of 77,112 on revenues of 1,224,000. In 20x2, the company earned a net profit of 98,952 on revenues of 1,596,000. Calculate the profit margin, asset turnover, return on assets, and return on equity for 20x1 and 20x2. Comment on the apparent cause of the increase or decrease in profitability. (Round the percentages and other ratios to one decimal place.)

E 14-9.
LO 6 *Long-Term Solvency and Market Strength Ratios*

An investor is considering investing in the long-term bonds and ordinary shares of Companies X and Y. Both companies operate in the same industry. In addition, both companies pay a dividend per share of 4 and a yield of 10 per cent on their long-term bonds. Other data for the two companies follow:

	Company X	Company Y
Total Assets	2,400,000	1,080,000
Total Liabilities	1,080,000	594,000
Net Profit before Taxes	288,000	129,600
Interest Expense	97,200	53,460
Earnings per Share	3.20	5.00
Market Price of Ordinary Shares	40	47.50

Calculate the debt to equity, interest coverage, and price/earnings (P/E) ratios, and the dividends yield, and then comment on the results. (Round calculations to one decimal place.)

E 14-10.
LO 6 *Cash Flow Adequacy Analysis*

Using the data below, taken from the financial statements of Furri Corporation, calculate the cash flow yield, cash flows to sales, cash flows to assets, and free cash flow.

Net Sales	3,200,000
Net Profit	352,000
Net Cash Flows from Operating Activities	456,000
Total Assets, Beginning of Year	2,890,000
Total Assets, End of Year	3,120,000
Cash Dividends	120,000
Net Capital Expenditures	298,000

E 14-11.
LO 6 *Preparation of Statements from Ratios and Incomplete Data*

On the following page are the income statement and balance sheet of Pandit Corporation, with most of the amounts missing.

Pandit's only interest expense is on long-term debt. Its debt to equity ratio is .5, its current ratio 3:1, its quick ratio 2:1, the receivable turnover 4.5, and its inventory turnover 4.0. The return on assets is 10 per cent. All ratios are based on the current year's information.

Complete Pandit Corporation's financial statements using the information presented. Show supporting calculations.

Pandit Corporation
Income Statement
For the Year Ended December 31, 20x1
(in Thousands)

Net Sales		18,000
Cost of Goods Sold		?
Gross Profit		?
Operating Expenses		
Selling Expenses	?	
Administrative Expenses	234	
Interest Expense	162	
Income Taxes Expense	620	
Total Operating Expenses		?
Net Profit		?

Pandit Corporation
Balance Sheet
December 31, 20x1
(in Thousands)

Assets

Cash	?	
Accounts Receivable (net)	?	
Inventories	?	
Total Current Assets		?
Property, Plant, and Equipment (net)		5,400
Total Assets		?

Liabilities and Shareholders' Equity

Current Liabilities	?	
Bonds Payable, 9% interest	?	
Total Liabilities		?
Ordinary Shares—20 nominal value	3,000	
Share Premium	2,600	
Retained Earnings	4,000	
Total Shareholders' Equity		9,600
Total Liabilities and Shareholders' Equity		?

Problem Set

P 14-1.

LO 4 *Effect of Alternative*
LO 6 *Accounting Methods*

Albers Company began operations this year. At the beginning of the year the company purchased plant assets of 900,000, with an estimated useful life of ten years and a salvage value of 130,000. During the year, the company had sales of 1,300,000, salary expense of 200,000, and other expenses of 80,000, excluding depreciation. In addition, Albers Company purchased inventory as follows:

January 15	400 units at 400	160,000
March 20	200 units at 408	81,600
June 15	800 units at 416	332,800
September 18	600 units at 412	247,200
December 9	300 units at 420	126,000
Total	2,300 units	947,600

At the end of the year on December 31, a physical inventory disclosed 500 units still available. The managers of Albers Company know that they have a choice of accounting methods, but are unsure how these methods will affect net profit. They have heard of the FIFO and LIFO inventory methods and the straight-line and double-declining-balance depreciation methods.

REQUIRED
1. Prepare two income statements for Albers Company, one using the FIFO and straight-line methods, the other using the LIFO and double-declining-balance methods.
2. Prepare a schedule accounting for the difference in the two net profit figures obtained in **1**.
3. What effect does the choice of accounting methods have on Albers's inventory turnover? What conclusions can you draw?
4. How does the choice of accounting methods affect Albers's return on assets?

Use year-end balances to calculate the ratios. Assume that the only asset other than plant assets and inventory is 80,000 cash. Is your evaluation of Albers's profitability affected by the choice of accounting methods?

P 14-2.

LO 5 *Horizontal and Vertical Analysis*

The condensed comparative income statements and balance sheets of Mariano Corporation follow. All figures are given in thousands.

Mariano Corporation
Comparative Income Statements
For the Years Ended December 31, 20x2 and 20x1

	20x2	20x1
Net Sales	3,276,800	3,146,400
Cost of Goods Sold	2,088,800	2,008,400
Gross Profit	1,188,000	1,138,000
Operating Expenses		
Selling Expenses	476,800	518,000
Administrative Expenses	447,200	423,200
Interest Expense	65,600	39,200
Income Taxes Expense	62,400	56,800
Total Operating Expenses	1,052,000	1,037,200
Net Profit	136,000	100,800

Mariano Corporation
Comparative Balance Sheets
December 31, 20x2 and 20x1

	20x2	20x1
Assets		
Cash	81,200	40,800
Accounts Receivable (net)	235,600	229,200
Inventory	574,800	594,800
Property, Plant, and Equipment (net)	750,000	720,000
Total Assets	1,641,600	1,584,800
Liabilities and Shareholders' Equity		
Accounts Payable	267,600	477,200
Notes Payable	200,000	400,000
Bonds Payable	400,000	—
Ordinary Shares—10 nominal value	400,000	400,000
Retained Earnings	374,000	307,600
Total Liabilities and Shareholders' Equity	1,641,600	1,584,800

REQUIRED   Perform the following analyses. Round percentages to one decimal place.

1. Prepare schedules showing the amount and percentage changes from 20x1 to 20x2 for Mariano's comparative income statements and balance sheets.
2. Prepare common-size income statements and balance sheets for 20x1 and 20x2.
3. Comment on the results in **1** and **2** by identifying favourable and unfavourable changes in the components and composition of the statements.

P 14-3.

LO 6   *Analysing the Effects of Transactions on Ratios*

Straits Corporation engaged in the transactions listed in the first column of the following table. Opposite each transaction is a ratio and space to indicate the effect of each transaction on the ratio.

REQUIRED   Place an X in the appropriate column to show whether the transaction increased, decreased, or had no effect on the indicated ratio.

			Effect	
Transaction	Ratio	Increase	Decrease	None
a. Sold goods on account.	Current ratio			
b. Sold goods on account.	Inventory turnover			
c. Collected on accounts receivable.	Quick ratio			
d. Wrote off an uncollectible account.	Receivable turnover			
e. Paid on accounts payable.	Current ratio			
f. Declared cash dividend.	Return on equity			
g. Incurred advertising expense.	Profit margin			
h. Issued share dividend.	Debt to equity ratio			
i. Issued bond payable.	Asset turnover			
j. Accrued interest expense.	Current ratio			
k. Paid previously declared cash dividend.	Dividends yield			
l. Purchased treasury stock	Return on assets			
m. Recorded depreciation expense.	Cash flow yield			

P 14-4.

LO 6   *Comprehensive Ratio Analysis of Two Companies*

Will Rowe is considering buying the ordinary shares of either Allison Corporation or Marker Corporation, department store chains whose income statements and balance sheets follow.

During the year, Allison Corporation paid a total of 100,000 in dividends. The market price per share of its shares is currently 60. In comparison, Marker Corporation paid a total of 228,000 in dividends, and the current market price of its shares is 76 per share. Allison Corporation had net cash flows from operations of 543,000 and net capital expenditures of 1,250,000. Marker Corporation had net cash flows from operations of 985,000 and net capital expenditures of 2,100,000. Information for prior years is not readily available. Assume that all notes payable are current liabilities and all bonds payable are long-term liabilities.

	Allison Corporation	Marker Corporation
Net Sales	25,120,000	50,420,000
Cost of Goods Sold	12,284,000	29,668,000
Gross Profit	12,836,000	20,752,000
Operating Expenses		
Sales Expense	9,645,200	14,216,400
Administrative Expense	1,972,000	4,868,000
Interest Expense	388,000	456,000
Income Taxes Expense	400,000	600,000
Total Operating Expenses	12,405,200	20,140,400
Net Profit	430,800	611,600
Earnings per share	4.31	10.19

	Allison Corporation	Marker Corporation
Assets		
Cash	160,000	384,800
Marketable Securities (at cost)	406,800	169,200
Accounts Receivable (net)	1,105,600	1,970,800
Inventory	1,259,600	2,506,800
Prepaid Expenses	108,800	228,000
Property, Plant, and Equipment (net)	5,827,200	13,104,000
Intangibles and Other Assets	1,106,400	289,600
Total Assets	9,974,400	18,653,200
Liabilities and Shareholders' Equity		
Accounts Payable	688,000	1,145,200
Notes Payable	300,000	800,000
Accrued Liabilities	100,400	146,800
Bonds Payable	4,000,000	4,000,000
Ordinary Shares—20 nominal value	2,000,000	1,200,000
Share Premium	1,219,600	7,137,200
Retained Earnings	1,666,400	4,224,000
Total Liabilities and Shareholders' Equity	9,974,400	18,653,200

REQUIRED Conduct a comprehensive ratio analysis for each company using the available information and compare the results. Round percentages and ratios to one decimal place, and consider differences of .1 or less to be indeterminate. This analysis should be done in the following steps:

1. Prepare an analysis of liquidity by calculating for each company the (a) current ratio, (b) quick ratio, (c) receivable turnover, (d) average days' sales uncollected, (e) inventory turnover, and (f) average days' inventory available.
2. Prepare an analysis of profitability by calculating for each company the (a) profit margin, (b) asset turnover, (c) return on assets, and (d) return on equity.
3. Prepare an analysis of long-term solvency by calculating for each company the (a) debt to equity ratio and (b) interest coverage ratio.
4. Prepare an analysis of cash flow adequacy by calculating for each company the (a) cash flow yield, (b) cash flows to sales, (c) cash flows to assets, and (d) free cash flow.
5. Prepare an analysis of market strength by calculating for each company the (a) price/earnings ratio and (b) dividends yield.
6. Compare the two companies by inserting the ratio calculations from **1** through **5** in a table with the following column heads: Ratio Name, Allison Corporation, Marker Corporation, and Company with More Favourable Ratio. Indicate in the right-hand column which company had the more favourable ratio in each case.
7. How could the analysis be improved if prior years' information were available?

Critical Thinking and Communication

Conceptual Mini-Case

CMC 14-1.

LO 4   *Quality of Earnings*

On Tuesday, January 19, 1988, *International Business Machines Corp.* (IBM), the world's largest computer manufacturer, reported greatly increased earnings for the fourth quarter of 1987. Despite this reported gain in earnings, the price of IBM's shares on the New York Stock Exchange declined by $6 per share to $111.75. In sympathy with this move, most other technology shares also declined.

IBM's fourth-quarter net earnings rose from $1.39 billion, or $2.28 a share, to $2.08 billion, or $3.47 a share, an increase of 49.6 per cent and 52.2 per cent over the year-earlier period. Management declared that these results demonstrated the effectiveness of IBM's efforts to become more competitive, and that, despite the economic uncertainties of 1988, the company was planning for growth.

The apparent cause of the share price decline was that the huge increase in profit could be traced to nonrecurring gains. Investment analysts pointed out that IBM's high earnings stemmed primarily from factors such as a lower tax rate. Despite most analysts' expectations of a tax rate between 40 and 42 per cent, IBM's rate was a low 36.4 per cent, down from the previous year's 45.3 per cent.

In addition, analysts were disappointed in IBM's revenue growth. Revenues within the United States were down, and much of the growth in revenues came through favourable currency translations, increases that might not be repeated. In fact, some estimates of the fourth-quarter earnings attributed $.50 per share to currency translations and another $.25 to tax-rate changes.

Other factors contributing to the rise in earnings were one-time transactions, such as the sale of Intel Corporation shares and bond redemptions, along with a corporate share buyback programme that reduced the amount of shares outstanding in the fourth quarter by 7.4 million shares.

The analysts were concerned about the quality of IBM's earnings. Identify four quality of earnings issues reported in the case and the analysts' concern about each. In percentage terms, what is the impact of the currency changes on fourth-quarter earnings? Comment on management's assessment of IBM's performance. Do you agree with management? Be prepared to discuss your answers to the questions in class.

Cultural Mini-Case

CLMC 14-1.
LO 4   *Quality of Earnings and*
LO 6   *International Comparisons*

Euro Disney operates Disneyland Paris in France, which opened in 1992 with a theme park, hotels, entertainment centre, and golf course. Following a disastrous net loss of 5,297 million French francs in 1993 and a reduced net loss of 1,797 million French francs in 1993, Euro Disney recovered to report net profits of 114 and 202 million French francs in 1995 and 1996 respectively. However, in a note to the financial statements, Euro Disney disclosed the following reconciliation from French accounting standards for generally accepted accounting principles (GAAP) to U.S. GAAP as follows (in millions of French francs):

	Year Ended September 30	
	1996	1995
Reconciliation of Net Income (Loss)		
Net income, as reported under French GAAP	202	114
Lease and interest adjustments	(1,215)	(1,213)
Other	(8)	(7)
Net Loss under U.S. GAAP	(1,021)	(1,106)

REQUIRED

Under U.S. GAAP, leases, which may be treated as operating leases under French rules, must be capitalised and amortised with consequent additional expense.

1. Calculate the return on equity for 1996 under French GAAP and U.S. GAAP. Note: Shareholders' equity under French GAAP for 1996 is FFr 5,813 million and for 1995 is FFr 5,610 million. Under U.S. GAAP, shareholders' equity for 1996 is FFr 2,286 million and for 1995 is FFr 3,305 million.
2. How can users make useful comparisons across countries when accounting differences can be so great?

Ethics Mini-Case

EMC 14-1.
LO 4   *Management of Earnings*

In 1993, the *Wall Street Journal* reported that **H. J. Heinz**, the famous maker of tomato sauce and many other food products, earned a quarterly profit of $.75 per share, including a gain on sale of assets of $.24 per share. Profit from continuing operations was only $.51 per share, or 16 per cent below last year's figure. The paper was critical of Heinz's use of a one-time gain to increase earnings: "In recent years, H. J. Heinz Co. has been spicing up its earnings with special items. The latest quarter is no exception." An analyst is quoted as saying that Heinz has not admitted the slump in its business but has "started including nonrecurring items in the results they were showing. That created an artificially high base of earnings that they can no longer match".[9] Do you think it is unethical for a company's management to increase earnings periodically through the use of one-time transactions, such as sales of assets, on which it has a profit? What potential long-term negative effects might this practice have for Heinz?

Decision-Making Case

DMC 14-1.
LO 4   *Effect of Alternative*
Accounting Methods on
Executive Compensation

At the beginning of 20x1, Victor Scribe retired as chief executive and principal shareholder in *Scribe Corporation,* a successful producer of personal computer equipment. As an incentive to the new management, Scribe supported the board of directors' new executive compensation plan, which provides cash bonuses to key executives for years in which the company's earnings per share equal or exceed the current dividends per share of 4.00, plus a .40 per share increase in dividends for each future year. Thus, for management to receive the bonuses, the company must earn per-share profit of 4.00 the first year, 4.40 the second, 4.80 the third, and so forth. Since Scribe owns 500,000 of the one million ordinary shares outstanding, the dividend income will provide for his retirement years. He is also protected against inflation by the regular increase in dividends. Earnings and dividends per share for the first three years of operation under the new management were as follows:

	20x3	20x2	20x1
Earnings per share	5.00	5.00	5.00
Dividends per share	4.80	4.40	4.00

During this time, management earned bonuses totalling more than 2 million under the compensation plan. Scribe, who had taken no active part on the board of directors, began to worry about the unchanging level of earnings and decided to study the company's annual report more carefully. The notes to the annual report revealed the following information:

a. Management changed from the LIFO inventory method to the FIFO method in 20x1. The effect of the change was to decrease cost of goods sold by 400,000 in 20x1, 600,000 in 20x2, and 800,000 in 20x3.
b. Management changed from the double-declining-balance accelerated depreciation method to the straight-line method in 20x2. The effect of this change was to decrease depreciation by 800,000 in 20x2 and by 1,000,000 in 20x3.
c. In 20x3, management increased the estimated useful life of intangible assets from five to ten years. The effect of this change was to decrease amortisation expense by 200,000 in 20x3.

REQUIRED

1. Calculate earnings per share for each year according to the accounting methods in use at the beginning of 20x1. (Use ordinary shares outstanding.)
2. Have the executives earned their bonuses? What serious effect has the compensation package apparently had on the net assets of Scribe Corporation? How could Scribe have protected himself from what has happened?

Basic Research Activity

RA 14-1.

LO 3 *Use of Investment Services*

In your library, find an investment guide. Locate the reports on three corporations. You may choose the corporations at random or choose them from the same industry, if directed to do so by your teacher. (If you did a related exercise in a previous chapter, use the same three companies.) Write a summary of what you learn about each company from the reference works and be prepared to discuss your findings in class.

Financial Reporting and Analysis

Interpretation Cases from Business

ICB 14-1.

LO 4 *Quality of Earnings*

The Walt Disney Company is a famous American entertainment company that produces films and operates theme parks, among other things. The company is also well known as a profitable and well-managed business. On November 15, 1984, the *Wall Street Journal* ran the following article by Michael Cieply, under the title "Disney Reports Fiscal 4th-Period Loss After Taking $166 Million Write-Down".

Walt Disney Productions reported a $64 million net loss for its fiscal fourth quarter ended Sept. 30, after writing down a record $166 million in movies and other properties.

In the year-earlier quarter, Disney had net income of $24.5 million, or 70 cents a share. Fourth-quarter revenue this year rose 28% to $463.2 million from $363 million.

In the fiscal year, the entertainment company's earnings rose 5% to $97.8 million, or $2.73 a share, from $93.2 million, or $2.70 a share, a year earlier. Revenue rose 27% to $1.66 billion from $1.31 billion.

The company said it wrote down $112 million in motion picture and television properties. The write-down involves productions that already have been released as well as ones still under development, but Disney declined to identify the productions or projects involved.

"This just reflects the judgment of new management about the ultimate value of projects we had under way," said Michael Bagnall, Disney's executive vice president for finance. . . .

The company also said it charged off $40 million to reflect the "abandonment" of a number of planned projects at its various theme parks. An additional $14 million was charged off as a reserve to cover possible legal obligations resulting from the company's fight to ward off a pair of successive takeover attempts last summer, Mr. Bagnall said.

Disney said its full-year net included a $76 million gain from a change in its method of accounting for investment tax credits. The change was made retroactive to the fiscal first quarter ended Dec. 31, and will boost that quarter's reported net to $85 million, from $9 million.

Mr. Bagnall said the $76 million credit stemmed largely from construction of Disney's Epcot theme park in Florida. By switching to flow-through from deferral accounting, the company was able to take the entire credit immediately instead of amortizing it over 18 years, as originally planned, Mr. Bagnall said. Flow-through accounting is usual in the entertainment industry.[10]

REQUIRED

1. What two categories of issues does the user of financial statements want to consider when evaluating the quality of a company's reported earnings? Did Disney have one or both types of items in 1984?

2. Compare the fourth-period earnings or losses for 1983 and 1984 and full year 1983 and 1984 earnings or losses before and after adjusting for the item or items described in **1.** Which comparisons do you believe give the best picture of Disney's performance?

ICB 14-2.

LO 4 *International Financial*
LO 6 *Statement Analysis*

Cadbury Schweppes is a major global beverage and confectionery company, with such well-known brands as Dr. Pepper, Schweppes, Sunkist, Canada Dry, Dairy Milk, and Roses. This United Kingdom-based company publishes its financial statements in accordance with accounting standards in the United Kingdom but includes in its annual report a very interesting summary of the differences that would result if selected financial data were presented in accordance with generally accepted accounting principles (GAAP) in the United States, as follows:[11]

	Per U.K. GAAP		Per U.S. GAAP	
Effect of Differences	1994 £m	1995 £m	1994 £m	1995 £m
Operating profit	504	**600**	457	**524**
Profit before tax	478	**526**	437	**442**
Net profit (as below)	262	**300**	222	**217**
Shareholders' equity	1,499	**1,316**	2,284	**2,626**

	1994 £m	1995 £m
Net Profit for Ordinary Shareholders **per U.K. GAAP**	262	300
U.S. GAAP adjustments (net of tax):		
Goodwill/intangibles	(37)	(88)
Capitalisation of interest	(2)	(2)
Elimination of revaluation surplus	2	5
One-time credits/(charges)	6	12
Pension costs	(9)	(9)
Other items	—	(1)
Taxation on above adjustments	2	3
Deferred taxation	(2)	(3)
Net per U.S. GAAP profit	222	217

Calculate return on equity for 1994 and 1995 under U.K. GAAP and U.S. GAAP. Which country's accounting standards show the best results? What role does goodwill and intangibles play in this difference? Do accounting standards appear to be more prudent in the U.K. or U.S.? How can the users of financial statements cope with international accounting differences? Should all companies follow international accounting standards?

Nestlé Case

NC 14-1.

LO 6 *Comprehensive Ratio* *Analysis*

Refer to the Annual Report in the appendix on Nestlé, and conduct a comprehensive ratio analysis that compares data from 1996 and 1995. If you have been calculating ratios for Nestlé in previous chapters, you may prepare a table that summarises the ratios for 1996 and 1995 and show calculations only for the ratios not previously calculated. If this is the first time you are doing a ratio analysis for Nestlé, show all your calculations. In either case, comment on Nestlé's performance after each group of ratios. Round your calculations to one decimal place. Prepare and comment on the following categories of ratios:

Liquidity analysis: Current ratio, quick ratio, receivable turnover, average days' sales uncollected, inventory turnover, and average days' inventory available.

Profitability analysis: Profit margin, asset turnover, return on assets, and return on equity.

Long-term solvency analysis: Debt to equity and interest coverage.

Cash flow adequacy: Cash flow yield, cash flows to sales, cash flows to assets, and free cash flow.

Market strength analysis: Price/earnings ratio and dividends yield. (For market price, use year-end prices.)

ENDNOTES

1. "Unilever Seeks £6 Billion from Speciality Chemicals Sale", *Financial Times*, February 12, 1997.
2. International Accounting Standard, IAS14, *Segment Reporting* (London: IASC, revised 1997).
3. Cadbury Schweppes, *Annual Report*, 1995.
4. "Accounting Rule Change Will Erase AT&T Earnings", *Chicago Tribune*, January 15, 1994.
5. John R. Wilke, "Lotus Net Rises 40% on One-Time Gain While Operating Earnings Plunge 66%", *Wall Street Journal*, October 16, 1992.
6. Volvo, *Annual Report*, 1995. Reprinted courtesy of Volvo Cars of North America, Inc.
7. Apple, *Annual Report*, 1993.
8. William H. Beaver, "Alternative Accounting Measures as Indicators of Failure", *Accounting Review*, January 1968; and Edward Altman, "Financial Ratios, Discriminant Analysis and the Prediction of Corporate Bankruptcy", *Journal of Finance*, September 1968.
9. "Heinz's 25% Jump in 2nd-Period Masks Weakness", *Wall Street Journal*, December 8, 1993.
10. "Disney Reports Fiscal 4th-Period Loss After Taking $166 Million Write-Down", *Wall Street Journal*, November 15, 1984. Reprinted by permission of *Wall Street Journal,* © 1984 Dow Jones & Company, Inc. All Rights Reserved Worldwide.
11. Cadbury Schweppes, *Annual Report*, 1995.

Appendix A

Management Report 1996

Table of contents

Letter to the shareholders

Ladies and Gentlemen,

1996 was a good year for Nestlé. Our sales increased by 7.1%, we managed to maintain our operating margin at 9.7% and our profits grew by 16.6% to 3.4 billion francs, i.e. 5.6% of sales as compared to 5.2% in the previous year. Only the progression of the sales volume remained below expectations at 2.7%. As for the evolution of foreign exchange, it had a moderately positive effect on sales and profits for the first time since 1993.

For this year, we expect an acceleration in the growth of sales volumes and good progress in both sales and profits. This development will be even more pronounced if the present currency levels are maintained.

Our optimism for 1997 and for the years to come is based on the efforts made since the beginning of the eighties. The strategy followed over the past years has given a new dimension to Nestlé. At the beginning of this period, the Group depended heavily on its European business and half of its profits came from coffee. Since then, we have extended our presence into other regions of the world where we now hold strong and promising positions. For our products, too, we have developed a more balanced distribution of risks and better prospects for growth. In addition, I would like to highlight the increase in research and development spending, the strengthening of the Group's image and that of its brands, the major efforts made in management development as well as in controlling and mastering our costs.

We made significant acquisitions in the last 15 years which have greatly helped us to reach the objectives that we fixed for our Group. While we remain open to the possibility of seizing strategic opportunities if they arise, acquisitions will play a lesser role in the Group's development which will be driven mainly by internal growth.

As for our organisation, we have adapted it to better respond to the challenges that we will have to meet. For example, in order to reflect the growing globalisation of the world economy, we have – apart from its functional responsibilities – focused the structure of the Group's General Management on the three major geographical regions – Europe; the Americas; Asia, Oceania, Africa and the Near East.

At the next General Meeting of June 5, 1997, the Board of Directors will propose the election of Mr. Peter Brabeck-Letmathe, presently Executive Vice-President, as a member of the Board. Provided this election goes through, I will propose to the Board that Mr. Brabeck-Letmathe be appointed Managing Director (Chief Executive Officer) while I will continue in my duties as Chairman.

These decisions further strengthen the confidence I have in Nestlé's future and the continuation of its development.

Finally, I would like to take this opportunity to thank – also on your behalf – the management and the employees for their contribution to the results we have achieved.

Vevey, 26th March 1997

Helmut O. Maucher, Chairman of the Board and Chief Executive Officer

Key figures (consolidated)

In millions of Swiss francs (except for per share data)		**1996**	1995
Sales		**60 490**	56 484
Trading profit		**5 862**	5 498
as % of sales		**9.7%**	9.7%
Net profit		**3 401**	2 918
as % of sales		**5.6%**	5.2%
as % of average shareholders' funds		**17.0%**	16.7%
Expenditure on tangible fixed assets		**3 054**	3 056
Shareholders' funds [a]		**21 938**	17 989
Market capitalisation, end December		**56 518**	50 303
Per share			
Net profit	Fr.	**86.4**	74.4
Shareholders' funds [a]	Fr.	**557**	459
Dividend	Fr.	**30.0** [b]	26.5

Principal key figures in US$ [c]
In millions of US$ (except for per share data)

		1996	1995
Sales		**45 481**	48 693
Net profit		**2 557**	2 516
Shareholders' funds [a]		**16 495**	15 508
Market capitalisation, end December		**42 495**	43 365
Per share			
Net profit	US$	**65.0**	64.1
Shareholders' funds [a]	US$	**419**	396
Personnel	Number at year end	**221 144**	220 172
Factories	Number at year end	**489**	489

[a] Before proposed appropriation of profit of Nestlé S.A.
[b] As proposed by the Board of Directors of Nestlé S.A.
[c] Figures translated at the year end rate.

Sales

Trading profit

Net profit

Market capitalisation

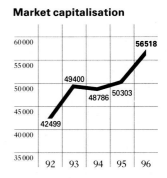

The business policies which the Nestlé Group applies in its home country and abroad are largely in line with the OECD guidelines for multinational enterprises. In this management report the guidelines concerning the disclosure of information have been observed wherever possible.

Directors and Officers

Sitting, from left to right:
Peter Brabeck-Letmathe
Helmut O. Maucher
José Daniel
Standing, from left to right:
Mario A. Corti
Carlos E. Represas
Brian Suter
Michael W.O. Garrett
Rupert Gasser
Philippe Véron

Group Management	as of 31st December 1996
Helmut O. Maucher	Chairman of the Board and Chief Executive Officer
† Ramón Masip	President & Chief Operating Officer-Food
Direct responsibilities:	Africa, the Middle East, Mineral Water, Joint Ventures,
(until 16.9.1996)	Nestlé Nutrition Center

General Managers

Peter Brabeck-Letmathe	Strategic Business Group 2 (Food, Chocolate, Confectionery & Ice Cream, Buitoni, Petcare), Communication, Marketing, Corporate Affairs, Nestlé Nutrition Center*
Mario A. Corti**	Finance, Control, Legal, Taxes, Information Systems & Logistics, Export, Purchasing
José Daniel	Pharmaceutical and cosmetic products, Liaison with L'Oréal, Human Resources, Center Administration
Michael W. O. Garrett	Asia, Oceania, Africa*, the Middle East*
Rupert Gasser	Strategic Business Group 1 (Milk & Nutrition, Coffee & Beverages, Foodservice), Technical Coordination, Quality Management, Environment
Carlos E. Represas	United States of America, Canada, Latin America***
Philippe Véron	Europe, Mineral Water*
Brian Suter	Research & Development (Nestec Ltd.)

* As of 17.9.1996
** Reto F. Domeniconi,
    until 30.5.1996
*** Felix R. Braun,
    until 31.10.1996

Board of Directors of Nestlé S.A.

Term expires[1]

○ Helmut O. Maucher	Chairman and Chief Executive Officer	2000
○ Rainer E. Gut	Vice-Chairman	2001
○ Fritz Leutwiler	Vice-Chairman	1997
○ Fritz Gerber		2001
Paul A. Volcker		1998
Stephan Schmidheiny		1998
Jean-Pierre Meyers		2001
Vreni Spoerry		1997
Lucia Santa Cruz Sutil		1997
Robert Studer		1997
Peter Böckli		1998
David de Pury		1998
Arthur Dunkel		1999
Georges Blum		1998
Reto F. Domeniconi		2001

Secretary to the Board

Bernard Daniel — Secretary general

Auditors of the annual financial statements of Nestlé S.A. and of the Group accounts

KPMG Klynveld Peat Marwick Goerdeler SA — 1999
London and Zurich

[1] On the date of the General Meeting of the Shareholders
○ Members of the Committee to the Board

Business review
General comments

Sales

In millions of Swiss francs

Net profit

In millions of Swiss francs

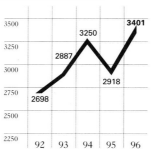

In 1996, Nestlé's sales and net profit reached record levels. Sales growth returned to a normal rate after several years in which the figures expressed in Swiss francs had been negatively affected by foreign exchange rates. The increase in sales of over 7% was accompanied by an even more satisfying rise in net profit, which increased by 17%.

Improvement in Europe

The 1990s have been marked by a gloomy economic climate in Europe, which has had a certain impact on the consumption of food products. In 1996, however, Nestlé's sales volumes in Europe grew at a faster pace than expected, thanks in particular to their strong development in Germany and in Eastern Europe.

Innovation, together with good marketing and competitive pricing, was the principal factor contributing to the increase in Germany. This increase occurred mainly in segments with high value added. Through dynamic research and efficient manufacturing Nestlé is able to offer consumers new specialities at attractive prices.

Sales in the countries of Eastern and Central Europe are continuing to make good progress, having almost doubled over the past two years. As a result of the acquisitions policy implemented since the early 1990s, the Group now possesses a local base for a large variety of products. At the same time imports, especially of soluble coffees into Russia, have become very significant.

A balanced portfolio

In the course of the past decade and a half, Nestlé has taken advantage of both internal growth and acquisitions to assemble an extensive portfolio of food and beverage products, thereby diversifying its risks and laying a solid foundation for future growth. The range includes products which are still relatively unfamiliar in many emerging countries, and which therefore offer considerable scope for development. The acquisitions of recent years have also given the Group a strong presence in certain sectors – ice cream and mineral water – while rounding out its existing activities in other sectors – e.g. pet food – which offer strong growth potential in both industrialised and emerging countries. Moreover, through the joint venture with General Mills (CPW), Nestlé continues to increase its sales of breakfast cereals in many countries of the world.

Nestlé has become the world leader in mineral water. In the United States, where it has a market share of 25%, water sales showed double-digit growth in 1996. The consumption of mineral water per US inhabitant is still only half the European average, so there are good prospects for the years ahead. Meanwhile, Nestlé is continuing to acquire springs in emerging countries. During 1997, new bottling centres will be inaugurated in China and Romania. In the future, demand for pure water will be on the increase everywhere in the world.

In the pet food sector, the Group had already consolidated its position in the United States by taking over Alpo in 1994. In Europe during 1996, a marketing campaign aimed at internal growth resulted in a substantial increase in sales volumes and significant gains in market share. Nestlé has a good position in a number of Western European countries where the consumption of pet food is still relatively low, having not yet reached the level of the United States or United Kingdom, and the prospects for growth are therefore very encouraging. The Group also plans to extend its pet food activities in Eastern Europe and in other emerging markets.

In every product category, research and development remain a crucial factor to sales growth. In the industrialised countries, they ensure innovation and constant renewal of the product range; in emerging countries, they stimulate growth by finding ways to adapt products to local tastes.

**Increasing importance
of emerging markets**
The importance of emerging countries to the Group's sales has grown steadily; increasing from 26% in 1995 to 28% in 1996. While this rise is due in part to the entry into new markets, like those of Eastern Europe, Nestlé also has the advantage of a longstanding presence in many Latin American and Asian countries. In these markets, the Group's products and brands are closely associated with local consumption habits. They are therefore well positioned to benefit from the continuing growth in demand, which is linked not only to demographics but also to increased purchasing power. Nestlé's extensive knowledge of these countries facilitates the integration of local acquisitions and the launch of new products.

Political and economic developments offer fresh opportunities for expansion. Following the opening-up of Middle Eastern markets, Nestlé has been actively reinforcing its local presence in the region. This illustrates the strategy of targeting a stronger presence in all the countries neighbouring the Mediterranean; the Group already has factories in Morocco, Tunisia, Egypt, Turkey, Greece and, thanks to the recent purchase of a participation in Osem, in Israel.

Key figures by product group

Sales

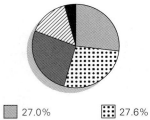

27.0%	27.6%
26.4%	14.9%
4.1%	

Trading profit

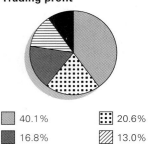

40.1%	20.6%
16.8%	13.0%
9.5%	

Capital expenditure

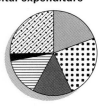

19.2%	24.0%
14.7%	14.2%
2.7%	25.2%

Sales

In millions of Swiss francs	1996	1995	1994
Beverages	**16 348**	16 215	16 125
Milk products, dietetics and ice cream	**16 697**	15 239	15 398
Prepared dishes and cooking aids (and miscellaneous activities)	**15 960**	14 655	14 907
Chocolate and confectionery	**9 034**	8 217	8 261
Pharmaceuticals	**2 451**	2 158	2 203
	60 490	56 484	56 894

Trading profit

In millions of Swiss francs	1996	1995	1994
Beverages	**2 352**	2 151	2 258
Milk products, dietetics and ice cream	**1 206**	1 264	1 282
Prepared dishes and cooking aids (and miscellaneous activities)	**984**	904	872
Chocolate and confectionery	**765**	743	726
Pharmaceuticals	**555**	436	490
	5 862	5 498	5 628

Capital expenditure

In millions of Swiss francs	1996	1995	1994
Beverages	**586**	618	574
Milk products, dietetics and ice cream	**732**	667	620
Prepared dishes and cooking aids (and miscellaneous activities)	**450**	446	501
Chocolate and confectionery	**433**	378	461
Pharmaceuticals	**84**	147	115
Investments in factories	**2 285**	2 256	2 271
Investments in research and development centres, distribution and administration	**769**	800	758
	3 054	3 056	3 029

Principal activities of the Group

Beverages

Nestlé invented soluble coffee in Switzerland in 1938, and sales of *Nescafé* have been growing steadily ever since. With more than 3000 cups consumed every second, *Nescafé* is by far the world's leading brand of coffee. Ready-to-drink coffees are also sold under this brand.

The Group also occupies the number one position worldwide in mineral and spring waters. Its presence is strongest in Europe, with such brands as *Vittel*, *Contrex*, *Perrier*, *Valvert*, *Fürst Bismarck* and *Vera*, and in the United States, with *Arrowhead*, *Poland Spring*, *Zephyrhills* and *Ozarka*.

Nestlé leads the world market for chocolate-based and malted drinks. Its best known brands, *Nesquik/Nestlé Quik*, *Milo* and *Nescau* are very popular

with a growing number of young people in both developed and emerging countries.

The Group's other beverage products include roasted coffees, like *Hills Bros.* and *MJB* in the United States and *Dallmayr Prodomo* in Germany; the *Libby's* fruit juices; and tea-based drinks, notably soluble and ready-to-drink *Nestea*.

Milk products, dietetics and ice cream

Nestlé is continuing to consolidate its excellent worldwide positions in condensed, evaporated and powdered milk. Its range of chilled dairy products is constantly being enlarged and renewed. Sustained efforts are being made to ensure the geographic expansion of these lines in the future.

As the oldest manufacturer of foods for infants and young children, Nestlé offers a complete range, extending from start-up and follow-up formulas and growing-up milk, to cereals, baby

foods (dehydrated or in jars) and dietetic specialities.

In ice cream, Nestlé has continued to expand and to strengthen its worldwide presence.

The terms in italics on pages 9 to 11 of this report are registered trademarks of the Nestlé Group.

Clintec, the joint venture with Baxter in clinical nutrition, was dissolved on 30th September 1996, with each partner taking back its own products. The new organisation, Nestlé Clinical Nutrition, is carrying on the business in enteral products (those taken orally).

CPW, the joint venture with General Mills for breakfast cereals outside North America, is confirming its progress in the many countries where it is already established while continuing its geographic expansion.

Prepared dishes and cooking aids (and miscellaneous activities)

Nestlé's frozen products (mainly prepared dishes) are sold under three principal brands: *Stouffer's* in the United States and *Findus* or *Maggi* in other parts of the world.

A diversified range of soups, bouillons, sauces and culinary preparations is sold under the *Maggi* and *Crosse & Blackwell* labels. The range is adapted to suit the tastes, recipes and local ingredients of each individual country.

Maggi instant oriental noodles are sold not only in the Far East/Pacific region, but also in Europe, Africa and Latin America.

In the area of Italian cuisine, Nestlé offers long-life and refrigerated sauces under the *Buitoni* brand (*Contadina dalla Casa Buitoni* in the United States). The *Buitoni* product range also includes a complete line of pizzas and frozen dishes.

In Europe, the Group sells a full range of *Herta* delicatessen products and cold meats; it also manufactures *Thomy* sauces and condiments in several countries.

Chief among Nestlé's miscellaneous activities is pet food. Nestlé is well known for its cat and dog foods sold under the *Friskies* and *Alpo* brands, along with pet accessories.

Chocolate and confectionery

Nestlé is the world's leading producer of chocolate and confectionery. The *Nestlé* range of chocolate bars, count-lines, specialities and boxed chocolates includes not only such strategic international brands as *Nestlé, Crunch, KitKat, Smarties, Lion, After Eight, Quality Street* and *Baci*, but also brands specific to a single geographic region or country, like *Butterfinger, Baby Ruth, Charge, Femina* and *Especialidades*. Some of the Group's chocolate brands are also brands for chocolate-based drinks or ice cream.

The principal varieties of sugar confectionery are *Polo* and *Fruit Pastilles*. Biscuits (sweet and plain) are produced mainly in South America, where the Group's brands include *São Luiz, McKay* and *La Rosa*.

Pharmaceutical products

In 1977, Nestlé diversified into pharmaceuticals through the acquisition of Alcon Laboratories, a group which has since become the world leader in ophthalmology. Alcon's activities are divided into three segments: ophthalmic therapeutic drugs, such as *Betoptic, Iopidine, Ciloxan, Alomide* and *Tobradex*; solutions for contact lens care, including *Opti-Free, Opti-Clean, Opti-One* and *Soaclens*; instruments and equipment for ocular surgery, as well as intraocular lenses and preparations used during surgery, particularly cataract operations: *Legacy, AcrySof, BSS, Viscoat* and *Provisc*.

In 1989, Nestlé and L'Oréal formed Galderma, a joint venture in dermatology, which has a research and development centre in Sophia Antipolis in France.

Key figures by geographic area

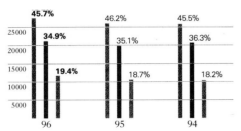

Sales

In millions of Swiss francs	1996	1995	1994
Europe	27 630	26 104	25 891
North and South America	21 110	19 797	20 639
Other regions of the world	11 750	10 583	10 364
	60 490	56 484	56 894

Trading profit

In millions of Swiss francs	1996	1995	1994
Europe	2 284	2 202	2 067
North and South America	2 285	2 083	2 286
Other regions of the world	1 293	1 213	1 275
	5 862	5 498	5 628

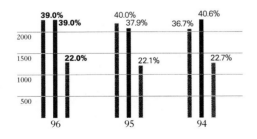

Capital expenditure

In millions of Swiss francs	1996	1995	1994
Europe	1 372	1 417	1 521
North and South America	1 016	1 039	1 037
Other regions of the world	666	600	471
	3 054	3 056	3 029

Sales

Exceeding the 60 billion mark

Nestlé's sales rose by 7.1% in 1996 to Fr. 60.5 billion, with **internal sales volume growth** of 2.7%. Volume growth was satisfactory in every region except North America, where it was mainly affected by temporary problems in the beverage division in the United States. These problems are largely resolved.

External growth – contribution resulting from acquisitions net of disinvestments – amounted to 0.6%.

The **net monetary effect**, which primarily reflects increased selling prices and variations in exchange rates, was 3.8%. After several years in which their impact had been unfavourable, exchange rate variations had a positive effect in 1996, contributing 1.4% to sales growth. The most important change was the appreciation of the U.S. dollar, especially during the last quarter, but the majority of the principal European currencies also gained in value against the Swiss franc. On the other hand, the yen, the Brazilian real and the Mexican peso weakened.

Further improvement in Europe, vigorous expansion in the rest of the world

Internal sales volume growth in **Europe** accelerated for the second consecutive year despite disappointing summer weather, which hampered sales of ice cream and mineral water. As already mentioned, Eastern and Central Europe contributed to the progression of sales in Europe. Growth also improved in the developed markets of Western Europe, especially in Germany following the launch of new products.

Growth in **North America** was affected by difficulties in the US beverage division. On the other hand, several product groups, including mineral water, pet food and pharmaceutical products, made good progress. **Latin American** sales again rose faster than the average for the Group, in spite of a slowdown in Brazil, which was inevitable after a period of spectacular expansion.

In **Asia** the emerging markets continue to record good growth rates. Among the mature markets, Japan consolidated the recovery noted at the end of 1995. Sales in **Africa** and the **Middle East** have entered a new phase of expansion.

1996 Sales in principal markets

In millions of Swiss francs

	Differences 1996/1995 in francs	in local currency	
USA			11 843
+ 3.1%	– 1.9%		
France			6 646
+ 1.9%	– 0.2%		
Germany			6 406
+ 2.4%	+ 2.8%		
Brazil			3 998
+ 9.9%	+14.3%		
United Kingdom			3 165
+ 5.7%	+ 1.4%		
Italy			3 128
+14.5%	+ 3.0%		
Japan			2 831
– 8.8%	0.0%		
Spain			2 112
– 1.6%	– 4.5%		
Australia			1 473
+25.0%	+13.0%		
Mexico			1 392
+21.7%	+36.6%		
Philippines			1 356
+23.3%	+20.1%		
Switzerland			1 040
– 0.7%	– 0.7%		
Canada			1 026
+ 8.2%	+ 1.6%		
Other markets			14 074
+15.5%	(a)		

(a) Not comparable.

Trading profit

**Breakdown of trading
expenses by category**

In percent

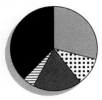

	1996	1995
Raw materials	**26.5**	27.8
Packaging	**9.4**	9.6
Salaries and welfare expenses	**16.4**	16.7
Depreciation	**4.1**	4.0
Other trading expenses	**33.9**	32.2
Total trading expenses	**90.3**	90.3
Trading profit	**9.7**	9.7

Higher trading profit

Trading profit increased from Fr. 5498 million in 1995 to Fr. 5862 million in 1996. The trading margin remained stable at 9.7% of sales.

The stability of the margin reflects contrasting trends in costs. As a percentage of sales, the cost of raw materials – particularly green coffee – and of packaging materials decreased. On the other hand, marketing expenditure was increased to support the introduction of new products and to strengthen the Group's market shares.

Distribution costs rose slightly as a percentage of sales, owing to the expansion of such categories as ice cream and pet food, for which these costs are proportionally higher. Research and development spending was unchanged as a percentage of sales.

The increase in restructuring charges – which nevertheless remain well below the level of the years prior to 1995 – reflects ongoing efforts to maintain competitiveness. Amortisation of intangible assets, representing an annual charge for all acquisitions made since 1st January 1995, also increased.

Differing trends in margin

In **Europe**, the trading margin was fractionally lower, owing mainly to higher restructuring charges in certain Western European countries. The profitability of Eastern European operations increased.

The improvement of the trading margin in **North and South America** reflects, in particular, the successful rationalisation programmes carried out in the United States and Canada over recent years.

In the **other regions of the world**, the decline in margin is mainly due to costs linked to the integration of acquisitions in the Australian ice cream and chilled dairy sectors. Margins improved in a large number of emerging countries in Asia, Africa and the Middle East.

Net profit

Strong progression in net profit

Group **net profit** rose by 16.6% in 1996 to Fr. 3401 million. The net margin increased from 5.2% to 5.6%. This improvement is due to a decrease in net non-trading expenses and in the tax charge, as well as to an increase in the contribution of associated companies.

Net financing costs, expressed in Swiss francs, remained virtually stable. The favourable impact of lower interest rates for the currencies in which the Group's borrowings are denominated was offset by the appreciation of these currencies against the Swiss franc. Moreover, interest rates also declined on Swiss franc deposits, which represent a large part of the Group's liquidity.

The reduction in **net non-trading expenses** is due to positive exchange rate differences arising during the year for most foreign currencies against the Swiss franc.

The **tax charge** fell from 35% of profit before taxation to 31%, reflecting a lower charge in several countries, particularly Brazil.

The **share of profit attributable to outside interests** rose by more than the net profit of consolidated companies. These interests mainly relate to companies operating in markets where the currency is linked to the dollar, which rose in value against the Swiss franc. The companies in question are frequently located in fast-growing regions of the world.

The improved performance of **associated companies**, especially the further rise in profit achieved by L'Oréal, caused the Group's share in their results to increase.

Earnings per share

Net profit per share rose by 16.1% to Fr. 86.4. The increase is slightly less than for the Group's global profit, owing to a small increase in the average number of shares. This increase is a result of the exercise in 1995 of the last remaining options linked to Group borrowings.

Net profit per share

In Swiss francs

Capital expenditure

Acquisitions and disinvestments

Capital expenditure

In billions of Swiss francs

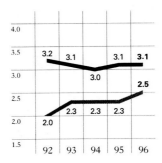

■ Capital expenditure

■ Depreciation of fixed assets

In 1996 capital spending in absolute terms was stable at Fr. 3054 million. It represented 5% of sales compared with 5.4% in 1995.

Capital expenditure in Europe continued to decline. The Group pursued its investment programme in Eastern Europe but restricted expenditure in Western Europe, where its manufacturing capacity is already well developed.

In North and South America, capital spending decreased slightly. In the other regions of the world, there was an increase of more than 10%, in order to keep pace with the expansion of sales.

489 factories in 77 countries

The number of factories worldwide is unchanged compared with 1995, as acquisitions and new constructions were balanced by disposals and closures. Of the four factories opened during 1996, three are in emerging countries (two in China and one in Syria).

The total of 489 includes 49 bottling plants for mineral water and 16 factories for pharmaceutical or dermatological products.

The Group's policy is oriented to internal growth and ongoing expansion in strategic sectors. In 1996, spending on acquisitions and participations declined to Fr. 1194 million from Fr. 1617 million in 1995. Proceeds from disinvestments totalled Fr. 96 million, so that net expenditure amounted to Fr. 1098 million, compared with Fr. 1162 million in 1995.

Nestlé continued to strengthen its position in mineral water and ice cream. The principal transactions in mineral water were the increase of the Group's interest in Perrier Group of America from 61% to 100%, and the purchase of 34% of Mineralbrunnen Überkingen in Germany. In ice cream, Nestlé acquired Premier/Eventyr in Denmark and the activities of Zhukowsky in Russia.

At the geographic level, Nestlé is currently extending its presence in the Middle East. Acquisitions in this region during 1996 included both ice cream and mineral water businesses, but the most important operation was the purchase of a 40% interest in Osem, one of the leaders in the Israeli market. This company, where Nestlé now has management control, sells a wide variety of beverages, culinary products and biscuits.

Proceeds from disinvestments came primarily from the sale of two non-strategic activities: canned pasta and beans in Canada and the fresh meat business in Germany.

More detailed information about new acquisitions, participations and disinvestments will be found in the sections on the various product groups on pages 20 to 38.

Financial position

Shares, stock exchange

Operating cash flow

Operating cash flow progressed at a satisfactory rate in 1996. Excluding exceptional elements, it increased by 26%, mainly owing to higher profit and depreciation. The increase in cash flow was close to 50% taking into account exceptional elements. In 1995, the latter included a settlement with the tax authorities in the United States of more than US$ 500 million.

Debt

The Group's net financial debt (short, medium and long term financial debt, net of liquid assets) rose from Fr. 6.3 billion at the end of 1995 to Fr. 6.8 billion. The increase is due to the trend in exchange rates, as most borrowings are contracted in currencies which have appreciated against the Swiss franc. This appreciation accelerated in the final quarter of 1996, and therefore had a pronounced effect on the Group's debt, as the balance sheet is prepared on the basis of year-end exchange rates. It was positively reflected in the level of shareholders' funds. The ratio of net debt to equity (including outside interests) was 29.6%, compared with 33.4% in December 1995 and 37.1% in December 1994.

The price of the Nestlé registered share increased by 12.6% in 1996. The share, which climbed steadily during the first half of the year, surged ahead at the beginning of July following a wave of speculative rumours in stock market circles. Although the price dropped a little when these rumours were dispelled, it resumed its upward movement during the fourth quarter, accelerating at the end of the year in response to the favourable trend in exchange rates.

The slight underperformance of the share against the SBC general index reflets the creation of Novartis, which strongly influenced the index.

Evolution of the Nestlé registered share in 1996

(compared with the Swiss stock market index)

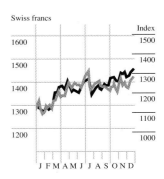

Registered share

SBC Index

Environment

Since 1990, Nestlé has systematically furthered its efforts in favour of the protection of the environment. New measures taken at the international headquarters and in Group operating companies include: the appointment of environmental officers, the publication of the Nestlé Policy on the Environment and the completion of an environmental survey of the factories. Particular attention has been given to packaging issues and to the reinforcement of training. All over the world, Nestlé conforms to legal requirements as a minimum standard. If these do not exist, the Group applies its internal rules, adjusted to local conditions.

The development of the Nestlé Environmental Management System

In 1996, a decision was made to integrate these measures into the Nestlé Environmental Management System, a management tool to support Nestlé's competitive efforts. The main objectives of the system are to ensure operational compliance with the Group's environmental strategies and to achieve compatibility with the international voluntary Standards on Environmental Management Systems. It also allows Nestlé continually to improve its environmental performance.

This system has been implemented in the packaging area in a highly effective manner. Between 1991 and 1996, Nestlé saved, worldwide, a total of 107 500 tons of packaging material, while at all times maintaining the high quality of its products. These efforts resulted in cost savings of Fr. 178 million.

Biotechnology

New and creative solutions are required to feed an ever-growing world population with affordable and wholesome foods in an environmentally sustainable way. Biotechnology is one of the tools available to meet these challenges. Mankind has a long tradition of using biotechnology; plant and animal breeding are examples of traditional biotechnology. Modern biotechnology, including gene technology, has evolved from these traditional processes, and allows improvements to be made more rapidly, precisely and safely. During 1996, agricultural raw materials such as soya, maize and oilseed rape improved by gene technology were introduced into the world's commodity markets. Although Nestlé does not produce its own raw materials, the Group is convinced that the responsible use of this technology will bring substantial benefits for consumers. It will help to improve the food supply for the world population and will be an important factor everywhere in the fight against hunger.

Transparency and information

Consumers ask legitimate questions about any new development, and gene technology is no exception. As a responsible and responsive company, Nestlé encourages transparency and welcomes open dialogue with consumers. The Group is committed to provide information through all appropriate channels, and indicates the use of genetically modified ingredients on product labels wherever reasonable and practicable.

Personnel

The number of people employed by the Group rose from 220 172 at the end of 1995 to 221 144 at 31st December 1996, a modest increase of 0.4%.

As always, the variation in personnel is the net result of several factors: increases occur in rapidly growing regions and because of acquisitions; decreases are due to the disinvestment of businesses and to necessary restructuring, usually following acquisitions.

Recruitment, training and development

Behind the net change in the workforce caused by the opposing trends described above lies a systematic effort to recruit people with strong development potential. This effort extends to all regions of the world, including those where business has slowed down as the result of a depressed economic environment. It favours the pursuit of a policy encouraging long-term career development, especially through promotion within the Group.

Once again, a key role in this process was played by the Rive-Reine International Training and Conference Centre, which celebrated its 25th anniversary in 1996. This occasion was marked by the completion of projects to expand the Centre's training facilities and residential capacity.

In 1996, Rive-Reine organised 71 seminars and welcomed 1705 participants. Of equal importance to the professional training offered by the Centre is the opportunity it provides to transmit the "Nestlé spirit" through personal relationships formed by participants from all over the world, and through the contacts they make with members of Management from the Vevey headquarters.

In addition to Rive-Reine's activities, 9955 people participated in the 640 seminars organised during 1996 by the five residential training centres in the United Kingdom, France, Spain, Brazil and Mexico.

To complete the picture, it should be noted that the operating companies around the world have their own internal training structures, which enabled them to organise numerous courses at their headquarters, in their factories and at suitable hotels, with tens of thousands of participants.

The Nestlé principles of management and leadership

In 1996, an important document was drafted summarising the basic principles governing management, leadership and executive commitment, in order to involve the personnel more deeply in the active life of the business. The same document also outlines the Nestlé culture and will enable people to grasp more easily the meaning of the "Nestlé spirit". This applies particularly to employees everywhere in the world who have joined the Company in the past few years. The document will be communicated in due course to every level of the organisation during 1997. It replaces, updates and supplements the concept of Management Commitment/ Employee Involvement that was introduced some years ago.

Geographic distribution

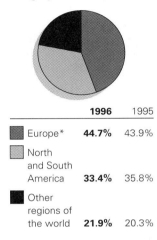

	1996	1995
Europe*	**44.7%**	43.9%
North and South America	**33.4%**	35.8%
Other regions of the world	**21.9%**	20.3%

* 6460 employees in Switzerland in 1996.

Distribution by activity

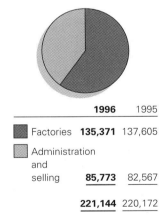

	1996	1995
Factories	**135,371**	137,605
Administration and selling	**85,773**	82,567
	221,144	220,172

Product group development
Beverages

The terms in italics on pages 20 to 38 of this report are registered trademarks of the Nestlé Group.

Millions of Swiss francs	**1996**	1995	1994
Sales	**16 348**	16 215	16 125
Trading profit	**2 352**	2 151	2 258
Capital expenditure	**586**	618	574

Green coffee prices

Average monthly prices expressed in US¢ per lb

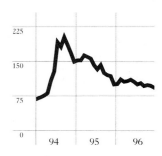

Green Coffee

The prospect of steadily improving supply as the year progressed, which was reinforced once the 1996 southern hemisphere winter had passed without causing damage to the Brazilian coffee plantations, resulted in prices easing. The decline might have been more significant had it not been for a determined attempt by some producers to limit their exports, leading to a further reduction in stocks held in consuming countries. The roasters displayed a very cautious attitude, which was reflected in a general tightening of the coffee supply chain. The result was a permanent, albeit limited, nearby demand for green coffee which in turn supported prices, especially for mild washed coffees. The continued expansion of robusta coffee cultivation in the Far East, combined with a strong recovery in African production – both a consequence of the higher market experienced since mid-1994 – caused prices for this coffee type to weaken significantly.

Sales

The increase in selling prices that stemmed from the sharp rise in the price of green coffee during 1994 caused a decrease in coffee consumption in 1995.

Throughout 1996, both green coffee prices and retail selling prices were on a downward trend; consumption picked up, and sales of *Nescafé* were highly satisfactory, as the product consolidated its leading position in the market for **soluble coffee**:

– The quality of coffee offered to consumers has been enhanced still further, owing to the more widespread use of technologies to preserve aromas and flavour.

– The new *Nescafé* specialities accelerated their geographic expansion. In Asia, products like *Nescafé 1+2*,

The new *Nescafé*
Espresso Roast in the United States.

Nescafé Gold has been introduced in Russia to satisfy the growing demand for a more sophisticated coffee.

Nescafé 1+2 in individual sachets, sold in China.

which combine coffee, milk and sugar, continued to make good progress.

– Eastern Europe is becoming increasingly important for *Nescafé*; in volume terms, Russia is now its fifth largest market in the world.

– In the United States, *Nescafé* has been relaunched in a test market. Its new quality, with more body and a taste modelled on the roasted coffees served in fashionable coffee bars, effectively differentiates it from competitors. *Nescafé Espresso Roast* is being sold in a new patented packaging with a double clasp and "click-lock" closure.

Sales of **roasted coffees** advanced in Europe, but decreased in the United States, owing to a strategic restructuring of the coffee business there.

Nespresso, a top-of-the-range espresso in capsules, continued to expand its sales, confirming its market leadership. The Group is also intensifying its presence in high quality Office Coffee Service through the introduction of *Caffèpresso*, a new system for preparing coffee in portions which is designed specially for offices. The originality of the concept and the convenience it offers gives the system a decided advantage over the competition.

Under the agreement with Coca-Cola, sales of *Nestea* **ready-to-drink teas** are moving rapidly ahead, particularly in the United States, where *Nestea* holds second place. Efforts are being made to develop *Nescafé* **ready-to-drink coffees**, with major launches in test markets in the United States, Canada and Spain.

Sales of **chocolate- and malt-based drinks** increased at a brisk pace. Good growth rates were recorded for *Nesquik* in Eastern Europe and for *Nescau* and *Nesquik* in Latin America. *Milo*'s position improved further in Asia, where the brand was already very strong, as well as in Latin America and Africa. Building on the strength of the *Lion* confectionery brand in

Nespresso. **Mastering the art of the espresso.**

The world leader in chocolate drinks for children.

France, a new chocolate-based drink aimed primarily at teenagers has been introduced under that name.

Fruit juices and nectars sold well in the United States, a particularly important market for these products.

Sales growth continued in **mineral** and **spring waters**, as a poor summer in Europe was offset by vigorous expansion in the United States and in new markets, including Mexico, Vietnam and Poland. The continuing rise in consumption of bottled water, and the positions acquired by the Group on an international level, augur well for further progress in 1997.

Profit
Trading profit rose by 9.3%, signifying a substantial increase in the margin. This improvement mainly reflects good results in the coffee sector.

Capital expenditure
Capital expenditure totalled Fr. 586 million, compared with Fr. 618 million in the previous year. Two production units for *Milo* began operation: one in China (Shanghai) and the other in India (Nanjangud). For soluble coffee, production facilities at Panjang in Indonesia were enlarged. New packaging lines were installed in the United Kingdom, Canada and Brazil, the latter to satisfy the increased demand for exports of *Nescafé* to Eastern Europe. A fruit juices and nectars factory began production in Mexico. For mineral water, additional PET bottling lines were set up in Germany and the United States.

New and increased participations
The Group continued to expand its geographic presence in mineral water, acquiring 49% of Sohat in Lebanon. Nestlé also took a 34% stake in Mineralbrunnen Überkingen in Germany, and raised its participation in the US subsidiary Perrier Group of America to 100%.

A delicious source of energy with a malted taste, very popular with young people.

Perrier and *Vittel* **continue to be the Group's strategic brands.**

Milk products, dietetics and ice cream

		1996	1995	1994
Millions of Swiss francs	Sales	**16 697**	15 239	15 398
	Trading profit	**1 206**	1 264	1 282
	Capital expenditure	**732**	667	620

Nestlé mio, "Petits
Suisses" with fruit introduced in Australia.

Increased milk production

Having stabilised in 1995, world milk production increased in 1996 as a result of continuing growth in developing countries, a record season in Oceania, and a reversal of the declining trend recently experienced in some Central European countries. Of the world's major dairy nations only the United States experienced a production decline, provoked by poor climatic conditions and high feed prices. The BSE or "mad cow disease" scare in Europe, which negatively impacted beef consumption, had a certain spill-over effect in the dairy sector. Calf numbers declined and certain importing countries banned dairy products originating from the European Union, despite independent official declarations endorsing the safety of milk and milk products. On the international market, the high prices prevailing at the end of 1995 for both powder and butterfat led to widespread consumer resistance particularly in the Middle and Far East, and resulted in prices weakening.

Sales

Sales volumes of milk remained stable, thanks to an outstanding performance in Asia and in Brazil, which made up for a slight decline in Europe and for the weakness of the Mexican economy.

Good sales increases were recorded for **unconcentrated milk**, while **condensed milk** slowed down and sales volumes of **powdered milk** held steady.

Products for **infant nutrition** showed strong growth in Europe, particularly in

A dehydrated food with
cereals plus meat,
fish or fruit, for children
aged 1 to 3.

A delicious
novelty adding to the *Nestlé* range
of refrigerated desserts in France.

A small jar with two separate layers of meat and vegetables, to help children distinguish tastes.

the East. Gains were also achieved in Asia, but Latin American sales stagnated as a result of the economic situation in Mexico. Product innovations in this segment include the *Petits Pots*, a baby food in two layers introduced in France, which has been enthusiastically received by consumers.

The good progress made by **chilled dairy products** was based on higher volumes in both Latin America and Europe. Business in the Far East/Pacific region is expanding at a gratifying rate. Less than a year after the introduction of its chilled products in Australia, Nestlé's market share stands at 16%.

During 1996, the use of the new Nestlé Refrigerated logo was extended throughout the world. A notable new introduction was a range for toddlers under the *P'tit Gourmand* brand in France. Baked specialities, including profiteroles, were added to the range.

Sales of *LC¹*, a speciality fermented with a strain of lactobacillus acidophilus selected at the Nestlé Research Centre, continued their expansion in Germany and Brazil.

In **adult nutrition**, the trend in the United States towards long-term healthy eating stimulated sales of *Nestlé Sweet Success*, repositioned as a wholesome nutritional supplement. On the other hand, weight-control products, such as *Nestlé Slender*, were less in demand.

The business of Cereal Partners Worldwide (CPW), the joint venture with General Mills in breakfast cereals, continues to expand rapidly. CPW increased its market share in this fast-growing segment and enlarged its presence in Argentina and Brazil.

Ice cream consumption is growing rapidly in Asia and Africa. Nestlé's sales continue to progress strongly, thanks to the contribution of recent acquisitions and to the start-up of operations in new markets such as China and Russia. In Europe, however, the weather in 1996 was not favourable for the ice cream business.

The development of international brands accelerated with *Maxibon* in Europe and *Sin Parar/Non Stop* in Latin

Nestlé fruit yogurts in Australia.

For figure and fitness, flakes of whole wheat with a high content of essential vitamins and minerals.

America and Asia. The Group successfully introduced a number of new products, such as the *Milo* ice lolly in Thailand and the *Fantasmikos* miniatures in Spain.

Profit

The reduction in trading profit reflects transitional costs linked to the integration of recent acquisitions in ice cream and refrigerated dairy products. Profits were satisfactory for milk and infant nutrition.

Capital expenditure

Capital expenditure rose to Fr. 732 million from Fr. 667 million in 1995. New production centres for powdered milk were built in South Africa (Harrismith) and in Pakistan (Kabirwala). At Laixi in China, two new units began operation for condensed milk and ice cream. At Echuca in Australia, production facilities for refrigerated dairy products were enlarged. For breakfast cereals,

production capacity was increased in the United Kingdom, Poland, the Philippines and Mexico.

Acquisitions

The acquisition of the Danish company *Premier Eventyr* marks Nestlé's entry into the Scandinavian ice cream market. In Russia, the newly-formed Nestlé Ice Cream Zhukowsky LLC will produce both traditional flavours and Western specialities for distribution in the Moscow region. Through the formation of a company with Galadari, Nestlé has taken over the latter's ice cream division, which is market leader in Dubai. This acquisition will make it possible to develop sales throughout the Arabian Peninsula.

In milk products, the participation in Mis Süt in Turkey was increased from 25% to 34%.

The rich satisfaction
of *Extrême*,
with its varied flavours.

Launched in Italy:
the mini version of *Mega*, tasting
just as good.

Maxibon, the ice cream
sandwich favoured
by young people in Europe.

Chocolate and confectionery

		1996	1995	1994
Millions of Swiss francs	Sales	9 034	8 217	8 261
	Trading profit	765	743	726
	Capital expenditure	433	378	461

Cocoa prices

Average monthly prices expressed in US¢ per lb

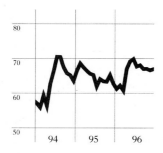

Cocoa

A record crop in the Ivory Coast and the highest production level in Ghana for more than two decades kept prices on the defensive during the first quarter. This was despite the continuing production decline in the Brazilian state of Bahia where more than 90% of the cocoa farms have now been affected by "witch's broom", a disease which severely reduces the pod-bearing ability of the tree. Strong grind figures, the commonly accepted indicator of the underlying chocolate consumption trend, failed to change market sentiment, which remained very much supply-oriented. In the second quarter, prices rallied sharply as the market came to terms with the probability that 1996/97 West African production was unlikely to reach the previous season's levels. However, from mid year divergent opinion on the supply/demand outlook for 1996/97, and the strength of the pound sterling against the US dollar, caused renewed pressure on prices.

Sales

Sales of chocolate and confectionery are continuing to increase particularly fast in Asia. A significant factor is the expansion of *KitKat* in several countries of the region. In Japan, the successful introduction of *KitKat Stick* in 1995 has been followed by two new lines: almond-flavoured *KitKat Stick* and *Crunch Stick*.

In Italy and the United Kingdom, the strong position of *Polo* – the "Sweet with the hole" – served as a basis for the launch of *Polo* "Holes", a mouth refresher in a small, convenient format.

Allen's Classic Coffee Candy has been introduced in the Philippines. This sweet is a delicious-tasting pocket cup of coffee which makes an ideal pick-me-up in the stress of daily life.

The *Lion* brand is still registering double-digit growth rates and is extending its presence in Eastern Europe, especially Russia and Poland.

New products introduced in Europe include *Eclat Noir* in France and *Nestlé Gold de Luxe* in Switzerland. *Eclat Noir*, a premium dark chocolate tablet with the addition of crisp rich fragments of

The new version of *KitKat Stick* in Japan.

***Smarties* – chocolates filled with fun.**

Nestlé Gold de Luxe,
the best in both chocolate and coffee.

over three consecutive years. This reflects marketing expenses linked to the launch of new products and to geographic expansion.

Capital expenditure
Capital expenditure rose to Fr. 433 million from Fr. 378 million in 1995. New production lines were installed in China (Tianjin) and Japan (Kasumigaura). Production capacity was increased in several factories such as Kargowa in Poland, Samara in Russia and Chembong in Malaysia.

Acquisitions
Nestlé expanded its operations in Latin America by acquiring Ecuador's leading biscuit manufacturer. This acquisition will strengthen the Group's position in the Andean region. In Russia, Nestlé purchased Konditer, a chocolate and confectionery company in Samara. In Canada, the Group acquired the confectionery company O'Pee Chee.

**The polar freshness of *Polo*
in a new format.**

the best cocoa beans, is a unique treat for connoisseurs of chocolate. *Nestlé Gold de Luxe*, in the form of filled tablets and napolitains, is a combination of the best in both chocolate and coffee – the renowned taste of Nestlé chocolate and the exquisite aroma of *Nescafé Gold de Luxe*.

Nesquik, the Group's chocolate drink brand, continues its successful extension to the milk chocolate category, as new products were added to the range and new markets were entered.

Profit
Trading profit rose by 3%. The trading margin declined slightly after increasing

Nesquik **chocolate bars –
with lots of good milk inside.**

Nestlé Eclat Noir, **a striking
innovation in dark chocolate.**

Prepared dishes and cooking aids (and miscellaneous activities)

		1996	1995	1994
Millions of Swiss francs	Sales	**15 960**	14 655	14 907
	Trading profit	**984**	904	872
	Capital expenditure	**450**	446	501

Buitoni Express **dry pasta: real Italian "al dente" bite in only five minutes.**

Increase in sales

Sales increased substantially compared with 1995, reflecting the good performance of frozen and dehydrated products and cold sauces. Thanks to many innovations and improvements, *Buitoni* products recorded an overall sales gain of 9%, with growth in every category.

The manufacture of **canned products** has ceased in Great Britain, but elsewhere there are growth segments such as *Buitoni* ravioli and pasta sauces which, after an overhaul of the range, have regained leadership in France, Europe's largest market. In the United States, Mexican products sold under the *Ortega* brand benefited from the introduction of a new line of refried beans and sauces for "enchiladas".

The increase in sales of **traditional dehydrated products** – bouillons, soups and sauces – is due in part to the opening up of new markets in Eastern Europe. Sales also rose in the major Western European countries, thanks to product renovation and successful new launches.

Buitoni **pastas** made from durum wheat have continued to post strong gains in Germany, Great Britain and Japan. The "Express" pastas were launched in Great Britain with great success. They take only five minutes to cook and have a perfect "al dente" consistency. Nestlé has patented these new forms of pasta, thus obtaining a strong advantage over the competition.

Sales of **oriental noodles** showed further growth, with the launch of noodles under the *Maggi* brand in Indonesia and Turkey. In Europe, *Maggi* dehydrated snacks based on pasta, rice or potatoes benefited from the trend towards less formal, lighter meals.

The range of **cold sauces** under the *Maggi* brand continued to grow, especially in the Middle East and Asia.

Frozen foods had a good year both in the United States and in Europe, where prepared dishes in sealed bags sold particularly well. *Buitoni* achieved notable gains in Italy with its frozen pizzas: in 1996 it became the market leader, thanks in particular to "Bella Napoli" with its attractive, home-made quality. "Bella Napoli" has also been introduced in France, to consolidate the success of "La Grandiosa".

First on the French market – a range of high quality sauce bases from *Maggi*.

For tasty, fast and simple meals: "Taco Dinner Kit" from *Ortega*, **a Mexican classic.**

I Fagottini from *Buitoni Fresco*: a big success thanks to innovation.

Maggi innovation in Germany: a range of dehydrated potato snacks – a tasty light meal in ten minutes.

In **chilled products**, *Buitoni*'s share of the Italian market for filled pasta increased sharply following the launch of *Fagottini*, with their exclusive shape and recipe. Other important introductions included a base for American-style pizza in France and Belgium, and a croissant base in France under the *Herta* brand.

Pet food sales rose strongly in almost every market, with satisfying increases in market share. The strongest performances were recorded in Japan, in Australia and in Europe, where the Group has established a new organisation under the name Friskies Europe.

The *Gourmet Gold* range of super-premium cat food was successfully launched throughout Europe and achieved leadership of the single-serve wet cat food segment in many countries. *Friskies Suprême* wet cat food in an aluminium pouch was launched in selected European markets. In the United States *Fancy Feast Filet & Pâté*, a new premium wet cat food made with proprietary technology, was introduced with a very good reception. Japan launched a super-premium wet dog food for small dogs under the *Friskies Wan Petit* brand.

Profit
Trading profit increased by 8.8%. The trading margin was stable, whilst continuing its improvement in frozen foods and pet food.

Capital expenditure
Capital expenditure was virtually unchanged at Fr. 450 million. The Group inaugurated its first factory in Syria at Khan Al-Sheih, which will manufacture culinary products. In China, a production centre for liquid seasonings began operation at Chashan.

Participation and disinvestments
Nestlé acquired a 40% stake in Osem, which manufactures a wide range of culinary products in Israel. Before signing a distribution agreement with Osem in 1995, the Group had been virtually absent from the Israeli market, where it is now in a position to sell its own brands.

In line with its strategic direction, the Group sold its canned beans and pasta operations in Canada, its fresh meat business in Germany and its cold meat activities in Sweden.

A new convenient packaging alternative for wet pet foods.

Foodservice

Although the sales of Nestlé's foodservice activities are divided among the four major categories of food products discussed on the previous pages, it is desirable, as in previous years, to devote a separate section to them, as they concern a special group of customers: professionals in the restaurant and hotel industries.

Nestlé is the world's largest and most diversified supplier of food and beverages to the out-of-home sector, which encompasses not only restaurants, hotels and fast-food chains but also company restaurants, airlines and private or government institutions such as hospitals, schools and senior-citizen homes. These institutions increasingly delegate the provision of meals and other services to specialised caterers. In most markets where Nestlé is present *Nestlé FoodServices* is also active, and the products and services offered take into account the diversity and specific requirements of the professional food operators.

Food products

The range of products is very wide, and varies from partially prepared ingredients and kitchen aids used by skilled chefs to ready-to-heat meal components and fully prepared meals used in kitchens which work using less qualified labour. In the United States, L.J. Minor continued to build on its success with major operators through innovative solutions. The *Minor's* and *Chef* brands are well known to professional chefs for food bases used mainly in the more traditional kitchens, whereas *Stouffer's*, *Findus* and *Davigel* are known for their frozen food products and meals. Dehydrated products sold under the worldwide *Maggi* brand now include many "exotic" dishes, as well as recipes which have been specially developed for specific preparation methods such as cold rehydration, preferred by caterers in central kitchens.

Coffee and beverages

Focus has been put on carrying the *Nescafé*, *Nestea* and *Milo* brands to the consumer using alternative channels such as vending machines and fast food chains.

To this end, a branding programme has been launched in France in conjunction with a major event grouping all professional circles involved in the vending industry. In Italy, a vending machine sponsorship activity led to the placement of several hundred *Nescafé* branded machines on various sites, including subways.

Nestlé beverages continue to extend their presence in emerging markets. In Asia, major fast food chains have adopted Nestlé's beverage programme for coffee, iced tea and malted beverages. The equipment proposed by Nestlé offers convenience of service and contributes to consumption growth.

Assaisonnement de Cuisson Maggi seasoning, a new range of tasty multi-purpose products suitable for all cooking methods.

Nescafé Sélection: an example of the range of coffees for vending machines.

Pharmaceutical products

Also included among pharmaceutical products are the infant cosmetics sold by pharmacies in several countries and, since 1993, the Group's share in the sales and results of Galderma, which was formerly treated as an associated company.

Millions of Swiss francs		**1996**	1995	1994
	Sales	**2 451**	2 158	2 203
	Trading profit	**555**	436	490
	Capital expenditure	**84**	147	115

Alcon

Alcon continued to make good progress in 1996, with sales reaching Fr. 2.2 billion. The 12% increase is due notably to several new product introductions and to the favourable evolution of exchange rates.

The use of expensive new technologies, the battle against new diseases and a rapidly ageing population have caused the costs of health care to soar over the past few decades. The resulting intervention by governments and health care organisations has maintained pressure on the pharmaceutical industry's pricing policies. These constraints have driven Alcon to increase efficiency and to reduce both prices and costs.

Alcon has continued its strategy of focusing exclusively on the needs of vision care specialists, supplying them with a full range of products and developing innovative specialities. At the same time the company has maximised its worldwide penetration.

Highlights of the year include the introduction in the United States of *Supra Clens*, a daily liquid protein remover which is revolutionising the care of soft contact lenses. The generic ophthalmic products launched by the Falcon subsidiary in the United States have also met with success.

In the **Surgical** division sales of the *AcrySof* intraocular lens have more than doubled, making it Alcon's third US$ 100 million product. Delivery of surgical kits and packs, which have been very successful in the United States, has begun in Europe.

Galderma

1996 was another year of significant progress for the joint venture of Nestlé and L'Oréal. Sales surpassed the one

Supra Clens, a new contact lens cleaner. *Betoptic S,* beta-blocker for the treatment of glaucoma.

Différine, a new treatment for moderate acne.

MetroCream,
as extension of the range
for rosacea.

billion French franc mark for the first time, increasing by 38% compared with the previous year. Turnover includes the dermatology activities previously managed by Alcon in several Latin American countries, in South Africa and in the Philippines, which were transferred to Galderma at the beginning of the year.

The major event of 1996 was the approval by the Food and Drug Administration in the United States of *Différine*, a new medication for local use in the treatment of moderate acne based on research conducted by Galderma's International Dermatological Research Centre. The product was introduced in the United States in October. In the course of the year, *Différine* was successfully launched in Germany, Switzerland, Canada and Argentina. As has been the case in France since 1995, it has met with an excellent response from doctors.

Numerous registrations for various specialities were obtained during the year, which will lead to launches in all major countries in 1997.

Profit
Trading profit rose by 27.3%, and the margin increased from 20.2% to 22.6%. This progression mainly reflects an excellent performance by Alcon, which benefited from productivity improvements and from good cost control.

Capital expenditure
Capital expenditure totalled Fr. 84 million compared with Fr. 147 million in 1995. In the United States, production capacity for surgical packs was increased, and the research and development centre was extended.

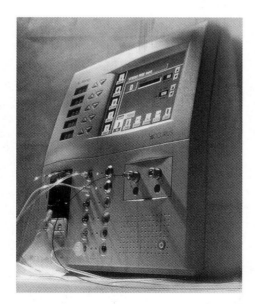

Equipment
for ophthalmic surgery.

Associated companies

Millions of Swiss francs		**1996**	1995	1994
	Nestlé's share in the sales of associated companies	**4 523**	3 948	4 467
	Nestlé's share in the results of associated companies	**233**	168	201

In these companies, Nestlé holds a minority interest of at least 20%, without exercising management control. The companies are included in the financial statements by the equity method. Their results appear, in proportion to Nestlé's participation, in the Group's consolidated income statement under "Share of results of associated companies". The Group's share of their net assets is shown in the consolidated balance sheet under "Financial assets".

L'Oréal

L'Oréal – which is controlled by the Gesparal holding company, of which Nestlé owns 49% and the Bettencourt family 51% – continued its very satisfactory development. L'Oréal's annual report presents detailed information about its activities and results. Consolidated sales rose by 13% in 1996, to 60.3 billion French francs. As the world leader in cosmetics, L'Oréal again reported a significant increase in net profit.

The company improved its position in all its markets, especially in America and Asia. In Japan, Nihon L'Oréal has been co-ordinating and promoting the French group's activities in consumer cosmetics and hair products since July 1996. Jade Kosmetic, the German leader in mass market make-up, was acquired by L'Oréal in 1995 and has been consolidated since January 1996.

In February 1996, L'Oréal gained full control of Maybelline and, as a result, has become the leader in mass market make-up in the United States. In the autumn the group opened a Maybelline factory in China, where it expects to grow rapidly in the major cosmetics segments.

Compagnie Financière du Haut-Rhin

Following a capital increase at San Pellegrino, the operating company of this group, the stake held by the Compagnie Financière du Haut-Rhin has risen to 90%. Nestlé now has a 6% direct stake in San Pellegrino (21% in 1995), while retaining its 49% share of the holding company.

In 1996, San Pellegrino continued the rationalisation programme started in 1995. The group, which is the leader in the Italian mineral water market, recorded sales of Fr. 724 million for 1996.

Great Lash from Maybelline, acquired by L'Oréal. The top-selling mascara in the United States.

Acqua di Giò for men, in the Parfums Armani range.

General information

Manufacture and sale of products

Position in 1996 in markets manufacturing and selling products
under Nestlé processes and trademarks.

Number of factories

	1996	1995
Europe	**211**	220
Africa	**28**	28
North and South America	**159**	159
Asia	**68**	58
Oceania	**23**	24
Total	**489**	489

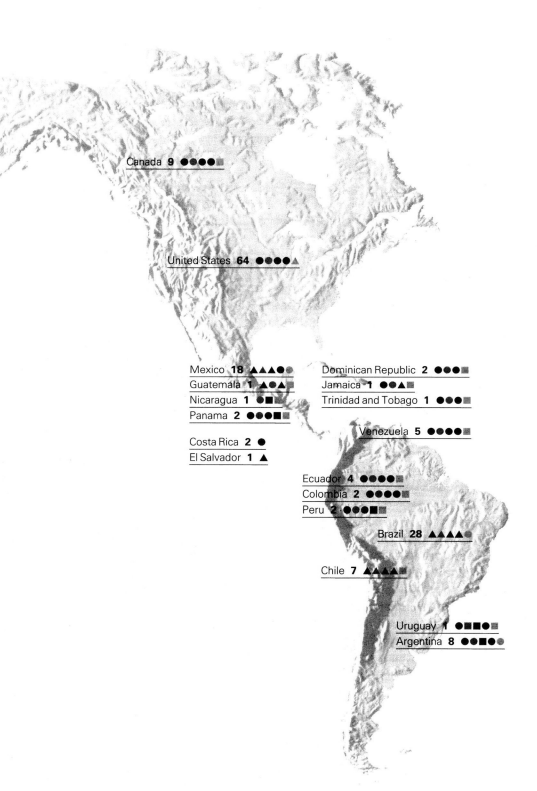

The figure in bold after the country
denotes the number of factories.

◼ Beverages

▨ Milk products, dietetics
and ice cream

◼ Prepared dishes and
cooking aids

◼ Chocolate and confectionery

▨ Pharmaceuticals

▲ Local production (may
represent production in
several factories)

● Local production and imports

▨ Imports (may, in a few
particular cases, represent
purchases from third parties
in the market concerned)

Norway **4** ●▲●■
Sweden **7** ●▲●■
Finland **2** ■●●■
Denmark **3** ■●■■

Russia **2** ■●●●

Republic of Ireland **3** ●■●
United Kingdom **22** ●●●
Netherlands **6** ■●●●
Belgium **5** ■●■●

Poland **7** ●●●●
Czech Republic **11** ●■■●
Slovakia **1** ■■●■
Hungary **2** ●■●●

France **39** ●●●●
Switzerland **9** ●●●●
Italy **21** ●●●●
Portugal **6** ●●●■
Spain **23** ▲●●●

Germany **29** ●●●●
Austria **2** ●■●●
Bulgaria **1** ■■■●

Greece **5** ●●●●
Turkey **1** ●■▲▲

People's Rep. of China **8** ●●●●

Republic of Korea **1** ●▲●■
Japan **4** ●●●●

Morocco **1** ●●●
Tunisia **1** ●●■■

Syria **1** ●
Israel **7** ●●●
Egypt **4** ●●▲

United Arab Emirates **1** ●
Saudi Arabia **1** ■●▲■

Taiwan **2** ●●●●
Hong Kong **1** ●●■■

Pakistan **2** ●●▲●
Bangladesh **1** ■●
India **5** ▲▲▲▲
Sri Lanka **2** ●●▲

Thailand **8** ●●●▲
Vietnam **1** ●
Philippines **8** ▲●●●

Senegal **1** ■●●
Guinea **1** ■■▲
Ivory Coast **2** ▲●▲
Ghana **1** ●●●■

Nigeria **2** ●●▲
Cameroon **1** ■■▲
Kenya **1** ●●●■

Malaysia **9** ●●●●
Singapore **1** ●●●■
Indonesia **5** ●●●●

Zimbabwe **1** ●●●■
South Africa **12** ●●●▲

Australia **15** ●▲●●
Pacific Islands **4** ●●●●
New Zealand **4** ●▲●●

History

Henri Nestlé
Founder of Farine lactée
Henri Nestlé

Nestlé can trace its origins back to 1866, when the first European condensed milk factory was opened in Cham, Switzerland. The founder of this factory, Anglo-Swiss Condensed Milk Company, was merged in 1905 with Farine lactée Henri Nestlé.

The latter company had made itself known in Switzerland in 1867 when it introduced the first infant formula. At the same time Henri Nestlé created the symbol of the "Nest", a graphic translation of his name, which personifies the business. This symbol, which is universally understood, simultaneously evokes security, maternity and affection, nature and nourishment, family and tradition. Today, it is the central element in Nestlé's corporate identity.

While the original business was based on milk and dietetic foods for children, numerous other food products have been added to the line over the years: chocolate, instant beverages (the *Nescafé* process was developed in

1867	1905	1929	1936	1938	1947
Farine lactée Henri Nestlé	**Nestlé & Anglo-Swiss Condensed Milk Co.**		**Nestlé & Anglo-Swiss Holding Co. Ltd**		**Nestlé Alimentana S.A.** (new name after the merger with Maggi)

**Peter-Cailler-Kohler
Chocolats Suisses S.A.**
(Merger with Nestlé)

1867
Farine lactée
Henri Nestlé

1866
Anglo-Swiss
Condensed Milk Co.

1819
Chocolats F.L. Cailler

1831
Chocolats Amédée Kohler

1875
Chocolats Daniel Peter

1938
Development
of *Nescafé*

1883
Potages Jules Maggi
(Alimentana S.A.)

1938), culinary, refrigerated and frozen products, ice cream, mineral water and pet foods. Nestlé is still primarily concerned with the field of nutrition, but it has also acquired interests in pharmaceutical specialities, with Alcon, and in the cosmetics industry, through its substantial participation in L'Oréal.

From 15 factories in 1900 to 489 today – that's how Nestlé's production has grown. As for distribution, the Nestlé brands have long been known on all five continents, and certain flagship products, like *Nescafé*, are sold in more than 100 countries.

1977

Nestlé S.A.

1960
Crosse & Blackwell

1969
Vittel

1973
Stouffer

1978
Chambourcy

1986
Herta

1992
Perrier

1961
Locatelli

1970
Libby

1974
L'Oréal
(minority interest)

1985
Hills Brothers
Coffee

1988
Buitoni-Perugina

1993
Finitalgel

1962
Findus

1971
Ursina-Franck

1977
Alcon

1985
Carnation

1988
Rowntree

1994
Alpo

Group accounts

Consolidated income statement for the year 1996

In millions of Swiss francs	Notes	**1996**	1995
Sales to customers	1	**60 490**	56 484
Cost of goods sold		**(31 495)**	(30 047)
Distribution expenses		**(4 037)**	(3 676)
Marketing and administration expenses		**(18 027)**	(16 387)
Research and development costs		**(710)**	(657)
Restructuring costs		**(257)**	(177)
Amortisation of intangible assets		**(102)**	(42)
Trading profit	1	**5 862**	5 498
Net financing costs	2	**(915)**	(911)
Net non-trading expenses	3	**(9)**	(96)
Profit before taxation	4	**4 938**	4 491
Taxation	5	**(1 552)**	(1 561)
Net profit of consolidated companies		**3 386**	2 930
Share of profit attributable to outside interests		**(218)**	(180)
Share of results of associated companies	6	**233**	168
Net profit for the year	7	**3 401**	2 918
As percentages of sales			
Trading profit		**9.7%**	9.7%
Net profit for the year		**5.6%**	5.2%

Consolidated balance sheet at 31st December 1996
before appropriations

In millions of Swiss francs	Notes	**1996**	1995
ASSETS			
Current assets			
Liquid assets	8	**5 860**	5 124
Trade and other debtors	9	**9 650**	8 918
Inventories	10	**6 843**	6 164
Prepayments and accrued income		**717**	721
Total current assets		**23 070**	20 927
Fixed assets			
Tangible fixed assets	11	**22 307**	19 266
Financial assets	12	**3 642**	3 010
Intangible assets	13	**2 017**	1 058
Total fixed assets		**27 966**	23 334
Total assets		**51 036**	44 261
LIABILITIES AND SHAREHOLDERS' FUNDS			
Current liabilities			
Trade and other creditors	14	**7 661**	7 185
Financial creditors	15	**9 248**	7 802
Provisions for taxation		**713**	792
Accrued liabilities and deferred income		**2 237**	1 631
Total current liabilities		**19 859**	17 410
Medium and long term liabilities			
Financial creditors	16	**3 443**	3 591
Provisions	17	**4 684**	4 481
Total medium and long term liabilities		**8 127**	8 072
Total liabilities		**27 986**	25 482
Outside interests		**1 112**	790
Shareholders' funds			
Share capital	20	**404**	404
Share premium and reserves	21	**21 802**	17 742
		22 206	18 146
Less:			
Own shares	22	**268**	157
Total shareholders' funds before appropriations	23	**21 938**	17 989
Total liabilities and shareholders' funds		**51 036**	44 261

Consolidated cash flow statement for the year 1996

In millions of Swiss francs	Notes	1996	1995
OPERATING ACTIVITIES			
Net profit of consolidated companies		**3 386**	2 930
Depreciation of tangible fixed assets	11	**2 496**	2 263
Amortisation of intangible assets	13	**102**	42
Increase/(decrease) in provisions and deferred taxes		**(276)**	(767)
Decrease/(increase) in working capital	24	**(83)**	(580)
Other movements		**8**	(49)
Operating cash flow [(a)]		**5 633**	3 839
INVESTING ACTIVITIES			
Expenditure on tangible fixed assets		**(3 054)**	(3 056)
Sale of tangible fixed assets		**180**	225
Acquisitions	25	**(1 122)**	(1 576)
Disposals	26	**96**	448
Income from associated companies		**69**	28
Other movements		**12**	33
Cash flow from investing activities		**(3 819)**	(3 898)
FINANCING ACTIVITIES			
Dividend for the previous year		**(1 043)**	(1 040)
Exercise of warrants to purchase shares		**—**	310
Purchase of own shares (net)		**(111)**	—
Movements with outside shareholders		**(137)**	(119)
Bonds issued		**786**	291
Bonds repaid		**(397)**	(300)
Increase/(decrease) in other medium/ long term financial creditors		**(88)**	(142)
Increase/(decrease) in short term financial creditors		**(399)**	858
Decrease/(increase) in marketable securities and other liquid assets		**(183)**	12
Decrease/(increase) in short term investments		**(332)**	(379)
Cash flow from financing activities		**(1 904)**	(509)
Translation differences		**11**	318
INCREASE/(DECREASE) IN CASH AND CASH EQUIVALENTS		**(79)**	(250)
Cash and cash equivalents at beginning of year		**2 698**	3 043
Effects of exchange rate changes		**167**	(95)
Cash and cash equivalents retranslated at beginning of year		**2 865**	2 948
Cash and cash equivalents at end of year	8	**2 786**	2 698

[(a)] Taxes paid amount to Fr. 1 721 million (1995: 1 504 million). Interest received/paid does not differ materially from interest shown under note 2 "Net financing costs".

Annex to the Group accounts

Accounting policies

Accounting convention and accounting standards

The Group accounts are prepared in accordance with International Accounting Standards (IAS) issued by the International Accounting Standards Committee (IASC).

The accounts have been prepared under the historical cost convention, modified by the inclusion of the revaluation of tangible fixed assets to net replacement value The accounts are prepared on the accruals basis. All significant consolidated and associated companies have a 31st December accounting year end. All disclosures required by the 4th and 7th European Union company law directives are provided.

Scope of consolidation

The Group accounts comprise those of Nestlé S.A. and of its affiliated companies, including joint ventures, and associated companies (the Group). Details of Nestlé Group companies are given on page 70.

Consolidated companies

Companies in which the Group has a participation, usually a majority, and where it is responsible for the management (formally licenses the use of its trademarks and, if applicable, its production technology) are fully consolidated. This applies irrespective of the percentage of the participation in the share capital. Outside shareholders' interests in the shareholders' funds, as well as in the net results, are shown separately in the Group accounts.

Proportional consolidation is applied for companies owned, controlled and managed jointly with partners. The individual assets, liabilities, income and expenditure are consolidated in proportion to the Nestlé participation in the equity (usually 50%).

Newly acquired companies are consolidated from the effective date of acquisition, using the purchase method.

Associated companies

Those companies where the Group has a participation of 20% or more but does not exercise management control are dealt with according to the equity method. The Group's share of the net assets is included under "Financial assets" whilst its share of net results is included under "Share of results of associated companies". The net assets and results are recognised on the basis of the associates' own accounting policies, which may differ from those of the Group.

Foreign currencies

In individual companies, transactions in foreign currencies are recorded at the rate of exchange at the date of the transaction or, if hedged forward, at the rate of exchange under the related forward contract. Assets and liabilities in foreign currencies are translated at year end rates. Any resulting exchange differences are taken to the income statement.

On consolidation, assets and liabilities of Group companies denominated in foreign currencies are translated into Swiss francs at year end rates. Income and expense items are translated into Swiss francs at the annual average rates of exchange or, where known or determinable, at the rate on the date of the transaction for significant items.

Differences arising from the translation of opening net assets of Group companies, together with differences arising from the restatement of the net results for the year of Group companies from average or actual rates to year end rates, are taken to reserves.

The balance sheet and net results of Group companies operating in hyper inflationary economies are restated for the changes in the general purchasing power of the local currency, using official indices at the balance sheet date, before translation into Swiss francs at year end rates.

Hedging

The Group uses derivatives to manage operational exposures to foreign exchange, interest rate and commodity price risks. The instruments used to hedge foreign currency flows and positions mainly include forward foreign exchange contracts, options, currency futures and currency swaps. Foreign exchange gains and losses on hedging instruments are matched with foreign exchange gains and losses on the underlying asset or liability. When an anticipated future transaction has been hedged and the underlying position has not been recognised in the financial statements any change in the fair value of the hedging instrument is not recognised in the income statement for the period.

Where derivatives are held for the long-term and are used to manage interest rate risks, they are accounted for on the cost basis (where the underlying asset or liability is accounted for on the cost basis) and payments and receipts relating to the instrument are recognised under net financing costs as they accrue. In other cases the instruments are carried at fair value and changes in the market value are taken to income.

Commodity instruments are used to ensure the Group's access to raw materials at an appropriate price. Outright purchase transactions are recorded at the contracted rates. Changes in the fair value of open commodity instruments are not recognised until the actual purchase transactions are recognised in the financial statements.

Valuation methods and definitions

Sales to customers

Sales to customers represent the sales of products and services rendered to third parties, net of sales rebates and sales taxes.

Research and development costs

Research and development costs are charged to the income statement in the year in which they are incurred.

Net financing costs

This item includes the interest payable on borrowings from third parties as well as the interest receivable on funds invested outside the Group. Exchange differences and the results of foreign exchange and interest hedge operations linked to external loans, intra-Group short term loans and deposits in foreign currencies are also included under this heading.

For hyper-inflationary economies, only the real net financing costs appear under this heading. The inflationary portion relating to the financing of the net working capital, which represents a trading expense, is included under "Marketing and administration expenses". The balance of the inflationary portion, relating to the financing of fixed assets, is treated as an exchange difference and shown under "Net non-trading expenses" since it is offset by a devaluation in the exchange rate of the domestic currency.

Taxation

This includes taxes on profit and other taxes such as taxes on capital. Also included are actual or potential withholding taxes on current and expected transfers from Group companies and tax adjustments relating to prior years.

Deferred taxation is the tax attributable to the timing differences arising from the inclusion of items of income and expenditure in tax computations in periods different from those in which they are included in the financial statements. Deferred tax assets or liabilities are recognised to the extent that they are expected to crystallise in the foreseeable future. Deferred taxes are calculated under the liability method at the rates of tax expected to prevail when the timing differences reverse.

Liquid assets

Liquid assets include cash at banks and in hand, cash equivalents, marketable securities and other liquid funds and short term investments. Cash equivalents consist of bank deposits and fixed term investments whose maturities are three months or less from the date of acquisition. Short term investments consist of bank deposits and fixed term investments whose maturities are higher than three months from the date of acquisition.

Marketable securities are valued at the lower of cost and market value.

Inventories

Raw materials and purchased finished goods are valued at purchase cost. Work in progress and manufactured finished goods are valued at production cost. Production cost includes direct production costs and an appropriate proportion of production overheads and factory depreciation.

Movements in the most important raw materials stocks and purchased finished goods are accounted for using the FIFO (first in, first out) method. The weighted average cost method is used for other stocks.

A provision is established when the net realisable value of any inventory item is lower than the values calculated above.

Prepayments and accrued income

Prepayments and accrued income comprise payments made in advance relating to the following year, and income relating to the current year which will not be received until after the balance sheet date, together with prepayments of pension and retirement benefits.

Accrued liabilities and deferred income

Accrued liabilities and deferred income comprise expenses relating to the current year which will not be paid until after the balance sheet date and income received in advance, relating to the following year.

Leased assets

Assets acquired under finance leases are capitalised and depreciated in accordance with the Group's policy on tangible fixed assets. The associated financial liabilities are included in financial creditors.

Rentals payable under operating leases are charged to the income statement as incurred.

Tangible fixed assets

Tangible fixed assets are shown in the balance sheet at their net replacement values arrived at as follows:
- Land: market value on a prudent basis.
- Other tangible fixed assets: replacement new value (the amount which theoretically would have to be invested in order to replace an asset by a similar new asset duly installed and rendering the same service) less the accumulated depreciation calculated on this value. Replacement new value is computed on the basis of coefficients determined by official or professional bodies. These amounts are recalculated each year.

Depreciation is provided on the straight-line method so as to amortise the replacement new values of tangible fixed assets over their estimated useful lives, which are as follows:

Buildings .... 25-50 years
Plant and machinery .... 10-15 years
Tools, furniture and other equipment.............. 3-5 years
Vehicles... 5 years

Once tangible fixed assets have reached the end of their estimated useful lives, no net replacement value is attributed to them. Land is not depreciated. Premiums capitalised for leasehold land or buildings are amortised over the length of the lease. Depreciation of tangible fixed assets is allocated to the appropriate expense headings in the income statement.

Financial assets

Other investments primarily comprise unquoted participations of minor importance in various companies where the Nestlé Group does not exercise management control as well as some securities. They are carried at cost less provisions for any permanent impairment in value.

Long term receivables included under this heading are discounted to their net present value at the date of inception. Net recoveries are included under "Non-trading income".

Intangible assets

As from 1st January 1995, the excess of the cost of an acquisition over the fair value of the net tangible assets is capitalised. Previously these amounts had been written off through reserves. This value comprises intangible assets acquired, in particular trademarks and industrial property rights, as well as business goodwill. The different components are not separately identified and valued.

Intangible assets are amortised on a straight line basis over their anticipated useful life but not exceeding 20 years. However, the Group considers that the useful life of intangible assets will in many cases exceed this period.

The unamortised balance is reviewed annually. Where the balance exceeds the value of expected future benefits, the difference is charged to the income statement.

Intangible assets are usually recorded in the currency of the acquiring entity.

Current liabilities

These include current or renewable liabilities due within a maximum period of one year. The provisions for taxation also include the withholding tax on expected transfers from Group companies.

Provisions

This item includes provisions for pensions and restructuring costs, as well as contingencies which may arise and which have been prudently provided.

Pensions and retirement benefits
The majority of Group employees are eligible for retirement benefits under defined benefit and defined contribution plans provided through separate funds, insurance plans or unfunded arrangements.

For defined benefit plans the amount charged to the income statement consists of current service cost which includes the normal cost of financing benefits in respect of future years of service and net interest on the net assets or obligations. If the case arises, variations from the current service cost are spread over the expected working lives of employees or recognised immediately in the case of retirees. Contributions to defined contribution pension schemes are charged to the income statement as incurred.

Liabilities arising under defined benefit schemes are either externally funded, with the assets of the scheme held separately from those of the Group in independently administered funds or are unfunded but with provisions maintained in the Group balance sheet. Any difference between the charge to the income statement in respect of funded schemes and the contributions payable to each scheme is recorded in the balance sheet as a prepayment or a provision.

Post retirement health care and other employee benefits
Group companies, principally in the United States and Canada, maintain health care and life assurance benefit plans which cover eligible retired employees. Based on actuarial assumptions these obligations are charged to the income statement so as to spread the estimated cost over the expected working lives of the employees. An interest charge on accumulated liabilities is also made.

The obligations for other employee benefits are recognised on the basis of local legislation. They consist mainly of end of service indemnities, which do not have the character of pensions.

Dividends

In accordance with Swiss law and the Company's Articles of Association, dividends are treated as an appropriation of profit in the year in which they are ratified at the Annual General Meeting and subsequently paid, rather than as an appropriation of the profit in the year to which they relate.

Changes in accounting policies and modification of the scope of consolidation

Changes in accounting policies

The accounting policies are unchanged but disclosure concerning financial instruments has been implemented in accordance with IAS 32 Financial Instruments: Disclosure and Presentation. The transitional provision of this standard states that comparative figures should be shown only where they are available.

Modification of the scope of consolidation

The scope of the consolidation has been affected by the acquisitions and disposals made in 1996. The principal companies which operate in the food sector are detailed below.

Fully consolidated companies

Newly included:
Premier/Eventyr, Denmark, 100% (1.1.1996)
Osem, Israel, 39.7% (1.8.1996)
Biscuit activities of La Universal, Ecuador, 100% (1.12.1996)

Associated company

Newly included:
Mineralbrunnen Überkingen Teinach, Germany, 34.3% (1.1.1996)

Notes to the Group accounts

1. Segmental information

In millions of Swiss francs	1996	1995
Sales		
By geographic area:		
Europe	**27 630**	26 104
North and South America	**21 110**	19 797
Other regions of the world	**11 750**	10 583
	60 490	56 484
By major business:		
Beverages	**16 348**	16 215
Milk products, dietetics and ice cream	**16 697**	15 239
Prepared dishes and cooking aids	**15 960**	14 655
Chocolate and confectionery	**9 034**	8 217
Pharmaceutical products	**2 451**	2 158
	60 490	56 484

The analysis of sales by geographic area is stated by customer destination. Inter-segment sales are not significant.

Trading profit	1996	1995
By geographic area:		
Europe	**2 284**	2 202
North and South America	**2 285**	2 083
Other regions of the world	**1 293**	1 213
	5 862	5 498
By major business:		
Beverages	**2 352**	2 151
Milk products, dietetics and ice cream	**1 206**	1 264
Prepared dishes and cooking aids	**984**	904
Chocolate and confectionery	**765**	743
Pharmaceutical products	**555**	436
	5 862	5 498

Expenditure on tangible fixed assets is given in the "Business Review" on page 16 and by major business on page 8 and by geographic area on page 12.

2. Net financing costs

In millions of Swiss francs	1996	1995
Interest income	**307**	353
Interest expense	**(1 222)**	(1 264)
	(915)	(911)

Net financing costs include Fr. 2 million (1995: Fr. 3 million) in respect of dividends received from other investments, but no material amount resulting from gains or losses on securities.

3. Net non-trading expenses

In millions of Swiss francs	1996	1995
Non-trading expenses		
Loss on disposal of fixed assets	**(48)**	(59)
Loss on disposal of activities	**(18)**	—
Provisions for risks	**(92)**	(65)
Other	**(332)**	(488)
	(490)	(612)
Non-trading income		
Profit on disposal of fixed assets	**29**	18
Profit on disposal of activities	**18**	29
Release of provisions for risks	**40**	232
Other	**394**	237
	481	516
	(9)	(96)

4. Profit before taxation

Profit is stated after charging the following items:

In millions of Swiss francs	1996	1995
Depreciation of tangible fixed assets	**2 496**	2 263
Salaries and welfare expenses	**9 948**	9 411
Defined contribution pensions	**93**	61
Defined benefit pensions	**370**	322
Remuneration of the executive management and statutory remuneration of the Directors	**19**	18
Auditors' remuneration	**22**	20
Rental charges	**456**	424
Exchange differences	**(168)**	186

5. Taxation

In millions of Swiss francs	1996	1995
Taxes on profit and other taxes	(1 624)	(1 576)
Deferred taxes	72	15
	(1 552)	(1 561)
Total tax charge as a percentage of profit before tax	31%	35%

6. Share of results of associated companies

In millions of Swiss francs	1996	1995
Share of profit before taxation	393	284
Less share of taxation	(160)	(116)
Share of profit after taxation	233	168

7. Net profit per share

In Swiss francs	1996	1995
Registered share	86.4	74.4

Net profit per share is based on the weighted average number of shares outstanding during the year (see page 68).
The fully-diluted net profit per share assuming the exercise of all outstanding options is the same as the net profit per share.

8. Liquid assets

In millions of Swiss francs	1996	1995
Cash at bank and in hand	1 065	1 042
Cash equivalents	1 721	1 656
Cash and cash equivalents per cash flow statement	2 786	2 698
Marketable securities and other liquid funds	1 782	1 570
Short term investments	1 292	856
	5 860	5 124

Liquid assets are mainly denominated in Swiss francs (43%) and US dollars (35%). Rates of annual interest on interest bearing instruments range from $2^1/_2$% to $7^3/_4$%.
The market value of marketable securities, comprising mainly short term promissory notes, and other liquid funds at 31st December 1996 amounted to Fr. 1 820 million (1995: Fr. 1 599 million).

9. Trade and other debtors

In millions of Swiss francs	1996	1995
Trade debtors	7 865	7 223
Other debtors	1 785	1 695
	9 650	8 918
Amounts included above which are due after more than one year	65	61

10. Inventories

In millions of Swiss francs	1996	1995
Raw materials, work in progress and sundry supplies	2 775	2 669
Manufactured goods	4 123	3 541
Provisions	(55)	(46)
	6 843	6 164

Inventories amounting to Fr. 111 million (1995: Fr. 113 million) are pledged as security for financial creditors.

11. Tangible fixed assets

In millions of Swiss francs	Land and buildings	Plant and machinery	Tools, furniture and other equipment	Vehicles	Total 1996	Total 1995
Gross value:						
1st January	15 746	23 655	4 570	831	44 802	46 676
Currency retranslation and inflation adjustment	1 701	2 971	549	93	5 314	(4 625)
Expenditure	535	1 780	582	157	3 054	3 056
Disposals	(150)	(503)	(291)	(108)	(1 052)	(1 485)
On acquisition and disposal of Group companies	78	140	92	31	341	496
Revaluations	(91)	310	38	20	277	684
At 31st December	17 819	28 353	5 540	1 024	52 736	44 802

In millions of Swiss francs	Land and buildings	Plant and machinery	Tools, furniture and other equipment	Vehicles	Total **1996**	Total 1995
Accumulated depreciation:						
1st January	(7 187)	(14 515)	(3 304)	(530)	**(25 536)**	(26 457)
Currency retranslation and inflation adjustment	(629)	(1 801)	(409)	(67)	**(2 906)**	2 632
Annual depreciation	(394)	(1 471)	(516)	(115)	**(2 496)**	(2 263)
Disposals	59	438	254	91	**842**	1 100
On acquisition and disposal of Group companies	(32)	(95)	(63)	(20)	**(210)**	(227)
Revaluations	4	(98)	(15)	(14)	**(123)**	(321)
At 31st December	**(8 179)**	**(17 542)**	**(4 053)**	**(655)**	**(30 429)**	(25 536)
Net at 31st December	**9 640**	**10 811**	**1 487**	**369**	**22 307**	19 266

At 31st December 1996 net tangible fixed assets included Fr. 533 million (1995: Fr. 559 million) of assets under construction. Net tangible fixed assets held under finance leases at 31st December 1996 were Fr. 130 million (1995: Fr. 147 million). Net tangible fixed assets of Fr. 414 million (1995: Fr. 187 million) are pledged as security for financial creditors.

The revaluation reserve included in the carrying value of net tangible fixed assets at net replacement value is as follows:

In millions of Swiss francs	Land and buildings	Plant and machinery	Tools, furniture and other equipment	Vehicles	Total **1996**	Total 1995
Net replacement value	9 640	10 811	1 487	369	**22 307**	19 266
Net book value	7 253	8 592	1 552	320	**17 717**	14 929
Revaluation reserve	**2 387**	**2 219**	**(65)**	**49**	**4 590**	4 337
Share attributable to outside interests					**(153)**	(116)
Revaluation reserve attributable to shareholders					**4 437**	4 221
Cumulative translation difference					**131**	448
Revaluation surplus as per note 21					**4 568**	4 669

Fire insurance values are reflected in the net replacement value of tangible fixed assets. Net replacement values provide a fair representation of the value of tangible fixed assets.

12. Financial assets

(a) The indirect participation in L'Oréal, Paris, is included at a value of Swiss francs 1020 million (1995: 753 million). The stock exchange market value at 31st December 1996 amounted to Swiss francs 8831 million (1995: 4962 million).

In millions of Swiss francs	1996	1995
Participations in associated companies (a)	1 229	851
Loans to associated companies	—	2
Other investments	246	414
Medium and long term receivables	1 529	1 287
Deferred tax assets (note 19)	638	456
	3 642	3 010

13. Intangible assets

(b) Intangible assets have been capitalised for the first time from 1st January 1995, in accordance with the revised requirements of IAS 22. Previously they were written off through reserves.

In millions of Swiss francs	1996	1995 (b)
Gross value:		
At 1st January	1 093	—
Currency retranslation	128	—
On acquisition	950	1 093
Other	(21)	—
At 31st December	2 150	1 093
Amortisation:		
At 1st January	(35)	—
Currency retranslation	(4)	—
Annual amortisation	(102)	(42)
Other	8	7
At 31st December	(133)	(35)
Net at 31st December	2 017	1 058

14. Trade and other creditors

In millions of Swiss francs	1996	1995
Trade creditors	4 521	4 171
Other creditors	3 140	3 014
	7 661	7 185

15. Short term financial creditors

In millions of Swiss francs	1996	1995
Commercial Paper	2 497	3 241
Overdrafts	1 372	1 155
Other short term financial creditors	4 006	2 895
	7 875	7 291
Current portion of medium and long term financial creditors	1 373	511
	9 248	7 802

Short term financial creditors are mainly denominated in major European currencies (36%) and in US dollars (24%). Rates of annual interest range from $3^{1}/_{2}$% to $16^{1}/_{4}$%.

16. Medium and long term financial creditors

In millions of Swiss francs	1996	1995
Loans from financial institutions	531	539
Bonds	4 197	3 470
Obligations under finance leases	88	93
	4 816	4 102
Current portion of medium and long term financial creditors	(1 373)	(511)
	3 443	3 591

Loans from financial institutions are mainly denominated in major European currencies (43%) and in US dollars (23%). Annual interest rates range from $3\frac{1}{4}$% to $17\frac{1}{2}$%. The majority of the loans are at fixed rates. Currencies and interest rates on bonds are disclosed below.

The above medium and long term financial creditors are repayable as follows:

In millions of Swiss francs	1996	1995
in the second year	1 420	1 361
in the third to fifth year inclusive	1 146	1 581
after the fifth year	877	649
	3 443	3 591

The following bonds were in issue at 31st December 1996 and 1995:

In millions of Swiss francs	1996	1995
USD 100 million 5% bonds with warrants 1987-1997 [a] [b]	133	116
CHF 300 million 2% bonds with warrants 1987-1997 [a] [b]	300	300
USD 200 million 6% bonds with warrants 1991-1998 [a]	266	232
USD 200 million $5\frac{7}{8}$% bonds with warrants 1991-1998 [a]	266	232
USD 200 million $7\frac{1}{8}$% bonds 1991-1996	—	232
CHF 300 million $6\frac{3}{4}$% bonds 1992-2002 [b] [c]	300	300
USD 200 million $6\frac{1}{8}$% bonds 1992-1997	266	232
USD 250 million $3\frac{5}{8}$% bonds with warrants 1992-1999 [a]	333	290
FRF 1500 million $6\frac{1}{2}$% bonds 1993-1998	381	351
CAD 300 million $6\frac{1}{4}$% bonds 1993-1998 [d] [e]	293	263
USD 300 million $6\frac{1}{2}$% bonds 1994-1997 [b]	399	348
ITL 150 billion 11% bonds 1994-1996 [b]	—	119
GBP 75 million $8\frac{3}{4}$% bonds 1994-1997 [b]	167	134
USD 250 million $7\frac{3}{8}$% bonds 1995-2005	333	290
DEM 500 million $5\frac{1}{8}$% 1996-2001 [c]	429	—
CHF 300 million 3% 1996-2000 [f]	300	—
Other bonds	31	31
Total	4 197	3 470
Due within one year	(1 269)	(373)
Due after one year	2 928	3 097

[a] The rights to exercise the warrants attached to these bonds have expired.
[b] Subject to an interest rate swap against variable rate.
[c] Subject to various interest rate and currency swaps against US$.
[d] Subject to an interest rate and currency swap against US$.
[e] Subject to various interest rate swaps against variable rates.
[f] Subject to an interest rate and currency swap against Austr.$.

The market value of the above bonds amounted to Fr. 4 311 million at 31st December 1996.

17. Provisions

(a) During 1996 an amount of Fr. 372 million has been paid to an externally funded plan.

In millions of Swiss francs	1996	1995
Pensions and retirement benefits (note 18)	**911** (a)	1 250
Post retirement health care and other employee benefits	**1 096**	931
Taxes payable	**84**	44
Deferred tax liabilities (note 19)	**256**	138
Other provisions (for contingencies and restructuring costs)	**2 337**	2 118
	4 684	4 481

18. Pensions and retirement benefits

In millions of Swiss francs	1996	1995

At the beginning of the year the assets and liabilities were as follows:
Defined benefit plans:
Actuarial present values of retirement benefits:

	1996	1995
Funded plans	**9 505**	9 626
Unfunded plans	**751**	808
Fair value of amount set aside for retirement benefits:		
Plan assets of funded plans at latest valuation date	**9 030**	8 949
Provisions for pension liabilities in the Group balance sheet	**1 250**	1 287

Actuarial assumptions used for the main benefit plans:
Interest rate less rate of salary increase   1% to 4.5%
Interest rate less rate of pension increase   3% to 8%

Actuarial valuations of the individual pension arrangements of the Group are performed at not more than three-yearly intervals. The actuaries use either the projected unit credit or attained age method of valuation in accordance with local practice and statutory requirements Contributions to funded schemes are determined for each plan separately based on actuarial advice in accordance with local practice and legislation. Any surpluses or deficits are absorbed by prospective modification of contributions over a period of years.

19. Deferred taxes

In millions of Swiss francs	1996	1995
Provided deferred taxes:		
Tax assets on timing differences	**633**	449
Tax assets on losses available for future relief	**5**	7
	638	456
Tax liabilities on timing differences	**256**	138
Unprovided deferred taxes:		
Tax assets on timing differences	**671**	550
Tax assets on losses available for future relief	**161**	160
	832	710
Tax liabilities on timing differences	**1 900**	1 832

The deferred tax on the difference between the net replacement and the net book values of tangible fixed assets is included under unprovided tax liabilities. Withholding tax on profits retained in affiliated companies is not provided where such profits form part of the financing of the companies concerned and are not intended to be distributed.

20. Share capital of Nestlé S.A.

	1996	1995
Number of registered shares of nominal value Fr. 10 each	**40 352 000**	40 352 000
In millions of Swiss francs	**404**	404

Additional information is given in the annex to the Annual report of Nestlé S.A., note 18 on page 83.
The share capital includes the nominal value of own shares (see note 22).

21. Share premium and reserves

In millions of Swiss francs	1996	1995
Reserves of Nestlé S.A.:		
General reserve [a]	**6 124**	6 235
Reserve for own shares [b]	**268**	157
Special reserve [c]	**5 537**	5 480
Earned surplus	**1 252**	1 104
	13 181	12 976
Other reserves:		
Revaluation surplus [d]	**4 568**	4 669
Other shareholders' funds [e]	**3 808**	628
Cumulative translation difference	**245**	(531)
	21 802	17 742

[a] The general reserve of Nestlé S.A. consists mainly of the legal reserve, the principal element of which is the share premium account. The legal reserve is distributable to the extent that it exceeds 50% of the nominal value of the share capital.
[b] This reserve relates to own shares as per note 22.
[c] The special reserve of Nestlé S.A. substantially consists of amounts appropriated from annual profits in accordance with resolutions passed at Annual General Meetings. The special reserve is substantially distributable at the discretion of shareholders.
[d] The revaluation surplus covers the difference between the net replacement and net book values of tangible fixed assets. This surplus is not distributable.
[e] Other shareholders' funds consist mainly of the reserves of Group companies (other than Nestlé S.A.) which are substantially distributable.

22. Own shares

This item includes the cost of own shares (of Nestlé S.A.) held by:
- an affiliated company: 928 940 freely available shares;
- Nestlé S.A.: 92 393 shares in order to allow the exercise of option rights by members of the Group's management.

The movement of these shares is described in the annex to the Annual report of Nestlé S.A., note 20 on page 84.

23. Movement of consolidated shareholders' funds

In millions of Swiss francs	1996	1995
Shareholders' funds at 1st January	17 989	16 944
Currency retranslation	1 476	(1 231)
Net profit	3 401	2 918
Exercise of warrants to purchase shares	—	310
Purchase of own shares (net of sales)	(111)	—
Revaluation of fixed assets	124	252
Dividend for previous year	(1 043)	(1 040)
Amortisation of intangible assets arising from acquisitions of companies, participations and trademarks [a]	—	(135)
Recovery of intangible assets on disposals charged to shareholders' funds prior to 1st January 1995	40	2
Other movements	62	(31)
Shareholders' funds at 31st December	**21 938**	17 989

[a] This item relates to adjustments on acquisitions made prior to 1st January 1995.

24. Decrease/(increase) in working capital

In millions of Swiss francs	1996	1995
Inventories	74	(34)
Trade debtors	(46)	(463)
Trade creditors	(128)	298
Other	17	(381)
	(83)	(580)

25. Acquisitions

In millions of Swiss francs	1996	1995
Fair value of net assets acquired:		
Tangible fixed assets	184	507
Financial assets	7	60
Provisions	(38)	(34)
Outside interests	(179)	(23)
Purchase of outside interests in existing participations	52	28
Net working capital	105	122
Financial creditors	(32)	(177)
Liquid assets	145	41
	244	524
Intangible assets	950	1 093
Total acquisition cost	1 194	1 617
less:		
Cash and cash equivalents acquired	(49)	(41)
Consideration payable	(23)	—
Cash outflow on acquisitions	1 122	1 576

26. Disposals

In millions of Swiss francs	1996	1995
Net assets disposed of:		
Tangible fixed assets	53	238
Financial assets	—	3
Net working capital	3	176
Financial creditors	—	—
Liquid assets	—	7
	56	424
Intangible assets previously charged to shareholders' funds	40	2
Profit/(loss) on disposals	—	29
Total sale consideration	96	455
less:		
Cash and cash equivalents disposed of	—	(7)
Cash inflow on disposals	96	448

27. Dividends

Dividends payable are not accounted for until they have been ratified at the Annual General Meeting. At the meeting on 5th June 1997, the following dividend in respect of 1996 will be proposed:

(a) Number of shares with right to dividend: see Annual report of Nestlé S.A. page 85.

Dividend per share	Fr.	30.–
resulting in a total dividend of (a)	Fr.	1 181 587 680.–

The accounts for the year ended 31st December 1996 do not reflect this resolution, which will be treated as an appropriation of profit in the year ending 31st December 1997.

28. Foreign exchange hedge instruments

Forward foreign currency sales

(b) See remark under changes in accounting policies, page 52.

In millions of Swiss francs	Recognised transactions		Anticipated future transactions	
	1996	1995 (b)	**1996**	1995 (b)
Contractual values	**4 873**	3 513	**348**	111
Fair values	**5 030**		**343**	
Unrealised gains	**2**		**5**	
Unrealised losses	**159**		**—**	

The hedge instruments consist mainly of forward foreign exchange contracts. Recognised transactions relate to balance sheet positions resulting from export debtors and liquid assets while anticipated future transactions refer to expected export sales and other cash flows.
Due to the nature of the Group's operations, most of the transactions have maturities of less than one year. They are denominated mainly in US Dollars.

Forward foreign currency purchases

In millions of Swiss francs	Recognised transactions		Anticipated future transactions	
	1996	1995 (b)	**1996**	1995 (b)
Contractual values	**1 376**	2 907	**725**	673
Fair values	**1 416**		**725**	
Unrealised gains	**43**		**4**	
Unrealised losses	**3**		**4**	

The hedge instruments consist mainly of forward foreign exchange contracts. Recognised transactions are related to balance sheet positions such as suppliers and financial creditors while anticipated future transactions refer to commitments for commodity and machinery imports. Due to the nature of the Group's operations, most of the transactions have maturities of less than one year. They are denominated mainly in US Dollars and other major European currencies.

29. Commodity hedge instruments

In millions of Swiss francs	1996	1995 [a]
Contractual values	402	
Fair values	375	
Unrealised gains	1	
Unrealised losses	28	

[a] See remarks under changes in accounting policies, page 52.

Commodity instruments consist essentially of futures on terminal markets related to the supply of coffee and cocoa used for the manufacture of finished goods.

30. Interest instruments

Interest rate exposures on liquid assets are hedged by interest rate swaps and interest rate futures. The notional amounts of the these instruments outstanding at 31st December 1996 are Swiss francs 1668 million and 147 million respectively. These instruments have maturity dates between one to five years and annual interest rates ranged from $1^1/_2$% to $8^1/_2$%. They are essentially denominated in Swiss francs. At 31st December 1996 the revaluation of these instruments at market rates resulted in unrealised gains of Swiss francs 29 million and unrealised losses of Swiss francs 21 million.

Interest rate exposures on financial creditors are hedged by means of the following financial instruments. The notional amounts of these instruments and the unrealised gains and losses on revaluation at market rates at 31st December 1996 are given below:

	1996		
In millions of Swiss francs	Notional amounts	Unrealised gains	Unrealised losses
Interest rate swaps	2 097	26	5
Interest rate and currency swaps	1 304	13	49
Forward rate agreements	669	71	—
Interest rate futures	133	—	—

These instruments have maturity dates comprised between one to six years and annual interest rates ranged from 2% to $8^3/_4$%. They are denominated mainly in US Dollars, in Australian Dollars and in major European currencies.

31. Guarantees

In the normal course of business, the Group has given guarantees totalling Fr. 476 million to third parties (1995: Fr. 523 million).

32. Commitments for expenditure on tangible fixed assets

At 31st December 1996, the Group was committed to expenditure amounting Fr. 275 million (1995: Fr. 270 million).

33. Commitments under irrevocable operating leases

The following charges arise from these commitments:

In millions of Swiss francs	1996	1995
within one year	187	164
in the second year	151	134
in the third to fifth year inclusive	365	308
after the fifth year	832	616
	1 535	1 222

34. Contingent liabilities

The Group has provided for all significant contingent liabilities which are probable of assertion and success.

35. Post balance sheet events

No material events.

36. Transactions with related parties

The Group has not entered into any material transaction with related parties.

37. Nestlé Group Companies

The list of companies appears in the section "Companies of the Nestlé Group".

Principal exchange rates

Swiss francs per	Year end rates 1996	Year end rates 1995	Average annual rates 1996	Average annual rates 1995
1 US Dollar	1.33	1.16	1.24	1.18
100 French Francs	25.40	23.40	24.20	23.70
100 Deutsche Mark	85.90	80.50	82.10	82.40
1 Pound Sterling	2.23	1.79	1.94	1.86
100 Italian Lira	0.087	0.073	0.08	0.072
100 Brazilian Reais	128.—	120.—	123.—	128.—
100 Spanish Pesetas	1.02	0.949	0.975	0.947
100 Japanese Yen	1.17	1.13	1.14	1.25
100 Mexican Pesos	17.—	15.20	16.30	18.30
1 Canadian Dollar	0.976	0.846	0.914	0.858
1 Australian Dollar	1.06	0.86	0.967	0.874

Report of the Group auditors
to the General Meeting of Nestlé S.A.

As Group auditors we have audited the Group accounts (balance sheet, income statement, cash flow statement and annex) of the Nestlé Group on pages 46 to 66 for the year ended 31st December 1996.

These Group accounts are the responsibility of the Board of Directors. Our responsibility is to express an opinion on these Group accounts based on our audit. We confirm that we meet the legal requirements concerning professional qualification and independence.

Our audit was conducted in accordance with auditing standards promulgated by the profession, and with International Standards on Auditing issued by the International Federation of Accountants (IFAC), which require that an audit be planned and performed to obtain reasonable assurance about whether the Group accounts are free from material misstatement. We have examined on a test basis evidence supporting the amounts and disclosures in the Group accounts. We have also assessed the accounting principles used, significant estimates made and the overall Group accounts presentation. We believe that our audit provides a reasonable basis for our opinion.

In our opinion, the Group accounts give a true and fair view of the financial position, the result of operations and the cash flows in accordance with International Accounting Standard (IAS) and comply with the law.

We recommend that the Group accounts submitted to you be approved.

KPMG Klynveld Peat Marwick Goerdeler SA

W. M. Tannett   B. A. Mathers
Chartered accountant   Chartered accountant
                    Auditors in charge
London   Zurich
            26th March 1997

Financial information – ten year review

In millions of Swiss francs (except for per share data)		**1996**	1995	
Results				
Consolidated sales		**60 490**	56 484	....
Trading profit		**5 862**	5 498	....
as % of sales		**9.7%**	9.7%	....
Taxation		**1 552**	1 561	....
Consolidated net profit		**3 401**	2 918	....
as % of sales		**5.6%**	5.2%	....
as % of average shareholders' funds		**17.0%**	16.7%	....
Total amount of dividend		**1 182** (a)	1 043	....
Depreciation of tangible fixed assets		**2 496**	2 263	....
as % of sales		**4.1%**	4.0%	....
Amortisation of intangible assets		**102**	42	....
Balance sheet				
Current assets		**23 070**	20 927	....
of which liquid assets		*5 860*	*5 124*	....
Fixed assets		**27 966**	23 334	....
Current liabilities		**19 859**	17 410	....
Medium and long term liabilities and outside interests		**9 239**	8 862	....
Shareholders' funds		**21 938**	17 989	....
Expenditure on tangible fixed assets		**3 054**	3 056	....
as % of sales		**5.0%**	5.4%	....
Data per share				
Weighted average number of shares in issue (b)		**39 363 637**	39 220 756	....
Consolidated net profit (c)	Fr.	**86.4**	74.4	....
Shareholders' funds (c)	Fr.	**557**	459	....
Dividend (c)	Fr.	**30.0** (e)	26.5	....
Pay-out ratio	%	**34.7%** (e)	35.6%	....
Stock exchange prices (high/low) (c)	Fr.	**1487/1250**	1298/1090	....
Yield (d)	%	**2.0/2.4** (e)	2.0/2.4	....

(a) As proposed by the Board of Directors of Nestlé S.A. This amount includes dividends payable in respect of shares with right to dividend at the balance sheet date (Fr. 1 180 million) as well as those potentially payable on the shares covering options (Fr. 2 million).

(b) The figures prior to 1990 represent the number of shares with right to dividend.
(c) Figures prior to 1993 adjusted in order to make comparable the data per share, following rights issues in June 1993 and in June 1989.

(d) Calculated on the basis of the dividend for the year concerned but which is paid out in the following year.
(e) As proposed by the Board of Directors of Nestlé S.A.

	1994	1993	1992	1991	1990	1989	1988	1987
. . . . . .	56 894	57 486	54 500	50 486	46 369	48 036	39 502	34 183
. . . . . .	5 628	5 591	5 384	4 783	4 484	4 660	4 270	3 654
. . . . . .	9.9%	9.7%	9.9%	9.5%	9.7%	9.7%	10.8%	10.7%
. . . . . .	1 647	1 669	1 745	1 605	1 404	1 538	1 267	1 374
. . . . . .	3 250	2 887	2 698	2 470	2 272	2 412	2 058	1 879
. . . . . .	5.7%	5.0%	5.0%	4.9%	4.9%	5.0%	5.2%	5.5%
. . . . . .	19.9%	19.5%	18.4%	17.2%	16.6%	19.1%	15.1%	11.8%
. . . . . .	1 040	972	870	793	736	735	612	510
. . . . . .	2 321	2 283	2 038	1 863	1 688	1 667	1 307	1 184
. . . . . .	4.1%	4.0%	3.7%	3.7%	3.6%	3.5%	3.3%	3.5%
. . . . . .	—	—	—	—	—	—	—	—
. . . . . .	21 420	20 982	20 670	19 195	18 460	17 985	17 117	16 359
. . . . . .	*5 132*	*5 084*	*4 688*	*4 888*	*5 528*	*4 231*	*4 244*	*6 961*
. . . . . .	23 807	24 178	23 803	19 795	17 116	17 421	16 024	12 138
. . . . . .	17 297	18 166	20 019	14 889	14 381	13 981	14 082	7 533
. . . . . .	10 986	11 334	10 524	8 731	7 781	7 486	7 678	5 037
. . . . . .	16 944	15 660	13 930	15 370	13 414	13 939	11 381	15 927
. . . . . .	3 029	3 093	3 191	2 815	2 538	2 446	1 950	1 588
. . . . . .	5.3%	5.4%	5.9%	5.6%	5.5%	5.1%	4.9%	4.6%
. . . . . .	38 838 376	37 759 826	36 938 374	36 800 050	36 750 000	36 750 000	35 000 000	34 000 000
. . . . . .	83.7	76.5	72.2	66.4	61.1	64.9	57.3	53.9
. . . . . .	436	415	373	413	361	375	316	456
. . . . . .	26.5	25.0	23.2	21.3	19.8	19.8	17.0	14.6
. . . . . .	31.7%	32.7%	32.2%	32.0%	32.4%	30.5%	29.8%	27.1%
. . . . . .	1437/1063	1294/1015	1 162/857	876/651	913/650	867/623	658/380	536/378
. . . . . .	1.8/2.5	1.9/2.5	2.0/2.7	2.4/3.3	2.2/3.0	2.3/3.2	2.6/4.5	2.7/3.9

Companies of the Nestlé Group

Operating companies

Principal affiliated companies which operate in the food sector, with the exception of those marked with an asterisk which are engaged in the pharmaceutical sector.

Countries within the continents are listed according to the alphabetical order of the French names.

1. Affiliated companies for which full consolidation treatment is applied (see page 49, "Scope of consolidation").

Europe

GERMANY Nestlé Deutschland AG *Frankfurt* 97.2% • Blaue Quellen Mineral- und Heilbrunnen AG *Rhens am Rhein* 90.6% • Trinks GmbH *Goslar* 90.6% • Alcon Pharma GmbH* *Freiburg/Breisgau* 100% • Alois Dallmayr Kaffee OHG *München* 48.6% • Heimbs & Sohn GmbH & Co. KG *Braunschweig* 48.6% • Motta Eiskrem GmbH & Co. KG *Schwanewede* 100% • Vittel Mineralwasser GmbH *Frankfurt* 100% • Nestlé Clinical Nutrition GmbH *Weinheim* 100% • **AUSTRIA** Öster-reichische Nestlé GmbH *Wien* 100% • **BELGIUM** Nestlé Belgilux S.A. *Bruxelles* 100% • Friskies Service Merchandising S.A. *Zaventem* 100% • Perrier Vittel Belgilux S.A. *Etalle* 100% • Alcon-Couvreur N.V.* *Puurs* 100% • **BULGARIA** Nestlé Sofia A.D. *Sofia* 99% • **DENMARK** Nestlé Danmark A/S *København* 100% • Premier Is A/S *Odense* 100% • **SPAIN** Nestlé España S.A. *Barcelona* 100% • Productos del Café S.A. *Reus* 100% • Conservas La Tila S.A. *Esplugas de Llobregat* 100% • EYCAM Perrier S.A. *Barcelona* 100% • Alcon Iberhis S.A.* *Madrid* 100% • Laboratorios Cusi S.A.* *Barcelona* 100% • Helados y Congelados S.A. *Araya* 100% • Compañia del Frio Alimentario S.A. *Araya* 100% • Avidesa-Luis Suñer S.A. *Alzira* 99.43% • Alimentos Con-gelados S.A. *Marcilla* 100% • **FINLAND** Suomen Nestlé Oy *Helsinki* 100% • **FRANCE** Nestlé France S.A. *Noisiel* 100% • France Glaces-Findus S.A. *Noisiel* 100% • Chambourcy S.A. *Noisiel* 99.9% • Herta S.A. *Noisiel* 100% • Davigel S.A. *Martin-Eglise* 99.9% • Vittel S.A. *Vittel* 100% • Générale de Grandes Sources *Paris* 100% • S.A. des Eaux Minérales de Ribeauvillé *Ribeauvillé* 98.1% • Société Conditionnement et Industrie S.A. *Bernay* 77.9% • Eau Minérale Naturelle de Plancoët «Source Sassay» S.A. *Plancoët* 100% • Société des Eaux Minérales de Quezac *Ispagnac* 100% • Nestlé Coffee Specialties France S.A. *Levallois-Perret* 100% • Clintec Nutrition Clinique S.A. *Sèvres* 100% • Laboratoires Alcon S.A.* *Rueil-Malmaison* 100% • **GREECE** Nestlé Hellas S.A.I. *Maroussi* 85.4% • Loumidis S.A. *Peristeri* 100% • Alcon Laboratories Hellas E.P.E.* *Alimos Attikis* 100% • **ITALY** Nestlé Italiana S.p.A. *Milano* 99.9% • SO.GE.AM. S.p.A. *Padova* 100% • SO.GE.PLAST S.p.A. *Padova* 100% • Fonti San Bernardo S.p.A. *Torino* 100% • Alcon Italia S.p.A.* *Milano* 100% • **HUNGARY** Nestlé Hungaria Kft *Budapest* 100% • **NORWAY** A/S Nestlé Norge *Asker-Oslo* 100% • **NETHER-LANDS** Nestlé Nederland B.V. *Amsterdam* 100% • Alcon Nederland B.V.* *Gorinchem* 100% • Artland Nederland B.V. *Houten* 100% • **POLAND** Goplana S.A. *Poznan* 76.97% • Nestlé Polska Sp. z.o.o. *War-saw* 100% • Naleczowianka Spolka z.o.o. *Naleczov* 33.3% • Winiary S.A. *Kalisz* 80.2% • **PORTUGAL** Nestlé Portugal S.A. *Linda-a-Velha* 100% • Longa Vida S.A. *Matosinho* 100% • Sociedade das Aguas de Pisoes Moura S.A. *Lisboa* 100% • **REPUBLIC OF IRELAND** Nestlé (Ireland) Ltd *Tallaght-Dublin* 100% • **CZECH REPUBLIC** Nestlé Food S.r.o. *Praha* 100% • **UNITED KINGDOM** Nestlé UK Ltd *Croydon* 100% • Perrier Vittel UK Ltd *Rickmansworth* 100% • Buxton Mineral Water Company Ltd *Rickmansworth* 100% • Alcon Laboratories (UK) Ltd* *Watford* 100% • **RUSSIA** JSC Rossiya *Samara* 91% • Nestlé Food LLC *Moscou* 100% • **SLOVAKIA** Nestlé Food S.r.o. *Prievidza* 99.9% • **SWEDEN** Svenska Nestlé AB *Bjuv* 100% • Jede AB *Mariestad* 100% • Zoégas Kaffe AB *Helsingborg* 100% • **SWITZERLAND** Société des Produits Nestlé S.A. *Vevey* 100% • Maggi AG *Kempttal* 100% • Thomi & Franck AG *Basel* 100% • Frisco-Findus AG *Rorschach* 99.8% • Dyna S.A. *Fribourg* 100% • Leisi AG Nahrungsmittelfabrik *Wangen bei Olten* 100% • Perrier Vittel Suisse S.A. *Mies* 100% • Alcon Pharmaceuticals Ltd* *Cham* 100% • Nestlé World Trade Corporation *La Tour-de-Peilz* 100% • Food Ingredients Specialities S.A. *Villars-sur-Glâne* 100% • Nestlé Coffee Specialties S.A. *Pully* 100% • **TURKEY** Nestlé Türkiye Gida Sanayi A.S. *Istanbul* 99.6%.

Africa

SOUTH AFRICA Nestlé (South Africa) (Pty) Ltd *Randburg-Johannes-burg* 100% • Alcon Laboratories Pty Ltd* *Randburg* 100% • **CAMEROON** Nestlé Cameroun *Douala* 99.6% • **IVORY COAST** Nestlé Côte-d'Ivoire *Abidjan* 80.9% • **EGYPT** Dolce S.A.E. *Cairo* 100% • Indus-trie du Froid S.A.E. *Kaliub-Cairo* 100% • Société des eaux minérales Vittor S.A.E. *Cairo* 88.5% • **GABON** Nestlé Gabon *Libreville* 90% • **GHANA** Nestlé Ghana Ltd *Tema-Accra* 51% • **GUINEA** Nestlé Guinée *Conakry* 99% • **KENYA** Nestlé Foods Kenya Ltd *Nairobi* 100% • **MAURITIUS** Nestlé's Products (Mauritius) Ltd *Port Louis* 100% • **MOROCCO** Nestlé Maroc S.A. *El Jadida* 93.4% • **NIGERIA** Nestlé Foods Nigeria PLC *Ilupeju-Lagos* 57% • **SENEGAL** Nestlé Sénégal *Dakar* 100% • **TUNISIA** Nestlé Tunisie *Tunis* 59.2% • **ZIMBABWE** Nestlé Zimbabwe (Pvt) Ltd *Harare* 100%.

North and South America

ARGENTINA Nestlé Argentina S.A. *Buenos Aires* 100% • Alcon Labo-ratorios Argentina S.A.* *Buenos Aires* 100% • **BOLIVIA** Nestlé Bolivia S.r.l. *La Paz* 100% • **BRAZIL** Nestlé Industrial e Comercial Ltda. *São Paulo* 100% • Companhia Produtora de Alimentos *Itabuna* 100% • Tostines Industrial e Comercial Ltda. *São Paulo* 100% • INSOL – Industria de Sorvetes Ltda. *São Paulo* 100% • SURAMIC Sucos Refri-gerantes Aguas Minerais Indústria e Comercio Ltda. *Rio de Janeiro* 100% • Alcon Laboratorios do Brasil S.A.* *São Paulo* 100% • **CANADA** Nestlé Canada, Inc. *Don Mills-Toronto (Ontario)* 100% • Midwest Food Products, Inc. *Toronto (Ontario)* 50% • Laura Secord, Inc. *Scarborough*

(Ontario) 100% · The Perrier Group of Canada Ltd *Toronto (Ontario)* 100% · Alcon Canada, Inc.* *Mississauga (Ontario)* 100% · **CHILE** Nestlé Chile S.A. *Santiago de Chile* 99.5% · **COLOMBIA** Nestlé de Colombia S.A. *Bogotá* 100% · Laboratorios Alcon de Colombia S.A.* *Santafé de Bogotá* 100% · **COSTA RICA** Nestlé Costa Rica S.A. *San José* 100% · **EL SALVADOR** Nestlé El Salvador S.A. *San Salvador* 100% · **ECUADOR** Nestlé Ecuador S.A. *Quito* 74.7% · **UNITED STATES** Nestlé Food Company *Los Angeles (California)* 100% · Nestlé Beverage Company *San Francisco (California)* 100% · Nestlé Brands Food-Services Company *Los Angeles (California)* 100% · Nestlé Frozen, Refrigerated & Ice Cream Companies, Inc. *Solon (Ohio)* 100% · Great Spring Waters of America, Inc. *Wilmington (Delaware)* 100% · Nestlé Clinical Nutrition Inc. *Deerfield (Illinois)* 100% · Nestlé Puerto Rico, Inc. *San Juan (Puerto Rico)* 100% · Nestlé Trading Corporation *Stamford (Connecticut)* 100% · Alcon Laboratories, Inc.* *Fort Worth (Texas)* 100% · Alcon (Puerto Rico), Inc.* *San Juan (Puerto Rico)* 100% · **GUATEMALA** Nestlé Guatemala S.A. *Guatemala* 100% · **HONDURAS** Nestlé Hondureña S.A. *Tegucigalpa* 100% · **JAMAICA** Nestlé-JMP Jamaica Ltd *Kingston* 100% · **MEXICO** Compañia Nestlé S.A. de C.V. *México* 100% · Alimentos Findus S.A. de C.V. *México* 100% · Industrias Alimenticias Club S.A. de C.V. *México* 100% · Manantiales La Asuncion, S.A. de C.V. *México* 50% · Alcon Laboratorios S.A. de C.V.* *México* 100% · **NICARAGUA** Productos Nestlé (Nicaragua) S.A. *Managua* 100% · **PANAMA** Nestlé Panamá S.A. *Panamá City* 100% · Nestlé Caribbean, Inc. *Panamá City* 100% · **PERU** Nestlé Perú S.A. *Lima* 93.1% · **DOMINICAN REPUBLIC** Sociedad Dominicana de Conservas y Alimentos S.A. *Santo Domingo* 70% · **TRINIDAD AND TOBAGO** Nestlé Trinidad and Tobago Ltd *Port of Spain* 100% · **URUGUAY** Nestlé del Uruguay S.A. *Montevideo* 100% · **VENEZUELA** Nestlé Venezuela S.A. *Caracas* 100% · Chocolates Nestlé S.A. *Caracas* 100% · Caramelos Royal C.A. *Barquisimeto* 100%.

Asia

SAUDI ARABIA Saudi Food Industries Co. Ltd *Jeddah* 51% · **BANGLADESH** Nestlé Bangladesh Ltd *Dhaka* 60% · **UNITED ARAB EMIRATES** Nestlé Ice Cream L.L.C. *Dubai* 49% · **HONG KONG** Nestlé China Ltd *Hong Kong* 100% · Nestlé Dairy Farm Ltd *Hong Kong* 51% · **INDIA** Nestlé India Ltd *New Delhi* 51% · **INDONESIA** P.T. Nestlé Indonesia *Jakarta* 57.6% · P.T. Indofood Jaya Raya *Jakarta* 70% · P.T. Nestlé Confectionery Indonesia *Jakarta* 100% · P.T. Nestlé Asean

(Indonesia) *Jakarta* 60% · P.T. Supmi Sakti *Jakarta* 95% · **ISRAEL** OSEM Investments Ltd *Petach-Tikva* 39.7% · **JAPAN** Nestlé Japan Ltd *Kobe* 100% · Nestlé-Mackintosh K.K. *Tokyo* 66% · Perrier Japon K.K. *Tokyo* 100% · Alcon Japan Ltd* *Tokyo* 100% · **JORDANIA** Nestlé Jordan Trading Co. Ltd *Amman* 49% · **KUWAIT** Nestlé Kuwait General Trading Co. W.L.L. *Kuwait* 49% · **LEBANON** Société pour l'Exportation des Produits Nestlé S.A. *Beyrouth* 100% · **MALAYSIA** Nestlé (Malaysia) Sdn. Bhd. *Petaling Jaya* 51% · Malaysia Cocoa Manufacturing Sdn. Bhd. *Petaling Jaya* 49% · Nestlé Asean (Malaysia) Sdn. Bhd. *Petaling Jaya* 60% · Nestlé Cold Storage (Malaysia) Sdn. Bhd. *Petaling Jaya* 51% · **PAKISTAN** Milkpak Ltd *Lahore* 56.2% · **PHILIPPINES** Nestlé Philippines, Inc. *Cabuyao* 55% · **REPUBLIC OF KOREA** Nestlé Korea Ltd *Cheongju* 100% · **PEOPLE'S REPUBLIC OF CHINA** Nestlé Shuangcheng Ltd *Shuangcheng* 90% · Nestlé Dongguan Ltd *Dongguan* 95% · Maggi Dongguan Ltd *Dongguan* 95% · Nestlé Tianjin Ltd *Tianjin* 100% · Nestlé Qingdao Ltd *Qingdao* 100% · Nestlé Shanghai Ltd *Shanghai* 60% · Nestlé Dairy Farm Tianjin Ltd *Tianjin* 38.25% · Nestlé Dairy Farm Qingdao Ltd *Qingdao* 51% · **SINGAPORE** Nestlé Singapore (Pte) Ltd *Singapore* 100% · Nestlé Asean Singapore (Pte) Ltd *Singapore* 60% · **SRI LANKA** Nestlé Lanka Ltd *Colombo* 90.8% · **TAIWAN** Nestlé Taiwan Ltd *Taipei* 100% · Nestlé Distributors Ltd *Taipei* 100% · Foremost Foods (Taiwan) Ltd *Taipei* 100% · Alcon Pharmaceuticals Ltd* *Taipei* 100% · **THAILAND** Nestlé Products Thailand, Inc. *Bangkok* 100% · Nestlé Asean (Thailand) Ltd *Bangkok* 60% · Quality Coffee Products Ltd *Bangkok* 49% · Nestlé Foods (Thailand) Ltd *Bangkok* 100% · Nestlé Trading (Thailand) Ltd *Bangkok* 49% · Nestlé Manufacturing (Thailand) Ltd *Bangkok* 100% · Nestlé Dairy Farm (Thailand) Ltd *Bangkok* 46.3% · **VIETNAM** Nestlé Vietnam Ltd *Bien Hoa* 100% · Long An Mineral Water Joint Venture Company *Tan An* 33.2%

Oceania

AUSTRALIA Nestlé Australia Ltd *Sydney* 100% · Nestlé Confectionery Ltd *Sydney* 100% · Petersville Australia Ltd *Melbourne* 100% · Nestlé Echuca Pty Ltd *Melbourne* 100% · Alcon Laboratories (Australia) Pty Ltd* *French Forests (NSW)* 100% · **FIJI** Nestlé (Fiji) Ltd *Ba* 67% · **NEW CALEDONIA** Nestlé Nouvelle-Calédonie S.A. *Nouméa* 100% · **NEW ZEALAND** Nestlé New Zealand Ltd *Auckland* 100% · **PAPUA-NEW GUINEA** Nestlé (PNG) Ltd *Lae* 100% · **FRENCH POLYNESIA** Nestlé Polynesia S.A. *Papeete* 100%.

2. Affiliated companies for which the method of proportionate consolidation is used (see page 49, "Scope of consolidation").

Europe

GERMANY C.P.D. Cereal Partners Deutschland GmbH & Co. OHG *Frankfurt* 50% · **SPAIN** Cereal Partners España AEIE *Esplugas de Llobregat* 50% · **FRANCE** Cereal Partners France *Noisiel* 50% · Laboratoires Galderma S.A.* *Levallois-Perret* 50% · **POLAND** Torun

Pacific Sp. z.o.o. *Torun* 50% · **PORTUGAL** Cereal Associados Portugal AEIE *Oeiras* 50% · **CZECH REPUBLIC** Cokoladovny a.s. *Praha* 40.6% · **UNITED KINGDOM** Cereal Partners UK *Welwyn Garden City* 50% · **SWITZERLAND** CCNR Europe S.A. *Lausanne* 50%.

Africa

SOUTH AFRICA Dairymaid-Nestlé (Pty) Ltd *Johannesburg* 50%.

North and South America

BRAZIL Galderma Brasil Ltda* *São Paulo* 50% · **UNITED STATES** Coca-Cola Nestlé Refreshments Company, USA *Atlanta (Georgia)* 50% · Galderma Laboratories, Inc.* *Fort Worth (Texas)* 50% · **CHILE** CP Chile *Santiago de Chile* 50% · **MEXICO** CPW México S.A. de C.V. *México* 50%.

Asia

PHILIPPINES Magnolia Nestlé Corporation *Manila* 50% · **REPUBLIC OF KOREA** Coca-Cola Nestlé Refreshments Korea *Seoul* 50% · **TAIWAN** Coca-Cola Nestlé Refreshments Taiwan Ltd *Taipei* 50%.

Principal associated companies which operate in the food sector, with the exception of those marked with an asterisk which are engaged in the cosmetics and dermatology sectors.

(For which the equity method is used – see page 49, "Scope of consolidation").

Europa

GERMANY Mineralbrunnen Überkingen-Teinach AG *Bad Überkingen* 33% · **SPAIN** Various cosmetics companies* (% varies) · **FRANCE** L'Oréal S.A.* *Paris* 26.3% · Houdebine S.A. *Noyal-Pontivy* 50% · S.B.E.C.M. Société de Bouchages Emballages Conditionnement Moderne S.à.r.l. *Lavardac* 50% · **ITALY** San Pellegrino S.p.a. *Milano* 6%.

Asia

MALAYSIA Premier Milk (Malaysia) Sdn. Bhd. *Kuala Lumpur* 25% · **PEOPLE'S REPUBLIC OF CHINA** Guangzhou Refrigerated Foods Ltd *Guangzhou* 22.4%.

Sub-holding, financial and property companies

FRANCE Nestlé Entreprises S.A. *Noisiel* 100% · Nestlé Finance France S.A. *Noisiel* 100% · Perrier Vittel S.A. *Paris* 100% · Société Immobilière de Noisiel *Noisiel* 100% · **LUXEMBOURG** Compagnie Financière du Haut-Rhin *Luxembourg* 49% · **POLAND** Nestlé Polska Holding Sp.z.o.o. *Warszawa* 100% · **UNITED KINGDOM** Nestlé Holdings (U.K.) PLC *Croydon* 100% · **SWITZERLAND** Entreprises Maggi S.A. *Kempttal* 100% · Nestlé Finance S.A. *Cham* 100% · Rive-Reine S.A. *La Tour-de-Peilz* 100% · S.I. En Bergère Vevey S.A. *Vevey* 100% · **BAHAMAS** Nestlé's Holdings Ltd *Nassau* 100% · Food Products (Holdings) Ltd *Nassau* 100% · **UNITED STATES** Nestlé Holding, Inc. *Stamford (Connecticut)* 100% · Nestlé Capital Corporation *Stamford (Connecticut)* 100% · **PANAMA** Unilac, Inc. *Panama City* 100%.

Technical assistance, research and development companies

Nestec Ltd., Vevey (Switzerland)

Technical assistance company for Nestlé products whose units, specialised in all areas of the business, supply permanent support to companies in the Group within the framework of technical assistance contracts. It is also responsible for all scientific research and technological development, which it undertakes itself or has done on its behalf by affiliated companies. The units involved are:

Scientific research centre

SWITZERLAND Nestlé Research Center *Lausanne*

Technological development centres

GERMANY Nestlé R&D Center Lebensmittelforschung GmbH *Ludwigsburg* · *Weiding* · **SPAIN** Nestlé R&D Center S.A. *Badajoz* · **FRANCE** Nestlé R&D Centre *Beauvais* · *Lisieux* · Centre de Recherche Nestlé *Tours* · Centre R&D Friskies S.A. *Amiens* · **ITALY** Casa Buitoni S.r.l. *Sansepolcro* · **UNITED KINGDOM** Nestlé R&D Center *York* · **SWEDEN** Nestlé R&D Center A.B. *Bjuv* · **SWITZERLAND** Nestlé R&D Center *Broc* · *Kempttal* · *Konolfingen* · *Orbe* · **IVORY COAST** Centre R&D Nestlé *Abidjan* · **ECUADOR** Nestlé R&D Center S.A. *Quito* · **UNITED STATES** Nestlé R&D Center, Inc. *Connecticut* · *Ohio* · Friskies R&D Center *Missouri* · **MALAYSIA** Nestlé R&D Center Sdn. Bhd. *Petaling Jaya* · **SINGAPORE** Nestlé R&D Center (Pte) Ltd *Singapore*.

130th Annual report of Nestlé S.A.

Administration

At the General Meeting held on 30th May 1996, Mr. Helmut O. Maucher, Chairman of the Board and Chief Executive Officer expressed his gratitude to the two directors whose terms of office expired and who were not standing for re-election, namely Messrs. Bruno de Kalbermatten and Pierre Lalive. The Chairman of the Board also extended thanks to Mr. Walter Frehner, who resigned.

The Meeting then re-elected Mr. Helmut O. Maucher until the year 2000 and Messrs. Rainer E. Gut, Fritz Gerber and Jean-Pierre Meyers for a period of five years. In accordance with the proposals of the Board of Directors, Messrs. Georges Blum and Reto F. Domeniconi were elected as new directors at the Meeting. Finally, the Meeting renewed for three years the term of office of the auditors of the annual financial statements of Nestlé S.A. and the Group accounts, the firm KPMG Klynveld Peat Marwick Goerdeler SA.

At the General Meeting to be held on 5th June 1997, the terms of office of Mr. Fritz Leutwiler (Vice-Chairman), Mrs. Vreni Spoerry, Mrs. Lucia Santa Cruz Sutil and Mr. Robert Studer expire. In accordance with the Board's statutes on retirement age, Mr. F. Leutwiler will not stand for re-election. Furthermore, Mrs. L. Santa Cruz Sutil has decided not to stand for re-election. However, the other two directors whose terms of office expire, Mrs. V. Spoerry and Mr. R. Studer, may be re-elected for a further period of five years.

In addition, the Board of Directors proposes the election, as a new director, of Mr. Peter Brabeck-Letmathe, who has been a General Manager of Nestlé S.A. since 1st January 1992. If Mr. P. Brabeck-Letmathe is elected, the Board of Directors will appoint him Chief Executive Officer. Mr. H. O. Maucher will continue as Chairman.

In September 1996, Nestlé mourned the death of Mr. Ramón Masip, President and Chief Operating Officer – Food since 1st January 1993. His direct responsibilities have been allocated between several General Managers (see page 4 of the Management Report).

On 31st May 1996, Mr. Mario A. Corti, who was appointed General Manager by the Board, assumed the duties of Mr. Reto F. Domeniconi who was elected to the Board of Directors.

On 31st October 1996, Mr. Felix R. Braun, who was appointed as General Manager in 1993, retired. The Latin American zone of which he was in charge has been merged with the North American zone under the responsibility of Mr. Carlos E. Represas, who will henceforth head the zone comprising the Americas as a whole. In this respect, we should also note the regrouping under Mr. Michael W. O. Garrett of Africa and the Middle East, in addition to Asia and Oceania.

This new tripartite structure for zone general management (Europe; Americas; Asia, Oceania, Africa and the Middle East) is a fitting response to the challenges posed by the increasing globalisation of the world economy.

During the year 1996, and also at 31st December 1996, no director had a personal interest in any transaction significant to the business of the Group.

Income statement for the year 1996

In millions of Swiss francs	Notes	1996	1995
Income			
Income from Group companies	1	**2 032**	2 135
Interest income	2	**591**	54
Profit on disposal of fixed assets	3	**66**	35
Other income		**27**	44
Total income		**2 716**	2 268
Expenses			
Investment write downs	4	**1 152**	706
Administration and other expenses	5	**114**	107
Interest expense	6	**22**	241
Provision for uninsured risks		**15**	15
Total expenses before taxation		**1 303**	1 069
Profit before taxation		**1 413**	1 199
Taxation	7	**165**	100
Profit for the year	19	**1 248**	1 099

The appropriation of profit proposed by the Board is set out on page 85.

Balance sheet at 31st December 1996

before appropriations

In millions of Swiss francs	Notes	1996	1995
ASSETS			
Current assets			
Liquid assets	8	**1 613**	1 445
Debtors	9	**1 538**	1 593
Prepayments and accrued income		**31**	20
Total current assets		**3 182**	3 058
Fixed assets			
Financial assets	10	**11 518**	11 498
Intangible assets	13	**—**	—
Tangible fixed assets	14	**—**	—
Total fixed assets		**11 518**	11 498
Total assets		**14 700**	14 556
LIABILITIES AND SHAREHOLDERS' FUNDS			
Liabilities			
Short term creditors	15	**88**	34
Accrued liabilities and deferred income		**44**	5
Long term creditors	16	**262**	516
Provisions	17	**721**	621
Total liabilities		**1 115**	1 176
Shareholders' funds			
Share capital	18/19	**404**	404
Legal reserves	19	**6 392**	6 392
Special reserve	19	**5 537**	5 480
Retained earnings	19	**1 252**	1 104
Total shareholders' funds	19	**13 585**	13 380
Total liabilities and shareholders' funds		**14 700**	14 556

Annex to the annual accounts of Nestlé S.A.

Accounting policies

General

Nestlé S.A. (the Company) is the ultimate holding company of the Nestlé Group which comprises subsidiaries, associated companies and joint ventures throughout the world. The accounts are prepared in accordance with accounting principles required by Swiss law. They are also prepared under the historical cost convention and on the accruals basis. There have been no changes in accounting policies during the year.

Foreign currency translation

Transactions in foreign currencies are recorded at the rate of exchange at the date of the transaction or, if hedged forward, at the rate of exchange under the related forward contract. Assets and liabilities in foreign currencies are translated at year end rates. Any resulting exchange differences are included in the respective income statement captions depending upon the nature of the underlying transactions. The aggregate unrealised exchange difference is calculated by reference to original transaction date exchange rates and includes hedging transactions. Where this gives rise to a net loss, it is charged to the income statement whilst a net gain is deferred.

Hedging

The Company uses forward foreign exchange contracts, options, financial futures and currency swaps to hedge foreign currency flows and positions. Unrealised foreign exchange differences on hedging instruments are matched and accounted for with those on the underlying asset or liability. Long term loans, in foreign currencies, used to finance investments in participations are generally not hedged.

The Company also uses interest rate swaps to manage interest rate risk. The swaps are accounted for at fair value at each balance sheet date and changes in the market value are recorded in the income statement.

Income statement

Income due at the balance sheet date, but not currently transferable is recognised only upon receipt. Dividends paid out of pre-acquisition profits are not included under income from Group companies; instead they are credited against the carrying value of the participation, with any remaining balance credited to reserves.

In accordance with Swiss law and the Company's articles of association, dividends are treated as an appropriation of profit in the year in which they are ratified at the Annual General Meeting and subsequently paid, rather than as an appropriation of profit in the year to which they relate.

Taxation

This caption includes taxes on profit, capital and withholding taxes on transfers from Group companies.

Financial assets

The carrying value of participations and loans comprises the cost of investment, excluding the incidental costs of acquisition, less any write downs.

Participations located in countries where the political, economic or monetary situation might be considered to carry a greater than normal level of risk are carried at a nominal value of one franc.

Participations and loans are written down on a conservative basis, taking into account the profitability of the company concerned.

Marketable securities are valued at the lower of cost and market value.

Intangible assets

Trademarks and other industrial property rights are written off on acquisition or exceptionally over a longer period. In the Group accounts this item has a different treatment (see page 51).

Tangible fixed assets

The Company owns land and buildings which have been depreciated in the past to one franc. Office furniture and equipment is fully depreciated on acquisition.

Provisions

Provisions recognise contingencies which may arise and which have been prudently provided. A provision for uninsured risks is constituted on a Group-wide basis to cover general risks not insured with third parties, such as consequential loss. Provision for Swiss taxes is made on the basis of the Company's taxable capital, reserves and profit for the year. A general provision is maintained to cover possible foreign taxation liabilities.

Pensions

Employees are eligible for retirement benefits under a defined benefit plan provided through separate funds.

For the defined benefit plan the amount charged to the income statement consists of current service cost which includes the normal cost of financing benefits in respect of future years of service. If the case arises, variations from the current service cost are spread over the expected working lives of employees or recognised immediately in the case of retirees.

Liabilities arising under the defined benefit scheme are externally funded, with the assets of the scheme held separately from the Company in independently administered funds.

Prepayments and accrued income

Prepayments and accrued income comprise payments made in advance relating to the following year, and income relating to the current year which will not be received until after the balance sheet date (such as interest receivable on loans or deposits). Revaluation gains on open forward exchange contracts at year end rates are also included in this caption.

Accrued liabilities and deferred income

Accruals and deferred income comprise expenses relating to the current year which will not be paid until after the balance sheet date and income received in advance, relating to the following year. Revaluation losses on open forward exchange contracts at year end rates are also included in this caption.

Notes to the annual accounts

1. Income from Group companies
This represents dividends for the current and prior years and other net income from Group companies.

2. Interest income

In millions of Swiss francs	1996	1995
Net result on loans to Group companies	557	—
Other	34	54
	591	54

The significant improvement in interest income results mainly from the strengthening of most foreign currencies against the Swiss Franc and its impact on the net result on loans to Group companies. Last year, the opposite situation led to substantial unrealised exchange losses and the net charge was included under "Interest expense" (see note 6). Interest income from deposits with Swiss banks was affected by the general decrease in interest rates.

3. Profit on disposal of fixed assets
This represents mainly the net gain of Fr. 66 million (1995: Fr. 35 million) recorded on the sale of some trademarks and other industrial property rights previously written down, as well as minor participations.

4. Investment write downs

In millions of Swiss francs	1996	1995
Participations and loans	1 056	163
Trademarks and other industrial property rights	96	543
	1 152	706

The write downs of participations and loans in 1996 derive from the conservative policy of valuation, based on the political, economic and monetary situation of the countries where the participations are located, as well as on the profitability situation of the companies concerned.

5. Administration and other expenses

In millions of Swiss francs	1996	1995
Salaries and welfare expenses	65	57
Other expenses	49	50
	114	107

6. Interest expense

In millions of Swiss francs	1996	1995
Net result on loans to Group companies (see note 2)	—	203
Interest on long term debentures	20	15
Other interest	2	23
	22	241

7. Taxation

The increase of the tax charge as compared with 1995 results mainly from withholding taxes on income from foreign sources. An adequate provision has been set up to cover Swiss taxes. Last year there was no taxation charge relating to Swiss corporation tax as the Company had sufficiently provided in previous years.

8. Liquid assets

In millions of Swiss francs	1996	1995
Cash	33	132
Short term deposits with Swiss banks	1 580	1 313
	1 613	1 445

9. Debtors

In millions of Swiss francs	1996	1995
Amounts owed by Group companies		
Short term treasury loans	1 262	1 181
Current accounts	230	210
Provision for accounts not currently transferable	—	—
	1 492	1 391
Other debtors (including withholding tax)	46	202
	1 538	1 593

Short term treasury loans are advanced to Group companies with the intention of investing liquid funds at competitive rates, thus replacing external borrowings. The amount owed to the Company in respect of withholding tax was received after the year end.

10. Financial assets

In millions of Swiss francs	1996	1995
Participations in Group companies (see note 11)	**7 869**	7 724
Finance loans to Group companies (see note 12)	**3 497**	3 655
Own shares	**111**	—
Other investments	**41**	119
	11 518	11 498

Own shares of the Company have been acquired in order to allow the exercise of option rights by members of the Group's Management (77 654 options were outstanding at the close of 1996, of which 55 589 may be exercised from 1st January 1997 and the balance in later years).

11. Participations in Group companies

In millions of Swiss francs	1996	1995
At 1st January	**7 724**	6 716
Increase	**989**	1 164
Write downs	**(844)**	(156)
At 31st December	**7 869**	7 724

The increase in participations represents in particular:
—   additional funding, through capital increases, of a number of Group companies mainly in France, Poland, China, Korea and Russia;
—   acquisition of participations in various companies, mainly in Israel (Osem).
The carrying value of participations continues to represent a conservative valuation having regard to both the income received by the Company and the net assets of the Group companies concerned.
A list of the most important companies held, either directly by Nestlé S.A. or indirectly through other Group companies, with the percentage of the capital controlled, is given on pages 70 to 72 in the section "Group accounts".
A Canadian affiliate has been granted options to purchase shares in certain Group companies situated outside Continental Europe.

12. Finance loans to Group companies

In millions of Swiss francs	1996	1995
At 1st January	**3 655**	3 455
New loans	**235**	850
Repayments and write downs	**(953)**	(257)
Realised exchange differences	**19**	(70)
Unrealised exchange differences	**541**	(323)
At 31st December	**3 497**	3 655

Finance loans are usually for the long term and finance investments in participations.

13. Intangible assets
All intangible assets have been fully written off.

14. Tangible fixed assets
These are principally the land and buildings at Cham and at La Tour-de-Peilz. Nestlé Suisse S.A., the principal operating company in the Swiss market, is the tenant of the building at La Tour-de-Peilz. The En Bergère head office building in Vevey is held by a property company, which is wholly owned by Nestlé S.A.

The fire insurance value of buildings, furniture and office equipment amounted to Fr. 22 million at 31st December 1996 and 1995.

15. Short term creditors

In millions of Swiss francs	1996	1995
Amounts owed to Group companies	59	5
Other creditors	29	29
	88	34

16. Long term creditors

In millions of Swiss francs	1996	1995
Amounts owed to Group companies	234	488
Other creditors	28	28
	262	516

Amounts owed to Group companies represent a long term bond issued in 1989, whose carrying value increased by Fr. 46 million to Fr. 234 million as a result of an unrealised exchange loss arising in 1996. The 1995 deposit of Fr. 300 million from a subsidiary company has been repaid during the year.

17. Provisions

In millions of Swiss francs	1996	1995
Provision for uninsured risks	430	415
Provision for exchange risks	197	—
Provision for Swiss and foreign taxes	64	103
Provision for pensions covering additional benefits for employees in other Group companies	—	79
Other provisions	30	24
	721	621

The provision for exchange risks includes the unrealised net exchange gains on the revaluation of foreign exchange positions and any associated forward cover at year end.

Since liabilities related to additional benefits for employees in other Group companies have been taken over by a separate fund, the amount of Fr. 79 million provided for at the end of 1995 has actually been paid to this fund during the year.

18. Share capital	1996	1995
Number of registered shares of nominal value Fr. 10.– each	40 352 000	40 352 000
In millions of Swiss francs	404	404

According to article 6 of the Company's articles of association, no natural person or legal entity can be registered as a shareholder with voting rights for shares held directly or indirectly for more than 3% of the share capital. In addition, article 14 provides that, on exercising the voting rights, no shareholder, through shares owned or represented, may aggregate, directly or indirectly, more than 3% of the total share capital.

At 31st December 1996, the Share Register showed 146 204 registered shareholders. If unprocessed applications for registration and the indirect holders of shares under American depository receipts are also taken into account, the total number of shareholders probably exceeds 200 000. The Company was not aware of any shareholder holding, directly or indirectly, 3% or more of the share capital.

Conditional increase in share capital

According to the articles of association, the share capital can be increased, by the exercise of conversion or option rights, by a maximum of Fr. 10 000 000 through the issue of a maximum of 1 000 000 registered shares with a nominal value of Fr. 10.– each, fully paid-up. Thus the Board of Directors has at its disposal a flexible instrument enabling it, if necessary, to finance the activities of the Company through convertible or option loans.

19. Movements in shareholders' funds

In millions of Swiss francs	Share capital	General reserve [a]	Reserve for own shares [a] [b]	Special reserve	Retained earnings	Total
At 1st January 1996	404	6 235	157	5 480	1 104	**13 380**
Appropriation of profit to special reserve				55	(55)	
Profit for the year					1 248	**1 248**
Dividend for 1995					(1 043)	**(1 043)**
Own shares acquired/sold		(111)	111			
Dividend on own shares acquired before payment date of 1995 dividend				2	(2)	
At 31st December 1996	404	6 124	268	5 537	1 252	**13 585**

[a] The general reserve and the reserve for own shares constitute the legal reserves.
[b] See note 20.

20. Reserve for own shares

At 31st December 1995, the reserve for own shares amounted to Fr. 157.1 million, representing the acquisition value of 929 313 shares issued by Nestlé S.A. and acquired by a Group company. During 1996, 373 shares in respect of which corresponding option rights were not exercised at their expiry date in 1995 have been sold on the market. At 31st December 1996, the Group company held 928 940 shares (at an acquisition cost of Fr. 156.7 million). These shares are available to be used in any way which, in the opinion of the Board of Directors, would be in the best interests of the Company and its shareholders. As long as these shares are held by the Group company, they will be recorded in the Share Register as being without voting rights and will not rank for dividends.

Moreover, during 1996, the Company has acquired, at a cost of Fr. 111.2 million, a total of 92 668 shares reserved to cover option rights in favour of members of the Group's Management. 275 options having been exercised during the year 1996, a total of 92 393 shares were held at balance sheet date. As long as the options are not exercised, these shares are also recorded in the Share Register as being without voting rights and do not rank for dividends.

The total of 1 021 333 own shares held at 31st December 1996 represents 2.5% of Nestlé S.A. share capital.

21. Contingencies

At 31st December 1996 and 1995, the total of the guarantees for credit facilities granted to Group companies, together with the buy-back agreements relating to notes issued, amounted to Fr. 2976 million and Fr. 3820 million, respectively.

Proposed appropriation of profit

In Swiss francs	1996	1995
Retained earnings		
Balance brought forward	**4 674 108**	4 967 764
Profit for the year	**1 247 622 632**	1 099 407 549
	1 252 296 740	1 104 375 313
We propose the following appropriations:		
Allocation to the special reserve	**70 000 000**	55 000 000
Dividend for 1996, Fr. 30.– per share on 39 330 667 shares (1995: Fr. 26.50 on 39 422 687 shares)	**1 179 920 010**	1 044 701 205
Dividend for 1996, Fr. 30.– per share on 55 589 shares reserved for the option rights which may be exercised as from 1st January 1997 [a]	**1 667 670**	—
	1 251 587 680	1 099 701 205
Balance to be carried forward	**709 060**	4 674 108

[a] The dividends on those shares for which the option rights will not have been exercised by the date of the dividend payment will be transferred to the special reserve.

If you accept this proposal, the gross dividend will amount to Fr. 30.– per share. After deduction of the federal withholding tax of 35%, a net amount of Fr. 19.50 will be payable as from Wednesday, 11th June 1997 by bank transfer to the shareholder's account or by cheque, in accordance with the instructions received from the shareholder.

Cham and Vevey, 26th March 1997
The Board of Directors

Report of the statutory auditors
to the General Meeting of Nestlé S.A.

As statutory auditors, we have audited the accounting records and the financial statements (balance sheet, income statement and annex) of Nestlé S.A. on pages 75 to 84 for the year ended 31st December 1996.

These financial statements are the responsibility of the Board of Directors. Our responsibility is to express an opinion on these financial statements based on our audit. We confirm that we meet the legal requirements concerning professional qualification and independence.

Our audit was conducted in accordance with auditing standards promulgated by the profession, which require that an audit be planned and performed to obtain reasonable assurance about whether the financial statements are free from material misstatement. We have examined on a test basis evidence supporting the amounts and disclosures in the financial statements. We have also assessed the accounting principles used, significant estimates made and the overall financial statement presentation. We believe that our audit provides a reasonable basis for our opinion.

In our opinion, the accounting records, financial statements and the proposed appropriation of retained earnings comply with the law and the company's articles of incorporation.

We recommend that the financial statements submitted to you be approved.

KPMG Klynveld Peat Marwick Goerdeler SA

W.M. Tannett   B.A. Mathers
Chartered accountant   Chartered accountant
                     Auditors in charge
London   Zurich

26th March 1997

**130th Ordinary General Meeting
of the Nestlé S.A.**

Thursday 5th June 1997,
at 3.00 p.m. at the "Palais de Beaulieu", Lausanne

Agenda

1a Annual report, annual financial statements 1996
of the Company and report of the auditors
1b Consolidated financial statements 1996 of the Group
and report of the Group auditors

2 Release of the Board of Directors and of the Management

3 Decision on the appropriation of profits resulting from the
balance sheet of the Company

4 Elections to the Board of Directors:
Vreni Spoerry (terms of office for 5 years)
Robert Studer (terms of office for 5 years)
Peter Brabeck-Letmathe (terms of office for 5 years)

Next Ordinary General Meeting:
Thursday 28th May 1998 at the "Palais de Beaulieu", Lausanne

Important dates:

11th June 1997	Payment of the dividend
September 1997	Publication of the half-yearly report January/June 1997
18th November 1997	Autumn meeting with the press (Vevey)
January 1998	Announcement of 1997 sales figures
26th March 1998	Announcement of 1997 results
29th April 1998	Press conference (Zurich)
28th May 1998	131st Ordinary General Meeting, "Palais de Beaulieu", Lausanne

Stock exchange listings

Switzerland:	Swiss Exchange
Abroad:	Amsterdam, Brussels, Frankfurt, London, Paris, Tokyo, Vienna

Registered Offices:

Nestlé S.A.
Avenue Nestlé 55
CH-1800 Vevey (Switzerland)
Telephone (021) 924 21 11

Nestlé S.A.
(Share Transfer Office)
Zugerstrasse 8
CH-6330 Cham (Switzerland)
Telephone (041) 780 20 22

For any additional information about the management report, please contact Nestlé S.A., Investor Relations, Avenue Nestlé 55, CH-1800 Vevey (Switzerland), telephone (021) 924 28 42, telefax (021) 924 28 13.

As to information concerning the share register (registrations, transfers, address changes, dividends, etc.), please contact Nestlé S.A., Share Transfer Office, Zugerstrasse 8, CH-6330 Cham (Switzerland), telephone (041) 780 20 22, telefax (041) 780 20 58.

© 1997, Nestlé S.A., Cham and Vevey (Switzerland)
Concept and design: Nestec Ltd., Vevey (Switzerland)
Printed by Genoud, Entreprise d'arts graphiques S.A., Le Mont-sur-Lausanne, Switzerland
CV 4240 GB   TGAOO-T-LG

Appendix B

GLOSSARY OF
INTERNATIONAL
ACCOUNTING TERMS

This glossary is based on the International Accounting Standards that are effective for financial statements covering periods beginning on or after 1 January 1997.

Referencing is by Standard number and paragraph number. References to IAS 12 are identified as the original or revised versions. References to the Framework for the Preparation and Presentation of Financial Statements are preceded by F. References set out below in brackets indicate minor variations in wording.

accounting policies   The specific principles, bases, conventions, rules and practices adopted by an enterprise in preparing and presenting financial statements.   8.6, (1.6)

accrual basis of accounting   The effects of transactions and other events are recognised when they occur (and not as cash or its equivalent is received or paid) and they are recorded in the accounting records and reported in the financial statements of the periods to which they relate.   F22

International Accounting Standards, Exposure Drafts, and other IASC documents are copyright of the International Accounting Standards Committee, 166 Fleet Street, London EC4A 2DY, United Kingdom. Telephone: +44 (171) 353-0565, Fax: +44 (171) 353-0562: E-mail: iasc@iasc.org.uk Internet: http://www.iasc.org.uk All rights reserved. No part of these publications may be translated, reprinted or reproduced or utilised in any form either in whole or in part or by any electronic, mechanical or other means, now known or hereafter invented, including photocopying and recording, or in any information storage and retrieval system, without the prior express permission of IASC in writing.

The various extracts from *International Accounting Standards 1997,* namely the "Glossary of International Accounting Terms", are reproduced in this textbook by Houghton Mifflin Company (USA) with permission from IASC. Copies of the complete original English language texts of IASC publications may be obtained direct from IASC.

accrued benefit valuation methods   Actuarial valuation methods that determine the cost of providing retirement benefits on the basis of services rendered by employees to the date of the actuarial valuation.   19.43

acquisition   A business combination in which one of the enterprises, the acquirer, obtains control over the net assets and operations of another enterprise, the acquiree, in exchange for the transfer of assets, incurrence of a liability or issue of equity.   22.9

actuarial present value of promised retirement benefits   The present value of the expected payments by a retirement benefit plan to existing and past employees, attributable to the service already rendered.   26.8, 19.41

asset   A resource controlled by an enterprise as a result of past events and from which future economic benefits are expected to flow to the enterprise.   F49(a)

associate   An enterprise in which an investor has significant influence and which is neither a subsidiary nor a joint venture of the investor.   28.3

bank   A financial institution one of whose principal activities is to take deposits and borrow with the objective of lending and investing and which is within the scope of banking or similar legislation.   30.2

basic earnings per share   The amount of net profit for the period that is attributable to ordinary shareholders divided by the weighted average number of ordinary shares outstanding during the period.   33.10

borrowing costs   Interest and other costs incurred by an enterprise in connection with the borrowing of funds.   23.4

business combination   The bringing together of separate enterprises into one economic entity as a result of one enterprise uniting with or obtaining control over the net assets and operations of another enterprise.   22.9

capital   Under a financial concept of capital, such as invested money or invested purchasing power, the net assets or equity of the enterprise. The financial concept of capital is adopted by most enterprises.
  Under a physical concept of capital, such as operating capability, the productive capacity of the enterprise based on, for example, units of output per day.   F102

capitalisation   Recognising a cost as part of the cost of an asset.   23.11

carrying amount   The amount at which an asset is included in the balance sheet after deducting any accumulated depreciation or amortisation thereon.   16.7

cash   Cash on hand and demand deposits.   7.6

cash equivalents   Short-term, highly liquid investments that are readily convertible to known amounts of cash and which are subject to an insignificant risk of changes in value.   7.6

cash flow risk   The risk that future cash flows associated with a monetary financial instrument will fluctuate in amount.   32.43(d)

cash flows   Inflows and outflows of cash and cash equivalents.   7.6

class of assets   Grouping of assets of a similar nature and use in an enterprise's operations.   16.37, (32.46)

closing rate   The spot exchange rate of two currencies at the balance   21.7
sheet date.

consolidated financial statements   The financial statements of a   27.6
group presented as those of a single enterprise.

construction contract   A contract specifically negotiated for the con-   11.3
struction of an asset or a combination of assets that are closely
interrelated or interdependent in terms of their design, technology
and function or their ultimate purpose or use.

contingency   A condition or situation, the ultimate outcome of   10.3
which, gain or loss, will be confirmed only on the occurrence, or
non-occurrence, of one or more uncertain future events.

contingent rental   A rental that is not fixed in amount but is based on   17.3
a factor other than just the passage of time (e.g. percentage of sales,
amount of usage, price indices, market rates of interest).

contract   An agreement between two or more parties that has clear   32.6
economic consequences that the parties have little, if any, discretion to avoid, usually because the agreement is enforceable at law.
Contracts may take a variety of forms and need not be in writing.

control   The power to govern the financial and operating policies of an   22.9, 27.6,
enterprise so as to obtain benefits from its activities.   28.3, (24.5,
31.2)

cost method   A method of accounting for investments whereby the   28.3
investment is recorded at cost. The income statement reflects
income from the investment only to the extent that the investor
receives distributions from accumulated net profits of the investee
arising subsequent to the date of acquisition.

cost of an item of property, plant and equipment or of an intan-   16.7, 16.16
gible asset   The amount of cash or cash equivalents paid or the
fair value of the other consideration given to acquire an asset at the
time of its acquisition or construction.

cost of an acquisition   The amount of cash or cash equivalents paid   22.22
or the fair value, at the date of exchange, of the other purchase consideration given by the acquirer in exchange for control over the
net assets of the other enterprise, plus any costs directly attributable to the acquisition.

cost of an asset acquired in exchange or part exchange for dissimilar   16.22
asset   The fair value of the asset received, which is equivalent to
the fair value of the consideration given adjusted by the amount of
any cash or cash equivalents received or paid.

cost of an asset acquired in exchange or part exchange for similar asset   16.23
The carrying amount of the asset given up. However, the fair value
of the asset received may provide evidence of an impairment in the
asset given up. Under these circumstances the asset given up is
written down and this written down value assigned to the new
asset.

cost of an investment   The cost includes acquisition charges such as   25.15,
brokerages, fees, duties and bank fees.   25.16
     If an investment is acquired, or partly acquired, by the issue of
shares or other securities, the acquisition cost is the fair value of the
securities issued and not their nominal or par value.

cost of conversion   Costs directly related to the units of production,   2.10
such as direct labour together with a systematic allocation of fixed
and variable production overheads that are incurred in converting
materials into finished goods.

cost of inventories   All costs of purchase, costs of conversion and   2.7
other costs incurred in bringing the inventories to their present
location and condition.

cost of purchase   All of the purchase price, import duties and other   2.8
taxes (other than those subsequently recoverable by the enterprise
from the taxing authorities), and transport, handling and other
costs directly attributable to the acquisition of the item. Trade discounts, rebates and other similar items are deducted in determining the costs of purchase.

cost plus contract   A construction contract in which the contractor is   11.3
reimbursed for allowable or otherwise defined costs, plus a percentage of these costs or a fixed fee.

cost plus method   A pricing method which seeks to add an appropriate   24.15
mark-up to the supplier's cost.

credit risk   The risk that one party to a financial instrument will fail   32.43(b)
to discharge an obligation and cause the other party to incur a
financial loss.

currency risk   A price risk—the risk that the value of a financial   32.43(a)(i)
instrument will fluctuate due to changes in foreign exchange rates

current assets   Assets that will be realised in the near future.   13.5, 13.13
Among the items included in current assets should be:

  (a) cash and bank balances available for current operations. Cash
or bank balances whose use for current operations is subject to
restrictions should be included as a current asset only if the
duration of the restrictions is limited to the term of an obligation that has been classified as a current liability or if the
restrictions lapse within one year;

  (b) securities not intended to be retained and capable of being
readily realised;

  (c) trade and other receivables expected to be realised within one
year of the balance sheet date. Trade receivables may be
included in their entirety in current assets, provided that the
amount not expected to be realised within one year is disclosed;

  (d) inventories;

  (e) advance payments on the purchase of current assets; and

  (f) expense prepayments expected to be used up within one year of
the balance sheet date.

current cost   The amount of cash or cash equivalents that would   F100(b)
have to be paid if the same or an equivalent asset was acquired
currently.
    The undiscounted amount of cash or cash equivalents that
would be required to settle an obligation currently.

current cost approach   In general, methods which use replacement   15.12
cost as the primary measurement basis. If, however, replacement
cost is higher than both net realisable value and present value, the
higher of net realisable value and present value is usually used as
the measurement basis.

current investment   An investment that is by its nature readily realisable and is intended to be held for not more than one year.   25.4

current liabilities   Liabilities that will be liquidated in the near future.   13.5, 13.15, 13.16
Among the items included in current liabilities should be obligations payable at the demand of the creditor and those parts of the following obligations whose liquidation is expected within one year of the balance sheet date:

(a) bank and other loans. If a loan is repayable in accordance with a schedule of repayment agreed with the creditor, the loan may be classified in accordance therewith, notwithstanding a right of the creditor to demand current payment;
(b) the current portion of long-term liabilities, unless the enterprise intends to refinance the obligation on a long-term basis and there is reasonable assurance that the enterprise will be able to do so;
(c) trade liabilities and accrued expenses;
(d) provision for taxes payable;
(e) dividends payable;
(f) deferred revenues and advances from customers; and
(g) accruals for contingencies.

current service cost   The cost to an enterprise under a retirement benefit plan for the services rendered in the current period by participating employees.   19.5

curtailment   Occurs either when there is a significant reduction in the number of employees covered by a retirement benefit plan or when an element of future service in respect of existing employees will no longer qualify for benefits.   19.34

date of acquisition   The date on which control of the net assets and operations of the acquirer is effectively transferred to the acquirer.   22.9

dealing securities   Marketable securities that are acquired and held with the intention of reselling them in the short term.   30.25

defined benefit plans   Retirement benefit plans under which amounts to be paid as retirement benefits are determined by reference to a formula usually based on employees' remuneration and/or years of service.   19.5, 26.8

defined contribution plans   Retirement benefit plans under which amounts to be paid as retirement benefits are determined by reference to contributions to a fund together with investment earnings thereon.   19.5, 26.8

depreciable amount   The cost of an asset, or other amount substituted for cost in the financial statements, less its residual value.   4.4, 16.7, E50.11

depreciable assets   Assets which: 4.4

(a) are expected to be used during more than one accounting period;
(b) have a limited useful life; and
(c) are held by an enterprise for use in the production or supply of goods and services, for rental to others, or for administrative purposes.

depreciation   The systematic allocation of the depreciable amount of an asset over its useful life.   4.4, 16.7

derivative financial instruments   Financial instruments, such as financial options, futures and forwards, interest rate swaps and currency swaps, which create rights and obligations that have the effect of transferring between the parties to the instrument one or more of the financial risks inherent in an underlying primary financial instrument. Derivative instruments do not result in a transfer of the underlying primary financial instrument on inception of the contract and such a transfer does not necessarily take place on maturity of the contract.   32.9, 32.10

development   The application of research findings or other knowledge to a plan or design for the production of new or substantially improved materials, devices, products, processes, systems or services prior to the commencement of commercial production or use.   9.6

development costs   All costs that are directly attributable to development activities or that can be allocated on a reasonable basis to such activities.   9.11

diluted earnings per share   The amount of net profit for the period that is attributable to ordinary shareholders divided by the weighted average number of ordinary shares outstanding during the period, both adjusted for the effects of all dilutive potential ordinary shares.   33.24

dilutive potential ordinary shares   Potential ordinary shares whose conversion to ordinary shares would decrease net profit per share from continuing ordinary operations or increase loss per share from continuing ordinary operations.   33.38

direct method of reporting cash flows from operating activities   A method which discloses major classes of gross cash receipts and gross cash payments.   7.18(a)

discontinuing operation   The sale or abandonment of an operation that represents a separate, major line of business of an enterprise and of which the assets, net profit or loss and activities can be distinguished physically, operationally and for financial reporting purposes.   8.6

dividends   Distributions of profits to holders of equity investments in proportion to their holdings of a particular class of capital.   18.5

equity   The residual interest in the assets of the enterprise after deducting all its liabilities.   F49(c)

equity instrument   Any contract that evidences a residual interest in the assets of an enterprise after deducting all of its liabilities.   32.5, 33.9

equity method   A method of accounting whereby the investment (an interest in a jointly controlled entity) is initially recorded at cost and adjusted thereafter for the post acquisition change in the investor's (the venturer's) share of net assets of the investee (the jointly controlled entity). The income statement reflects the investor's (the venturer's) share of the results of operations of the investee (the jointly controlled entity).   28.3, 31.2

events occurring after the balance sheet date   Those events, both favourable and unfavourable, that occur between the balance sheet date and the date on which the financial statements are authorised for issue. Two types of events can be identified: 10.3

(a) those that provide further evidence of conditions that existed at the balance sheet date; and

(b) those that are indicative of conditions that arose subsequent to the balance sheet date.

exchange difference   The difference resulting from reporting the same number of units of a foreign currency in the reporting currency at different exchange rates.   21.7

exchange rate   The ratio for exchange of two currencies.   21.7

expenses   Decreases in economic benefits during the accounting period in the form of outflows or depletions of assets or incurrences of liabilities that result in decreases in equity, other than those relating to distributions to equity participants.   F70(b)

experience adjustments   Adjustments arising from the differences between the previous actuarial assumptions as to future events and what has actually occurred.   19.5

extraordinary items   Income or expenses that arise from events or transactions that are clearly distinct from the ordinary activities of the enterprise and therefore are not expected to recur frequently or regularly.   8.6

fair value   The amount for which an asset could be exchanged, or a liability settled, between knowledgeable, willing parties in an arm's length transaction.   16.7, 17.3, 18.7, 20.3, 21.7, 22.9, 25.4, 32.5, 33.9, E50.11

FIFO (first-in, first-out)   The assumption that the items of inventory which were purchased first are sold first, and consequently the items remaining in inventory at the end of the period are those most recently purchased or produced.   2.22

finance lease   A lease that transfers substantially all the risks and rewards incident to ownership of an asset. Title may or may not eventually be transferred.   17.3

financial asset   Any asset that is: 32.5

(a) cash;

(b) a contractual right to receive cash or another financial asset from another enterprise;

(c) a contractual right to exchange financial instruments with another enterprise under conditions that are potentially favourable; or

(d) an equity instrument of another enterprise.

financial instrument   Any contract that gives rise to both a financial asset of one enterprise and a financial liability or equity instrument of another enterprise.   32.5, 33.9

financial liability   Any liability that is a contractual obligation: 32.5

(a) to deliver cash or another financial asset to another enterprise; or

(b) to exchange financial instruments with another enterprise under conditions that are potentially unfavourable.

financial position   The relationship of the assets, liabilities, and equities of an enterprise, as reported in the balance sheet.   F.47

financial statements   The term covers balance sheets, income statements or profit and loss accounts, cash flow statements, notes and other statements and explanatory material which are identified as being part of the financial statements.   1.2, (F7)

financing activities   Activities that result in changes in the size and composition of the equity capital and borrowings of the enterprise.   7.6

fixed price contract   A contract in which the contractor agrees to a fixed contract price, or a fixed rate per unit of output, which in some cases is subject to cost escalation clauses.   11.3

fixed production overheads   Those indirect costs of production that remain relatively constant regardless of the volume of production, such as depreciation and maintenance of factory buildings and equipment, and the cost of factory management and administration.   2.10

foreign currency   A currency other than the reporting currency of an enterprise.   21.7

foreign currency transaction   A transaction which is denominated in or requires settlement in a foreign currency.   21.8

foreign entity   A foreign operation, the activities of which are not an integral part of those of the reporting enterprise.   21.7

foreign operation   A subsidiary, associate, joint venture or branch of the reporting enterprise, the activities of which are based or conducted in a country other than the country of the reporting enterprise.   21.7

forgivable loans   Loans which the lender undertakes to waive repayment of under certain prescribed conditions.   20.3

fundamental errors   Errors discovered in the current period that are of such significance that the financial statements of one or more prior periods can no longer be considered to have been reliable at the date of their issue.   8.6

funding   The transfer of assets to an entity (the fund) separate from the enterprise to meet future obligations for the payment of retirement benefits.   19.5, 26.8

future economic benefit   The potential to contribute, directly or indirectly, to the flow of cash and cash equivalents to the enterprise. The potential may be a productive one that is part of the operating activities of the enterprise. It may also take the form of convertibility into cash or cash equivalents or a capability to reduce cash outflows, such as when an alternative manufacturing process lowers the costs of production.   F53

gains   Increases in economic benefits and as such are no different in nature from revenue.   F75

general purchasing power approach   The restatement of some or all of the items in the financial statements for changes in the general price level.   15.11

geographical segments   The distinguishable components of an enterprise engaged in operations in individual countries or groups of countries within particular geographical areas as may be determined to be appropriate in an enterprise's particular circumstances.   14.5

going concern   The enterprise is normally viewed as a going concern, that is, as continuing in operation for the foreseeable future. It is assumed that the enterprise has neither the intention nor the necessity of liquidation or of curtailing materially the scale of its operations. — 1.4(a), F.23

goodwill   Any excess of the cost of the acquisition over the acquirer's interest in the fair value of the identifiable assets and liabilities acquired as at the date of the exchange transaction. — 22.40

government   Government, government agencies and similar bodies whether local, national or international. — 20.3

government assistance   Action by government designed to provide an economic benefit specific to an enterprise or range of enterprises qualifying under certain criteria. — 20.3

government grants   Assistance by government in the form of transfers of resources to an enterprise in return for past or future compliance with certain conditions relating to the operating activities of the enterprise. They exclude those forms of government assistance which cannot reasonably have a value placed upon them and transactions with government which cannot be distinguished from the normal trading transactions of the enterprise. — 20.3

grants related to assets   Government grants whose primary condition is that an enterprise qualifying for them should purchase, construct or otherwise acquire long-term assets. Subsidiary conditions may also be attached restricting the type of location of the assets or the periods during which they are to be acquired or held. — 20.3

grants related to income   Government grants other than those related to assets. — 20.3

gross investment in the lease   The aggregate of the minimum lease payments under a finance lease from the standpoint of the lessor and any unguaranteed residual value accruing to the lessor. — 17.3

group   A parent and all its subsidiaries. — 27.6

historical cost   Assets are recorded at the amount of cash or cash equivalents paid or the fair value of the consideration given to acquire them at the time of their acquisition. Liabilities are recorded at the amount of proceeds received in exchange for the obligation, or in some circumstances (for example, income taxes), at the amounts of cash or cash equivalents expected to be paid to satisfy the liability in the normal course of business. — F100(a)

imputed rate of interest   The more clearly determinable of either: — 18.11

(a) the prevailing rate for a similar instrument of an issuer with a similar credit rating; or
(b) a rate of interest that discounts the nominal amount of the instrument to the current cash sales price of the goods or services.

inception of a lease   The earlier of the date of the lease agreement or of a commitment by the parties to the principal provisions of the lease. — 17.3

income   Increases in economic benefits during the accounting period in the form of inflows or enhancements of assets or decreases of liabilities that result in increases in equity, other than those relating to contributions from equity participants. — F70(a)

incremental borrowing rate of interest (lessee's) The rate of interest a   17.3
lessee would have to pay on a similar lease or, if that is not determinable, the rate that, at the inception of the lease, the lessee
would incur to borrow over a similar term, and with a similar
security, the funds necessary to purchase the asset.

indirect method of reporting cash flows from operating activities   7.18(b)
Under this method, net profit or loss is adjusted for the effects of
transactions of a non-cash nature, any deferrals or accruals of past
or future operating cash receipts or payments, and items of income
or expense associated with investing or financing cash flows.

industry segments The distinguishable components of an enterprise   14.5
each engaged in providing a different product or service, or a different group of related products or services, primarily to customers
outside the enterprise.

intercompany balances or transactions Balances or transactions   5.12(b)
between:

(a) a parent and its subsidiaries; and
(b) a subsidiary and its parent or other subsidiaries in the group.

interest rate implicit in a lease The discount rate that, at the incep-   17.3
tion of the lease, causes the aggregate present value of:

(a) the minimum lease payments, from the standpoint of the
lessor; and
(b) the unguaranteed residual value

to be equal to the fair value of the leased asset, net of any grants
and tax credits receivable by the lessor.

interest rate risk A price risk—the risk that the value of a financial   32.43(a)
instrument will fluctuate due to changes in market interest rates.   (ii)

inventories Assets: 2.4, 2.5

(a) held for sale in the ordinary course of business;
(b) in the process of production for such sale; or
(c) in the form of materials or supplies to be consumed in the production process or in the rendering of services.

Inventories encompass goods purchased and held for resale
including, for example, merchandise purchased by a retailer and
held for resale, or land and other property held for resale.
Inventories also encompass finished goods produced, or work in
progress being produced, by the enterprise and include materials
and supplies awaiting use in the production process. In the case of
a service provider, inventories include the costs of the service for
which the enterprise has not yet recognised the related revenue.

investing activities The acquisition and disposal of long-term assets   7.6
and other investments not included in cash equivalents.

investment An asset held by an enterprise for the accretion of wealth   25.4
through distribution (such as interest, royalties, dividends and
rentals), for capital appreciation or for other benefits to the
investing enterprise such as those obtained through trading relationships.

investment property An investment in land or buildings that are not   25.4
occupied substantially for use by, or in the operations of, the
investing enterprise or another enterprise in the same group as the
investing enterprise.

investment securities Securities acquired and held for yield or capital growth purposes, usually held to maturity. — 30.25

investor in a joint venture A party to a joint venture that does not have joint control over that joint venture. — 31.2

joint control The contractually agreed sharing of control over an economic activity. — 31.2

joint venture A contractual arrangement whereby two or more parties undertake an economic activity which is subject to joint control. — 31.2

jointly controlled entity A joint venture which involves the establishment of a corporation, partnership or other entity in which each venturer has an interest. The entity operates in the same way as other enterprises, except that a contractual arrangement between the venturers establishes joint control over the economic activity of the entity. — 31.19

lease An agreement whereby the lessor conveys to the lessee in return for rent the right to use an asset for an agreed period of time. — 17.3

lease term The non-cancellable period for which the lessee has contracted to lease the asset together with any further terms for which the lessee has the option to continue to lease the asset, with or without further payment, which option at the inception of the lease it is reasonably certain that the lessee will exercise. — 17.3

legal merger Usually a merger between two companies in which either: — 22.6

(a) the assets and liabilities of one company are transferred to the other company and the first company is dissolved; or

(b) the assets and liabilities of both companies are transferred to a new company and both the original companies are dissolved.

liability A present obligation of the enterprise arising from past events, the settlement of which is expected to result in an outflow from the enterprise of resources embodying economic benefits. — F49(b)

LIFO (last-in, last-out) The assumption that the items of inventory which were purchased or produced last are sold first, and consequently the items remaining in inventory at the end of the period are those first purchased or produced. — 2.24

liquidity The availability of sufficient funds to meet deposit withdrawals and other financial commitments as they fall due. — 30.7, (F16)

liquidity (enterprise's) The enterprise's ability to carry on its activities on a day to day basis without encountering financial stringencies. — 13.4

liquidity risk The risk that an enterprise will encounter difficulty in raising funds to meet commitments associated with financial instruments. Liquidity risk may result from an inability to sell a financial asset quickly at close to its fair value. — 32.43(c)

long-term investment An investment other than a current investment. — 25.4

losses Decreases in economic benefits and as such they are no different in nature from other expenses. — F79

market risk A price risk—the risk that the value of a financial instrument will fluctuate as a result of changes in market prices whether those changes are caused by factors specific to the individual security or its issuer or factors affecting all securities traded in the market. — 32.43(a) (iii)

market value   The amount obtainable from the sale, or payable on the   25.4, (32.5)
acquisition, of a (financial) instrument in an active market.

marketable   There is an active market from which a market value (or   25.4
some indicator that enables a market value to be calculated) is
available.

master netting arrangement   An arrangement providing for an enter-   32.41
prise that undertakes a number of financial instrument transactions with a single counterparty to make a single net settlement of
all financial instruments covered by the agreement in the event of
default on, or termination of, any one contract.

matching of costs with revenues   Expenses are recognised in the in-   F95
come statement on the basis of a direct association between the
costs incurred and the earning of specific items of income. This
process involves the simultaneous or combined recognition of revenues and expenses that result directly and jointly from the same
transactions or other events. However, the application of the
matching concept does not allow the recognition of items in the
balance sheet which do not meet the definition of assets or liabilities.

materiality   Information is material if its omission or misstatement   F30
could influence the economic decisions of users taken on the basis
of the financial statements.

measurement   The process of determining the monetary amounts at   F99
which the elements of the financial statements are to be recognised
and carried in the balance sheet and income statement.

minimum lease payments   The payments over the lease term that the   17.3
lessee is or can be required to make (excluding costs for services
and taxes to be paid by and be reimbursable to the lessor) together
with:

(a)   in the case of the lessee, any amounts guaranteed by the lessee
or by a party related to the lessee; or

(b)   in the case of the lessor, any residual value guaranteed to the
lessor by either:
(i)   the lessee;
(ii)   a party related to the lessee; or
(iii) an independent third party financially capable of meeting this guarantee.

However, if the lessee has the option to purchase the asset at a
price which is expected to be sufficiently lower than the fair value at
the date the option becomes exercisable that, at the inception of the
lease, it is reasonably certain that the option will be exercised, the
minimum lease payments comprise the minimum rentals payable
over the lease term and payment required to exercise this purchase
option.

minority interest   That part of the net results of operations and of net   22.9, 27.6
assets of a subsidiary attributable to interests which are not owned,
directly or indirectly through subsidiaries, by the parent.

monetary items (monetary financial assets and financial liabilities;   21.7, 29.12,
monetary financial instruments)   Money held and assets (finan-   (32.5)
cial assets) and liabilities (financial liabilities) to be received or
paid in fixed or determinable amounts of money.

negative goodwill   Any (remaining) excess, as at the date of the exchange transaction, of the acquirer's interest in the fair values of the identifiable assets and liabilities acquired over the cost of the acquisition.   (22.49), 22.51

net assets available for benefits   The assets of a plan less liabilities other than the actuarial present value of promised retirement benefits.   26.8

net cash investment   The balance of the cash outflows and inflows in respect of the lease excluding flows relating to insurance, maintenance and similar costs rechargeable to the lessee. The cash outflows include payments made to acquire the asset, tax payments, interest and principal on third party financing. Inflows include rental receipts, receipts from residual values, and grants, tax credits and other tax savings or repayments arising from the lease.   17.3

net current assets   The excess of current assets over current liabilities.   13.3

net investment in a foreign entity   The reporting enterprise's share in the net assets of that entity.   21.7

net investment in a lease   The gross investment in the lease less unearned finance income.   17.3

net profit or loss   Comprises the following components: 8.10

(a)   profit or loss from ordinary activities; and
(b)   extraordinary items.

net realisable value   The estimated selling price in the ordinary course of business less the estimated costs of completion and the estimated costs necessary to make the sale.   2.4, 15.13

neutrality   Freedom from bias of the information contained in financial statements.   F.36

non-cancellable lease   A lease that is cancellable only: 17.3

(a)   upon the occurrence of some remote contingency;
(b)   with the permission of the lessor;
(c)   if the lessee enters into a new lease for the same or an equivalent asset with the same lessor; or
(d)   upon payment by the lessee of an additional amount such that, at inception, continuation of the lease is reasonably certain.

normal capacity of production facilities   The production expected to be achieved on average over a number of periods or seasons under normal circumstances, taking into account the loss of capacity resulting from planned maintenance.   2.11

obligation   A duty or responsibility to act or perform in a certain way. Obligations may be legally enforceable as a consequence of a binding contract or statutory requirement. Obligations also arise, however, from normal business practice, custom and a desire to maintain good business relations or act in an equitable manner.   F60

offsetting   See **set-off, legal right of**

operating activities   The principal revenue-producing activities of an enterprise and other activities that are not investing or financing activities.   7.6

operating cycle   The average time between the acquisition of materials entering into the process and the final cash realisation.   13.5

operating lease   A lease other than a finance lease.   17.3

option   A financial instrument that gives the holder the right to pur-   33.6
chase ordinary shares.

ordinary activities   Any activities which are undertaken by an enter-   8.6
prise as part of its business and such related activities in which the
enterprise engages in furtherance of, incidental to, or arising from
these activities.

ordinary share   An equity instrument that is subordinate to all other   33.6
classes of equity instruments.

parent   An enterprise that has one or more subsidiaries.   22.9, 27.6

participants   The members of a retirement benefit plan and others   26.8
who are entitled to benefits under the plan.

past service cost   The cost to an enterprise under a retirement benefit   19.5
plan for services rendered in prior periods by participating
employees and resulting from:

(a) the introduction of a retirement benefit plan; or
(b) the making of amendments to such a plan.

percentage of completion method   A method by which contract re-   11.25
venue is matched with the contract costs incurred in reaching the
stage of completion, resulting in the reporting of revenue, expenses
and profit which can be attributed to the proportion of work completed.

performance   The relationship of the income and expenses of an   F.47
enterprise, as reported in the income statement.

potential ordinary share   A financial instrument or other contract   33.6
that may entitle its holder to ordinary shares.

present value   A current estimate of the present discounted value of   F100(d),
the future net cash flows in the normal course of business.   15.13

price risk   There are three types of price risk: currency risk, interest   32.43(a)
rate risk and market risk. The term "price risk" embodies not only
the potential for loss but also the potential for gain.

primary financial instruments   Financial instruments such as receiv-   32.9
ables, payables and equity securities, that are not derivative finan-
cial instruments.

profit   The residual amount that remains after expenses (including   F105, F107
capital maintenance adjustments, where appropriate) have been
deducted from income. Any amount over and above that required
to maintain the capital at the beginning of the period is profit.

projected benefit valuation methods   Actuarial valuation methods   19.45
that determine the cost of providing retirement benefits on the
basis of service both rendered and to be rendered by employees as
at the date of the actuarial valuation.

property, plant and equipment   Tangible assets that: 16.7

(a) are held by an enterprise for use in the production or supply of
goods or services, for rental to others, or for administrative
purposes; and
(b) are expected to be used during more than one period.

proportionate consolidation   A method of accounting and reporting whereby a venturer's share of each of the assets, liabilities, income and expenses of a jointly controlled entity is combined on a line-by-line basis with similar items in the venturer's financial statements or reported as separate line items in the venturer's financial statements.   31.2

prospective application   Application of a new accounting policy to the events and transactions occurring after the date of the change.   8.45

provision   A present obligation which satisfies the rest of the definition of a liability, even if the amount of the obligation has to be estimated.   F64

prudence   The inclusion of a degree of caution in the exercise of the judgements needed in making the estimates required under conditions of uncertainty, such that assets or income are not overstated and liabilities or expenses are not understated.   F37

realisable value   The amount of cash or cash equivalents that could currently be obtained by selling an asset in an orderly disposal.   F100(c)

recognition   The process of incorporating in the balance sheet or income statement an item that meets the definition of an element and satisfies the following criteria for recognition: F82, F83

    (a)   it is probable that any future economic benefit associated with the item will flow to or from the enterprise; and

    (b)   the item has a cost or value that can be measured with reliability.

recoverable amount   The amount which an enterprise expects to recover from the future use of an asset, including its residual value on disposal.   16.7

related parties   Parties are considered to be related if one party has the ability to control the other party or exercise significant influence over the other party in making financial and operating decisions.   24.5

related party transaction   A transfer of resources or obligations between related parties, regardless of whether a price is charged.   24.5

relevance   Information has the quality of relevance when it influences the economic decisions of users by helping them evaluate past, present or future events or confirming, or correcting, their past evaluations.   F26

reliability   Information has the quality of reliability when it is free from material error and bias and can be depended upon by users to represent faithfully that which it either purports to represent or could reasonably be expected to represent.   F31

replacement cost of an asset   Normally derived from the current acquisition cost of a similar asset, new or used, or of an equivalent productive capacity or service potential.   15.13

reporting currency   The currency used in presenting the financial statements.   21.7

reporting enterprise   An enterprise for which there are users who rely on the financial statements as their major source of financial information about the enterprise.   F8

research   Original and planned investigation undertaken with the   9.6
prospect of gaining new scientific or technical knowledge and
understanding.

residual value   The net amount which an enterprise expects to obtain   16.7
for an asset at the end of its useful life after deducting the expected
costs of disposal.

retirement benefit plans   Arrangements whereby an enterprise pro-   19.5, 26.8
vides benefits for its employees on or after termination of service
(either in the form of an annual income or as a lump sum) when
such benefits, or the employer's contributions towards them, can
be determined or estimated in advance of retirement from the provisions of a document or from the enterprise's practices.

retrospective application   Application of a new accounting policy to   8.45
events and transactions as if the new accounting policy had always
been in use.

revaluation   Restatement of assets and liabilities.   F81

revalued amount of an asset   The fair value of an asset at the date of   16.30
a revaluation less any subsequent accumulated depreciation.

revenue   The gross inflow of economic benefits during the period   18.7
arising in the course of the ordinary activities of an enterprise
when those inflows result in increases in equity, other than
increases relating to contributions from equity participants.

reverse acquisition   An acquisition when an enterprise obtains own-   22.13
ership of the shares of another enterprise but as part of the
exchange transaction issues enough voting shares, as consideration, such that control of the combined enterprise passes to the
owners of the enterprise whose shares have been acquired.

rewards associated with a leased asset   The expectation of profitable   17.5
operation over the asset's economic life and of gain from appreciation in value or realisation of a residual value.

risks associated with a leased asset   Possibilities of losses from idle ca-   17.5
pacity or technological obsolescence and of variations in return
due to changing economic conditions.

sale and leaseback transaction   The sale of an asset by the vendor and   17.56
the leasing of the same asset back to the vendor. The rentals and
the sale price are usually interdependent as they are negotiated as a
package and need not represent fair values.

segment assets   All tangible and intangible assets that can be identi-   14.19
fied with a particular segment. Assets shared by two or more segments may be allocated between or among those segments if a
reasonable basis exists for such allocation.

segment expense   Expense that is directly attributable to a segment or   14.5
the relevant portion of an expense that can be allocated on a reasonable basis to the segments.

segment result   The difference between segment revenue and segment   14.17
expense. This generally reflects operating profit, although other
bases are sometimes found to be more appropriate. Interest
income and interest expense are not normally included in segment
result unless the segment's operations are primarily of a financial
nature. Also taxes on income, minority interest and extraordinary
items are not usually included in segment result.

segment revenue   Revenue that is directly attributable to a segment, or the relevant portion of revenue that can be allocated on a reasonable basis to a segment, and that is derived from transactions with parties outside the enterprise and from other segments of the same enterprise.   14.5

set-off, legal right of   A debtor's legal right, by contract or otherwise, to settle or otherwise eliminate all or a portion of an amount due to a creditor by applying against that amount an amount due from the creditor.   32.36

settlement   Occurs when an enterprise discharges its retirement benefit obligation.   19.36

settlement value   The undiscounted amounts of cash or cash equivalents expected to be paid to satisfy the liabilities in the normal course of business.   F100(c)

shares outstanding   Shares other than those held as "treasury stock".   5.17(a)

significant influence   The power to participate in the financial and operating policy decisions of an economic activity but is not control or joint control over those policies.   28.3, 31.2, (24.5)

solvency   The availability of cash over the longer term to meet financial commitments as they fall due.   F16

subsidiary   An enterprise that is controlled by another enterprise (known as the parent).   22.9, 27.6, 28.3

substance over form   The principle that transactions and other events are accounted for and presented in accordance with their substance and economic reality and not merely their legal form.   F35, 1.7(b)

treasury stock   A company's shares which have been acquired by the issuing company or a consolidated subsidiary company and are legally available for reissue or resale.   5.17(a)

understandability   Information provided in financial statements has the quality of understandability when [it] is comprehensible to users who have a reasonable knowledge of business and economic activities and accounting and a willingness to study the information with reasonable diligence.   F.25

unearned finance income   The difference between the lessor's gross investment in the lease and its present value.   17.3

unfunded benefit plan   A retirement benefit plan where the enterprise retains the obligation for the payment of retirement benefits under the plan without the establishment of a separate fund.   19.9

unguaranteed residual value   That portion of the residual value of the leased asset (estimated at the inception of the lease), the realisation of which by the lessor is not assured or is guaranteed solely by a party related to the lessor.   17.3

uniting of interests   A business combination in which the shareholders of the combining enterprises combine control over the whole, or effectively the whole, of their net assets and operations to achieve a continuing mutual sharing in the risks and benefits attaching to the combined entity such that neither party can be identified as the acquirer.   22.9

useful life   Either: 4.4, 16.7, 17.3

   (a) the period over which a depreciable asset is expected to be used by the enterprise; or

(b) the number of production or similar units expected to be obtained from the asset by the enterprise.

venturer A party to a joint venture that has joint control over that joint venture. 31.2

vested benefits Benefits, the rights to which, under the conditions of a retirement benefit plan, are not conditional on continued employment. 26.8

warrant A financial instrument that gives the holder the right to purchase ordinary shares. 33.6

weighted average cost method Under this method, the cost of each item is determined from the weighted average of the cost of similar items at the beginning of a period and the cost of similar items purchased or produced during the period. The average may be calculated on a periodic basis, or as each additional shipment is received, depending upon the circumstances of the enterprise. 2.22

weighted average number of ordinary shares outstanding during the period Number of ordinary shares outstanding at the beginning of the period, adjusted by the number of ordinary shares cancelled, bought back or issued during the period multiplied by a time-weighting factor. 33.15

INTERNATIONAL
ACCOUNTING STANDARDS
COMMITTEE

The International Accounting Standards Committee (IASC) is an independent private sector body, with the objective of achieving uniformity in the accounting principles which are used by businesses and other organisations for financial reporting around the world. It was formed in 1973 through an agreement made by professional accountancy bodies from Australia, Canada, France, Germany, Japan, Mexico, the Netherlands, the United Kingdom and Ireland and the United States of America. Since 1983, IASC's members have included all the professional accountancy bodies that are members of the International Federation of Accountants (IFAC). As at January 1997, that is 119 members and 6 associate members in 88 countries. Many other organisations are now involved in the work of IASC and many countries that are not members of IASC make use of International Accounting Standards.

The objectives of IASC as stated in its Constitution are:

(a) to formulate and publish in the public interest accounting standards to be observed in the presentation of financial statements and to promote their world-wide acceptance and observance;

(b) to work generally for the improvement and harmonisation of regulations, accounting standards and procedures relating to the presentation of financial statements.

The work of IASC is made possible by financial support from the professional accountancy bodies and other organisations on its Board, by IFAC, and by contributions from companies, financial institutions, accounting firms and other organisations. IASC also generates revenue from the sale of its publications.

International Accounting Standards, Exposure Drafts, and other IASC documents are copyright of the International Accounting Standards Committee, 166 Fleet Street, London EC4A 2DY, United Kingdom. Telephone: +44 (171) 353-0565, Fax: +44 (171) 353-0562: E-mail: iasc@iasc.org.uk Internet: http://www.iasc.org.uk All rights reserved. No part of these publications may be translated, reprinted or reproduced or utilised in any form either in whole or in part or by any electronic, mechanical or other means, now known or hereafter invented, including photocopying and recording, or in any information storage and retrieval system, without the prior express permission of IASC in writing.

The various extracts from *International Accounting Standards 1997*, are reproduced in this textbook by Houghton Mifflin Company (USA) with permission from IASC. Copies of the complete original English language texts of IASC publications may be obtained direct from IASC.

BOARD

The business of IASC is conducted by a Board comprising representatives of accountancy bodies in thirteen countries (or combinations of countries) appointed by the Council of IFAC, and up to four other organisations with an interest in financial reporting. Each Board Member may nominate up to two representatives and a technical adviser to attend Board meetings. IASC encourages each Board Member to include in its delegation at least one person working in industry and one person who is directly involved in the work of the national standard setting body. For the two and a half year term ending 31 December 1997, the Board members are:

Australia

Canada

France

Germany

India

Japan

Malaysia

Mexico

Netherlands

Nordic Federation of Public Accountants

South Africa

United Kingdom

United States of America

and representatives of the International Co-ordinating Committee of Financial Analysts' Associations, the Federation of Swiss Industrial Holding Companies and the International Association of Financial Executives Institutes (IAFEI). The Indian and South African delegations also include a representative from Sri Lanka and Zimbabwe respectively. Representatives of the European Commission, the United States Financial Accounting Standards Board (FASB) and the International Organization of Securities Commissions (IOSCO) attend Board meetings as observers.

CONSULTATIVE GROUP

In 1981, the IASC Board established an international Consultative Group that includes representatives of international organisations of preparers and users of financial statements, stock exchanges and securities regulators. The group also includes representatives or observers from development agencies, standard setting bodies and intergovernmental organisations. The current members of the Consultative Group are:

Fédération Internationale des Bourses de Valeurs (FIBV)

International Association for Accounting Education and Research (IAAER)

International Banking Associations

International Bar Association (IBA)

International Chamber of Commerce (ICC)

International Confederation of Free Trade Unions (ICFTU), and World Confederation of Labour

International Valuation Standards Committee (IVSC)

International Finance Corporation (IFC)

The World Bank

Organisation for Economic Co-operation and Development (OECD)*

United Nations Division on Transnational Corporations and Investment*

The Consultative Group meets periodically to discuss with the Board the technical issues in IASC projects, IASC's work programme and IASC's strategy. This group plays an important part in IASC's due process for the setting of International Accounting Standards and in gaining acceptance for the resulting Standards.

ADVISORY COUNCIL

In 1995, IASC established a high level, international Advisory Council of outstanding individuals in senior positions from the accountancy profession, business and the other users of financial statements. The role of the Advisory Council is to promote generally the acceptability of International Accounting Standards and enhance the credibility of IASC's work by, among other things:

(a) reviewing and commenting on the Board's strategy and plans so as to satisfy itself that the needs of IASC's constituencies are being met;

(b) preparing an annual report on the effectiveness of the Board in achieving its objectives and in carrying out its due process;

(c) promoting participation in, and acceptance of, the work of IASC by the accountancy profession, the business community, the users of financial statements and other interested parties;

(d) seeking and obtaining funding for IASC's work in a way that it does not impair IASC's independence; and

(e) reviewing IASC's budget and financial statements.

The Advisory Council ensures that the independence and objectivity of the Board in making technical decisions on proposed International Accounting Standards are not impaired. The Advisory Council does not participate in, nor seek to influence, those decisions.

IASC STAFF

The Board is supported by a small staff based in London, headed by the Secretary-General. The technical staff and other project managers currently include people from Canada, France, Germany, Malaysia, New Zealand, the United Kingdom and the United States of America.

THE DEVELOPMENT OF INTERNATIONAL ACCOUNTING STANDARDS

Board Representatives, Member Bodies, members of the Consultative Group, other organisations and individuals and the IASC staff are encouraged to submit suggestions for new topics which might be dealt with in International Accounting Standards.

IASC's due process ensures that International Accounting Standards are high quality standards that require appropriate accounting practices in particular economic circumstances. The due process also ensures, through consultation with the Consultative Group, IASC's Member Bodies, standard setting bodies and other interested groups and individuals on a worldwide basis, that International

*Observers

Accounting Standards are acceptable to the users and preparers of financial statements.

The procedure for the development of an International Accounting Standard is as follows:

(a) the Board sets up a Steering Committee. Each Steering Committee is chaired by a Board Representative and usually includes representatives of the accountancy bodies in at least three other countries. Steering Committees may also include representatives of other organisations that are represented on the Board or the Consultative Group or that are expert in the particular topic;

(b) the Steering Committee identifies and reviews all the accounting issues associated with the topic. The Steering Committee considers the application of IASC's Framework for the Preparation and Presentation of Financial Statements to those accounting issues. The Steering Committee also studies national and regional accounting requirements and practice, including the different accounting treatments that may be appropriate in different circumstances. Having considered the issues involved, the Steering Committee may submit a Point Outline to the Board;

(c) after receiving comments from the Board on the Point Outline, if any, the Steering Committee normally prepares and publishes a Draft Statement of Principles or other discussion document. The purpose of this Statement is to set out the underlying accounting principles that will form the basis for the preparation of the Exposure Draft. It also describes the alternative solutions considered and the reasons for recommending their acceptance or rejection. Comments are invited from all interested parties during the exposure period, usually around three months. For revisions to an existing International Accounting Standard, the Board may instruct the Steering Committee to prepare an Exposure Draft without first publishing a Draft Statement of Principles;

(d) the Steering Committee reviews the comments on the Draft Statement of Principles and normally agrees a final Statement of Principles, which is submitted to the Board for approval and used as the basis for preparing an Exposure Draft of a proposed International Accounting Standard. The final Statement of Principles is available to the public on request, but is not formally published;

(e) the Steering Committee prepares a draft Exposure Draft for approval by the Board. After revision, and with the approval of at least two-thirds of the Board, the Exposure Draft is published. Comments are invited from all interested parties during the exposure period, a minimum of one month and usually at least three months; and

(f) the Steering Committee reviews the comments and prepares a draft International Accounting Standard for review by the Board. After revision, and with the approval of at least three-quarters of the Board, the Standard is published.

During this process, the Board may decide that the needs of the subject under consideration warrant additional consultation or would be better served by issuing a Discussion Paper for comment. It may also be necessary to issue more than one Exposure Draft before developing an International Accounting Standard.

BENCHMARK AND ALLOWED ALTERNATIVE TREATMENTS

In some cases where International Accounting Standards permit two accounting treatments for like transactions and events, one treatment is designated as the benchmark treatment and the other as the allowed alternative treatment. The Board's 1990 Statement of Intent on the Comparability of Financial Statements gave the following explanation:

The Board has concluded that it should use the term "benchmark" instead of the proposed term "preferred" *[the term proposed in E32, Comparability of Financial Statements]* in those few cases where it continues to allow a choice of accounting treatment for like transactions and events. The term "benchmark" more closely reflects the Board's intention of identifying a point of reference when making its choice between alternatives.

INTERPRETATIONS

In 1996, the IASC Board approved the formation of a Standing Committee on Interpretations (SIC) to consider, on a timely basis, accounting issues that are likely to receive divergent or unacceptable treatment in the absence of authoritative guidance. Its review will be within the context of existing International Accounting Standards and the IASC Framework. In developing interpretations, the SIC will consult similar national committees which have been nominated for the purpose by Member Bodies. The SIC will meet for the first time in the first half of 1997.

The SIC will deal with issues of reasonably widespread importance, and not issues of concern to only a small set of enterprises. The interpretations will cover both:

- mature issues (unsatisfactory practice within the scope of existing International Accounting Standards); and
- emerging issues (new topics relating to an existing International Accounting Standard but not considered when the Standard was developed).

The SIC has twelve voting members from various countries, including individuals from the accountancy profession, preparer groups and user groups. IOSCO and the European Commission are non-voting observers. To ensure adequate liaison with the Board, two Board Representatives will attend SIC meetings.

If no more than 3 of its voting members have voted against an interpretation, the SIC will ask the Board to approve the interpretation for issue; as for International Accounting Standards, this will require three-quarters of the Board to vote in favour. Interpretations will be formally published after approval by the Board.

IASC's Operating Procedures do not allow IASC staff to give advice on the meaning of International Accounting Standards.

IASC's ACHIEVEMENTS

IASC currently has 31 International Accounting Standards. These Standards deal with topics that affect the financial statements of business enterprises.

The Board has also issued a Framework for the Preparation and Presentation of Financial Statements. The Framework assists the Board:

(a) in the development of future International Accounting Standards and in its review of existing International Accounting Standards; and
(b) in promoting the harmonisation of regulations, accounting standards and procedures relating to the presentation of financial statements by providing a basis for reducing the number of alternative accounting treatments permitted by International Accounting Standards.

International Accounting Standards have done a great deal both to improve and harmonise financial reporting around the world. They are used:

(a) as a basis for national accounting requirements in many countries;
(b) as an international benchmark by countries which develop their own requirements (including major industrialised countries as well as an increasing number

of emerging markets such as China and many other countries in Asia, Central Europe and the CIS);

(c) by stock exchanges and regulatory authorities which allow foreign or domestic companies to present financial statements in accordance with International Accounting Standards;

(d) by supra-national bodies such as the European Commission, which announced in 1995 that it is relying heavily on IASC to produce results that meet the needs of capital markets; and

(e) by a growing number of companies themselves.

The International Organisation of Securities Commissions (IOSCO) is looking to IASC to provide mutually acceptable International Accounting Standards for use in multinational securities offerings and other international offerings. Already, a number of stock exchanges require or allow foreign issuers to present financial statements in accordance with International Accounting Standards. As a result a growing number of companies disclose the fact that their financial statements conform with International Accounting Standards.

In 1993, IOSCO agreed a list of core standards for use in financial statements of companies involved in cross-border offerings and listings. International Accounting Standards already deal with most of the core standards. IOSCO has already endorsed IAS 7, Cash Flow Statements, and has indicated to IASC that 14 of the existing International Accounting Standards do not require additional improvement, providing that the other core standards are successfully completed. All the projects, other than Agriculture, on the Work Plan relate to IOSCO's list of core standards.

In 1995, IOSCO's Technical Committee agreed that successful completion of the Board's current Work Plan will mean that International Accounting Standards comprise a comprehensive core set of standards. Completion of comprehensive core standards that are acceptable to the Technical Committee will allow the Technical Committee to recommend endorsement of International Accounting Standards for cross-border capital raising and listing purposes in all global markets. The Work Plan is scheduled for completion in early 1998.

INTERNATIONAL ACCOUNTING STANDARDS (AS OF OCTOBER 1997)

IAS 1   Presentation of Financial Statements (revised 1997)

IAS 2   Inventories

IAS 4   Depreciation Accounting

IAS 5   Information to be Disclosed in Financial Statements

IAS 7   Cash Flow Statements

IAS 8   Net Profit or Loss for the Period, Fundamental Errors and Changes in Accounting Policies

IAS. 9   Research and Development Costs

IAS 10   Contingencies and Events Occurring after the Balance Sheet Date

IAS 11   Construction Contracts

IAS 12   Income Taxes (revised 1996) *effective 1 January 1998*

IAS 13   Presentation of Current Assets and Current Liabilities

IAS 14   Segment Reporting (revised 1997)

IAS 15   Information Reflecting the Effects of Changing Prices

IAS 16   Property, Plant and Equipment

IAS 17   Accounting for Leases

IAS 18   Revenue

IAS 19   Retirement Benefit Costs

IAS 20   Accounting for Government Grants and Disclosure of Government Assistance

IAS 21   The Effects of Changes in Foreign Exchange Rates

IAS 22   Business Combinations

IAS 23   Borrowing Costs

IAS 24   Related Party Disclosures

IAS 25   Accounting for Investments

IAS 26   Accounting and Reporting by Retirement Benefit Plans

IAS 27   Consolidated Financial Statements and Accounting for Investments in Subsidiaries

IAS 28   Accounting for Investments in Associates

IAS 29   Financial Reporting in Hyperinflationary Economies

IAS 30   Disclosures in the Financial Statements of Banks and Similar Financial Institutions

IAS 31   Financial Reporting of Interests in Joint Ventures

IAS 32   Financial Instruments: Disclosure and Presentation

IAS 33   Earnings Per Share

Exposure Drafts

E48   Financial Instruments *(now partly superseded by IAS 32)*

E54   Employee Benefits

E55   Inpairment of Assets

E56   Leases

E57   Interim Financial Reporting

E58   Discontinuing Operations

E59   Provisions, Contingent Liabilities and Contingent Assets

E60   Intangible Assets

E61   Business Combinations

For further information about the IASC, please contact them at the following address:

166 Fleet Street
London EC4A 2DY
United Kingdom
Telephone: +44 171 353-0565
Fax: +44 171 353-0562
E-mail: iasc@iasc.org.uk
Internet: http://www.iasc.org.uk

COMPANY NAME INDEX

SUBJECT INDEX

Note: **Boldface** type denotes key terms.